Dr. Sim

MW01550495

Counterterrorism

Counterterrorism

From the Cold War to the War on Terror

Volume 1: Combating Modern Terrorism (1968–2011)

FRANK SHANTY, EDITOR

Praeger Security International

 PRAEGER

AN IMPRINT OF ABC-CLIO, LLC
Santa Barbara, California • Denver, Colorado • Oxford, England

Copyright 2012 by ABC-CLIO, LLC

All rights reserved. No part of this publication may be reproduced, stored in
a retrieval system, or transmitted, in any form or by any means, electronic,
mechanical, photocopying, recording, or otherwise, except for the inclusion of brief
quotations in a review, without prior permission in writing from the publisher.

Library of Congress Cataloging-in-Publication Data

Counterterrorism : from the Cold War to the war on terror / Frank Shanty, editor.
    v. cm. — (Praeger security international)
  Includes bibliographical references and index.
  Contents: v. 1. Combating modern terrorism (1968–2011) — v. 2. Twenty-first
century global counterterrorism measures.
  ISBN 978-1-59884-544-0 (hardcopy : alk. paper) — ISBN 978-1-59884-545-7
(ebook : alk. paper) 1. Terrorism—Prevention. I. Shanty, Frank, 1950–
  HV6431.C69143 2012
  363.325'16—dc23   2012006425

ISBN: 978-1-59884-544-0
EISBN: 978-1-59884-545-7

16 15 14 13 12   1 2 3 4 5

This book is also available on the World Wide Web as an eBook.
Visit www.abc-clio.com for details.

Praeger
An Imprint of ABC-CLIO, LLC

ABC-CLIO, LLC
130 Cremona Drive, P.O. Box 1911
Santa Barbara, California 93116-1911

This book is printed on acid-free paper ∞

Manufactured in the United States of America

Contents

Preface

This two-volume set addresses counterterrorism issues from the days of the Cold War to the current global campaign. Although historically terrorism has been a tactic in anticolonialist struggles, national resistance movements, and conventional wars, and has also been used by governments against their own citizens, this publication will primarily address terrorism by subnational or nonstate groups in the period post-1968.

Hence, this two-volume set provides a comprehensive examination of modern nation-state legislative, military, and nonmilitary attempts to combat terrorism by these groups within and outside state borders. Special emphasis is placed on the counterterrorism efforts of the international community, post-911. Issues relative to the "global war on terrorism" and "lessons learned" from these events as well as other prior counterterrorism campaigns are also addressed.

Counterterrorism: From the Cold War to the War on Terror includes articles that discuss global, regional, and state counterterrorism issues, policies, and events, as well as problems that are inherent in state and global efforts to combat international and state-based domestic terrorism. With extraordinary expenditures within national budgets going towards anti- and counterterrorism efforts, the question we need to ask is, Have these programs worked? Indeed, few empirically based studies have been initiated that examine the effectiveness of existing state and global counterterrorism strategies. While this work is not intended to serve as a comprehensive assessment of various state counterterrorism policies, some of the articles will address the success or failure of these actions. Articles that address these issues include state actions taken to manage the threat/ event and the outcome of these actions.

Volume 1 consists of six parts. Part I is devoted largely to definitional issues and serves as a foundation for further discussion in subsequent sections on the 21st-century terrorist threat. Part II addresses the evolution and effectiveness of select nation-state counterterrorism policies. Parts III and IV address key issues that impact counterterrorism strategy and the post-9/11 global counterterrorism campaign respectively. Regional counterterrorism efforts and an agenda for future research are discussed in parts V and VI.

Volume 2 provides a section containing articles on some of the world's elite counterterrorism forces and a chronology of major global counterterrorism operations. Volume 2 also includes a compilation of national and international treaties, laws, conventions, agreements, and protocols that have been implemented in an attempt to counter this ongoing threat to public safety and international security. Volume 2 concludes with an appendix containing organizational and individual profiles. This two-volume set provides a useful and easy-to-read discussion of these and other vital issues. A comprehensive index is also provided for easy browsing and quick reference.

Frank Shanty, PhD

Acknowledgments

Composing a two-volume reference work on a specific topic is a challenging, time-consuming, and often frustrating endeavor. This two-volume reference work on counterterrorism was no different. Without the combined efforts and feedback of many individuals during the course of this project this two-volume set would not have been written. Moreover, many contributors' specific areas of expertise broadened the scope and expanded the subject matter of this reference work. Consequently, seldom-discussed but nevertheless important topics in current and future global counterterrorism efforts were addressed.

I thank all those who contributed their expertise, time, and writing skills to bring this important work to fruition. I also thank my family for their understanding and acceptance of my personal dedication to completing this project, which often impacted other "life priorities." Special thanks go to Dr. Jeffrey Ian Ross, University of Baltimore, for his valuable assistance in contacting potential qualified writers and informing them of this project. He also provided valuable assistance in directing me to individuals with varied expertise in some of the covered topics within these pages.

My appreciation is also extended to Dr. Rohan Gunaratna, Dr. Arabinda Acharya, Dr. John Harrison, and Kay Floyd, Nanyang Technological University, Singapore; Dr. Joshua Sinai, Virginia Tech; Michael Kraft, Institute for Bioscience and International Security Policy; Brian Blodgett, American Public University System; Sajjad Rahman, University of Chittagong, Bangladesh; Sarah Eastlake-Smith, CHD Partners, Australia; Dr. Hank Prunckun, Australian Graduate School of Policing; Dr. Taberez Ahmed Neyazi, Kyoto University; Dr. James Perry, Northrop Grumman

Corporation; Hans Brun, King's College, Department of War Studies; Dr. Xavier Stewart, colonel, U.S. Army; and Jamie Walsh, University College Cork (UCC) School of History, for their efforts at soliciting qualified scholars and/or their willingness to contribute their time and knowledge writing entries that otherwise would probably not have been included in this work.

I am also grateful to those contributors who provided comments and insights regarding some of the entries chosen for inclusion in this reference work. This valuable and constructive feedback has given this two-volume reference work global significance.

I thank Steve Catalano, senior editor for military history and security issues at Praeger Publishers, for his valuable insights and assistance. Steve is a professional and has been great to work with throughout this project.

Finally, I dedicate these two volumes to the men and women in the U.S. and allied armed forces and those civilian personnel who have provided and continue to provide frontline defense against international terrorism and violent extremism at home and abroad.

Frank Shanty, PhD

Introduction

Frank Shanty

Terrorism in the 21st century has morphed into a unique and serious challenge to state, regional, and international security. During the late 1960s through the 1980s terrorism was primarily confined within state borders, and attacks largely resulted from nationalist issues (e.g., in Spain, Sri Lanka, Northern Ireland, and Turkey), in addition to attacks (e.g., aircraft hijackings and bombings) perpetrated by the Palestine Liberation Organization (PLO) against Israeli targets within and outside of Israel and sporadic attacks by left- and right-wing organizations in Europe during the 1980s.

However, while terrorism created much civil unrest in various individual states, it did not impact or threaten the foundations of secular democracies, nor did it directly challenge global security. The revolution in Iran and the Soviet invasion of Afghanistan, both in 1979, ushered in a new era of terrorism and spawned the current global threat. This new terrorism, couched in religious precepts, would dominate the global landscape during the 1990s and launch a global effort to defeat it in the beginning years of the 21st century.

TERRORISM: HISTORICAL PROBLEM

Since antiquity terrorism has impacted states' domestic security and in the past 50 years has evolved from a state-specific threat to a global security challenge. From the 1st-century Sicarii of Judea, the 11th-century Brotherhood of the Assassins, the 13th-century Thugs of India, and the 19th-century anarchists in Europe and America, to the 20th-century ethnonationalist and religious terrorism, state security, and the post–Cold War era, international security has and will continue to be negatively impacted by a phenomenon that has for much of its history been confined within national borders. Post–Cold War terrorism has been characterized by an increase in the number of successfully perpetrated attacks and a concomitant increase in lethality with many attacks killing and injuring large numbers of people.

Moreover, the illicit trade in arms and drugs adds a new dimension to the problem by amplifying the destructive capability of these groups. Terrorist groups have employed various tactics such as car bombings, commercial aircraft hijackings, improvised explosive devices, kidnappings, suicide bombings, and shootings against high-traffic-area targets where the body count is guaranteed to be high and media exposure intense. Thus, efforts to rid the world of this lethal phenomenon will require proactive strategies and the collective action and cooperation of all concerned states.

During the past half century members of the international community have taken individual and collective action in an attempt to mitigate this ongoing threat to global order and public safety. However, in the second decade of the 21st century the international community confronts a problem not easily understood or even amenable to a universally acceptable definition. Hence, there are no quick and easy solutions for many of the issues discussed within these pages. Terrorism, crime, violence, and conflict do not occur in a vacuum. Underlying causes that spawn these activities and the concomitant human misery are very difficult to isolate. Frequently, many interrelated and overlapping issues shape the foundation of a problem.

TERRORISM IN THE 21ST CENTURY

The pages within these two volumes contain much information regarding terrorism and its past and current threat to global security. However, as many of the articles in this two-volume work suggest, terrorism in the 21st century has the potential to further proliferate and become more dangerous as groups seek to acquire weapons capable of killing and maiming hundreds of thousands of people in a single attack. Such a stark scenario would no doubt launch a global nuclear war that would destroy civilization as we know it. There is no single approach that will rid the world of a problem that has existed since antiquity. Solving problems with violence is as old as humankind.

We live in a world of varied cultures and beliefs. Moreover, real or perceived injustices and historical grievances cannot be resolved with empty words or economic incentives. Some of the grievances that have been articulated over the years are legitimate and therefore need to be addressed in a constructive and nonthreatening way. This will be an arduous and lengthy process. It will take a multidimensional and multinational approach to begin to successfully address these issues.

Terrorism in the second decade of the 21st century will not be defeated by attempting to beat it into submission militarily. That said, a police or military action in response to events such as the 9/11 attacks is a logical and understandable response in order to bring the perpetrators to justice and to convey the message that attacks on innocent civilians will not be tolerated in a civil society but rather will bring a swift and overwhelming counteraction.

The establishment of trust through open dialogue and domestic and international policies and initiatives designed to address differences and develop understanding between cultures will take years, not days. Actions rather than words can alter perceptions over the long term. This difficult and protracted course of action needs to be initiated to circumvent an escalation of current global tensions and violence.

GLOBAL WAR ON TERRORISM

The global war on terrorism launched by the United States and its allies following the events of September 11, 2001, engaged the United States and its coalition partners in a fight with a new and more deadly strain of terrorism: a global movement of like-minded Islamists who seek the total destruction of the West and moderate Arab states. Pakistan, particularly the Federally Administered Tribal Areas (FATA) in the north of the country, is the epicenter of this new breed of extremism and an area that breeds militancy and crime and provides a safe haven to some of the world's most dangerous groups.

One such group, al-Qaeda, responsible for the 9/11 attacks on America, justifies its actions on religious tenets and a desire for one world government ruled by an extremist interpretation of one of the world's major religions. It remains to be seen how the killing of Osama bin Laden in Abbottabad, Pakistan, on May 1, 2011, by U.S. Special Operations Forces will impact this organization. Whether some of the objectives of al-Qaeda and other organizations and individuals that comprise this global movement of extremists can be reached will depend in part on proactive and unified international measures designed to discredit the ideology that drives this movement's recruitment and financial and logistical support efforts.

According to a research brief issued by the RAND Corporation in 2006, a sound and inclusive counterterrorism policy "needs to move beyond the boundaries of conventional counterterrorism theory and practice to address the ideological and political factors that motivate much of the threat" (2006, 2).

A similar view is taken by Rohan Gunaratna, head of the International Centre for Political Violence and Terrorism Research at Nanyang Technological University in Singapore. He notes, "The real strength of al Qaeda is not its membership per se but in its overarching, highly appealing ideology" (2006, 3). This extremist mindset has killed and injured thousands of people, and unless effective multinational counterstrategies can be developed, this dangerous ideology will no doubt continue to proliferate and could potentially involve the acquisition of weapons systems capable of annihilating large population centers and critical national infrastructure.

This mindset presents the counterterrorism community with an additional challenge that will not be defeated on the battlefield. Islamists and other religiously based terrorist groups believe that they have the moral high ground, that their actions are sanctioned by a higher authority. Many of these individuals—usually young, disenfranchised, and without much hope for upward mobility—are highly susceptible to the propaganda and rhetoric espoused through Internet chat rooms and other communication channels. These vulnerable individuals oftentimes are seeking to become part of something significant. Hence, becoming part of a group that shares a common belief system provides the individual with an identity and a sense of self-worth (Kershaw 2010).

It is important to note that individuals who gravitate toward these types of groups do not emanate solely from Middle Eastern and South Asian countries; successful recruitment for potential terrorists has also taken place in many Western countries. This creates additional problems for counterterrorist operatives and law enforcement officials.

INTERNATIONAL COOPERATION

From an operational perspective better synchronization is needed between various agencies charged with countering the terrorist threat. To this end state intelligence agencies need to organize their efforts to develop timely and actionable intelligence and coordinate these efforts with other state and international intelligence and law enforcement agencies. Timely and factual information is the most vital component of sound counterterrorism policies and proactive measures. Moreover, detailed assessments and analytic efforts need to be applied to this information. This is a critical component of the intelligence-gathering process if lives are to be saved, the enemy's objectives derailed, and proper judgments made regarding specific actions that need to be taken to mitigate the threat.

Indeed, the attacks of 9/11 have raised new issues and challenges, generated new thinking, and added a new dimension to the security threats presented by terrorism that in many cases transcends national borders. Collectively, the international community needs to acquire a broader understanding of violent extremism and its underpinnings. There also needs to be a mutual sharing of information between various agencies within individual state governments and, as already stated, an effort to establish relevant information sharing between affected states.

Counterterrorism involves numerous strategies including legislative and diplomatic initiatives and humanitarian, economic, and military responses. Depending on the immediate or anticipated threat one or a combination of these strategies may be employed to proactively mitigate the threat or respond to a successfully launched attack. As often is the case, specifically in the past two decades, the response has been reactive. It is very difficult to predict with 100 percent accuracy the next target that an individual or group will attack. Terrorists, particularly Islamist extremists and insurgents on the battlefield in Southwest Asia have a trait that we in the West have not fully developed; that attribute is patience.

The Afghan Taliban has a saying, "NATO has all the watches, but we have all the time" (Shinn 2009). This statement reveals much about the enemy we are fighting. It also reveals a lot about the culture for which we lack a proper understanding. Al-Qaeda was determined to attack a significant target on U.S. soil. In February 1993 Ramzi Yousef attempted to destroy the Twin Towers at the World Trade Center in Manhattan, New York, using a chemical explosive and a rented van; he did not succeed. Eight years later this plot was successfully launched.

CONCLUSION

Finally, we need to rethink the terrorism problem, which ultimately impacts humanity as a whole. It is the opinion of this author that extremism and acts of terrorism will unfortunately not be eliminated in our lifetimes. Military actions, diplomatic initiatives, and economic incentives alone or together will not defeat an enemy who is willing to strap on a suicide vest or hijack a plane and kill thousands of innocents. Ideologies that spawn acts designed to intimidate, maim, and kill need to be examined, and new approaches need to be adopted and put into action. The situation that we are presently involved in, specifically in Afghanistan and Pakistan, is very serious and has wider regional and global implications. Although the global war on terrorism is being fought on many fronts—financial, diplomatic, social, and military—the ongoing war in Afghanistan and insurgent activity in Pakistan's Federally Administered Tribal Areas and other places throughout the country are a direct and immediate threat to the Pakistani government. This is a country with major political and social problems and a country that also possesses nuclear armaments.

There are no easy answers or quick fixes. Although it will be a difficult, time-consuming task, the challenges we face at this moment in history can be confronted successfully. It will take an international coalition of concerned states (Western and non-Western) to formulate strategies aimed at initiating dialogue between disparate and competing cultures. Ultimately, it is the responsibility of each one of us to ensure that the situations that currently exist in Southwest Asia and other global "hotspots" do not escalate to the point that events rather than humans control the outcome. Finally, the global community has over time created many of these problems. Thus, the solutions rest squarely on our collective shoulders.

REFERENCES

Gunaratna, Rohan. "Strategic Counterterrorism: Getting Ahead of Terrorism, Part 1: Understanding the Threat." The Jebsen Center for Counter-terrorism Studies Research Briefing Series, vol. 1, no. 1, December 2006.

Kershaw, Sarah. "The Terrorist Mind: An Update." *New York Times,* January 9, 2010. http://www.nytimes.com/2010/01/10/weekinreview/10kershaw.html.

RAND Corporation. "U.S. Counterterrorism Strategy Must Address Ideological and Political Factors at the Global and Local Levels." Research Brief, Project Air Force, 2006. http://www.rand.org/pubs/research_briefs/2006/RAND_RB202.pdf.

Shinn, James. "'NATO Has the Watches, We Have the Time.'" *Wall Street Journal,* October 26, 2009. http://online.wsj.com/article/SB1000142405274870433590457449712054893455.html.

I

Terrorism: A Global Security Challenge

Defining Terrorism: Issues and Problems

Łukasz Kamieński

The word *terrorism* (from Latin *terrere*, "to frighten") received its political meaning during the French Revolution when Maximilien Robespierre created the *regime of terror* (1793–1794) to consolidate the revolutionary state. Although the oppositionists were guillotined, the term had a positive connotation because the goal was to prevent a counterrevolution. In the 19th century, however, due to the activities of the anarchists, *terrorism* began to be pejoratively associated with antistate violence. Because the term has undergone many changes in meaning and refers to a multifaceted phenomenon, it remains disputed, slippery, abused, and misunderstood.

THE CONCEPT OF TERRORISM

Its historical evolution apart, the concept is ideologically, politically, and emotionally loaded and implies negative moral judgment because, depending on one's point of view, the same activity may be referred to as either terrorism or a liberation movement. The former indicates exclusion and political illegitimacy, while the latter implies unconventional violence against a victimizing regime or innocent civilians. The attackers label themselves as freedom fighters, while the attacked call them terrorists. This problem of subjectivity is captured by the phrase "One man's terrorist is another man's freedom fighter." Furthermore, terrorism is but one type of violence, often difficult to distinguish from other forms, such as crime, war, and guerrilla actions.

Diverse legal systems, various government agencies, and scholars adopt different definitions. The one most widely used, proclaimed by the U.S. Department of State in 1983, and also recognized by the 2002 National Security Strategy, describes this phenomenon as "premeditated, politically motivated violence perpetrated against noncombatant targets by subnational groups or clandestine agents, usually intended to influence the audience" (U.S. Code, Section 2656f(d), Title 22). The British Prevention of Terrorism Act of 1974 states that terrorism is "the use of violence for political ends, and includes any use of violence for the purpose of putting the public or any section of the public in fear" (Prevention of Terrorism Act (Northern Ireland) 1974, part III, 9(1)). Walter Laqueur defines terrorism as the "illegitimate use of force to achieve a political objective when innocent people are targeted" (2001, 3), while Bruce Hoffman identifies it as "the deliberate creation and exploitation of fear through violence or the threat of violence in the pursuit of political change" (2006, 40).

Faced with a variety of attempts to define the phenomenon as well as with the disagreement on what constitutes a terrorist act, the solution might be to investigate its main characteristics. First, it is the use of violence or the threat of violence, which may involve diverse methods (assassination, kidnapping, skyjacking, hostage taking, suicide bombing, etc.). Second, its aims are mainly political. Hoffman reveals that terrorism is "ineluctably about power: the pursuit of power, the acquisition of power, and the use of power to achieve political change" (2006, 2). Third, it is not ordinary violence but rather acts designed to intimidate and frighten a larger audience than the immediate victims of the attack. Brian Jenkins observed that "terrorism is theatre" since there is a message underneath the brutal violence (cited in Hoffman 2006, 38). For the 19th-century German revolutionary John Most, it was propaganda by deeds. With the global mass media this aspect gained great importance because images can empower the weak. Thus, terrorism, being not only instrumental but essentially performative, is a lethal communication strategy. Fourth, its effect is indirect, as already stated. Physical destruction is less important than the psychological impact, and, as observed by Raymond Aron, "a violent action is deemed terrorist when its psychological effects are disproportionate to its purely physical results" (cited in Chaliand and Blin 2007, 6). The terrorist's goal is to create anxiety in an "enemy" society, thus disrupting its normal functioning; the old maxim "Kill one, scare ten thousand" applies. Fifth, terrorism is a weapon of the weak, used by nonstate actors against states, societies, and individuals.

DEFINED BY STATES

States can adapt two basic approaches when dealing with terrorism and, accordingly, have different counterterrorism policies. They can regard it as a crime or as an act of war. The Europeans tend to view terrorism as a crime that has to be managed through law enforcement efforts. Alternatively, Americans perceive terrorism as war and, apart from homeland security measures, have waged a war against it. This variance is due to different experiences with terrorism but also partly to the degree of remoteness of the terrorists, which is vast for the Americans (Afghanistan, Iraq, Pakistan, etc.) and almost nonexistent for Europeans, who have been producing their own suicide bombers (three out of four terrorists in the 2005 London bombing were born in Britain). To deal with such a challenge the European governments must use domestic law and police forces instead of cruise missiles.

Overall, terrorism is more than a crime but less than a war; therefore, any sound counterterrorist strategy requires a balanced combination of police and military countermeasures. Alex Schmid captured this crime-versus-war ambiguity when he defined terrorism as the "peacetime equivalent of war crimes" (Schmid 1993, 11–13).

What separates terrorism from a common crime is its political nature and, to some degree, its legitimization. Criminal acts are usually motivated by financial or material gain, while terrorism uses violence for political and/or social change. Unlike terrorism, criminal acts are not intended to influence public opinion, nor do they usually seek a psychological impact. The criminal's motive is money, while the terrorist fights for an imagined community of ideas and brotherhood in faith. Konrad Kellen famously stated that a "terrorist without a cause is not a terrorist" but an ordinary criminal (Kellen 1982, 10).

Terrorism as such is not a form of war. It is rather a technique or tactic that should be seen as part of an irregular or asymmetrical warfare strategy, where the weak challenge the strong. Here we face yet another problem, because the terms *terrorism* and *guerrilla* are often interchanged, as the war in Iraq has recently demonstrated. Therefore, the distinctions in Table 1 might be one path to a definition of terrorism.

Table 1
Guerrilla Warfare versus Terrorism

Guerrilla Warfare	Terrorism
Seeks a change through force of arms, usually by an attempt to overthrow the government	Attempts to popularize a cause but rarely results in political change; often aims to provoke a governmental response
Is a defensive form of asymmetric warfare using violence on its own territory	Is an offensive form of asymmetric warfare using violence on the enemy's territory

(Continued)

Table 1 (*Continued*)

Guerrilla Warfare	Terrorism
Seeks to establish control over territory	Does not strive for control over territory
Measures success in terms of physical damage	Measures success in terms of psychological effect
Relies on the support of the local population	Does not need such support from the local population
Is characterized by violence extended in time, hit-and-run tactics, and a protracted struggle to exhaust the enemy	Is characterized by violence concentrated in time; uses spectacular and symbolic strikes to shock and fear the enemy
Operates as a military unit	Does not function in the open as armed units
Consists of a larger group of armed individuals	Consists of small units, often a single assassin
Uses ordinary military-type arms	Uses various forms of weapons, often in an innovative way
Attacks the military and the innocents ("hard" and "soft" targets)	Usually attacks the innocents ("soft" targets)

INSURGENCY OR TERRORISM

However, even such a distinction might be of little help because insurgents often turn to terrorist tactics. In a number of anticolonial wars after World War II, terrorism proved to be a successful method of guerrilla warfare. The mixed character of some subnational violent groups has posed one of the greatest challenges to the definition of terrorism, for example, the Lebanese Hezbollah. Responsible for spectacular acts of terrorism including the suicide bombing in Beirut (1983), it also fought a protracted guerrilla campaign against the Israeli military, finally forcing them to withdraw from southern Lebanon.

The terms have been further blurred with 9/11 and its aftermath. As Christopher Coker notes, al-Qaeda "is a movement that is engaged not in terrorism so much as a *global insurgency*, the first networked war. . . . [So is] the insurgency in Iraq" (2008, 82). Insurgents have been increasingly using the most spectacular terrorist technique, suicide bombing, while many jihadist groups have been sending their members to fight in Iraq, Afghanistan, and elsewhere (for example, it is estimated that 3,000 foreign volunteers have gone to Iraq, and approximately 700 Somali fighters flew to Lebanon to assist Hezbollah in its 2006 war with Israel). Thus, terrorism has become a form of insurgency.

Another controversial problem is the issue of *state terrorism*. Some academics (e.g., Hoffman) and governments (e.g., the United States) rightly consider the concept as unsound and argue that state-sanctioned violence against its citizens is not terrorism but *oppression*. *Terrorism* instead refers to violence committed by nonstate actors (bottom-up), while a government's killing (top-down) should be called *terror*. Others, however, insist on referring to the mass repressions of the totalitarian regimes in the 1930s and 1940s as well as of many right-wing dictatorships, particularly in Latin America, during the 1970s and 1980s, as *state terrorism*. Their goal was to strengthen the government's control by absolute intimidation of a society. Their basic characteristics were secrecy and government denial of responsibility. The "disappearing" citizens, "death squads," and torture in Argentina, Chile, and Peru are good examples. Yet *state terrorism* might have a double meaning, also encompassing the support provided by certain governments (such as Libya, Iran, Pakistan, and Saudi Arabia) to terrorist groups.

The meaning and the usage of *terrorism* have been regularly blurred. In the 1990s the term *narco-terrorism* became customary, meaning the use of drug trafficking as a source of revenues to support the activities of terrorist organizations and to protect the illicit business, a practice dating back to the 1970s. The beginning of the 21st century witnessed a new, post-9/11 debate on postmodern terrorism, which, motivated by religion, knows no limits and aims to cause massive, indiscriminate human casualties and physical destruction. Since the 1970s there has been a worrying tendency—terrorist attacks have declined in number but increased in lethality, and today the ultimate threat becomes terrorism using weapons of mass destruction, particularly the nuclear option. Also, the contemporary meaning of the term includes *cyberterrorism*. Although it has not yet materialized, the threat is becoming serious. Interference with or disruption of electronic systems might become the nightmare of many Western states and societies, as evidenced by the 2007 cyberattack against Estonia. These manifestations of various trends must be incorporated into a meaningful universal definition of terrorism and what constitutes a terrorist act.

CONCLUSION

Anyone wishing to find a comprehensive, essential, and agreed definition of terrorism will be disappointed because the phenomenon is getting increasingly complex and therefore harder to define. However, such attempts are necessary because counterterrorism and its strategies are dependent on the term as defined and understood.

See also: **Volume 1, Part I:** Defining the Enemy; Global Terrorism Post-9/11; Insurgent Terrorism; The Terrorist Threat in the 21st Century: A Global Security Problem

REFERENCES

Chaliand, Gerard, and Arnaud Blin. *The History of Terrorism: From Antiquity to Al Qaeda*. Berkeley and Los Angeles: University of California Press, 2007.

Coker, Christopher. *Ethics and War in the 21st Century*. London and New York: Routlege, 2008.

Hoffman, Bruce. *Inside Terrorism*. New York: Columbia University Press, 2006.

Kellen, Konrad. *On Terrorists and Terrorism*. N-1942-RC. Santa Monica, CA: RAND Corporation, 1982.

Laqueur, Walter. *The New Terrorism: Fanaticism and the Arms of Mass Destruction*. London: Phoenix Press, 2001.

Laqueur, Walter. *No End to War: Terrorism in the Twenty-First Century*. New York: Continuum, 2003.

Schmid, Alex P. "The Response Problem as a Definition Problem." In *Western Responses to Terrorism*, edited by Alex P. Schmid and Ronald D. Crelingsten, 7–13. New York: Frank Cass Publishers, 1993.

Schmid, Alex Peter, and Albert J. Jongman. *Political Terrorism: A New Guide to Actors, Authors, Concepts, Data Bases, Theories, and Literature*. New Brunswick, NJ: Transaction Books, 1988.

Definition and Dimensions of Counterterrorism

Tatyana Kelman

This section explores the definition, dimensions, and challenges associated with counterterrorism. Since the aftermath of the 9/11 terrorist attacks, the U.S. government, European Union (EU), United Nations (UN), and other organizations have changed how they view and counter terrorism. With the development of new technologies, the advent of the Internet as a tool of communication and base of support, and ease of transportation, terrorism has become more complex and dangerous (Alexander 2006, 3). Especially since the end of the Cold War, as new forms of terrorism have emerged, counterterrorism efforts have become more advanced. In order to prevent and respond successfully to terrorist attacks, counterterrorism efforts continue to evolve to stay ahead of the changing facets of terrorism.

DEFINITION OF COUNTERTERRORISM

Counterterrorism can be viewed as a set of measures that states apply in response to acts of terrorism. According to the *Oxford English Dictionary*, *counterterrorism* is defined as "political or military actions or measures intended to combat, prevent, or deter terrorism, sometimes (in early use) with the implication that the methods utilized resemble those of the terrorists." These measures are not simple and are often multidimensional policies that involve many agencies located within various national governmental departments spanning many countries.

Counterterrorism can also be thought of as "a mix of public and foreign policies designed to limit the actions of terrorist groups and individuals associated with terrorist organizations in an attempt to protect the general public from terrorist violence" (Omelicheva 2007). Furthermore, in line with the General Assembly's adoption of the UN's Global Counter-terrorism Strategy resolution in 2006, counterterrorism can be described using 47 measures that are categorized under four types of strategies that deal with how to counter terrorism: (1) addressing the conditions conducive to the spread of terrorism; (2) preventing and combating terrorism; (3) building states' capacity to prevent and combat terrorism and to strengthen the role of the UN's system in this regard; and (4) ensuring respect for human rights for all and the rule of law as the fundamental basis of the fight against terrorism (United Nations 2006b). Additionally, the UN has 13 international conventions listing all types of known terrorist activities. These conventions act as "manuals" for member states to enact legislation that prevents terrorist groups from flourishing (United Nations 2006a). However, none of these instruments and strategies can fully address the ever-growing and complex phenomenon of terrorism.

CHALLENGES OF COUNTERTERRORISM

In order to grasp the full extent of counterterrorism measures, it is important to look at some of the challenges that counterterrorism faces. Like terrorism, counterterrorism is a complex and multifaceted undertaking. Each organization that deals with combating terrorism has its own approach in viewing and defining this phenomenon. As such, tension between these groups in the way they combat terrorism occurs. Furthermore, the context of terrorist activities can also have an impact on the outcome of counterterrorism methods from one country to the next. Hence, to counter terrorist activities it is beneficial to consider methods employed by other states to ascertain which policies and protocols have been successful in combating terrorism.

The international community, for the most part, requires that counterterrorism measures maintain a balance between being effective and acceptable (i.e., democratic; Steven and Gunaratna 2004, 102). For example, counterterrorism measures must adhere to human rights by placing limits on military power during combat operations. Countries must "constantly evaluate" their actions "in accordance with international law" (Guiora 2008, 66). Additionally, state counterterrorism units also encounter difficulties and challenges in distinguishing between legitimate targets and civilians (Guiora 2008, 67). Some militants can resort to using civilians as shields, and the issue of human rights becomes a central focus during such operations (Guiora 2008). Hence, this is a constant dilemma that is widely seen in wars, such as in the war between Lebanon and Israel in 2006.

In terms of technology and resources, terrorist groups often know how to deflect counterterrorism measures (Steven and Gunaratna 2004, 41). Over time terrorist groups become more technologically advanced. They are "known for their ability and willingness to adapt, diversify, and embrace new technology, links, and operations" (Steven and Gunaratna 2004, 125). Hence, it is important to know what measures can better thwart terrorist attacks; therefore, counterterrorism efforts must keep up with the changing nature of terrorist groups. Counterterrorism can be best understood only if terrorism is understood, especially since counterterrorism measures will not be 100 percent effective until terrorism is fully understood (Alexander 2006, 2).

In keeping with the EU's formulated four strands of how to deal with terrorism, counterterrorism measures can be clearly viewed in terms of preventing, protecting, pursuing, and responding (i.e., preventive policies: policies that prevent individuals from resorting to terrorism; protective policies: policies that protect citizens and infrastructure from terrorist attacks; pursuing policies: policies that pursue terrorists and disrupt their groups and their networks; and responsive policies: policies that respond successfully to terrorist attacks). These measures work together to meet the EU's strategic commitment to "combat terrorism globally while respecting human rights, and making Europe safer, allowing its citizens to live in an area of freedom, security and justice" (*Europa* 2005). Since there is no single strategy that can defeat terrorism, it would be useful to look at these four strands to better define and understand the multifaceted problem of combating terrorism.

DIMENSIONS OF COUNTERTERRORISM

Literature on counterterrorism has widely referred to Ronald Crelinsten's classification of counterterrorism policies via the following dimensions: the criminal justice model (CJM), the war model (WM), and a combination of both models. The CJM includes measures that follow democratic principles and is viewed as more acceptable within the international community. Most Western countries pursue this model in dealing with terrorism (Crelinsten 2009). This model closely follows the rule of law, in which institutions such as the police, courts, and prisons are utilized in punishing terrorists. Unlike the CJM, the WM can infringe on democratic principles and human rights. In this model, countermeasures are more direct and often spawn more violence with unknown repercussions and unknown costs and benefits. Specifically, this model views terrorism as an "act of war" and calls on military forces to fight terrorism (Crelinsten 2009, 72). Since wars are fought with states, this model views terrorist groups as entities that can be attacked and defeated.

The combination of both models occurs when governments and organizations that institute policies aim for these measures to be both effective (i.e., successful) and acceptable (i.e., democratic). It has been said that the Bush administration overcame the risk of being seen as antidemocratic by the U.S. public as well as the international community by adopting this model. For example, President Bush simultaneously supported policies that brought criminals to justice and declared a war on terror. This is one of the big challenges that counterterrorism efforts continue to encounter (Crelinsten 2009).

However, these models do not allow for an empirical comparison of policies and only reflect "ideas" (COT Institute for Safety, Security and Crisis Management 2008). The EU's counterterrorism strategy that classifies counterterrorism policies as preventing, protecting, pursuing, and responding provides a framework for such empirical research. Policies under this classification can quantitatively explain which efforts are the most successful in combating terrorism.

CONCLUSION

Although much information and data on terrorist incidents exist, there is a shortage of empirical research that analyzes states' counterterrorism policies. Scholars argue that empirical research on states' responses to terrorism is needed to account for the differences and similarities of counterterrorism policies across countries (Omelicheva 2007).

Effective research in this area should assess the methods these countries use to identify terrorism, their counterterrorism responses and the impact of these responses on terrorist activities. Currently, the National Counterterrorism Center provides the U.S. Department of State with data on terrorism. This statistical information is then provided to the U.S. Congress in an annual report issued by the U.S. secretary of state. The center also posts that information in the Worldwide Incidents Tracking System, which is available to the general public. Empirical research on counterterrorism is necessary, especially since terrorist groups continue to grow and acts of terrorism have become more advanced as new technologies are being developed and become available.

See also: **Volume 1, Part I:** Defining Terrorism: Issues and Problems; Defining the Enemy; The Terrorist Threat in the 21st Century: A Global Security Problem. **Part III:** Counterterrorism Training; Defensive Measures against Terrorism: Military Preemption and Retaliation; Evolution of Global Counterterrorism Initiatives

REFERENCES

Alexander, Yonah. *Counterterrorism Strategies: Successes and Failures of Six Nations.* Dulles, VA: Potomac Books, 2006.

COT Institute for Safety, Security and Crisis Management (NL, Project Coordinator), Netherlands Organisation for Applied Scientific Research, Transnational Terrorism, Security and the Rule of Law. "Mapping Counterterrorism: A Categorization of Policies and the Promise of Empirically-Based, Systematic Comparisons." June 17, 2008. http://www.transnationalterrorism.eu/tekst/publications/WP6%20Del%2011.pdf.

Crelinsten, Ronald. *Counterterrorism.* Cambridge, UK: Polity, 2009.

Europa. "Counterterrorism Strategy." *Europa: Summaries of EU Legislation,* November 30, 2005. http://europa.eu/legislation_summaries/justice_freedom_security/fight_against_terrorism/l33275_en.htm.

Guiora, Amos N. *Fundamentals of Counterterrorism.* New York: Aspen, 2008.

Omelicheva, Mariya Y. "Counterterrorism: The State of Scholarship, Directions for Future Data Collection and Analysis." *Perspectives on Terrorism* 1, no. 2 (2007). http://www.terrorismanalysts.com/pt/index.php/pot/article/view/7/html.

Oxford English Dictionary. "Counterterrorism." http://dictionary.oed.com/entrance.dtl.

Steven, Graeme C.S., and Rohan Gunaratna. *Counterterrorism: A Reference Handbook.* Santa Barbara, CA: ABC-CLIO, 2004.

United Nations. "UN Action to Counter Terrorism." September 6, 2006a. http://www.un.org/terrorism/ruperez-article.html.

United Nations. "United Nations General Assembly Adopts Global Counterterrorism Strategy." September 8, 2006b. http://www.un.org/terrorism/strategy-counter-terrorism.shtml.

Defining the Enemy

Donathan Lawrence Brown

In efforts to respond to, prevent, or mitigate terrorist threats, both real and imagined, it is imperative to both define and articulate the enemy. If elected officials, for instance, are to respond to such threats, whether protecting our homeland or responding to an overseas threat, a defined and common enemy must first exist, one who represents the threatening menace among us. The rhetorical construction of who we are as a people along with who we are not, not only concerns itself with establishing our common identity but also involves the creating, defining, naming, and maintaining of who we view as our threats, or the enemy. After all, in order to define who we are, whether as a nation, citizenry, group, or otherwise, we must first be able to articulate not only who we are but also who we are not.

WHO IS THE ENEMY?

Enemies are understood as aggressors, always defined and named in opposition to how we view ourselves. By eliminating the possibility for resemblance, enemy construction shelters itself within the confines of division, creating an us-versus-them mentality. American political history is replete with examples of naming and defining enemies; these include the "axis of evil" and the "evil empire," all constructed in opposition to how Americans saw and defined themselves. Of the various political examples, the Cold War and America's war on terror are two noteworthy illustrations that represent rather identical ways of defining the enemy.

While more words than actions were exchanged amid the Cold War, examples of defining the enemy were plentiful. With the looming belief that nuclear annihilation was a credible threat, Presidents Dwight Eisenhower and Ronald Reagan both sought to construct the enemy, the Soviet Union, as a polar opposite to how they defined Americans. Through President Eisenhower's construction of "true Americans," we were able to comprehend who and what true Americans were in comparison to the Soviet Union, those whom we were not. In his 1955 State of the Union address, President Eisenhower sought discursive means to frame America and true Americans as exemplary and identical in their beliefs and values, whereas the Soviet Union existed outside this realm of resemblance and therefore existed as the forces of darkness. As Eisenhower uttered in his 1955 State of the Union address, the Cold War was "not a struggle merely of economic theories, or of forms of government, or military power. At issue is the true nature of man" (Eisenhower 2004, 40). This "true nature of man" would become the dividing force President Eisenhower would build on to define America's enemy. In President Eisenhower's words, "freedom is pitted against slavery; lightness against darkness" (Statler and Lyon 2006, xii). Here, the division is rather clear: true Americans believe in freedom and therefore are on the side of light, whereas the barren darkness that embodies immorality represents the Soviet Union.

Continuing along similar threads as Eisenhower, President Reagan cast the Cold War as a righteous battle between good and evil, light and dark, as illustrated in his 1983 "Evil Empire" address delivered before the annual meeting of the National Association of Evangelicals in Orlando, Florida. Here, Reagan famously uttered, "We will never compromise our principles and standards. We will never give away our freedom. We will never abandon our belief in God. And we will never stop searching for a genuine peace." Here, the Soviet Union, akin to Eisenhower's framing, does not reflect the values and principles "Americans" cherish—ideals we will never compromise. Our freedom, belief in God, and quest for peace represent who we are as Americans, whereas the enemy is drawn to fit the build of everything we are not. As the evil of the modern world, Reagan attempted to decivilize the Soviet Union, through which he, as a result, sought to strengthen American solidarity against a common opponent and allegiance to a common goal. The ability to define an enemy, whether real or imagined, is only as successful as the message it arouses. To define an enemy, whether it be a specified group or person, relies heavily on how the message identifies or unites "us" and divides us from "them." Whether defining our common enemy occurs via presidential war messages or otherwise, this task is vital not only for arousing sentiments of national unity but also when seeking to either craft or legitimize a proposed or present course of political action.

More recently, the war on terror under President George W. Bush provides various illustrations of defining the enemy. Without question, terrorist networks, specifically al-Qaeda, pose the greatest threat to America's national security, an argument President Bush made on numerous occasions, especially following September 11, 2001. At 9 P.M. on September 20, 2001, President Bush addressed not only a joint session of Congress but also an anxiously awaiting nation in need of guidance and answers. In an address that would begin his "war on terror" campaign, President Bush carefully constructed and defined America's enemy or, in his words, America's "enemies of freedom." As President Bush explained in his address, "The enemy of America is not our many Muslim friends; it is not our many Arab friends. Our enemy is a radical network of terrorists and every government that supports them." America's enemies, as President Bush explained, do not cherish the same values that unite "us"; rather, America's "enemies of freedom" represent all that "we" are not, threatening our ways of being. Their beliefs and way of being not only counter what we hold to be sacred but also threaten our existence and security. Because "America's enemies of freedom" exhibited menacing actions on September 11, 2001, by means of destroying New York's Twin Towers and taking the lives of many Americans, President Bush was able to justify his war on terror as the requisite policy response regarding America's enemy.

CONCLUSION

The Cold War and America's war on terror have demonstrated an uncanny similarity and staunch adherence to enemy construction. Defining and articulating who or what the common enemy is so that it is readily made available for public consumption requires an in-depth understanding of the situation's context along with the available means of political actions.

REFERENCES

Eisenhower, Dwight D. *State of the Union Addresses*. Whitefish, MT: Kessinger Publishing, 2004.

Engels, Jeremy. "Friend or Foe? Naming the Enemy." *Rhetoric and Public Affairs* 12 (2009): 37–64.

Ivie, Robert. "Images of Savagery in American Justification for War." *Communication Monographs* 47 (1980): 279–94.

Medhurst, Martin J., Robert L. Ivie, Philip Wander, and Robert L. Scott. *Cold War Rhetoric: Strategy, Metaphor, and Ideology.* East Lansing: Michigan State University Press, 1990.

Statler, Kathryn C., and Andrew L. Lyon. *The Eisenhower Administration, the Third World, and the Globalization of the Cold War.* Lanham, MD: Rowman & Littlefield, 2006.

Concept of Islamist Jihad

Brittany Bounds

The notion of *jihad* has endured transformations in understanding throughout history. Writings on jihad date back to the Quran and have been redefined through the centuries by hadith (reports or narrations of the sayings and actions of Muhammad) written by Muslim jurists in the Middle East. Radical activities have appeared at historical points of extreme socioeconomic and political change, even though these activities breach the letter and spirit of traditional Islam.

EVOLUTION OF JIHAD

Jihad originated around the time of the rise of Islam, but the doctrine of jihad as we recognize it today came relatively late in the eighth century; the long series of dynastic states that arose and succeeded one another in the Islamic world had an effect on the outcome and practice of jihad. This term *jihad* does not historically mean "holy war" or "just war"; it literally means "striving" or fighting for the sake of God. The "greater" jihad is not interpreted as combat against exterior enemies; rather, it referred to an internal spiritualized war to purify the self against humanistic impulses. However, the "lesser" jihad of waging war has become more important to many Muslims in recent history. Islam grew in an environment where warfare was characteristic of everyday life; martial valor usually topped the list of virtues, and in poems war typically appears as necessary for revenge. Further, martyrs were held in high esteem: if someone fought against a Muslim political rebel (*baghi*), apostate (*murtadd*), or brigand (*muharib*) and died, he was honored as a martyr.

There is a difference in approach between Sunni and Shiite jurists on the topic of jihad. Jihadist texts and documents can include the following: law governing the conduct of war, declaration and cessation of hostilities, doctrine of martyrdom, and the jihad's derivation from the Quran and the sunna. These jurists disagreed with each other on many matters, which caused the dissolution of the religion into four main classical schools of thought. Primary Sunni collections include *Sahih al-Bukhari, Sahih Muslim, Sunan an-Nasa'I al-Sugra, Sunan Abu Dawood, Sunan al-Tirmidhi,* and *Sunan Ibn Maja.* The Shia Twelver collections contain *Al-Kutub Al-Arb'ah* ("The Four Books"), *Kitab al-Kafi* of Kulainy, *Man la yahduruhu al-Faqih* of Shaikh Saduq, *Tahdhib al-Ahkam* of Shaikh Tusi, and *al-Istibsar* of Shaikh Tusi. The main Sunni jurists support defensive warfare as a way of requiring submission to God; Shiites validate offensive war when the authorities sanction it. Another recent school of thought, fundamentalism, harbors a more radical and progressively more violent vision of jihad.

In the traditional version of jihad, restrictions were placed on when and against whom jihad could be used. Qadi al-Numan, a 10th-century Muslim jurist, wrote a treatise titled *The Pillars of Islam.* In this work al-Numan argues for fighting in the name of God but only after the opponent has been given the opportunity to accept God and Muhammad as holy. The people on whom war was waged could not be forced to convert to Islam, but if they did not convert they were required to give the poll tax (*jizya*) readily and submissively. All texts were very specific that warriors not kill or mutilate children, elderly men, or women if they do not offer any resistance. The "People of the Book"—Christians, Zoroastrians, and Jews— were also required to pay jizya, as fighting them was unlawful due to their shared basic beliefs. Muslims were allowed to fight only those set against Islam; al-Mawardi, another Muslim jurist, writing in the 11th century described them as renegades, oppressors, or public offenders. Al-Farabi, a medieval Islamic philosopher, believed warfare fit into the overall concept of a well-ordered regime. The ability to wage war is one of the qualities of those fit to rule the virtuous city, and a moral ruler would avoid such violence.

The turning point of relations between the Islamic world and Western Europe occurred in 1798, when Napoleon and his army arrived in Egypt. Gradually, mystical brotherhoods in Algeria and Daghestan began to build an organization to stand up against the invading forces of the French. In response to the invaders, Islam and its role against outsiders were reevaluated in the 19th century. Some thinkers, like the reformer Sayyid Ahmad Khan, maintained that jihad was valid only in the case of outright oppression or the prevention of the practice of faith. Rashid Rida, a noted jurist, writing at the turn of the 19th century, condoned jihad if used as a tool to uphold the sharia (holy law) and to defend Islam against persecution with the support of a strong leader; he did not consider jihad legitimate if used only to convert others to Islam. In the 19th century, a body of juridical and apologetic work surfaced that redefined jihad as defensive warfare to control Arab modernity that had fallen behind in comparison to world development. This is a key purpose of the rebellion of many contemporary jihadists in the modern age.

In response, Sayyid Qutb, an educator and author, stirred up something close to his own revolution in the 1940s. In his book *Milestones*, Qutb argued that the modernization process stimulated an Islamic resurgence, which has both encouraged and opposed modernization. He supported freedom of religion, especially the dynamic message of Islam, and implementation of the sharia of God. This mission led to his instrumental role in the development of the secret Muslim Brothers, which became a major political force in the 1940s with its call for an Islamic order. They formed into an organization under the pressures of nationalist agitation, to defend Islam and the Brotherhood regardless of the national leadership. In 1949, six months of terror and tyranny at the hands of the Muslim Brothers came to a close with the assassination of Mahmud Fahmi al-Nuqrashi, the prime minister of Egypt.

In the 1970s, Muslim governments began downplaying religion to focus on nationalism and modernity. In reaction, an essentially defensive Islamic revival was kicked off against modernity, specifically applied to the "pollution" of sexually explicit references on television and radio. In 1979, activist militants called for the overthrow of the House of Saud in Saudi Arabia, denouncing the corruption of their government's "infidel" regime by the corrosive impact of the West, seeking a return to traditional Islam. The further Soviet occupation of Afghanistan provided a new enemy and mission, as the call for a jihad offered a shared Islamic religious identity and source of inspiration. In the Gulf War (1990–1991) American forces defended the House of Saud, forever turning the religious extremists against the new occupying force.

The rise of Osama bin Laden and al-Qaeda represent a watershed, due to their power and influence to effect the first Muslim attacks on American soil. Recent terrorists are able to skew the traditional Muslim tenets of jihad to legitimate terrorism, as many modern Arabs are uneducated with respect to various concepts contained in Islamic texts. Additionally, Taliban students have been influenced by the militant neo-Deobandi movement in Pakistan, transformed by the Jamiat Ulema-e-Islam (JUI), a religious party with a rigid, militant, anti-American, and anti–non-Muslim culture. The traditional Islamic belief in jihad as a defense of Islam and the Muslim community against aggression was transformed into a militant jihad culture and worldview that targets nonbelievers, including Muslims and non-Muslims alike.

These movements, which rise up in different locations, with diverse ideologies, agendas, and support bases, are becoming united in their struggle against governmental repression of even the most moderate Islamic states. Many of these groups have adopted principles and methods similar to the Taliban and al-Qaeda. This mindset spreads quickly, in part because local governments and the international community have largely failed to modernize and provide for the people, thus giving an incentive for some of them to become terrorists.

CONCLUSION

Today's global movements have strayed from the traditional interpretation of the Quran and have created their own path to redemption. They disregard the greater jihad of internal spiritual war advocated by Muhammad and instead implement the lesser jihad of violence as a complete political and social philosophy. The modernization of the Islamic world is needed to minimize the terrorist threat but may also be viewed as a primary reason why many Muslim nations are experiencing so much discontent and violence.

REFERENCES

Bonner, Michael. *Jihad in Islamic History*. Princeton, NJ: Princeton University Press, 2006.

Crone, Patricia. *Medieval Islamic Political Thought*. Edinburgh: Edinburgh University Press, 2005.

Deringil, Selim. *The Well-Protected Domains: Ideology and the Legitimation of Power in the Ottoman Empire 1876–1909*. New York: I. B. Tauris, 1999.

Esposito, John L. *Unholy War: Terror in the Name of Islam*. New York: Oxford University Press, 2002.

Johnson, James Turner, and John Kelsay, eds. *Cross, Crescent, and Sword: The Justification and Limitation of War in Western and Islamic Tradition*. New York: Greenwood, 1990.

Rashid, Ahmed. *Jihad: The Rise of Militant Islam in Central Asia*. New Haven, CT: Yale University Press, 2002.

Sivan, Emmanuel. *Radical Islam Medieval Theology and Modern Politics*. New Haven, CT: Yale University Press, 1985.

Global Terrorism: Post-9/11

Chamila S. Liyanage

A new manifestation of terrorism has taken root in the post–Cold War world. The impact of globalization, growing global interactions, the global economy, and communication networks have created unprecedented opportunities for civil society as well as international terrorists and criminals. During the 1990s and the first decade of the 21st century, global terrorism has been able to adapt and exploit the new global realities more rapidly than other major international actors such as nation-states and national and international statutory organizations. Radical Islam as well as other nefarious nonstate entities has benefited greatly from globalization.

CYBERSPACE

Jihadists use global networks as a means to reach their ends. Consequently, global terrorism is a highly adaptable, fluid, and dispersed phenomenon. It is based on loosely knit networks of cells and relies on readily available knowledge, technology, and information accessible through modern communication mediums.

Communication channels such as the worldwide web, web 2.0, mass media, and telecommunications are important tools utilized by the new global terrorism. Terrorist groups utilize these channels to spread propaganda and to recruit and instruct terrorists and those inclined to join such groups. The interactive worldwide web increases collaborative virtual spaces. Transnational terrorist organizations have penetrated these spaces to establish virtual gathering spaces where they can formulate strategy, share knowledge, and plan future actions. Terrorist organizations have adapted relatively easily to the virtual environment. Furthermore, less regulated national borders and the mass movement of people across these borders increase the ability of global terrorism to expand its operational capacity. Thus, terrorism has been able to proliferate by utilizing contemporary technological advancements.

The organizational structure of certain group's terrorism has undergone a profound change since the events of 9/11. The new terrorism has structurally adapted to better survive in continually changing contexts. Adaptability and agility are prerequisites for terrorist group survival in the era of transformation that began at the end of the Cold War. Increasingly open frontiers create a dynamically connected world; many people began to migrate across national boundaries. Subsequently, many countries provided fertile ground for terrorism, specifically states in Central, Southeast, and Southwest Asia. A state's relative inability to regulate national borders provides more autonomy and freedom for many diverse actors. Global developments are significant when one is trying to understand terrorist group capabilities in the 21st century.

CHARACTERISTICS OF TERRORISM

Terrorism has existed throughout history and has played an integral part in many forms of warfare. It gains an advantage by employing asymmetrical tactics such as targeting unarmed civilians and humanitarian agencies to create psychological trauma. Alex Schmid has referred to

Vladimir I. Lenin's maxim "The purpose of terrorism is to produce terror" (2005, 137), while John Horgan notes that "terrorism attempts to use the threat of violence to achieve an effect, which is political in context" (2005, 1). According to Walter Laqueur terrorism is the "substate application of violence or threatened violence intended to sow panic in a society" (1996, 24). These general characteristics of terrorism remain unchanged in the contemporary era, which is marked by rising Islamist fundamentalism. Additionally, current forms of terrorism are more lethal and intense than its previous manifestations. Global terrorism can also be identified as an empowered form of terrorism, and its ability to adapt globally creates crucial policy challenges for global counterterrorism efforts.

RADICAL ISLAM

Rising Islamist extremism is in many aspects the new face of terrorism. As a convenient modus operandi, a fundamentalist interpretation of Islam, a seventh-century monotheistic religion with more than one billion followers, is utilized by various extremist groups to provide justification for their violent acts. Extremist interpretations are further justified by centuries-old prejudices, the present conflicts in Afghanistan and Iraq, U.S. policies in the region, and the U.S.-initiated war on terrorism. Globalization and the information age have unsettled many Islamic religious tenets and have created hostility among many of its followers. The danger is that religion can provide, and often has provided, the cohesion and unity that terrorist organizations strive to achieve. As a result, the target population that post-9/11 global terrorism aims to exploit is the worldwide followers of Islam. The younger generation of Muslims is more vulnerable to indoctrination. Global terrorist organizations utilize the straightforward foundation that the religion provides to demarcate their followers. First, terrorist organizations are trying to communicate their radical message to a specific targeted population. This is relatively uncomplicated as they can easily use global communication networks. Second, they are trying to influence younger generations to establish networks and initiate a self-radicalization process. Terrorist organizations, specifically al-Qaeda, have been relatively successful in their global recruitment drives. It remains to be seen how the killing of Osama bin Laden by U.S. Joint Special Operations Forces and Central Intelligence Agency (CIA) operatives on May 1, 2011, will impact that organization. While democracies are battling terrorism in various places throughout the world, diaspora Muslim youths in Western industrialized democracies often create environments that global terrorism can silently penetrate. The homegrown terrorism phenomenon, which suddenly surfaced in the wake of the London bombings on July 7, 2005, continues to present policy challenges and security concerns for the West.

CHALLENGES OF COUNTERTERRORISM

The growing lethality of contemporary weapons and the increasing knowledge of and expertise in the production of chemical, biological, radiological, and nuclear (CBRN) weapons add a crucial dimension to the dangers of post-9/11 global terrorism. Groups such as al-Qaeda have sought such weapons, and if successful in this endeavor they would not hesitate to use them. Indeed, the chemical agent sarin was released in a subway in Tokyo, Japan, in 1995 by the apocalyptic group Aum Shinrikyo. The situation is challenging as states' ability to control globally oriented nonstate actors is declining. The rapid shift of scope from mainly national security considerations to global security threats produces a dilemma for the nation-state. Thus, terrorism using chemical, biological, radiological, and nuclear weapons inevitably demands more agile counterterrorism measures and out-of-the-box thinking regarding the direction and scope of future counterterrorism measures, initiatives, and policies.

The scope of terrorism is expanding, and hence counterterrorism must rise to the challenges posed by this amorphous and growing threat. Terrorism, as evidenced by recent developments, dynamically explores options and adapts in order to seize opportunities. Thus far, post-9/11 global terrorism finds its strength and fluidity through the evolving forces of contemporary history.

Nevertheless, while global terrorism is adaptive to contemporary structural dynamics, it contains crucial inconsistencies. Though globalization is an uneven process, it develops global perspectives. There are plenty of dogmas, divisions, and demarcations, but the post-9/11 world is not short of prospects to reclaim the universal values and common grounds that are more or less shared by many nations. The information age helps the process by delivering knowledge, understanding, and rationality. Global structural dynamics offer unifying as well as divisive factors.

Throughout history terrorism has exploited vulnerable communities and individuals to garner support for their perceived or genuine grievances. Terrorism has considerably less ability to penetrate knowledgeable, rational, and empowered individuals or communities than to exploit vulnerable individuals and masses. Furthermore, the current dynamics for more free and open societies in the Middle East and North Africa could hinder or enhance the wave of terrorism experienced in the past decade. At this point in time it remains an open question how these political dynamics will evolve. Therefore, the best countermeasures to combat global terrorism are empowered communities and innovative bottom-up approaches. Empowered communities can tackle terrorism from within, while states that are actively addressing the problem need to formulate alternative strategies that mitigate violence as a way to solve difficult global issues.

CONCLUSION

The era of globalization opens up unexplored potentials for knowledge, innovation, and growth. It is the ground that contemporary counterterrorism needs in order to evolve successfully. Most important, it is counterterrorism's ability to explore and push its own boundaries in order to find radical new measures that crucially defines the survival of global terrorism. Therefore, the contemporary era provides innumerable opportunities for innovative counterterrorism measures.

See also: **Volume 1, Part I:** Defining Terrorism: Issues and Problems; Definition and Dimensions of Counterterrorism; Concept of Islamist Jihad; Insurgent Terrorism; The Terrorist Threat in the 21st Century: A Global Security Problem; War on Terror. **Part III:** Identifying and Combating Sources of Terrorist Financing; Ideology That Spawns Islamist Militancy; Information Technologies to Combat Terrorism; Multidisciplinary Approach to Combating Terrorism; Organizational Resilience and Counterterrorism; Role of the International Community; Terrorism, Counterterrorism, and the Internet. **Part IV:** Eliminating Terrorist Support Networks; Global Initiative to Combat Nuclear Terrorism; United Nations Global Counterterrorism Strategy: Significance and Limitations

REFERENCES

Horgan, John. *The Psychology of Terrorism.* Abingdon, Oxon, UK: Routledge, 2005.
Laqueur, Walter. "Postmodern Terrorism." *Foreign Affairs* 75 (1996): 24–36.
Schmid, Alex. "Terrorism as Psychological Warfare." *Democracy and Security* 1 (2005): 137–46.

Insurgent Terrorism

John P. Sullivan

Insurgency and terrorism are two interrelated forms of political violence. Essentially, they are both means of influencing political processes. Both seek to change the political equation and employ instrumental and symbolic violence to varying degrees. The distinction between insurgency and terrorism is complex. No universal definition of the two varieties of political violence exists, and the distinction between the two has varied over time and according to the political influences of the analyst examining them.

INSURGENCY AND TERRORISM

Defining the problem or nature of the conflict is an essential element of solving what Boaz Ganor has called the "counter-terrorist puzzle." For

Ganor, international terrorism had crossed the Rubicon after the 9/11 attacks. Defining the problem and bridging interdisciplinary, ideological, bureaucratic, and regional (or national) perspectives are essential to crafting viable responses.

Insurgent terrorism can be seen through two lenses: one is the use of political violence to cause political or social change, and the other is the use of terrorism by insurgents as a tactical or strategic choice. In the first view, prevalent during the 1970s–1980s, insurgent terrorism is violence used by actors seeking to challenge or overthrow existing social or political structures. In this view, insurgent terrorists oppose established authority, such as a government or colonial or postcolonial occupation force. This could include both revolutionary and separatist terrorism, although some analysts preferred to narrow insurgent terrorism to the radical variety employed by revolutionary movements or terrorist bands like the Baader-Meinhof Group/Red Army Faction, Red Brigades, and so on. More recent views look at insurgent terrorism as the use of targeted attacks against civilians and military forces during an insurgency or global insurgent campaign.

Insurgent terrorism could simply be described as violence directed against public authorities for the purpose of bringing about radical political change. In this earlier view, as exemplified by Alex Schmid and Albert Jongman, insurgent terrorism was distinguished by the desire of the terrorists to forge a sense of identity to inspire action. Here, terrorism is a form of combat where random or symbolic victims are selectively targeted in an instrumental manner. The aim is to trigger chronic fear that amplifies the impact of a specific attack and draws attention to the terrorists' movement. Violence is directed against the class of person targeted and is intended to be outside the normative expectations of those attacked (and the broader audience they represent). Hence, an attack on civilians, or persons hors de combat, at an unexpected place—that is, off the battlefield— amplifies the impact of the attack, ensuring an audience for the group's cause and attracting support for their movement. Here, insurgent terrorism is a tool intended to yield multiple benefits. It could trigger negotiations for tactical and strategic gains and mobilize support for the group's demands, hastening acceptance of the group's political platform.

Schmid and Jongman saw insurgent terrorism as an indirect means of creating an attentive audience. The goals of this action were either to immobilize their adversary by creating fear or terror, thereby producing disorientation or compliance, or to mobilize secondary audiences. The secondary audiences could be targets of demands (i.e., governments) or targets of attention (i.e., public opinion). As such, insurgent terrorism seeks to become political theater driven by "propaganda of the deed." Attacks are instrumental and are intended to influence an audience (or multiple audiences). They are not (or not solely or primarily) means of retaliation or revenge.

In this formulation, insurgent terrorism is "symbolic politics" where terrorist attacks are inherently rational, political acts that seek to influence the political calculus. The terrorist attack relies on the media to spread and amplify its message. As Jorge Nef has stated (1986, 8), "A barbarous and dramatic deed, such as a hostage-taking, or a skyjacking, is ideal media fodder. So is the attempt at a rescue. They will both make the 6 o'clock news. The multiplier takes effect: acts—news—response—more news; a ripple with an ever-widening audience." Here we see insurgent terrorism as more than brutality, posturing, and theatrics. The attack or act of kidnapping or hostage taking is, rather, a core element of a subtle political process. According to Nef (1986, 8), "In its basic sense, terrorism is the management, or politics, of scare-mongering. Its logic is fairly simple. It aims to create obedience (or disobedience) by profoundly altering the political frame of reference and circumstances of human behaviour through acute fear and uncertainty."

Nef noted that terrorism is deeply linked to psychological warfare or what we now call "information operations." In this formulation, all terrorist acts are "staged" for maximum impact. In his view, "Doing the unthinkable, committing especially callous and immoral acts, is oriented to achieve maximum effect: 'more bang for the buck'. There is always an enormous discrepancy between the actual military damage resulting from a terrorist outrage and its wider psychological effects. In fact, most victims are non-combatants symbolically associated with an 'adversary out there' " (1986, 9). The goal is to undermine the legitimacy and credibility of the established political order or a specific regime through the manipulation of fear and uncertainty.

Nef observed that insurgent terrorism's revolutionary variant is rarely successful. He notes that not a single instance of insurgent terrorism has stimulated social revolution. On the contrary, the opposite is often the result. Insurgent terrorism has historically triggered a backlash, increased government repression, and security measures. Nevertheless, insurgent terrorism is attractive to some of those outside the established circles of power. In Nef's formulation, "Terrorism is inherently political. It is about power—the influence over the actions of individuals and groups within a given system of rules. However, by altering these rules through violent, disorienting behaviour, terrorists force their targets to operate within a radically altered environment. This constitutes a more pervasive form of power, what some analysts call metapower—the ability to manipulate an outcome in the power game by altering the very language of politics" (1986, 9).

Prior to the 1970s and the rise of social/revolutionary terrorism, terrorism was largely viewed as a tactic used within insurgencies. Thus, *terrorists* was a term used to delegitimize the participants in localized/separatist or anticolonial insurgencies or "wars of national liberation." This formulation was seen in the British use of the term *terrorists* to describe guerrillas operating in Northern Ireland, Malaya, and Cyprus. The rise in the 1970s of international revolutionary movements characterized by "disembodied" small cells of alienated individuals without broad, popular support (such as the Baader-Meinhof Group/Red Army Faction in Germany, the Red Brigades in Italy, and the Japanese Red Army) led to a separation of terrorism and insurgency in public and academic discourse. Insurgent terrorism became a goal of the social revolutionary, but the phenomenon was separated from mass movements and public grievances. The 9/11 attacks once again changed the formulation and reconnected the links between terrorism and insurgency.

The concept of insurgent terrorism in the post-9/11 era is focused not only as a lens for understanding and addressing criminal, ideology-based social revolutionaries but once again as a means for addressing insurgents that employ terrorism in insurgencies with (potential or actual) mass support. From a counterterrorism perspective, this broadens the response from a primarily police and law enforcement focus to a whole-of-government approach. On the face of it, views of terrorism and insurgency have come full circle.

COUNTERINSURGENCY AND GLOBAL JIHAD

The counterinsurgency (COIN) view of terrorism-insurgency interaction makes responding to insurgent terrorism a strategic imperative. Terrorist attacks are no longer solely tactical events aimed at shaping perceptions and strengthening vague social/revolutionary movements; they are potentially strategic events influencing a broader global political architecture and the relations within, among, and between states. The 9/11 attacks brought to light a globally integrated movement—*Salafist Jihadis*—that seeks to serve as the vanguard for a global caliphate. This movement, exemplified by al-Qaeda and its affiliates, is multinational in scope, has religious as well as social imperatives, and seeks to operate as a global insurgency.

In the view of David Kilcullen the contemporary security environment embodied by the global jihad can be viewed in four conceptual models: (1) a backlash against globalization, (2) a globalized insurgency, (3) a civil war within Islam, and (4) asymmetrical warfare. These views are neither exhaustive nor mutually exclusive. Indeed, they only overtly describe one threat stream within contemporary terrorist and insurgent threats. Nevertheless, they accurately describe a significant component of the new insurgent terrorism. These models together describe the complexity of terrorism within the broader context of insurgency. Here the current thrust is to use terrorism as an insurgent tactic and to stimulate mass revolt or social (and religious) change through tactical use of terrorist violence to stimulate strategic ends. In this postmodern formulation, insurgent terrorism remains a form of combat: one that embraces the targeting of civilians, indiscriminate attacks, hostage taking, and perfidy.

CONCLUSION

While *insurgent terrorism*, like *terrorism* itself, does not have a recognized and agreed legal meaning, it is a feature of contemporary conflict. It has both descriptive and normative implications, especially considering the systematic, organized use of violence directed against civilians to influence political outcomes. Here both views of insurgent terrorism are in sync.

See also: **Volume 1, Part I:** Global Terrorism: Post-9/11; The Terrorist Threat in the 21st Century: A Global Security Problem; War on Terror. **Part III:** Safe Havens and Weak and Failing States; Terrorists, Criminals, and Drug Cartels. **Part IV:** Eliminating Terrorist Support Networks; Lessons of Afghanistan and Iraq; Pakistan's Federally Administered Tribal Areas (FATA). **Part VI:** Global Jihad Movement; Sun Tzu's *Art of War:* Lessons for 21st-Century Counterterrorism Practitioners

REFERENCES

Ganor, Boaz. *The Counter-terrorism Puzzle: A Guide for Decision Makers.* New Brunswick, NJ: Transaction, 2005.

Kilcullen, David. *The Accidental Guerilla: Fighting Small Wars in the Midst of a Big One.* New York: Oxford University Press, 2009.

Kilcullen, David. *Counterinsurgency.* New York: Oxford University Press, 2010.

Nef, Jorge. "Symbolic Politics." *New Internationalist,* no. 161 (July 1986): 8–9. http://www.newint.org/features/1986/07/05/symbolic/.

Schmid, Alex P., and Albert L. Jongman. *Political Terrorism: A New Guide to Actors, Authors, Concepts, Data Bases, Theories, and Literature,* 2nd ed. New Brunswick, NJ: Transaction, 2005.

The Terrorist Threat in the 21st Century: A Global Security Problem

Philip C. Aka

Terrorism has been defined as "any action . . . intended to cause death or serious bodily harm to civilians or non-combatants, when the purpose of such act, by its nature or context, is to intimidate a population, or to compel a Government or an international organization to do or to abstain from doing any act" (United Nations High-Level Panel on Threats, Challenges, and Change [UN Panel] 2004, 52). September 11, 2001, marked a watershed in our understanding of the relationship, or lack thereof, between terrorism and global security. Before 9/11, terrorism used to be a second-order foreign policy issue whose connection to global security few people dwelled on. That orientation changed after 9/11 when terrorism was catapulted to the top of the global agenda, as well as in U.S. national security doctrine.

TERRORISM AND GLOBAL SECURITY

Terrorism impairs global security. The United Nations High-Level Panel on Threats, Challenges, and Change, set up by then UN secretary-general Kofi Annan to assess global threats to international peace and security and advise him on collective action to address those challenges, reached this conclusion. Its report assessed that "terrorism attacks the values that lie at the heart of the Charter of the United Nations: respect for human rights; the rule of law; rules of war that protect civilians; tolerance among peoples and nations; and the peaceful resolution of conflict" (UN Panel 2004, 47). The panel comprised 16 eminent and experienced persons drawn from different parts of the world, including Brent Scowcroft of the United States, a distinguished military officer and former national security adviser.

The conclusion of the high-level panel deserves careful analysis. Terrorism poses both objective (material) and subjective threats to global security. Beginning with the objective threats, although states do *not* today face the "mutual assured destruction" they were exposed to during the Cold War era, nevertheless the threat arising from terrorist acts remains substantial. The costs in human lives (nearly 3,000 persons killed) and infrastructure (amounting to billions of U.S. dollars) that accompanied the attacks against the United States on September 11, 2001, are a testament to this position. The scale in costs and lethality could go higher if terrorists have access to weapons of mass destruction (WMD) that they then use in their operations. The UN panel probably had this threat in mind when it identified the "mass casualties" caused by terrorists among the "new dynamics" that lend urgency today to the terrorist threat.

The subjective threat terrorism poses to global security is no less worrisome than the objective threat. The threat may be divided into impacts on the general public and effects on governments. In essence, what makes terrorism a potent threat for ordinary citizens is the uncertainty arising from the unpredictable nature of the phenomenon. Terrorism often targets civilians going about their daily business, and the time, place, and identity of the terrorist present victims with a gratuitous surprise. Even seemingly minor acts of terrorism constantly draw to mind the public's vulnerability. Such reminders are not painless, given that even threats by themselves carry weight. Unlike the far-fetched threat of nuclear attack that characterized the Cold War, the threat of a terrorist attack is real, particularly for residents of Western societies used to the relative stability these societies afford, compared to denizens of many developing countries. Through their framing of terrorism, the modern media, especially television, amplify the perception of risk and nurture sensitivity to the threat. Through instantaneous coverage, they can also make the audience for terrorism global and make it difficult for persons to escape the awareness of danger.

Similarly, terrorism poses a threat to governments because, if nothing else, it can impair the security of their territories and populations. Compared to previous waves of terrorism (involving nationalists, revolutionaries, and right-wing extremists), the threat of contemporary terrorism has a longer territorial reach in various aspects, including diversity of attack location, plot sites, and the nationalities of the terrorists. Contributing to this reach factor is the fact that the threat could be both domestic and international. The horror of the 9/11 attacks permanently altered expectations of what terrorists could accomplish as well as creating widespread fear that al-Qaeda and its affiliates, who executed the 9/11 attacks, would acquire WMD that they could use for more catastrophic operations. Lastly, as the U.S. experience bears out, a country could view a terrorist attack against it as an attack on its identity (rather than its interests) and one designed by the perpetrators to undermine values reflective of that identity—in the case of the United States, as a threat to democracy, freedom, and toleration. It was a position decipherable in the refrain of the U.S. government, rightly or wrongly, that the terrorists hated Americans because of who they were.

NEW TERRORISM

Since the 1990s, the principal driving force behind terrorism worldwide has been al-Qaeda and its affiliates, offshoots, imitators, and sympathizers. Together, these groups constitute the *jihadi* (or "holy war") movement. Its leaders included Osama bin Laden, a wealthy Saudi Arabian agitator, who helped fund the organization and mobilized recruits from the Muslim world. Bin Laden was killed by U.S. forces in Abbottabad, Pakistan, on May 1, 2011. His second in command, Ayman al-Zawahiri, has since assumed leadership of the organization. The movement is mainly antidemocratic, intolerant of opposing viewpoints (including those of certain Muslims), and vehemently anti-Western, anti-American, and anti-Israeli. It perceives U.S. and Western influence as a threat to Islam and strives to diminish that influence. Its other goals include a campaign for a return to a purer form of Islam that would restore the Muslim community, supposedly now damaged by U.S. domination, to greatness. Assessment of this group as active worldwide is based on attacks that the movement has conducted in a variety of countries since 9/11, including (alphabetically) Afghanistan, Egypt, Great Britain, Indonesia, Iraq, Jordan, Kenya, Morocco, Pakistan, Saudi Arabia, Spain, Tunisia, and Turkey.

However, al-Qaeda is not the only terrorist group, whether based domestically or internationally, that threatens global security in the 21st century.

Others include the Revolutionary Armed Forces of Colombia (FARC), Hezbollah, and Hamas, among others. Also, although terrorism is considered primarily the province of nonstate actors, governments can passively or actively support them and occasionally sponsor terrorism directly through official agents. State actors accused of supporting or sponsoring terrorism include Pakistan (over the region of Kashmir), as well as Iran and Syria, alleged to be assisting al-Qaeda and Hamas. Finally, the current "jihadist" terrorism, represented by al-Qaeda and its affiliates, is differentiable from the "old" terrorism of nationalists, revolutionaries, and right-wing extremists. Despite this distinction, scholars such as Martha Crenshaw maintain that the fundamental process of terrorism has not changed. She notes that although today's jihadist terrorism varies from terrorism in the past along the three dimensions of goals, methods, and forms of organization, the main difference is one of degree rather than kind.

The definition that starts this entry is not a universally accepted definition of terrorism. No such universally accepted definition exists. Instead, different legal systems define terrorism differently. The definition cited earlier is the one recommended by the UN panel set up by then secretary-general Kofi Annan. The lack of a comprehensive definition for terrorism does not come from a lack of trying. Actually, there have been two such attempts. The first, the Convention for the Prevention and Punishment of Terrorism, proposed by the League of Nations in 1937, never entered into force. The second, a proposed Comprehensive Convention on International Terrorism, has been under negotiations since 2000. A major reason impeding consensus on a generally accepted definition of terrorism is the politically and emotionally charged nature of the term, evident in the saying that "one person's terrorist can be another person's freedom fighter." The UN panel sought to override the disagreement by concluding that terrorism is never acceptable, no matter how legitimate or popular the cause it purports to serve. The panel's suggested definition includes two other elements that I discuss next: (1) the existing conventions on aspects of terrorism, and (2) UN Security Council Resolution 1566 (2004).

UN CONVENTIONS AND UN SECURITY COUNCIL RESOLUTION 1566

The existing conventions on aspects of terrorism refer to the 13 sectoral multilateral treaties on counterterrorism that, in the absence of a comprehensive treaty on the topic, the UN and affiliated agencies developed in the period from 1961 to 2005. These treaties define and criminalize particular categories of terrorist activities; they focus on the wrongful nature of terrorist activities rather than on their intent. They are as follows:

1. Vienna Convention on Diplomatic Relations (1961)
2. Vienna Convention on Consular Relations (1963)

3. Convention on Offences and Certain Other Acts Committed On Board Aircraft (1963)

4. Convention for the Suppression of Unlawful Seizure of Aircraft (1970)

5. Convention for the Suppression of Unlawful Acts against the Safety of Civil Aviation (1971)

6. Convention on the Physical Protection of Nuclear Material (1979)

7. Protocol for the Suppression of Unlawful Acts of Violence at Airports Serving International Civil Aviation (1988)

8. Convention for the Suppression of Unlawful Acts against the Safety of Maritime Navigation (1988)

9. Protocol for the Suppression of Unlawful Acts against the Safety of Fixed Platforms Located on the Continental Shelf (1988)

10. Convention on the Marking of Plastic Explosives for the Purpose of Identification (1991)

11. International Convention for the Suppression of Terrorist Bombings (1997)

12. International Convention for the Suppression of the Financing of Terrorism (1999)

13. International Convention for the Suppression of Acts of Nuclear Terrorism (2005)

In its Resolution 1566, unanimously adopted on October 8, 2004, the UN Security Council noted that "acts of terrorism seriously impair the enjoyment of human rights and threaten the social and economic development of all States and undermine global stability and prosperity." Therefore, "terrorism in all its forms and manifestations constitutes one of the most serious threats to peace and security." Acts of terrorism that target civilians are not justifiable under any circumstances. Resolution 1566 called on states to prosecute or extradite for prosecution anyone who aided and abetted terrorists. Yet states "must ensure that any measures taken to combat terrorism comply with all their obligations under international law, and should adopt such measures in accordance with international law in particular international human rights, refugee, and humanitarian law" (UN Security Council Resolution 1566). A stream of terrorist strikes, additional to the 9/11 attacks against the United States, gave impetus to this resolution. One of these attacks occurred in Besian, Ossetia, in which hundreds of students and their teachers were killed by Chechen separatists who held them hostage in a school.

In its own way, each of the preceding materials—the work of the high-level panel, UN Security Council Resolution 1566, and even the 13 existing conventions on various aspects of terrorism—contributes importantly to the search for a commonly accepted definition of terrorism. To this range of materials should be added the series of resolutions on the topic by the UN Security Council and the strings of regional conventions, such as those of Africa, Asia, the Commonwealth of Independent States, the European Union, the League of Arab States, and the Organization of

American States. It should also include antiterrorist laws passed by numerous countries.

UNIVERSAL DEFINITION

A final addition to the list in the movement for a comprehensive definition of terrorism is former UN secretary-general Kofi Annan's contribution, from a keynote address at the International Summit on Democracy, Terrorism, and Security in March 2005 in Madrid, Spain. Annan highlighted the main elements of a "principled, comprehensive strategy" for combating terrorism. They are the five Ds: (1) dissuading disaffected groups from choosing terrorism as a means for achieving whatever goals they seek to achieve, (2) denying terrorists the means to carry out their attacks, (3) deterring states from supporting terrorists, (4) developing the capacity of states to prevent terrorism, and (5) defending human rights in the struggle against terrorism. For the first D, all possible moral and political authorities must clearly state that terrorism is unacceptable under any circumstance and in any culture. For him, this means that none of the old arguments impeding a universal definition makes sense. The work of the UN panel indicates that, under the rules of international law, states may not deliberately use their armed forces against civilians, and the right to resist occupation, in its true meaning, cannot include the right to deliberately kill or maim civilians. Turning to the second D, this can be accomplished by making it difficult for terrorists to travel, receive financial support or launder money, or acquire weapons of mass destruction (like nuclear or radiological materials). For the third D, the Security Council has repeatedly used sanctions for states that support or sponsor terrorists, but this tool could be strengthened to include even coercive measures. The fourth D, making states more capable and responsible to prevent terrorism, could be achieved through promoting good governance, particularly the rule of law, including the establishment of professional police and security forces who respect human rights. For poor countries unable to build the capacity they need, the UN will provide technical assistance. It will also help provide education that will make it difficult for terrorist groups to recruit society's most vulnerable people. On the last D, Annan stated that compromising human rights cannot serve the struggle against terrorism.

CONCLUSION

Restricting human rights in order to combat terrorism facilitates achievement of the terrorist's objective by ceding to the terrorist the moral high ground and provoking tension, hatred, and mistrust of government in those parts of the population where the terrorist is most likely to find recruits. Annan is convinced that upholding human rights is an essential element of a successful counterterrorism strategy.

See also: **Volume 1, Part I:** Defining Terrorism: Issues and Problems; Global Terrorism: Post-9/11; War on Terror. **Part III:** Countering WMD Terrorism; Identifying and Combating Sources of Terrorist Financing; International Law, Human Rights, and Counterterrorism; Multidisciplinary Approach to Combating Terrorism; Threat Perception and Multinational Cooperation. **Part IV:** International Legal Framework to Eliminate Terrorism against Civil Aviation and Maritime Targets; United Nations Global Counterterrorism Strategy: Significance and Limitations; United Nations Security Council Resolution 1540. **Part VI:** Multilateral Approach to Counterterrorism: Issues, Problems, Responses; Preemptive Counterterrorism: The Need for a Global Integrated Approach; Threat Convergence

REFERENCES

Annan, K. Keynote address to the Closing Plenary of the International Summit on Democracy, Terrorism, and Security, Madrid, Spain, March 10, 2005. http://www.un.org/News/ossg/sg/stories/statements_search_full.asp?statID=16.

Crenshaw, M., ed. *The Consequences of Counterterrorism.* New York: Russell Sage Foundation, 2010.

Crenshaw, M. *Explaining Terrorism: Causes, Processes, and Consequences.* New York: Routledge, 2010.

Crenshaw, M. "Terrorism and Global Security." Stanford Alumni Association, June 14, 2006. http://www.stanfordalumni.org/leadingmatters/pdf/terrorism_global_security.pdf.

Imre, Robert, T. Brian Mooney, and B. Clark. *Responding to Terrorism: Political, Philosophical, and Legal Perspectives.* Burlington, VT: Ashgate, 2008.

Laqueur, Walter. *The New Terrorism: Fanaticism and the Arms of Mass Destruction.* New York: Oxford University Press, 1999.

Nesi, Giuseppe, ed. *International Cooperation in Counter-terrorism: The United Nations and Regional Organizations in the Fight against Terrorism.* Burlington, VT: Ashgate, 2006.

United Nations High-Level Panel on Threats, Challenges, and Change. *A More Secure World: Our Shared Responsibility.* New York: United Nations, 2004. http://www.un.org/secureworld/report2.pdf.

United Nations Security Council. Resolution 1566 (2004). http://www.mideastweb.org/1566.htm.

War on Terror

Philip C. Aka

Few events in recent U.S. history have had as much influence on the country's domestic and foreign affairs as the campaign dubbed, colloquially or literally, the war on terror. The "war" signifies the U.S. government's boldest attempt in the 21st century to tackle the problem of domestic and international terrorism. It is also, as it has shaped up, a challenging experience. Although it benefited him politically with a second term in office, the campaign marred the presidency of George W. Bush and could cast a shadow over the tenure of Bush's successor, Barack Obama, if he fails to keep his promises, made when he ran for president, to redress the fallout from the "war." The campaign's conduct made a mockery of the country's famed distinctive socioeconomic human rights culture. The war on terror also put a question mark on the country's presumed strength in political and civil rights. Finally, judging by its noncompliance with the Geneva Conventions and hostility toward the International Criminal Court, the campaign also exposed the U.S. government's infidelity to international law.

POST-9/11

The war on terror originated as a response to the terrorist attacks of September 11, 2001. This was the day that 19 Middle Eastern nationals, affiliated with al-Qaeda, hijacked several commercial U.S. airliners and then crashed them into symbols of U.S. military-political and economic might. Two of the targets hit were the Pentagon building in Arlington, Virginia, near the seat of the U.S. government in Washington, D.C., and the World Trade Center twin towers in New York City. A fourth airliner crashed in Pennsylvania when several passengers attacked the terrorists manning the cockpit.

Founded toward the end of the Soviet-Afghan war (1988–1989), al-Qaeda (Arabic for "the base") is a Muslim organization committed to a global jihad, or "holy war," against presumed enemies of Islam. Prior to his death at the hands of U.S. forces in May 2011 the group was led by Osama bin Laden, a Saudi national, who used his vast personal wealth to finance it. For several years before the attacks, bin Laden vociferously objected to U.S. policy in the Middle East, which he and many Arabs perceived as favoring Israel, to the detriment of Arabs. He also bitterly opposed the continued presence of U.S. troops in Saudi Arabia after the U.S.-Iraqi war of 1991. Driven from Saudi Arabia for his extremism, bin Laden initially found refuge in Sudan and later in Afghanistan among the Taliban, an Islamist militia group, which allowed him and al-Qaeda to use their country as a base for the recruitment and training of terrorists.

The set of coordinated attacks on September 11, 2011, produced the dramatic effect its sponsors craved; it claimed the lives of nearly 3,000 civilians and inflicted damages running into billions of dollars that impaired the health of the U.S. economy at least in the short term. The attacks had many life-changing effects on U.S. residents, including the way they travel and the general management of their personal safety. Coming in the wake of the Oklahoma City bombing disaster of April 19, 1995, the attacks erased any doubts that terrorist activities could occur on U.S.

soil. As the first successful attack inside the country by a foreign group since the Japanese attack on Pearl Harbor on December 7, 1941, the attacks confirmed the United States' vulnerability to attacks by a determined group of extremists outside its borders. During the Cold War between the United States and the former Soviet Union, Americans contemplated and prepared for the eventuality of a deadly attack within U.S. borders by outside forces propagating a different political and economic system. Now, in the euphoric aftermath of that ideological competition, the country had been hit by vicious attacks that, thanks to the emergence of cable television, were broadcast and watched across the globe, at the very moment that those attacks were taking place.

As with the invasion of Pearl Harbor, the 9/11 attacks spawned another U.S. war. However, the situations are starkly different. In World War II, the enemy was a nation-state with easily identifiable standing armies, whereas the enemy in the present conflict is a nonstate entity employing asymmetrical tactics. World War II had a marked endpoint after which hostilities ceased and rebuilding occurred, whereas the current conflict in Afghanistan seems to drag on indefinitely with no clear end in sight. Finally, unlike a conventional war, this is a "war" that, to be won, must be waged through a variety of instruments that, in addition to military force, include intelligence gathering, law enforcement, foreign aid, international cooperation, and immigration control. The war on terror calls to mind the propensity of the U.S. government going back to the 1960s and the days of the Great Society to target a national problem, whether poverty or addiction, by declaring "war" on that problem.

Now approaching its 11th anniversary, the war on terror is being waged on several fronts. One of these is the USA PATRIOT Act of 2001. The acronym stands for Uniting and Strengthening America by Providing Appropriate Tools Required to Intercept and Obstruct Terrorism. The law overturned many of the counterintelligence program (COINTELPRO) reforms some U.S. officials blamed for the intelligence failures that preceded 9/11. COINTELPRO refers to the Federal Bureau of Investigation's (FBI) counterintelligence program, which dates from the era of the civil rights movement and was designed to disrupt civil rights advocates, including opponents of the Vietnam War. The USA PATRIOT Act allowed greater sharing of intelligence information and broadened the ability of law enforcement personnel to tap telephone and e-mail communications. It is underscored by other institutional changes, among them the first major reorganization of the U.S. national security bureaucracy since the formation of the Department of Defense in 1947, signified by the creation of the Department of Homeland Security in 2003. One of the larger objectives of this law and other regulations patterned after it, such as the United Nations antiterrorism instruments, is to cut off the financial lifeline that nurtures and maintains terrorist networks.

INTERNATIONAL EFFORT

Another battlefront in the war on terror is the U.S. invasion and occupation of Afghanistan on October 7, 2001, which overthrew the Taliban regime that was harboring Osama bin Laden and al-Qaeda. A third battlefront is Iraq, which the United States invaded in March 2003. Like in Afghanistan, the United States overthrew the Iraqi leadership, headed by the brutal dictator Saddam Hussein. The invasion and subsequent occupation of Iraq marked an expanded—and controversial phase—in the war on terror. The Bush administration found justification for this invasion in the allegation that the Iraqi leadership possessed and was engaged in the production of biological and chemical weapons, which the U.S. government feared could end up in the hands of terrorists, who could in turn use such weapons to attack Americans. Following a diligent search, facilitated by the U.S. occupation of the country, no such weapons were found. Serious questions arose regarding the earmarking of Iraq, to use the language of President Bush, as a "central front" in the war on terror. This severely undermined the legitimacy of the U.S. campaign against terror. This was particularly true in Great Britain where former prime minister Tony Blair, a key Bush ally, was forced out of office by the leaders of his own Labor Party over his policy on Iraq.

OCCUPATION OF AFGHANISTAN AND IRAQ

In Afghanistan and Iraq, the U.S. government had a difficult time maintaining stability, much less accomplishing its touted goal of building democracy. In both countries, even those individuals who initially welcomed U.S. intervention resented occupation. The resistances took their toll on American and allied troops and drew criticism at home with respect to U.S. objectives in these two countries. With U.S. military power focused on two countries simultaneously, al-Qaeda and its sympathizers globalized their attacks, indiscriminately hitting targets in Europe and Asia, including Britain, Indonesia, Spain, and Yemen, and even in the United States, where as recently as Christmas 2009, a man linked to al-Qaeda tried unsuccessfully to blow up an airplane over Detroit with chemicals hidden in his underwear.

Some of the major dilemmas impacting the war on terror arose from the appellation of "war" tagged to the campaign. The appellation sent a clear message regarding the United States' resolve to confront the scourge of terrorism and the priority that it assigned the problem. But denominating the campaign a "war" meant that the United States had to comply with rules on war in the U.S. Constitution and relevant laws. These include treaties, such as the Geneva Conventions, that the United States is party to. The treaties mandate that state parties treat captured prisoners humanely and set them free at the end of hostilities.

Additionally, the campaign against terror sired many ugly monuments. One obvious one is the detention center at the U.S. naval base at Guantánamo Bay in Cuba, which houses numerous individuals suspected of terrorism. The United Nations assessed the facility as a torture center and recommended it be closed. During his campaign for president, Obama promised to close the facility but has yet to fully implement this option since he took office. Other dubious monuments include prisoner abuse scandals, such as the one that broke out at the detention center in Abu Ghraib in Iraq; a warped definition of *torture* that allowed techniques like waterboarding; and the practice of extraordinary rendition (transfer of prisoners to third-party states where they are tortured), among others. To avert the possibility of U.S. troops being called to account for offenses committed during the war on terror, President Bush strongly opposed U.S. membership in the International Criminal Court, even though U.S. officials participated strongly in the negotiations leading to the establishment of the court. The situation has not changed under President Obama. However, Obama has wound down the U.S. occupation in Iraq while still maintaining high troop levels in Afghanistan.

The United States–led war on terror morphed into an international campaign that the United States could have benefited from but did not for two reasons. The first, as already indicated, was the unwillingness of the U.S. government, under former president Bush, to conduct its "war" consistent with the strictures of the Geneva Conventions. The second was the decision of the U.S. government to go it alone rather than forge an international coalition, under the United Nations, as the United States did in the first Gulf War in 1990. While maintaining some of the Bush-era policies, Obama has also staked his own unique path in the war on terror. This distinctiveness is evident in his insistence on conducting an antiterrorism campaign bound by the rule of law.

CONCLUSION

Specifically, Obama pledges to conduct a campaign against terrorism that seeks a balance between liberty and security, premised on the argument that, in the fight against terrorism, Americans can have both, rather than sacrifice liberty on the altar of security. The practical effect of this new policy is to minimize the importance of the "war" component in the campaign. In his pronouncements, including, importantly, the speech he gave in Cairo, Egypt, soon after taking office, the president has made it clear that the U.S. campaign against terror is against terrorists who killed U.S. residents on American soil on 9/11, rather than a war against Islam.

See also: **Volume 1, Part I:** Defining the Enemy; Global Terrorism: Post-9/11; The Terrorist Threat in the 21st Century: A Global Security Problem. **Part III:** Defensive Measures against Terrorism: Military Preemption and Retaliation; Just War

Doctrine; Military Force: Effective against Terrorists?; Preemption: Moral and Ethical Considerations. **Part IV:** Eliminating Terrorist Support Networks; Lessons of Afghanistan and Iraq. **Part VI:** Afghanistan: Present and Future Challenges; Sun Tzu's *Art of War:* Lessons for 21st-Century Counterterrorism Practitioners

REFERENCES

Aka, Philip C. "Analyzing U.S. Commitment to Socioeconomic Human Rights." *Akron Law Review* 39 (2006): 417–63.

Baker, Peter. "Obama's War over Terror." *New York Times,* January 17, 2010. http://www.nytimes.com/2010/01/17/magazine/17Terror-t.html?page wanted=all.

Clarke, Richard A. *Against All Enemies: Inside America's War on Terror.* New York: Free Press, 2004.

Danner, Mark. *Torture and Truth: America, Abu Ghraib, and the War on Terror.* New York: New York Review Books, 2004.

Hoge, James F., and Gideon Rose, eds. *Understanding the War on Terror.* New York: Foreign Affairs, 2005.

Woodward, Bob. *Plan of Attack.* New York: Simon & Schuster, 2004.

Woodward, Bob. *Obama's War.* New York: Simon & Schuster, 2010.

II

Historical Look at the Evolution and Effectiveness of State Counterterrorism Strategies: Laws, Policies, and Operational Tactics Post-1945

Algeria

Taibi Ghomari

The September 11, 2001, tragedy was a significant event for Algerians, not only because the disaster was of such great magnitude but also because on that day the most powerful global states became aware of the imminent threat of terrorism to international peace and security. During the 1990s Algerians were victims of both terrorism and world isolation.

ALGERIAN WAR ON TERROR

The Algerian war on terror began in 1991 as a reaction to terrorist attacks against the National Popular Army soldiers in Guemmar (El Oued in southeastern Algeria). It was a difficult war because of two primary factors: The first was religious. When terrorists use religious discourse to justify their actions, they present themselves as defenders of Islam. This makes for a very dangerous adversary. On the other hand, the government faced a very difficult situation, that is, convincing society that this war was unholy. Algerian terrorists were supported for more than 10 years by the tenets of Salafism, a radical form of Islam. At the outset of the conflict well-known Saudi imams assisted the Algerian terrorists by issuing fatwas (religious rulings) that legitimatized their acts. The events of September 11, 2001, helped the Algerian government in its policies toward combating domestic terrorism.

The second element was political. Initially, Algeria's approach to domestic terrorism was rejected by much of the international community since it was viewed as antidemocratic and infringed on human rights. Hence, in many respects the Algerian government was isolated by the international community. However, the events of September 11 and the subsequent actions taken by the world's most powerful Western countries (e.g., the USA PATRIOT Act, the United Kingdom's Anti-terrorism, Crime and Security Act, and France and Germany's antiterrorism legislation) strengthened and justified Algeria's resolve in its efforts to fight domestic extremism. According to certain experts, provisions in some of the laws of the Western nations represent an extensive attack on fundamental democratic rights. Some of the initiatives adopted by various states were more severe than what Algeria had experienced during more than 10 years of war against terrorists, and thus counterterrorism actions taken by the major powers provided the Algerian government with an aura of legitimacy in its attempts to combat internal violence and terrorism. The following government actions define Algeria's counterterrorism policy: military operations, political decisions, and social actions.

MILITARY OPERATIONS

Algeria experienced its first terrorist attack while under martial law (military rule), decreed after the civil rebellion by the Islamic Salvation Front (Front Islamique du Salut) in the summer of 1991. By instituting martial law the army became directly responsible for state security and administration.

To give legitimacy to this repressive action the government declared a state of emergency on February 9, 1992. The United Nations was informed of this impending action on February 2, 1992. On the battlefield, other actions became necessary. For example, civilians were disarmed. The majority of Algerian adults owned sporting guns used for hunting. When terrorist groups were formed they armed themselves by modifying these types of firearms into deadlier weapons that would better serve their hostile intentions. To counteract this situation, the government began disarming all civilians. These confiscated weapons were reregistered and stocked in civilian and military police offices and stations.

The disarmament operation caused the civilian population, especially those living in remote areas, to become easy targets for terrorist organizations, mainly the Armed Islamic Group (GIA). This action also increased the government's responsibilities toward its citizens. To honor these obligations and protect the population, the government created new military and paramilitary forces. The Communal Guard, a government-backed security force, was implemented in small villages and rural areas, and its members were generally assisted by soldiers of the National Popular Army. The Patriots paramilitary forces were comprised of living members of the former National Liberation Army, who fought against French colonization. These individuals were experienced in guerrilla tactics and warfare. These paramilitaries provided assistance to government forces in forests and mountainous areas.

Another paramilitary group, the Auto Defense Groups, is comprised of citizen volunteers who are commanded by military officers. Their primary purpose is the protection of villages and surrounding populated areas. Following the September 11, 2001, attacks on the United States, the government reissued previously confiscated weapons to the civilian volunteers in order to arm and empower the Auto Defense Groups.

In addition to these new forces there was the official army, the gendarmerie, and the police. In order to coordinate operations between all of these forces, the government created what was called the "combined forces," formed from the forces already mentioned and commanded by a military officer. The combined forces were mobilized for a specific operation, that is, fighting terrorists, and when this objective was met, each unit returned to its respective base. In order to protect the population, the government secured remote regions by deploying permanent military forces in forests and rural areas. This strategy helped to secure local areas and slowed down the movement of the terrorists, thereby making their efforts less successful.

POLITICAL DECISIONS

The main political action adopted by the government to support the military actions was the amendment of the constitution in 1996. This reform banned all Islam-based political parties and revised the fundamental laws for state political parties. Islam could no longer be used for political purposes. As a result, all existing and legal "Islamic" parties were compelled to change their statutes and designations. The aim of this law was to institute a low level of secularism throughout the Algerian political and cultural system in an effort to eradicate the sources of fundamentalists' mobilization.

On another level the government nationalized religious institutions. In the past the majority of the mosques and the Quranic schools used to be under the control of Islamist parties or at least under the control of the Salafist imams; consequently, the religious institutions were a real threat to state security due to their ability to attract a large and unified following. To mitigate this threat, religious institutions became state controlled; religious leaders of these institutions were prohibited from preaching or engaging in associated activity without the permission and authorization of the state. This action helped the government control religious discourse, thus reducing Islamist radicalism.

SOCIAL ACTIONS

While the preceding efforts proved fruitful, the Algerian government was convinced that military and political actions were not enough. Following this logic, the government combined these actions with social initiatives that could further enhance stability and state security. The first action was a media appeal to terrorists to hand in their weapons and reintegrate back into society. On July 13, 1999, the Civil Concord Law was promulgated. This law was accepted by the whole population following a referendum. This law authorized the government to forgive terrorists for all crimes and atrocities committed and accept them as ordinary citizens if they put down their weapons.

Strategically, the Civil Concord Law isolated terrorists and generated confusion and conflicts among terrorist groups, especially between the radicals and the more moderate factions. Moreover, Saudi religious scholars reviewed their opinions on Algeria and declared that Islamist violence in that country was unholy. However, terrorist groups that remained active became more violent and aggressive, especially in their targeting of civilians. This provided the government with a legitimate opportunity to forcibly strike the remnants of Algeria-based extremism.

In 2005, the government pushed the Civil Concord Law further to a National Reconciliation and Peace Charter, which helped neutralize the Islamic Salvation Army, an important and active terrorist organization. In this new law, which was instituted by a referendum, terrorists who did not participate in massacres, slaughters, or murders were forgiven and integrated back into society with all of their fundamental civil rights restored; some of them received financial aid to begin a new life. In essence, this law granted a general pardon to all terrorists who surrendered and furthermore abandoned all judicial actions that had previously been taken against them. This also included sentence reductions and in some instances the granting of freedom for imprisoned terrorists.

The National Reconciliation and Peace Charter helped the government concentrate its military efforts against the GIA; consequently, it succeeded in marginalizing and virtually eradicating it. The majority of GIA members were killed; some of them accepted the terms of National Reconciliation; and the remaining ones created the Salafist Group for Preaching and Combat and later joined al-Qaeda in the Islamic Maghreb.

Finally, it is worth noting that the Civil Concord Law and the National Reconciliation and Peace Charter succeeded in rehabilitating repentant terrorists back into society. Additionally, both of these initiatives gave the government the legal means to take care of and provide for the victims of terrorism. These actions became possible when the government succeeded in convincing the Algerian people, particularly those who had been tragically affected by the terrorists' crimes, to forgive repentant terrorists.

After applying the National Reconciliation pact, the government began repopulating the rural areas by encouraging people to rebuild their houses and exploit their properties. To achieve this, a large program of rural housing, financial support to agriculture, and several developmental programs were launched. All of these actions were designed to alleviate some of the problems encountered by the rural population who decided not to leave their lands. These policies also persuaded those who migrated to urban areas to return to their previous dwellings.

CONCLUSION

The Algerian government's military, political, and social policies were necessary and complementary. The military operations were necessary to consolidate state authority; the political actions were necessary to stabilize state structures; and the social initiatives were necessary to strengthen state infrastructures.

See also: **Volume 1, Part I:** Concept of Islamist Jihad; Insurgent Terrorism

REFERENCES

Alexander, Yonah, and Michael B. Kraft. *Evolution of U.S. Counterterrorism Policy.* Vol. 3. London: Praeger Security International, 2007.

Jasparro, Christopher. "Socio-cultural, Economic, and Demographic Aspects of Counterterrorism." In *Countering Terrorism and Insurgency in the 21st Century,* Vol. 2: *Combating the Sources and Facilitators,* edited by James J. F. Forest, 420–50. London: Praeger Security International, 2007.

Lutz, James M., and Brenda J. Lutz. *Global Terrorism.* 2nd ed. New York: Routledge, 2008.

Volpi, Frédéric. *Islam and Democracy: The Failure of Dialogue in Algeria.* London: Pluto, 2003.

Wald, General Charles. "New Initiatives with African Countries." Foreign Press Center Roundtable, Washington, DC, 2008.

Australia

Augustine Meaher

The evolution of Australian counterterrorism strategy has been shaped by three key factors: (1) Australia's federal system, (2) Australian encounters with terrorism, most of which have been aimed at non-Australians and were inspired by the actions of third countries in other areas of the world, and (3) the fact that terrorism has been and remains rare in Australia. Counterterrorism nevertheless has become increasingly important to Australian governments in the last three decades, with a noted increase in governmental activity since September 11, 2001, which has resulted in substantial increases in Commonwealth authority.

CROATIAN REVOLUTIONARY BROTHERHOOD

Postwar migration turned Australia from an overwhelmingly Anglo-Celtic nation into a multicultural though still predominantly European nation. A tiny minority of those new Australians brought with them extreme ideologies and the will to further those ideologies violently. The most important of these transplanted extremists were Croatian nationalists who created the Croatian Revolutionary Brotherhood, which sought to create an independent Croatia. Most of their operations occurred in Yugoslavia, but Yugoslavian interests in Australia were also targeted. In 1970, the Yugoslav consulate in Melbourne was bombed, and the following year a Serbian Orthodox Church was targeted, but there were no casualties and these incidents were left to state police organizations to deal with under normal criminal laws.

The September 1972 attack on the Yugoslav General Trade and Tourist Agency wounded 16, including 2 critically. The casualties and Yugoslav prime minister Dzemal Bijedic's upcoming visit greatly alarmed the newly elected Whitlam government. The attorney general, Lionel Murphy, aware that Croatians in Australia were planning protests during Bijedic's visit, suspected that the Australian Security and Intelligence Organisation (ASIO) had not given him the information he needed to guarantee Bijedic's safety. ASIO was a Cold War creation, and although it monitored organizations such as the Croatian Revolutionary Brotherhood, counterterrorism was not its primary focus nor even in its official remit.

In March 1973, the Office of the Attorney General raided ASIO offices to obtain all ASIO files related to Croatian nationalists in Australia. The raid gravely damaged ASIO morale and tarnished its reputation at home and with allied intelligence agencies. The following year the Australian government established the Royal Commission on Intelligence and Security with New South Wales Supreme Court justice Robert Hope as royal commissioner. The commission's 1977 report confirmed the need for an Australian security and intelligence agency and urged expanding ASIO's jurisdiction to include sabotage and terrorism, and giving ASIO lawful authority to open mail, enter premises, use listening devices, and intercept electronic communications.

EVOLUTION OF AUSTRALIAN COUNTERTERRORISM POLICY

Despite increased powers, and with terrorism now officially in its remit, ASIO and the Australian government remained unprepared. On the morning of December 13, 1978, an undetected bomb in a rubbish bin exploded as the bin was being placed into a rubbish truck outside the Sydney Hilton, which was hosting the first Commonwealth Heads of Government Regional Meeting. Two rubbish collectors and a policeman guarding the hotel were killed. The New South Wales Special Branch was given responsibility for apprehending the terrorists, and while it is generally believed that the Universal Proutist Revolutionary Federation—the military wing of the Indian-based Ananda Marga organization—was behind the bombing, the case remains unsolved.

The Hilton bombing spurred the development of Australia's first comprehensive counterterrorism strategy. The Standing Advisory Committee on Commonwealth/State Cooperation for Protection against Violence (SAC-PAV) was at the center of this new strategy. Reflecting Australia's federal nature SAC-PAV consisted of the commissioners and/or deputy police commissioners of all Australian states and territories, a representative of each state's premier, and representatives from a variety of Commonwealth, state, and territory law enforcement agencies. SAC-PAV was chaired by the head of the Protective Security Coordination Center, which coordinates protective security for diplomatic and consular premises and personnel in Australia. SAC-PAV met at least twice a year to offer advice to the Commonwealth, states, and territories on protection against terrorism.

For most of its existence SAC-PAV and Australian counterterrorism efforts were focused on terrorism with its roots outside of the region and targeting non-Australians. The first threat SAC-PAV encountered was the arrival of Phillip McCullough, a self-confessed member of the Irish Republican Army, on a speaking and fund-raising tour. After considerable public debate McCullough was deported. Six months later the Turkish consul general in Sydney, Sarik Ariyak, was gunned down along with his bodyguard while driving in Sydney. The assassination was attributed to Armenian nationalists, but no arrests were made. No one was convicted following the 1982 bombing of the Israeli consul general in Sydney, which was attributed to the Palestine Liberation Organization (PLO).

Terrorism gradually faded from the public eye in the 1980s and 1990s. The events in the United States on September 11, 2001, made counterterrorism a central political issue as Australian citizens were soon implicated in various Islamic organizations and plots, some of which targeted Australia itself because of Australia's intervention in East Timor and its close alliance with the United States. The primary instrument for the development of domestic counterterrorism became the Council of Australian Governments (COAG), which brings together the Commonwealth, state, and territory governments for regular meetings. At the April 2002 COAG, a new four-pronged counterterrorism framework was agreed to that substantially increased Commonwealth power and responsibility:

1. The Commonwealth has responsibility for "national terrorist situations," including attacks on Commonwealth targets, multijurisdictional attacks, threats against civil aviation, and those involving chemical, biological, radiological, and nuclear materials.
2. The Commonwealth will consult and seek the agreement of the affected states and territories before a national terrorist situation is declared, and the states and territories will not unreasonably withhold their agreement.
3. All governments agree to take whatever action is necessary to ensure that terrorists can be prosecuted under the criminal law.
4. SAC-PAV will be reconstituted as the National Counter-terrorism Committee (NCTC) with a broader mandate.

NATIONAL COUNTER-TERRORISM PLAN

The NCTC coordinates the nationwide cooperative framework to counter terrorism. The Commonwealth government, which chairs NCTC meetings, is represented by the Department of the Prime Minister and Cabinet, the Attorney General's Department, the Department of Transport and Regional Services, the Australian Federal Police, ASIO, the Department of Defence, the Department of Finance and Administration, Emergency Management Australia, and the Department of Foreign Affairs and Trade. State and territory representatives include senior officials of the premiers' and chief ministers' departments, as well as deputy police commissioners. Senior New Zealand representatives observe the meetings.

The NCTC developed, modifies, and maintains the National Counter-terrorism Plan (NCTP). The NCTP is updated and reviewed periodically by the NCTC. These reviews often lead to the passage of new counterterrorism laws such as the 2005 Anti-terrorism Act, which allowed control orders for up to a year, preventive detention for up to 48 hours, and expanded stop, question, search, and seize powers at airports and Commonwealth places.

By 2006, the Australian government felt that its counterterrorism efforts warranted the publication of *Protecting Australia against Terrorism*, which provides an excellent insight into the National Counter-terrorism Plan. The report provides the most valuable insight into contemporary

Australian counterterrorism policy available. The report revealed that Australia spent A$8.3 billion in five years on counterterrorism. The report also laid out a revised four-pronged approach to counterterrorism: prevention, preparedness, response, and recovery. Prevention and preparedness are considered the most crucial, encompassing counterterrorism legislation; intelligence; law enforcement; critical infrastructure protection; border security; transport security; identity security; e-security; chemical, biological, radiological, and nuclear security; and security-related science and technology research.

In 2010, the Australian government declared that terrorism continued to pose a serious security challenge to Australia, but that Australia now had a slightly modified four-pronged approach to counterterrorism based on analysis, protection, response, and resilience. As part of this new four-pronged intelligence-centered approach the government established the Counter Terrorism Control Centre to set and manage counterterrorism priorities, identify intelligence requirements, and ensure the harmonization of counterterrorism information. The government also established the ambassador for counterterrorism, reflecting an appreciation that terrorism was a transnational challenge.

The ambassador for counterterrorism coordinates Australia's international counterterrorism efforts by building international linkages and ensuring that the separate efforts of Australian government agencies are consistent, prioritized, well focused, and effective. The ambassador negotiates counterterrorism agreements with partner countries and advises on international developments to ensure that Australia has access to the best international practices.

CONCLUSION

Australia's counterterrorism strategy will continue to evolve in the years to come as governments seek to craft a national strategy that acknowledges Australia's federal system and the public perception that terrorism is a serious but remote threat to Australia.

REFERENCES

Chulov, Martin. *Australian Jihad: The Battle against Terrorism from Within and Without.* Sydney, Australia: Macmillan, 2006.

Commonwealth Government. *Protecting Australia against Terrorism 2006.* Canberra, Australia: Commonwealth Publisher, 2006.

Commonwealth Government. *Counter-terrorism White Paper.* Canberra, Australia: Commonwealth Publisher, 2010.

National Counter-terrorism Committee. *National Counter-terrorism Plan.* Canberra, Australia: Commonwealth Publisher, 2008.

Austria

Anna Pechenina

In 1850 Emperor Franz Joseph I created the first Austrian gendarmerie. Its goal was to prevent and subdue the disorder and looting that accompany uprisings ("Austria" 2010). After World War II and before 1955, when Austria regained its freedom from the Soviet Union through the Austrian State Treaty, Austria was forced to protect itself from Soviet postwar activities as well as the threat of new invasions. This prompted the nation to form a postwar gendarmerie (U.S. Department of State, Bureau of European and Eurasian Affairs 2011).

Gendarmeriekommando Bad Voeslau (GBV) was formed in 1973. It dealt with a Palestinian group of terrorists known as El Saika. This unit opposed the wave of Jewish immigrants from the Soviet Union, who used the town of Bad Voeslau as a stop on their way to Israel. These immigrants arrived on trains and had to be protected. In order to be close to the railroad line that was of interest to terrorists the unit was temporarily posted at the Castle of Bad Schoneau (Weiss and Davis 2009, 49).

GENDARMERIE-EINSATZKOMMANDO

In the 1970s a wave of terrorism shocked the Austrian community. In one particular case two armed Palestinian terrorists took an old Jewish couple and an Austrian customs officer hostage. In another instance a terrorist named Ilich Ramirez Sanchez, also known as Carlos the Jackal, led a team that took 42 Organization of Petroleum Exporting Countries (OPEC) ministers hostage in Vienna, Austria. They were subsequently released in exchange for a multimillion-dollar ransom. On September 5, 1978, the president of the German Employers Federation, Hanns Martin Schleyer, was abducted by the Red Army Faction's (RAF) Siegfried Hausner Commando. His driver and three bodyguards were killed on the spot. The president himself was later executed after the German government refused to meet the kidnappers' demands ("Chronology of Events" n.d.). By 1978, Austria had overhauled the GBV and created a special antiterrorism unit, called Gendarmerie-einsatzkommando (GEK), which in English means "Gendarmerie Operations Command."

Members of the GEK are trained by the best counterterrorism units available—Germany's Grenzschutzgruppe 9 (GSG 9) and Israel's Sayeret Mat'kal. To this day the GEK utilizes these same resources. In 1993, the GEK was placed in charge of special operations in the field of public law enforcement and recruited officers mostly from the GBV (Weiss and Davis 2009, 50). The GEK mission was to resolve hostage situations, arrest armed and dangerous criminals, protect people and property at risk, and provide air marshal service to Austrian Airlines.

STATE POLICE

Parallel to the GEK, the Austrian Federal Police force established its own branch, called the *Staatspolizei* or *Stapo* (in English, the State Police), which specializes in counterterrorism and counterintelligence. This secret service branch conducts security investigations for various government agencies and is "responsible for measures to protect national leaders and prominent visiting officials" ("Austria" 2010).

ISSUES WITH SPECIAL POLICE FORCES

In 1990, it was revealed that the Austrian State Police had violated the laws protecting personal data collection by the government and public institutions as well as constitutional protection of the secrecy of the mail and phone lines. It was found that about 20 percent of 11,000 public inquiries had actually been monitored. Thus, the State Police had monitored the activities of citizens without sufficient justification. This gave rise to a restructuring of the State Police, which included the reduction of its staff by half. The Police Law of 1993 introduced parliamentary control of the State Police and the military secret police "with oversight to be exercised by separate parliamentary subcommittees" ("Austria" 2010).

The September 11, 2001, terrorist attacks in the United States prompted the Austrian leadership to reevaluate its counterterrorism strategy. Identification and disruption of the channels through which terrorism was funded became the central goal of Austrian counterterrorism strategy (Council of Europe 2005, 5). The Austrian Ministry of Interior "has begun to investigate suspicious and possible links between non-profit organizations and terrorism" (Kellman 2003, 2). During these investigations it was discovered that the most important money-laundering problems faced by Austria were money remittance systems and offshore businesses.

At the same time, the Austrian minister of the interior initiated a review of Austria's special police units. The results of this review identified several areas for concern. They included the police forces' slow response to emergencies due to the distances that they had to travel, as well as large numbers of management levels within the police structure. Different levels within the police hierarchy meant different training and equipment levels, in addition to conflicting jurisdictions, which posed a problem.

EINSATZKOMMANDO COBRA

In 2002, the GEK became "Einsatzkommando" (EKO) COBRA, known in English as the Special Operations Command. As a special operations task force it was directly subordinate to the Ministry of the Interior and consisted of both the police and gendarmerie officers of Austria's law enforcement. This brought about integration of the existing city and rural regions' SWAT teams and the creation of five locations of operation as well as three operational field offices. This change ensured that a single unit could be present at any point in the country within an hour's notice. Additionally, EKO COBRA took over all VIP protection and bodyguard services in Austria as well. The rest of their responsibilities remained the same (Weiss and Davis 2009, 51).

In 2005 a national research program on terrorism prevention was launched. That same year Austrian law enforcement reform abolished the gendarmerie and divided the policing duties between the federal police, state security, and Interpol. The federal police incorporated the duties previously divided between public security, criminal investigation service, and the gendarmerie.

CONCLUSION

Internationally, Austria has signed several bilateral and multilateral treaties of mutual legal assistance in criminal matters and extradition. These treaties include the European Convention on Mutual Assistance in Criminal Matters of January 1, 1977, and its First Additional Protocol of May 15, 2003; the European Convention on Extradition of December 13, 1957, and its Second Additional Protocol of March 17, 1978; and the European Convention on Suppression of Terrorism of April 20, 1959 (Council of Europe 2005, 7).

The main national legislation on international cooperation is contained in the Federal Law of December 4, 1979, on Extradition and Mutual Assistance in Criminal Matters (Extradition and Mutual Assistance Law [ARHG]), and it applies to all cases involving states that are not European Union members. In it, Austria will only "grant assistance in proceedings in respect of offences also punishable under Austrian law and the punishment of which, at the time of the request for assistance, falls within the jurisdiction of the judicial authorities" (Council of Europe n.d., 1).

REFERENCES

"Austria." *Crime and Society: A Comparative Criminology Tour of the World.* February 5, 2010. http://www.rohan.sdsu.edu/faculty/rwinslow/europe/aus tria.html.

"Chronology of Events. History of the RAF, and the Context of Anti-imperialist Movements, Liberation Movements in the 'Third World', Student Revolts." Rote Armee Fraktion—Documents, compiled by Ron Augustin. *Labour History Resources.* n.d. http://labourhistory.net/raf/chronology.php.

Council of Europe. "Austria." *Country Profiles on Counterterrorist Capacity.* 2005. http://www.coe.int/T/E/Legal_Affairs/Legal_co-operation/Fight_against_terrorism/4_Theme_Files/Country_Profiles/.

Council of Europe. "Austria." *National Procedures for Mutual Legal Assistance in Criminal Matters.* n.d. http://www.coe.int/t/e/legal_affairs/legal_co-operation/transnational_criminal_justice/2_PC-OC/Mutual%20legal%20assistance%20in%20criminal%20matters.asp.

Kellman, Barry. "Austria." *National Laws and Measures: Counter-terrorism Regulation of Biology,* May 2003. http://www.interpol.int/Public/BioTerrorism/NationalLaws/.

U.S. Department of State, Bureau of European and Eurasian Affairs. "Background Note: Austria." December 9, 2011. http://www.state.gov/r/pa/ei/bgn/3165.htm.

Weiss, Jim, and Mickey Davis. "COBRA: Austria's Special Police Commandos." *Law and Order,* July 2009, 48–52.

Bangladesh

Mohammad Sajjadur Rahman

On August 17, 2005, within less than an hour, over 450 bombs exploded in 63 of Bangladesh's 64 districts. Instead of causing mass casualties (three people lost their lives), this sensational string of attacks, conducted by Jamaat-ul-Mujahideen, was, in part, aimed at attracting the attention of the state and the populace. Almost a year before this incident, on August 21, 2004, unprecedented violence, in the form of grenade attacks, was unleashed against the high-profile opposition leadership, leaving 21 people dead and 200 injured. With these events the long-assumed relative stability of Bangladesh became questionable. These acts of violence came as a surprise to many who strongly believed that the country's secular past would be able to contain the tide of Islamist sentiment in the post-9/11 era.

RADICAL ISLAMISM

Radical Islamism in Bangladesh developed through three distinctive, yet connected, stages. The first era (1971–1975) is very crucial for understanding the basic difference between the Islamist experience of Bangladesh and those of other Muslim-dominated countries. During this period Islamist groups were immensely unpopular due to their opposition to the creation of Bangladesh and their collaboration with the Pakistani army in the genocide of 1971. Moreover, during this era tensions arose within nationalist and secular discourse that would ultimately open the door to future Islamists. The second era (1976–1990), which was dominated by military rulers, witnessed the reemergence of political Islam within the mainstream political arena. The third era (1991–present) can be identified as an age in which the emergence of radical Islamist groups with militant features became a political reality. Therefore, Bangladesh's counterterrorism efforts in regards to Islamist radicalism are a very recent phenomenon.

With the fall of General Ershad in 1990, Bangladesh entered into the democratic era. The Bangladesh Nationalist Party (BNP) came out victorious in the first democratic election in the post-1975 era. In order to secure the necessary parliamentary seats to form the government, the BNP's leader, Begum Khaleda Zia, was prepared to initiate an alliance with the Jamaat-i-Islami, whose leaders are alleged to have participated in the genocidal activities of 1971. Thus, for the first time in Bangladesh's history, Jamaat-i-Islami gained the opportunity to play a vital role in power politics. It needs to be pointed out that Bangladeshi mujahideens, who went to Afghanistan in the 1980s, began to return home in the early 1990s. Some of these individuals would play crucial roles in organizing militant organizations in later years.

Law enforcement agencies in Bangladesh were not taking this issue seriously at the time, and militant Islamism was yet to become a threat to state security. The secular Awami League (AL) understood the importance of Jamaat-i-Islami and succeeded in attracting their support during their antigovernmental movement in 1995–1996. Once again, Jamaat proved themselves useful to another major political party (this time, the AL), and these events ultimately legitimized their existence in the political arena. Sheikh Hasina of the AL began to use Islamic symbols in her outlook, and her frequent visits to Saudi Arabia were intended to prove that she was a good Muslim and that AL was not a threat to Islam. In 1996, AL won the election, and Sheikh Hasina became the prime minister. The Islamists issued several death threats against her, but the government was more interested in portraying those threats as conspiracies of the BNP, the main opposition party at the time. Thus, the Islamist threat was not addressed properly. Moreover, interparty political violence and killings became more common, and the law-and-order situation deteriorated.

STATE SUPPORT

The period 1991–1996 also witnessed other incidents that indicated that Bangladesh was becoming more intolerant toward secular ideals and multicultural values. A female writer, Taslima Nasreen, was declared a heretic by some clerics because of her "anti-Islamic" novel titled *Lajja* (Shame), and pressure mounted on the government to place her under arrest. Consequently, Nasreen had to seek refuge in another country. It was quite disturbing that even though the head of the government and the leader of the main opposition party were women, a female writer could not feel secure in her own country. Fatwas were also declared against the activities of nongovernmental organizations (NGOs) that were instrumental in poverty-alleviation programs and the empowerment of rural women. Several prominent secular writers including poets and university professors were threatened and declared to be heretics during this period. An organization called the Ahle-Hadith Movement also received attention for their violence against a tiny minority sect of Ahmadiyya, who are regarded as non-Muslim by the ulema. Additionally, with state support the madrassa education system expanded during this period, and it was becoming clear that people were becoming more interested in religious education. The increasing number of unskilled Bangladeshi migrants working in Middle Eastern countries made Bangladesh's economy somewhat dependent on foreign currencies. At the same time various Islamic nongovernmental organizations based in Saudi Arabia began to operate in Bangladesh.

In 2001, BNP and its main ally Jamaat-i-Islami again came to power, and two top leaders from Jamaat, who are famous for their alleged war crimes in 1971, became ministers. This period (2001–2006) saw unprecedented state support for the Islamist cause. Following the election in 2001, Hindus in various parts of Bangladesh were attacked for their alleged support of the AL, and many Hindus fled to India for fear of persecution. A number of terrorist incidents occurred within this period; most were portrayed as antigovernment activities of the AL. Additionally, the rise of homegrown terrorist organizations with international linkages became a particular concern during this period.

COUNTERTERRORISM

Islamism in Bangladesh also acquired a new flavor through the emergence of Hizb-ut-Tahrir in the late 1990s, which called for the creation of the Khilafat (governance by Islamic principles). This transnational Islamist group became somewhat popular among university students. Therefore, by the end of the 1990s, Islamism in Bangladesh acquired many diverse and complicated features. The infamous Jamaat-ul-Mujahideen Bangladesh (JMB) and Jagrata Muslim Janata Bangladesh (JMJB), mostly supported by illiterate and poverty-ridden rural people, made headlines through their terrorist activities. Tensions mounted when reports of the existence of the Bangladesh chapter of the Pakistani terrorist organization Harakat ul-Jihad-I-Islami were published. The BNP-Jamaat government at first tried to deny the existence of terrorist organizations in Bangladesh and criticized the news reports as part of a "global conspiracy" and "anti-Bangladesh campaign" supported by the AL and India. However, following the terrorist attacks of August 2005, the government, under increased international pressure, had to react and began a crackdown on selected organizations and individuals. The Rapid Action Battalion, an elite paramilitary force created in 2004 by the BNP government, along with National Security Intelligence and Directorate General Forces Intelligence, was mobilized to counter terrorist activities, and by 2006 six senior leaders of JMB and JMJB were arrested.

The military-backed caretaker government of 2007–2008 made significant progress on the issue of terrorism. In this period, most of the top leaders of JMB, who had already faced trials, were executed, and the government also commissioned a report that included suggestions on how to address the problem of terrorism more effectively. Furthermore, the new AL government, which came to power through winning the December 2008 election, has already taken notable steps to curb Islamist extremism in Bangladesh. The Rapid Action Battalion, along with other law enforcement agencies, has proven its efficiency in dismantling homegrown terror networks and in uncovering terrorists' plots. The new government, led by Prime Minister Sheikh Hasina, has asserted its commitment to secular and democratic principles on several occasions.

In February 2009, the government enacted the Anti-terrorism Act and the Money Laundering Prevention Act. Bangladesh also applied for membership in the Egmont Group to operate its newly established financial intelligence unit to combat money laundering. A 17-member-strong National Committee on Militancy Resistance and Prevention headed by the state minister for home affairs was also created by the government to tackle terrorism and mobilize public opinion against extremist activities. Furthermore, in order to better coordinate various intelligence agencies, an eight-member National Committee for Intelligence Coordination was formed, with the prime minister as the chairperson. The government also announced that it was forming a National Police Bureau of Counterterrorism. In October 2009, the organization Hizb ut-Tahrir was banned for its alleged antistate activities. It became the fifth organization to be outlawed since 2001. Moreover, for the first time, the capital Dhaka has shown a serious interest in regional cooperation regarding intelligence sharing to fight terrorist networks operating within South Asia.

CONCLUSION

The counterterrorism measures taken by the current regime and the absence of any serious terror events for the last few years suggest that Bangladesh has become quite successful in combating terrorism. However, recent reports by WikiLeaks and local investigations have revealed that a number of individuals from various intelligence agencies were in fact collaborating with high-profile terrorists during the last BNP regime. Thus, experts believe that the success of counterterrorism efforts in Bangladesh rests on the efficient management of its intelligence agencies.

See also: **Volume 1, Part I:** The Terrorist Threat in the 21st Century: A Global Security Problem. **Part VI:** Global Jihad Movement. **Volume 2, Part I:** Rapid Action Battalion (Bangladesh)

REFERENCES

Rahman, Mohammad Sajjadur. "Islamism in Bangladesh." *Journal of International Relations* 8, no. 1 (2010): 71–82.
Rahman, Mohammad Sajjadur. "Foreign Relations and Identity Politics in Bangladesh." *South Asian Journal* 32 (April–June 2011): 47–54.
Riaz, Ali. *God Willing: The Politics of Islamism in Bangladesh.* Oxford: Rowman & Littlefield, 2004.
Sobhan, Faiz. "Bangladesh's Recent Efforts at Countering Terrorism." *Dhaka Courier,* April 22, 2011. http://www.bei-bd.org/files/file/Bangladesh's%20 recent%20efforts%20at%20countering%20terrorism.pdf.

Belgium

Samaya L. S. Chanthaphavong

The Kingdom of Belgium is located in Western Europe and shares borders with France, Germany, Luxembourg, and the Netherlands. It is a federated state with three main regions, Wallonia in the south (French speaking), Flanders in the north (Dutch speaking), and the capital area of Brussels. With a population nearing 11 million it is a constitutional monarchy with a bicameral parliament (U.S. Department of State, Bureau of Public Affairs 2011) and a founding member of the European Union (EU). Home to the headquarters of the EU as well as the North Atlantic Treaty Organization (NATO), Belgium is often viewed as one of the early adopters of counterterrorism policies, and it continues to be a strong advocate for antiterrorism and counterterrorism laws and strategies.

BACKGROUND

Historically, Belgium's geographic position in Europe meant that it was often occupied by countries seeking to take advantage of its strategic position. Due to the consistent influx of peoples, Belgium is viewed as a melting pot of nationalities, with Austrian, Celtic, Dutch, Germanic, French, Roman, and Spanish influences at one time or another over the area since 100 BC (Bunson 1994, 169). Major occupation occurred with the Spanish from 1519 to 1713 and the Austrians from 1713 to 1794. In 1795, Belgium was annexed to France under Napoleon, and following his defeat at the Battle of Waterloo, the country was made part of the Netherlands in 1815.

Belgium is considered to have a high migrant population with modest estimates indicating that just over 25 percent of Belgium's population is not native Belgian. A high migrant intake has, at times, spawned wide sociopolitical issues, which during the 1970s to late 1980s fed into a political landscape predominantly dominated by right-wing and extreme right-wing movements.

The high levels of postwar immigration into the country disenfranchised a significantly large segment of the population. Belgium soon became peppered with strong anti-immigration and pro-Belgian nationalist groups whose ideological foundations were usually drawn from Communist or Socialist manifestos. Public bombings and threats were frequent, with groups such as the People's Socialist Movement of Germany/ Workers Party (Schmid and Jongman 2005, 557), the National Front for the Liberation of Belgium (Schmid and Jongman 2005, 508), and the Westland New Post group and Communist Combatant Cells creating public disharmony.

ISLAMIST EXTREMISM AND COUNTERTERRORISM

During the late 1980s and into the early 1990s Belgium witnessed a shift away from right-wing political extremist groups toward Islamist extremist groups. Criminal activity shifted away from concerted efforts at destabilizing the local sociopolitical landscape toward internationally significant crimes such as intracountry money laundering, arms trafficking, and falsification of national passports. Belgium's corresponding shift to focus on crimes that have henceforth been believed to be terrorist activities resulted in it being viewed as at the forefront of counterterrorist activities both domestically and internationally (Levy 2007, 5). Recently there has been a concerted push (in line with Europe and the United States) to make sure that terrorism-related behavior was criminalized so that, legally, all suspicious financial transactions are reported. One such example is the Belgian Financial Intelligence Processing Unit, which is responsible for enforcement of the anti–money-laundering bill (1993). The introduction of strong antiterrorism laws and the increasing and widening of the powers of Belgian counterintelligence groups further cemented this viewpoint.

The late 1990s and 2000s saw Belgian authorities becoming more and more concerned with Islamic extremists and breakaway groups such as the Kurdistan Workers Party, which appeared to use Belgium as an inroad into Europe. The country is able to maintain and submit a national list of terrorist organizations that is distinct and separate from that of the United Nations and the EU; the list relies heavily on Belgium's domestic intelligence network.

Belgium has fruitful relationships with its internal counterterrorism and intelligence-gathering communities. Two intelligence groups serve to protect the state, the Belgium State Security Service (Veiligheid van de Staat, or Sûreté de l'État) and the Belgium General Information and Security Service (Algemene Dienst Inlichting en Veiligheid, or Service Général du Renseignement et de la Sécurité) The Belgium State Security Service is administered by the Ministry of Justice and is tasked with antiterrorism, espionage, religious and political extremism, and social and political interference. It is a civilian agency, unlike the Belgium General Information and Security Service, which is administered by the Ministry of Defence. The Belgium General Information and Security Service focuses on intelligence gathering, terrorist threats, and counterstrategies and is broken up into four divisions: intelligence, security, security intelligence, and support. Like most states, Belgium has a federal police force that can also assist with terrorism-related intelligence gathering.

Two additional groups that deal predominantly with counterterrorism are the Mixed Anti-terrorist Group, whose focus is independent intelligence gathering (Rheinheimer 2006, 4) and the relatively newly formed (2007) Threat Analysis Coordination Body (OCAD/OCAM [Organe de coordination pour l'analyse de la menace or Coördinatieorgaan voor de dreigingsanalyse]), whose job it is to analyze the nature of the terrorist threat by triangulating information gathered from all state agencies.

As well as exhibiting strong domestic relationships between intelligence communities, Belgium has strong international intelligence ties. Belgium's Ministry of Defence has a reciprocal relationship with the United States via the Office of Defense Cooperation, Belgium-Luxembourg, which, among other vital defense-related matters, actively oversees security cooperation and assistance, particularly in relation to counterterrorism. In 2009, Belgium ratified the U.S. and EU multilateral legal assistance and extradition agreements, which further increases its ability to provide, and be provided with, counterintelligence.

Belgium's intelligence community is now governed by the Organic Law on the Intelligence and Security Services, passed on November 30, 1998 (Belgium Standing Intelligence Agencies Review Committee). Since 1991, Belgium's laws surrounding counterterrorism and security have strengthened and increased so that progressive acts were passed with relatively little fanfare. Prior to this time the state's security agencies worked with little legal framework in that their functions were considered to be outside of the scope of the existing Belgium law. The 1998 act provided a legal framework that strengthened intelligence gathering so that information collection and sharing were enhanced domestically with an eye toward international cooperation. An example of this would be the successful intelligence gathering that identified Belgium's national passport as vulnerable to forgery and subsequent use by terrorists. In March 2001, a new passport that incorporated antifraud measures was introduced by Belgian authorities (U.S. Department of State 2002).

Following the terrorist attacks in the United States on September 11, 2001, Belgium's counterterrorism strategies coincided with a general strengthening of counterterrorism strategy globally. In recognition of the United Nations Security Council Resolution 1386, and operating as part of the International Security Assistance Force, Belgium sent troops to Afghanistan. Belgium actively participated in Operation Enduring Freedom by way of naval support and counterterrorism surveillance (under NATO). Furthermore, in 2001 Belgium was one of the first countries to support the adoption of a European Union Arrest Warrant, which allows EU states to extradite persons for crimes such as terrorism. Belgium is a party to the European Convention for the Suppression of Terrorism, and the Belgium Anti-terrorism Act of 2003 was introduced to amend the criminal code and thus criminalize terrorism and terrorist-related acts.

CONCLUSION

Over the decades Belgium has implemented a strong domestic antiterrorism framework and has also supported international counterterrorism efforts. Belgium's intelligence capabilities will undoubtedly evolve to further protect and defend against terrorism.

See also: **Volume 1, Part I:** The Terrorist Threat in the 21st Century: A Global Security Problem. **Part VI:** Afghanistan: Present and Future Challenges. **Volume 2, Part II:** Operation Enduring Freedom (2001)

REFERENCES

Belgium Standing Intelligence Agencies Review Committee. Organic Law on the Intelligence and Security Services. http://www.comiteri.be/index.php?option=com_content&view=article&id=3&Itemid=7&lang=EN.

Bunson, Matthew. *Encyclopaedia of the Roman Empire.* New York: Facts on File, 1994.

Coolsaet, R., and Struye de Swielande. *Belgium and Counterterrorism Policy in the Jihadi Era (1986–2007),* Brussels: Egmont Royal Institute for International Relations, 2007.

Grignard, Alain. "The Islamist Networks in Belgium: Between Nationalism and Globalisation." In *Jihadi Terrorism and the Radicalisation Challenge in Europe,* edited by Rik Coolsaet, 85–94. Aldershot, UK: Ashgate, 2007.

Levy, Janine. *Terrorism Issues and Developments.* Hauppauge, NY: Nova Science, 2007.

Rheinheimer, Francis. "Counterterrorism in the European Union, A Who's Who of the Agencies Involved." Center for Defense Information, Joint Publication of the Center for Defense Information and the Brussels Office of the World Security Institute, August 2, 2006. http://www.cdi.org/program/issue/document.cfm?DocumentID=3607&IssueID=45&StartRow=1&List

Rows=10&appendURL=&Orderby=DateLastUpdated&ProgramID=39& issueID=45.

Schmid, Alex, and A. J. Jongman. *Political Terrorism: A New Guide to Actors, Authors, Concepts, Databases, Theories and Literature.* 2nd ed. New Brunswick, NJ: Transaction, 2005.

U.S. Department of State. *Patterns of Global Terrorism 2001—Belgium.* Refworld. May 21, 2002. http://www.unhcr.org/refworld/country,,,ANNUALREPO RT,BEL,,4681077f23,0.html

U.S. Department of State, Bureau of Public Affairs. *Background Notes: Belgium.* February 2011. http://www.state.gov/r/pa/ei/bgn/2874.htm.

U.S. Department of State, Office of the Coordinator for Counterterrorism. *Country Reports on Terrorism.* n.d. http://www.state.gov/s/ct/.

Bulgaria

Zornitza Grekova

Bulgaria is a parliamentary democracy and a member of both the North Atlantic Treaty Organization (NATO) and the European Union (EU). Bulgaria's attitude toward the problem of international terrorism and the questions regarding adequate measures to prevent and fight against terrorist activities originated during the Cold War. Small in scope but comprehensive in tools, counterterrorism policy in Communist Bulgaria was primarily aimed at protecting the Communist regime; therefore, foreign residents and foreign guests were often the targets of Bulgaria's counterterrorist operatives.

BACKGROUND

The first full account of the structure of the counterintelligence section (CIS), which comprises counterterrorism, dates from 1946 in a Report to the Director of the People's Militia. During the first years of Communist rule CIS was part of the larger State Security department under the rule of the People's Militia. In the 1950s the CIS was transformed into a department that reflected the growing importance of this activity to the Communist government. In 1950, under the presidency of Vylko Chervenkov, the department of State Security (SS) became an independent agency within the Ministry of Internal Affairs. The new Communist leader Chervenkov wanted SS to become the Communist Party's "eyes and ears." This is the period (1953) when the final structure of SS had been established. Accordingly, the counterintelligence department was constituted as an independent department within SS under the denomination of the "Second

Agency." Its main objective and concern was counterterrorism. The next step in reforming the structure of SS occurred in July 1962, but the Second Agency remained tasked with counterterrorist operations until 1989.

Bulgaria identified and responded to two distinct threats to state security during the 1960s and 1970s. In the 1960s counterterrorism involved the protection of Socialism and its state institutions against the influences and acts of sabotage by enemy forces within the Bulgarian diasporas in Western Europe and the United States, as well as internal criminal hubs. This trend reflected the adoption of the Stalinist political model, which was applied in the ideologically based analysis of security threats. Toward the end of the 1970s the political establishment in Communist Bulgaria changed its attitude and took a more pragmatic point of view, having in mind the possible spread in Eastern Europe of terrorist activities based in Western Europe and the Middle East. On January 21, 1978, four leading members of the Red Army Faction (Baader-Meinhof Group), a German terrorist organization, were arrested in the Sea Resort, Sunny Beach, in Bulgaria, and extradited to Germany. Cooperation was further improved in February 1979 when the deputy director of the counterintelligence service of the Bulgarian State Security Agency visited the Federal Criminal Police Office of Germany in Wiesbaden. In January 1980 the Ministry of the Interior adopted MZ No. 1–2 (Ministerial Order for the Measures for Detection, Prevention and Fight against Terrorist Acts), stipulating that "terrorism acquires highly organized profile" (Kostadinov 2010) and could pose an immediate threat to state security. This order authorizes the formation of special units within the central bureaus of the SS.

Three main security concerns existed in Bulgaria in the 1980s. The first was the threat of terrorist acts on Bulgarian territory. A vivid example of this trend was the assassination of Bora Suelkan, the administrative attaché at the Turkish Consulate General in Bourgas, on September 9, 1982, by a branch of the Combat Units of Justice against the Armenian Genocide. The second trend was exemplified by the "Bulgarian trace" in the assassination attempt on Pope John Paul II on May 13, 1983, which made the Bulgarian secret service reconsider the practice of hosting international terrorists and using them for their own nefarious purposes. The assassination attempt seriously questioned their ability to fully control terrorist activity. The third trend had its origin in the assimilation campaign directed toward Bulgaria's Turkish minority since 1984. This campaign intended to eradicate their cultural and religious identity. As a result there was an organized and unprecedented bombing campaign that killed 30 Bulgarians in public places during 1984 and 1985. Therefore, during the second part of the 1980s, counterterrorism and counterintelligence became the primary concern of Bulgaria's secret services. In all three cases tensions between the policymakers within the Bulgarian Communist Party and the professionals in the secret services were more or less visible. The first visible change can be detected in the enhanced but concealed cooperation with West Germany.

POST–COLD WAR

In the post–Cold War period the international system underwent major transformations in domestic state and international relations. Several remarkable events occurred, one of which was the changing attitude of the former Eastern European Socialist/Communist states regarding counterterrorism policy. This trend was exemplified by the willingness of the Bulgarian government to join both NATO (it has been a member state since 2004) and the EU (since 2007). These decisions marked a tremendous shift in the country's foreign policy and security threat perceptions.

The September 11, 2001, terrorist attacks in the United States prompted Bulgaria to formulate policies that address new security challenges. Bulgaria is an active supporter of and participant in the antiterrorist coalition formed after September 11, 2001. Having ratified and promulgated all basic international agreements on the prosecution and punishment of various forms of terrorism, the country has implemented the basic conditions for these policies. Clauses regarding cooperation in combating international terrorism and transnational organized crime are included in a number of bilateral and multilateral international agreements to which the Republic of Bulgaria is a party.

In the course of implementing national counterterrorism policy Bulgarian agencies and institutions directly involved in combating terrorism implemented a National Plan of Detection and Prevention of Terrorist Activities in the Territory of the Republic of Bulgaria (United Nations [UN] Security Council 2001). The plan, instituted in November 2001, aimed at improving the interaction among various Interior Ministry services with a view to acquiring information and intelligence on potential and significant targets including diplomatic missions. The protection of these important sites was provided by security guards assigned to various agencies within the Ministry of the Interior and licensed security companies. Within the Ministry of the Interior, a headquarters for the detection and prevention of terrorist acts was established whereby information was collected, analyzed, processed, and transmitted to the appropriate agencies. The antiterrorism agencies held meetings with analogous organizations from the major antiterrorist coalition states. Consequently, the exchange of information and cooperation in this area have been substantially increased.

On November 28, 2001, the Withdrawal of the Reservation Concerning the European Convention on the Suppression of Terrorism Act was adopted. On December 12, 2001, the Bulgarian Council of Ministers adopted Decree No. 277 for the implementation of UN Security Council Resolution 1373 of September 28, 2001. During the implementation of Resolution 1267

(1999) and 1373 (2001) practical measures were undertaken to update legislation relative to combating terrorism and its financing. In March 2001 Bulgaria became a signatory to the International Convention for the Suppression of the Financing of Terrorism. This instrument entered into force on April 10, 2002. Another piece of legislation was the adoption of articles amending Bulgaria's Penal Code. On September 13, 2001, the National Assembly adopted the Law on the Amendments to the Penal Code, which contains special criminal provisions on terrorism and the financing of terrorism (Second Supplementary Report 2007, 2). Additionally, the amendments envisaged punishments related to the establishment, leadership of, and participation in a terrorist group; the preparation to commit terrorist acts; instigations by verbal pronouncements to commit terrorism; and the threat to commit terrorism. Confiscation of all or part of the assets of the perpetrators of terrorist acts and the persons who finance their activities were also envisaged. On February 5, 2003, the National Assembly adopted the Law on the Measures against Financing of Terrorism, which entered into force on February 21, 2003 (Second Supplementary Report 2007, 1). These new amendments aimed at achieving full compliance with European norms in the fight against money laundering.

CONCLUSION

Countering terrorism is an important element of Bulgarian membership within the EU and NATO. The steady policy toward suppression of terrorist acts within the territory of the country was a constant element of the national program for NATO membership and parts of Bulgaria's counterterrorism policy after its accession to NATO. The contemporary counterterrorism policy of the Republic of Bulgaria includes legislative amendments, coordination mechanisms such as national plans and guidelines, and active international cooperation at the regional and international level.

See also: **Volume 1, Part I:** Global Terrorism: Post-9/11; The Terrorist Threat in the 21st Century: A Global Security Problem. **Part III:** Intelligence/Information Sharing between U.S. Government Agencies; Intelligence Sharing and Law Enforcement Cooperation between Nations; Role of the International Community. **Part V:** European Union

REFERENCES

Committee for Disclosing the Documents and Announcing Affiliation of Bulgarian Citizens to the State Security and Intelligence Services of the Bulgarian National Army. http://www.comdos.bg/p/language/en/.
Council Directive 91/308/EEC of 10 June 1991 on Prevention of the Use of the Financial System for the Purpose of Money Laundering. *Official Journal* L 166

(June 28, 1991): 0077–0083. http://eur-lex.europa.eu/LexUriServ/LexUri
Serv.do?uri=CELEX:31991L0308:EN:HTML.

Directive 2001/97/EC of the European Parliament and of the Council of 4 December 2001 Amending Council Directive 91/308/EEC on Prevention of the Use of the Financial System for the Purpose of Money Laundering—Commission Declaration. *Official Journal* L 166 (December 28, 2001): 76–82. http://eur-lex.europa.eu/smartapi/cgi/sga_doc?smartapi!celexplus!prod!CELEXnumdoc&numdoc=32001L0097&lg=EN.

Ismailov, Orhan, and Tatyana Kiruakova, eds. *State Security Services—Structure and Basic Documents, Collection of Records.* Sofia: Committee for Disclosing the Documents and Announcing Affiliation of Bulgarian Citizens to the State Security and Intelligence Services of the Bulgarian National Army, 2010.

Kostadinov, Evtim, ed. *International Terrorism in the Bulgarian State Security Files, Documentary Volume.* Sofia: Committee for Disclosing the Documents and Announcing Affiliation of Bulgarian Citizens to the State Security and Intelligence Services of the Bulgarian National Army, 2010.

Metodiev, Momchil. *Legitimacy Machine: State Security in the Power Strategy of Bulgarian Communist Party.* Sofia: The Institute for Studies of the Recent Past, Open Society Institute, CIELA Publishers, 2008.

Second Supplementary Report to the National Report on the Activities of the Republic of Bulgaria to Counteract Terrorism in Implementation of Resolution 1373 (2001) of the UN Security Council on Measures That the UN Member States Need to Take in the Fight against Terrorism. June 2007. Republic of Bulgaria, Ministry of Interior. http://www.mvr.bg/NR/rdonlyres/D3172AEC-99FB-48D7-B375-8AAC65444238/0/ReportIII.doc.

State Agency for National Security, Republic of Bulgaria. History of Bulgarian Special Services. http://www.dans.bg/index.php?option=com_content&view=article&id=9%3Ahistory-art-bul&catid=11%3Ahistory-cat-bul&Itemid=9&lang=en.

United Nations Security Council. "Letter Dated 27 December 2001 from the Chairman of the Security Council Committee Established Pursuant to Resolution 1373 (2001) Concerning Counter-terrorism Addressed to the President of the Security Council." December 27, 2001, p. 3, http://www.unhcr.org/refworld/pdfid/46d571320.pdf.

Canada

Irwin M. Cohen and Raymond Corrado

With the successful terror attacks in New York City and Washington, D.C., on September 11, 2001, the Canadian government concluded that it was facing a new terror threat, one that its traditional approach to counterterrorism was ill prepared to deal with. Throughout its history, and certainly since the Cold War, Canada has not been a frequent target of either domestic or international terrorism and certainly had not experienced the type of terror attack used against the United States on September 11. Instead, in Canada, acts of terrorism since the Cold War have been rooted in environmental or animal-rights issues, designed to compel the government, an industry or corporation, or an individual to change their position or behavior on a specific issue, such as clear-cutting forests, performing abortions, or testing pharmaceuticals on animals, rather than to achieve the mass killing of civilians. It could be argued that since the terror campaign of the ethnic nationalist organization Front de Liberation du Quebec (FLQ) in the late 1960s and early 1970s, and the still-unresolved Air India bombing, allegedly by a Khalistani (Sikh nationalist) international terrorist group, on June 23, 1985, which resulted in the deaths of 329 passengers, mostly Canadian citizens, there have been very few major acts of political terrorism in Canada.

COUNTERTERRORISM AND CIVIL RIGHTS

Preventing and responding to terrorism in Canada is complex and challenging primarily because counterterrorism strategies must be consistent with constitutional principles and several federal laws governing police and national security agencies. As in other liberal democracies, the overwhelming issue is that more aggressive antiterrorism polices increase the likelihood of violations of the civil rights, freedoms, and liberties of Canadian citizens, especially immigrants from countries considered to harbor terrorist organizations (Bolz, Dudonis, and Schulz 2002). Specifically, because intelligence-gathering operations employ a variety of methods, from electronic voice and data capture to human operatives, basic privacy rights can be transgressed. Yet these tactics are legal if the appropriate legislative-defined procedures are followed. However, there inevitably are cases where national security and police agencies conduct their operations in a manner that violates either legal procedures or the spirit of the law more generally. In effect, without proper oversight and accountability, even routine antiterrorism tactics can result in violations of privacy rights, as well as a large number of other basic rights and freedoms in Canada. Similarly, there are antiterror programs involving either Canadian agencies alone or joint activities with parallel agencies from other allied countries that attempt to deter terrorist activities through increased physical security, increased public awareness, and the pursuit, interception, incapacitation, and sometimes elimination of those responsible for acts of terrorism, as well as those who are planning, funding, training people for, or otherwise assisting in acts of terrorism, regardless of nationality and whether they are in Canada (Bolz, Dudonis, and Schulz 2002). The latter clandestine and often violent acts against suspected terrorists can violate Canadian law or international conventions, treaties, or declarations that

Canada has signed. A recent example involved a Canadian citizen, Maher Arar, who was detained at the U.S. border based on information provided by the Royal Canadian Mounted Police (RCMP). Arar was renditioned to Syria by the Federal Bureau of Investigation; there, he was imprisoned and tortured for one year by Syrian security agents before being returned to Canada, cleared of all terrorist suspicions, given an official public apology by the Canadian prime minister, and provided a large multimillion-dollar financial settlement (Murphy 2007).

HISTORICAL OVERVIEW

From the Cold War until 1984, Canada utilized a number of different federal agencies; however, collecting and acting on information related to domestic security in Canada involved the RCMP. In effect, as Canada's federal police force, the RCMP alone was responsible for preventing and responding to domestic acts of terrorism outside of wartime situations. However, because of the widely perceived exigencies or hysteria of the Cold War and the use of wartime emergency legislation, invoked in 1970 by the federal government to defeat the Front de Liberation du Quebec's "apprehended insurrection" involving a campaign of kidnappings and the killing of a major Quebec government official, when it came to counterterrorism, the RCMP functioned without any independent legislative oversight or control (Chalk and Rosenau 2004). By the 1980s, there was a strong media and public reaction to "illegal acts" by the RCMP security agency uncovered in detail by separate federal and Quebec provincial inquiry committees (Corrado 1992). The overriding issue was having an unaccountable security organization that served an intelligence function and also had broad powers of arrest (Chalk and Rosenau 2004). In response, in 1984, the federal government created a new civilian intelligence organization, the Canadian Security Intelligence Service (CSIS). Unlike the RCMP, CSIS does not have the ability to detain or arrest suspects. Instead, it is responsible for advising the federal government about activities that threaten the domestic security of Canada (Jacoby 2004). More specifically, the main activities of CSIS are to provide time-sensitive evaluations of terror threats by groups or individuals to municipal, provincial, and federal governments and police agencies; to use case officers to gather information and intelligence in relation to threats to Canada and Canadians; to provide input to the Enforcement Information Index that places alerts on known and suspected terrorists who might try to enter Canada; and to coordinate counterterrorist activities with municipal, provincial, and federal governments and police agencies to respond to terror threats or incidents. In effect, CSIS works on files with national security implications, including terrorism, but they operate closely with the RCMP, who retained exclusive authority for investigating all crimes (Chalk and Rosenau 2004). While the formal processes connecting the two security agencies were only in effect for several years before the largest terrorist attack in Canadian history, the Air India bombings, a recent federal inquiry revealed a fundamental lack of coordination by CSIS and the RCMP that led to major mistakes in uncovering the long-planned terrorist plot (Major 2010). It is within this context that the response to the next generation of antiterrorist policies developed in Canada in the first decade of the 21st century.

A NEW APPROACH

The terror attacks on September 11 fundamentally changed Canada's approach to counterterrorism. Within three months of the attacks, Canada introduced the Anti-terrorism Act (Bill C-36) (Goldsmith 2008). As will be discussed in greater detail in the following, this act provided the police with new and enhanced security powers. A second major change was the reorganization of the federal government's security structures in a parallel manner to the then newly created U.S. Department of Homeland Security. In Canada too, the main theme for the nascent national security policy was to integrate national policing and security/intelligence. To achieve this objective, a new federal ministry was created, Public Safety and Emergency Preparedness Canada. This ministry is responsible for coordinating all of the new and existing agencies associated with security governance, including the RCMP, CSIS, the Communications Security Establishment, and the Canada Border Services Agency (Murphy 2007).

The Anti-terrorism Act amended several federal acts, such as the Criminal Code of Canada, the Security of Information Act, the National Defence Act, and the Proceeds of Crime (Money Laundering) Act (Jacoby 2004). The specific objectives of Bill C-36 are stopping terrorists from entering Canada and protecting Canadians from terrorist acts; providing security agencies and the criminal justice system with the tools to identify, prosecute, convict, and punish terrorists; securing the Canadian-U.S. border and the Canadian economy; and cooperating with the international community in bringing terrorists to justice and addressing the root causes of terrorism (House of Commons of Canada 2001). Bill C-36 gave the security apparatus of Canada, most critically the RCMP, expanded powers including the authority to conduct investigative hearings, to engage in preventive arrests, to list groups as terrorist, and to criminalize participation in or support of a terrorist group (French 2007).

Given these broad powers, Bill C-36 gave the RCMP the authority to label individuals or groups a threat to national security, arrest these defined people using security certificates, and hold them without charge well beyond the limits of habeas corpus (French 2007). Importantly, these police powers have extended not just to federal police officers but also to municipal police forces as well as provincial police forces that are not

RCMP. In effect, given that Bill C-36 entrenched terrorism under the penal jurisdiction of the Criminal Code of Canada, punishment of these offenses also became the responsibility of local and provincial police forces (Chalk and Rosenau 2004). And while this might add enormous resourcing strains to already tight municipal police budgets, much of Canada's domestic terrorism concerns are located in the larger metropolitan cities of Toronto, Montreal, and Vancouver, given their multicultural and multiracial character. Thus, these police departments have had to add counterterrorism units or officers to their organizations and their mandate.

To date, the government has declared its counterterrorism strategies a success since there have been no successful al-Qaeda–style terror attacks in Canada, and there have been several highly publicized operations. Most recently, in June 2006, 17 young males were arrested in Toronto and charged with a variety of offenses, allegedly a terrorist conspiracy that included beheading the prime minister along with blowing up the federal parliament building in Ottawa. There were several other cases where Canadian residents were involved with terrorist plots in Britain and other countries, and they too were considered resolved without damage in Canada. However, critics of the act point to the Arar case and the 2003 case of 23 Muslim citizens and residents who were arrested and charged with a variety of terrorism-related offenses, only to have all allegations of terrorism dropped within two weeks, as evidence of the fact that the act is too sweeping and increases the risk of racial profiling, especially related to the use of security certificates (i.e., detention without immediate trial) against ethnic minorities (Murphy 2007; Jacoby 2004).

CONCLUSION

Since the Cold War, counterterrorism in Canada has evolved from developing strategies and legislation to keep Canada safe from foreign spies and domestic ethnic-nationalist terrorists, to responding to single-issue extremists, to actively deterring real or alleged religious fundamentalist terrorists. Canada has adopted legislation that has expanded the power of the public police, increased information sharing between all security agencies, and increased the ability of the criminal justice system to respond punitively against terrorists. The challenge in Canada, as with all liberal democracies, is to safeguard all Canadians without sacrificing the fundamental principles and values on which Canada has been built and without adopting the repressive methods of authoritarian states in the name of national security.

REFERENCES

Bolz, F., K. J. Dudonis, and D. Schultz. *The Counterterrorism Handbook: Tactics, Procedures, and Techniques.* Boca Raton, FL: CRC Press, 2002.

Chalk, P., and W. Rosenau. *Confronting the "Enemy Within": Security Intelligence, the Police, and Counterterrorism in Four Democracies*. Santa Monica, CA: Rand Corporation, 2004.

Corrado, R. "Political Crime in Canada." In *Criminology: A Canadian Perspective*, edited by R. Linden, 419–50. Toronto: Holt, Rinehart, & Winston, 1992.

French, M. "In the Shadow of Canada's Camps." *Social and Legal Studies* 16, no. 1 (2007): 49–69.

Goldsmith, A. "The Governance of Terror: Precautionary Logic and Counterterrorist Law Reform after September 11." *Law and Policy* 30, no. 2 (April 2008): 141–67.

House of Commons of Canada. "Bill C-36: An Act to Amend the Criminal Code, the Official Secrets Act, the Canada Evidence Act, the Proceeds of Crime (Money Laundering) Act and Other Acts, and to Enact Measures Respecting the Registration of Charities, in Order to Combat Terrorism." October 15, 2001. http://www.law.utoronto.ca/c-36/resources/c36summary.htm. Jacoby, T.A. "Terrorism versus Liberal Democracy: Canadian Democracy and the Campaign against Global Terrorism." *Canadian Foreign Policy* 11, no. 3 (Spring 2004): 65–79.

Major, John C. "Air India Flight 182: A Canadian Tragedy." Ottawa: Commission of Inquiry into the Investigation of the Bombing of Air India Flight 182 (Canada). 2010. http://publications.gc.ca/collections/collection_2010/bcp-pco/CP32-89-4-2010-eng.pdf; http://publications.gc.ca/collections/collection_2010/bcp-pco/CP32-89-2-2010-1-eng.pdf; http://publications.gc.ca/collections/collection_2010/bcp-pco/CP32-89-2-2010-2-eng.pdf.

Murphy, C. "Securitizing Canadian Policing: A New Policing Paradigm for the Post 9/11 Security State?" *Canadian Journal of Sociology* 32, no. 4 (2007): 449–75.

China

Philip C. Aka

Prior to the terrorist attacks against the United States on September 11, 2001, China maintained the semblance of a counterterrorism policy. Although avowedly aimed at the "three evils" of separatism, terrorism, and religious extremism, which the Chinese government pledged to extirpate using "maximum pressure," in actuality, the policy targeted mostly terrorism.

SEPARATISM IN CHINA

Consistent with the opaque character of the regime, China implemented a low-profile program designed to suppress ongoing separatist agitations in various minority regions of the country. Much unrest preceded the installation of Communist rule in China in 1949. The goal of this limited policy was to persuade countries and regimes patronizing these separatists and their organizations to refrain from extending assistance. The policy fit well with the outlook of Chinese leaders who guarded the sovereignty of their country jealously and strove strenuously not to give outsiders, especially the United States and other Western countries, reason to meddle in China's internal affairs, in the guise of criticizing their human rights practices, as Beijing sees it.

The sources of the separatist agitations in China, in order of magnitude, were and still are Xinjiang, Tibet, and Inner Mongolia. The last of these areas borders Mongolia, with whom China seeks to maintain good relations. Tibet is the home of numerous Buddhist clergies whose challenge to the legitimacy of Chinese rule has benefited immensely from the popularity and personal appeal of the Dalai Lama, the region's traditional and spiritual leader. Xinjiang is a region in the western portion of the country, about the size of Alaska, with a population of about 20 million people. The region is rich in mineral resources, accounting for nearly 80 percent of the coal, gold, jade, and precious metal reserves in China, and about one-third of the country's production of petroleum and natural gas. It is bordered by eight countries: Afghanistan, India, Kazakhstan, Kyrgyzstan, Mongolia, Pakistan, Russia, and Tajikistan; as the only region with major roads leading to these countries, it is the nation's gateway to Central Asia. Because of these economic and strategic values, which also include Xinjiang's capacity to absorb high population growth from the central and coastal regions of the country, Chinese leaders place high priority on the stability of this region and fear that its loss would lead to the possible secession of Tibet and Taiwan.

The ethnic group identified with the separatist agitations in Xinjiang is the Uighur, a Turkic Muslim ethnic group, with a population of about 8–10 million. The Uighur were previously an ethnic majority, but increased in-migration of Han Chinese (the majority group in China) to the region turned the Uighur into a minority group in their own region. The influx, which followed the installation of Communist rule in China, was designed to facilitate integration of this and other groups in the new Socialist society Chinese leaders sought and are still seeking to build. The largest incident of separatist unrest involving the group occurred in 1997 when about 100 people were killed during a pro-independence uprising in the town of Ili. To date, the Chinese government maintains a strong presence in Xinjiang, evident in the stationing of about one million Chinese troops throughout the region.

COUNTERTERRORISM MEASURES

The measure described in the preceding morphed into a more vibrant and complicated policy in the aftermath of September 11 and the global war on terror that ensued. With the onset of the global war on terror, China broadened its definition of *terrorism* and criteria for the offense. Under the new dispensation, separatist activities that in the past the Chinese leadership had downplayed as criminal (rather than religious or terrorist) acts suddenly became "terrorism." The definition of terrorism grew in scope to encompass even "ideological attacks." Testament to the recalibration is the publication of data on ethnic conflicts in the region that Chinese officialdom had previously denied existed or had characterized as rare. For example, in January 2002, the Chinese government released a white paper that provided specific details about the political unrests in Xinjiang, which it now denominated terrorism. Among other things, the report provided a list of terrorist organizations that Beijing asked the assistance of the international community in prosecuting. Since September 11, the Chinese government has released information that claims that organizations operated by Uighurs received training and funding from foreign terrorist organizations, such as the Taliban and al-Qaeda.

There have also been reports about raids, arrests of thousands of terrorist suspects, and news regarding the discovery of large caches of weapons and documents pointing to future acts of violence. There have also been reports of Uighur terrorists who Chinese authorities indicate have collaborated with the Taliban or al-Qaeda. Finally, on December 15, 2003, the Chinese Ministry of Public Security released its first list of terrorists and terrorist organizations. The announcement identified four terrorist organizations. These organizations, which the Chinese government also banned, were the Eastern Turkestan Islamic Movement, the Eastern Turkestan Information Center, the East Turkestan Liberation Organization, and the World Uighur Youth Congress. Signs of the changing times include the progressive prosecution of "spiritual terrorism," consisting of public dissent, expressions of dissatisfaction, or even the airing of messages critical of the Chinese government. The overall effect of all this, facilitated by the huge number of troops, suggestive of foreign occupation, is that Xinjiang now has the highest number of executions per week in China.

To critics' charge that terrorist activities in the region had declined steadily since the pro-independence uprising in 1997 (described earlier), which predated September 11, Chinese authorities have responded that "separate thought" is the new technique followed by the same terrorist organizations that previously used violent methods. In support of this thesis of declining separatist violence, critics have observed that of the hundreds of Uighur terrorists the Chinese government claims have collaborated with the Taliban or al-Qaeda, only 22 were ever detained by the United States at Guantánamo Bay, and of that number only 5 were determined to have engaged in terrorist activities. The remaining 17 were released following their acquittal of any terrorist crimes by a U.S. military commission (Munro-Nelson 2011).

Commentators like Martin Wayne have praised Chinese counterterrorism strategies as successful and have suggested that the United States learn from them in its own campaign. In their approach to counterterrorism, the Chinese adopt a "stick and carrot" approach, built up and expanded considerably since September 11, 2001. One component of this approach is border cooperation designed to promote security along China's borders with other countries. Border countries with which China maintains this cooperation include Afghanistan, Kazakhstan, and India. Elements of this cooperation include summit meetings on issues of mutual interest, including antiterrorism, between Chinese leaders and their counterparts in the cooperating countries. One such cooperative activity with Kazakhstan's leaders involved a three-day joint counterterrorism drill in August 2006. Another, a summit meeting held in Delhi, India, in February 2007, covered a range of issues, including curbing financing of terrorism and the nature of the relationship between terrorism financing and drug trafficking.

SOCIAL AND ECONOMIC INITIATIVES

Chinese authorities strive to maintain cordial relations with Muslim nations. Thus, in 2006, in a move aimed at influencing both foreign Muslim nations and China's vast domestic population of Muslims (at 100 million the largest outside the Middle East), the Chinese government officially condemned a Danish cartoon that Muslims considered an insult to the Prophet Muhammad. China has also striven not to do anything that would suggest that its suppression of Uighurs is anti-Muslim. The Chinese government cannot afford to alienate nations that, in addition to religion, share a common language and culture with the Uighurs. This is not an idle concern given that following an ethnic riot in 1997 (different from the one discussed earlier) where nine Uighur Muslims died and hundreds were arrested, Turkey and Saudi Arabia, both Muslim nations, complained about the violations of the human rights of Uighur Muslims. On this point, China, although officially an atheist state, has a State Bureau of Religious Affairs that works to improve relations with leaders both abroad and within China.

Another strategy that Beijing uses in its campaign against terrorism is economic development. In an attempt to promote better living standards for its ethnic minorities and eliminate the economic conditions that can feed separatist agitation, the Chinese leadership maintains a development program for Xinjiang, including opportunities in employment and education, which was operative long before September 11, 2001.

CONCLUSION

Many observers agree that this program has served to minimize separatist unrest. Chinese leaders appear to point to this outcome when, in criticism of the U.S. approach to the war on terror, they advise Washington to focus more on relieving the economic and social conditions that can create a breeding ground for terrorism.

One area in need of attention in China's post–September 11 counterterrorism strategy is an antiterrorism law, which Chinese authorities have spoken about but are yet to enact. Such a law is sorely needed to put some rein on the present loose definition of terrorism, which opportunistically lumps all kinds of violent activities, including criminal, separatist, and religious acts, as terrorism.

See also: **Volume 1, Part IV:** China's Xinjiang Province. **Volume 2, Part I:** Snow Leopard Commando Unit (China)

REFERENCES

Chung, Chien-peng. "Confronting Terrorism and Other Evils in China: All Quiet on the Western Front." *China and Eurasia Forum Quarterly* 4 (2006): 75–87.

Clark, Michael. "China's 'War on Terror' in Xinjiang: Human Security and the Causes of Violent Uighur Separatism." Griffith Asia Institute. Regional Outlook Paper No. 11, 2007, pp. 1–32. http://www.griffith.edu.au/_data/assets/pdf-file/0005/18239/regional-outlook-volume- 11.pdf.

Millward, James. "Violent Separatism in Xinjiang: A Critical Assessment." *Policy Studies* 6 (2004): 1–41.

Munro-Nelson, Janet. "Uighurs in Guantanamo Bay Prison: Innocents or Terrorists?" *Beacon*, July 18, 2011. http://the-beacon.info/countries/united-states/uighurs-in-guantanamo-bay-prison-innocents-or-terrorists-2/.

Shen, Simon, ed. *China and Antiterrorism.* Hauppauge, NY: Nova, 2007.

Van Wie Davis, Elizabeth, and Rouben Azizian, eds. *Islam, Oil, and Geopolitics: Central Asia after September 11.* Lanham, MD: Rowman & Littlefield, 2007.

Wayne, Martin I. "Five Lessons from China's War on Terror." *Joint Force Quarterly* 47 (2007): 42–47.

Wayne, Martin I. *China's War on Terrorism: Counter-insurgency, Politics and Internal Security.* New York: Routledge, 2008.

Wayne, Martin I. "Inside China's War on Terrorism." *Journal of Contemporary China* 18 (2009): 249–61.

Colombia

Anna Kaganiec-Kamieńska

For the last several decades Colombia has been engaged in an internal conflict involving several actors: the government, leftist guerrilla groups, paramilitary units, and drug traffickers. The war has led to large-scale human rights abuses, assassinations, and internal displacement. Further complicating Colombia's problem is the fact that guerrilla groups as well as paramilitaries are often engaged in the drug trade. Hence, it is important to look at the conflict in Colombia as a very complex and multifaceted war. The policies of the Colombian government have been to address these many issues and problems simultaneously.

COLOMBIA'S REVOLUTIONARY FORCES AND PARAMILITARIES

Colombia became a striking example of what may be called *narcoterrorism*. The relationship between terrorism and drugs has taken different forms. Drug profits have been used to fund political violence (e.g., the Revolutionary Armed Forces of Colombia [Fuerzas Armadas Revolucionarias de Colombia, or FARC]), or violence and intimidation have been used by powerful drug traffickers (e.g., Pablo Escobar) to protect illegal drug production and trafficking.

FARC is the largest and the oldest guerrilla group in Colombia. It was founded in the 1960s by Manuel Marulanda as a Communist organization. Since the 1980s FARC has been engaged in and funded by drug production and trafficking.

The National Liberation Army (Ejército de Liberación Nacional [ELN]), formed in 1964, was inspired by the Cuban revolution but also has Christian roots and rejects accusations of having links to the illegal drug trade. The group is mainly financed by income from retentions and kidnappings, as well as "war taxes" imposed on private companies. The most spectacular operations by the ELN were the 1999 retention of the passengers and crew of an Avianca jetliner, the 1999 retention of a church congregation in Cali, and the 2000 bombing of the Medellín power grid.

Another insurgent group in Colombia was the 19th of April Movement (M-19). This urban guerrilla movement is noted for its Dominican embassy siege in 1980 and the Palace of Justice siege in Bogotá in 1985, which left at least 100 people dead, including 12 Supreme Court judges. M-19 signed a peace agreement with the government in the early 1990s and transformed itself into a "legitimate" political party. Finally, the People's Liberation Army (Ejército Popular de Liberación [EPL]) was the country's weakest leftist guerrilla group; its members were finally absorbed by FARC or the ELN.

Another threat to the Colombian state is right-wing paramilitary groups, which emerged due to the weakness of the state and formed mainly to protect different local social, economic, and political interests of civilians and landowners. They often have links to the drug trade, which serves as a source of revenue and funding. Paramilitaries often served as proxy forces of the government in their ongoing battle with leftist guerrillas.

Many of these groups are extremely violent and have turned into a real threat to Colombian state and public order. For example, paramilitaries were responsible for about 75 percent of all politically motivated extrajudicial killings in the first nine months of 1998.

The most formidable self-defense organization—designated a terrorist organization by the United States and the European Union—was the United Self-Defense Forces of Colombia (Autodefensas Unidas de Colombia [AUC]). The AUC formed in 1997, spawned out of local paramilitary and self-defense groups. They engaged in selective assassinations, kidnappings, rapes, civilian displacements, and other human rights violations. Between 2003 and 2006 over 31,000 members were demobilized under the Disarmament, Demobilization and Reintegration program. However, the AUC's successor groups (e.g., Black Eagles) still remain violently active in some regions. This creates new problems for Colombia, as noted in the 2010 Human Rights Watch report.

NARCO-TERRORISM

The term *narco-terrorism* refers to the use of violence and intimidation by powerful narcotics traffickers to protect illegal drug production and trafficking. The Medellín cartel engaged the government in an extremely violent war in the 1980s and sought to influence and change the country's drug policies and law enforcement efforts by means of political violence, bombings, and assassinations. The cartel is believed to have caused the death of thousands of people, including prominent figures such as the minister of justice Rodrigo Lara Bonilla in 1984, three presidential candidates (e.g., Luis Carlos Galán in 1989), and dozens of judges. The violence led to some concessions from the government; for example, Pablo Escobar negotiated his surrender in 1991.

Another powerful Colombian cartel, Cali, was active from the late 1980s till the mid-1990s. This group preferred nonviolent methods of running the drug business, such as bribes. It could, however, be as violent and ruthless as the Medellín cartel when it was considered necessary for business. Since the fall of these two major cartels the drug business in Colombia has been run by a number of smaller groups.

The Colombian government has employed various strategies to stabilize the country. The first steps were taken by President Alfonso López Michelsen (1974–1978) and were continued by his successor, Julio César Turbay Ayala (1978–1982). Turbay ordered a two-year blockade of the Guajira Peninsula, which helped seize about 6,000 tons of marijuana. He also signed an extradition treaty with the United States in 1979. However, during his tenure, increasing guerrilla activity led to repressions and human rights abuses under the state's 1978 Security Statute (in force 1978–1982). Nonetheless, the Trubay Ayala government is credited with introducing the Amnesty Law of 1981 and the first Commission of Peace.

PEACE EFFORTS

President Belisario Betancur (1982–1986) continued the idea of the Commission of Peace (1982) and also approved the General Amnesty Law (1982). It was a significant step in the negotiation process. In March 1984 the government and the FARC signed the so-called Acuerdos de la Uribe, which brought a bilateral cease-fire. Thanks to these attempts the Unión Partiótica (UP) emerged in 1985. This leftist political party formed by FARC gained 14 seats in the national congressional elections of 1986. These former guerrilla members became targets of right-wing paramilitary death squads, some of which were linked to the government. In the late 1980s and the early 1990s, some 4,000 UP leaders and supporters may have been assassinated, including two UP presidential candidates (Jaime Pardo Leal and Bernardo Jaramillo). This experience caused FARC to end the truce, believing that it could not function in the political process. Betancur intensified the war on the drug czars and refused to negotiate their possible reincorporation into the society, which in turn led to increased violent attacks on the Colombian judiciary (some 50 judges were assassinated in 1981–1986).

Under President Virgilio Barco Vargas (1986–1990) the dialogue between the government and FARC was minimal, since his administration focused mainly on peace negotiations with M-19 and EPL. Barco significantly intensified the fight against drug czars (e.g., the 1987 capture of Carlos Lehder and the 1989 killing of Jose Gonzalez Rodriguez Gacha—both of the Medellín cartel), which further intensified drug violence.

The next administration, that of President César Gaviria Trujillo (1990–1994), is sometimes considered a step backward in the peace process. Negotiations with FARC, held in 1991–1992 in Caracas and Tlaxcala, as well as those with the ELN, were unsuccessful. Under Gaviria, however, Pablo Escobar was tracked down by Colombian forces after his escape from his "private" prison and killed in December 1993.

President Ernesto Samper (1994–1998) was accused of accepting $6 million from the Cali cartel to fund his presidential campaign. Nonetheless, six out of seven leaders of the Cali cartel were arrested during his tenure. In the meantime, FARC launched a new strategy, taking advantage of the weak position of the government.

Andrés Pastrana (1998–2002) made peace negotiations with guerrillas his priority. The initial negotiations with FARC led to the 1998 creation of a demilitarized *zona de distención*—a Switzerland-size territory in southern Colombia—as a "laboratory of peace." Negotiations with FARC were, however, unsuccessful. Violence, terrorist incidents, and kidnappings by FARC increased. In February 2002 the zone was taken over by the military. However, under Pastrana some important initiatives that later helped to enhance public security were instituted, such as a significant increase in defense and security expenditures; the 1999 adoption of Plan

Colombia—an ambitious plan to stabilize the situation in the country, with several billion dollars in aid from the United States for the struggle against narcotics (eradication of coca crops, improvement of technology, training and intelligence, etc.); and far-reaching military reforms (started by the new military leadership).

MILITARY AND POLICE REFORMS

Thomas Marks, a researcher for the U.S. Army War College, states, "Colombia's counterinsurgency approach under President Álvaro Uribe Velez built upon a foundation already put in place by the armed forces, a foundation upon which a national as opposed to a virtually stand-alone armed forces campaign could be constructed" (2005, v).

The administration of Álvaro Uribe Vélez (2002–2010) developed a new long-term strategy ("Democratic Security and Defense Policy"), which assigned the cutting-edge role to the Colombian armed forces. The Uribe administration increased expenditures for the military, carried out intensified military and police operations, supported the development of local forces (Soldados de mi Pueblo) trained by the armed forces, formed the Coordination Center for Integrated Action (CCAI), and introduced a "war tax" to increase the Colombian army. It also implemented Plan Patriota, which led to an enhanced offensive against the guerrillas, and implemented a demobilization process for the AUC. The last successful operations of the Colombian government (as of 2008) included the rescue of former Colombian presidential candidate and senator Ingrid Betancourt, the rescue of three U.S. Department of Defense contractors, the deaths of FARC Secretariat members Raúl Reyes and Iván Ríos, the reduction of FARC-controlled territory and the group's financial resources through counternarcotics and other security operations, the captures of midlevel FARC leaders, and the extradition in 2008 of as many as 208 defendants to the United States for prosecution. Another sign of a weakened FARC position is the desertion of a huge number of FARC members, including midlevel and senior FARC leaders (e.g., Nelly Ávila Moreno "Karina"). Progress is also being made as far as drug seizures and the destruction of drug laboratories. For example, in 2009 over 200 metric tons of cocaine and coca base were seized, and over 3,000 drug laboratories were destroyed.

CONCLUSION

Overall, Colombia has made steady progress in establishing the rule of law, increasing public security, and reducing violence. Between 2002 and 2008 kidnappings decreased by 88 percent, and terrorist attacks declined by 79 percent. However, the drug economy continues to pose serious problems and remains a challenge for present and future Colombian governments.

See also: **Volume 1, Part III:** Terrorists, Criminals, and Drug Cartels. **Part VI:** Narco-terrorism: How Real Is the Threat? **Volume 2, Part II:** Colombia Palace of Justice Siege (1985)

REFERENCES

Marcella, Gabriel. *Democratic Governance and the Rule of Law: Lessons from Colombia.* Carlisle, PA: Strategic Studies Institute, U.S. Army War College, 2009.

Marks, Thomas. *Sustainability of Colombian Military/Strategic Support for "Democratic Security."* Carlisle, PA: Strategic Studies Institute, U.S. Army War College, 2005.

Medina Gallego, Carlos. *Conflicto armado y procesos de paz en Colombia. Memoria de casos FARC-RP y EZLN.* Bogotá: Universidad Nacional de Colombia, 2009.

National Consortium for the Study of Terrorism and Responses to Terrorism (START). http://www.start.umd.edu/start/.

Rochlin, James F. *Vanguard Revolutionaries in Latin America.* Boulder, CO: Lynne Rienner, 2003.

Egypt

Nabil Ouassini

Modern terrorism in Egypt has its origins in some of the more radical elements of the Muslim Brotherhood. The Muslim Brotherhood was founded in 1928 by the schoolteacher Hassan al-Banna as a religious, political, and social movement. The movement worked to achieve social justice and political power in Egyptian society by opposing British imperialism and the corrupt monarchy of King Farouk. While al-Banna was committed to nonviolent mobilizing mechanisms toward social change, a number of oppositional figures within the Brotherhood preferred systematic violence to address their grievances. The ensuing violence by this rebellious fringe and the growth of the movement in Egypt as well as neighboring Arab nations led to the Brotherhood's dissolution by the Egyptian prime minister Mahmud Fahmi Nokrashi. The heavy-handed policy of the government eventually provoked the assassinations of both the prime minister (by a member of the Muslim Brotherhood) and al-Banna (by government supporters).

MUSLIM BROTHERHOOD

As an illegal organization, the Muslim Brotherhood found refuge in Gamal Abdel Nasser's Association of Free Officers and its revolutionary ideologies; this group successfully overthrew the Egyptian monarchy.

However, because of its oppositional attitudes toward the officers' secular orientation, the Muslim Brotherhood found itself at odds with the new junta. Nasser had no plans of sharing power and in 1954 abolished the movement after a failed assassination attempt on his life. Through the rest of Nasser's hegemonic reign in Egypt, thousands of members of the Brotherhood were either held in prison, tortured, or executed.

Nasser's repressive policies further radicalized many Brotherhood members and transformed Egypt into the ideological center for extremist Islamic thought. During this contentious period, the intellectual father of Islamic fundamentalism, Sayyid Qutb, produced his exegesis of the Quran and his manifesto in his book *Milestones*. Because of various formulations from Milestones, Nasser's regime convicted Qutb of conspiring against the state and executed him by hanging. In Egypt, as his death elevated his status among Islamists as a *shaheed*, or martyr, his work became widely distributed domestically and internationally. Regarded as one of the most influential works of prison literature, Qutb's Milestones continues to inspire Islamic terrorists all over the world and gave birth to two of the most violent terrorist groups in Egypt's history.

TERRORISM IN EGYPT

Qutb's work and execution prompted many members of the Muslim Brotherhood who disagreed with its position of nonviolence to break away and form organizations that completely embraced violence as a method to bring about change. In the 1970s, these organizations declared the state as an illegitimate un-Islamic entity and preached the use of violence as a means to create political opportunities to establish an Islamic state. The two largest organizations were al Gama al Islamiyah al Masri (GI) and the Egyptian Islamic Jihad (EIJ). After Nasser's death, President Anwar el-Sadat made a significant shift in policy that led to the release of many members of these extremists groups from prison as a political means of countering the growth of communism in Egypt. President Sadat also credulously believed that members of these organizations could be integrated into the state by addressing their grievances and opening up institutional avenues of power. The implications became apparent in an unsuccessful coup attempt in 1974 and the subsequent assassination of Sadat in 1981 for his peace agreement with Israel.

As political opportunities became even more limited as a result of state repression, members of these organizations sought to link their grievances and resources internationally. In the 1980s many members of these organizations participated in the jihad against the Soviet Union in Afghanistan. Like other allies of the United States, Egypt contributed significantly to the mujahideen's resistance to the Soviets, and under the Mubarak regime the Egyptian government pursued both Nasser's unyielding tactics and also Sadat's accommodating approach in dealing with the Islamists. Unfortunately, Mubarak's renewal of the emergency law after Sadat's assassination extended the government's power and control. The law's restriction on any nongovernmental political activity pushed many Islamic radicals to declare an open war against the Egyptian government in the 1990s.

It was in the early 1990s that Egypt experienced the pinnacle of terrorist attacks. Numerous attacks were aimed at the destabilization of society through assassinations, bombings, and shootings of various political and economic targets. There was the assassination of the parliamentary Speaker Rifaat el-Mahjoub, and the attempts on Zaki Badr, the interior minister, in 1989; Safwat Sharif, the information minister in 1993; Hassan al-Alfi, the interior minister, in 1993; and Atef Sedky, the prime minister, in 1993; as well as numerous attempts on President Mubarak himself, including one on a trip to Addis Ababa, Ethiopia.

GOVERNMENT'S RESPONSE TO TERRORISM

The Egyptian government responded with a brutal counterterrorism policy that included many excesses in abuses reminiscent of the Nasser years. This uncompromising approach by the government, along with other experiential and regional factors, pressured the leadership of GI, the organization that was responsible for most of the terrorism in the period, to revise its use of violence (Rashwan 2009, 122–26). Although the leaders of GI declared an end to the use of violence, other radicals, including the second in command in al-Qaeda, Ayman al-Zawahiri, opposed the initiative and organized an attack on the Temple of Hatshepsut in Luxor. The massacre of over 60 people in Luxor by six gunmen, who also held hostages in exchange for Sheikh Abdul Rahman, the man convicted for conspiracy in the first World Trade Center bombing in 1993, infuriated the Egyptian public to the point that Islamic radicals were denying responsibility and losing their appeal. Although the amount of terrorist attacks increased 10-fold in the Muslim world in the following years, Egypt was exempt from this trend apart from the al-Qaeda-inspired Sinai bombings in 2004, the bombings in Sharm el-Shiekh in 2005, and the bombings in Dahab in 2006.

Egypt's success in its counterterrorism strategies can be attributed to the government's uncompromising internal policies and its efforts in external diplomacy. The Egyptian government has evolved in its counterterrorism policies by embracing a mix of strategies used by previous regimes. The current regime adopts a no-concessions policy in dealing with terrorists, and every case of terrorism is tried in either military tribunals or emergency courts that prohibit any plea bargaining (Abou-el-Wafa 2006, 142–43). Along with this firm approach, the Egyptian government has authorized a dynamic deradicalization policy used as an outlet for low-key members of terrorist organizations by accepting their repentance once they renounce the use of violence. The Egyptian government has also remained proactive in its antiterrorism campaigns by countering radical ideology through the use of the media and religious scholars from Al-Azhar University, the center of Sunni Islamic learning in the Muslim world.

Throughout the years of terrorism in Egypt the government has also used external diplomacy at both the regional and international levels as a means of countering terrorism. Egypt has hosted many conferences and signed on to most of the international treaties on terrorism including the Geneva Convention for the Prevention and Suppression of Terrorism. In 1998, Egypt along with other states in the Arab League signed the first regional antiterrorism pact in Cairo. The agreement promised cooperation between Arab states in exchanging information and denying support for terrorist groups with the exception of Palestinian organizations. Egypt, however, continues to work with Israel on marginalizing Hezbollah. Egypt has also worked with Israel in undermining Hamas by cracking down on the smuggling routes in the border areas between Gaza and Egypt, a policy that has drawn widespread criticism from the Muslim world. Egypt adopted the Africa Convention on the Prevention and Combating of Terrorism in a 1999 meeting with the former Organization of African Unity (OAU). As a member of the Organization of the Islamic Conference (OIC) Egypt signed the Convention on Combating Terrorism in 1999. Egypt also maintains close relations and cooperation on numerous issues in counterterrorism with the United States. Following the attacks on September 11, Egypt has cooperated completely with the United Nations Security Council Counter-terrorism Committee (CTC) and tenaciously supported George W. Bush's war on terror. Along with the exchange of intelligence, the United States also continues to train law enforcement personnel from Egypt in the State Department's Antiterrorism Assistance Program. The U.S. government also helped Egypt establish a financial intelligence unit after the Egyptian Parliament passed strong legislation against money laundering.

CONCLUSION

Overall, the Egyptian government has been quite successful in its counterterrorism strategies despite its historical reputation as the center of Islamic extremist thought. Egypt's success is accredited to its domestic no-tolerance policy, its effectual deradicalization campaigns in the media, and its successful cooperation with the international community. Egypt has also created one of the most innovative counterterrorism programs in its promotion of the renunciation of violence by terrorist groups, adopted primarily by the leaders of GI and EIJ. In spite of its comprehensive success with some of the political and religious causes of terrorism, it will be essential for the government's future counterterrorism strategy to address some of the potential manifest political and socioeconomic root causes of terrorism in Egypt (Alexander 2006, 214). Since the 2011 revolution that drove President Mubarak and his regime from power, Egypt has been under military rule, and there remains political unrest in the country.

REFERENCES

Abou-el-Wafa, Ahmed. "Egypt." In *Counterterrorism Strategies: Successes and Failures of Six Nations*, edited by Yonah Alexander, 127–51. Dulles, VA: Potomac Books, 2006.

Alexander, Yonah, ed. *Counterterrorism Strategies: Successes and Failures of Six Nations*. Dulles, VA: Potomac Books, 2006.

Rashwan, Diaa. "The Reunification of Violence by Egyptian Jihadi Organizations." *Leaving Terrorism Behind: Individual and Collective Disengagement*, edited by Tore Bjorgo and John Horgan, 113–32. New York: Routledge, 2009.

France

James McIntyre

France is the country of origin for the term *terrorism*, coined by members of the government during the radical phase of the French Revolution of 1789. At that time, *terrorists* were those who supported and implemented the policies of the radical government. Throughout the 19th and early 20th centuries, the country experienced many of the same types of terrorist acts as other European states, including bombings and assassinations. In the more modern sense, the French experience with terrorism began in the aftermath of World War II, specifically during France's war of decolonization in Algeria (1954–1962). In addition to terrorism by the groups associated with Algerian independence, France has struggled with attacks from internal groups devoted to both right-wing extremist political views and the extreme left of the political spectrum. By the same token, various state-sponsored and nonstate actors with origins in the Middle East have targeted France on a number of occasions.

ALGERIA (1954–1962)

France's first experience of something approaching international terrorism in the period following World War II came during the conflict in Algeria. From the outset of this conflict, members of the Algerian resistance, the Front Liberation Nationale (FLN), began to target French civilians living in Algiers. Since Algiers was considered to be a part of France, these attacks could be considered to have been carried out on French soil. In addition, members of the FLN attempted to bring the war to French soil as well. Numerous campaigns and specific attacks were plotted, but few reached the stage of implementation. The plans that were carried out resulted in failure. While their terrorist activities were poorly orchestrated and unsuccessful, the group did experience a great deal of success in raising funds in France for the struggle in Algeria. In responding to the various threats posed by the FLN, the French government created special security courts. These courts were not bound by the same rules of evidence as regular French criminal courts.

In the aftermath of the Algerian War, France experienced a lull in terrorist activity. This respite was short-lived. The peace was shattered by the activities of several groups in the 1970s. Among the most potentially devastating was the attack on Mt. d'Arree Nuclear Power Station on August 15, 1975. Two bombs exploded, damaging sections of the facility that at the time were shut down for inspection. For the most part, the terrorist activity in France during the 1970s stood as the work of various internal separatist groups. In addition, some still held onto resentments that stemmed from the war in Algeria. Throughout the decade, the French government's reaction to these attacks was one of neutrality. Under this policy, France attempted to take no stance on issues that could conceivably generate terror attacks and at the same time did little to interdict the activities of various groups working within its borders. This approach had a reverse effect in that it succeeded in creating fresh difficulties due to the fact that many groups made France a base of their operations against other powers, who grew to resent the French policy. As a result of the international climate as well as domestic factors French authorities moved to a different set of policies. Much of this occurred due to new threats France encountered in the 1980s.

FRENCH VULNERABILITY

Since 1980, France has experienced terrorist attacks from three distinct types of political groups. The first encompassed groups that espoused an extreme leftist ideology and sought the overthrow of the French government. A good example of this type of group would be Action Directe, which posed a significant security threat between 1979 and 1987. Initially, the group focused its attention on material targets. As the decade wore on, it began to support political assassination as well. In the end, however, the group never secured a following large enough to sustain it, and French authorities succeeded in breaking its back by the end of the 1980s. A second source of terrorism in France in the 1980s derived from various regional separatist groups that sought independence from France. Groups such as these were most prevalent in the Basque country, Brittany, and Corsica.

The last source of terrorist threats to France was international terrorism, predominantly Middle Eastern in origin. Much of the reason for the upsurge in attacks from Middle Eastern groups lay in the fact that in the 1980s French policy began to work at odds with the policies of the governments of Syria, Iran, and Libya, all known to be state sponsors of various terrorist groups at the time. For example, a series of attacks occurred in the mid-1980s. These were most likely inspired by the Iranian government and were directed at France as punishment for its continued military and financial backing of Saddam Hussein.

The initial response of government agencies to this new threat lacked both energy and direction. Much of this lethargy derived from the inexperience of existing agencies in dealing with the challenge of international terrorism. These government organs likewise seemed uninterested in learning about the new threat. Many factors contributed to the weakness of the French counterterrorism response. These factors included the policy France had followed in regards to terrorists during the 1970s. In addition, there was the political environment engendered by Socialist Party's coming to power in France in 1981.

All of the preceding issues combined to make France the European country that was most often targeted by various terrorist groups through the 1980s. For a brief period during the presidency of Socialist François Mitterand there even appeared to be an attempt to negotiate with the terrorists and attempt some sort of agreement with the various groups targeting France. On coming to power, Mitterand closed the security courts that had been created to meet the threats arising during the Algerian War; however, he failed to replace them with any comparable agency. While it fell in line with the president's politics, this action had the effect of leaving France particularly vulnerable and ill equipped to meet terrorist attacks.

REFORMS

The French response to terrorism underwent a dramatic shift as the result of a series of attacks that targeted numerous transportation and shopping venues in Paris in 1986. Responsibility for most of the attacks was claimed by a new group known as the Committee for Solidarity of Near Eastern Political Prisoners. Their goal encompassed the release of three unrelated terrorist prisoners then incarcerated in French jails. The attacks launched by this group, in turn, generated a substantive transformation in the government policy for dealing with terrorists. As a result, new laws were passed in September 1986, and agencies were created that retained broad powers for the investigation and prosecution of terror suspects. The laws also succeeded in coordinating the various police and intelligence-gathering agencies within France in order to make them more effective. Among the agencies created at this time was the Unite Coordination de La Lutte Anti-Terroriste and, at the Justice Ministry, the Service Pour Coordination de La Lutte Anti-Terroriste, both of which were housed in the Ministry of the Interior. Rather than create new courts, the measures of the

1980s centralized the trials of terrorism suspects in the trial court of Paris. The cumulative effect of this reform was that it allowed agencies within France for the first time to assemble a complete picture of terrorist groups and their activities on a national scale.

The new system created by the 1986 legislation received its first true test with the spillover of actions from the Algerian Civil War into France. On the whole, the new agencies proved very effective. The next major terrorist event in France was the hijacking of flight 8969 from Algiers to Paris on December 25, 1994. The plane was retaken the next day by French commandos, who killed the hijackers. In a clear contrast to the experience of the 1980s, the French government was able to track down the remaining members of the responsible network within four months. The enhanced security measures soon bore fruit as French authorities were increasingly able not only to respond to threats but also to abort some attacks before they were launched.

As the new agencies created by the legislation of 1986 gained experience, they began to focus to a greater degree on the financial lifelines of various terrorists groups. The change of focus drove a change in policy to one that targets interdiction. This approach gained institutional support with the passage of a 1996 law that made it a crime to conspire to commit a terrorist act, regardless of whether any action was ever taken.

CONCLUSION

Since 1974, over 3,500 people have been killed in France as a result of various attacks by different terrorist groups. Clearly, the French experience with terrorism in the late 20th century has been a painful one. At the same time, it has led to the development of one of the most aggressive response systems for confronting terrorism in the world today.

See also: **Volume 1, Part IV:** Counterterrorism Policy in France. **Part V:** European Union. **Volume 2, Part I:** Groupe d'Intervention de la Gendarmerie Nationale (GIGN) (France); Groupes d'Intervention de la Police Nationale (GIPN) (France). **Part II:** Air France Flight 8969 (1994)

REFERENCES

Andress, David. *The Terror: The Merciless War for Freedom in Revolutionary France.* New York: Farrar, Straus and Giroux, 2005.

Gerecht, Marc Reuel, and Gary Schmitt. "France: Europe's Counterterrorism Powerhouse." *American Enterprise Institute for Public Policy Research* 3 (November 2007): 1–6.

Horne, Alistair. *A Savage War of Peace: Algeria 1954–1962.* New York: New York Review Books, 2006. (Orig. pub. 1977.)

Shapiro, Jeremy, and Bénédicte Suzan. "The French Experience of Counterterrorism." *Survival* 45, no. 1 (Spring 2003): 67–98.

Tlemcani, Rachid. "Islam in France: The French Have Themselves to Blame." *Middle East Quarterly* 6, no. 1 (March 1997): 31–38.

Germany

Hans Brun

Germany's current legal and constitutional structure is, of course, a direct consequence of its troubled past. The German Constitution (Grundgesetz) was created in 1949 and includes a number of rules particularly aimed at preventing minority parties from seizing control and, by doing so, acquiring the right to introduce emergency powers (as happened at the beginning of the 1930s when the National Socialists came to power). Unlike many other constitutions, the German Constitution's first section contains a very detailed listing of the rights of the individual (e.g., the right to free speech, the right of assembly, and the right of association, just to name a few). Another interesting aspect of the German Constitution is the balance between the protection of the civil liberties of the individual and the prevention of possible abuse of these civil liberties by violent extremists. That is, the German Constitution guarantees and protects the rights of the individual, but it also allows for the limitation of those rights if necessary to promote and protect the democratic order and community rights. The German Federal Court, which oversees and controls the actions of the German Parliament and its government, has also chosen to include "community security" as a civic right, which means that the government's antiterrorism measures, undertaken to protect society as a whole, might be more important than individual claims (Beckman 2007, 90–91).

POLITICAL VIOLENCE

West Germany started to experience political violence and terrorism during the late 1960s when student protests gradually morphed into terrorism. From 1968 to 1977, several extreme left-wing terrorist groups attacked individuals and property labeled as symbols of capitalism and American imperialism. A number of right-wing terrorist groups also started to attack various targets, in one instance killing 13 people with an explosive device during the Oktoberfest in Munich in 1980 (Schneckener 2006, 73–80; Rau 2004, 313).

West Germany has experienced not only domestic but also foreign terrorism. Several foreign terrorist groups started to operate in West Germany during the 1970s. One well-known terrorist attack perpetrated by foreign terrorist groups is, of course, the attack on the Israeli Olympic Team during the 1972 Olympics that was carried out by the Palestine group known as Black September. The German authorities tried to liberate the Israeli hostages with force at an airfield but were unsuccessful. This failed rescue attempt was the reason for the creation of the elite antiterrorist unit Grenzschutzgruppe 9 (GSG 9; Tophoven 1984).

In reaction to attacks by various terrorist groups, the German Parliament enacted new legislation, that is, three major antiterrorism acts (*Anti-Terror-Gesetze*) in 1974, 1976, and 1978 (Schneckener 2006, 82–83). The formation of terrorist organizations and the support and encouragement of serious violent crimes were criminalized. This was an effort to discourage individuals from forming or joining radical organizations, since a number of leading politicians perceived various political movements as the main source of political violence. Under this legislation, the authorities did not need a reasonable suspicion of criminal activity in order to launch an investigation. The new legislation also strengthened the powers of the prosecution and introduced regulations that specifically targeted the rights of the defense. It became possible for a court to exclude defense attorneys from the courtroom at the request of the police, the prosecutor, or the court itself, if the attorney in question was the subject of the proceedings or was obstructing justice (Boyne 2004, 58–59, 60–61).

The political response to political violence in Germany was influenced and affected not only by particular events but also by the political situation in the German Parliament and different constraints facing legislators. One of the more controversial policies introduced by the German government was the so-called Termination of the Radicals Policy (*Berufsverboten*). This policy made it possible to bar from employment civil servants who engaged in "anti-constitutional behavior" or belonged to an organization that engaged in such activities. It has been estimated that at least 1.3 million civil servants were screened between 1973 and 1980 and that approximately 1,300 were barred from public sector employment (Boyne 2004, 55, 57).

The German Parliament also enacted the Law for the Protection of Communal Peace, which made it a crime to support "violence by means of words, publications, and films that could disturb the 'public peace'" (Boyne 2004, 62; Beckman 2007, 99). This law made it possible for the authorities to investigate the area between conduct and behavior on one side and the right to freedom of expression and speech on the other. In a well-known case, author Bommi Bauman was charged and convicted for a book he had written about his earlier experiences as a terrorist, even though the book contained a severe critique of some of the methods used by left-wing terrorists (Boyne 2004, 62–63; Beckman 2007, 99).

LAW ENFORCEMENT

The German police introduced new working methods in order to fight terrorism as effectively as possible. They modernized their computer systems and introduced new methods of gathering and analyzing vast amounts of information. Several databases were created, and new legislation made it possible to store personal data. Most databases were used to identify overlapping clusters of interesting traits in the population. These clusters were deduced from profiles of known Rote Armee Fraktion (RAF) members and identified using a search method known as grid search (*Ras-terfahndung*; Schneckener 2006, 83–84).

The German authorities began to successfully arrest members of the most notorious left-wing group, the RAF (also known as the Baader-Meinhof group), in 1970. The five leading members of the RAF were arrested in 1972. These arrests were spawned by surveillance operations and information from the public. In prison, one of the leading members, Holger Meins, starved himself to death during a hunger strike in December 1974. Criminal proceedings were initiated against the other four members in 1975. They were all sentenced to life imprisonment and died in prison, most likely due to suicide. The imprisonment and death of the RAF leadership led to a significant decrease in RAF operations and left-wing terrorism in West Germany (Groenewold 1993, 137; Rau 2004, 313–15).

COUNTERTERRORISM POST-9/11

The German government introduced a number of additional counterterrorism measures after 9/11. The most controversial measure was the use of military force. According to German legislation, the government needs the approval of the Parliament to send military forces abroad. German support of Operation Enduring Freedom caused a political crisis and forced the chancellor to link the commitment to military operations in Afghanistan with the question of whether the cabinet should stay in power in order to achieve a majority support in the Parliament for sending military forces to Afghanistan (Schneckener 2006, 85; Rau 2004, 319–20).

Just eight days after 9/11, the German government approved the so-called first security package (*Anti-Terror-Pakete*), which was primarily focused on the abolishment of so-called religious privilege (*Religionsprivileg*) and the criminalization of support for or membership in criminal or terrorist organizations based outside of Germany. Up until this revision, religious organizations had enjoyed special rights under German law. It now became possible to ban religious organizations if their activities or purposes were incompatible with the German Constitution or criminal legislation. Using this provision, German authorities have banned at least three religious organizations linked to violent Islamists. The package also contained additional funding of €1.5 billion earmarked for the German military, the intelligence community, and the Federal Border Guard (Schneckener 2006, 86; Rau 2004, 316).

The second package was introduced in January 2002 and dealt mainly with the effectiveness of law enforcement and the security services. Efforts were made to strengthen the rights and capabilities of these agencies and to improve information flow between various agencies within the law enforcement and intelligence community. It also became easier to collect information from public and private sources (e.g., telephone records). The use of armed air marshals was also permitted on German airliners (Schneckener 2006, 87–88; Rau 2004, 317, 339–44). The second security package also provided for increased collection of social information from public and private sources in order to conduct more efficient grid searches. As mentioned earlier, grid searches were used in the 1970s during an ongoing terrorist campaign. Today, grid searches are used as a preventive measure for identifying possible sleeper cells that may or may not exist. That is, the authorities use this method without any concrete suspicions that individuals have committed or are planning to commit acts of terrorism (Schneckener 2006, 84, 87–88; Rau 2004, 317, 339–44).

CONCLUSION

The German government has also introduced a number of additional reforms. One is an immigration law making it possible to issue deportation orders against persons with suspected links to terrorism. Another is an aviation security law introduced to allow the German Air Force to use force against civilian aircraft inside German airspace. New regulations have also been introduced for banks and credit institutes in order to stop terrorist financing and money laundering (Schneckener 2006, 88–89).

See also: **Volume 1, Part IV:** Counterterrorism in Germany: Post-9/11; **Volume 2, Part I:** Grenzschutzgruppe 9 (Germany); Special Operations Command/Mobile Task Force (SEK/MEK) (Germany). **Part II:** West German Embassy Siege (1975); Lufthansa Flight 181 (1977)

REFERENCES

Alexander, Yonah, ed. *Counterterrorism Strategies. Successes and Failures of Six Nations.* Dulles, VA: Potomac Books, 2006.

Beckman, James. *Comparative Legal Approaches to Homeland Security and Anti-Terrorism.* Farnham Surrey, UK: Ashgate, 2007.

Boyne, Shawn. "Law, Terrorism, and Social Movements: The Tension between Politics and Security in Germany's Anti-terrorism Legislation." *Cardozo Journal of International and Comparative Law,* no. 41 (2004): 41–82.

Groenewold, Kurt. "The German Federal Republic's Response and Civil Liberties." In *Western Responses to Terrorism,* edited by Alex P. Schmid and Ronald D. Crelinsten, 136–50. London: Frank Cass, 1993.

Rau, Markus. "Country Report on Germany." In *Terrorism as a Challenge for National and International Law: Security versus Liberty?* edited by Christian Walter, Silja Vöneky, Silja Röben, and Frank Schorkopf, 311–62. Heidelberg, Germany: Springer, 2004.

Schmid, Alex P., and Ronald D. Crelinsten, eds. *Western Responses to Terrorism.* London: Frank Cass, 1993.

Schneckener, Ulrich. "Germany." In *Counterterrorism Strategies: Successes and Failures of Six Nations,* edited by Yonah Alexander, 72–98. Dulles, VA: Potomac Books, 2006.

Tophoven, Rolf. *GSG 9: German Response to Terrorism.* Koblenz, Germany: Bernard & Graefe, 1984.

Walter, Christian, Silja Vöneky, Silja Röben, and Frank Schorkopf, eds. *Terrorism as a Challenge for National and International Law: Security versus Liberty?* Heidelberg, Germany: Springer, 2003.

Greece

Anthony Nicolopoulos

Terrorism in Greece was virtually unknown before 1975 because the Greek Communist Party had renounced violence after its crushing defeat in the 1945–1949 civil war. The extreme repression of the 1967–1974 dictatorship of the colonels in Greece, also known as the junta, caused the Communist movement to splinter into violent radical groups, which blossomed into full-blown terrorist organizations in the post-1975 security vacuum. It took Greece more than 25 years after the fall of the junta to rebuild its security forces and establish effective laws and policies to combat terrorism in a manner consistent with democratic principles.

REPRESSION AND POLITICAL DISSENT

Whereas pre-junta regimes had been content to stymie the spread of the left in politics, the colonels sought to control and censor every form of human expression, leaving no outlet for restless students to vent their frustrations. These repressive policies effectively politicized every form of expression, thus creating political dissidents where there were none to begin with. Creative expression, however, cannot be stopped; it can only be driven underground. The membership of secret student organizations, all of them Communist fronts, swelled during the junta.

The frustrating initial failure to mobilize the Greek public through peaceful demonstrations and propaganda prompted talk of violent resistance in order to create loud, self-evident actions proving the regime's vulnerability. But the Communists had abandoned violence as the means to power in favor of infiltration and subversion. This caused loud disagreements within the anti-junta movement between the indoctrinated party members and the younger impatient and restless neophytes. Several groups advocating political violence split from the Communist organizations, creating what became known as the far left: radicals outside the sphere of control of the Communist Party.

The security services quickly rounded up these prototerrorists thanks to mistakes they made due to inexperience and a lack of training. Prosecution and sentencing were swift and orderly as no charges had to be invented in these cases since the law had actually been broken. When the junta fell in 1974 after a military debacle in Cyprus, all political prisoners were freed and resistance fighters achieved instant celebrity status.

Some resistance members used their anti-junta credentials to win election to political office, especially with the newly formed Panhellenic Socialist Movement (PASOK). Others, however, rejected the post-junta democratic system and continued their underground revolutionary armed struggle. They were the founders of the two most notorious Greek terrorist groups, the November 17 Revolutionary Organization (17N), a direct reference to the anti-junta struggle, and the Popular Revolutionary Struggle (ELA).

ANTITERRORISM LEGISLATION

By 1978, terrorist assassinations and bombings prompted the first Greek attempt at creating antiterrorism legislation. Law 774/1978, inspired by contemporaneous Italian and German legislation, criminalized the organization of and participation in terrorist groups and provided severe penalties including life imprisonment or death for serious crimes such as murder and kidnapping.

In 1981, PASOK won the elections, bringing many former freedom fighters into the government and into the security services through political appointments. This was the year terrorism became a full-fledged social phenomenon in Greece. The PASOK government undermined the antiterrorist law of 1978 and finally abolished it altogether in 1983 because many, if not most, Socialist deputies were opposed in principle to the concept of a state with strong coercive powers.

Terrorism reached new heights in Greece between 1983 and 1990. Terrorist groups were idolized like rock bands, while the PASOK government emasculated the security services through legislation curtailing police powers, budget reductions, and rampant cronyism. In the late 1980s the seemingly deliberate bungling of a series of terrorism cases by police and intelligence officials led many observers to speculate that PASOK members were providing top cover for their former comrades or even directing them behind the scenes. Many of the terrorists' victims were considered threats to the PASOK government. They included publishers, journalists, and parliament members, as well as the star prosecution witness in a corruption scandal that could have destroyed PASOK as a political party.

A series of political scandals eventually brought down PASOK and returned the center right to power in 1990 after nearly a decade on the opposition bench. One of the first orders of business was the drafting of antiterrorism legislation that was immediately voted into law. The new law, 1916/1990, avoided the word *terrorism*, using *organized crime* as a euphemism. In practice, the law was a reincarnation of the previous 774/1978 law without the death penalty provision. The 1990 law broadened police jurisdiction and forbade the publication of terrorist communiqués by the press.

In 2001, PASOK, back in power but under new and more moderate leadership, proposed a new antiterrorism bill under international pressure following the assassination of the British military attaché by leftist terrorists. The new law retained the term *organized crime* as catchall to include terrorism. This was the first bill to gain bipartisan support in the fight against terrorism, and it proved to be a very effective tool for the police, who managed to dismantle both 17N and ELA within the next two years.

Three years later, under international pressure concerning the safety and security of the 2004 Athens Olympic Games, the Greek Parliament approved a new antiterrorism law (3251/2004) that defined terrorist actions according to European Union guidelines as the performance of one or more crimes in a way or on a scale, or under such conditions, that the fundamental constitutional, political, financial, or social structure of a state or an international organization are harmed or seriously destabilized or destroyed. The following activities were specifically excluded from the definition of terrorism: demonstrations, including violent demonstrations; membership in antiglobalization movements or political organizations; exercise of the right to free speech; ideological support of terrorism without participation in terrorist acts or organizations; and violent activities such as clashes with police during demonstrations.

The 2004 law also raised the statute of limitations to 30 years, but a clause of the Greek Constitution prohibited its retroactive application. In order to close the loophole it was decided that old terrorists would be prosecuted for membership in a terrorist group, which would be considered ongoing until the time of arrest, and would automatically receive the maximum sentence.

LAW ENFORCEMENT MEASURES

The Counterterrorist (CT) Service (officially designated the Special Violent Crimes Squad) is a secret police organization with handpicked members. In 2002, the CT Service was led by a police lieutenant general and consisted of 250 police officers split into six specialized sections in constant synergy with each other: coordination, investigations, identification, operations, intelligence, and internal affairs. The CT Service has access to a modern crime lab that was set up with assistance from the Federal Bureau of Investigation and the New Scotland Yard.

The CT Service and the Serious Organized Crime branch of the police share a special supervising prosecutor, assigned by the Ministry of Justice, who can grant immediate access to classified files as well as databases protected by privacy laws and can issue search or wiretap warrants. A supervising prosecutor with similar duties is also assigned to the National Intelligence Service (EYP) to grant access to information protected by privacy laws and to perform intelligence oversight functions. EYP, however, has no arrest authority so any actionable information must be passed to law enforcement agencies. In 1999, in order to strengthen information sharing with law enforcement agencies, EYP was subordinated to the Ministry of Public Order (renamed the Ministry of Citizen Protection in 2010).

In support of the CT Service, the Greek police maintain a separate SWAT-type unit called the Special Antiterrorist Unit (EKAM). EKAM spearheaded the apprehension of terrorist suspects during the dismantling of the 17N and ELA terrorist organizations in 2002. In March 2003, unit members successfully resolved a hijacking situation at the Athens International Airport. During the security ramp-up for the 2004 Olympic Games, the unit's strength was raised to 200 men; they must requalify in their specialty every three months. EKAM's missions include hostage rescue, high-risk arrests, VIP protection, and chemical, biological, radiological, and nuclear (CBRN) responses.

In 2004, after the Olympic Games, the center right returned to power and began the customary reshuffling of privileged assignments within the government, and the CT Service was no exception. Its special pay incentives and the perception that little real work was left to be done invited political cronyism that seriously diluted the capabilities of the CT Service even as it nearly doubled in size to 460 personnel. In 2009, at a time when domestic terrorism was making a comeback, insider information leaks exposed the severity of the situation in the CT Service, prompting the resignation of key officers and the reevaluation of previous policy decisions.

Approximately half of the veteran CT officers who had been transferred to the provinces following the dismantling of 17N and ELA were returned to senior postings in the CT Service, and all terrorism cases from 2002 on were reevaluated for missed clues. Furthermore, closer ties were forged between the National Intelligence Service (EYP), and the CT Service while carefully delineating each service's responsibilities. In order to achieve this and avoid interservice rivalries, a senior officer of the CT Service was appointed as the new director of EYP and a former director of EYP counterintelligence was appointed as the new head of the CT Service.

CONCLUSION

Although Greece has successfully dealt with its major domestic terrorist groups, there seems to be a never-ending supply of would-be terrorists to take their place. The culture of impunity when it comes to political street violence and vandalism has created a fringe element in Greek society that attracts rebellious and frustrated young people into the manipulative clutches of the radical extraparliamentary left. Additionally, the lack of upward mobility in Greek society, a disproportionate tax burden on the poor and middle classes due to outrageous tax evasion by the wealthy, and institutional government corruption that is seldom (if ever) punished all add to the frustrations of the younger generations, who are increasingly losing faith in their country's political system.

See also: **Volume 1, Part I:** Global Terrorism: Post-9/11; The Terrorist Threat in the 21st Century: A Global Security Problem

REFERENCES

Apogevmatini (Athens), July 17, 2002.

Center for Security Studies. http://www.kemea.gr/main.php?lid=2.

Gatopoulos, Derek. "Police Scour Greece for 'Man of a Thousand Faces.'" Athens News Agency (Athens), August 9, 2002. http://www.athensnews.gr/old_issue/12974/8473.

Gilson, George. "Police Nab Suspected 17N Leader." Athens News Agency (Athens), July 19, 2002. http://www.athensnews.gr/old_issue/12971/8372.

Gilson, George. "Will the Mystery of 17N Arms Depot Theft Be Solved?" Athens News Agency (Athens), July 19, 2002. http://www.athensnews.gr/old_issue/12971/8374.

Gilson, George. "The Rights and Wrongs of 17N Suspects." Athens News Agency (Athens), August 9, 2002. http://www.athensnews.gr/old_issue/12974/8474.

Greek Ministry of Public Order Press Office. "Special Anti-terrorist Unit." July 2004, http://www.astynomia.gr/images/stories/DOCS/Attachment11479_ENHMEROTIKO_EKAM_28-7-04.pdf.

Greek National Intelligence Service. http://www.nis.gr/portal/page/portal/NIS/.

Greek National Television. *Ρεπορτάζ Χωρίς Σύνορα—Η ΑΛΗΘΙΝΗ ΙΣΤΟΡΙΑ ΤΗΣ 17 ΝΟΕΜΒΡΗ* [Reporters without borders: The true story of 17 November] (documentary). December 15, 2008. http://www.youtube.com/user/graikylos.

"Junta Supporters in Action in the Police" (*"Χουντικοί εν δράσει στην Αστυνομία"*). *Rizospastis* (*Ριζοσπάστης*), November 11, 1997. http://www2.rizospastis.gr/wwwengine/story.do?id=3704558&publDate=11/11/1997.

Migdalovitz, Carol. "Greece: Threat of Terrorism and Security at the Olympics." Congressional Research Service, Report RS21833, July 9, 2004.

"The New Super Wiretap System of EYP and the CT Service." *News Kosmos*, April 15, 2010. http://www.newskosmos.com/index.php?option=com_content&view=article&id=4240:2010-04-15-17-20-49&catid=37:greece&Itemid=56.

Papahellas, Alexis, and Tasos Telloglou. *Φάκελος 17 Νοεμβρη* [File 17 November]. Athens: Estia, 2002.

Research Institute for European and American Studies. "Mapping the Development of Anti-terror Legislation in Greece in the Aftermath of 9/11." November 20, 2007. http://www.rieas.gr/index.php?option=com_content&view=article&id=485&catid=21&Itemid=63.

"Revolutionary Organization 17 November." Wikipedia. March 14, 2012. http://en.wikipedia.org/wiki/Revolutionary_Organization_17_November.

Simeonidou-Kastanidou, E. *Organized Crime and Terrorism.* Athens and Thessaloniki: Sakkoula, 2005.

"The Trajectory of 17N–29 May, Cubans, Lambros, ELA" (Η διαδρομή της «17N»). *Kathimerini* (Athens), Sunday edition, July 21, 2002.

India

Patit Paban Mishra

India achieved independence on August 15, 1947, following the end of British colonial rule. On January 26, 1950, it became a sovereign democratic republic when the Indian Constitution entered into force. In its history of more than five decades, the country has made tremendous progress under a democratic political system. However, the specter of terrorism has become a major national security concern as various groups and nonstate actors endeavor to achieve their various violent agendas. Internal security is the responsibility of the Ministry of Home Affairs of the government of India. For the first few decades after independence, the ministry focused on law and order and crime control. But gradually its scope expanded and encompassed the eastern states, Kashmir, Punjab, and others, which had become a hotbed of terrorism and insurgency. Indeed, since independence India has become one of the most terrorism-afflicted countries in the world.

TERRORIST ATTACKS

India has experienced violence from separatist movements within its borders and cross-border terrorism from various extremist factions based in Pakistan. Some of India's most devastating attacks were the assassination of Prime Minister Indira Ghandi by her Sikh bodyguards in 1984, an attack on the Indian Parliament in December 2001, an attack on the Akshardam Temple in 2002, the Mumbai blasts in 2003, the Ayodhya and Delhi attacks in 2005, the Doda armed attack in 2006, and the Varanasi bombing in 2010. Many of these attacks attracted international attention.

Homegrown Islamist movements have also grown in recent years. After Indonesia India has the largest Muslim population in the world. Many of these individuals have formed jihadist organizations to redress the real and perceived grievances of the Islamic community in India. Their cadre is drawn from Muslim youth, students, mullahs, professionals, and even criminals. For example, the Students Islamic Movement of India, established in 1977, has an agenda of rejecting nationalism and secularism. They are based in North India and the province of Kerala and are purportedly linked to jihadist elements in Pakistan. The cadres are influenced by the rhetoric of Osama bin Laden and seek to convert India into an Islamic theocracy. Additionally, the Indian Mujahideen emerged as a terrorist group in 2007 and perpetrated numerous attacks throughout various Indian cities; they were responsible for a series of bombings in Ahmedabad in July 2008. Other groups contributing to instability in India are the Naxalites and the United Liberation Front of Assam among others. The groups mentioned here pose an ongoing threat to the Indian state.

KASHMIR

Kashmir has been a flashpoint for over 60 years. Militancy in Kashmir is one of India's major security problems as the country has claimed sovereignty over the entire region. Civil unrest and terror in this region have taken the lives of both Hindus and Muslims. Over the years there have been reports of human rights abuses by terrorists as well as the Indian army. The problem in Kashmir is not about religion as reported by much of the news media. Three states lay claim to territory in Kashmir: India, Pakistan, and China. A portion of Kashmir designated as Azad Kashmir is occupied by Pakistan. Many of India's terrorism problems have been spawned by the conflict with Pakistan over control of this area. In fact, Kashmir is one of the major issues between the two neighbors, which have fought four wars over the region since 1947.

From the mid-1980s, a changed situation had confronted India regarding Kashmir. A sizable number of the people of Kashmir desired independence. An insurgency movement began, which changed its position from independence for Kashmir to a merger with Pakistan. Islamist militants from Pakistan as well as Afghanistan, Iran, Bangladesh, and Sudan unleashed a reign of terror on the region. The support from the Pakistani government was obvious, with terrorists getting training in various camps in Afghanistan and Pakistan. The All Parties Hurriyat Conference and the Jammu and Kashmir Liberation Front opted for an independent Kashmir. Terrorist groups operating in the region—Lashkar-e-Taiba, Jaish-e-Mohammed, Harakat ul-Mujahadeen, and Harakat ul-Jihad-I-Islami—openly advocate violence to further their aims. These groups, many of whom fought in the Soviet-Afghan War, went to Kashmir to continue the jihad following the withdrawal of Soviet forces from Afghanistan in 1989.

ANTITERRORIST LEGISLATION

Counterterrorism in India has been criticized for lacking a unified approach to the problem and for the failures of its intelligence agencies. Nevertheless, over the years the Indian government has armed itself with an array of legislation designed to curtail and combat the terrorist threat from internal as well as external forces.

The Prevention of Violent Activities Act of 1970 was enacted to curb the activities of the leftist Naxalite movement, which originated in West Bengal in the late 1960s. After the Indo-Pakistani War of 1971, the infamous Maintenance of Internal Security Act (1971) was passed by Parliament to maintain domestic security. Additionally, beginning in 1978 a series of antiterrorist laws were passed by the Indian Parliament. Some of these instruments were the Jammu and Kashmir Public Safety Act (1978), the National Security Act (1980, amended 1984 and 1987), the Anti-hijacking Act (1982), the Punjab Disturbed Areas Act (1983), the Terrorist and Disruptive Activities Prevention Act (1985, amended 1987), the National Security Guard Act (1986), and the Special Protection Group Act (1988). Many of these legislative actions were repressive, and the government often received widespread criticism in the implementation of these laws due to the misuse of power by Indian security forces. For example, the Prevention of Terrorism Act, 2002, became very controversial and was viewed by many as a violation of basic and fundamental rights enshrined in the Indian Constitution. It came under scathing criticism by the opposition in the Indian Parliament, the Indian public, and various human rights groups for its infringement of democratic values. With the change of government, the coalition led by the Congress repealed the act, and the president promulgated the Prevention of Terrorism (Repeal) Ordinance, 2004, on September 21, 2004. Some of India's provinces such as Rajasthan, Orissa, Gujarat, Andhra Pradesh, and Uttar Pradesh had their own laws in place to address terrorism.

SECURITY AGENCIES

Indian counterterrorism efforts span several intelligence agencies, the Indian military, special security units, and law enforcement agencies. These organizations often work at cross-purposes as information is not always shared between these various agencies. The Research and Analysis Wing and the Intelligence Bureau collect external and internal intelligence on terrorist activities and potential actions. The Central Industrial Security Force is responsible for security at airports and other sensitive sites. The Central Reserve Police Force and the Border Security Force assist police personnel in counterterrorism operations. In a hijacking or hostage rescue mission, the National Security Guards (NSG) are ordered into action. The NSG was established in 1984 and works under the Ministry of Home Affairs. This unit is considered one of the country's most important counterterrorism agencies. Modeled after the German elite unit Grenzschutzgruppe 9, the NSG has two components: the Special Action Group and Special Rangers Group. Over the years they have been involved in several important assignments such as Operation Black Thunder II in the Golden Temple (1986), the freeing of the hijacked Indian Airlines Boeing 737 (1993), Operation Vajra Shakti to free captives at the Akshardham temple in Ahmedabad, Gujarat (2002), and the response to the Mumbai attacks (2008).

The India Army has been engaged in Jammu and Kashmir, Maoist hit areas, and northeastern India. It also supervised the erection of a fence along the Line of Control to check terrorist infiltration from Pakistan into Indian-controlled Kashmir. The Indian Coast Guard was established in 1978 to safeguard the nation's maritime interest. Working closely with the Indian Navy, it expanded considerably after the Mumbai attacks in November 2008. Additionally, some Indian states have their own counterterrorism agencies and capabilities. The Anti Terrorism Squad of the government of Maharashtra is perhaps the most famous. It was mired in controversy after its chief, Hemant Karkare (1954–2008), lost his life fighting terrorists during the 2008 Mumbai attacks.

CONCLUSION

The development of counterterrorism strategy in India is a reflection of the cultural and political ethos of the country. As a secular nation, it cannot alienate minorities by repressive measures. Moreover, many politicians do not want to adopt tough measures for fear of losing support among different groups, and the judicial system has become a lengthy and burdensome process. Human rights organizations contribute a great deal to protecting the rights of citizens, but sometimes their appeals hamper the work of the various security agencies. To effectively combat terrorism, India must implement sound and comprehensive counterterrorism policies that do not infringe on basic human rights and freedoms. These measures should include development initiatives for improving its people's living conditions. Moreover, assistance should be sought from the international community, and a dialogue with Pakistan regarding the issue of Kashmir needs to occur sooner rather than later.

See also: **Volume 1, Part IV:** Counterterrorism in India. **Volume 2, Part I:** National Security Guard (India); Para Commandos (India). **Part II:** Golden Temple, Amritsar, India (1984); Air India Flight 182 (1985); Mumbai, India, Attacks (2008)

REFERENCES

Barapind, Buta S. *Rise and Fall of Khalistan Movement*. Jalandhar, India: International Research Centre, 2007.

Bhuta, Nihal. *Back to the Future: India's 2008 Counterterrorism Laws*. Edited by Meenakshi Ganguly and Brad Adams. New York: Human Rights Watch, 2010.

Ganguly, D. K. *Law of National Security, Control of Goondas, Gangsters, and Anti-terrorism*. Allahabad, India: Dwivedi Law Agency, 2009.

Gupta, Ranjit K. *The Crimson Agenda: Maoist Protest and Terror*. Delhi: Wordsmiths, 2004.

Hegde, H. P. *India under Shadow of Terrorism*. New Delhi: Kaveri Books, 2005.

Jama, Arshad. *Shadow War: The Untold Story of Jihad in Kashmir*. Brooklyn: Melville House, 2009.

Kanwal, Gurmeet, and N. Manoharan. *India's War on Terror.* New Delhi: KW, 2010.

Lahiri, Prateep K. *Decoding Intolerance Riots and the Emergence of Terrorism in India.* New Delhi: Lotus Collection, 2009.

Mehta, R. S. *Encyclopedia of Anti-terrorism and Security Laws of India.* New Delhi: Pentagon Press, 2009.

Mishra, Patit P. "India, a Profile." In *Encyclopedia of Modern Asia,* edited by D. Levinson & K. Christensen, 3:22–25. New York: Charles Scribner's Sons, 2002.

Mishra, Patit P. "India." In *Encyclopedia of World History,* edited by Marsha E. Ackermann and Michael Schroeder, 6:201–4. New York: Facts on File, 2008.

Mukherjee, Aditya, Mridula Mukherjee, and Aditya Mukherjee. *India after Independence 1947–2000.* New Delhi: Penguin Books India, 2000.

Pandey, Swati. *Law and Counterterrorism: The Prevention of Terrorism Act in a Strategic Dimension.* New Delhi: Institute of Peace and Conflict Studies, 2004.

Rabasa, Angel. *The Lessons of Mumbai.* Santa Monica, CA: RAND Corporation, 2009.

Raman, B. "Evolution of India's Counter-terrorism Capabilities." International Terrorism Monitor, South Asia Analysis Group, May 10, 2006. http://www.southasiaanalysis.org/%5Cpapers18%5Cpaper1793.html.

Raman, P. V. *The Naxal Challenge: Causes, Linkages, and Policy Options.* New Delhi: Pearson Education, 2008.

Shankar, Shylashri. *Scaling Justice: India's Supreme Court, Anti-terror laws, and Social Rights.* New York: Oxford University Press, 2009.

Singh, Surat, and Hemraj Singh. *Law Relating to Prevention of Terrorism.* Delhi: Universal Law Publications, 2003.

Singh, Ujjwal K. *The State, Democracy and Anti-terror Laws in India.* New Delhi: Sage, 2007.

Upadhyay, Archana. *India's Fragile Borderlands: The Dynamics of Terrorism in North East India.* London: I. B. Tauris, 2009.

Indonesia

Jamie Morgan

Although most commonly known as the country with the largest population of Muslims, it is Indonesia's transition through four different forms of government in the past 60 years, each with a different approach to Islam as a political force within a secular state, that makes it particularly instructive for examining counterterrorism strategy. This paper will analyze four phases of Indonesian strategy in combating terrorism through the comparative theoretical frameworks of counterterrorism (CT) and counterinsurgency (COIN) theories. As space does not permit a full discussion of the distinctions between these two strategies and their variants here, a simplified version of these two umbrella terms will be used, defined as follows: *CT* is an enemy-centric approach, with the primary strategic objective being to disrupt and dismantle terrorist organizations and their ability to execute an attack on the opponent. In contrast, *COIN*, in its modern form, refers to a population-centric strategy in which the primary goal is to control the physical, human, and information aspects of the battle space, creating conditions such that the local populace accepts the legitimacy of the government mounting COIN or the government on behalf of which COIN is mounted. Excluding very recent debates (Rineheart 2010; Boyle 2010), CT has typically denoted a strategy focused on military or kinetic tools and will be defined as such within this paper (Rineheart 2010, 36, 43), while the more expansive focus of COIN has called for the use of both military and nonmilitary tools and will also be defined accordingly herein (John Nagl, quoted in Smith 2009; U.S. Department of Defense 2010). Various elements of these theories have also been termed *enemy-centric* and *population-centric* COIN strategies (Kilcullen 2007) and more recently *direct* and *indirect* CT and COIN strategies (Rineheart 2010; Olson 2009).

HISTORICAL PERSPECTIVES

In 1949, through the unified efforts of an array of militias across the 17,000-island archipelago, Indonesia officially became independent from its Dutch colonizers. However, after independence the country's unity fractured along ideological and regional lines, and several militias turned to fight the newly minted Indonesian Armed Forces (Angkatan Bersenjata Republik Indonesia, or ABRI). One of these groups was Darul Islam ("House of Islam," abbreviated DI), which sought to make Indonesia an Islamic state and would go on to serve as the general ideological foundation for Indonesia's future "terrorist" organizations.

To the extent to which the central government had a coherent counterterrorism strategy toward DI during this period, it could be considered a classic CT strategy, with some efforts at engaging in the human space. From 1949 to the early 1950s, Communist, nationalist, and Islamist political parties, as well as members of the ABRI, all fought for political power under the weak parliamentary system, which left little political leadership over military strategy. Initially, ABRI's CT work was mostly reactionary, as the force was overwhelmed with insurgent threats on multiple fronts and also had not yet developed the capabilities necessary in responding to guerrilla warfare (Conboy 2006, 5–11). However, its strategy evolved into a more systematic one by the early 1960s, at which point the ABRI was conducting town-by-town sweeps of villages known to house DI members. The sweeps were thorough, aimed at eliminating any and all DI affiliates and thus making a statement to the surrounding population. In what some consider an innovation for the time, the ABRI involved citizens in operations as human blockades (Conboy 2006, 10; Friend 2003, 55).

What is unclear is whether this was an attempt to empower citizens and gain their support via participation (K. Conboy, pers. comm., July 12, 2010) or whether it was a coercive tactic borne out of convenience or necessity (Friend 2003, 55). Regardless, by the late 1960s most DI members had been arrested or killed.

Islam was given only a nominal role in politics at this time. By 1957, Sukarno, with the support of the ABRI, had taken control of the government. He ruled from that point onward under quasi-authoritarian rule, veiled in the notion of "guided democracy." In 1960, he banned the strongest Muslim party, Masyumi, which advocated creating an Islamic state. Sukarno professed to consult Islamic leaders and the leaders of other factions before making political decisions, but in practice Islam was virtually absent from politics.

REPRESSIVE COIN STRATEGY UNDER AUTHORITARIAN RULE

In 1965 tensions within the ABRI and the political elites came to a head. The ensuing violence across the country claimed between 300,000 and 500,000 lives. General Suharto eventually took power and established a highly centralized, military-backed autocratic regime. Suharto's approach to controlling violent Islamist groups, although much more oppressive than Sukarno's, was also more comprehensive and coherent. His governance was aimed at complete control of the population and mimicked the physical, human, and informational aspects of a COIN strategy. It was top driven, with Suharto coordinating various tools of suppression, cooption, propaganda, and accommodation.

The Suharto regime controlled the physical security space via intimidation and the use of force by the ABRI, as well as co-option of minor threats. During the Sukarno period the ABRI had developed an extensive territorial command structure, which it used to maintain military and intelligence officers at nearly every level of society (Chalk et al. 2009, 149–51). The ABRI used this structure to closely monitor the populace and identify antiregime activity. The more benign members of DI and other groups were offered entrée into the Suharto government (Conboy 2006, 14–19), while those who posed a visible threat to the government were either arrested or killed. A few of the most prominent arrests include those of 185 members of Komando Jihad (Holy War Command, one of the most hard-line successors to DI) in 1977 (Conboy 2006, 18) and those of Abu Bakar Bashir and Abdullah Achmad bin Sungkar, two Islamic preachers calling for the creation of an Islamic state, in 1977 and 1978. By the mid-1980s most terrorist organizations had vanished. Those supporting DI and Komando Jihad had either been scared into silence or had become too old to continue (Conboy 2006, 19, 26), and Bashir and Sungkar fled to Malaysia, where they continued their work and formed a group later known as Jemaah Islamiyah (Islamic Community, abbreviated JI).

The government controlled the human and information spaces through military surveillance, co-option, propaganda, and minor measures of accommodation. Suharto's policy of *dwifungsi* (dual function) made the military responsible for ensuring domestic stability through taking an active role in political as well as security affairs (Chalk et al. 2009 149–50). This policy, accompanied by the expansive military intelligence network, laws outlawing Islam as a basis of political activity and prohibiting Muslim dress, and the continual demonization of ideologies that differed from the *pancasila* (official national philosophy) was used to control the information space (Schwarz 2004, 171–73). However, despite these extensive controls, popular support for political Islam grew stronger in the 1980s (Schwarz 2004, 173–76). Suharto began making concessions to the Islamists, such as allowing the establishment of the Indonesian Association of Muslim Intellectuals, which was meant to serve as a vehicle for Muslim intellectuals to provide input on government policy (Schwarz 2004, 173–88; Hafidz 2003).

In May 1998, violent protests triggered by the economic fallout of the 1997 Asian economic crisis, and fueled by long-standing social and political tensions, broke out all over Indonesia and eventually brought about Suharto's resignation. As the country began to build new political structures and governing roles, combating terrorism was a low priority. Perhaps more important, public anti-American sentiment and the reemergence of Islam as a political force put pressure on some administrations, Megawati Sukarnoputri's in particular, to distance themselves from the United States and its war on terror (Hafidz 2003, 5–8). Each of the presidents during this period, B. J. Habibie, Abdurraham Wahid, and Megawati Sukarnoputri, denied the presence of violent Islamist groups in Indonesia.

COIN STRATEGY AND CT OPERATIONAL APPROACH

In October 2002, JI set off three bombs in major tourist areas on the island of Bali. The scale of the attack, which left 202 dead and injured 189, forced the Megawati administration to acknowledge the presence of terrorist organizations in Indonesia and quickly establish a CT program. Megawati built several institutions to combat terrorism, including the elite counterterrorism unit known as Densus 88 (Detachment 88) under the newly constituted Indonesian National Police. However, it was not until Noordin Top and members of JI launched a second attack in Bali in 2005 that the Indonesian government, under President Susilo Bambang Yudhoyono, sought to build a strategy behind its efforts. The result has been a strategy that is disconnected from the institutional and legal infrastructure supporting it.

At the strategic level, President Yudhoyono's terrorism strategy is rooted in COIN principles, but at the operational and tactical level, it is largely based on CT principles. The strategy, as declared by Yudhoyono in a speech in 2005, aims to combat terrorist networks while still maintaining legitimacy with the citizenry. It plans to employ direct, offensive measures to stop terrorist networks and to use indirect actions to support civil society and promote moderate religious organizations (Waluyo 2007, 128–29). Operationally and tactically, however, the majority of resources and attention have been directed at the offensive operations conducted by Densus 88.

The Yudhoyono administration has sought to maintain legitimacy for CT operations by treating terrorism the same way all crime is treated under a democracy, as a law enforcement issue (Waluyo 2007, 128–29). As such, the administration has maintained the primary responsibility for counterterror operations within the Indonesian National Police, despite calls by the Tentara Negara Indonesia (Military of Indonesia), the successor of ABRI, for a larger military role. Both the Indonesian and foreign governments have poured a considerable amount of resources into developing the capabilities of Densus 88. Despite major terrorist attacks in 2004, 2005, and 2009, the organization has been relatively successful in reducing the operating ability of what was previously the largest terrorist threat in the region, JI (Jones 2010a, 2010b). The raid of a major terrorist camp in Aceh in February 2010 was largely hailed as a success, although the camp's initial discovery showed holes in the organization's intelligence capabilities (International Crisis Group 2010a).

Although Yudhoyono professed to use indirect actions to counter extremist ideology in his 2005 speech, this effort has been much more poorly resourced and coordinated. The majority of efforts to promote tolerance and interfaith understanding have been from civil society organizations, which at times are overlapping or even competing due to the lack of government coordination (Morgan 2011). In addition, antitolerant religious activity has risen in recent years (International Crisis Group 2010b), and critics decried the Yudhoyono administration's failure to take decisive action to protect citizens ("Indonesian Intolerance Rising" 2010) against mob violence from conservative Islamic groups such as the Front Pembela Islam (Islamic Defenders Front). Experts maintain that a small but not inconsequential number of Islamic schools that teach extremist ideology still exist in Indonesia (Jones 2010a; Morgan 2011). In addition, extremist groups continue to publish literature espousing *takfiri* ideology (strict adherence to the tenets of Islam as espoused in the original teachings and doctrines of the Prophet Muhammad) and to recruit new members via the launch events for such material and other more informal meetings (Jones 2010a; International Crisis Group 2008; Morgan 2011). The most critical space where the government has failed to control information is in prisons, where arrested terrorists are allowed to use cell phones to communicate with their counterparts outside, hold meetings with co-conspirators, and lead Friday prayer sessions for the entire prison (International Crisis Group 2007; Arnaz 2010). Despite deradicalization programs that were highly acclaimed in the past, Indonesian government experts now admit that the programs were ad hoc and driven mainly by a desire to obtain information from detainees, not to dissuade them from violence (Morgan 2011; Nivell Rayda & Agencies 2010).

LESSONS LEARNED

Three major lessons can be drawn from the Indonesian transition through CT and COIN models of combating terrorism. First, promulgating a CT/COIN program that adheres to the basic rights championed under the democratic ideal is critical to preserving general public support for the effort and for the proponent government, as well as to delegitimizing terrorist organizations. Sungkar and Bashir's rise to national prominence after they were held by the administration in prison for four years is a direct example of the potential backfire effect of overly draconian policies (Conboy 2006, 29). In addition, although world events, particularly the Iranian Revolution, surely played a role in the Indonesian Islamic revivalism of the 1980s, many scholars maintain that Suharto's tight control over political dialogue in normal settings pushed youth and activists toward Islam in hope for political change and into mosques as a space to have such dialogue (Schwarz 2004, 173–76). Finally, the relative success of the Yudhoyono administration in maintaining legitimacy for CT operations and relegating terrorist ideology to the fringes has been largely due to the criminal justice approach it has taken to CT.

A second, corollary lesson is that once suspected terrorists are convicted, their activities must be strictly monitored and controlled while in prison, and later monitored through a postrelease guidance program. This must be done through a unified, cohesive government program that involves thorough training and messaging to all levels of government employees dealing with terrorists. The planning and recruitment that have occurred in Indonesian prisons in recent years have greatly undermined all other CT and COIN efforts. The lack of comprehensive, nationwide basic religious education for prison officials makes them vulnerable to charismatic and persuasive extremist preachers, the lack of training on methods for dealing with high-risk prisoners makes it difficult for them to serve as support systems for prisoners vulnerable to terrorist recruiters, and the lack of enforcement of antibribery rules gives terrorist prisoners free rein within prisons.

Third, the collective experiences in each of the periods examined demonstrate the importance of allowing a space for Islam in the mainstream political dialogue. Arguably one of the greatest achievements of the Republic of Indonesia has been the country's ability to incorporate and accommodate the aspirations of political Islamists while maintaining a secular state and combating violent Islamist organizations.

CONCLUSION

The Indonesian experience demonstrates the importance of the moderated use of force in pursuing terrorists and of incorporating Islam into mainstream politics. Even the most effective of CT/COIN programs will not endure in the long term if not supported by a more comprehensive effort to accommodate the Islamist aspirations of society while simultaneously quelling its most radical manifestations.

See also: **Volume 2, Part II:** Bali, Indonesia (2002)

REFERENCES

Arnaz, Farouk. "Antiterror Chief Calls for Change in Game Plan." *Jakarta Globe,* June 3, 2010.
Boyle, Michael. "Do Counterterrorism and Counterinsurgency Go Together?" *International Affairs* 86, no. 2 (2010): 333–53.
Chalk, Peter, Angel Rabasa, William Rosenau, and Leanne Piggott. "Counterterrorism and National Security in Indonesia." In *The Evolving Terrorist Threat to Southeast Asia: A Net Assessment*, chap. 8. Arlington, VA: RAND Corporation, 2009. http://www.rand.org/pubs/monographs/2009/RAND_ MG846.pdf.
Conboy, Ken. *The Second Front: Inside Asia's Most Dangerous Terrorist Network.* Jakarta: Equinox (Asia), 2006.
Friend, Theodore. *Indonesian Destinies.* Cambridge, MA: Harvard University Press, 2003.
Front Pembela Islam. "Tentang FPI" [About FPI]. Front Pembela Islam website, n.d. http://www.fpi.or.id/?p=tentangfpi&mid=1.
Hafidz, Tatik S. "The War on Terror and the Future of Indonesian Democracy." Working Paper Series no. 46, Institute of Defense and Strategic Studies, Nanyang Technological University, Singapore, 2003. http://dr.ntu.edu.sg/ handle/10220/4448.
"Indonesian Intolerance Rising." *Asia Sentinel,* October 15, 2010.
International Crisis Group. "'Deradicalization' and Indonesian Prisons." Asia Report no. 142, November 19, 2007. http://www.crisisgroup.org/en/ regions/asia/south-east-asia/indonesia/142-deradicalisation-and-indonesian-prisons.aspx.
International Crisis Group. "Indonesia: Jemaah Islamiyah's Publishing Industry." Asia Report no. 147, February 28, 2008. http://www.crisisgroup.org/en/ regions/asia/south-east-asia/indonesia/147-indonesia-jemaah-islami yahs-publishing-industry.aspx.
International Crisis Group. "Indonesia: Jihad Surprise in Aceh." Asia Report no. 189, April 20, 2010a. http://www.crisisgroup.org/en/regions/asia/south-east-asia/indonesia/189-indonesia-jihadi-surprise-in-aceh.aspx.
International Crisis Group. "Indonesia: Christianization and Intolerance." Asia Briefing no. 114, November 24, 2010b. http://www.crisisgroup.org/en/regions/ asia/south-east-asia/indonesia/B114-indonesia-christianisation-and-intoler ance.aspx.

Jones, Sidney. "Radicalization and Counter-radicalization in Indonesia: Taking Stock." Presentation given at the Center for Strategic Studies, Washington, D.C., May 24, 2010a. http://csis.org/event/radicalization-and-counter-radicalization-indonesia-taking-stock.

Jones, Sidney. "After Aceh: The Evolution of Terror Networks in Indonesia." Presentation given for the United States–Indonesia Society, Jakarta, November 2, 2010b.

Kilcullen, David. "Two Schools of Classical Counterinsurgency." *Small Wars Journal* blog, January 27, 2007. http://smallwarsjournal.com/blog/2007/01/two-schools-of-classical-count/.

Morgan, Jamie R. Forthcoming research on counter-radicalization initiatives, supported by the U.S.-Indonesia Society, 2011.

Nivell Rayda & Agencies. "Terrorist 'Rehabs' a Failure: Minister." *Jakarta Globe,* June 26, 2010.

Olson, Eric T. "A Balanced Approach to Irregular Warfare." *Journal of International Security Affairs* 16 (Spring 2009). http://www.securityaffairs.org/issues/2009/16/olson.php.

Rineheart, Jason. "Counterterrorism and Counterinsurgency." *Perspectives on Terrorism* 4, no. 5 (2010): 31–47. http://www.terrorismanalysts.com/pt/index.php?option=com_rokzine&view=article&id=138&Itemid=54.

Schwarz, Adam. *A Nation in Waiting: Indonesia's Search for Stability.* Singapore: Talisman, 2004.

Smith, Emily Esfahani. "The Battle on Capital Hill." *Weekly Standard,* September 29, 2009. Accessed via Center for a New American Security website, http://www.cnas.org/node/3382.

U.S. Department of Defense. *Joint Publication 1–02 DOD Dictionary of Military and Associated Terms.* As amended through May 30, 2008. http://www.militarynewsnetwork.com/publications/militaryterms.pdf.

U.S. Department of Defense. *Joint Publication 1–02 DOD Dictionary of Military and Associated Terms.* As amended through September 30, 2010. http://www.dtic.mil/doctrine/new_pubs/jp1_02.pdf.

Waluyo, Sapto. "Indonesia's Predicament on Counterterrorism Policy in the Era of Democratic Transition." *UNISCI Discussion Papers* no. 15 (October 2007): 111–56.

Widjajanto, Andi. "After Aceh: The Evolution of Terror Networks in Indonesia." Presentation given for the United States–Indonesia Society, Jakarta, November 2, 2010.

Ireland

Jamie Walsh

Ireland has a long and complex history of dealing with terrorism. It might even be said that on one level the establishment of the Irish Free State in December 1922 was due to the conclusion of a successful insurgent campaign. Since then, successive Irish governments have been challenged by the actions of organizations that do not recognize the legitimacy of the state and seek the unification of North and South through armed violence. Ireland's domestic antiterror laws were fashioned to address this threat.

DOMESTIC COUNTERTERRORISM LAWS

When the current Constitution of Ireland came into force on December 29, 1937, the state was already familiar with "special" antiterror laws, owing to the civil war that immediately followed independence and threatened the stability of the fledgling Free State. The emergency laws, passed under the 1922 Constitution of the Irish Free State, granted authorities, inter alia, the power of internment without trial and established the Constitution (Special Powers) Tribunal consisting of military officers with power to impose such punishment as they saw expedient (including the death penalty) following conviction.

The 1937 Constitution, which is the fundamental law of the Irish state, repealed the Constitution of the Irish Free State and its draconian provisions contained in the amended Article 2A for Military Tribunals and other measures. Characterizing Article 2A as "grotesque," the drafters of the new constitution were determined to examine new ways of dealing with the threats posed by paramilitary violence. In this context, the relevant provisions in the 1937 Constitution include Article 15.6, which exclusively vests the right to raise and maintain military or armed forces with the Oireachtas (National Parliament), and Article 28, which allows the government to pass laws for the purpose of securing public safety and the preservation of the state in a "time of war or armed rebellion." Article 40.6.1 guarantees freedom of expression and assembly but limits these rights in certain circumstances where the material is deemed seditious or treasonable.

The new constitution enhanced the power of judicial review and carefully protected a more extensive range of personal rights, as compared with its predecessor. However, while the 1937 Constitution was clearly intended to represent a fresh start so far as political violence and other features of public life were concerned, renewed Irish Republican Army (IRA) activity and the growing threat of war in Europe led to the enactment of the first of the Offences against the State Acts 1939–1998, the main body of Irish law dealing with offenses that, broadly speaking, could be classified as terrorism.

EMERGENCY POWERS

Pursuant to the emergency powers contained in Article 28.3.3 of the Constitution, a state of emergency was declared on September 2, 1939. However, this "emergency" was not rescinded until 1976, and then only to be immediately replaced with a fresh state of emergency arising from the conflict in Northern Ireland. The latter was rescinded in February 1995 following the IRA cease-fire. The 1976 emergency was used to justify the introduction of the Emergency Powers Act, 1976, the principal feature of which was to permit detention in Garda (police) custody for seven days. These powers lapsed in 1977 and were not renewed.

INTERNMENT WITHOUT TRIAL

Internment without trial operated between 1940 and 1945 and again between 1957 and 1962. However, internment was not used during the most recent conflict in Northern Ireland. The power to intern without trial may be exercised pursuant to Part II of the Offences against the State (Amendment) Act, 1940. The provisions contained therein come into force pursuant to a government proclamation to the effect that internment powers "are necessary to secure the preservation of public peace and order." While the provisions permitting internment without trial are still on the statute book, they are not currently in force.

SPECIAL COURTS

Part V of the Offences against the State Act 1939 provides for "special criminal courts." In order for special criminal courts to be established the government must first issue a proclamation declaring that the ordinary courts are inadequate to secure the effective administration of justice and the preservation of public peace and order. Special criminal courts have been established on three occasions: between 1939 and 1946, between 1961 and 1962, and from 1972 to the present. At present, special criminal courts try offenses scheduled under the Offences against the State Acts, the Criminal Justice (Amendment) Act 2009, the Firearms Acts, and the Explosive Substances Acts. During World War II, black-market profiteering cases were dealt with in the special criminal court as well as cases involving the IRA. Since 1972, most cases have concerned terrorism; however, during the 1990s a number of high-profile organized crime cases have come before the court.

CRIMINAL STATUTE-LAW DIRECTED AGAINST
TERRORIST ORGANIZATIONS

The Offences against the State Acts 1939–1998 do not define or refer to *terrorism* per se. Instead, the acts principally focus on the concept of an unlawful organization. The acts also make special provision in relation to evidentiary matters connected with the question of membership in such organizations. While the right of citizens to form associations is guaranteed by the Constitution, the acts expressly prohibit any organization that engages in, promotes, encourages, or advocates the commission of treason or any activity of a treasonable nature. The dissemination of publications relating to unlawful organizations is also governed under this legislation. The government may declare an organization to be illegal by means of a suppression order (Offences against the State Act 1939). Since 1939, a number of suppression orders have been issued declaring a wide variety of subversive organizations on both sides of the conflict in Northern Ireland to be illegal.

The Criminal Law Act 1976 makes it an offense to recruit another person for an unlawful organization or to incite or invite another person to join an unlawful organization or to take part in or support or assist its activities. Other relevant offenses include the offense of directing an unlawful organization and of training persons in the making or use of firearms or explosives, for which provision was made in the Offences against the State (Amendment) Act 1998. Enacted following the Omagh bombing, the act also provides for inferences to be drawn from a person's failure to answer certain questions.

INTERNATIONAL TERRORISM

The September 11, 2001, attacks on the United States marked a watershed in Irish law on terrorism. Prior to September 11, the emphasis focused on those actors intent on usurping the functions of the government of Ireland, state institutions, and the Irish Constitution. Irish law had little to say about organizations that directed their activities against governments abroad. Indeed, Ireland took account of terrorism outside the state only to the extent that it was required to do so by virtue of a limited number of international treaties and conventions. The response of the international community to the September 11 attacks was swift, and both the United Nations (UN) and the European Union (EU) effected a number of legally binding measures to tackle terrorism. These have had a significant impact on Irish law.

The EU Framework Decision on Combating Terrorism was agreed on in June 2002. Its objective was to harmonize the definition of terrorist offenses (Article 1) in all member states and ensure that proportionate and dissuasive criminal penalties are established for those who commit, incite, aid, abet, or attempt to commit such offenses. It sets out jurisdictional rules to guarantee that terrorist offenses may be effectively prosecuted and adopts specific measures with regard to victims of terrorist offenses. In 2008, another significant framework decision was agreed on in order to harmonize national provisions on public provocation to commit a terrorist offense, recruitment for terrorism, and training for terrorism and to ensure that these forms of behavior are punishable. The 2008 decision also means that individuals disseminating terrorist propaganda and bomb-making expertise through the Internet can be prosecuted and sentenced to prison insofar as such dissemination amounts to public provocation to commit terrorist offenses, recruiting for terrorism, or training for terrorism and is committed intentionally.

The European Framework Decision took effect in Ireland through the Criminal Justice (Terrorist Offences) Act 2005. Section 6 of the act creates a new offense of engaging in terrorist activity. Under the terms of the act, specified offenses will become terrorist offenses when committed with intent to seriously intimidate a population, unduly compel a government or international organization to perform or abstain from performing an act, or seriously destabilize or destroy the fundamental political, constitutional, economic, or social structures of a state or an international organization. Moreover, terrorist groups that commit terrorist offenses within or outside the state are deemed unlawful organizations for the purposes of the Offences against the State Acts 1939–1998. Thus, the relevant provisions of those acts, including the offenses of membership in and direction of an unlawful organization, now apply with equal force to terrorist organizations both inside and outside the state.

The 2005 act also incorporates into Irish domestic law four antiterrorist conventions acceded to or ratified by Ireland, namely, the Convention on the Prevention and Punishment of Crimes against Internationally Protected Persons, including Diplomatic Agents, 1973; the International Convention against the Taking of Hostages, 1979; the International Convention for the Suppression of Terrorist Bombings, 1997; and the International Convention for the Suppression of the Financing of Terrorism, 1999. The offenses created by these four conventions are established as offenses in domestic law in Sections 9, 10, 11, and 13, respectively, of the 2005 act.

TERRORIST FINANCING

The Criminal Justice (Money Laundering and Terrorist Financing) Act 2010 transposes the Third EU Money Laundering Directive (2005/60/EC), and the associated implementing directive (2006/70/EC), into national law. The act also ensures compliance with the recommendations of the third mutual evaluation report on Ireland of the Financial Action Task Force. The act repeals and reenacts the current anti–money-laundering provisions contained in other statutes, principally the provisions relating to money laundering contained in the Criminal Justice Act 1994. In doing so, the act consolidates all of Ireland's anti–money-laundering legislation in a single statute. The act also increases the obligations of a wide range of legal persons, including credit and financial institutions, lawyers, accountants, estate agents, trust and company service providers, tax advisers, and others, in relation to money laundering and terrorist financing. Contained in the act are requirements on the part of designated bodies covered by the legislation to identify customers, to report suspicious transactions to An Garda Síochána (Irish National Police) and the Revenue Commissioners, and to have specific procedures in place to provide to the fullest extent possible for the prevention of money laundering and terrorist financing.

CONCLUSION

The growing threat of terrorist networks acquiring weapons of mass destruction led to the adoption of UN Security Council Resolution (UNSCR) 1540, which legally obliges states to adopt and enforce appropriate effective laws that prohibit any nonstate actor from manufacturing, acquiring, possessing, developing, transporting, transferring, or using nuclear, chemical, or biological weapons. Ireland fully supports the aims and objectives of UNSCR 1540 and has pursued a progressive policy to ensure compliance with its obligations. In 2010, Ireland established an Interdepartmental Committee on Non-proliferation of Weapons of Mass Destruction, with membership drawn from all relevant government departments and agencies. The committee was established to ensure coherent implementation of the state's obligations arising from UNSCR 1540 and the different international treaties and initiatives to which the state is a party, including the Biological and Toxin Weapons Convention, the Chemical Weapons Convention, the Nuclear Non-proliferation Treaty, the Proliferation Security Initiative, the Global Initiative to Combat Nuclear Terrorism, and the G8 Global Partnership as well as the various export-control regimes (relating to both military and dual-use goods).

REFERENCES

Council Framework Decision of 13 June 2002 on Combating Terrorism, 2002 O.J. (L 164) 3.

Council Framework Decision 2005/222/JHA on attacks against information systems, 2005 O.J. (L 069) 67.

Council Framework Decision 2008/919/JHA of 28 November 2008 amending Framework Decision 2002/475/JHA on Combating Terrorism, 2008 O.J. (L 330) 21.

Department of Justice and Law Reform. "Terrorism." n.d. http://www.irishstatute book.ie/ResultsTitle.html?q=Terrorism&Simple_Search=Acts&Simple_Search=SIs.

Department of Justice and Law Reform. "Report of the Committee to Review the Offences against the State Acts, 1939–1998 Dublin, 2002." http://www.justice.ie/en/JELR/hederman%20report.pdf/Files/hederman%20report.pdf.

Director of Public Prosecutions. "The Interplay between EU and Domestic Counter-terrorism Laws." November 2, 2007. http://www.dppireland.ie/filestore/documents/ERA-ICEL_Seminar_Speech_021107_Amended.pdf.

Hogan, G., and G. Whyte, *Kelly's Irish Constitution*. 4th ed. Dublin: Butterworths, 2003.

Kissane, B. "Defending Democracy? The Legislative Response to Political Extremism in the Irish Free State, 1922–39." *Irish Historical Studies* 34, no. 134 (November 2004): 156–74.

Ó Longaigh, Seosamh. *Emergency Law in Independent Ireland 1922–48*. Dublin: Four Courts, 2006.

Israel

Bart Schuurman

The state of Israel was declared on May 14, 1948. It was immediately set upon by its Arab neighbors but managed to fend off the poorly coordinated conventional assault. During this War of Independence and the civil strife that preceded it, hundreds of thousands of Palestinian civilians fled to neighboring countries. Large refugee camps were established in Jordan and Egypt, and these quickly became bases of operation for incursions into Israel by Palestinian militants. Anti-Israeli terrorism increased over the next two decades, especially after Israel's victory in 1967's Six-Day War and its subsequent occupation of the West Bank and the Gaza Strip.

Driven out of Jordan in 1970 after angering its leader, King Hussein, the various militant groups aligned under Yasser Arafat's Palestine Liberation Organization (PLO) took refuge in southern Lebanon, expanding the geographic dimensions of Israel's struggle with terrorism. In 1982, wishing to destroy the terrorist threat on its northern border, Israel launched a full-scale invasion of Lebanon. Although successful in driving the PLO from its headquarters in Beirut, the invasion contributed to the formation of a new and highly competent enemy. The Lebanese Shiite militants of Hezbollah proved too tough to defeat outright, leading to Israel's withdrawal in 2000.

During the 1980s, Islamic fundamentalism also rapidly gained popularity in the occupied territories, leading to the formation of such groups as Hamas and Palestinian Islamic Jihad. These terrorist organizations played a key role in destabilizing the 1993–2000 Israeli-Palestinian peace process, which followed on the heels of the first intifada, a massive Palestinian uprising that began in 1987. As tensions between the negotiating partners reached critical levels and public confidence in the talks plummeted, all-out conflict returned with the 2000–2005 al-Aqsa intifada.

COUNTERTERRORISM, 1948–2010

During the 1950s, Israel relied on a policy of reprisals, responding to incursions by conducting punishment raids on Arab villages in Jordan and Egypt. The aim of these attacks was to coerce Arab citizens into restraining the terrorist elements operating from their midst. To conduct these operations a special commando force, Unit 101, was established under the command of future prime minister Ariel Sharon. However, the reprisal raids were unable to reduce the number of attacks against Israeli targets. After the 1953 Qibya incident, where 60 Arab civilians lost their lives, international outcry led to an Israeli policy shift. From that point on, the reprisals were aimed at the terrorists themselves instead of their presumed supporters, but the policy's effectiveness did not noticeably improve.

Between the 1957 Suez Crisis and the 1967 Six-Day War, the number of terrorist attacks against Israel dropped to record lows. United Nations (UN) peacekeepers established a buffer between Egypt and Israel, and the latter's recently demonstrated willingness to use military force acted as a powerful deterrent to Egyptian, Syrian, and Jordanian militancy. Nevertheless, rising tensions led to the 1967 war, which resulted in another overwhelming victory for Israeli forces. As the Arab states proved themselves consistently unable to champion the Palestinian cause, the guerrilla groups became the new bearers of Arab hopes for a liberated Palestine. Foremost among them was Arafat's Fatah organization, which gained massive popularity and a swell of new recruits when it withstood Israeli forces during the Battle of Karameh in 1968. This propaganda victory allowed Arafat to exert his control over the recently established PLO, which subsequently became one of Israel's prime irregular adversaries.

In the years leading to the 1973 Yom Kippur War, airplane hijackings, a tactic initiated by the Marxist-oriented Popular Front for the Liberation of Palestine (PFLP), added a new dimension to the terrorist threat. Israel's response was to greatly increase airport and in-flight security, policies that over time were very successful. During this time frame, the struggle against terrorism also gained a larger international aspect after Palestinian terrorists murdered Israeli athletes at the 1972 Olympic Games in Munich. In response, Israel launched Operation Wrath of God, assassinating those responsible for the massacre. This operation underlined Israel's preference for responding to terrorism with reprisals, a policy that continued into the 1970s with attacks on targets in Jordan and Lebanon.

Similar to the 1950s, however, the continued reliance on reprisals did not lead to a reduction of terrorist attacks against Israel. What did have an effect on the Palestinian militants' operational capabilities was Jordan's decision to violently oust the PLO from its territory in 1970. The guerrillas then relocated to Lebanon, and after Israel had recovered from the surprise attack launched on it in 1973 by Egypt and Syria, Israeli counterterrorism efforts started to focus heavily on Lebanon and became more warlike in nature. Air strikes, artillery barrages, special forces operations, and the 1982–2000 invasion of southern Lebanon were the methods Tel Aviv chose in its attempt to destroy the PLO, methods that were subsequently used against Hezbollah. While PLO remnants fled Lebanon in defeat in 1983, Hezbollah was able to outlast the Israel Defense Forces (IDF) because the Israeli focus on high-intensity military operations led to large numbers of Lebanese civilian casualties. These provided Hezbollah with the legitimacy and recruits it needed to keep up its resistance to a militarily more powerful opponent.

Additionally, in the occupied territories, meanwhile, more than a decade of life under Israeli military rule had laid the basis for a popular uprising. Ongoing Israeli settlement construction, economic decline, increasing violence from radical Jewish settlers, and harsh Israeli policies such as deportations, house demolitions, and large-scale curfews, aimed at reducing terrorists' operational capabilities, enraged many Palestinians. Moreover, Israel's attempt to weaken the PLO's influence by aiding the formation of religious groups had backfired, as Hamas and Palestinian Islamic Jihad were in many ways more radical than Arafat's organization and enjoyed rapidly growing support. Israel's initial response to the 1987 intifada was to use lethal force, but international criticism soon led to the slightly less violent policy of "force, might and beatings" and the intensification of restrictive and punitive policies.

While none of these responses succeeded in containing the uprising, behind-the-scenes talks managed to bring the increasingly war-weary parties to the negotiating table. With the first Oslo Accord in 1993, the peace process got underway. Israel hoped to gain Palestinian guarantees for an end to terrorism, while the PLO wanted to establish a viable independent state in the occupied territories. The Palestinian Islamic Jihad and Hamas, however, saw the PLO's willingness to talk as a betrayal of the Palestinian cause and sought to derail the negotiations with an intense campaign of terrorism, utilizing suicide attacks on a hitherto-unseen scale. In response, Israel imposed extensive curfews and placed heavy restrictions on the movement of people and goods. The use of force was remarkably restrained in order to give the peace process a chance of success. Israel did greatly increase its use of "targeted killings," assassinating operatives and leaders of terrorist groups in an attempt to render these organizations incapable of further action. More often than not, Israel's chosen responses led to a further escalation of violence as Palestinian factions launched revenge attacks against Israeli citizens.

During the al-Aqsa intifada, the large-scale use of targeted killings, military incursions into the occupied territories, and the abundant use of force were combined with a novel policy: the construction of a security wall around the West Bank. The security wall, despite its controversial nature, does appear to have measurably improved Israel's safety, reducing the number of terrorists that succeed in reaching their targets, if not the number of those who try. The second intifada is generally viewed to have come to an end in 2005, influenced by such factors as Arafat's death in 2004 and his succession by Palestinian Authority president Mahmoud Abbas, Israel's unilateral withdrawal from Gaza, Hamas's tentative acceptance of a two-state solution, and general war-weariness among most parties.

Nevertheless, terrorism still threatens Israel, which has continued to answer threats to its security with high-powered military responses such Operation Cast Lead (2008–2009), during which the IDF launched an invasion of the Gaza Strip. At the same time, Hamas and Fatah have been engaged in a vicious battle for control over Gaza, which has made post-2005 international efforts at mediation even more difficult. In 2006, violence also escalated along Israel's northern border after Hezbollah abducted Israeli soldiers and launched rockets into northern Israel. The month-long showdown between the IDF and Hezbollah ended in a UN-mediated cease-fire with both sides claiming victory.

CONCLUSION

Throughout the period under investigation, Israel has shown a marked preference for repressive and violent counterterrorism measures. The IDF has been at the forefront of the fight against terrorism, emphasizing the warlike nature of the conflict. Israeli perceptions of being a small, vulnerable country surrounded by hostile Arab nations and devoid of reliable international allies appear to have played a large role in shaping this preference for the use of force. Yet despite undeniable regional military superiority, Israel's fight against terrorism has yet to yield strategic results because the root causes of the conflict have not been successfully addressed. However, for a country that sees itself as being under perpetual existential threat, merely surmounting individual crises has come to be seen as a strategic goal in itself.

REFERENCES

Catignani, Sergio. *Israeli Counter-insurgency and the Intifadas: Dilemmas of a Conventional Army.* London: Routledge, 2008.
Cronin, Audrey Kurth. *How Terrorism Ends: Understanding the Decline and Demise of Terrorist Campaigns.* Princeton, NJ: Princeton University Press, 2009.
Ganor, Boaz. "Israel, Hamas, and Fatah." In *Democracy and Counterterrorism: Lessons from the Past,* edited by Robert J. Art and Louise Richardson, 261–303. Washington, DC: U.S. Institute of Peace Press, 2007.
Lustick, Ian S. "Terrorism in the Arab-Israeli Conflict: Targets and Audiences." In *Terrorism in Context,* edited by Martha Crenshaw, 514–52. University Park: Pennsylvania State University Press, 1995.

Maoz, Zeev. *Defending the Holy Land: A Critical Analysis of Israel's Security and Foreign Policy.* Ann Arbor: University of Michigan Press, 2006.

Smith, Charles D. *Palestine and the Arab-Israeli Conflict: A History with Documents.* Boston: Bedford/St. Martin's, 2007.

Italy

Bart Schuurman

Italy's most notable experience with terrorism took place between 1969 and 1983. During these "Years of Lead" the country suffered "4,362 events of political violence, 6,153 unclaimed bombings against property; 2,712 attacks for which terrorist groups claimed responsibility, 324 of which were against people, with 768 injured and 351 killed" (Della Porta 1995, 106). As violence peaked between 1978 and 1981, roughly seven acts of terrorism occurred per day. While extremists on both sides of the political spectrum conducted terrorist campaigns, the Years of Lead have come to be almost exclusively associated with the left-wing Brigate Rosse (BR), or Red Brigades, an organization that fought for vaguely defined revolutionary change.

The roots of Italian terrorism were manifold. Pervasive social changes during the 1950s and 1960s, the onset of an economic crisis at the end of the latter decade, violent student and worker activism, the unpopular American intervention in Vietnam, and Italy's equally unpopular membership in the North Atlantic Treaty Organization (NATO) all played important roles in shaping a volatile political atmosphere, as did an instable political system tainted by the remnants of fascism; many governments lasted less than a year, and it left large numbers of citizens feeling disenfranchised. In the late 1960s sizable left- and right-wing extraparliamentary opposition groups were formed. Neofascist extremists believed a Communist coup to be imminent and strove for a return to a "strong state," while their opposites felt betrayed by the Italian Communist Party's move to constitutional politics and feared a return to fascism.

The incident that put the spark to this powder keg was the December 1969 Piazza Fontana bombing in Milan, which left 16 civilians dead and many more injured. The event was framed to look like a left-wing action, as the neofascist perpetrators carried it out as part of their "strategy of tension," which was intended to provoke left-wing violence, thus paving the way for the public's acceptance of a right wing–backed military coup. Indeed, the government's initial response was to target left-wing individuals. This convinced many on the left that the time had come to take up arms against what they saw as the state's collusion with neofascism, and in 1970 the infamous BR made their first appearance.

COUNTERTERRORISM MEASURES

It was not until 1974, when the BR started attacking state representatives, and right-wing groups once again indiscriminately bombed public places, that an actual counterterrorism policy began to take shape. At that point public outrage over the increasing violence and the state's ineffective response to it prompted several developments. Two dedicated counterterrorism inspectorates were established: one within the state police, which focused on neofascist groups, and one within the *carabinieri* (military police), which sought to tackle left-wing terrorism. Despite interservice rivalries and inadequate coordination, by late 1976 many neofascists had been arrested as well as all but one of the founding members of the BR.

Believing success had been achieved, the Italian government promptly and prematurely dissolved both specialized inspectorates. However, as their predecessors were being put behind bars, a new and more violent generation of mainly left-wing terrorists took center stage. The rise of the so-called 77 Movement resulted in the conflict's highest levels of violence. New recruits and leadership brought the BR back from the brink, and the organization subsequently launched some of its most infamous attacks, killing Prosecutor General Francesco Coco in 1976 and abducting and murdering former prime minister Aldo Moro in 1978.

The shock caused by Moro's death quickly led to the reinstatement of the successful *carabinieri* general Carlo Alberto Dalla Chiesa. Once again skillfully and patiently using surveillance and infiltration techniques, Dalla Chiesa and his team secured the arrests of large numbers of BR militants. The high-profile Moro operation had garnered the BR the respect and limited assistance of the German Rote Armee Fraktion, the French Action Directe, and the Popular Front for the Liberation of Palestine. Indiscriminate government measures against left-wing groups had also increased the supply of new recruits. But by 1980 the BR had nevertheless been severely weakened, with many members killed in shoot-outs or imprisoned by increasingly effective police work. Critically, by murdering Moro the *brigatisti* lost whatever mainstream public support they had still enjoyed.

In late 1981 the BR sought to regain the initiative by capturing American NATO general James Dozier. Although Dozier was successfully abducted, a recently formed Italian elite police unit, the Central Security Operations Service, secured the general's release in early 1982, capturing all the hostage takers in the process. This demonstrated the effectiveness of increased police efficiency combined with legal counterterrorism measures. The captured terrorists provided the authorities with extensive information on their comrades still at large in return for reduced sentences. Hundreds of BR members were subsequently arrested, signaling the end for the movement and Italian left-wing terrorism in general. While individuals claiming allegiance to the BR murdered two government economic advisers in 2002 and 2003, politically motivated terrorism has virtually ceased to exist when compared to the Years of Lead.

The legal reform in question was the 1982–1983 Penitence Law, which allowed repentant terrorists to receive significantly reduced sentences in return for cooperating with the authorities. It was highly effective in undermining the BR, who by 1980 led an increasingly isolated underground life, having lost virtually all public support and increasingly harassed by the police. The Penitence Law provided thoroughly demoralized terrorists a last chance of a way out. As more and more militants provided information to the authorities (including some who were already imprisoned), the BR and other left-wing fringe groups were decimated. The 1987 Disassociation Law allowed those terrorists still at large to be considered for reduced sentences merely for renouncing their violent pasts, bringing in hundreds who had refused to inform against their comrades. By that time, Italian terrorism had virtually been defeated.

While effective against terrorism these laws met with severe public criticism because they allowed even convicted murderers to get away with very light sentences. Somewhat less controversial were the other legal counterterrorism measures enacted since 1974, which generally increased the police's powers of arrest, seizure, and detainment while reducing suspects' ability to protest their incarceration. The 1975 Reale Law, for example, reduced judges' ability to grant provisional liberty to suspects and loosened the restrictions on police officers' use of firearms. Following Moro's abduction, the penalty for kidnapping was increased, and the 1980 Cossiga Law made it possible to pass extralong sentences on those found guilty of association with terrorism. The effectiveness of these legal reforms as counterterrorism measures is questionable, especially when their detrimental effects on civil rights and public confidence in the justice system are taken into account. Strikingly, most of these judicial countermeasures were used against left-wing groups, with very few convictions of neofascist terrorists occurring throughout the Years of Lead.

Another questionable aspect of the Italian counterterrorism effort concerns the role of the security services. While effective police counterterrorism directorates were eventually established, the military and civil intelligence services continued to suffer from widespread corruption and ongoing allegations of collusion with right-wing paramilitaries. Successive reforms undertaken during the 1970s to improve these organizations' effectiveness and democratic accountability failed to produce significant results.

Conspiracy theories about the Italian state's collusion with right-wing terrorists abound, and while many of them are hard to substantiate, it seems likely that neofascist sympathizers in all levels of government contributed to the high levels of violence and that they obstructed the course of justice. The 1981 discovery of a secret Masonic Lodge called

Propaganda Due revealed that high-ranking members of government and society were involved in anti-Communist subversive activities. In 1990, the existence of a secret NATO "stay-behind network" of anti-Communist partisans, to be activated in case of a Soviet invasion, was discovered in Italy and other European countries. Both Propaganda Due and the so-called Gladio network have subsequently been implicated in acts of right-wing terrorism and state collusion with neofascist groups.

Yet despite allegations of government collusion, right-wing terrorism also declined in the early 1980s, although it is not completely apparent what caused this downward trend. It appears likely, however, that the deadly 1980 Bologna train station bombing, carried out by right-wing terrorists, and the 1982 electoral success of a neofascist party contributed to the movements' fragmentation and decline into obscurity.

CONCLUSION

From a purely instrumental perspective the combination of penitence legislation and specialized police inspectorates produced a very effective synergy between "carrots and sticks." But while these measures proved their efficacy by virtually eliminating left-wing terrorism between 1978 and the early 1980s, Italy's response to violent extremism was also in many ways lacking. Not only did the state fail to address the grievances feeding the violence, it was also slow to formulate a response. Finally, allegations of collusion between elements of the state and neofascist terrorist groups undermined Italy's democratic credentials and appear to have contributed to the biased prosecution of left-wing extremists despite several high-profile and deadly indiscriminate bombings carried out by right-wing terrorists.

REFERENCES

Della Porta, Donatella. "Left-Wing Terrorism in Italy." In *Terrorism in Context*, edited by Martha Crenshaw, 105–59. University Park: Pennsylvania State University Press, 1995.

Ganser, Daniele. *NATO's Secret Armies: Operation Gladio and Terrorism in Western Europe*. London: Frank Cass, 2005.

Hoffman, Bruce, and Jennifer Morrison Taw. *A Strategic Framework for Countering Terrorism and Insurgency*. Santa Monica, CA: RAND, 1992.

Meade, Robert C., Jr. *Red Brigades: The Story of Italian Terrorism*. Basingstoke, UK: Macmillan, 1990.

Parker, Tom. "Fighting an Antaean Enemy: How Democratic States Unintentionally Sustain the Terrorist Movements They Oppose." *Terrorism and Political Violence* 19 (2007): 155–79.

Weinberg, Leonard. "The Red Brigades." In *Democracy and Counterterrorism: Lessons from the Past*, edited by Robert J. Art and Louise Richardson, 25–62. Washington, DC: U.S. Institute of Peace Press, 2007.

Japan

Salvador Jimenez Murguia and Ayumi Hidaka

As the global war on terrorism has proliferated, nations involved in counterterrorism, security maintenance, and prevention have developed policies for dealing with a variety of threat levels. The nation of Japan hosts several geopolitical flashpoints and ever-growing ideological movements that employ terrorism as a tactic. Terrorism, however, is not new to Japan, and although the policies for dealing with terror have varied, the Japanese have nevertheless sought to deal both openly and strategically with the problem.

RED ARMY FACTION

In general, the motivations for major terror plots in Japan have been either political or religious. During the 1970s and 1980s the Japanese Communist League-Red Army Faction and its splinter group, the Japanese Red Army, were responsible for several acts of terrorism worldwide including shootings, bombings, hijackings, and hostage taking for ransom. In March 1970, for example, nine members of the Japanese Communist League-Red Army Faction hijacked a plane in Tokyo carrying 122 people en route to the southern city of Fukuoka. The hijackers rerouted the plane to Seoul, Korea, where the hostages and seven crew members were released. The hijackers then continued on to Pyongyang, North Korea, where they received asylum.

In a similar incident in September 1977, the Japanese Red Army hijacked a flight from France to Japan carrying 156 people. Unlike in the hijacking seven years earlier, the Japanese Red Army carried out a successful ransom deal involving the freedom and safety of the hostages for an alleged $6 million and the release of Japanese Red Army prisoners. In a controversial decision, then prime minister Takeo Fukuda agreed to exchange the money and six of the nine requested prisoners for the hostages.

After this 1977 hijacking, Japan unofficially established an armed antiterrorism unit called the Special Assault Team. This unit would go on to be involved in hindering several domestic terrorism plots throughout country; however, it proved to fall short of resolving Japan's most infamous incident, involving a rogue organization driven to violence that used nerve gas.

AUM SHINRIKYO

From 1989 to 1995, Japan dealt firsthand with religious terrorism orchestrated by a new religious movement known as Aum Shinrikyo. Led by founder Shoko Asahara, an alias for Chizuo Matsumoto (b. 1955), Aum Shinrikyo was at odds with Japanese media and legal and governmental institutions over their interpretation of its controversial beliefs and practices. In a series of violent attacks predicated on maintaining its image as a religious organization, the Aum Shinrikyo killed 27 people and injured thousands more through physical beatings and the use of chemical weapons. In perhaps the deadliest act of terrorism on Japanese soil by a domestic organization, five members of Aum Shinrikyo executed a sarin gas attack on a Tokyo subway line, killing 12 people and injuring thousands more. This attack generated speculation about Japan's preparation and policy for response in dealing with terrorism. Although the National Police Agency was involved in a larger effort to investigate and even conduct massive raids on a number of Aum Shinrikyo operations just prior to the subway incident, the end result proved much too late.

LEGISLATION TO COUNTER TERRORISM

The Japanese Parliament, however, took action by passing legislation entitled Law Related to the Prevention of Bodily Harm Caused by Sarin and Similar Substances, which would prohibit the manufacturing and possession of this type of weaponry and substances. In addition, Japan moved to loosen restrictions on monitoring of "dangerous religious organizations" in 1995, effectively revising the Religious Corporations Law.

Shortly after the September 11, 2001, terrorist attacks in the United States, then prime minister Junichiro Koizumi offered support to the United States, United Kingdom, and their military efforts in Afghanistan. Koizumi strategically demonstrated this support by advancing legislation that would allow the Japanese military, or Self-Defense Forces (SDF), to engage in support capacities during wartime—a controversial act that encountered little resistance. In contrast to the passive use of the SDF, the Japanese government passed counterterrorism legislation in less than a month establishing laws governing Japanese involvement in the war on terror.

Despite this gesture of support, Japan refrained from military intervention through force in both Afghanistan and Iraq in accordance with constitutional restrictions gleaned from Japan's history of war. Since the end of World War II, there has been a fine line between the security of the nation and the pacifist image that accompanied a restructured Japan. Perhaps the most integral intervening factor that has contributed to this divide is the interpretation of Article 9 of the Constitution. Introduced in 1947 as part of the postwar Constitution, Article 9 prohibits the use of force and war by Japan.

Notwithstanding this constitutional framework, Japan has ordered SDF personnel to participate in disaster relief and peacekeeping missions. In 2001, Japan passed the Anti-terrorism Special Measures Law, a law enabling Japanese forces to take measures in cooperation with and support of activities undertaken by "foreign forces" in the suppression of terrorism. In addition, under the Humanitarian Relief and Iraqi Reconstruction Special Measures Law, passed in December 2003, Japan prepared itself to send troops into a war zone where major combat missions had reportedly ended. In 2004, Japan deployed SDF personnel into Samawah, Iraq, as well as providing airlift support to assist with the U.S.-led occupation. However, Japan began withdrawing SDF troops from Iraq in 2006.

By 2010, Japan had cultivated an international record of maintaining security in the region of South Asia and abroad. In March 2007, the Japanese prime minister, Shinzo Abe, and the Australian prime minister, John Howard, signed a security pact entitled the Japan–Australia Joint Declaration on Security Cooperation, which serves to enhance cooperative efforts in a number of areas such as border security, counterterrorism, and control of the illegal weapons trade, as well as sea and air security. Once again, in October 2008, a similar pact entitled Joint Declaration on Security Cooperation between Japan and India was signed by prime ministers Taro Aso of Japan and Manmohan Singh of the Republic of India. This pact was geared toward improving cooperation in several areas including counterterrorism and the suppression of transnational crime.

CONCLUSION

In addition to these security pacts and changes to foreign policy, Japan will have served as an elected member of the United Nations Security Council a total of 20 times by the close of the year 2010, as well as actively seeking to secure a permanent seat on this council. Japan's domestic counterterrorism efforts to control immigration have also adapted to the challenges of terrorism. In addition to the implementation of new inspection technologies for safeguarding ports of entry, Japan has also made efforts to ensure its domestic policies run parallel with those of its allies. For example, Japan has improved the lines of communication among international agencies in an effort to share pertinent information about terrorism and terror suspects. In accordance with UN Security Council Resolution 1267, Japan has also established policies to prevent the entry of designated Taliban and al-Qaeda members.

REFERENCES

Kaplan, David, and Andrew Marshall. *The Cult at the End of the World: The Terrifying Story of the Aum Doomsday Cult, from the Subways of Tokyo to the Nuclear Arsenals of Russia.* New York: Crown, 1996.

Katzenstein, Peter. *Rethinking Japanese Security: Internal and External Dimensions.* New York: Routledge, 2008.

Midford, Paul. *Japanese Public Opinion and the War on Terrorism: Implications for Japan's Security Strategy.* Washington, DC: East-West Center, Washington, 2006.

Samuels, Richard J. *Securing Japan: Tokyo's Grand Strategy and the Future of East Asia.* Ithaca, NY: Cornell University Press, 2008.

Shinoda, Tomohito. *Koizumi Diplomacy: Japan's Kentei Approach to Foreign and Defense Affairs.* Seattle, WA: University of Washington Press, 2007.

Jordan

Nicholas E. Swails

The modern state of Jordan originated in the aftermath of World War I when the United Kingdom was given the mandate over the area known as Transjordan from the dissolved Ottoman Empire. The state known officially as the Hashemite Kingdom of Jordan was given independence in 1946. The state was led by the pragmatic King Hussein ibn Talal (1953–1999) and later his successor and son, King Abdullah II.

The history of Jordan's counterterrorism policies is based on Jordan's central geographic location in the Middle East. Jordan borders on Israel, Syria, Iraq, Saudi Arabia, and the Palestinian occupied West Bank, which places Jordan at the center of geopolitics in the region. Jordan's geographic location also places it between two conflicts, one long-standing and one more recent: (1) the Israeli-Palestinian conflict and (2) the more recent Iraqi and Gulf conflicts. The history of Jordan's counterterrorism policies can be summed up in King Hussein ibn Talal's role in the Jordanian Civil War (1970–1971), with the events of Black September at center stage, and more recent developments that place Jordan at the center of the "Iraqi resistance" movements under King Abdullah.

FEDAYEEN

Under the leadership of Yasser Arafat—the head of Fatah and chairman of the Palestine Liberation Organization (PLO)—the Jordanian state was occupied by an ever larger number of "freedom fighters," known as the fedayeen, following the swift Arab defeat at the hands of Israel in the 1967 Six-Day War. The fedayeen had virtually created a "state within a state" as King Hussein and his military struggled to deal with the increased violence in Jordan. Fighting between the Jordanian military and the fedayeen broke out in June 1970. This rise in violence would reach epoch proportions in September 1970 as simultaneous terrorist events threatened the stability of the Jordanian state and Hussein's rule. However, due to his diplomatic and political brilliance Hussein was able to counter the terrorist violence in his state through military efforts and Cold War–era diplomacy between the United States and Israel.

ASSASSINATION ATTEMPTS

On September 1, 1970, Hussein and his motorcade came under heavy fire on the way to meet his daughter Princess Alia. The failed ambush by the Popular Front for the Liberation of Palestine (PFLP) was one of a series of attacks on his life being waged by the fedayeen (Ashton 2008, 144; Shlaim 2008, 326). This event and the events to follow represented a long history of terrorist attacks against the Jordanian state (Cooley 1973, 133–56). George Habash (a Palestinian Christian), the leader of the PFLP, argued that attacks on Jordan represented a stepping-stone for attacks on Israel. Habash believed that attacks on the Hashemite government should represent an "Arab Hanoi" (Laqueur and Rubin 2001, 145–49). On September 6, 1970, Jordan was challenged as the PFLP hijacked four airliners, three of which landed at Dawson's Field (renamed Revolution Field by the terrorists) near Zarqa. In a jubilant display the PFLP blew up the aircraft before the media on September 12 (Ashton 2008, 145; Shlaim 2008, 327).

This event triggered Hussein to take a more militant stand toward the fedayeen when he dismissed his civilian government and created a military government. During the early morning hours of September 17, the 60th Armored Division of the Jordanian army entered Amman and began conducting offensive operations on refugee camps where fedayeen fighters were headquartered. Fears of external attacks were realized on September 18 when Syrian tanks rolled across the border toward the village of Irbid, which would later fall to the Syrian forces (Shlaim 2008, 147–48).

JORDANIAN CIVIL WAR

These events became known as Black September but are also known as the Jordanian Civil War (1970–1971), in which Hussein struggled to maintain power over his Hashemite kingdom. Hussein had important decisions to make to combat the terrorists' occupation of his country: whether to seek the aid of the United States and potentially Israeli air support and intelligence. During the following days Hussein considered the benefits of Israeli air strikes but was concerned about the fallout of Israeli involvement in his battle against the fedayeen forces. On September 22, Hussein was approached by Arab leaders to arrange a meeting with Arafat in Cairo that would be mediated by Sudanese president Jaafar Muhammad al-Nimeiry. A cease-fire agreement between Arafat and Hussein was signed on September 27 at the Cairo Hilton with the stipulation that at 19:25 GMT the fedayeen and Jordanian forces were to cease all military actions.

However, violence continued between Hussein and the fedayeen as Hussein pursued additional political agreements with Arafat, which culminated in the October 13, 1971, agreement in which the fedayeen fighters were to recognize Hussein and the Jordanian state. Unfortunately, this agreement was not recognized by the fedayeen, and violence persisted until the Jordanian army crushed the PLO in July 1971 and forced them to flee to Lebanon.

Hussein's success in the civil war only satisfied his immediate goal of removing the fedayeen from his country and reestablishing his authority and his state in the region. Hussein was congratulated on his successes by the Nixon administration, which gave him millions in aid to combat the regime's enemies. Hussein also viewed his struggle with the fedayeen as a tragedy in that this confrontation between "brothers" should have been avoided due to their ongoing struggle with their common enemy, Israel.

IRAQI RESISTANCE MOVEMENTS

More recent counterterrorism efforts in the Jordanian state involve King Abdullah's struggle against terrorists who support Iraqi resistance movements after the U.S.-led invasion of Iraq in 2003. The most recent attacks have involved challenges from Islamist groups including members of al-Qaeda. Until his death in 2006, the dominant al-Qaeda figure in Jordan was Abu Musab al-Zarqawi (Ahmad Fadel Khalyla), who was of Jordanian birth. A petty criminal in Jordan during his youth, he went to Afghanistan to fight the Soviets in 1989 but arrived as the Soviet forces were leaving. However, in Afghanistan he met his al-Qaeda mentor, Abu Zubaydah (Terrill 2008, 35).

Al-Zarqawi returned to Jordan in 1993 and was subsequently followed by Jordanian security forces because he was a known terrorist. He was arrested and convicted by a Jordanian court in 1994 but was released in 1999 as part of a traditional amnesty offered after a new king comes to power. Shortly after his release al-Zarqawi began to work with Abu Zubaydah on the "millennium plots," which involved attacking Jordanian tourist sites and the Los Angeles LAX airport. Through successful Jordanian and U.S. intelligence cooperation the plots were prevented.

Al-Zarqawi's group was involved in the October 2002 murder of U.S. diplomat Laurence Foley in Amman and the August 7, 2003, truck bombing of the Jordanian embassy in Iraq. The Jordanian state took a stand against al-Qaeda in 2004 when it convicted eight terrorists involved in the Foley murder and sentenced Abu Zubaydah and al-Zarqawi to death in absentia. Beginning in 2004 increased numbers of supporters of the resistance movement began to leave Jordan for Iraq, especially from the towns of Salt and Zarqa, even as the state made efforts to prevent this (Terrill 2008, 36–38).

In a unique response to this situation plans were underway for a subsidized housing project near Zarqa, funded by the Saudi Arabian government with Jordanian banks subsidizing the houses. In addition to these efforts the Jordanian state continued to create ties with the new Iraqi government to combat terrorism, kidnapping, smuggling, and other border crimes. The goal was for the state to obtain essential Iraqi intelligence (Terrill 2008, 39–40).

AL-ZARQAWI AND AL-QAEDA

Al-Zarqawi's group is also alleged to be part of the 2004 plan to attack the head of the Jordanian General Intelligence Directorate (GID), the prime minister's Office, and the U.S. embassy in Amman. Jordanian security and intelligence forces prevented the attacks, and allegations soon followed of Syrian financial support for the attack (Terrill 2008, 41).

The most important and serious al-Qaeda terrorist attack in Jordan occurred on November 9, 2005—a day that will be remembered as Jordan's 9/11—when simultaneous suicide bombers attacked the Radisson SAS, Grand Hyatt, and Day's Inn hotels in Amman, killing four Americans and two non-Jewish Israelis. Al-Zarqawi supported the attacks on the Amman hotels by stating that they were "playgrounds" for Jews and Jewish terrorists.

In response to these attacks King Abdullah appointed his national security advisor, Marouf al-Bakhit, as the new prime minister. Al-Bakhit was ordered to wage an "all-out war" against terrorism. Abdullah and al-Bakhit, according to numerous media sources, began to wage their war by creating the "Knights of God" to hunt down al-Zarqawi's group. In November 2005 the Jordanian state began to work more closely with U.S. government intelligence agencies and allegedly sent Jordanian intelligence officials to Iraq to find al-Zarqawi and his group. On June 7, 2006, al-Zarqawi was killed in a U.S. air strike on his headquarters about 30 miles north of Baghdad. According to Jordanian officials this action would not have been possible without the help of Jordanian intelligence (Terrill 2008, 42–45).

CONCLUSION

It remains to be seen what King Abdullah and his state will do in the aftermath of the U.S. withdrawal from Iraq. With Jordan's substantial population of Iraqi refugees and supporters of the resistance crossing the border, it will be up to the Jordanian monarch, government, and security forces to effectively address this issue. In the shadow of U.S. and Iraqi cooperation with Jordan against al-Zarqawi, it is most likely that King Abdullah will continue similar counterterrorism policies and tactics.

See also: **Volume 2, Part I:** Royal Special Forces (Jordan)

REFERENCES

Ashton, Nigel John. *King Hussein of Jordan: A Political Life.* New Haven, CT: Yale University Press, 2008.

Cooley, John K. *Green March, Black September: The Story of the Palestinian Arabs.* London: Cass, 1973.

Laqueur, Walter, and Barry M. Rubin. *The Israel-Arab Reader: A Documentary History of the Middle East Conflict.* 6th ed. New York: Penguin Books, 2001.

Shlaim, Avi. *Lion of Jordan: The Life of King Hussein in War and Peace.* 1st ed. New York: Alfred A. Knopf, 2008.

Terrill, W. Andrew. *Jordanian National Security and the Future of Middle East Stability.* Carlisle, PA: Strategic Studies Institute, U.S. Army War College, 2008. http://www.strategicstudiesinstitute.army.mil/pdffiles/pub838.pdf

Mexico

Anna Kaganiec-Kamieńska

Probably the most important threat to Mexican national security today is the escalation of drug-related violence. Drug-trafficking organizations employ terrorist strategies such as bombings, targeted killings, and kidnappings to facilitate their illegal activities. Terrorist acts carried out by groups involved in the illegal drug business are referred to as *narco-terrorism*. Even though insurgency groups at the present seem to pose a lesser threat to Mexico's national security than narco-terrorism, they need to be addressed.

BACKGROUND

Since 2006, drug-related violence in Mexico has increased substantially. One of the factors that contributed to Mexico's instability is its growing role since the 1980s as a transit country for the transport of cocaine to the United States. According to the U.S. Department of State's 2009 *International Narcotics Control Strategy Report*, about 90 percent of the cocaine entering the United States transits through Mexico. Consequently, the level of violence has reached unprecedented rates. The number of drug-related killings increased from about 2,220 in 2006 to about 6,000 in 2008, and it is rising. Some of the incidents are spectacularly violent (including torture and decapitations, etc.) to ensure the maximum psychological impact. Unfortunately, the violence has also affected innocent civilians (e.g., eight people were killed in Morelia on Independence Day 2008).

The drug problem has also led to widespread corruption. For many years politicians have been suspected of either protecting or being directly involved in the trade. Some recent striking examples are the 2008 arrests and dismissals of at least 35 officials and agents of an elite organized crime unit, Subprocuraduría de Investigación Especializada en Delincuencia Organizada (SIEDO); the 2008 arrest of the former head of SIEDO, Noé Ramírez Mandujano; and the 2008 arrest of two former heads of Interpol in Mexico. The armed forces, which are generally respected and perceived as more honest than the police, are also vulnerable to luring "job offers" from the cartels or paramilitaries (in 2000–2006 about 100,000 desertions took place).

As of 2009 the dominant drug organizations are the Sinaloa Federation and Cartel, Gulf Cartel, Beltrán Leyva Organization, Arrellano Felix Organization/Tijuana Cartel, and the Vicente Carillo Fuentes Organization/Juárez Cartel. According to the U.S. Drug Enforcement Agency, La Familia Michoacana, once a criminal group affiliated with the Sinaloa Cartel, is an "emergent cartel." Alliances among the cartels tend to be temporary, which leads to widespread bloodshed. The cartels often recruit former military and police officials, criminals, and security guards to serve in their own private armies. The most dangerous and perfectly trained group is Los Zetas (formerly linked to the Gulf Cartel), considered by U.S. officials to be "the most technologically advanced, sophisticated, and violent" (National Drug Intelligence Center 2007) private army in Mexico. The group formed in the late 1990s out of deserters from the Mexican Army's Airborne Special Forces Groups (elite counternarcotics units), and it also recruited *Kaibiles* (former Guatemalan counterinsurgency specialists). Los Zetas pose a serious threat, as they have expanded their activities (kidnapping, arms trafficking, money laundering, and access to cocaine sources).

The monopoly of political power since the 1920s facilitated the development of the drug business. The Partido Revolucionario Institucional government tolerated illegal drug traffic, while prominent political figures, especially in the northern states on Mexico, were believed to discreetly control the business. Drug traffickers became more autonomous with the deterioration of the political system and Partido Revolucionario Institucional's monopoly in the 1980s and 1990s.

In the 1940s more attention was given to combating the drug trade. In 1947, President Miguel Aleman transferred the antidrug policy from the Department of Health to the Attorney General's Office (Procuraduría General de la República [PGR]). During that year the Federal Security Directorate (Dirección Federal de Seguridad) was created and also given the authority to act in the antidrug area. The Federal Security Directorate and the Federal Judicial Police (Policía Judicial Federal, depending on the PGR) became the institutions responsible for fighting the forbidden trade (links between both institutions and drug traffickers were later found). In 1948, the government announced a "Great Campaign" to destroy the illegal plants, and the army became more openly involved in destroying the crops. However, crop eradication had a limited effect. Its effectiveness grew in the 1960s with the introduction of new technology acquired from the United States (e.g., airplanes, jeeps, weapons, helicopters).

RISING DEMAND AND COUNTERNARCOTICS INITIATIVES

Greater demand for drugs in the United States in the 1960s had a significant impact. In 1969, President Nixon launched Operation Intercept, which consisted in meticulous car inspection for drugs at the border northeast of Mexico. In 1977, during an impressive military operation against drug plantations and traffickers, Operation Condor, 10,000 soldiers were sent to the sierra of Sinaloa, Durango, and Chihuahua.

An incident that marked the beginning of a new period in antidrug policy was the kidnapping and death of a Drug Enforcement Agency agent, Enrique Camarena, in 1985. The U.S. government put more political pressure on Mexico, and the names of high-ranking officials linked to the drug trade came to light. In 1986, U.S. president Ronald Reagan launched his "war on drugs," declaring that drugs were a threat to national security, and started the "certification" of drug-producing countries. Mexico (under President Miguel de la Madrid) complied and, under American influence, began to "militarize" its war on drugs. This led to increased cooperation with the United States (e.g., Operation Alliance in 1986).

Under President Ernesto Zedillo (1994–2000), the head of the Gulf Cartel, Juan García Abrego, was arrested and extradited to the United States. Zedillo also conducted a massive purge of the Federal Judicial Police. Following the visit of U.S. Defense Secretary William Perry, U.S.-Mexico cooperation in the areas of counternarcotics and border security was further increased.

Vicente Fox Quesada (2000–2006) adopted a more aggressive, militarized approach to the drug problem. He increased military presence in federal police agencies; military officers were assigned important positions within the PGR under the new attorney general. Additionally, there was greater coordination between the PGR and the military. U.S.-Mexico cooperation improved considerably. Militarization resulted in significant advances such as the capture or death of many high-ranking drug traffickers, increased seizures of drug shipments, and the replacement of the corrupt Federal Judicial Police with the Agencia Federal de Investigación in 2002. However, corruption continued to be a major challenge, and many members of the military and the Agencia Federal de Investigación were investigated and sentenced. Another problem was accusations of human rights abuses by the military.

President Felipe Calderón's administration (2006–) has been even more committed to national security and more aggressive in its counternarcotics actions. Under President Calderón combating drug trafficking organizations (DTOs) became a priority. His policies include increased spending on security, aggressive military offensives against drug traffickers, deployment of thousands of soldiers and federal police into various hot spots, and unprecedented cooperation with the United States (e.g., the extradition of 83 persons in 2007, including the head of the Gulf Cartel), in addition to fighting corruption and reforming the police and judiciary. These measures resulted in the apprehension of more than 14,000 suspects, the seizures of large quantities of drugs, and the detention of 10 mayors and 18 other officials, including heads of state, municipal police, and state prosecutors, in Michoacan in May 2009. In October 2007, the Merida Initiative, a three-year, $1.4 billion counternarcotics program for Mexico and Central America, was implemented. It provided aid for counternarcotics, counterterrorism, border and public security, and law enforcement institution building. Some critics argue that the overall effects of counternarcotics policies are relatively small because of lack of manpower and firepower, weak coordination between police forces, and good training and armament of paramilitary groups.

EJÉRCITO ZAPATISTA DE LIBERACIÓN NACIONAL AND EJÉRCITO POPULAR REVOLUCIONARIO

The Zapatista Army of National Liberation (Ejército Zapatista de Liberación Nacional [EZLN]) gained international attention when it started an armed rebellion in Chiapas on January 1, 1994 (the date coincided with the launch of the North American Free Trade Agreement [NAFTA]). The rebellion took the lives of approximately 150 people in a two-week period before the cease-fire. Since then the group has generally refrained from using violence. Although EZLN began as an armed guerrilla group, it turned into a postmodern antiglobalization force that uses new technology and the Internet to further its objectives. While it does not pose a military challenge, "it is the product of a convergence of economic, social and political problems that exist not only in Chiapas but in much of rural Mexico" (Wager and Schulz 1994, v). Although EZLN maintains some characteristics of a terrorist group (such as wearing ski masks in public and retaining military capabilities) and has been labeled a "terrorist" organization by some researchers and politicians (including Ernesto Zedillo), it is not officially considered as such by the United States, the European Union, or other states. Zapatistas consider themselves an indigenous insurgency movement.

EZLN is one of over a dozen insurgency groups operating in Mexico. Another important organization is the People's Revolutionary Army (Ejército Popular Revolucionario [EPR]), active mainly in Guerrero, Oaxaca, and Chiapas. EPR made its first public statement on June 28, 1996, at the memorial of 17 citizens killed by the police in the so-called Aguas Blancas massacre in Guerrero. Unlike EZLN it uses violent methods, such as attacks on public and military installations and bomb attacks.

Insurgency groups have also required some reaction from the state. The conflict in Chiapas has been deeply militarized. In the first seven days of the rebellion in Chiapas, 17,000 Mexican troops were sent to the conflict area. On January 12, President Salinas called for a unilateral cease-fire and offered to negotiate with the rebels. On February 16, 1996, after two years of on-and-off negotiations and low-intensity conflict, an agreement that addressed the indigenous people's rights and culture (San Andrés Accords) was signed but never implemented. Up until 2001 the situation remained unchanged, while the counterinsurgency war by paramilitary groups and the military intensified. Paramilitary groups are also responsible for many deaths (e.g., the 1997 massacre of 45 Tzotzil indigenous people in the community of Acteal) and internal displacement in Chiapas. After President Fox took office in December 2000 the situation seemed to change. However, in April 2001, the Congress approved a law, the Ley Indigena, which did not meet the expectations of the Zapatistas.

As for the EPR, following the 2007 attacks on Mexico's gas and oil pipelines, President Calderón sent special troops to secure the infrastructure. In 2008, the EPR proposed to negotiate with the government but later rejected the conditions set by the authorities. Some analysts suggest that groups like EPR may pose a threat to Mexico's security in the future. With drug-related violence escalating, more resources are being allocated to this problem, and less effort is being allocated to combating insurgent groups.

CONCLUSION

Counterterrorism in Mexico is a complex issue and involves combating narco-terrorism as well as political violence perpetrated by insurgents. The Mexican state is also struggling with other problems, such as organized crime, including migrant smuggling, human trafficking, and weapons smuggling, especially in the border areas.

See also: **Volume 1, Part III:** Terrorists, Criminals, and Drug Cartels

REFERENCES

Astorga, Luis. "Organized Crime and the Organization of Crime." In *Organized Crime: Democratic Governability, Mexico and the U.S.-Mexican Borderlands,* edited by John Bailey and Roy Godson, 58–82. Pittsburgh: University of Pittsburgh Press, 2001.

Beittel, June S. *Mexico's Drug-Related Violence.* Congressional Research Service Report for Congress, May 27, 2009. http://www.fas.org/sgp/crs/row/ R40582.pdf.

Brands, Hal. *Mexico's Narco-insurgency and U.S. Counterdrug Policy.* Carlisle, PA: Strategic Studies Institute, U.S. Army War College, 2009.

Freeman, Laurie, and Jorge Luis Sierra. "Mexico: The Militarization Trap." In *Drugs and Democracy in Latin America: The Impact of U.S. Policy,* edited by Coletta Youngers and Eileen Rosin, 263–302. Boulder, CO: Lynne Rienner, 2005.

Longmire, Sylvia. "Mexico's EPR 'Guerrillas': A Nuisance or a Threat in 2010?" Mexidata.Info. August 24, 2009. http://mexidata.info/id2376.html.

National Drug Intelligence Center. *National Drug Threat Assessment 2008, Southwest Border Region-Drug Transportation and Homeland Security Issues.* October 2007. http://www.justice.gov/ndic/pubs25/25921/border.htm.

Rochlin, James F. *Vanguard Revolutionaries in Latin America: Peru, Colombia, Mexico.* Boulder, CO: Lynne Rienner, 2003.

U.S. Department of State. *International Narcotics Control Strategy Report 2009.* Released by the Bureau of International Narcotics and Law Enforcement Affairs, U.S. Department of State, Washington DC, issued February 27. http://www.state.gov/documents/organization/120054.pdf.

Wager, Stephen J., and Donald E. Schulz. *The Awakening: The Zapatista Revolt and Its Implications for Civil-Military Relations and the Future of Mexico.* Carlisle, PA: Strategic Studies Institute, U.S. Army War College, 1994.

Williams, Phil. *Drug Trafficking, Violence, and the State in Mexico.* Carlisle, PA: Strategic Studies Institute, U.S. Army War College, 2009.

Nepal

James Perry

The Nepalese Civil War was a struggle between the government of Nepal and the Communist Party of Nepal (Maoist). The Maoists initiated armed struggle in 1996, and the war formally ended with Maoist victory after the signing of the Comprehensive Peace Accord in 2006. About 12,000 people were killed, and over 100,000 were displaced during the course of the 10-year struggle.

INSURGENCY IN NEPAL

In the 1990s, Nepal was ripe for insurgency. The country had an extremely high population density in the arable areas of the country, with 90 percent of the population working on very small farms. The country had little or no industry, and thus the per capita gross domestic product (GDP) was (and remains) one of the lowest in the world, roughly equivalent to that of Haiti. The country was divided along caste, ethnic, and linguistic lines, and the insurgents exploited these divisions. About half the population was within the Hindu caste system; the rest belonged to tribal groups or other religious communities. The top two castes, about 29 percent of the population, controlled the nation's important institutions. About half the nation spoke Nepali; the rest spoke 31 other languages. Inability to speak Nepali was an obstacle to employment in government or the tourist industry, which were essentially the only options other than farming.

Politically, the British ruled Nepal from 1815 to 1950. King Mahendra began ruling the country directly in 1960, and his son Birendra succeeded him in 1972. Birendra agreed in 1990 to install a multiparty parliamentary democracy. This made little difference in the lives of the people, particularly because the state failed to implement land reform. The Communist Party secured seats in Parliament in the 1991 election, but more extreme elements argued that armed struggle was necessary because the Communists were a small minority in Parliament. The extremists boycotted the 1994 election and coalesced under the Communist Party of Nepal (Maoist), or CPN(M), in 1995. The CPN(M) issued 40 demands to the government and threatened to begin fighting if the demands were not met. The demands included an end to "Indian imperialism" in Nepal, an end to the monarchy and the caste system, land reform, and measures to address rural poverty. The government ignored these demands, and the CPN(M) declared the "people's war" on February 13, 1996.

The CPN(M) modeled itself on two extremely brutal groups: Peru's Shining Path and India's Naxalites (another Maoist group). The insurgency began with attacks on rural police stations, an effective tactic because rural police were poorly armed and were the main representatives of the central government in a given area. The police quickly abandoned isolated stations in favor of larger, more defensible, less isolated stations, but this conceded control of rural areas to the guerrillas. The guerrillas drove away village leaders and destroyed transportation and communications infrastructure. The guerrillas managed to establish rural base areas in which to recruit and sustain their forces while indoctrinating villagers and denying resources to the government. The guerrillas enjoyed safe havens and training areas in India, which the Indian government tolerated until 2001.

GOVERNMENT RESPONSE

The government response to the insurgency was weak and counterproductive. Initially, the government viewed the insurgency as a law enforcement problem, and heavy-handed police tactics alienated the population and drove many people to join the guerrillas. For example, Operation Kilo Sierra Two in 1998 focused on killing Maoists, but poorly trained police killed, looted, raped, and tortured many innocent people. The government failed to address any of the underlying political issues in order to undermine the CPN(M)'s appeal, and it likewise failed to implement an effective information campaign to counter Maoist propaganda or to develop a unified, long-term political and military counterinsurgency strategy. Moreover, Nepal's police and military intelligence organizations were weak and underresourced, and they lacked the confidence of the government. They could not analyze information effectively or provide useful, timely support to units in the field. In general, government forces never established effective, legitimate governance and security in guerrilla-controlled areas and consequently failed to secure popular support.

On June 1, 2001, the heir to the throne, Prince Dipendra, killed King Birendra and eight other members of the royal family in a drunken rage and then shot himself. After he died, his brother Gyanendra was crowned king. The royal massacre damaged the government's image and strengthened the CPN(M)'s argument that Nepal should become a secular republic. Meanwhile, the CPN(M) felt sufficiently secure in rural base areas to instigate revolt in Nepal's cities, including the capital, Kathmandu. The guerrillas engaged the government in peace talks and, when these talks failed, launched a major assault on police stations. The guerrillas also attacked an army barracks for the first time. In response, in November 2001, Parliament declared a state of emergency, proclaimed that the guerrillas were terrorists, and committed the Royal Nepalese Army (RNA) to the counterinsurgency fight.

Until 2001, the RNA was primarily used for peacekeeping abroad. While many soldiers were somewhat familiar with counterinsurgency principles, most were unused to actual combat. High casualties in the wake of the 2001 Maoist offensive shocked the nation. The RNA lacked transport and was thus unable to outmaneuver the guerrillas, and it failed to coordinate effectively with the police, whom the RNA distrusted. The RNA attempted some rural development projects but on too small a scale to make much difference. Most important, the RNA operated without clear political support and direction from Parliament or the monarchy. Despite these problems, the RNA prevented the guerrillas from seizing control of Nepal in early 2002, as they seemed on the verge of doing.

Political turbulence that began in 2002 undermined the overall government effort. The king dissolved the Parliament in May, due to its opposition to extending the state of emergency, and in October, the king deposed the prime minister, assumed executive authority, and postponed elections indefinitely. As the king's legitimacy was itself in question, his puppet government provoked immediate opposition from ousted parliamentarians and, of course, from the guerrillas. In June 2004, the king restored his former prime minister, only to dissolve the government again in February

2005, when he also cracked down on journalists, union leaders, opposition politicians, and other democratic forces.

From January 2003 through 2006, the Maoists pursued a dual-track strategy of fighting and negotiating. The fighting, as before, focused on attacking police stations, security forces, and government offices in order to secure and expand guerrilla-controlled base areas. Politically, the Maoists sought to turn their enemies against one another and, in particular, to form a common front with the ousted political parties to end the monarchy and remove the puppet government. The Maoists believed they would emerge triumphant through democratic processes if the king abdicated, and their demand that he do so enhanced the international image of their struggle as a pro-democracy movement.

NATIONWIDE PROTESTS AND PEACE ACCORD

After the king dissolved the Parliament again in February 2005, the ousted political leaders formed the Seven Party Alliance (SPA) and launched strikes and protests throughout the country against the king's rule. After talks with the SPA, the CPN(M) joined it in November 2005. The SPA accepted the Maoist demand for election of a constituent assembly to rewrite the constitution. In return, the Maoists agreed to support multiparty democracy and freedom of speech. The Maoists contributed to the nationwide strikes, protests, and political agitation in 2006. After massive protests in April 2006, including a protest of 300,000 to 500,000 people in Kathmandu itself, King Gyanendra requested that the SPA nominate a prime minister and form a government. The SPA declined, demanding instead the reinstitution of the old parliament and election of a constituent assembly to rewrite the constitution. The CPN(M) declared a truce and announced they would accept the results of the elections if they were free and fair. In May, the restored parliament voted to strip the king of many of his powers.

The CPN(M) and the government initiated peace talks in May 2006 and signed the Comprehensive Peace Accord in November 2006, formally ending the civil war. Both sides agreed to cease attacking one another and to accept a United Nations (UN) mission to monitor the disarmament and demobilization of both the Maoists and the RNA. The king was stripped of his political rights, and his property was nationalized. The Maoists agreed to scrap the separate political structures they had established within the zones they controlled.

CONCLUSION

In January 2007, Nepal established an interim constitution and parliament, which the Maoists joined in March. In April 2008, the Maoists won a large majority of the seats in the constituent assembly, and in May,

Parliament officially abolished the monarchy. The leader of the CPN(M) became prime minister of the new secular republic in August 2008. A lengthy UN-monitored peace process ensued, as the nation struggled to finalize the constitution, rehabilitate Maoist guerrillas and integrate them into the new Nepalese security forces, ensure human rights, and meet humanitarian needs. The UN Security Council voted in September 2010 to remove the UN mission in Nepal in January 2011, judging that by then the final tasks of the peace process would be complete.

See also: **Volume 1, Part I**: Insurgent Terrorism

REFERENCES

Crane, S. D. "The Maoist Insurgency in Nepal, 1996–2001." Carlisle, PA: U.S. Army War College, 2002. http://smallwarsjournal.com/documents/crane1.pdf.

Kreuttner, Timothy R. *The Maoist Insurgency in Nepal, 1996–2008: Implications for U.S. Counterinsurgency Doctrine.* Fort Leavenworth, KS: U.S. Army Command and General Staff College, 2009. http://www.dtic.mil/cgi-bin/GetTRDoc?AD=ADA505200.

Marks, Thomas A. *Insurgency in Nepal.* Carlisle, PA: Strategic Studies Institute, U.S. Army War College, 2003. http://www.strategicstudiesinstitute.army.mil/pdffiles/pub49.pdf.

Subba, Dil Bikram. "Government's Strategy against the Maoist Insurgency in Nepal." Master's thesis. Fort Leavenworth, KS: U.S. Army Command and General Staff College, 2010. http://www.dtic.mil/cgi-bin/GetTRDoc?AD=ADA524135.

Netherlands

Teun van Dongen and Rob de Wijk

In the 1970s the Netherlands was confronted with several types of terrorism. First, there was the Rode Jeugd (Red Youth), a leftist group with a violent wing that modeled itself after the Rote Armee Fraktion (Red Army Faction), although its attacks never produced more than material damage (Dekkers and Dijksman 1988). Second, several foreign terrorist groups were active on Dutch soil. These groups, including the Euskadi Ta Askatasuna (Basque Homeland and Freedom), the Irish Republican Army, Black September, and the Japanese Red Army, almost exclusively targeted foreign interests in the Netherlands (Muller 2008, 230–33).

The most serious terrorist challenge, however, emanated from violent Moluccan activists. After the Dutch recognized Indonesian independence in 1949, some Moluccans ended up in the Netherlands, where they lived in camps under poor conditions, isolated from the rest of society. Unemployment was high, and educational levels were low. Out of discontent with their situation and the Dutch reluctance to press for Moluccan independence at the United Nations, a group of Moluccans occupied the Indonesian ambassador's residence near the Hague in 1970. The Moluccan action took the country by surprise. There were no crisis mechanisms that could be applied during terrorist hostage situations or hijackings. The division of responsibilities was unclear. To end the uncertainty, Prime Minister De Jong went down to the site to personally deal with the crisis. The hostage takers gave themselves up after they had been worn down by lengthy negotiations, and the crisis was resolved without bloodshed.

EVOLUTION OF DUTCH COUNTERTERRORISM

At the time of the occupation of the ambassador's residence, the Netherlands did not have a counterterrorism policy, nor did the incident trigger one. Dutch counterterrorism was initiated only after Black September's widely televised action at the Munich Olympics of 1972, where the Palestinian organization took several Israeli athletes hostage and eventually killed them. In reaction to this event, Dutch prime minister Barend Biesheuvel wrote the so-called *Terror Letter* (*Terreurbrief*), which can be considered the founding document of Dutch counterterrorism. The letter, which announced the Dutch counterterrorism policy to Parliament, suggested that terrorism should be perceived as a law enforcement problem rather than as a political problem. Consequently, the Netherlands did not introduce counterterrorist legislation. Instead, the government set up an interdepartmental coordination group and created a national public prosecutor for terrorist cases. On a more operational level, the Dutch government created the Bijzondere Bijstands Eenheden (Special Assistance Units), which consisted of military and civilian personnel specialized in close combat and sharpshooting (Janse 2005, 65–66; Graaf 2010, 28–33). Finally, an arrangement for the management of hostage crises and hijackings was adopted (Schmid 1993, 92–93). An interesting feature of Dutch counterterrorism at this point was its secretive nature. Dutch policymakers felt that a salient and clearly visible counterterrorism policy would only cause alarm among the population. For instance, care was taken not to publish information about terrorist attacks that were disrupted (Graaf 2010, 44).

Following the implementation of these new policies the Netherlands faced a series of Moluccan terrorist attacks. Between 1974 and 1979, Moluccan groups took hostages on two occasions—in a provincial government building and in an elementary school—and twice hijacked a train. On three of these occasions, the government, using the Bijzondere Bijstands Eenheden, ended the crisis by force, leading to the deaths of several Moluccan terrorists. However, there was also a softer side to Dutch counterterrorism at the time. The government provided better housing, improved treatment of drug addiction, and put effort into lowering unemployment among the Moluccan community. Also, it allowed Moluccan media airtime on Dutch television, founded a Dutch-Moluccan consultation platform, and organized trips to the Moluccas to show Dutch-Moluccan activists that independence was no longer on the Moluccans' minds (Rasser 2005, 487–88). The decline of Moluccan terrorism can thus be attributed to the combination of both hard and soft measures. Some former activists later claimed that the violent disruption of their actions by the government and the increasing integration of the Moluccan community in Dutch society made them see the pointlessness of their armed struggle (Demant et al. 2008, 32–34).

After the decline of Moluccan violence, the Dutch approach to counterterrorism did not change essentially until 9/11, even though the Netherlands was no stranger to political violence in the 1980s. Radical leftist groups like the Revolutionaire Anti-Racistische Actie (Revolutionary Anti-racist Action) firebombed political and corporate targets that maintained ties with the South African apartheid regime. Also, Kurdish groups and leftist Turkish groups bombed Turkish targets on Dutch soil. The Irish Republican Army and the Euskadi Ta Askatasuna (Basque Homeland and Freedom) committed attacks in the Netherlands during this period as well, albeit only sporadically (Bakker 2009, 225). Throughout the 1980s and 1990s, the Dutch security service Binnenlandse Veiligheidsdienst (Domestic Security Service) pressed for restraint and stuck to the label *political violent activism,* still of the position that using the label *terrorism* would only lead to further hostility and would hamper the pacification of violent groups (Bakker 2009, 331). In the absence of political interest in terrorism, it was easy for the Binnenlandse Veiligheidsdienst to enforce this line, as it was the only major actor involved in counterterrorism (Abels 2007, 127–28). Unsurprisingly, this changed after 9/11.

POST-9/11

The 9/11 attacks made a big impression in the Netherlands. Less than a month later, the Dutch government started expanding its counterterrorism policy. Also, in the first years after 9/11, the Netherlands became aware of the existence of homegrown terrorism, which had its most dramatic manifestation in the murder of filmmaker Theo van Gogh by a member of the Hofstad Group. These threats were countered by a wide range of measures in different spheres. First, several adjustments in the laws and legal procedures were made. The Netherlands adopted a legal definition of *terrorism* and has penalized preparation for and financing of terrorist acts and membership in a terrorist organization (Boer 2007, 294–96). To facilitate the prosecution of terrorist suspects, new laws expanded the possibilities for using intelligence reports in court and widened the investigative powers—surveillance, infiltration, wiretapping, and so on—of the police for investigations into upcoming terrorist attacks (Council of Europe 2008, 1). On a more institutional level, Dutch counterterrorism since 2005 has been overseen by the Nationaal Coördinator Terrorismebestrijding (National Coordinator for Counterterrorism), which also produces terrorist threat assessments on the basis of information from intelligence agencies (Minister van Binnenlandse Zaken en Koninkrijksrelaties and Minister van Justitie 2005). The Counterterrorism Infobox has been created to give all relevant players—for example, intelligence agencies, the police, and the immigration service—access to all available terrorism-related information (Review Commission for the Intelligence and Security Services 2007, 2–3). Finally, an interdepartmental forum and a forum for operational services—for example, police and customs—were created to facilitate regular consultation on terrorism and related matters (Minister van Justitie 2004). The Dutch government claims its counterterrorism efforts follow the so-called broad approach. Although nowhere officially codified as a strategy, the broad approach suggests that all steps in the terrorist chain, that is, from recruitment to preparation to the actual attack, should be addressed by appropriate countermeasures (Algemene Inlichtingen- en Veiligheidsdienst [AIVD] 2004, 6).

CONCLUSION

A 2009 government report concluded that the effectiveness of the new measures has not been determined. It also observed that Dutch counterterrorism lacks internal coherence and leans too heavily on judicial measures (Commissie Evaluatie Antiterrorismebeleid 2009, 86–87). On the other hand, a few months after the release of this report, the Algemene Inlichtingen- en Veiligheidsdienst (AIVD; General Security and Intelligence Service, formerly the Binnenlandse Veiligheidsdienst) noted that the threat of homegrown terrorist groups to Dutch national security has declined. The AIVD claimed that these groups have fallen apart as a result of a lack of cohesion and focus but also as a result of the government's broad approach (AIVD 2009, 6–9).

See also: **Volume 2, Part I:** Unit Interventie Mariniers (Netherlands). **Part II:** Holland Train Seizure (1977)

REFERENCES

Abels, P. "'Je wilt niet geloven dat zoiets in Nederland kan!' Het Nederlandse contraterrorismebeleid sinds 1973." In *Terroristen en hun bestrijders: vroeger en nu*, edited by I. Duyvesteyn and B. de Graaf, 121–28. Amsterdam: Boom, 2007.

Algemene Inlichtingen- en Veiligheidsdienst (AIVD). *Van dawa tot jihad: de diverse dreigingen van de radicale islam tegen de democratische rechtsorde.* The Hague: Algemene Inlichtingen- en Veiligheidsdienst, 2004. http://www.crethip lethi.com/download/notavandawatotjihad.pdf.

Algemene Inlichtingen- en Veiligheidsdienst (AIVD). *Lokale jihadistische netwerken in Nederland: veranderingen in het dreigingsbeeld.* The Hague: Algemene Inlichtingen- en Veiligheidsdienst, 2009.

Bakker, E. "Terrorisme en politiek gewelddadig activisme in Nederland." In *Jaarboek Vrede en Veiligheid 2008,* edited by B. Bomert, Th. van den Hoogen, and R.A. Wessel, 221–36. Center for International Conflict Analysis and Management (CICAM). Amsterdam, The Netherlands: Rosenberg Publishers, 2009.

Boer, M. den. "Wake-Up Call for the Lowlands: Dutch Counterterrorism from a Comparative Perspective." *Cambridge Review of International Affairs* 20, no. 2 (2007): 285–302.

Commissie Evaluatie Antiterrorismebeleid. *Naar een integrale evaluatie van antiterrorismemaatregelen.* The Hague: Rijksoverheid, 2009.

Council of Europe. "Profiles on Counter-terrorist Capacity: The Netherlands." Committee of Experts on Terrorism, Council of Europe, 2008. http://www. coe.int/t/dlapil/codexter/Source/country_profiles/CODEXTER%20Pro file%20(2008)%20NETHERLANDS.pdf.

Dekkers, F., and D. Dijksman. *'n Hollandse stadsguerrilla: terugblik op de Rode Jeugd.* Amsterdam: Balans, 1988.

Demant, F., M. Slootman, F. Buijs, and J. Tillie. *Teruggang en uittreding: processen van deradicalisering en teruggang ontleed.* Amsterdam: Institute for Migration and Ethnic Studies (IMES), Universiteit van Amsterdam, 2008.

Graaf, B. de. *Theater van de angst: de strijd tegen terrorisme in Nederland, Duitsland, Italië en Amerika.* Amsterdam: Uitgeverij Boom, 2010.

Janse, R. "Fighting Terrorism in the Netherlands: A Historical Perspective." *Utrecht Law Review* 1, no. 1 (2005): 55–67.

Minister van Binnenlandse Zaken en Koninkrijksrelaties and Minister van Justitie. Regeling van de Ministers van Justitie en van Binnenlandse Zaken en Koninkrijksrelaties van 29 juni 2005, nr. DDS5357209, houdende instelling van de Nationaal Coördinator Terrorismebestrijding. 2005. http://www. nctb.nl/organisatie/wat_doet_de_NCTb/.

Minister van Justitie. Instellingsbesluit Gezamenlijk Comité Terrorismebestrijding. June 15, 2004. http://wetten.overheid.nl/BWBR0016870/geld igheidsdatum_15-05-2010.

Muller, E. "De geschiedenis van terrorisme in Nederland." In *Terrorisme: studies over terrorisme en terrorismebestrijding in Nederland,* edited by E.R. Muller, U. Rosenthal, and R. de Wijk, 217–41. Deventer: Kluwer, 2008.

Rasser, M. "The Dutch Response to Moluccan Terrorism, 1970–1978." *Studies in Conflict and Terrorism* 28, no. 6 (2005): 481–92.

Review Commission for the Intelligence and Security Services (CTIVD). *Toezichtsrapport inzake het onderzoek van de Commissie van Toezicht naar de Contra Terrorisme Infobox.* The Hague, The Netherlands: CTIVD, 2007.

Schmid, A.P. "Countering Terrorism in the Netherlands." In *Western Responses to Terrorism,* edited by Alex P. Schmid and Ronald D. Crelinsten, 79–109. London: Frank Cass, 1993.

Pakistan

Chris J. Kirkpatrick

Pakistan's internal tensions, weak government, and assertive military combined with a complex international environment have yielded a confused counterterrorism policy, one that has simultaneously combated and facilitated terrorist groups to legitimize the state. Pakistan was founded in 1947 by Muhammad Ali Jinnah, who envisioned a secular government. However, from the very beginning the government of Pakistan has focused on survival in the face of internal fragmentation and external pressures (Haqqani 2005, 313). This has led to a military with a vested interest in the domestic political situation that has intervened repeatedly; Pakistan has been ruled for half of its 64 years by the military presidents Ayub Khan (1958–1969), Yahya Khan (1969–1971), Zia-ul-Haq (1977–1988), and Pervez Musharraf (1999–2008) (Rizvi 2000, 2–12; Talbot 2009, 2–8). When the military is not actively in power, it has used the intelligence services of the state to counter popular political movements in the name of stability and security (Rizvi 2000, 192–93).

DOMESTIC-BASED THREATS AND THE DIRECTORATE FOR INTER-SERVICES INTELLIGENCE

The primary institutions responsible for counterterrorism efforts in Pakistan are the army and the Directorate for Inter-services Intelligence (ISI). Officially, the ISI is a partner of the U.S. intelligence services. In reality, the counterterror efforts of the ISI are complicated by their complicity in developing many of the groups they are responsible for eradicating. Many of these groups are still strategically and domestically valuable. In essence, the counterterrorism efforts of the ISI reflect the expediency of the moment (Tellis 2008, 4–5).

Much like many other institutions in Pakistan, the ISI was formed as a response to a crisis. The ISI was created in 1948 to facilitate interagency cooperation after perceived intelligence failures during the 1947 war in Kashmir (Ziring 2003, 105). The combination of a coordinated headquarters with access to cumulative intelligence resources and either weak civil governments or military coups led to an expansion of the ISI portfolio. For example, the growth of separatist sentiments in East Pakistan in the 1950s led President Khan to direct the ISI to infiltrate and investigate both the Intelligence Bureau and the center-left Pakistan People's Party (Talbot 2009, 180–83). After the humiliating secession of East Pakistan in

1971 and the invasion of neighboring Afghanistan by the Soviet Union in 1979, President Zia began a program of Islamization of Pakistani society in 1982. The combination of this program, a growing foreign Islamist population during the Soviet-Afghan War from 1979 to 1988, and an increasing number of conservative madrassas encouraged the development of fundamentalist ideologies within Pakistan. This focus on tradition and fundamentalism coupled with various ethnic and linguistic divisions allowed the ISI to develop organizations useful in influencing domestic politics, as well as the situations in Kashmir and Afghanistan (Rizvi 2000, 192–95; Ziring 2003, 170–73).

Pakistan faced four different but overlapping terrorist threats when called on as an ally of the United States in 2001. First were domestic groups such as the Sunni Sipah-e-Sahaba, responsible for thousands of sectarian deaths. See Table 2 for a list of major Pakistani terrorist groups and their affiliations. Originally many of these groups were encouraged by the ISI to divide and suppress domestic political movements, but they had become an embarrassment and a threat to internal order (Tellis 2008, 4).

The second set are Kashmiri resistance groups, labeled terrorist by the United States and other states but organized and armed by the ISI. These organizations operate primarily in Kashmir and were initially exempt from counterterrorism efforts (Siddiqa 2011, 154–55; Tellis 2008, 9). The attack on India's Parliament in 2001 and the Mumbai attacks in 2008 first

Table 2
Representative List of Terrorist Organizations Currently Active in Pakistan

Group	Ideology	Focus	TTP Affiliated?	ISI Linked?	Declared Terrorist?
Al Umar Mujahideen	Deobandi	Kashmir separatist	No	Yes	2002 (US)
Al-Qaeda	Salafi	Franchise terrorism	Franchised	Yes	Yes
Balochistan National Movement	Nationalist	Separatist	No	No	Yes
Harkat-ul-Jihad-Islami	Deobandi	Kashmir separatist	Yes	Yes	2008 (US)
Harkat-ul-Mujahideen	Deobandi	Kashmir separatist/ Transna-tional	Yes	Yes	1997 (US)

(Continued)

Table 2 (*Continued*)

Group	Ideology	Focus	TTP Affiliated?	ISI Linked?	Declared Terrorist?
Harkat-ul-Mujahideen Al-alami	Deobandi	Transnational	Yes	Yes	2002 (Pakistan)
Jaish-e-Mohammed	Deobandi	Kashmir separatist	Yes	Yes	2001 (US) 2002 (Pakistan)
Lashkar-i-Jhangvi	Deobandi	Sunni Islamization	Yes	Yes	2001 (Pakistan and US)
Lashkar-e-Taiba	Salafi	Kashmir separatist	Yes	Yes	2001 (US) 2002 (Pakistan)
Sipah-e-Mohammed Pakistan	Shi'i	Shi'i Islamization	No	No	2001 (Pakistan)
Sipah-e-Sahaba	Deobandi	Sunni Islamization	Yes	No	2002 (Pakistan)
Tehreek-e-Nafaz-e-Shariat-e-Mohammadi	Salafi	Sunni Islamization	Yes	Yes	2002 (Pakistan)
Tehreek-ul-Mujahideen	Deobandi	Kashmir separatist	Yes	Yes	2002 (US and Pakistan)
Tehrik-e-Jafria Pakistan	Shi'i	Shi'i Islamization	No	No	No, but arrests made

Note: ISI = Inter-Services Intelligence; TTP = Tehrik-e-Taliban.

inspired and then expedited an official effort to eliminate these groups. It is likely that these groups are still supported and resourced by the ISI (Ziring 2003, 344).

TALIBAN

The third set of groups in Pakistan can be broadly labeled as the Taliban. Pakistan was integral to the creation of the Taliban in both Pakistan and Afghanistan between 1979 and 1999, and it maintained ties with subunits to destabilize political movements, influence Afghanistan, and prevent Indian interference. Former president Musharraf proved reluctant to actively target the entire spectrum of the Taliban between 2001 and 2007 due to this close relationship. Only after the United States increased both pressure and aid beginning in 2005 did the efforts against the Taliban intensify (Tellis 2008, 12).

From a Pakistani perspective the Taliban are further subdivided into the ostensibly pacified Taliban of North Waziristan and the still violent Taliban of North and South Waziristan and Swat. This paradigm is further complicated by the franchise relationship between al-Qaeda and Tehrik-e-Taliban in Pakistan (TTP). The TTP is similar to al-Qaeda in that it serves as an umbrella organization that distributes scarce resources to an allied subset of ideologically similar groups. The army dealt with the unfriendly elements of the TTP groups in operations in the Federally Administered Tribal Area (FATA) in 2004, 2006, 2007, and 2009. These operations were intended to eliminate Taliban control but ended in negotiated settlements between the army and elements of the Taliban forces, which created friction between tribal and ideological elements rather than reasserting Pakistani rule (Siddiqa 2011, 150–52).

The fourth group, which was already mentioned, is al-Qaeda, which is officially opposed by Pakistan. Al-Qaeda serves as a franchise organization for other terrorist groups and uses the FATA of Pakistan as a safe haven for high-level members. Al-Qaeda is linked with the TTP and probably receives support from other groups as well. The ISI has arrested numerous al-Qaeda operatives, including Khalid Sheikh Mohammed in 2003, and the organization also likely provides intelligence for U.S. drone strikes on operatives (Siddiqa 2011, 157–58).

COUNTERTERRORISM

While the government of Pakistan has again become a parliamentary republic since the elections held in February 2008, it still faces the same problems Musharraf faced in 1999. The Zardari government is unable to focus its efforts and resources on the challenges of governance and instead must placate the Pakistani army and manage border, religious, and provincial tensions (Haqqani 2005, 313–16). Counterterrorism efforts in Pakistan face four primary problems in addition to the sociopolitical tensions within the government, military, and intelligence institutions.

First, the overlapping loyalties of various terrorist-affiliated organizations and their value to different state actors such as the army and ISI create a case-by-case and disjointed strategy. This dynamic is further complicated by the advent of civil government in 2008, which is often at odds with the security institutions of Pakistan.

Second, the nexus of terrorist groups is in the FATA. The operations mentioned earlier targeted the southern region of the FATA and were primarily a solution to internal political problems. Any benefit to the international counterterror effort was a secondary goal. Further, the northern region of FATA is a more difficult challenge for the Pakistani army due to the terrain, a higher concentration of terrorist groups, and the increasing complexity of ethnic and religious factors (Tellis 2008, 34–37).

Third, counterterrorism in Pakistan is one-dimensionally focused on using force. This does not address a wider need to respond to a growing socioeconomic gap or environmental crises such as the massive flooding in 2010. Similar to many other nations' efforts at counterterrorism, Pakistan fails to address the full spectrum of problems contributing to terrorist growth and success (Siddiqa 2011, 157–60).

Finally, Pakistan's counterterrorism efforts are hampered by a disproportionate focus on India. Certain groups are ignored because of perceived benefits in Kashmir. The ISI also protects or encourages certain groups in the FATA and Afghanistan because they are perceived to provide a bulwark against the burgeoning threat of Karzai's "India-friendly" foreign policy (Siddiqa 2011, 161; Tellis 2008, 4, 11–13).

CONCLUSION

Currently Pakistan is both one of the United States' most important allies and one of its largest threats. The agendas of the government of Pakistan, the army, and the ISI often work at cross-purposes, to the detriment of Pakistan's neighbors and the United States. A clear understanding of the intimate and seemingly paradoxical relationship between both terrorism and counterterrorism in Pakistan is key to understanding counterterrorism in a global context.

See also: **Volume 1, Part IV:** Pakistan's Federally Administered Tribal Areas (FATA). **Volume 2, Part I:** Special Service Group (Pakistan). **Part II:** Islamabad's Red Mosque (2007); Mumbai, India, Attacks (2008); Lahore (2009)

REFERENCES

Haqqani, Husain. *Pakistan: Between Mosque and Military.* Washington, DC: Carnegie Endowment for International Peace, 2005.
Rizvi, Hasan-Askari. *Military, State and Society in Pakistan.* New York: St. Martin's, 2000.
Siddiqa, Ayesha. "Pakistan's Counterterrorism Strategy: Separating Friends from Enemies." *Washington Quarterly* 34 (Winter 2011): 149–62.
Talbot, Ian. *Pakistan, a Modern History.* New York: Palgrave Macmillan, 2009.
Tellis, Ashley J. *Pakistan and the War on Terror: Conflicted Goals, Compromised Performance.* Washington, DC: Carnegie Endowment for International Peace, 2008. http://www.carnegieendowment.org/files/tellis_pakistan_final.pdf.
Ziring, Lawrence. *Pakistan: At the Crosscurrent of History.* Oxford: Oneworld, 2003.

Peru

Anna Kaganiec-Kamieńska

In some cases terrorism may be difficult to distinguish from guerrilla warfare, even though some criteria might help distinguish between the two (control of territory, tactics, targets, weapons, intended impact, use of uniforms, etc.). It is even more complex when insurgent groups combine the strategies of both. In Peru, Sendero Luminoso, a guerrilla group formed in the late 1960s in Ayacucho by Abimael Guzmán, employed guerrilla strategies in the Ayacucho region, while in the cities it carried out terrorist operations (kidnappings, bombings, assassinations, and attacks on public installations). For this reason Sendero Luminoso has been classified a terrorist group by the U.S. government and the European Union.

SENDERO LUMINOSO

Sendero Luminoso owed its success, on the one hand, to the specific structural problems of the state, such as rural poverty, maldistribution, and an unsuccessful land reform, and, on the other hand, to a Peruvian tradition of revolutionary and subversive actions (e.g., Tupac Amaru, Gonzalez Prada, Jose Mariategui, and the land invasions of the 1950s and 1960s). Its predominantly indigenous followers also liked the vision of the restored past glory of the group. As James Rochlin notes, "Sendero channeled centuries of indigenous hostilities and resentments into an angry rebel movement" (2003, 80). Another factor that partly contributed to the group's success was the initial ineffectiveness of the government's countersubversive actions.

Sendero Luminoso turned to violence in 1980, when they burned ballot boxes in the Andean town of Chuschi. Terrorism, assassinations, and sabotage of public sites whose destruction had an important impact on society (e.g., high-tension towers) were viewed as an important strategy to achieve their goal, namely, to destabilize the existing social order and replace it with one based on Guzmán's vision. Sendero Luminoso also engaged in drug trafficking as a source of funding. In 1988, the organization turned toward extreme violence.

In its peak years Sendero Luminoso was undoubtedly the most powerful and the most brutal guerrilla movement in the region. However, it was not the only guerrilla group in Peru in the 1980s and the 1990s. The Movimiento Revolucionario Tupac Amaru (MRTA; Tupac Amaru Revolutionary Movement)—not as numerous and powerful as Sendero Luminoso—originated from the Movimiento de Izquierda Revolucionaria (Revolutionary Left Movement), an insurgent group in the 1950s and

1960s. In 1991, MRTA was responsible for about 15 percent of terrorist attacks and 5 percent of assassinations. The group did not target civilians to attract support. It won international notoriety through the siege of the Japanese embassy in Lima (December 1996–April 1997), when 14 members of MRTA held 72 hostages, including President Alberto Fujimori's brother. This operation proved a failure, and after four months of unfruitful negotiations the embassy was stormed by Special Forces. All hostage takers were killed. Since the siege, the group is "finished politically" (Rochlin 2003, 75).

STATE ACTION AGAINST TERRORISM

State policy toward Sendero Luminoso evolved from total neglect toward counterinsurgency and intelligence. Ultimately, the latter proved to be the most successful strategy. Even though terrorist attacks had already taken place, at the beginning of the administration of President Fernando Belaunde Terry (1980–1985) the government did not take punitive actions against Sendero. At that time the military was focused on external threats from Ecuadorian troops. However, after the internal threat was acknowledged, the military turned to the opposite extreme. In December 1982 President Belaunde declared a state of emergency, and martial law was established in the departments of Ayacucho and Apurimac. The military action against Sendero Luminoso in 1983–1984 led to indiscriminate state terror in the form of extreme violence and human rights abuses. It is estimated that in 1984 over 4,000 civilians were killed as a direct consequence of state violence.

The first two years of the administration of Alan Garcia (1985–1990) brought state violence to an end. The president put emphasis on ending the "dirty war" and human rights abuses. However, Garcia's relation with the military was tense. He increased public investment in the Ayacucho region, which helped reduce local support for Sendero Luminoso. However, the number of terrorist attacks increased (from 1,760 in 1984 to 2,489 in 1987). The use of force against Sendero in this period was minimal, which gave the impression that the government was complacent in combating the guerrilla movement. In the final two years of his administration some changes were introduced, which proved effective a few years later. These initiatives included the reorganization of the police, the restructuring of the Sistema de Defensa Nacional (National Directorate Against Terrorism), and the creation in 1988 of the Dirección Nacional Contra el Terrorismo (DINCOTE) out of Dirección Contra el Terrorismo (DIRCOTE), outlined by former President Belaunde within the Policía de Investigacion del Peru (PIP). The creation of DINCOTE and its Grupo Especial de Inteligencia Nacional (GEIN) meant a change in approach toward the use of intelligence. In August 1989 the Comandante General del Ejercito approved the manual of countersubversive action ("Guerra no convencional. Contrasubversión"), which spawned a new strategy developed by the armed forces. The strategy involved combating guerrilla forces from a variety of fronts, for example, military, political, economic, and psychosocial. From this point on the counterinsurgency was focused primarily on intelligence. Subversive organizations as well as their strategy and tactics were thoroughly analyzed. The implementation of the new counterinsurgency policy brought significant results in 1989–2001, as substantial help came from self-defense units as well as increased input from DINCOTE and GEIN.

Peru's next president, Alberto Fujimori (1990–2000), supported the new strategy, regardless of the risks and costs that might be involved, and gave the armed forces a principal role. In November 1991 the Congress debated a package of far-reaching counterinsurgency decrees put forward by the executive. Some of these proposals addressed national intelligence and national defense and included provisions that would allow the armed forces to enter universities to eradicate terrorism. The Congress was strongly opposed to some of these proposals. The conflict between Fujimori and the Congress finally led to the presidential coup d'état (*autogolpe*) on April 5, 1992. In Decree 25418 Fujimori "temporarily" dissolved Congress, suspended the Constitution, and declared a state of emergency. His shift toward authoritarianism had wide public support, since it was viewed as a measure to restore public order.

COUNTERSUBVERSIVE ACTIVITY

Countersubversive activities under President Fujimori led to state terror, torture, disappearances, and human rights abuses (e.g., "faceless judges," sexual abuse). The intelligence service, the Servicio de Inteligencia Nacional, headed by Vladimiro Montesinos, carried out a series of brutal, repressive countersubversive actions such as the assassination by Grupo Colima (the death squad of the Servicio de Inteligencia Nacional) of a professor and nine students at the University of Cantuta. During this period intelligence-gathering efforts by DINCOTE and GEIN, the infiltration of the narco-trafficking business in relation to Sendero Luminoso and assistance from the U.S. Central Intelligence Agency in the form of equipment, training, transportation, and financial aid led to the capture of Guzmán at his hideout in Lima on September 12, 1992. Other key leaders of Sendero Luminoso were also arrested. The arrest of its leader and other senior members resulted in a significant decrease in its power base. Another important aspect of President Fujimori's success against Sendero Luminoso was actions taken by armed self-defense groups (*rondas campesinas*). The military *rondas* spread substantially under Fujimori; in 1984, there were about 200 *rondas,* and in 1991 this number reached 1,400. In 1992, the number of *ronderos* (individual members) armed by the government was over 230,000. *Rondas* were very effective security forces and also contributed to the reduction of human rights abuses by the armed forces.

Following his imprisonment, Guzmán ordered his followers to engage in peace talks with the government. This led Alberto Ramirez Durand

(Guzmán's successor) to form a new group called Sendero Rojo, which refused to negotiate. This small group did not, however, pose a serious threat to Peru. Ramirez Durand and other members of the group were captured in 1999. Other Senderistas were granted government amnesties. Presently, Peru's primary counterterrorism concern is fighting remnants of Sendero Luminoso.

The authoritarian rule of former president Fujimori also resulted in widespread corruption within the government. This was revealed also by the so-called Vladivideos, videotapes showing Montesinos, the head of the Servicio de Inteligencia Nacional, bribing selected high-ranking people (e.g., politicians, television station owners, etc.). Montesinos was also allegedly linked to the drug trade.

CONCLUSION

After Fujimori was forced to resign in 2000, the office of president was taken over by Alejandro Toledo, who called for the creation of the Comission de la Verdad y Reconciliacion (Truth and Reconciliation Commission), which investigated the 1980–2000 violence in Peru. The report, published in 2003, revealed an unprecedented scale of violence and extensive human rights abuses committed by the Senderistas or followers of the group and/or by the armed forces.

See also: **Volume 2, Part II:** Japanese Embassy Seizure (1996)

REFERENCES

Hidalgo Morey, Teodoro. *Subversion y contrasubversion. Historia y tragedia.* Lima: Aguilar, 2004
National Consortium for the Study of Terrorism and Responses to Terrorism (START). http://www.start.umd.edu/start/.
Rochlin, James F. *Vanguard Revolutionaries in Latin America: Peru, Colombia, Mexico.* Boulder, CO: Lynne Rienner, 2003.
Tapia, Carlos. *Las Fuerzas Armadas y Sendero Luminoso.* Lima: Instituto de Estudios Peruanos, 1997.

Philippines

Alastair Reed

The Philippines have suffered a long and bloody history of terrorism and insurgency in the postwar years. Since 1968, the Philippines have faced terrorism on two fronts: first from separatist groups within the Moro Muslim population on the southern island of Mindanao and, second, from the Communist Party of the Philippines.

THE MORO CONFLICT

The Moro conflict has deep historical roots going back to the Spanish colonization of the Philippines and the subsequent failure to integrate the southern Muslim population into the Christian-dominated nation-state. Successive influxes of Christian settlers from the 1900s on further aggravated the situation, and by the 1960s the Moros had become a minority in many of their traditional southern homelands. In 1972, the Moro National Liberation Front (MNLF) was formed to fight for an independent homeland for the Moro people; unlike future organizations the MNLF was at heart a secular organization.

From underlying communal violence between Muslim and Christian militias, the conflict escalated into a full-blown civil war with the declaration of martial law by the Marcos regime in 1972. The MNLF launched a bitter guerrilla campaign against the Armed Forces of the Philippines (AFP), in which over 100,000 people were killed and half a million displaced. By 1976, the conflict reached a de facto stalemate, with the bulk of the AFP engaged against the MNLF and the cost of the conflict threatening the economy and the stability of the Marcos regime. For the MNLF, the realization dawned that they would be unable to militarily drive the AFP from Mindanao. In December of that year the Organization of the Islamic Conference hosted talks in Libya that led to the signing of the Tripoli Accord and the prospect of an autonomous government in Mindanao. However, the Marcos regime soon set about undermining the agreement by creating its own regional government and appointing its leaders, seriously undermining MNLF's credibility. The accord should have ended the conflict; instead, it precipitated splits in the Moro movement, prolonging the conflict for decades to come.

In 1984, a faction led by MNLF's foreign minister, Salamat Hashim, broke away to form the rival Moro Islamic Liberation Front (MILF). This new organization, critical of the MNLF's left-leaning orientation, pursued a new Islamist direction, uncompromising on independence. Through Hashim the MILF had extensive contacts in the international jihadist community. Consequently, many recruits were sent to Afghanistan for training, and the MILF's ranks rapidly increased with disaffected MNLF fighters and Soviet-Afghan War veterans. Through the Afghanistan connection, the MILF is alleged to have established links to al-Qaeda, and later in the mid-1990s it developed a close working relationship with Jemaah Islamiyah, including running joint training camps in Mindanao.

The People Power Revolution of 1986 that swept aside the Marcos regime ushered in the prospect of peace as the new government embarked on fresh negotiations with the MNLF. The talks soon floundered as the Aquino administration insisted on forming an autonomous Muslim region without discussing the details with the group. In 1996, the MNLF reached a final agreement on the implementation of the Tripoli Accord and the establishment of the Autonomous Region of Muslim Mindanao. The settlement included a general amnesty and provisions for the integration of former fighters into the army and police, as well as for the creation of a regional development council.

The MILF meanwhile derided the cease-fire as a sellout, and many within the MNLF ranks defected to the MILF, which now picked up the torch of the Moro struggle and became the dominant group in the Muslim south. In September 1997 the MILF entered into an Agreement of General Cessation of Hostilities with the Philippine government, which has formed the basis of all ongoing talks since. The government has pursued a twin-track approach of attempting to win over the MILF moderates with promises of development, while simultaneously applying coercive force against the hard-liners. This has produced a cycle of negotiation and conflict, with the government ordering new offensives against the MILF in 2000 and 2003 when talks were failing to progress. In 2000, the Estrada government attempted to tackle the extreme poverty and unemployment that have fueled the conflict, with an extensive program funded by the World Bank and the European Union.

A new threat emerged during the 1990s with the formation of Abu Sayyaf Group (ASG). It pursued a far more radical Islamist agenda than the MILF, aiming to create a Muslim caliphate in the southern Philippines. The group had established strong international connections with al-Qaeda and Jemaah Islamiyah, but locally it had also forged working relationships with elements of MNLF and MILF. The group shot to worldwide notoriety with the kidnapping of foreign tourists from the holiday resorts of Sipadan and Dos Palmas in 2000 and 2001. In the latter an American businessman was infamously beheaded.

The timing of the ASG's Dos Palmas kidnapping of U.S. citizens in the months prior to 9/11 ensured the southern Philippines a place in President Bush's war on terror. This was to have two major implications. First, the United States was to actively support the AFP's counterterrorism efforts; by early 2002 the United States was sending military advisers and equipment. Second, significant pressure was placed on the MILF to disassociate itself from the more radical Islamist groups for fear of being placed on the U.S. list of foreign terrorist organizations. Central to the government's policy has the decoupling of MILF, with its essentially separatist agenda, from the Islamist terrorism of ASG and its associated groups. The Ad Hoc Joint Action Group was established in 2005 to coordinate between the MILF and the government, to share intelligence on terrorist groups, and to avoid accidental clashes when the AFP acts against such groups. This mechanism has enabled AFP operations across MILF territory that have successfully targeted the ASG.

Since 9/11 the United States has played a major role in supporting AFP's counterinsurgency efforts against the ASG: first, in providing training to professionalize the AFP and, second, in providing aid and funding to win the hearts and minds of the population. The subsequent counterinsurgency operations have been a paradigm of success, combining both soft and hard power, widely referred to as the "Mindanao Model." They have aimed to separate the terrorists from the mass support of the population through improving living conditions. The AFP has been successfully conducting civil-military operations such as building roads, bridges, and schools and providing free medical and dental services.

THE COMMUNIST INSURGENCY

In 1968 the Communist Party of the Philippines (CPP) was founded by Jose Maria Sison, a former university professor. A year later it linked up with disgruntled former "Huk" commanders, from the previous postwar Communist insurgency, to form its armed wing, the New People's Army (NPA). The CPP-NPA aims to seize power through armed revolution and install a Communist regime. The CPP-NPA adopted Mao's "protracted people's war" strategy and has been a predominantly rural-based insurgency, though in later years it has adopted urban insurgency tactics.

In 1972, the Marcos regime declared martial law, ostensibly to tackle the rising threat from the NPA, and began launching military operations. However, from 1972 to 1977, the AFP was predominantly occupied with operations against the MNLF in Mindanao. Following the Tripoli Accord, the AFP refocused on tackling the NPA. The AFP strategy was largely based on copying the unsuccessful search-and-destroy tactics deployed by the United States in Vietnam. An organization and equipment that were primarily meant for conventional war, combined with a lack of understanding of the NPA strategy, made for ineffective military operations. However, the AFP had some success as nearly the entire political and military leadership was killed or captured by 1978. Despite this, increasing poverty, official corruption, and army abuses continued to fuel the conflict. By the early 1980s the conflict was growing rapidly.

The People Power Revolution of 1986 that swept away the Marcos regime saw the CPP-NPA lose the political advantage—the return to democracy with Aquino undercut the appeal the CPP-NPA had enjoyed when fighting a corrupt and repressive dictatorship. Further, the CPP-NPA made a grave tactical error by boycotting the elections. Aquino initially pursued a conciliatory approach, releasing CPP-NPA political prisoners, including founder Sison, and entering into talks, which culminated in the first and only cease-fire agreement with the CPP.

When talks collapsed, the AFP relaunched military operations, this time pursuing a more holistic approach, unleashing a counterinsurgency campaign with a combined economic, political, psychological, and military strategy. Moreover, state-sponsored paramilitary groups were mobilized, and an effective policy of rewards for information on groups activities supplied actionable intelligence. Furthermore, the CPP-NPA was weakened by internal purges against suspected collaborators, which saw thousands of "comrades" tortured and killed.

The Ramos government of the 1990s brought structural reforms and economic development, which succeeded in eroding the CPP's moral and support base. This coincided with a renewed period of negotiations between the government and the CPP-NPA. Despite the signing of The Hague Joint Declaration in 1992—that negotiations should be pursued to end the armed conflict—no subsequent peace deal has materialized.

CONCLUSION

The year 2001 saw the formal suspension of talks, following the NPA's assassination of a provincial governor in June of that year. Following the terrorist attacks on America in September, the Philippine government reverted to a tough stance against terrorism and renewed attacks against NPA bases across the country. The U.S. government soon added the CPP-NPA to its list of foreign terrorist organizations, and successful lobbying by the Philippine government saw the Council of Europe add the NPA to its terror blacklist. Fresh negotiations resumed in Oslo in 2004, with Norway officially acknowledged as a "third-party facilitator," but a permanent peace agreement remains elusive.

See also: **Volume 1, Part I:** Global Terrorism: Post-9/11; The Terrorist Threat in the 21st Century: A Global Security Problem. **Part IV:** Combating Religiously Based Terrorism

REFERENCES

Ferrer, Miriam Coronel. "The Communist Insurgency in the Philippines." In *A Handbook of Terrorism and Insurgency in Southeast Asia,* edited by Andrew T. H. Tan, 405–36. Cheltenham, UK: Edward Elgar, 2007.

Gregor, A. James, and Jose P. Magno Jr. "Insurgency and Counterinsurgency in the Philippines." *Asian Survey* 26, no. 5 (1986): 501–17.

International Crisis Group. "Southern Philippines Backgrounder: Terrorism and the Peace Process." ICG Asia Report, no. 80, July 13, 2004.

International Crisis Group. "The Philippines: Counter-insurgency vs. Counterterrorism in Mindanao." Crisis Group Asia Report, no. 152, May 14, 2008.

Jones, Gregg R. *Red Revolution: Inside the Philippine Guerrilla Movement.* Boulder, CO: Westview, 1989.

Rodell, Paul A. "Separatist Insurgency in the Southern Philippines." In *A Handbook of Terrorism and Insurgency in Southeast Asia,* edited by Andrew T.H. Tan, 225–47. Cheltenham, UK: Edward Elgar, 2007.

Tan, Andrew T. H. "Old Terrorism in Southeast Asia: A Survey." In *A Handbook of Terrorism and Insurgency in Southeast Asia,* edited by Andrew T. H. Tan, 45–62. Cheltenham, UK: Edward Elgar, 2007.

Russia

Hans Brun

Domestic-based terrorism is the primary threat facing Russia. Since the mid-1990s, Russia has been fighting an insurgency and a terrorist campaign fought mostly by Chechens and supported by militant Islamists from other Muslim countries. The Russian government has relied on several policies in its struggle against Chechen separatism and terrorism.

BACKGROUND

Since the beginning of the First Chechen War, Russia has heavily relied on the use of force. In November 1991, the Chechen leader Dzokhar Dudaev unilaterally declared independence from Russia. President Yeltsin responded by announcing a state of emergency and dispatched troops to the borders of Chechnya, leading to the First Chechen War (1994–1996). This war resulted in de facto independence for the Chechen Republic of Ichkeria, which lasted until the fall of 1999, when the Second Chechen War began following a series of mysterious apartment building bombings. Russia succeeded in gaining control of Chechnya and installed a government loyal to Moscow (Deflem 2010, 102–3; Soldatov and Borogan 2010, 172). Both sides to this conflict used methods considered illegal under international law. The exact number of casualties continues to be disputed. Reliable sources estimate that at least 50,000 civilians were killed in the First Chechen War alone, and at least 5,500 Russian soldiers lost their lives.

According to the local Chechen government, which still remains loyal to Moscow, the two wars have caused the deaths of between 150,000 and 160,000 civilians and combatants (Center for Defense Information, 2003; "Chechen Officials Put Death Toll" 2005). Both the Interior Ministry and the Russian Federal Security Service were given the mission to counter Chechen separatism and terrorism. The Federal Security Service appears to have infiltrated Chechen groups of interest at various points by providing protection in exchange for information. The Russian authorities introduced new working methods at the beginning of the Second Chechen War in 1999, emphasizing extrajudicial operations carried out by clandestine units. A number of extrajudicial killings have been carried out in Chechnya and in neighboring regions by military units and security agencies. Often, the victims' bodies have not been found. In order to destroy evidence, the bodies were sometimes strapped to artillery shells and blown up, a method referred to as *pulverization*. These units are also known to make use of a method known as *countercapture*, which refers to the practice of capturing relatives of known or suspected terrorists in order to force the suspect to surrender. This tactic, though not allowed under Russian law, remains in use (Soldatov and Borogan 2010, 181–87).

ASSASSINATION AND LEGAL REFORMS

After a lethal terrorist attack against Russian diplomats in Baghdad in June 2006, new legislation was established in order to grant the president of Russia the authority to order the Russian military and security services to conduct operations in other countries. This legislation appears to have been used for the first time in August 2007, when a well-known Chechen leader was assassinated in Abkhazia. A series of assassinations of Chechens hiding in Turkey is also believed to have been carried out by Russian operatives under this legislation (Soldatov and Borogan 2010, 200–203).

In addition, Russia has also relied on several more traditional policies, such as a number of legal reforms. Current Russian counterterrorism legislation contains two definitions of terrorism. A legal framework was introduced in July 1998 by then president Yeltsin, containing guiding principles for the executive bodies and law enforcement agencies. According to this legislation:

1) measures to prevent terrorism will have priority; 2) punishment for those who commit terrorist acts will be inevitable; 3) the government will employ overt and covert methods of fighting terrorism; 4) the government will employ preventive measures to avoid terrorist acts, including the use of legal, political, socioeconomic and propaganda based measures; 5) the right of government to protect society and the rights of persons exposed to the danger of terrorism; 6) minimal concessions to apprehend terrorists; 7) a one-man command in the leadership of counter-terrorism security forces; and 8) minimal disclosure of technical methods and tactics for the conduct of counter-terrorism operations. (Beckman 2007, 128)

This legislation defines terrorism as:

violence or the threat of violence against individuals or organizations, and also the destruction (damaging) of or threat to destroy (damage) property and other materials, such as threatening to cause loss of life, significant damage to property, or other socially dangerous consequences, and implemented with a view to violating public security, intimidating the population, or influencing the adoption of decisions advantageous to terrorists by organs of power, or satisfying their unlawful material and (or) other interests; attempts on the lives of states-men or public figures perpetrated with a view to ending their state or other political activity or out of revenge for such activity. (Soldatov and Borogan 2010, 173)

This legislation also defines and regulates related offences, such as the taking of hostages, the organization of an illegal armed formation, and an attempt on the life of a public agent (Beknazar 2003, 475).

After 9/11, the Russian government strengthened its counterterrorism policies and legislation. President Vladimir Putin issued a number of pres-idential decrees regarding terrorism, and new legislation went into effect in 2006. This legislation was drafted after the violent hostage crisis at a Moscow theater in 2002 and the Beslan school massacre in 2004. The leg-islation required several years of negotiations, as many members of Par-liament were concerned that the proposed legislation would infringe on civil liberties and grant federal authorities too much power. This legisla-tion gives the president of Russia the authority to utilize the military and the Federal Security Service to fight terrorism, both in Russia and abroad (Beckman 2007, 129–33; Deflem 2010, 103). The 2006 legislation also rede-fined terrorism as "an ideology of violence and practice of influence on decision-making bodies by bodies of the government, institutions of local government, or international organizations, by means of intimidation of the population and (or) other forms of illegal violent actions" (Soldatov and Borogan 2010, 173).

Furthermore, the Russian authorities have consequently attempted to protect the political elite by avoiding transparency and assuming control of the media as much as possible. After the theater hostage disaster in 2002, Russian authorities initiated a criminal case against the few surviv-ing terrorists, but there was no official inquiry regarding the actions of the authorities and security forces during the hostage crisis. Relatives of the victims received no information about the events that actually took place during the siege. When the victims' relatives sued the Russian state to obtain this information, they were accused of attempting to profit from the deaths of their loved ones. These relatives never received informa-tion from the Russian authorities, who offered compensation only for the victims' belongings (Soldatov and Borogan 2010, 167). After the Beslan school massacre in 2004, Russian authorities and security services once again attempted to avoid an official inquiry regarding their actions and decisions. According to then president Putin, an internal investigation would suffice, as a parliamentary inquiry "could become the next political sideshow" (Soldatov and Borogan 2010, 168). Due to widespread protests in North Ossetia, President Putin later agreed to create an official commis-sion. The commission presented its findings two years later and largely confirmed and approved the official explanation (Soldatov and Borogan 2010, 169–70).

In June 2007, a special working group was created by the Russian National Anti-terrorism Committee in order to counter "the ideology of terrorism" (Soldatov and Borogan 2010, 170). One suggested action involved the creation of a special training course for journalists covering terrorism. According to Russian reporters, the training course "established by the security services is a sort of brainwashing for journalists, aimed at limiting journalistic coverage of scenes of a terrorist attack and counterterrorism operations" (Soldatov and Borogan 2010, 170). According to the Russian Interior Ministry, journalists who have not attended the course may not be granted access to the scene of a terrorism attack. This requirement is not supported by Russian media legislation (Soldatov and Borogan 2010, 170–71). Moreover, at least 52 Russian journalists have been killed in Russia, including the well-known reporter and writer Anna Politkovskaya. Several Russian sources claim that some 300 journalists have been killed since 1992 (Centre for Journalism in Extreme Situations n.d.; Committee to Protect Journalists n.d..

CONCLUSION

As already mentioned, Russia's counterterrorism practices are unusually harsh. However, Russia has also been successfully involved in a number of international counterterrorism initiatives. The 9/11 attack on the United States brought Russia and the United States closer and generated an understanding for each other's counterterrorism policies. The attack also led to a level of cooperation that has not existed between the two countries since World War II. A U.S.-Russia Working Group on Counterterrorism has been established as the primary bilateral mechanism for cooperation and coordination. Russia and the United States have also cooperated closely in the Global Initiative to Combat Nuclear Terrorism. In addition, Russia has established cooperation with a number of different international bodies, such as Interpol (Bolt, Changhe, and Cross 2008, 24–25; Deflem 2010, 103).

See also: **Volume 1, Part IV:** Russian Counterterrorism Efforts. **Volume 2, Part I:** Alpha Units (Russia); Spetsnaz (Russia); Vega Group (Russia). **Part II:** Nord-Ost Siege (2002); Beslan Massacre (2004); Moscow Metro Attacks (2004 and 2010)

REFERENCES

Beckman, James. *Comparative Legal Approaches to Homeland Security and Anti-terrorism*. Aldershot, UK: Ashgate, 2007.

Beknazar, Tigran B. "Country Report on Russia." In *Terrorism as a Challenge for National and International Law: Security versus Liberty?* edited by Christian Walter, Silja Vöneky, Silja Röben, and Frank Schorkopf, 517–56. Heidelberg, Germany: Springer, 2003.

Bolt, Paul J., Su Changhe, and Sharyl Cross. *The United States, Russia, and China: Confronting Global Terrorism and Security Challenges in the 21st Century.* Westport, CT: Praeger Security.

Center for Defense Information. "Casualty Figures." *Chechnya Weekly,* February 20, 2003. http://www.cdi.org/russia/245–14.cfm/.

Centre for Journalism in Extreme Situations. "Death of Journalists in Russia." n.d. http://journalists-in-russia.org/.

"Chechen Officials Put Death Toll for 2 Wars at Up to 160,000." *New York Times,* August 16, 2005. http://www.nytimes.com/2005/08/15/world/europe/15iht-chech.html?_r=1/.

Committee to Protect Journalists. "52 Journalists Killed in Russia since 1992/Motive Confirmed." n.d. http://cpj.org/killed/europe/russia/.

Deflem, Mathieu. *The Policing of Terrorism: Organizational and Global Perspectives.* London: Routledge, 2010.

Soldatov, Andrei, and Irina Borogan. *The New Nobility: The Restoration of Russia's Security State and the Enduring Legacy of the KGB.* New York: Public Affairs, 2010.

Walter, Christian, Silja Vöneky, Silja Röben, and Frank Schorkopf, eds. *Terrorism as a Challenge for National and International Law: Security versus Liberty?* Heidelberg, Germany: Springer, 2003.

Saudi Arabia

Kristian Alexander

The Saudi monarchy has long dealt with a series of internal challenges from a variety of actors. In 1979, a group of armed extremists led by Juhayman bin Muhammed bin Sayf al-Uteybi seized the Grand Mosque in Mecca. The Saudi government was faced with the problem that the Quran explicitly prohibits violence from being used within the confines of the mosque. The religious clergy had to issue a suitable fatwa (religious edict) to legitimize the use of violence by Saudi forces, with the help of French counterterrorism experts, to regain the holiest of mosques. It was only after a long standoff and intensive fighting as well as tremendous loss of life that the security forces were able to regain control of the mosque and that the radicals were captured. The rebels captured in the mosque were either publicly beheaded or executed in a secret setting.

TERRORISM AND COUNTERTERRORISM

In response to this event, the Saudi government placed new emphasis on religion and embarked on financial funding of religious causes abroad. One prime example of the strategy was the funding of Islamic mujahideen in Afghanistan in their quest to oust Soviet forces that had invaded their country. The Soviet-Afghan War (1979–1989) was one of the factors that spawned groups such as al-Qaeda, which have been responsible for numerous high-profile terrorist attacks over the past two decades:

- In 1995, there was a terrorist attack in the form of a car bomb exploding at a U.S. military headquarters in Riyadh, killing five U.S. servicemen.
- In 1996, certain elements struck again, this time targeting the Khobar Towers. A U.S. military compound was destroyed, killing 19 soldiers and injuring 350.
- In May 2003, bombings in the Saudi capital of Riyadh claimed 35 lives and injured over 160 persons, and in November of that year a suicide bomber killed 17 people at the Almohiya housing compound in Riyadh.

Additionally, it is worth noting that 15 of the 19 terrorists who were involved in the September 11, 2001, attacks on the United States were Saudi citizens. In the aftermath of September 11, some Saudi officials first reacted to the news by going into a state of denial, but in a sense these events also served as a wake-up call to the Saudi government. Once it realized the seriousness of the threat, it decided to enhance counterterrorism measures in a variety of areas.

Given Saudi Arabia's proximity to Iraq, several security analysts have warned that Saudi citizens were joining the jihadist fight in neighboring countries. Besides the fact that their involvement in Iraq might further radicalize them, it is feared that the surviving returnees will gain valuable fighting experience and that they might ignite further violence inside the kingdom. In turn, Saudi authorities have created a new security system along its borders with Iraq and are steadily improving the quality of the country's counterterrorism forces. They constructed a double-track barbed-wire fence equipped with remote sensors and thermal cameras in order to better monitor this congested area.

More specifically, there is a deep concern about the security of oil facilities and oil pipelines. Significant expenditures have been made to upgrade security by installing sophisticated monitoring devices to protect these facilities and other critical infrastructure. The most serious security threat in recent years has clearly emanated from al-Qaeda in the Arabian Peninsula (AQAP). AQAP and other radical groups have challenged the religious legitimacy of the ruling family. Osama bin Laden has accused the ruling family of not following the true Wahhabi line and has called for the overthrow of the Saudi regime. He has also said on a variety of occasions that the official ulema (religious clerics) were complicit in their defense of their employers, the al-Saud family.

More recently, AQAP has been using bases in Yemen to launch terror strikes on Saudi Arabia. In November 2009, al-Qaeda–affiliated groups in Yemen attempted to assassinate the top Saudi antiterror official, Prince Muhammad bin Nayef bin Abdel Aziz. Although AQAP managed to stage some small-scale attacks in the kingdom, it proved ineffective in achieving its main objectives for a number of reasons. For one, it failed to articulate a viable alternative to the existing government. It also lost a lot of its initial popularity due to the fact that some of this violence was killing innocent fellow Saudi citizens. Moreover, AQAP has also lacked the funding as well as manpower to seriously challenge the security forces in the kingdom. The Saudi state, on the other hand, has unlimited material resources and access to U.S. technical assistance. Prior to 2001 the Saudi state had limited experience in antiterrorism operations and advanced intelligence analysis. The biggest problem, however, was the "nonconfrontational" culture of policing, meaning that the authorities lacked the confrontational/aggressive and intrusive approach needed for effective counterterrorism work.

MULTIDIMENSIONAL APPROACH

The Saudi government has since used a multipronged approach in combating terrorism. Besides detaining, arresting, and imprisoning thousands of suspected terrorists, the authorities also provided exit options for militants as part of a one-month general amnesty declared in 2004 as well as 2006.

On the ideological front, the response has been to discredit Islamist challengers by issuing government-sanctioned fatwas by religious scholars who brand those who seek to use violence as deviating from the true tenets of Islam. The Saudi Ministry of Islamic Affairs removed hundreds of religious officials from their positions with the official justification that they no longer fulfilled the requirements set forth to work in mosques, and implemented regulations that would require many religious officials to undergo further training. In mid-2010, the Council of Senior Ulema in Saudi Arabia, the main body of the religious leadership, publicly denounced terrorism and stated that terrorism was criminal and against Islamic teachings.

Since 2001, the Saudi government has conducted a thorough review of its charitable organizations. New government regulations have sought to limit the way these organizations can operate and manage their funds. It has also reined in the activities of *hawala* networks, which are informal money-transferring agencies frequently used throughout the Arabian Gulf region. Many independent *hawalas* in Saudi Arabia have been forced to close down. In these cases they have been replaced with government-regulated establishments that perform basically the same services but with far greater oversight. These financial institutions began monitoring the flow of money to and from Saudi charities.

The kingdom has also undertaken measures to initiate a reform process that entails changes in the fields of education, the economy, and civil society. The Saudi king has pushed for an ambitious agenda in the areas of economic reform, corruption, and educational reform. Saudi textbooks were reviewed and revised in order to remove inflammatory material and substantially modernize the curriculum. A worldwide campaign was also launched by the Ministry of Information to emphasize the peace-loving and nonviolent nature of Wahhabi Islam and improve the "misguided image" of Islam in the world at large.

In August 2003, Saudi Arabia and the United States established a Joint Task Force that incorporates law enforcement and intelligence agencies, enabling them to share real-time intelligence and conduct joint operations in the fight against terrorism. Saudi authorities have also cooperated with the Federal Bureau of Investigation and the Central Intelligence Agency regarding al-Qaeda activities and cells. King Abdullah hosted 60 countries and international organizations in a conference on ways to improve counterterrorism efforts in 2009.

Saudi Arabia has also initiated efforts to rehabilitate citizens convicted of terrorism-related offenses. This program targets Islamists who have not yet committed a terrorist act but have shown an inclination to become involved in terrorist activities. The Prevention, Rehabilitation, and Aftercare program is designed to combat the intellectual and ideological tenets of violent extremism by characterizing them as deviations from true Islam. Sponsored by the Saudi Ministry of Interior and operational since 2003, this approach has had some success. As of September 2008, 3,000 prisoners had participated in the program, with 1,400 renouncing their past beliefs. Thus far, it appears that this strategy is working as the recidivism rate is only 1 to 2 percent. This unique "soft" counterterrorism approach is based on a mix of religious education, psychological techniques, and incentives to help potential graduates reintegrate into society.

According to Saudi authorities, many of the participants have only a limited knowledge of Islam and one that is heavily influenced by jihadist propaganda, which is easily accessed in online chat rooms and other Internet websites. This type of religious counseling is meant to correct the detainees' interpretation of Islam through open dialogue. Spiritual counseling is supplemented by a six-week course that covers a variety of issues. Additionally, part of the overall program may include financial incentives that can include monthly stipends and inducements like cars and the financing of marriages. Those released from detention are often required to stay in study circles, and their immediate family is tasked with the responsibility of keeping their family member on the right path.

CONCLUSION

The Prevention, Rehabilitation, and Aftercare program reflects an understanding that effective counterterrorism must, beyond the use of military means in responding to groups and cells, also include the use of persuasive mechanisms as well as financial provisions that address the underlying socioeconomic, political, and religious factors that motivate young men to join extremist organizations.

See also: **Volume 2, Part I:** Special Emergency Force (Saudi Arabia). **Part II:** Grand Mosque, Mecca, Saudi Arabia (1979)

REFERENCES

Ansary, Abdullah F. "Combating Extremism: A Brief Overview of Saudi Arabia's Approach." *Middle East Policy* 2 (2008): 111–42.
Asseri, A.S.A. *Combating Terrorism: Saudi Arabia's Role in the War on Terror.* Oxford: Oxford University Press, 2009.
Boucek, C. *Saudi Arabia's "Soft" Counterterrorism Strategy: Prevention, Rehabilitation and Aftercare.* Washington, DC: Carnegie Endowment for International Peace, 2008.
Cordesman, A. C. *Saudi Arabia: National Security in a Troubled Region.* Santa Barbara, CA: ABC-CLIO, 2009.
Gause, F. Gregory, III. "Saudi Arabia and the War on Terrorism." In *A Practical Guide to Winning the War on Terrorism,* edited by Adam Garfinkle, 89–102. Stanford, CA: Stanford University Press, 2004.
Hegghammer, T. *Jihad in Saudi Arabia: Violence and Pan-Islamism since 1979.* Cambridge: Cambridge University Press, 2010.

Spain

Alejandra Gómez-Céspedes

The Kingdom of Spain is a democracy organized in the form of a parliamentary government under a constitutional monarchy. Parliamentary democracy was restored following the death of General Francisco Franco, who had ruled since the end of the civil war in 1939. The Constitution of Spain was enacted after a referendum on December 6, 1978, and is thus regarded as the culmination of the Spanish transition to democracy. Spain joined the European Union in 1986 and since then has become a dynamic and rapidly growing economy, ranking 13th on the 2009 gross domestic product (GDP) list produced by the International Monetary Fund.

BASQUE HOMELAND AND FREEDOM

Today, terrorism in Spain is not considered a major threat to democratic stability but rather a recurrent violent phenomenon that systematically violates fundamental rights and restrains the free exercise of political and civil liberties (Alonso and Reinares 2005). Until the Madrid train bombings in 2004, the terrorism scenario in Spain was largely dominated by the terrorist organization ETA (standing for Euskadi Ta Askatasuna in Basque, or Euskera, or Basque Homeland and Freedom in English).

ETA was formed during the last years of Francoism as a radicalized expression of Basque ethnic nationalism, an ideology and movement dating back to the end of the 19th century. ETA was founded by young nationalists under the pillars of language, ethnicity, and independence of the territories that, according to ETA, belong to the Basque nation: Álava, Biscay, and Guipúzcoa (in Spain) and Lapurdi, Basse-Navarre, and Zuberoa (in France).

In its early years, ETA's activities seem to have consisted mostly of destroying technical infrastructure and Spanish symbols across the country. However, they soon embarked on a spiral of violence that escalated dramatically from the 1970s on. One of the most notorious assassinations occurring during Francoism was that of Admiral Luis Carrero-Blanco, Franco's chosen successor and president of the government. Within about six months of being named prime minister, Carrero-Blanco was assassinated on December 20, 1973, in a car bombing in Madrid. ETA placed around 220 pounds (100 kilograms) of explosives in a tunnel they had excavated under a street that the admiral used regularly. The blast catapulted the vehicle over the building in front of which it had been passing, and it landed on a second-floor balcony on the other side.

This killing, committed as a reprisal for the execution of Basque independents, was widely applauded by the Spanish opposition in exile and was seen by many as instrumental in the establishment of democracy. That is, by denying Franco his chosen successor, it forced him to hand the reins of power back to the monarchy, which in turn established the current democratic state.

Paradoxically, although the Spanish Constitution of 1978 granted the Basque Country the status of a historical region with an unprecedented degree of self-rule, the military faction of ETA carried on the armed struggle. However, ETA's growing radicalization resulted in a steady loss of social support. In recent years, ETA supporters have become a minority in the Basque region. In fact, surveys conducted by the University of the Basque Country have recurrently found in recent years that about 9 out of 10 Basques (88%) believe that any political objective in the Basque Country can be achieved without resorting to violence.

According to the Spanish Ministry of the Interior, as of March 16, 2010, ETA had killed a total of 829 victims in the name of their political struggle. Out of that total, 486 victims belonged to the armed forces and law enforcement agencies (58.6%), while the remaining 343 victims were civilians and politicians (41.3%). Most killings (551) have taken place in the Spanish Basque Country, although assassinations have also been perpetrated abroad, namely, in France (3). In any case, ETA's murderous campaign has progressively declined: 395 killings occurred between 1980 and 1989, 162 between 1990 and 1999, and 57 between 2000 and 2009.

POST-9/11 TERRORISM

As mentioned earlier, in 2004 Spain witnessed a new form of terrorism that urged authorities to rethink their counterterrorist strategy. On March 11, 2004, around 7:30 A.M., 10 bombs exploded on four commuter trains in the span of a few minutes. The attacks were the deadliest assault and the worst terrorist incident in modern Spanish history, as 191 people were confirmed dead, and over 1,500 were injured. The date appears to have been carefully selected because the events took place just three days before the general elections in which the party of the outgoing president Jose Maria Aznar (of the political right) was favored in opinion polls. In the elections on March 14, 2004, the victory went to the Socialist Party of Jose Luis Rodriguez Zapatero.

To date, the controversy over the real perpetrators of the attack has not yet ended. The suspicions of the media and of the majority of Spaniards turned immediately to ETA. However, despite ETA's history of violent attacks across the country, the modus operandi of this attack had not been seen in Spain before. Later evidence strongly pointed to the involvement of Islamic extremist groups of Moroccan, Syrian, and Algerian origin.

Three weeks after the bombings, on April 3, 2004, police finally located the terrorist group in an apartment in Leganes, a town outside Madrid. Surrounded by the police, seven North African suspects committed suicide by blowing up the apartment. The Grupo Especial de Operaciones (GEO; Special Operations Group of the Spanish national police) had launched an assault to try to capture the suspects. The police forced open the apartment door, and an explosion occurred that killed the seven suspects and a GEO police officer.

The investigative proceedings lasted more than two years. In February 2007 the bombing trial began. The courts upheld the premise of an Islamic attack, but the alleged organizers of the attack were acquitted. Only one defendant was found guilty of having planted bombs on the trains, and most of the other 29 defendants were convicted of being members of a jihadist group, not for being involved in the attack. The Supreme Court upheld that ruling in July 2008. Nevertheless, an intense controversy continues around the bombings, designated as 11-M. The foreign press has essentially abstained from reporting the polarization in the Spanish media on the topic.

Other Spanish-based terrorist organizations such as Grupo de Resistencia Antifascista Primero de Octubre (GRAPO; First of October Antifascist Resistance Group) and other anarchist groups have also been the subject of police intervention. However, today's efforts are largely concentrated in the fight against ETA and radical Islamic groups.

COUNTERTERRORISM STRATEGIES

Spain has developed and tested several counterterrorism strategies for over 30 years. However, none of them have been evaluated empirically. This reality prevents us from knowing what exactly really works in practice. What everybody should bear in mind, though, is that terrorist organizations are fluid and adaptable (Reinares 2004) and that certain counterterrorism policies may work well for a particular group in a particular time and in a particular place and may not necessarily work out well for similar circumstances in different locations and certainly over long periods of time.

Crimes of terrorism in Spain are outlined in the second section of the Spanish Criminal Code. Title XXI explicitly refers to crimes against the "public order," which defines the objective elements of terrorist crimes, that is, "belonging to, acting in the name of, or collaborating with an armed group or a terrorist organization." One should take into account that a direct relationship has to exist between the author of the crime and the armed group or terrorist organization. In 1988, the Spanish Supreme Court recognized an "armed group" as an association concentrating on armed action from which permanent links are born. Hierarchy and discipline are important to armed groups, whose actions are usually numerous and unpredictable and who attack with suitable instruments of violence provided by their criminal organizations. The trial of the suspected perpetrators of terrorist activities is carried out in the National Court (Audiencia Nacional), which is endowed with exclusive jurisdiction over terrorist crimes.

CONCLUSION

Counterterrorism policies in Spain have included negotiated solutions with the terrorists, short-lived truces, persuasion of militants to renounce their links to terrorist organizations in exchange for reduced sentences, dispersal of prisoners across the country, and the undermining of the cohesion of terrorist groups with coercive or intelligence tactics. Nevertheless, in general terms, the antiterrorist strategy has been undermined by improvisation, heterogeneous guidelines, and transient policies. Many experts consider the counterterrorism policy a violation of the fundamental principles of law, since it allows a certain type of crime to be dealt with in a fashion clearly different from other forms of violent crime.

REFERENCES

Alonso, Rogelio, and Fernando Reinares. "Terrorism, Human Rights and Law Enforcement in Spain." *Terrorism and Political Violence* 17 (2005): 265–78.

Reinares, Fernando. "Democratic Regimes, Internal Security Policy and the Threat of Terrorism." *Australian Journal of Politics and History* 44, no. 3 (1998): 351–71.

Reinares, Fernando. "Who Are the Terrorists? Analyzing Changes in Sociological Profile among Members of ETA." *Studies in Conflict and Terrorism* 27 (2004): 465–88.

Sri Lanka

Rohan Kumar Gunaratna

Sri Lanka defeated the world's first insurgency of the 21st century (Ahmed Hashim, pers. comm., June 13, 2010). On May 19, 2009, the country achieved a great strategic and moral triumph by militarily defeating the Liberation Tigers of Tamil Eelam (LTTE). The theory, articulated by Western theorists and scholars, that a political solution is a prelude to defeating an insurgency was shattered. After three decades of fighting a cruel and costly insurgency, peace finally returned to Sri Lanka. Whether peace and future prosperity will endure will depend on the ability and willingness of the political leaders of the country to work together across the party divide to build a new Sri Lanka.

POTENTIAL THREAT

The failure of Sri Lankan leaders to govern a multiethnic and a multireligious society since independence precipitated Sri Lanka's ethnopolitical conflict. Sri Lanka's political masters compromised Sri Lanka's long-term national and strategic interests for short-term political gain. Unless Sri Lankan politicians build the understanding that they should never again play ethnic- and religious-based politics, poison the ground by radicalizing the youth, and reinforce ethnic and religious divisions, the country is likely to suffer a repetition of its unfortunate past.

Sri Lanka celebrated the end of the war, but a segment of radicalized Sri Lankans both at home and overseas resents this victory. The terrorist threat to Sri Lanka has diminished but has not ended. The LTTE threat has declined in Sri Lanka, but it is increasing overseas. The LTTE had two organizational bases—the domestic, or territorial, base, from which it recruited, and the foreign, or diaspora, base, from which it generated funds. To prevent a disconnect, the LTTE exercised exceptional control over these two bases through intense and sustained propaganda and the punishment of dissent, at times brutally. After the LTTE was dismantled during a military confrontation on the banks of the Nandikadal lagoon, the group very quickly reorganized itself overseas. Once regarded as the world's most ruthless terrorist and guerrilla group, the LTTE, after one year, is steadily reemerging in Western cities. The LTTE is acting through three fronts—the Transnational Government of Tamil Eelam, led by Visuvanathan Rudrakumaran in New York; the Global Tamil Forum, led by Father S. J. Emmanuel in the United Kingdom; and the criminal faction, led by Perinbanayagam Sivaparan (alias Nediyawan) in Norway. The LTTE leaders, offices, and assets overseas are largely intact. The LTTE-controlled diaspora campaign contributions and carefully orchestrated pressure on elected officials compelled the United States, United Kingdom, Norway, and a few other countries to turn a blind eye to LTTE activities. Although the LTTE leadership in Sri Lanka has been dismantled, the LTTE's global network poses an enduring and long-term threat to the stability and security of the country. The LTTE ideology is intact, its financial infrastructure is operational, and its vicious propaganda machine is impactful. For sustainable peace and stability, the long-term ideological and operational threat posed by the LTTE will need to be carefully managed.

To harness the hard-earned gains from militarily defeating the LTTE, the government must quickly develop a strategy of working toward engaging both the international community and the resident and nonresident Sri Lankan populations. The government still needs a concept, a master plan, or a national road map for crafting a future of prosperity for all Sri Lankans. While security is essential to creating the conditions for such success, a lasting victory comes from a vibrant economy, broad-based political participation, and restored hope (U.S. Army Military Police School 2009, 15). The likely future trajectory of the LTTE will depend on the government's ability to continue to work with the Tamil population, to move fast and reach out to the Tamil diaspora, and to invest the time and resources to co-opt the Tamil political opposition both at home and abroad. The art of politics is to not only work with friends but also engage the opposition, pockets of adversaries, and even past, present, and future enemies—this includes even those infected with and still suffering from the Eelam ideology and seeking pathways to lead a respectable mainstream life. To craft a road map to unify the country through nation building will delegitimize and effectively kill the vicious ideology that spawned and sustained the violence that plagued Sri Lanka for 30 years. The government's highly visible strategy of attrition in the past must be replaced by a high-profile strategy of proactive engagement.

Today, the most dominant actors at play are the government, the international community, and the remnants of the LTTE. The LTTE remnants seeking to reorganize include three components: (1) the LTTE group (dismantled), (2) the LTTE network (active), and (3) the LTTE movement (active). Let us examine each of these components that took Sri Lanka backward for three decades. This presentation is drawn from a review of government and other documents on the LTTE and from information from several hundred LTTE leaders, members, and helpers who I have debriefed since 1984. In addition to an interview with Velupillai Prabhakaran, leader of the LTTE, in August 1987, I debriefed key leaders, including Selvarasa Pathmanathan (alias Kumaran Pathmanathan alias K.P.), who succeeded Prabhakaran, as well as the parents of Prabhakaran.

LTTE AS A GROUP

The LTTE as a group is militarily vanquished. Although its ideology is intact, the component that was physically based in Sri Lanka is no longer operational as a coherent group. The conduct of the LTTE leadership in the final phase of battle demonstrated its true face of willingness to sacrifice its own support base and potential support base. Although every Tamil family voluntarily or involuntarily provided a family member and resources, the Tamil public confidence the LTTE had meticulously built through years of systematic indoctrination was shattered. Instead of respecting the fifth No Fire Zone, the LTTE held nearly 280,000 Tamils as hostages. When the LTTE persisted and eventually started to shoot the civilians who wanted to flee, the Sri Lankan military was able to breach the LTTE human shield and launch an operation to rescue them. The angry Tamil civilians rescued by the Sri Lankan forces identified several thousand LTTE leaders, members, and helpers. While over 10,000 LTTE cadres were killed, a total of 12,500 LTTE leaders, cadres, and helpers who did not wish to fight either surrendered or were spotted by Tamil civilians in the welfare centers.

Although the government was highly criticized for holding and screening the civilians, its strategy of preventing a reinfiltration and reradicalization of the community worked. Today, except a few thousand civilians who are free to leave the open welfare centers, every Tamil civilian has been resettled. Ironically, one part of the United Nations (UN), lobbied by the LTTE, called for the early release of internally displaced persons and campaigned side by side with the LTTE fronts for this, while another part of the UN pressured the government to delay the releases because of the slow pace of mine removal. Some leaders of international organizations, foreign governments, nongovernmental organizations, and a segment of the press exposed to LTTE's powerful propaganda toed the LTTE line when they spoke of "concentration camps" and "internment camps." This includes some poorly informed think tanks in Colombo that even propagated this view.

Despite the economic status of a country recovering from conflict, the government even provided a resettlement allowance, and it continues to assist those internally displaced persons. In recent history, no country has resettled such a significant number of the displaced in such short period of time. The government appointed one of its ablest commanders, Major General Kamal Gunaratna, the general officer commanding the

54 Division, as the Competent Authority of the Internally Displaced Persons, a task he admirably accomplished. Likewise, the government skillfully launched a multifaceted rehabilitation program under the guidance of the former justice minister, Milinda Moragoda, and the secretary of defense, Gotabhaya Rajapaksa, to engage the LTTE followers (International Centre for Political Violence and Terrorism Research 2010). Away from the glare of the international media, the government has today released all the disabled and student rehabilitees and has started the process of releasing the women rehabilitees. Unless there is a terrorist attack, the government is likely to release over half of those undergoing rehabilitation within the next year. To prevent recidivism, it is paramount for the government to continuously engage this vulnerable segment of the population. To ensure complete reintegration back into the community, there should be a separate authority to monitor their reentry and maintain the engagement.

Although the commissioner general of rehabilitation and his dedicated staff have treated the rehabilitees in the most humane way, the government has yet to get the reentry into the community worked out, especially the long-term monitoring part. To prevent a relapse to the old ways, the government's reintegration staff should work with the families, community and religious leaders, business community, and nongovernmental organizations. Extensive interagency collaboration is necessary to ensure that every rehabilitee has a job and is never again trapped and misguided by the vicious and intolerant ideology of the LTTE. The LTTE network overseas, in partnership with a few Tamil political leaders at home, seeks to poison another generation of Tamil youth.

If the government is strategic in its thinking, the LTTE as a group is unlikely to reemerge in Sri Lanka in our lifetime. As long as the government continues to reorient its combat forces and expand its intelligence strength, it will be capable of detecting LTTE individual operatives and emerging support cells both at home and overseas, especially in Tamil Nadu. In addition to a focus on economic growth and stronger partnerships with Tamil parties, a powerful national and military intelligence service at home is the key to securing Sri Lanka in the coming years.

THE LTTE NETWORK OVERSEAS

The LTTE as a group has been rendered impotent at home. Nonetheless, the second component of the LTTE—its network overseas—has survived. The network's activities that supported the terrorist campaign in Sri Lanka have moved to the diplomatic and international arena. They lobby not only governments but also the UN, World Bank, International Monetary Fund, and other important stakeholders in international affairs. The network represents a short-term nuisance and irritant (for 1–2 years) and, depending on the government response, a mid- to long-term threat (in 5–10 years). Although it is factionalized into three entities, these factions cooperate and at times fight. To ensure compliance, the LTTE shadow leader Nediyawan, who heads the criminal network, threatens other LTTE leaders and activists and conducts acts of violence against them. The three factions are no longer genuinely interested in the welfare and well-being of Tamils, including those affected by the war. Their leaders, Nediyawan, Rudrakumaran, and Emmanuel, are interested in building their personal and political power and financial strength. As the activists and assets of the LTTE are located overseas, its network of front, cover, and sympathetic organizations are not within the reach of Sri Lankan law enforcement. Due to an inherent weakness in the Sri Lankan government's overall strategy, there was no fight overseas to parallel the work of the security forces and intelligence agencies that dismantled the LTTE in Sri Lanka. Like the Ministry of Defence, the Ministry of External Affairs must develop a vision and a mission; they too must play their role by making it their personal fight. The former foreign minister, Lakhman Kadirgarmar, PC, a Tamil himself, understood the threat from overseas and the need to counter it, as did the entire Ministry of Foreign Affairs during his tenure. Nonetheless, the working culture of the Sri Lankan Foreign Service and other associated systemic factors in the service meant that it did not make the dismantling of the LTTE overseas its single most important mission.

Unfortunately, in the run-up to the final Wanni operation, most career foreign service officers appeared in the shadows without forcefully representing Sri Lanka's interests and rebutting the LTTE and others influenced by its black and gray propaganda. There was no structure in place in the Ministry of External Affairs for appointing, promoting, and rewarding officials based on merit, ability, and performance in this domain. As such, most career foreign service officers and political appointees did not adequately understand the importance of, and hence did not embrace the responsibility of, working closely with key international partners. To ensure that the LTTE presence is dismantled in the countries to which they are appointed, they must proactively identify and build adequate working relationships with influential leaders in the political establishment, security and intelligence services, law enforcement authorities, human rights groups, think tanks, and media, as well as the Tamil community. To date, when the LTTE generates false reports, there is no established practice to monitor, counter, and rebut the adverse publicity within six hours. Because the government neglected this crucial dimension, the LTTE network was able to convince some host governments and host communities of "ethnocide," "genocide," and "war crimes," activities that were not perpetrated by the government and labels that Sri Lanka never deserved. Furthermore, the LTTE interfaced with, interlocked with, and galvanized a segment of the Tamil population overseas and used them as pawns to wage their vicious and malicious propaganda campaign.

The configuration of the LTTE network overseas evolved dramatically even before its defeat at home. The successor to K.P., Manivannan Veerakulasingham (alias Castro), has headed the LTTE's international network since 2003. Raising funds under the pretext of relief and rehabilitation, the LTTE has invested the bulk of its finances in arms procurement from North Korea and propaganda in the West. Although the bulk of the LTTE's ships have been destroyed, its propaganda network is still intact. Dismantling the LTTE infrastructure and countering the false propaganda can be accomplished by two principal methods.

First, the government should create platforms and institutions in northern and eastern Sri Lanka to engage LTTE leaders and their activists overseas. Ideally working with the parliamentary opposition, the government should build a mechanism to invite these misguided LTTE leaders to witness for themselves the unprecedented economic development in the north and east, as well as the humane treatment of the displaced and the rehabilitees, and the government should create opportunities for their participation. Furthermore, the president should grant amnesty to those who engaged in not-so-serious criminal activity in support of the LTTE. The government should build a mechanism through its missions abroad to ensure that travel for these individuals is facilitated and that they are engaged in a manner to facilitate others to reenter the Sri Lankan mainstream. The Sri Lankan political opposition should declare its support for the government for such a mechanism, including engaging with Rudrakumaran, Emmanuel, and Nediyawan. If they or other high-ranking figures of the LTTE's international network remain stubbornly uncooperative notwithstanding sincere attempts by the government, they should be totally left out of the political discourse and thereafter exposed to the law enforcement authorities of their countries of residence to be dealt with for their criminal activities.

Second, the government should expand the mandate of its national and military intelligence services to operate overseas to develop its coverage of terrorist support and operational activities. While the dominant strategy should be to engage, it is natural for Sri Lankans to think that the LTTE network overseas will not plan and prepare acts of terrorism to carry out in Sri Lanka. Although most Tamils, including the radicalized, see the sense of pursuing nonviolence to achieve their goals, a few fanatics within the three factions are determined to resort to violence. Already, LTTE cells in India and Malaysia that supported acts of terrorism in Sri Lanka have been detected. As an LTTE hard core is active overseas, they need to be closely monitored and appropriate actions taken. There should be dedicated desks for every country, not just for every region of the world, where there are LTTE personnel, infrastructure, and activities. Such desks should work closely with the diplomatic, political, intelligence, law enforcement (police, border control, and others), judicial, and other branches of government. After 9/11, if there is a will, there is sufficient political commitment and mechanisms available globally to bring to justice anyone who is seeking to spawn, support, and sustain terrorism.

PROSCRIPTION

Sri Lanka was fortunate that, by 2005, virtually all countries in the developed West and Europe had proscribed the LTTE. We will be failing in our duty if we fail to recall with gratitude the untiring efforts of the late minister Kadirgarmar with regard to successfully satisfying foreign leaders that the LTTE was no mere "liberation or freedom organization" but a "criminal-terrorist outfit." It is the international proscription of the LTTE that has made it difficult for any foreign government to directly criticize the government of Sri Lanka for its resolve to militarily demolish the LTTE. If we are serious in our current determination to continue to take all meaningful measures to eliminate the LTTE's remaining tentacles located overseas, it is of paramount importance that Sri Lanka ensures that countries that have proscribed the LTTE continue to do so and that countries such as Australia, New Zealand, and South Africa should proscribe the LTTE. It is vital that diplomatic measures aimed at achieving this objective should be implemented following a comprehensive understanding of the divergent mechanisms in place in such countries. In certain countries the authority to designate an organization as an "international terrorist organization" or "terrorist organization" (and thereby proscribe it) rests with the executive branch, that is, the head of state, the minister of defense, or some other official in the executive branch. In certain other countries, the designation of an organization and thereby its proscription should be achieved through legislative action, that is, by passing a law. In certain other countries, there is a need for both the state or regional government and the federal government and their respective parliaments to collaborate in this regard. Australia is one such example. This means that proscription, or designation as terrorist, is basically a political decision taken against the backdrop of factual circumstances such as the conduct of the organization. Under these circumstances, if we are to ensure that the LTTE remains proscribed, and that countries such as Australia that have not yet proscribed the LTTE come to proscribe it, Sri Lanka has to have a positive diplomatic and political relationship with such countries. Furthermore, apart from continuing to brief those governments regarding continuing activism by organizational manifestations of the LTTE in those countries (aimed at reactivating terrorist operations), Sri Lanka needs to have a better ground situation. This means that the government should in good faith necessarily address the genuine political needs of the Tamil minority. Foreign leaders should necessarily perceive that the government of Sri Lanka is acting reasonably and will effectively protect the interests of the Tamil people, in the aftermath of the full elimination of the LTTE.

Now that an armed conflict is no longer occurring, the only legally tenable way in which LTTE activists could be neutralized, and thereby prevented from continuing to engage in LTTE activities, is by successfully prosecuting them for their terrorist and other criminal activities. Sri Lankan authorities have been somewhat successful in that regard by launching successful prosecutions against hard-core LTTE activists in Sri Lankan courts, thereby getting them to serve terms of imprisonment, and by promoting investigations and prosecutions of LTTE activists who operated on foreign soil. Due to both keen interest shown by local authorities and the initiatives of foreign intelligence and law enforcement agencies, successful prosecutions have been launched against LTTE activists in Canada, the United States, the United Kingdom, France, Italy, India, and Australia. If LTTE activists are to be kept at bay and dissuaded from engaging in LTTE activities on foreign soil, these investigations and prosecutions have to continue. However, now that LTTE activists operating in developed countries appear to have satisfied foreign powers that they are no longer engaging in terrorist or other illegal activities on foreign soil and that their activities are limited to lobbying and political activism, the challenge for Sri Lanka becomes considerably more difficult.

CONCLUSION

Though we as Sri Lankans will steadfastly argue that a tiger never changes his stripes, and hence that LTTE activists would use political activism only to camouflage their determined efforts aimed at reviving the LTTE as a violent force, it is likely that foreign powers would prefer to adopt a wait-and-see attitude and not continue to arrest LTTE activists, particularly since LTTE activists no longer pose a threat to the normal law and order in the countries in which they presently operate. Therefore, Sri Lankan authorities would necessarily have to turn toward the Sri Lankan criminal justice system to have LTTE operatives investigated, arrested, prosecuted, and imprisoned. One major barrier in this regard appears to be that Sri Lankan courts do not have extraterritorial jurisdiction to try persons such as LTTE operatives who have committed offences overseas and are not engaged in any illegal activities on Sri Lankan soil. It would be important for Sri Lankan authorities to pay due regard to this weakness of the Sri Lankan criminal justice system and to adopt legislative reform so as to vest extraterritorial jurisdiction in Sri Lankan criminal courts and to amend the substantive criminal law of Sri Lanka to recognize as punishable offenses LTTE activism overseas.

See also: **Volume 1, Part I:** Defining the Enemy. **Part III:** Countering Terrorism: Law Enforcement or Military Problem? **Part V:** South Asian Association for Regional Cooperation. **Volume 2, Part I:** Special Boat Squadron (Sri Lanka); Special Task Force (Sri Lanka)

REFERENCES

Gunaratna, Rohan. *War and Peace in Sri Lanka*. Kandy, Sri Lanka: Institute of Fundamental Studies, 1987.

International Centre for Political Violence and Terrorism Research. "Rehabilitating Tamil Tigers." Singapore: Counter Terrorist Trends and Analysis (CTTA), May 2010.

U.S. Army Military Police School. "Counterinsurgency in Detention Operations for Military Police." Internment/Resettlement and Combat Support Battalions/Brigades, Version 2.0, p. 15, March 2009.

Turkey

Tim Jacoby

Turkey's position as the single Muslim-majority member of the North Atlantic Treaty Organization (NATO), its location on the crucial East Mediterranean southern flank, and its vast military reserves have tended to mean that its counterinsurgency policies, institutions, and initiatives have frequently been funded by, and are of particular interest to, strategists in Washington, D.C. Indeed, the overriding theme of President Truman's famous speech of March 1947, which was to influence much of U.S. foreign policy thenceforth, was the specific dangers of ignoring leftist agitation in Greece and Turkey. The subsequent extension of $225 million in economic and $553 million in military Marshall aid, and Turkey's eventual absorption into NATO in 1952 (which led to the transfer of a further total of $2.5 billion in aid between 1953 and 1961 under the Mutual Security Act), constituted the preliminary basis for Ankara's postwar internal security regime.

RADICAL LEFT AND DIRECT ACTION GROUPS

This rebuilding initially took the form of the Tactical Mobilization Committee (Seferberlik Taktik Kurulu). Founded in 1955, it principally focused on nurturing anti-Communist sentiment, with a particular eye on residual Greek networks following the crushing of the insurgency there in 1949. After the military coup of 1960, which created a military-dominated National Security Council (Milli Güvenlik Kurulu) with considerable executive powers, the Tactical Mobilization Committee was reorganized to become the Special Warfare Department (Özel Harp Dairesi). As the 1960s began to produce a growing number of left-wing direct action groups, this department began working closely with the newly restructured National Intelligence Agency (Milli Istihbarat Teşkilatı).

The primary object of their attentions during this period was the activities of a plethora of small cells and splinter groups that, in general, had their roots in the Turkish Workers' Party (Türkiye şçi Partisi) and the Federation of Revolutionary Youth (Dev-Genç). The largest and most well known of these, such as Dev-Sol and Dev-Yol, established military training camps during the 1970s and funded their activities with (often spectacular) robberies; they remain active today. Alongside the radical left, quasi-fascist direct action groups also emerged during the late 1960s. Organized by the Nationalist Action Party (Milliyetçi Hareket Partisi), these had founded around 150 "commando" training camps by 1968 and were extensively used as strikebreakers throughout the 1970s. Once party leader Alparslan Türkeş was appointed deputy prime minister with direct control over the National Intelligence Agency in 1975, the state's counterterrorism strategy became increasingly mired in what U.S. Senator Frank Church was later to describe as a "contra-guerrilla" force made up of rightists, clandestine units within the Turkish armed forces, and American intelligence officials. The range of activities and the true extent and changing form of these are only just coming to light through the recent Ergenekon investigations launched by the current Turkish government.

KURDISTAN WORKERS' PARTY

A key target of these covert networks was, and remains today, the activities of the Kurdistan Workers' Party (Partiya Karkareni Kurdistan [PKK]). Formed in 1978 and with its roots in the Dev-Genç spin-off the Revolutionary Eastern Cultural Society (Devrimci Doğu Kültür Ocakları), the PKK initially concentrated its attacks on "collaborators" and feudatories in the southeast of the country, accounting for around 400 of the 5,000 or so politically motivated murders between 1979 and 1980. By late 1980s, however, it had become the largest and most effective insurgent network in Turkey; up until its cease-fire in 1999, it had killed over 5,000 soldiers, injured a further 11,000, and absorbed $15 billion in counterterrorism expenditures. To fund such a response, between the military coup of 1980 and 2006, Ankara received military assistance from the United States worth more than $8.5 billion.

STATE RESPONSE

The primary institutional response to the PKK was the imposition of emergency rule (the infamous OHAL—Olağanüstü Hal—regime). Embarked on under Articles 119 and 122 of the Constitution, devised by the military in 1982, this system, which remained in place for much of the next 15 years, invested extraordinary dictatorial powers in provincial governors and in a regional "supergovernor." Decree 285 (1987), for instance, permitted the latter to evacuate and resettle civilian areas in the interest of the region's security, while Decree 430 (1990) granted the office of the supergovernor the power to exile people from the region without further recourse (Article 8), to detain suspects without charge for up to 10 days (Article 3), and to prohibit publications deemed to be provocative from entering, or being disseminated within, the region. According to Ankara's own figures, 3,216 settlements were emptied and then destroyed under these laws, displacing 362,915 people—although some put the figures at close to 9,000 settlements and nearly three million people displaced.

These measures were undergirded by constitutional statutes that greatly reinforced an ethnically Turkish understanding of citizenship. Articles 141 and 142 of the penal code, for instance, prohibited anything that might weaken "national sentiments," while Article 26 of the Constitution and Law 2932 combined to ensure that Turkish remained the country's only legal language—using Kurdish verbally, in writing, or even as a name could be deemed a breach of Article 3 of the Constitution, which enshrined a "national culture." Despite some legislative revisions in 1991 and 1995, terrorism continued to be equated with a broad range of activities, including the undefined charge of separatism. Jurisprudential control of this section of the statute also remained under the auspices of state security courts made up of a combination of centrally appointed military and civilian judges.

Kurds were also co-opted into the state's counterinsurgency strategy through a network of local village guards. Backed by elite commando units (many of which received instruction though the United States' Joint Combined Exchange Training Program), these were formed through a combination of payments, threats, and coercion and had, by March 2000, risen in number to a force of 65,000. In addition to regular troop support for these units, which could be arranged without civilian input, activists of the Nationalist Action Party (crushed following the 1980 coup) reappeared as members of a network of Uniformed Gangs (Üniformalı Çeteler). From the early 1990s on, these were supported by so-called Hezbollah contra-guerrillas as the coercive wing of a broader effort to undermine Marxism and minority identity with a universal exegesis of Islam.

This extraordinary militarization of society, combined with the National Intelligence Agency's growing use of American satellite technology in directing aerial bombardments, the PKK's conflict with Iraqi Kurds in 1995, and the fact that (according to official figures) over 23,000 of its operatives had been killed, led to a decline in PKK recruitment of around 40 percent between 1993 and 1998. Following Syria's decision to close the PKK's camps in the Bekar Valley (and the subsequent capture of its leader, Abdullah Öcalan, in 1999), there was a considerable decline in the intensity of violence and a greater acknowledgment of the Kurds' cultural and political claims through a series of constitutional reform packages during the early years of the new millennium.

By 2005, though, amid accusations that the Turkish state had neither significantly altered its military policies on the ground nor succeeded in narrowing the socioeconomic divide between the southeastern region and the rest of the country, the armed struggle had been resumed, leading to rapid revisions in the penal code. Highly punitive sanctions for those found guilty of incitement, loosely defined as "disobey[ing] laws" (Article 217) or "breed[ing] enmity" (Article 216), were reintroduced amid considerable dissent from domestic and international human rights observers. As the violence reintensified, further legislation followed. The Law to Fight Terrorism of 2006, for instance, gave the security services greater powers of surveillance and more authority to "establish special covert investigation teams." These are now administered through a new Directorate General of Security Affairs that incorporates a Higher Council for Anti-terrorism, which, with six senior members from the security forces and only five ministers under the chairmanship of the prime minister, represents an approximate return to the militarized response of the 1980s and 1990s.

CONCLUSION

Increasingly concerned that the return of the PKK's insurgency might destabilize its interests in northern Iraq, the United States helped to establish Ankara's Centre of Excellence: Defence against Terrorism in 2005 as one of NATO's three flagship training and research establishments (Norway and Germany are home to winter strategy and airpower centers, respectively). This was accompanied by the appointment of retired Air Force general Joseph Ralston as "special envoy for countering the PKK" and a marked increase in the International Military Education Training budget for Turkish officers, from under $1.5 million in 1997 (with fewer than 100 graduates) to over $3.5 million (and more than 350 graduates) in 2007, making Turkey, by some margin, the largest recipient in the world. From 2006 on, the International Military Education Training program has been augmented by a reciprocal arrangement with Israeli commandos that has been funded through the U.S. Department of Justice as part of a future shift from what is currently a largely conscripted deployment in the southeast to a specialized, six-brigade spearhead of fully professional soldiers.

REFERENCES

Alexander, Y., D. Brenner, and S. Tutuncuoglu Krause. *Turkey: Terrorism, Civil Rights, and the European Union.* Abingdon, UK: Routledge, 2008.

Fernandes, D., and İ. Özden. "United States and NATO Inspired 'Psychological Warfare Operations' against the 'Kurdish Communist Threat' in Turkey." *Variant* 12 (2001): 10–16.

Ismet, I. *The PKK.* Ankara: Turkish Daily News, 1992.

Mango, A. *Turkey and the War on Terror: For Forty Years We Fought Alone.* Abingdon, UK: Routledge, 2005.

United Kingdom

Bart Schuurman

Britain's principal experience with domestic terrorism lasted from 1968 to 1998 and revolved around the constitutional status of the province of Northern Ireland. The province's Protestant inhabitants wished to remain within the United Kingdom, while many of their Catholic compatriots sought a union with the Republic of Ireland. Tensions between the two communities were further raised by discriminatory policies that led the Catholic minority to suffer from lack of political representation, poor access to higher education, generally inadequate housing, and pro-Protestant favoritism on the job market. Until "the Troubles" started, Northern Ireland was ruled by devolved government from the Stormont area in Belfast. This meant that the province enjoyed substantial autonomy, but the Protestant-dominated government and its police force, the Royal Ulster Constabulary (RUC), formed key points of contention.

Feeling increasingly threatened by the Catholic-led civil rights movement that took to the streets in 1968, Northern Ireland's Protestant politicians used the considerable means at their disposal to safeguard their privileged position. The RUC actively and passively participated in attacking Catholic protestors. When reciprocal violence escalated to a level where the police force was no longer able to cope, London intervened. In 1969, the British Army was deployed to restore order in the province. Although initially welcomed by the Catholic community as neutral arbiters that would protect them from Protestant extremists, known as Loyalists, the army's presence soon functioned as a major catalyst for the violence.

COUNTERTERRORISM, 1968–1998

The deployment of the British Army seemed a decisive move, but it masked the critical absence of an overarching political plan and the lack of unified command and control; until direct rule was established in 1973, both London and Stormont attempted to guide the armed forces. Without a clear political strategy to guide it, and without the assistance of an effective police force, the army's inherent heavy-handedness soon provoked fear and resentment among the population it was meant to protect. As the general perception of policymakers on both sides of the Irish Sea was that the unrest was primarily being fomented by Catholic nationalists, the army focused the majority of its efforts on this population group. Shortly after the army's arrival, many Catholics had come to perceive it as no less biased against them than the RUC.

The early years of the Troubles predominantly saw the use of restrictive and violent counterterrorism measures. Roadblocks, curfews, the use of tear gas against protesters, and extensive house searches were intended to contain the violence and neutralize the Catholic paramilitary organizations. Because these searches did not target the Protestant community, the confiscated weapons and explosives came at the cost of alienating Catholic citizens, which in turn led to increased support for the revitalized Irish Republican Army (IRA).

The British decision in August 1971 to respond to the deteriorating security situation by using internment without trial proved disastrous. Not only was the operation poorly prepared and executed, leading to scores of innocent citizens being detained while most IRA members had been forewarned, but the measure once again solely targeted the Catholic community. Worsening an already bad situation and fueling the single largest spike of violence in the Troubles' history were the dramatic events of January 1972's "Bloody Sunday," when British troops killed 14 unarmed civil rights protestors in Londonderry.

In 1972, the struggle between the British government and the IRA took precedence over the conflict's intercommunal origins. Following the simultaneous detonation of 26 bombs in Belfast, public opinion turned against the terrorists long enough for the British Army to launch Operation Motorman. Conducted by some 28,000 troops, the operation succeeded in reestablishing government control over "no-go" areas in Belfast and Londonderry, forcing many paramilitaries to flee to the countryside and providing government forces with a wealth of low-level intelligence. As such, Motorman was an important operational success.

After Motorman, the rugged countryside along the border between Northern Ireland and the Republic of Ireland rose in strategic importance. Two factors allowed the British to concentrate their forces on the "border war" from the mid-1970s on: the improved security situation in the province's cities and the freedom of action that the policy of "normalization" brought the army. This policy rested on the recognition that the army's urban policing role was highly provocative. Through the institution of "police primacy," it was hoped that tensions within the province would subside. But as the army and the elite Special Air Service became increasingly entangled in a vicious and often controversial "secret war" on the border, the police forces initially proved unable to fulfill their new frontline roles.

Until the early 1980s, the RUC and the paramilitary Ulster Defense Regiment (established in 1970) lacked the necessary training and experience to cope with their new responsibilities. Police stations and officers became prime targets for IRA operations, and losses were considerable. The subsequent "militarization" of these organizations increased their operational effectiveness but raised doubts about the extent of "normalization." Controversial Special Air Service operations, such as the ambush of IRA personnel at Loughall police station (1987) and the assassination of Republican militants on Gibraltar (1988), only underlined these doubts, as did persistent allegations of collusion between Loyalist terrorists and the security forces, allegations that several official inquiries were unable to dispel. By the late 1980s very little had been actually normalized, and military operations had failed to bring the conflict closer to resolution.

Throughout the Troubles, various counterterrorism measures were used parallel to the repressive policies outlined thus far. The 1973 Sunningdale Agreement emphasized conciliation, as it attempted to implement a power-sharing executive for Northern Ireland that would grant the Catholic community greater political representation. However, intense Unionist opposition to the new executive caused the measure to fail, and direct rule was swiftly reestablished.

Around the same time, legislative reforms greatly expanded the police's powers of arrest and detainment, enabled the army to conduct house searches without a warrant, allowed for the prohibition of organizations, and limited terrorist groups' fund-raising abilities. Because they failed to address any of the conflict's underlying grievances and increased the potential for police abuse, the effectiveness of these measures was limited. Indeed, by primarily targeting the Catholic community, these reforms further delegitimized the British government and aided IRA recruitment.

Warranting specific attention are the Diplock Courts that were established in 1973 and the so-called supergrass trials that took place during the 1980s. The first measure replaced trial by jury with trial by a single judge, thus preventing the paramilitaries from influencing the proceedings by threatening the jury members or their families. Although the Diplock system emphasized the rule of law in countering extremism, it broke with long-standing British legal traditions, relied on confessions obtained under duress, and was seen to predominantly target Catholics. These factors ultimately made the Diplock system counterproductive.

Besides emphasizing police primacy, the normalization policy also attempted to criminalize the IRA to damage its popular image. The supergrass trials aimed to achieve this goal by emphasizing criminal proceedings over military action. The trials relied on informers willing to testify against their comrades in the IRA and the smaller Irish National Liberation Army. While the latter organization was severely affected, the IRA was not noticeably weakened. Crucially, virtually all convictions were overturned by an appeals court, and many informers revoked their statements. Although the supergrass trials failed, legal countermeasures continued to be used. In 1988, the paramilitary organizations and their political wings became subject to a controversial media ban that was not lifted until the start of the peace process in 1994.

The most significant negotiated settlement prior to the peace process was 1985's Anglo-Irish Agreement. This historic accord marked London's official recognition of the Republic of Ireland's role in the conflict and led to improved cooperation in security matters. Additionally, Britain reaffirmed that it did not oppose a united Ireland if a majority of the province's population voted in favor. This went some way toward stemming the electoral success that Sinn Fein, the IRA's political wing, had been enjoying since the prison strikes of the early 1980s.

By 1990, both the British government and the IRA realized they were militarily unable to defeat each other. Furthermore, to the Unionist population the Anglo-Irish Agreement had signaled that London would not maintain direct rule of the province forever. These factors contributed to the formation of a climate in which political solutions could be sought. The 1993 Downing Street Declaration promised Sinn Fein a part in multiparty peace negotiations if the IRA declared a cease-fire. Although the IRA did so in 1994, followed by the Loyalist paramilitaries, the peace process proved long and fraught with dangers. A return to violence in 1996 preceded the final signing of the Good Friday Agreement in April 1998.

Four months after the Good Friday Agreement was signed the Real IRA, an IRA splinter group, detonated a car bomb in Omagh but did not succeed in derailing the procedures. The agreement instituted a power-sharing executive for the province, led to the withdrawal of the majority of the British Army, ended emergency legislation, and reorganized the discredited police forces.

CONCLUSION

While the subsequent dearmament process has been slow, and despite various paramilitary groups' transition toward criminal enterprises and vigilantism, the Good Friday Agreement in many respects marked the end of 30 years of conflict.

REFERENCES

Coogan, Pat. *The Troubles: Ireland's Ordeal 1966–1996 and the Search for Peace*. London: Arrow, 1996.

Donohue, Laura K. *The Cost of Counterterrorism: Power, Politics, and Liberty*. New York: Cambridge University Press, 2008.

Kennedy-Pipe, Caroline. *The Origins of the Present Troubles in Northern Ireland*. New York: Longman, 1997.

Neumann, Peter R. *Britain's Long War: British Strategy in the Northern Ireland Conflict, 1969–98*. Houndmills, UK: Palgrave Macmillan, 2003.

Richardson, Louise. "Britain and the IRA." In *Democracy and Counterterrorism: Lessons from the Past*, edited by Robert J. Art and Louise Richardson, 63–104. Washington, DC: U.S. Institute of Peace Press, 2007.

Thornton, Rod. "Getting It Wrong: The Crucial Mistakes Made in the Early Stages of the British Army's Deployment to Northern Ireland (August 1969 to March 1972)." *Journal of Strategic Studies* 30 (2007): 73–107.

United States

Dhruba J. Bora

Arguably, the United States has been engaged in activities that can be labeled counterterrorism as far back as 1798, with the passage of the Alien Act and the Sedition Act. However, this early legislation fell under the scope of national security. Subsequently, the Force Act and the Ku Klux Klan Act of 1871 were added measures at fighting domestic terrorism, primarily by "expanding the powers of the government" (Fagan 2006, 51). At the dawn of the 20th century, the Espionage Act of 1917 and the Sedition Act of 1918 were passed to add to the repertoire of policies targeting subversive activities. Despite these early measures, the crux of U.S. counterterrorism strategy did not emerge until after World War II by way of numerous laws, policies, and directives.

EVOLUTION OF U.S. COUNTERTERRORISM POLICY

The postwar era was fraught with policies and strategies aimed at stopping the spread of Communism. By default, terrorism was included within that framework of political dissent. By 1950, Senator Joseph McCarthy began a nationwide campaign of weeding out Communist and terrorist activity, which ultimately culminated in the passage of the Communist Control Act in 1954 (Fagan 2006, 41). This legislation essentially stripped anyone identified as a Communist of his/her rights under the law. A few years later, the Federal Bureau of Investigation (FBI) launched its counterintelligence program (COINTELPRO), whose programs for the next two decades investigated radical political actions within the United States. The 1970s brought policies aimed at streamlining what the government could and could not do in the face of the Cold War. In 1976 and 1983, the U.S. attorney general's office issued the Levi Guidelines and Smith Guidelines, respectively, for the FBI in its authority to conduct domestic intelligence plus initiate investigations prior to the commission of criminal acts (Electronic Privacy Information Center n.d.).

COMBATING MODERN TERRORISM

With the demise of the Communist threat in the late 1980s came the beginning of modern terrorism. While much of the earlier legislation of the 19th and early 20th centuries focused on the prohibition of propaganda, deportation of enemies of the state, and expansion of governmental powers, the new focus would include laws and directives defining the role of government agencies that would be responsible for responding to and preventing various types of terrorist activities. Throughout the Reagan administration, a number of directives were issued to help organize the government's response to terrorism. The National Security Decision Directives 30, 179, 180, 205, and 207 would later go on to be enhanced during the current war on terrorism. The first of these, Directive 30, was aimed at the prevention of and response to the hijacking of commercial airlines. Directives 179 and 180 helped establish the Task Force on Combating Terrorism, which would be responsible for holding government agencies accountable in the event of an attack. These two directives had a hand in expanding the Federal Air Marshal Program that is currently in place to protect commercial aviation. The final two directives, 205 and 207, subtitled State-Sponsored Terrorism and Non-concessions Policy, took aim at nations that pose a threat to U.S. national security through state sponsorship of terrorism (Fagan 2006, 53–56). At the time Libya was the primary concern, but in the coming years Cuba, North Korea, Iran, Iraq, Sudan, and Syria would be added to the list of potential threats (U.S. Department of State 2004).

The basis of much of the existing counterterrorism strategy of the United States was formulated during the Clinton administration. Initially, domestic terrorism would be the focus. In 1994, the Freedom of Access to Clinic Entrances Act (FACE) was passed, which made it a criminal offense to obstruct and threaten individuals at entryways to such places as clinics, pregnancy centers, and physicians' offices where abortions were performed. On the heels of the Oklahoma City bombing, identifying the target vulnerability of the United States, both at home and on foreign soil, became the primary objective. Just as in the Reagan era, the use of legislation and presidential directives was the common method for inclusion of such policy (Fagan 2006, 59). Presidential Decision Directive 39, adopted in 1995, revisited the role of the federal agencies involved in the event of a terrorist attack. The directive not only expanded the number of agencies responsible—for example, the Department of Defense and the Central Intelligence Agency (CIA) now would have a more direct role—but addressed the need for planning and response in a scenario where weapons of mass destruction might be used.

In conjunction with Directive 39, Congress also passed the Omnibus Counterterrorism Act of 1995. The aim was to strengthen the government's ability to deal with both international and domestic terrorism. Nonetheless, it was quickly replaced by the Anti-terrorism and Effective Death Penalty Act of 1996, which was meant to be more comprehensive than its predecessor by including justice for victims of terrorism and mandating capital punishment at the federal level for acts of terrorism. The act did not come without criticism, however, due to possible infringement of civil liberties (Nacos 2006, 167). The Anti-terrorism and Effective Death Penalty Act of 1996 was, in actuality, several former legislative efforts merged together that dated back a decade, but it regained momentum through the World Trade Center bombing of 1993 and the bombing of the Alfred P. Murrah Federal Building in Oklahoma City in 1995. Most of the controversy centered on law enforcement at the domestic level, rather than foreign policy (Griset and Mahan 2003, 282). Regardless, the act served as the foundation for the extremely controversial Uniting and Strengthening America by Providing Appropriate Tools Required to Intercept and Obstruct Terrorism Act (USA PATRIOT Act) that would follow in the coming decade.

COUNTERTERRORISM AFTER SEPTEMBER 11

The terrorist attacks of September 11, 2001, without a doubt intensified counterterrorism efforts in the United States. Within two weeks, President George W. Bush issued Executive Order 13224, which, among other things, authorized the government to freeze and seize assets of individuals and organizations that provide material support to terrorist groups and their activities. Shortly thereafter two other controversial strategies would emerge from the Bush administration, the Enemy Combatant Executive Order and the USA PATRIOT Act. The first of these efforts, the executive order, was issued on November 13, 2001, and it climaxed with the detainment of close to 700 individuals at Guantánamo Bay, Cuba. In essence, the order authorized the indefinite detention of persons declared as enemy combatants by the president of the United States. With this label, detainees were not afforded their constitutional rights of due process, such as access to counsel or notification of charges, if any (Nacos 2006, 171). Several questionable aspects of the order include violation of the 1864 and 1949 Geneva Conventions' provision regarding capture and torture of prisoners of war in addition to presidential power to determine who is named an enemy combatant, thus making them subject to a military tribunal rather than a civilian trial in which the authority lies with the courts (Fagan 2006, 65). This was further complicated by the fact that adjudication in military venues cannot be appealed in civilian court, including the U.S. Supreme Court. Much of the criticism and controversy surrounding the Enemy Combatant Executive Order would also be carried over to the USA PATRIOT Act, passed in October 26, 2001, and amended in 2006.

The USA PATRIOT Act may indeed be the most significant piece of counterterrorism legislation in U.S. history while at the same time the most deeply contested. In fact, more than 150 local governments and several states passed various resolutions in objection to the act (Fagan 2006, 69). The act contains 10 titles dealing with issues ranging from money laundering and border protection to the provision of support to victims of terrorism. Yet the most controversial aspects involve Title II, Enhanced Surveillance Procedures. Civil libertarians fear that increasing the ability of government, through law enforcement, to gather information on private citizens and groups will expand the power of the executive branch, thereby destroying the system of checks and balances (Martin 2011, 286). Included in this argument is the fact that the police may not be required to inform individuals of an impending search, which lies at the heart of the Fourth Amendment to the U.S. Constitution. Despite these arguments, the government has continued to maintain that the act is necessary, and the fact that another attack on the United States has been avoided justifies its existence.

While the USA PATRIOT Act was the pinnacle of counterterrorism policy in the United States, efforts did not stop there. In May 2002, the U.S. attorney general introduced the Ashcroft Guidelines, which delineated further standards for the FBI in checking leads, conducting investigations, and allowing officials to utilize private databases in an effort to predict future attacks. Later that year, President Bush also signed the Homeland Security Bill, which was the catalyst for creating the Department of Homeland Security (DHS). The formation of DHS was the largest reorganization of federal agencies in the nation's history. Twenty-two agencies from across the federal level were shifted to DHS, including the Secret Service, Immigration and Naturalization Service, and Customs Service. There were initial plans to include the FBI and CIA in this restructuring, but they were allowed to stay within their present departments while still having a link to DHS (Nacos 2006, 199).

CONCLUSION

In terms of confronting terrorism, the United States is still in its infancy when compared to other nations; however, it is not alone when it comes to facing the challenges of dealing with global terrorism. Counterterrorism policy and legislation have progressed considerably over the last 60 years and will continue to evolve as the times and key players change.

REFERENCES

Electronic Privacy Information Center. "The Attorney General's Guidelines." n.d. http://epic.org/privacy/fbi/.

Fagan, James A. *When Terrorism Strikes Home Defending the United States*. Boston: Pearson, 2006.

Griset, Pamela L., and Sue Mahan. *Terrorism in Perspective*. Los Angeles: Sage, 2003.

Martin, Gus. *Essentials of Terrorism: Concepts and Controversies*. 2nd ed. Los Angeles: Sage, 2011.

Nacos, Brigitte. *Terrorism and Counterterrorism: Understanding Threats and Responses in the Post-9/11 World*. New York: Penguin Academics, 2006.

U.S. Department of State. *Patterns of Global Terrorism 2003*. Washington, DC: U.S. Department of State, 2004. http://www.state.gov/documents/organization/31944.pdf.

Yemen

Nabil Ouassini

Yemen represents an interesting case study for counterterrorism. During the last two decades, Yemen has experienced rebellion from armed tribal groups in the North, a threat of secession from former members of the previous government in the South, and a surge of attacks from al-Qaeda. A confluence of political, social, and economic factors has turned Yemen into one of the most fertile grounds for terrorism. Yemen's huge population explosion, high levels of unemployment, dwindling resources, tough geography, and weak central government are a few of the variables that demonstrate why terrorists are determined to turn Yemen into the next battleground in the fight against terrorism. These factors as well as the evolution of the government's relationship with terrorist organizations have complicated Yemen's counterterrorism policy.

HISTORICAL UNREST

Yemen has a long history of conflict stemming from the country's division during the Cold War. There was a strong contrast between the Yemen Arab Republic in the North and its predominantly Shiite tribes and the People's Democratic Republic of Yemen in the South, a Communist state dominated by secular Sunnis. Yemen's present-day predicament started in the 1980s as veterans of the Afghan jihad against the Soviet Union returned to Yemen. During the eventual unification of Yemen in 1990, the government permitted and at times assisted the settlement in Yemen of Arab Afghanis of both Yemeni and non-Yemeni origins at a time when other Arab countries denied them sanctuary. The Arab Afghanis were particularly useful for the government during an attempted secession by the South in 1994. Regrettably, many of these fighters soon turned against the republic as the Islamic state they envisioned did not materialize under President Ali Abdullah Saleh's rule.

It was during the 1990s that the modern wave of terrorism in the forms of bombings, kidnappings, shootings, and various other types of violence manifested itself in Yemen. Among the many attacks aimed at Yemen's fragile economy, government facilities, and religious minorities, as well as its relations with the West, were the kidnappings of British, American, and Australian tourists in 1998 that resulted in the death of four hostages. Along with killing some of the terrorists in the subsequent raid, the Yemeni government also successfully captured and executed the head of the terrorist group that orchestrated the attack. On the first anniversary of his execution, al-Qaeda operatives successfully perpetrated a suicide bombing on the U.S. Navy ship *Cole* in the port of Aden, killing 17 American sailors and injuring 39. There was also the 2002 al-Qaeda attack on a French oil tanker that killed one crew member and spilled over 90,000 barrels of oil into the sea. After a brief period of concord, terrorist activity resumed when 23 al-Qaeda operatives escaped from a prison in Sana'a in 2006. The escape was followed by numerous incidents of violence that included attacks on Spanish tourists in 2007, on the U.S. embassy in 2008, and on South Korean tourists in 2009.

COUNTERTERRORISM STRATEGIES

Yemen's counterterrorism strategies can be attributed to the government's domestic policies and its efforts in regional and international diplomacy. The Yemeni government has integrated a mix of traditional and innovative strategies in its domestic counterterrorism policies. In the traditional strategies of counterterrorism, the Yemeni government has stepped up its capabilities by revamping its armed forces with better training and equipment. The Yemeni government has also taken various measures to improve security along its extensive border with Saudi Arabia as well as its maritime capabilities to detect and respond to various illegal activities including the smuggling of people, money, drugs, weapons, and explosives. Security forces have worked on gaining citizens' support, especially those living in Yemen's remote tribal areas by rewarding them for their loyalty and denial of refuge to any extremists. The Yemeni government has also created a money-laundering intelligence unit in April 2003 and recently adopted a convention to monitor and combat the financing of terrorism (Saleh 2006, 4).

Some of the more innovative counterterrorism strategies in Yemen include the use of mass media in countering Islamic extremism. Recently the Yemeni government supported a new movie called *The Losing Bet* that was designed to educate Yemenis on the negative consequences of terrorism and extremist ideology. Moreover, the Yemeni government has given moderate scholars the power to address and challenge extremist Islamic ideologues through airtime on state-run television, and the delivery of sermons in most mosques, as well as in the creation of new curriculums for schools that advocate a more tolerant version of Islam that defies radical ideology. However, the most innovative component to Yemen's counterterrorism strategy is its program to pursue a path of dialogue and communication with terrorists, the first of its kind in the Arab world.

In 2003, the Yemeni government started to use its Islamic scholars to confront terrorists who were in prison through countrywide theological debates and symposiums. This effort was led by the Islamic scholar and judge Hamoud al-Hatar. Islamic scholars argued that if the terrorists can justify terrorism through the Quran, then they would enlist in their struggle. The debate gave Islamic scholars a chance to share their point of view on extremism with terrorists in an attempt to convince them to renounce terrorism. According to al-Hatar, the dialogues with terrorists center on their views of Yemen's constitutional and penal laws, international treaty obligations, roles and legitimacy of the president, and Muslim relations with non-Muslims (Boucek, Beg, and Horgan 2009, 181–92). After the dialogues, any prisoner who renounces violence becomes eligible to enter an amnesty program designed by President Saleh. The program did not cover the prisoners who were convicted of a terrorist attack. Prisoners sign a document before release and would receive help from the government in seeking employment and at times marriage while they were on probation. There are many criticisms of this program, including the allegation that terrorists simply tell the scholars what they want to hear to be released from prison. Others have argued that the government is really trying to convince terrorists not to launch any terrorist attacks in Yemen. Overall, the Yemeni government considers its innovative counterterrorism program a success.

REGIONAL COOPERATION

A large segment of Yemen's counterterrorism strategies includes regional and international diplomacy. Yemen works closely with neighboring countries on all security issues. Yemen and Saudi Arabia, for example, have established joint patrols to guard their borders. Yemen has signed numerous resolutions and agreements with other Arab governments including Resolution 257 in 1996, approved by the Arab Interior Ministers' Council in Tunis, and the first regional antiterrorism pact issued by the Arab Interior and Justice Ministers' Councils in Cairo in 1998, which promised cooperation between Arab states in exchanging information and denying support for terrorist groups with the exception of Palestinian organizations (Al-Bukaiti 2004). Hamas and the Palestinian Islamic Jihad are recognized by the Yemeni government as legal organizations that maintain offices in Yemen's capital. Yemen has also signed the Convention on Combating Terrorism as a member of the Organization of the Islamic Conference in 1999. Yemen continues to closely cooperate with the United States on a number of issues related to counterterrorism. After the September 11 attacks, the United States and Yemen worked together in a number of counterterrorism endeavors that included the exchange of intelligence as well as the pursuit of many terrorist organizations within Yemen through the use of American special forces, drones, and cruise missiles. Many of Yemen's armed forces continue to receive training in counterterrorism from American special forces. The United States has also given millions in military aid to the

Yemeni government and continues its direct involvement in numerous counterterrorism operations.

A young Nigerian's recent attempt to bomb an American airliner, and his contact with radical scholars in Yemen such as the American-Yemeni Anwar al-Awlaki, indicates the complicated circumstances that Yemen will continue to face. Yemen remains one of the most active training and recruiting grounds for al-Qaeda operatives. Many of these recruits have been found in Afghanistan and Iraq, and the more than 100 Yemenis imprisoned in Guantánamo Bay, Cuba, are an indication of that. Although the Yemeni government has taken a proactive stance against terrorism, its counterterrorism efforts have been complicated by numerous variables that it has yet to address.

CONCLUSION

Future counterterrorism policies need to address some of Yemen's political and socioeconomic problems. Yemen's economic crisis can easily transform it into a failed state, which would ensure al-Qaeda's presence in the country. Apart from its efforts in counterterrorism, the Yemeni government with the international community must work on improving education and human rights, fight unemployment and corruption, and work on political reform to counter the radicalization of a new generation of Yemenis. This is especially true since both the Saudi and Yemeni al-Qaeda groups have currently reconstituted themselves into the new organization al-Qaeda in the Arabian Peninsula.

See also: **Volume 1, Part I:** The Terrorist Threat in the 21st Century: A Global Security Problem; War on Terror

REFERENCES

Al-Bukaiti, Mohamed H. *Yemen's Fight against Terrorism.* Strategy Research Project. Carlisle PA: U.S. Army War College, May 3, 2004. http://www.dtic.mil/cgi-bin/GetTRDoc?AD=ADA424190.

Boucek, Christopher, Shazadi Beg, and John Horgan. "Opening up the Jihadi Debate: Yemen's Committee for Dialogue." In *Leaving Terrorism Behind: Individual and Collective Disengagement,* edited by Tore Bjorgo and John Horgan, 181–92. New York: Routledge, 2009.

Saleh, Taiseer. *Yemen National Strategy to Combat Global Terrorism.* Strategy Research Project. Carlisle, PA: U.S. Army War College, March 15, 2006.

III

Key Issues Impacting Counterterrorism Strategy

Border, Port, and Transportation Security

James Perry

Border, port, and transportation security involves protection of the U.S. land borders with Canada and Mexico, as well as protection of coasts, ports, airports, and the surface transportation system. Such security encompasses protecting against smuggling, interdicting narcotics and illegal aliens, collecting import duties, preventing terrorist acts, and stopping insect pests, plant and animal diseases, and weapons of mass destruction from entering the country. The Department of Homeland Security (DHS) is the federal department responsible for border, port, and transportation security, although federal, state, and local law enforcement agencies also are involved. DHS divides enforcement among the following agencies: Customs and Border Protection (CBP), Immigration and Customs Enforcement (ICE), Citizenship and Immigration Services (USCIS), the Coast Guard (USCG), and the Transportation Security Administration (TSA). Collectively these organizations employ almost 200,000 people and have an annual budget of over $50 billion.

SECURING THE NATION'S BORDERS

Border security primarily entails the monitoring of people and goods as they move through border crossings. This is a massive task. In fiscal year 2007, CBP officers at 326 ports of entry inspected 411 million travelers and more than 120 million cars, trucks, buses, trains, vessels, and aircraft. The land borders outside the official checkpoints are sparsely monitored, even though thousands of illegal aliens cross the border every day. As people from the Middle East have been caught crossing the Mexican and Canadian borders, borders are obvious potential avenues for terrorist infiltration. One jurisdictional problem is that the Department of the Interior, which controls 4.3 million acres of wilderness areas within 100 miles of the Mexican border, hinders CBP access to this land. In 2005, DHS created the Secure Border Initiative to improve border security and customs and immigration enforcement. The program seeks to acquire surveillance technologies to create a "virtual border fence," as well as software and communications to process and disseminate the surveillance information to command centers and vehicles. The Secure Fence Act of 2006 mandated the construction of 700 miles of a high-tech fence, which includes cameras and sensors, in various sectors of the California, Arizona, New Mexico, and Texas borders. CBP and the Coast Guard operate hundreds of vehicles, aircraft, and vessels to monitor land borders, coasts, and airspace, including six Predator B Unmanned Air Systems that began patrolling the northern and southern borders in 2005.

Aircraft and airports are highly attractive targets for terrorists due to the high concentration of people and the spectacular nature of a successful attack. Aviation security involves the security, in the United States alone, of 450 airports and 19,000 public airfields, and the screening of more than 700 million passengers and 550 million pieces of luggage per year. Furthermore, security requires checking the backgrounds of airport and airline employees, denying unauthorized access to airport grounds, and particularly to parked aircraft, and ensuring that air cargo is screened for explosives and other hazards. Aviation security received enormous attention and funding after the 9/11 attacks. The Aviation and Transportation Security Act of 2001 created the TSA, which made screeners federal employees (previously they were contractors hired by the airlines). TSA employs 45,000 screeners as well as air marshals, aviation inspectors, and cargo inspectors. TSA has spent some $800 million on screening technology to prevent passengers from carrying weapons or explosives onto aircraft. A particular concern, after a 2006 terrorist plot was frustrated in Britain, is the improvisation of explosives from small amounts of liquid. Passengers are now restricted in the amounts and types of liquids they can bring aboard an aircraft. In 2009, a Nigerian terrorist on a flight from Amsterdam to Detroit attempted to detonate explosives concealed in his underwear but failed to destroy the plane. In response, TSA installed a large number of "full-body" scanners—ostensibly able to detect bombs under clothing—at U.S. airports and announced that passengers traveling to the United States from 14 "high-risk" nations would undergo extra screening. Cynics have argued that the main effect of post-9/11 aviation security measures has been to provide, at great expense and inconvenience, the illusion of security without actually improving security.

Port security is extremely challenging for a number of reasons: seaports (like airports) are large, easily accessible, and located in cities; they have numerous employees and require a rapid throughput of people and goods. About 95 percent of U.S. foreign trade moves by sea, and more than 5,400 ships, with a total of six million containers, make over 60,000 port calls to the United States each year. Criminals bring narcotics and illegal aliens into the country via the ports. Terrorists could potentially bring chemical, biological, or nuclear weapons into the country though the ports, or they could attack the port system itself, its supporting transportation infrastructure such as bridges or railroads, or related targets such as cruise ships, naval vessels, or oil tankers. Port security jurisdiction is divided between numerous federal, state, and local agencies, which have widely different priorities and levels of expertise and funding.

POST-9/11 SECURITY

Port security measures initiated in the wake of the 9/11 attacks included vulnerability assessments, development of national standards for port security, inspection of containers, prescreening of cargoes, and tracking of ships at sea. As about 90 percent of nonbulk cargo moves by container, and over 12 million containers exist, container security is an obvious concern. In 2002, the CBP launched the Container Security Initiative (CSI) to protect containerized shipping while minimizing the disruption to peaceful trade. CSI identifies high-risk containers, prescreens containers before they are shipped, scans high-risk containers with X-ray machines and radiation detectors, and seeks to identify containers that have been opened in transit. As of 2010, 58 ports worldwide cooperate with CSI teams to inspect containers overseas before they are shipped. The Maritime Transportation Security Act of 2002 required U.S. ports and vessels to conduct vulnerability assessments and develop security plans, and established committees to coordinate federal, state, and local port security agencies. This act also required many types of vessels operating in the navigable waters of the United States to carry automatic identification systems that supply the vessel's identification, course, speed, and position to maritime authorities. The principal use of automatic identification systems is to prevent collisions. The 2006 SAFE Port Act included provisions for background checks of port workers, long-range vessel tracking, port security training and exercises, radiation detection and imaging, inspection of car ferries and containers, and the creation of the Domestic Nuclear Detection Office. In 2008, DHS launched the Small Vessel Security Strategy to reduce the vulnerability of large vessels to waterside attacks from small vessels and to detect nuclear materials on small vessels.

To defend against nuclear terrorism, the United States plans to install some 1,400 advanced detectors at 370 border crossings and ports; 825 scanners are operational in 2010. In 2007, Congress mandated the scanning of all U.S.-bound cargo containers at more than 600 foreign ports by July 2012. In 2009, 80 percent of incoming containers were scanned. Large-scale

X-ray and gamma ray machines and radiation detection devices can detect nuclear materials or other contraband without opening the container. Inspectors also use handheld radiation detection devices, as well as dogs capable of identifying narcotics, bulk currency, human beings, explosives, agricultural pests, and chemical weapons. Two major concerns with these detectors are reducing the number of "false positives" (the detector wrongly sounds the alarm when nothing suspicious is in the container) and "false negatives" (the detector fails to sound the alarm when something suspicious is in the container).

Transportation security relates not merely to airports and seaports but also to roads, railroads, bridges, tunnels, pipelines, and public transportation such as buses, subways, and ferries. There are hundreds of thousands of potential targets, both fixed and mobile (such as fuel tankers and HAZMAT trucks), and a wide range of federal, state, local, and private sector organizations with security responsibilities. The attacks on Madrid in 2004, London in 2005, and Mumbai in 2006 indicate that public transportation is an attractive terrorist target. Both the surface transportation network and the other networks that depend on it, such as energy, communications, and manufacturing, require maximum possible free movement of goods, services, and people. Given the practical impossibility of protecting every target and of screening passengers, workers, and cargo in surface transportation systems, only selected "high-value" transportation nodes can be hardened against attack.

CONCLUSION

For other targets, DHS seeks to share intelligence among security partners, increase security awareness, and enhance the resilience of the system to permit rapid recovery from a terrorist attack. Executive Order 13416 of December 2006 ordered DHS to assess the security of surface transportation, to identify security gaps, to draft security guidelines, and to develop a process for monitoring compliance with those guidelines. The 9/11 Commission Act of 2007 authorized TSA, among other measures, to deploy "visible response" teams to augment transportation security, to train "explosives detection canine teams," to develop transportation security plans and conduct training exercises, to evaluate the risks of terrorist attacks on railroads, to upgrade the security of the passenger and freight rail system, and to enhance the security of the pipeline and hazardous materials transportation systems. As of 2009, however, the Government Accountability Office considered that the TSA still faced considerable challenges in implementing the provisions of this act.

See also: **Volume 1, Part III:** Target Hardening; U.S. Immigration Policies: Impact on Moderate Muslims. **Part IV:** International Legal Framework to Eliminate Terrorism against Civil Aviation and Maritime Targets. **Part VI:** Protecting Critical Infrastructure: Government/Private Sector Alliance

REFERENCES

Haveman, Jon D., and Howard J. Shatz. *Protecting the Nation's Seaports: Balancing Security and Cost.* San Francisco: Public Policy Institute of California, 2006.

"Implementing Recommendations of the 9/11 Commission Act of 2007." Public Law no. 110-53. August 3, 2007. http://intelligence.senate.gov/laws/pl11053.pdf.

U.S. Customs and Border Protection. "Container Security Initiative 2006–2011 Strategic Plan." October 7, 2011. http://www.cbp.gov/xp/cgov/trade/cargo_security/csi/

U.S. Department of Homeland Security. "Transportation Systems: Critical Infrastructure and Key Resources." May 2007. http://www.dhs.gov/xlibrary/assets/nipp-ssp-transportation.pdf.

U.S. Government Accountability Office. "Transportation Security: Key Actions Have Been Taken to Enhance Mass Transit and Passenger Rail Security, but Opportunities Exist to Strengthen Federal Strategy and Programs." GAO-09–678, June 2009. http://www.gao.gov/new.items/d09678.pdf.

U.S. Government Accountability Office. "Maritime Security: DHS Progress and Challenges in Key Areas of Port Security." GAO-10–940T, July 2010. http://www.gao.gov/new.items/d10940t.pdf.

White House. "Surface Transportation Security Priority Assessment." March 2010. http://www.whitehouse.gov/sites/default/files/rss_viewer/STSA.pdf.

Combating Terrorist Recruitment, Propaganda, and Radicalization Campaigns

Nur Azlin Mohamed Yasin and Gloria Spittel

Recruitment, propaganda, and radicalization campaigns are the dissemination of information and knowledge by terrorists and their supporters and sympathizers. Terrorists use propaganda to convey their worldview or their ideology. Ideology is a simple way of describing the past, the present, and the desired future, and who is preventing that future from occurring. This is meant to attract people to support the cause and ultimately fight for it. Propaganda is also used to build a support base of sympathizers, financiers and other propagandists, and all the people who are essential for the survival of the terrorist organization. However, the ultimate end goal of propaganda is obtaining new recruits. This depicts a linear progression beginning with propaganda and leading to recruitment after radicalization. However, it is also likely that these processes are mutually dependent on each other and work in a continuous loop, thus supporting the claim that individuals who are influenced by terrorist propaganda are those who are already radicalized to some extent, thus ignoring the plethora of alternate views while seeking terrorist communiqués. Regardless of whether these components work in a linear or a cyclical manner, the main function is to inform the public. As such, we assert that a method to tackle terrorist propaganda, radicalization, and recruitment would be the use of a communication model to initially situate the threat, identify the weak points, and thereafter organize the best point at which to counter the threat of terrorist communication online.

SITUATING AND IDENTIFYING THE THREAT USING A COMMUNICATION MODEL

For al-Qaeda communications, the Internet is a particularly key facilitator of jihad. For them the message is that we are in a struggle ordained by God and we are winning. All good Muslims, those who follow al-Qaeda's understanding of Islam, should join the fight as it is their religious duty. The best way to understand what al-Qaeda is attempting is to apply Shannon's (1948) model of communication. The elements, which have been modified over time, consist of the source, message, signal, destination, transmitter/receiver, and noise; these have undergone various revisions in communication theory and include additional elements such as feedback, all of which are commonly utilized.

The feedback component in the model depicts the interactive communication heralded with the advent and avid use of the Internet for communication over multiple platforms such as chat services, e-mail, forums, and social networking sites, whose use has been popularized and effectively leveraged by jihadists. Extremist materials, from emotional poems glorifying those regarded as mujahideen to hacking manuals, are disseminated even more effectively with the availability of these forums. Extremist propaganda in Arabic, for instance, can influence people in Southeast Asia, the United States, and United Kingdom through English and Bahasa Indonesian forums. The interactive nature of forums overcomes language barriers as articles are shared, translated, and reposted, all by the forum participants. A collective understanding emerging from the forum helps crystallize the acceptance of the extremist message by an individual. The noise component of the model is usually a secondary technical glitch that impedes effective communication, assuming that the sender and receiver have similar skill sets in encoding and decoding messages across a reliable medium. However, *noise* is also an overarching term to describe the interrupter that prevents the sending of an effective message. As such, effective communication is concerned with the reduction of noise.

The message may be encoded in many formats including video and music and distributed over many media, but popularly over the Internet because of its accessibility, affordability, anonymity, and ease of use. Jihadist followers have also quickly adapted to a more interactive forum including individual blogs and chat rooms. They rally against free speech but exploit it by hosting their sites in the West on free international domains such as Wordpress, Blogspot, and Multiply.

ORGANIZED NOISE

Noise affects the sender, the receiver, and the message/medium; as such, it follows that combating terrorism in its communicative form could be conducted in each of these processes. This would be the first dimension considered. The second dimension is the nature of the material transferred, that is, whether the information is verbal or enhanced with multimedia including pictures and videos.

The goal in combating terrorism communication is to ensure an oppositional reading of the information, or a negotiated reading, against the dominant reading propagated by the sender of the message (Hall 2001, 174–75). The most effective way of countering terrorism would be to negate the source and prevent the sender from sending the message. Two issues are pertinent with this tactic: First, the sender will find alternate avenues including the media, pseudonyms, or simply the use of a proxy to send the message on his or her behalf. Second, in many democratic nations preventing individual communication is the prevention of free speech—a fundamental human right. The same issues are applicable to the receiver. It would be nearly impossible to prevent access to Internet content. Even in the unlikely event that the principle of free speech is abandoned the sender would have a plethora of media to choose from as computer technology becomes increasingly ubiquitous. Combating terrorism at this juncture and through such methods would not bring favorable results.

Combating terrorism at the message and medium can occur in two ways. The first is by creating multiple messages that are confusing, contradictory, or not germane. This is achievable only if the communications networks are identified and can be infiltrated. Second, while not strictly noise, one can block the message from leaving the source or from reaching the recipient. Again this assumes their network is known, or at least that there are complicated algorithms in place to detect suspicious communications even if the source is unknown. If it is, then there are issues of privacy violations and other potential infringement of rights. Excessive use of intercepts can and does cause community backlash and may create barriers to using communication monitoring and intercepts that will hamper security.

NOISY STRATEGY

Counterterrorism strategy needs to identify how to respond; that is, the source, medium, message, and potential receivers need to be understood and the nature of the message recognized. These two steps are necessary to design a preemptive or reactive countermeasure.

The reactive approach requires the countermeasures to provide material to counter claims made by the terrorists. This is usually termed *counterideology*. However, counterideology in itself would not succeed, as it may seem to pit itself one-on-one against the terrorist. Rather, the type of information that should be produced to counter claims should be integral and draw on the authority of reputed sources, factual to a point where it is not merely refuting terrorist claims. Engaging discussants on forums would also require patience and diplomacy. It would be important to refrain from acting superior but instead to engage in dialogue and "learning" discussions, a variant of "contaminating" the discussion forum with counterideology.

Preemptive measures would be harder to produce and may actually provide the sender of the message a "first-mover advantage" where the receiver's attention is up for grabs. Unlike in a physical security context, terrorist communication activity is largely nonviolent although the communiqués may espouse and herald violence. However, preemptive measures would revolve around the readiness of the counterterrorist to respond to messages and know the direction in which a particular forum or email thread is leading, or the responses to an article, video, or photograph. This is achieved by passively monitoring sites. Other preemptive measures to combat terrorist propaganda, recruitment, and radicalization may provide fodder for the terrorists, as mentioned previously, and are best employed as a part of a multipronged strategy involving military action, legislative initiatives, and law enforcement measures.

CONCLUSION

We have charted a course for combating terrorism propaganda, recruitment, and radicalization campaigns online by using a communication model to identify the best point at which to respond. Effective communication is necessarily the delivery of a message from the sender to the receiver in its intended form. Counterideology attempts in the past have been preemptive but rarely engage participants because they do not achieve the same technical efficacy as the terrorists. Disrupting effective communication is necessary to combat terrorism communication, and this is best done by employing a strategy of noise. A strategy of noise is best as it encompasses the communication process in its entirety, rather than only targeting the sender, receiver, or message. A strategy of noise requires the counterterrorist to provide a steady stream of factually correct information bolstered by a continuous process of engagement and dialogue, matching the efficacy and efficiency of terrorist communication. This ultimately should provide a steady and strong alternate viewpoint, readily accessible and al-lowing receivers to negotiate the sender's message with the intention of forming an oppositional reading.

See also: **Volume 1, Part I:** Concept of Islamist Jihad. **Part III:** Ideology That Spawns Islamist Militancy; Terrorism, Counterterrorism, and the Internet; Terrorist Recruitment in Correctional Institutions. **Part VI:** Rehabilitation of Extremists: Methods and Practice

REFERENCES

Bailey, Timothy D., and Grimaila, Michael R. "Running the Blockade: Information Technology, Terrorism, and the Transformation of Islamic Mass Culture." *Terrorism and Political Violence* 18, no. 4 (2006): 524–43.

Hall, Stuart. "Encoding/Decoding." In *Media and Cultural Studies Keyworks*, edited by Meenakshi Gigi Durham and Douglas Kellne, 166–77. Malden, MA: Wiley-Blackwell, 2001.

Martin, John L. "The Media's Role in International Terrorism. *Studies in Conflict and Terrorism* 8, no. 2 (1985): 127–46.

Nacos, Brigitte L. "Communication and Recruitment of Terrorists." In *The Making of a Terrorist: Recruitment, Training and Root Causes*, edited by James J.F. Forest, 41–52. Westport, CT: Praeger, 2005.

Shannon, C.E. "A Mathematical Theory of Communication." *Bell System Technical Journal* 27 (1948): 379–423, 623–56.

Weimann, Gabriel. "Terrorist Dot Com: Using the Internet for Terrorist Recruitment and Mobilization." In *The Making of a Terrorist: Recruitment, Training and Root Causes*, edited by James J.F. Forest, 53–65. Westport, CT: Praeger, 2005.

Whine, Michael. "Cyberspace—A New Medium for Communication, Command and Control by Extremists." *Studies in Conflict and Terrorism* 22, no. 3 (1999): 231–45.

Countering Terrorism: Law Enforcement or Military Problem?

Matthew C. DuPée and Nathan A. Minami

The emerging threat posed to the greater international community is char-acterized by a shifting dynamic in the global security environment, one that is increasingly fused with terrorism, crime, and weak or failed states whose financial ties are bound through local and global enterprise. Russian organized crime groups are transferring antiaircraft missiles, small arms, and ammunition to rebels in Colombia in exchange for tens of thousands of kilograms of cocaine for distribution in the former Soviet Union (Bagley 2001, 17–18). Mexican drug cartels are powerful enough to "purchase" an entire regiment of the Mexican armed forces to be used as enforcers and to assassinate rival cartel operatives (Manwaring 2009, 17–19). Several semiautonomous quasicriminal states like Ciudad de Este in Paraguay have emerged over the last decade, where drug traffickers, Chinese *triads*, Japanese *yakuza*, and international terrorist organizations like al-Qaeda and Hezbollah operate and conduct business together (Robinson 2000, 13).

COMPLEX SECURITY ENVIRONMENT

These are a few examples of the complex security environment in which terrorist movements are incubated and thrive. "Terrorist groups like Al Qaeda and Hezbollah are becoming hybrids: one part terrorist group, one part drug trafficking. It's all about the money," Michael Braun, the former assistant administrator and chief of operations at the Drug Enforcement Administration, told reporters in 2008. "It's meaner and uglier than anything law enforcement has ever encountered" (Fosson 2008).

Despite the emerging threat posed by asymmetrical intrastate war zones and hybrid terror-crime networks, there is a basic disagreement among academics and the professions of political science and criminology on whether counterterrorism is a law enforcement or a military priority. The ongoing symbiosis between transnational criminal organizations, terrorist movements, and domestic insurgent or revolutionary groups blurs the line where crime and war intersect. A similar conundrum faces policymakers, who struggle to agree on how to properly deal with the issues associated with terrorism: are military countermeasures better situated to handle the threat, or is terrorism better treated as a law enforcement issue?

Just as the illicit drug industry posed a series of challenges to sovereign governments in the 1970s and 1980s, terrorism creates a similar legal and military conundrum in today's contemporary environment, or, as some analysts suggest, the world functions as "a global village without a police department" (Buruma 2004 304). This divide manifests into "bureaucratic divisions between law enforcement and national security" (Cornell 2007, 211), creating "the perception that crime is a domestic problem, and that law enforcement and national security are based on very different philosophies, organizational structures, and legal frameworks" (Williams 1994, 96).

The type of asymmetrical threat to a state, in this case terrorism, also plays a major role in the delineation of responsibilities among military or law enforcement entities. The increasing symbiotic relationship between traditional terrorist organizations and transnational organized crime groups continues to pose a serious challenge to the global community, and the integration and cooperation among terrorist organizations and domestic insurgent or revolutionary movements have also muddied the waters for security and law enforcement efforts. The narco-terror nexus, or the broader crime-terror nexus, is an excellent example of the evolution of terrorism in the age of globalization. Beginning in the late 1970s, insurgent and terrorist connections to illicit activity like narcotics production emerged as a result of the worldwide expansion in the demand for drugs, which has opened up new opportunities for what might be considered nontraditional suppliers. This includes political parties, terrorist organizations, revolutionary movements, and even some sovereign governments (Steinitz 1985). Although the trend of criminal and drug trafficking organizations creating strategic partnerships with terrorist and armed political groups to boost profits or enhance military capabilities emerged in South America during the 1980s, the trend continues to hamper international efforts to combat the threat of global terrorism and is prevalent in several contemporary conflict zones such as Iraq and Afghanistan. For instance, the role of organized crime is a severely misunderstood dimension of the Iraq conflict, and as Williams (2009, 11) suggests, both criminal enterprises and criminal activities have a profound debilitating effect on reconstruction and development ventures. This acts as a political and economic spoiler and facilitates armed clashes over territory vital to criminal markets.

BUILDING MUTUAL COOPERATION

Within the parameters of a legal framework, cooperation between law enforcement agencies on both national and international levels is critical to counterterrorism operations because research has shown that most terrorist groups end either due to them joining the political process or due to the success of law enforcement and intelligence agencies in arresting or killing key leaders (Jones and Libicki 2008). While America and the international community have made some notable efforts to attack the growing threat of international terrorism, there has been only limited success. At best, current efforts are merely serving to disrupt the nexus and have failed to decisively neutralize it. In addition, there has not been a concerted international effort to attack the nexus specifically, as most programs focus on either criminals or terrorists but not the areas where these two types of organizations are linked together. The advantage of focusing at the point where criminals and terrorists intersect is that these efforts will have a synergistic affect against both criminals and terrorists, neutralizing the symbiotic relationship that exists between the two entities. In accomplishing this, cooperation between international and domestic law enforcement agencies is critical. There must be focus on the diplomatic level to build trust and strong international relationships between countries, which will establish the conditions for strong law enforcement partnerships and intelligence sharing. Mutual respect is critical in building this trust, and outreach and exchange programs on all levels can help to achieve this. Finally, more funding is needed to enhance the ability of U.S. law enforcement agencies to expand overseas and build the strong partnerships that are requisite to defeating the global criminal-terrorist nexus.

It logically follows that countering terrorism is neither a military nor a law enforcement problem; it is a national and international problem. In order to achieve success in thwarting terrorist efforts in their attacks against America, multiagency approaches are needed that combine the diverse skill sets available in the Department of Defense, Department of Homeland Security, Department of Justice, Central Intelligence Agency, local law enforcement, and many other agencies (Wise and Rania 2006). A strong argument can even be made that the Department of State should play a lead role in combating terrorism as in many ways this department is most capable of working with our international allies to address the root causes of terrorism such as the Middle East peace process and the perceived unfairness of U.S. and Western policies around the world, as well as poverty and a lack of political participation in many Muslim countries. The challenge in accomplishing this is overcoming traditional bureaucratic turf battles and competition over resources by promoting or assigning proven team players to key leadership positions within all of the pertinent agencies.

CONCLUSION

The activities of criminal syndicates, transnational mafias, revolutionary insurgent movements, and global terrorist groups continue to thrive off illegal activities and transactions while they harbor their assets in failed, failing, or weak states. Law enforcement assets responsible for maintaining internal security, stability, and social control play a key role in combating terrorism and organized crime in their own jurisdictions but still lack the necessary resources for increasing their cooperation with global partners and military assets. International and domestic intelligence operations have been separated from law enforcement and operate in separate spheres, and responses to failing, failed, or weak states have traditionally been the responsibility of the diplomatic and military services (Sullivan and Weston 2008, 293). Ultimately, this is a complex problem, and it will require both active and passive measures to solve it, if that is even possible. While the Constitution and common law have traditionally argued for a clear separation between law enforcement and the military, only a unified effort among agencies and a sense of cooperation will allow the United States to secure its borders against terrorism for the foreseeable future (Khademian 2006).

See also: **Volume 1, Part III:** Defensive Measures against Terrorism: Military Preemption and Retaliation; Intelligence Sharing and Law Enforcement Cooperation between Nations; Military Force: Effective against Terrorists?; Preemption: Moral and Ethical Considerations. **Part IV:** Ethical and Legal Issues in Democratic Societies: National Security and Civil Liberties. **Part VI:** Need for Empirical Research on the Effectiveness of Counterterrorism Strategies; Threat Convergence

REFERENCES

Bagley, Bruce M. "Globalization and Transnational Organized Crime: The Russian Mafia in Latin America and the Caribbean." Paper published by the School of International Studies at the University of Miami, November 15, 2001. http://www.as.miami.edu/international-studies/pdf/Bagley%20 GLOBALIZATION%202.pdf.

Buruma, Ybo. "Drugs and Transnational Organized Crime." In *The Political Economy of the Drug Industry: Latin America and the International System,* edited by Menno Vellinga, 306–18. Gainesville: University Press of Florida, 2004.

Cornell, Svante E. "Narcotics and Armed Conflict: Interaction and Implications." *Studies in Conflict and Terrorism* 30, no. 3 (2007): 207–27.

Fosson, Adam. "Confluence of Evil: The Smuggling-Terrorism Nexus." *Homeland Security Today* 5, no. 12 (2008): 24–29. http://www.hstoday.us/index. php?id=483&cHash=081010&tx_ttnews[tt_news]=6099.

Jones, Seth G., and Martin C. Libicki. *How Terrorist Groups End: Lessons for Countering Al Qaida.* Santa Monica, CA: RAND, 2008.

Khademian, Anne M. "The Politics of Homeland Security." In *The McGraw-Hill Homeland Security Handbook,* edited by David G. Kamien, 1091–114. New York: McGraw-Hill, 2006.

Manwaring, Max G. *A "New" Dynamic in the Western Hemisphere Security Environment: The Mexican Zetas and Other Private Armies.* Carlisle, PA: Strategic Studies Institute, 2009.

Robinson, Jeffery. *The Merger: The Conglomeration of International Organized Crime.* London: Olverlook, 2000.

Steinitz, Mark S. "Insurgents, Terrorists and the Drug Trade." *Washington Quarterly,* Fall 1985, 141–53.

Sullivan, John P., and Keith Weston. "Law Enforcement Response Strategies for Criminal States and Criminal Soldiers." In *Criminal States and Criminal Soldiers,* edited by Robert J. Bunker, 287–300. New York: Routledge, 2008.

Williams, Phil. "Transnational Criminal Organizations and International Security." *Survival* 36, no. 1 (1994): 96–113.

Williams, Phil. *Criminals, Militias, and Insurgents: Organized Crime in Iraq.* Carlisle, PA: Strategic Studies Institute, 2009.

Wise, Charles, and Nader Rania. "Accountability and Homeland Security." In *The McGraw-Hill Homeland Security Handbook,* edited by David G. Kamien, 1115–30. New York: McGraw-Hill, 2006.

Countering Weapons
of Mass Destruction (WMD)

Thomas E. Baker

On September 11, 2001, our nation witnessed two hijacked airliners crash into the twin towers of the New York World Trade Center. Only minutes later, a third hijacked plane struck the Pentagon, while a fourth hijacked airliner, United Airlines Flight 93, crashed in a remote Pennsylvania field. These terrorist attacks against the United States raised immediate concerns about future assaults involving chemical, biological, nuclear, or radiological weapons of mass destruction (WMD).

The threat of *atomic* WMD declined after the end of the Cold War and the collapse of the former Soviet Union. However, previous threats of nation-states linger, and weapons, including "suitcase" nuclear weapons, submarines, and missiles, remain available. However, most recently, the threat is emerging from nonstate actors, specifically terrorist organizations. Hence, biological, chemical, and radiological contamination agents are becoming more of a concern as possible terrorist weapons.

Accurate intelligence/criminal information is the first line of defense in protecting the United States against WMD attacks. Addressing WMD prevention and intervention strategies requires excellent intelligence analysis and antiterrorism and counterintelligence approaches. In addition, federal, state, local, and tribal governments must plan and train for exceptional incident responses and case investigations. Successful preparedness issues include crisis management planning, first-responder training, and the appropriate protective equipment. The majority of credible threat investigations center on biological and chemical agents.

DEFINING COUNTERTERRORISM

Confusion emerges regarding basic terrorism concepts. The counterterrorism model includes two phases: (1) proactive and (2) reactive. Effective *antiterrorism* demands a proactive planning approach, while *counterterrorism* is reactive and requires tactical applications. The proactive phase requires government and law enforcement antiterrorism intervention measures that reduce the probability of a terrorist action unfolding. During the proactive phase, intelligence gathering includes threat analysis and planning that sets the stage for prevention. Basic terrorist and crime prevention measures assist in target-hardening techniques to reduce target vulnerability. These procedures help implement corrective procedures. Proactive strategic planning and training represent essential components of the assessment strategies for countering terrorism.

Counterterrorism consists of remedial measures taken to respond to an ongoing terrorist incident. This activity is tactical; however, the success of the operation depends on effective intelligence. Successful execution during the terrorist event stage depends on proper planning and training prior to the event. Therefore, counterterrorism is the reactive and tactical phase of countering terrorism.

THREAT ANALYSIS

Threat assessment and analysis expose terrorist threat vulnerabilities. Threat analysis identifies security weaknesses, the means by which that vulnerability could lead to a successful terrorist operation, and the consequences. After the threat analysis, the development of potential scenarios and brainstorming are used to identify related problem-solving and planning outcomes. Analysts "think like terrorists," constantly updating intelligence/criminal information to improve the security posture. Nuclear power plants necessitate a first-priority status because terrorists could turn them into nuclear weapons.

State-sponsored and nonaligned terrorist groups represent the greatest potential nuclear threat to the United States. However, Iran and North Korea represent state nuclear threats. The range of terrorists capable of using WMD includes not only radical Islamist terrorists but also extremist elements of right-wing groups, lone wolf offenders, nonaligned terrorists, cult groups of the doomsday variety, and insurgent groups.

While terrorists are likely to use conventional strategies such as bombings, traditional weapons are available in the black market and through state sponsorship. State sponsors of terrorism and some nations continue to express interest in WMD. There, a concentration exists in acquiring nuclear weapons, as well as chemical and biological agents.

BIOLOGICAL, CHEMICAL, AND NUCLEAR WEAPONS

Biological agents are toxins capable of creating various diseases. Anthrax and bubonic plague are biological agents that can cause massive casualties and can be spread with diverse dissemination methods that are difficult to detect. In most cases of biological agents, symptoms do not unfold or appear for 24 to 60 hours after initial exposure. First responders would not detect obvious clues, making it initially difficult to respond to the terrorists' use of biological agents. There are many avenues for dispersion and easy access to vulnerable citizens.

Nuclear waste offers opportunities to contaminate large residential areas, which would cause a public panic. The deployment of an improvised nuclear device would be a likely secondary scenario. Radiation is colorless, tasteless, and odorless; moreover, its detection and identification require specialized instruments. Exposure to radiation does not produce immediate symptoms. Therefore, the radiation damage may be more insidious over a protracted period. The nuclear waste scenario is problematic for first responders. They could not respond properly to provide an immediate remedial response without prior knowledge and radiological equipment indicators.

Chemical agents are the WMD scenario where first responders are most likely to be reasonably able to recognize and react properly in a timely manner. The chemicals include sarin, as well as many of the chemical agents used during warfare. These chemicals are presently available in industry, including chlorine, phosgene, and cyanide. Most of these chemicals are colorless, odorless, and tasteless; however, the primary indicators are the immediate victim symptoms. Adequate first-responder training offers opportunities for prompt identification of the chemical and a fast remedial response.

Police, fire, and emergency personnel serve as first responders. Selected, trained, and equipped first-responder personnel are essential to meeting the WMD emergency. Their equipment would include protective clothing, agent-monitoring equipment, personnel decontamination equipment, and medical supplies for preliminary treatment of WMD exposure. Prior training would preferably include learning simulation scenarios, including establishing contamination control zones.

The crisis management mode requires front-end and consequence planning. Crisis management provides proactive measures to identify resources that are necessary to anticipate, prevent, or resolve a terrorist threat or incident. Resources and logistical supplies must have direct support applications. Consequence management requires estimating the damage, loss, and psychological hardship caused by the terrorist incident to citizens and property. In addition, consequence management necessitates measures to protect public health and safety. The goal is to restore essential government services and provide emergency relief to those affected: governments, businesses, and citizens.

First responders are in the best position for a proactive counterintelligence response. They provide the initial on-the-ground intelligence/criminal information. The flow of information allows law enforcement agencies to initiate the appropriate preplanned counterintelligence response.

INTELLIGENCE-LED POLICING

Intelligence data and analysis greatly enhance the mission of law enforcement. The threat of terrorism and diminished homeland security have driven intelligence-led policing (ILP) onto center stage. Occasionally, ILP is referred to as *intelligence-driven policing;* ILP forms the basis for formulating strategic intelligence. Strategic intelligence may lead to operational tactics that target specific domestic and international terrorist activities.

The ILP management philosophy centralizes intelligence reporting and serves as the primary mechanism for law enforcement executive decision making. ILP is a collaborative philosophy concerned with intelligence/criminal information that improves the understanding of the operational environment. The key components of this process include the creation of tactical, operational, and strategic intelligence products. These intelligence-reporting systems support immediate needs, promote immediate situational awareness, and provide the foundation for longer-term planning.

INTELLIGENCE ANALYSTS

Defining an analyst's role is complicated because the associated professional discipline continues to unfold. An analyst's position is associated with a variety of professional skills and talents. The development of ILP terrorist requirements mandates reorganization of law enforcement procedures and analyst role requirements. The framework for intelligence analysis answers three questions:

1. Who are the terrorists?
2. Where and when will the attacks take place?
3. How will the terrorists attack?

The analyst's role requires multitasking and thriving performance in a rapidly changing terrorist environment. The new role under the ILP philosophy suggests escalating responsibilities and collaboration throughout the law enforcement agency. Requirements for coordination with commanders, middle management, sergeants, officers, and detectives have increased considerably.

Analysts are primarily responsible for developing intelligence products that coordinate the information needs of internal and external customers. Strategic and tactical products require decisive thinking across staff and line operations. Intelligence products must assist in countering terrorist events and preventing successful terrorist strategies. Counterintelligence for tactical, operational, and logistical requirements must be succinct and timely.

This formidable terrorist test requires converting data into a useful format and convincing others of the significance and merits of ideas. Moreover, supplying intelligence to rightful customers is the eventual objective. Analysts refine the intelligence product and determine the needs of consumers through consultation and feedback. In addition, they brief commanders with reference to operational areas of terrorist activities and possible strategic and tactical outcomes.

Basic intelligence analyst responsibilities include collecting information or data from open and closed sources, followed by targeting known terrorist organizations and criminals. Raw data or information is not police intelligence. The *collection process* is the initial step, followed by *critical analysis*, conducted by a trained professional capable of critical thinking. *Problem solving* is the third step, and the final step is proper *dissemination* of intelligence, to those who have the need and right to acquire terrorist data.

The National Criminal Intelligence Sharing Plan recommends that every law enforcement agency incorporate the minimum standards for intelligence requirements for law enforcement agencies. This federal agency provides guidance for information sharing and the blueprint for building an intelligence system. In addition, the plan provides a model for intelligence-sharing procedures. Federal, state, local, and tribal law enforcement agencies serve as primary sources for terrorism intelligence. First responders are on the frontlines of the feedback loop. Once the WMD incident occurs, first responders are center stage.

CONCLUSION

The terrorist threat is imminent; intelligence analysts must think critically. Basic intelligence analysis strategies offer opportunities for preventing and countering acts of terrorism. Strategies for preempting terrorism require nontraditional investigative strategies and intelligence procedures. Knowledge is power; "knowing your enemy," including their strategies and tactics, applies to antiterrorism and counterterrorism planning. One must plan and train for possible WMD events. Terrorists will seize the initiative, if nations fail to seize the moment. ILP provides the means to prevent, intervene in, and respond to terrorism.

REFERENCES

Aman, Michael. *Preventing Terrorist Suicide Attacks*. Sudbury, MA: Jones and Bartlett, 2007.

Baker, Thomas E. *Intelligence-Led Policing: Leadership Strategies and Tactics*. New York: Looseleaf Law Publications, 2009.

Borgesson, Kevin, and Robin Valeri. *Terrorism in America*. Sudbury, MA: Jones and Bartlett, 2009.

Bunn, Mathew. *Nuclear Terrorism: A Strategy for Prevention*. Cambridge, MA: MIT Press, 2010.

Gallant, Brian J. *Essentials in Emergency Management: Including the All-Hazards-Approach*. Lanham, MD: Scarecrow, 2008.

Howard, Russell D., and James J.F. Forest, eds. *Weapons of Mass Destruction and Terrorism*. Guilford, CT: McGraw-Hill, 2007.

Sachs, Gordon M. *Terrorism Emergency Response: A Workbook for Responders*. Upper Saddle River, NY: Prentice-Hall, 2003.

Counterterrorism Training

Michael B. Kraft

A tremendous variety of training programs are conducted by the U.S. government to deter, defeat, capture, and prosecute terrorists. They range from SWAT teams being trained to use sophisticated techniques against hostage takers, to first responders at the scene of terrorist attacks, accidents, and major natural disasters, to dogs trained to sniff out explosives. Other programs train accountants and banking officials to counter terrorism financing, and scientists to detect dangerous biological agents, whether spread deliberately or not.

COUNTERTERRORISM TRAINING PROGRAMS

Some of the training programs predate the emergence of international terrorism in the 1970s and 1980s. These programs are "dual use," for example, training law enforcement officers to handle hostage situations regardless of the perpetrators' motivation since first responders' skills are useful in a wide variety of scenarios. Various U.S. government agencies have also developed specific counterterrorism training programs. Courses are offered at various levels for federal, state, and local officials and also for the security personnel of friendly foreign countries. The offices and training programs involved in this major domestic and international training effort are too numerous to list here; however, the following descriptions illustrate the scope and types of programs, many of them little known.

At the suggestion of the interagency Terrorism Training Working Group, a website titled *Counter-terrorism Training and Resources for Law Enforcement* was created to provide training and planning resource links for law enforcement officials to survey. A selected illustrative list of training programs and providers follows.

U.S. DEPARTMENT OF JUSTICE

The Department of Justice helps other countries that seek assistance in drafting legislation to criminalize money laundering and financial and other material support to terrorists. It also provides technical assistance and training to implement and enforce these laws. Key Justice Department components that contribute to this process include the Criminal Division's Asset Forfeiture and Money Laundering Section, the Office of Overseas Prosecutorial Development Assistance and Training, and the Counterterrorism Section.

The Office of Overseas Prosecutorial Development Assistance and Training, which receives funding through the State Department, is instrumental in the planning, staffing, and delivery of international training and technical assistance regarding financial crime. With State Department funding assistance, the office also placed Justice Department resident legal advisors in East Africa, the Horn of Africa, the Middle East, and South Asia.

The Asset Forfeiture and Money Laundering Section designs and delivers both training and technical assistance, particularly with respect to the threat of money laundering and asset-forfeiture issues. The Counterterrorism Section focus on terrorism issues and terrorist financing. These three offices often draw on the expertise of U.S. attorneys to help design and deliver the assistance. The Drug Enforcement Administration and Federal Bureau of Investigation (FBI) headquarters and field agents also participate in the design and delivery of both training and technical assistance in connection with financial crimes, including terrorist financing, money laundering, and asset forfeiture. Additionally, the FBI National Academy at Quantico, Virginia, provides courses for leaders and managers of state and local police, sheriffs' departments, military police organizations, and federal law enforcement agencies. Foreign law enforcement students also attend the academy, located on the grounds of the sprawling U.S. Marines base. Four classes a year of about 250 officers each take college and graduate-level courses in a variety of areas, such as law, behavioral science, forensic science, terrorism/terrorist mindsets, leadership development, and communications.

The Justice Department's State and Local Anti-terrorism Training program, funded by its Bureau of Justice Assistance, provides state, local, and tribal law enforcement personnel with specialized preincident training and resources to combat terrorism and extremist criminal activity. On-site, customized training is offered to about 10,000 participants annually. The program also provides online training and resources, including information on current terrorist and criminal extremist issues. Finally, the Justice Department's Bureau of Alcohol, Tobacco, Firearms and Explosives is the federal agency primarily responsible for enforcing federal laws pertaining to destructive devices (bombs), explosives, and arson. The bureau provides training in bomb detection, including the training of sniffer dogs, and the safe disposal of explosives. The bureau has also trained explosives detection dogs for foreign counties.

U.S. DEPARTMENT OF HOMELAND SECURITY

The Department of Homeland Security's training and technical assistance programs provide a variety of specialized training. The Federal Law Enforcement Center serves as an interagency law enforcement training organization for 88 federal agencies. The 40-year-old agency also provides services to state, local, tribal, and international law enforcement agencies. In 2009, the center provided training to 67,244 students, of whom 5,033 were from state and local agencies and 914 from other countries.

The main facility at Glynco, Georgia, is a 1,600-acre campus with 18 firearms ranges and a sprawling complex of driver training ranges, an explosives range, and a fully functional mock port of entry. The Federal Law Enforcement Center also has smaller U.S. facilities including one in Artesia, New Mexico, which was used to help provide training for 9,000 new law enforcement recruits for the Secure Border Initiative. Training courses include those relating to terrorism methodology, threat response and infrastructure protection, weapons of mass destruction and hazardous materials, physical security, weapons/explosives detection, operations security, and man-portable air defense systems. The center also develops and presents international law enforcement training and provides management direction for the International Law Enforcement Academy in Botswana and a similar one in El Salvador.

The Federal Emergency Management Agency's (FEMA) Emergency Management Institute provides courses for emergency management officials to cope with both natural disasters as well as other hazards, such as chemical spill issues or terrorist attacks using weapons of mass destruction. The FEMA National Training and Education Division offers more than 135 first-responder training programs including terrorism using weapons of mass destruction and catastrophic events; cyber, agricultural, and food security; and citizen preparedness. The division works with over 60 training partners, including the National Domestic Preparedness Consortium, which is comprised of seven institutions, including universities. Participants include state, local, and tribal officials involved in emergency prevention, protection, response, and recovery.

The FEMA Center for Domestic Preparedness is the Department of Homeland Security's only federally chartered weapons of mass destruction training center; it offers hands-on training for the nation's first responders. Additionally, the Community Emergency Response Teams program provides education and training about disaster preparedness and basic disaster response skills for volunteers, and the Critical Infrastructure Protection Training Program is for senior security managers or specialists who are responsible for critical infrastructure protection.

U.S. DEPARTMENT OF STATE

The United States operates programs specifically to train foreign students. The State Department's Antiterrorism Training Assistance program was authorized by Congress in 1983 to provide training and equipment to strengthen the capabilities of civilian officials from friendly nations to counter terrorism and to bolster bilateral working relations. The courses originally focused on meeting basic needs such as explosives detection, airport and seaport security, hostage negotiations, and VIP protection. As the threat evolved, the program added new courses, for example, on the countering of terrorism financing and medical crisis management. The program often uses various federal agencies, such as the FBI or Department of Justice, to provide the actual training.

TERRORISM FINANCING

Countering terrorism financing is a relatively new field. The Department of State, Department of the Treasury, and Department of Justice began developing counter-terrorism-financing courses for other countries before 9/11, but the scope greatly accelerated after that attack. In October 2001 the White House established the interagency Terrorist Finance Working Group to coordinate, develop, and provide counterterrorism training and technical assistance to foreign partners that the executive branch has identified as the most vulnerable to terrorist financing. Cochaired by the State Department's Office of the Coordinator for Counterterrorism and the Bureau for International Narcotics and Law Enforcement Affairs, it includes officials from the Treasury, Justice, and Homeland Security Departments and from regulatory agencies and the intelligence community.

Tailored interagency teams from the Treasury, State, and Justice Departments and other components visit participating countries to identify risks and vulnerabilities and determine the types of training and technical assistance needed to implement international anti–money-laundering and counter-terrorism-financing standards designed to counter terrorist and criminal abuse and to detect, disrupt, and dismantle international terrorist financial networks. About five teams are sent out annually, although this varies due to changing circumstances.

Interagency component groups include the Counterterrorism Finance Unit of the State Department's Counterterrorism Office. This unit coordinates the delivery of technical assistance and training to foreign governments to help them investigate, identify, and interdict the flow of money to terrorist groups. Along with the Bureau of International Narcotics and Law Enforcement Affairs, it funds and coordinates interagency training and technical assistance in the basic components of a comprehensive counter-terrorist-financing/anti–money-laundering regime: legal frameworks, financial regulatory systems, financial intelligence units, law enforcement, and judicial/prosecutorial development. It also provides funding support for Justice Department resident legal advisors in East Africa, the Horn of Africa, the Middle East, and South Asia.

The Treasury Department's Office of Technical Assistance Economics Crimes Program is also part of the interagency effort. This unit specializes in providing assistance to other countries for development of legal foundations, policies, and anticorruption entities. Combating terrorist financing, as well as money laundering, is one of the office's missions in addition to helping countries counter organized crime and complex international financial crimes. The office works with about 80 countries each year, although not always on directly terrorism-related assistance. The U.S. government's economic and trade sanctions are administered and enforced by the U.S. Treasury's Office of Foreign Assets Control. These sanctions target international narcotics traffickers, proliferators of weapons of mass destruction, terrorist support networks, and other malign foreign adversaries in countries such as Burma, the Democratic Republic of Congo, North Korea, and Somalia. The Office of Foreign Assets Control provides outreach programs and training assistance, both in the United States and overseas. Another agency, the Financial Crimes Enforcement Network, also works with international agencies and other countries in training officials to counter money laundering.

COUNTERING BIOTERRORISM

Biosecurity-related programs range from lab security and infectious disease detection and reporting to first-responder training, crisis management coordination, and investigative training. The providers include a wide range of government agencies. The Centers for Disease Control, under the Department of Health and Human Services, though domestically oriented, has more than 14,000 employees in 54 countries and is heavily involved in such health problems as malaria and AIDS. Its overseas activities, including training, are also related to biodanger concerns. Other agencies responsible for protection against biohazards are the Division of Bioterrorism Preparedness and Response, which provides technical assistance to public health agencies and other partners regarding bioterrorism detection and response, and the Federal Law Enforcement Center. The center runs a first-responder course related to biological weapons and other weapons of mass destruction. The course offers training and exercises for personnel who would be the first responders to an active and evolving threat or incident that involved radiological, biological, or chemical weapons of mass destruction and required a law enforcement response.

U.S. DEPARTMENT OF DEFENSE

In addition to its roles in training hostage rescue teams, counterinsurgency-related training, and the counterterrorism fellowship program, the Defense Department is involved in countering threats of weapons of mass destruction. The Global Emerging Infections Surveillance and Response System, in partnership with U.S. and non-U.S. public and private sector agencies, links the Defense Department response system with the overall U.S. and international system for addressing infectious disease threats worldwide. The programs include training for foreign health personnel, both civilian and military, in epidemiological methods, investigations of outbreaks, and preparedness response. Additionally, the Defense Threat Reduction Agency provides training in lab security as part of the Biological Threat Reduction Program, a disease surveillance and response program to enhance biosecurity programs at research facilities in Kazakhstan, Uzbekistan, Azerbaijan, Georgia, and Ukraine.

CONCLUSION

As noted in the preceding, a wide variety of agencies and programs are involved in counterterrorism training both for American and foreign officials, making coordination and prevention of duplication a challenge. At times there have been "teething" problems and turf issues, sometimes as a result of different perspectives. Although interagency contacts and other mechanisms attempt to minimize the difficulties, the effort needs to be consistent and persistent regardless of changes in leadership and/or program managers.

See also: **Volume 1, Part III:** Countering Terrorism: Law Enforcement or Military Problem; Countering Weapons of Mass Destruction (WMD); Defensive Measures against Terrorism: Military Preemption and Retaliation; Evolution of Global Counterterrorism Initiatives

REFERENCES

Counter-terrorism Training Coordination Working Group. *Counter-terrorism Training and Resources for Law Enforcement.* U.S. Department of Justice's (DOJ's) Office of Justice Programs. http://www.counterterrorismtraining.gov/mission/index.html.

Gottron, Frank, and Dana A. Shea. "Federal Efforts to Address the Threat of Bioterrorism: Selected Issues for Congress." Congressional Research Service, August 6, 2010. http://www.fas.org/sgp/crs/terror/R41123.pdf.

Government Accountability Office. "DOD and State Need to Improve Sustainment Planning and Monitoring and Evaluation for Section 1206 and 1207Assistance Programs." GAO-10-431. April 15, 2010. http://www.gao.gov/new.items/d10431.pdf.

Reese, Shawn. "Federal Counter-terrorism Training Issues for Congressional Oversight." Congressional Research Service, August 31, 2006. http://www.fas.org/sgp/crs/terror/RL32920.pdf.

Russell, Kevin L., Jennifer Rubenstein, Ronald L. Burke, Kelly G. Vest, Matthew C. Johns, Jose L. Sanchez, William Meyer, Mark M. Fukuda, and David L. Blazes. "Global Emerging Infections Surveillance and Response System (GEIS), a U.S. Government Tool for Improved Global Biosurveillance: A Review of 2009."" Center for Biosecurity of UPMC. http://www.biomedcentral.com/content/pdf/1471-2458-11-S2-S2.pdf. 2011.

Sabin, Barry M. "Acting Deputy Assistant Attorney General, Criminal Divisions, Investigation, Testimony on Counter-terrorism Financing Foreign Training and Assistance: Progress Since 9/11." U.S. House of Representatives Committee on Financial Services, Subcommittee on Oversight and Investigation, April 6, 2006. http://archives.financialservices.house.gov/media/pdf/040606bs.pdf.

U.S. Department of State. Counterterrorism Finance Unit, Office of the Coordinator for Counterterrorism. http://www.state.gov/j/ct/about/programs/ctfinance/index.htm.

U.S. Department of the Treasury Office of Technical Assistance (OTA) Economic-Crimes Program. http://treasuryota.us/index.php?option=com_content&task=view&id=33&Itemid=78.

Crisis Management: The Public Health System

Linda S. Watts

The public health profession must anticipate a wide range of emergencies, planning effective responses to those crises. Crisis management for terrorist incidents, while distinct in some respects, demands many of the same elements of disaster preparation required to address other categories of crises, such as floods, earthquakes, and tornadoes. Public health authorities must promote and maintain a state of readiness for immediate, intermediate, and extended responses to terrorist acts. It is through careful thinking about prevention, vulnerability assessment, consequence management, and restorative action that a nation proves most resistant to harm resulting from terrorist attacks.

ALL-HAZARDS APPROACH

Preparedness is a vital component of any public health crisis management system. Both emergency personnel and the general public should receive sufficient education and training that they may play their part in a constructive response to a terrorist act. For instance, if each household in the nation has an emergency kit, an evacuation route, and a communication plan for use in the event of a disaster, then emergency services may devote their time and energies to critical needs during a public health crisis. This is the premise of the "Three Days, Three Ways" campaign, urging the American public to keep at the ready all the materials they would need to shelter in place for a minimum period of three days following a disaster.

Although there is some debate about whether crisis management for the public health implications of terrorism should be addressed separately from other emergencies, the prevailing current practice is an all-hazards approach. This strategy takes a broad perspective on emergency management, setting in place basic frameworks for common responses to a wide range of crises. Such an approach helps focus planning, control costs, and address cases where the nature of the emergency is not immediately known. For instance, a fire may require initial action before its cause is identified. The emphasis within an all-hazards system is on those disasters most likely to occur and the actions most customarily taken in response. The all-hazards approach has four components: preparedness, mitigation, response, and recovery.

CRITICAL INFRASTRUCTURE AND DEFINED AUTHORITY

Typically, a robust public health system also relies on a sound infrastructure. This foundation includes adequate systems for storing, retrieving, and sharing data; sufficient organizational capacity; and suitable positioning of emergency personnel. Even the general public's level of emergency awareness contributes to a society's infrastructural strength. The "If you see something, say something" campaign, which originated in New York's public transit system following the 9/11 attacks, is an example of a program enlisting the public's cooperation in maintaining a climate of health and safety. Without these elements of infrastructure in place, the public health response to a terrorist incident may be weakened.

In addition, management of public health crises relies on clearly defined leadership and a widely understood chain of command. Although many agencies, civic organizations, and other entities may contribute to emergency response, their combined efficacy and agility depend on decisive command and thoughtful direction. For instance, in the United States, the secretary of the Department of Homeland Security functions as the principal federal officer when a domestic incident of terrorism occurs. That individual works with other leaders at the federal, state, and local levels to achieve an integrated response to a terrorist incident or threat.

Regardless of the nature of a terrorist attack, and even if its effects seem limited or local, its implications must be carefully assessed. Risk or damage perceptions, even among those on the scene, may not prove entirely accurate. Public health representatives must think systematically and work cooperatively to reach reliable judgments regarding the threat level, the damage sustained or anticipated, and the necessary plan for response. Only then can the public health system achieve coordination of services to address the needs of a society undergoing terrorist threats or attacks. Partnership not only among federal agencies but also among a wide range of community services may prove crucial to resilience and recovery. Examples include hospitals, medical labs, clinics, pharmacies, producers and distributors of vaccines, and entities charged with such functions as poison control or crisis counseling. Vulnerable populations, such as the elderly or the disabled, may demand particular attention within such hazard assessments.

INTERAGENCY COOPERATION AND PUBLIC AWARENESS

Crucial to public health crisis management is an effective communication model, both among emergency personnel and with the public. Immediately upon discovery of a public health attack or its threat, officials establish an incident command system. Such a provision creates a central base of operations. It also facilitates agency partnerships and coordination of services. There must also be a practical division of labor for first responders, and care taken to guard their safety during the emergency response. Following the 9/11 attacks, for example, the United States rethought its strategies for federal, state, local, and interagency interoperability, emphasizing rapid and efficient information relay among responders, as well as timely and accurate communication with the public. Messages delivered to the public during a health crisis must be frank enough to be taken seriously without alarming the population unduly.

Generally speaking, the trend in the United States has been a more fully reckoned notion of response, featuring the National Response Framework (2008) and National Incident Management System. In this way, national organizations such as the Department of Homeland Security, Department of Health and Human Services Centers for Disease Control, National Institute for Occupational Safety and Health, Substance Abuse and Mental Health Services Administration, and Department of Defense can work in concert to respond to terrorist incidents or other emergencies with consequences for the nation's public health.

A COMPREHENSIVE APPROACH

There are public health implications to almost every terrorist act, whether it involves small arms or weapons of mass destruction. The specific actions required in response to a terrorist incident will vary widely depending on its source and nature. A school or workplace shooting may call for a different course of action than a bridge collapse. A comprehensive public health crisis management plan will address the full spectrum of potential hazards. Included within such a framework are threats including bioterrorism (terrorism that targets physical well-being through such means as biological toxins, chemical weapons, or infectious agents) and agroterrorism (terrorist acts that target agriculture through such means as plant pathogens or livestock diseases). For example, the Public Health

Security and Bioterrorism Preparedness and Response Act of 2002 (also known as the Bioterrorism Act) speaks to potential terror-related risks to food safety and security. In addition, a thorough crisis management plan will help prevent or mitigate attacks with nuclear or radiation risks.

Whatever the nature of the terrorist incident, crisis management should account not only for physical effects but also for psychological and social impacts. Even those who do not sustain physical injuries in a crisis may, whether initially or subsequently, require mental health services as part of their recovery from the experience. Too often, emergency plans overlook or underestimate the crisis counseling needs associated with the anxiety, depression, or posttraumatic stress resulting from terrorist incidents. Even the worried-well population requires attention in such a crisis, ensuring that their concerns do not escalate or consume resources needed for those directly affected by a public health emergency. For instance, in 2001, when several U.S. government officials and news media representatives received envelopes by mail containing anthrax, the medical community needed to communicate to the public that it was neither practical nor necessary for the entire population to receive antibiotics such as Cipro on a preventive basis. Instead, it was sufficient for citizens to exercise caution in opening their mail, receiving antibiotic treatment only if there was confirmation of exposure to anthrax. While providers must recognize patient fears, they have a responsibility to meet such reactions with information rather than acquiescence. Had physicians not exercised professional judgment in this regard during the anthrax scare, the available supply of medication might have become dangerously depleted. In other words, the wrong response to a public health challenge can deepen a crisis or introduce new hazards.

Finally, care should be taken to ensure that public health responses to a terrorist incident do not divert resources that are (or might be) needed to address multiple crises, whether they are related or unrelated to terrorism. The public health system needs to remain ready in the event that multiple emergencies require attention, particularly at the same time and/or in the same area. Otherwise, convergence on one problem or site can itself endanger public health by needlessly limiting the ability to react to simultaneous or subsequent emergencies.

CONCLUSION

Crisis management of public health challenges related to terrorism requires a coordinated and integrated approach. Prevention and preparation lay the groundwork for a resilient nation. Clarity of leadership, communication, and interagency collaboration in response efforts helps ensure the best recovery from the public health consequences of terrorist incidents. Following 9/11, the public health profession refined its strategies for handling large-scale disasters, striving to increase the quality and consistency of disaster management. Enhanced methods for information sharing and coordination of services are among the improvements the United States has made in its national plan for handling a public health crisis related to terrorism. While the demands of each emergency should be assessed for its unique features, a comprehensive public health strategy with an all-hazards approach can anticipate many of the community needs that will accompany a terrorist threat or action.

See also: **Volume 1, Part I:** Defining Terrorism: Issues and Problems; Definition and Dimensions of Counterterrorism. **Part III:** Multidisciplinary Approach to Combating Terrorism; Psychological Operations. **Part VI:** Counterterrorism and the Forensic Sciences

REFERENCES

Grey, Michael R., and Kenneth R. Spaeth. *The Bioterrorism Sourcebook.* New York: McGraw-Hill, 2006.

Kellman, Barry. *Bioviolence: Preventing Biological Terror and Crime.* New York: Cambridge University Press, 2007.

Levy, Barry S., and Victor W. Sidel, eds. *Terrorism and Public Health: A Balanced Approach to Strengthening Systems and Protecting People.* New York: Oxford University Press, 2003.

Rowitz, Louis. *Public Health for the 21st Century: The Prepared Leader.* Boston: Jones and Bartlett, 2006.

Sauter, Mark A., and James Jay Carafano. *Homeland Security: A Complete Guide to Understanding, Preventing, and Surviving Terrorism.* New York: McGraw-Hill, 2005.

United States Congress, Senate, Committee on Health, Education, Labor and Pensions. *Terror Attacks: Are We Prepared?* Washington, DC: U.S. Government Printing Office, 2005.

Defensive Measures against Terrorism: Military Preemption and Retaliation

Thomas E. Baker

The concept of preemptive self-defense is anticipatory and reactive. According to the U.S. Department of Defense, preemptive attacks are possible and can become a reality "on the basis of incontrovertible evidence that an enemy attack is imminent" (Department of Defense [DoD] Dictionary of Military and Associated Terms 2011). The preemptive strike is a proactive countermeasure to prevent an attempted evasion or to gain an advantage in an inevitable offensive war.

SIGNIFICANCE

The modern moral questions concerning the right to self-defense are comparable to ancient Greek wars between Sparta and Athens. Preemptive attacks seek to protect the nation's defensive assets and infrastructure before total warfare becomes an inescapable reality. The obvious moral risk is that nation-states may justify an attack as a preemptive strike when the underlying motive is to validate political or territorial conquests.

Article 51 of the UN Charter declares that a nation-state can lawfully respond to an armed attack. However, preemptive acts represent a nation-state's decision to strike *before* an attack. Commanders who seek authorization for preemptive strikes must validate answers to four significant international law considerations other than a nation's self-defense needs: *alternatives, military necessity, proportionality,* and *collateral damage.*

ACCURATE AND TIMELY INTELLIGENCE

Philosophical, legal, and military deliberations intensify when global issues threaten world peace and preemptive self-defense tactics emerge as plausible options. The basic premise is that offensive military warfare is unavoidable because of the failure to resolve conflict through traditional political or diplomatic channels. The premise is that preemptive attacks ultimately prevent an unnecessary and lengthy war and protect the civilian population.

The employment of a preemptory attack carries a double-edged sword. In one case, a nation's decision to use preemptory attacks could be considered correct and an appropriate act of self-defense; however, in another case, it could be incorrect. The correct judgment that determines whether to use preemptory attacks depends on the accuracy of diverse intelligence sources.

In addition, is the intelligence timely, precise, reliable, credible, valid, and viable? The answers to those questions, and others, require considerable and thoughtful contemplation. Mistakes in judgment can cause substantial military and civilian human casualties. The dangers lie in failure to act in time or in overreaction and the initiation of hostile actions that lead to the escalation of violence and warfare.

Israel felt justified in launching the June 5, 1967, preemptory attack against Egypt because of credible intelligence information concerning Egypt's imminent attack. Surrounded by 22 Arab states, Israel seized the initiative to avoid total defeat and death as a nation. The Six-Day War also included troops and arms from Iraq, Saudi Arabia, Sudan, Morocco, and Algeria. This war required preemptive attacks to ensure Israel's survival. In stark contrast, the Arab nations denied Israel's accusations and were defiant when they denounced Israel's actions as unwarranted and illegal acts of aggression.

In 1981, Israel conducted another preemptive self-defense maneuver, destroying nuclear facilities in Iraq that were allegedly engaging in the development of nuclear weapons. The justification for a preemptive attack centered on the possibility that potential nuclear weapons could result in a devastating attack against Israel. The preemptive attack on Iraq would never find adequate justification or irrefutable evidence to support it on the world stage.

BUSH DOCTRINE

After the September 11, 2001, attacks, President George W. Bush announced the Bush Doctrine. The president stated before a joint session of Congress, "we will pursue nations that provide aid or safe haven to terrorism . . . any nation that continues to harbor or support terrorism will be regarded by the United States as a hostile regime" (Bush 2001). In December 2002, the National Strategy to Combat Weapons of Mass Destruction clarified that "the United States will continue to make clear that it reserves the right to respond with overwhelming force—including through resort to all of our options—to the use of WMD against the United States, our forces abroad, and friends and allies" (Arms Control Association 2002).

On March 16, 2006, President Bush reaffirmed his first-strike policy for targeting terrorists and rogue nations. This policy on preemptive strikes remains a core element of the United States's right of self-defense. He publicly stated to the nation,

To forestall or prevent such hostile acts by our adversaries, the United States will, if necessary, act preemptively in exercising our inherent right of self-defense. The United States will not resort to force in all cases to preempt emerging threats. Our preference is that nonmilitary actions succeed. And no country should ever use preemption as a pretext for aggression. (Bush 2006)

WAR ON TERRORISM

The goal of preemptive strikes is to fight the war forward, thereby keeping terrorists and other hostile entities in a defensive mode, restricting or minimizing their capability to plan and initiate aggressive and offensive operations. The attacks of September 11, 2001, raised intense fear and speculation regarding possible future attacks against innocent citizens in the homeland and abroad. Reports of thriving training camps that purportedly intended to use weapons of mass destruction and additional methods to create catastrophic loss of life and property filled the print media and airwaves. Terrorists adapt to changing environments, requirements, and circumstances.

Some officials and decision makers believe that preemptive strikes keep terrorists in a state of reorganization and "on the run" when they suffer losses in leadership, volunteers, financial support, and motivation. Others believe that these attacks serve to further the terrorists' propaganda and misinformation campaigns and therefore serve as tools for enlisting new participants to take the place of those lost.

Using crop dusters to disperse poisonous gases, making dirty bombs, targeting nuclear plants using conventional and nonconventional explosives, and spreading poisonous gases throughout office buildings using ventilation systems all seemed plausible and credible threats. Citizens and first responders now understand that the terrorists need to be right only *once*.

CONCLUSION

Problems in the Middle East during the Cold War were considerably different from those of the current war on terror. For example, during the Arab-Israeli conflict (Six-Day War), preemptive strikes decided the outcome of the war. Israel was able to attack command posts, air support, logistical supply lines, military troops, and armor/tank formations. In the current fight against terrorism preemptive cruise missile strikes have achieved limited success in targeting the terrorist leadership. However, when core leadership remain in place, and when leaders are targeted or killed, new appointments continue to fill the ranks of the leadership positions in al-Qaeda and the Taliban.

Terrorist targets are elusive. Military formations and logistical supply concentrations in asymmetrical warfare cannot be fought with traditional strategies and tactics. Therefore, the deterrent effect of weapons of mass destruction does not apply to terrorist groups. Traditional states have investments and the desire to protect their assets; terrorists would welcome the use of weapons of mass destruction to alienate moderates and build their political base.

In a limited way military preemption and retaliation serve to keep the war contained and enemy leadership less mobile. Terrorists want to escalate their war effort; the United States wants to contain and isolate terrorists. Thus far, the terrorists continue to struggle to achieve their goals; the United States continues to thwart their violence with deterrence, preemption, and retaliation. The security of the nation and its people depends on the principle that we must be right *every time* in the war against terror.

REFERENCES

Arms Control Association. "National Strategy to Combat Weapons of Mass Destruction." Washington, DC, December 2002. http://www.armscontrol.org/print/1184.

Bush, George W. "President George W. Bush's Address to Congress and the Nation on Terrorism." September 20, 2001. The White House, Washington, DC. http://www.whitehouse.gov.

Bush, George W. "The National Security Strategy of the United States of America." March 16, 2006. The White House, Washington, DC. http://www.presidentialrhetoric.com/speeches/nss2006.pdf.

Department of Defense (DoD) Dictionary of Military and Associated Terms. 2011. http://www.dtic.mil/doctrine/dod_dictionary/.

Flynn, Mathew J. *Preemptive War in Modern History*. New York: Routledge, Taylor Francis Group, 2008.

Howard, Russell D., and Reid L. Sawyer. *Defeating Terrorism: Shaping the New Security Environment*. Guilford, CT: McGraw-Hill, 2004.

Howard, Russell D., and Reid L. Sawyer. *Terrorism and Counterterrorism: Understanding the New Security Environment*. Guilford, CT: McGraw-Hill, 2004.

Mahan, Sue, and Pamala L. Griset. *Terrorism in Perspective*. 2nd ed. Thousand Oaks, CA: Sage, 2008.

Maniscalco, Paul M., and Hank T. Christen. *Understanding Terrorism and Managing the Consequences*. Upper Saddle River, NY: Prentice-Hall, 2002.

Mariani, Cliff. *Terrorism Prevention and Response*. 2nd ed. New York: Looseleaf Law Publications, 2004.

Martin, Gus. *Essentials of Terrorism: Concepts and Controversies*. Thousand Oaks, CA: Sage, 2008.

Poland, James M. *Understanding Terrorism: Groups, Strategies, and Responses*. 3rd ed. Upper Saddle River, NY: Pearson/Prentice-Hall, 2011.

Rodin, David. *War and Self Defense*. New York: Oxford University Press, 2003.

Spindlove, Jeremy R., and Clifford E. Simonsen. *Terrorism Today: The Past, the Players, the Future*. 4th ed. Upper Saddle River, NY: Pearson/Prentice-Hall, 2011.

Economics of Counterterrorism

Daniella Graves

Many financial resources are invested to fight the war on terrorism. Essentially, the war on terror is an economic war. This is because terrorism has hurt the world's financial systems, depleted natural resources, and damaged human capital. For counterterrorism to succeed, it must target the manner in which terrorists finance their organizations. Although the global community has invested heavily in fighting terrorism at its core, terrorists react to our attempts to eradicate them by shifting targets.

IMPACT ON THE GLOBAL ECONOMY

Terrorism has impacted the global economy and spawned a multitude of revisions and initiatives in the international financial network. The direct costs include loss of earnings and slower economic growth, while the indirect costs are a substantial loss of confidence and reduced demand for travel and tourism. Terrorist attacks impair productive capital especially in the transportation, tourism, and trade sectors. Some financial analyst believed that the airline industry was the sector that was hardest hit by the events of 9/11. These attacks had a profound and immediate impact on legislative initiatives and security measures undertaken by the government and the nation's airlines. Moreover, the enhancement of airport security reduced the convenience of air travel, in turn causing a decline in the demand for air travel. As a result, "the airline industry lost about $1.1 billion in revenues . . . a tenth of the projected revenue lost because of 9/11 itself" (Blalock, Kadiyali, and Simon 2008). Moreover, "it has been estimated that a one-day delay due to border controls costs 0.5% of the value of the delayed good" (Schneider, Bruck, and Meirrieks 2010, 83). These types of financial losses strike fear in investors and therefore have global repercussions

Abadie and Dermisi (2006, 1) note that the fear and uncertainty caused by terrorism "have large effects on the behavior of economic agents." For example, changes in demand are a result of risk aversion. Corporate investors rate terrorism as "one of the most important factors influencing their foreign direct investment decisions" (Abadie and Gardeazabal 2008, 5). By increasing uncertainty, terrorism reduces foreign direct investment as investors seek less violence-prone countries to invest in and conduct business. The tourism industry, particularly hard hit after 9/11, "will suffer from terrorism as a response to increased security measures or increased (perceived) vulnerability" (Schneider, Bruck, and Meirrieks 2010, 77). The fear that results from terrorism also affects consumer behavior. Fear of terrorism and weapons of mass destruction "are estimated to have lowered (US) consumption spending by 0.3 percent (equivalent to a cumulative US$ 40 billion) over the past two years" (Schneider, Bruck, and Meirrieks 2010, 37). Even if businesses are not directly exposed to the physical destruction of terrorism, it can impact them by "increasing their overall level of market risk" (Schneider, Bruck, and Meirrieks 2010, 38). This increased risk leads to more counterterrorism expenditures.

TERRORIST FINANCING

Terrorist financing has been a major concern; therefore, efforts that attack the economic hubs of terrorist groups are designed and implemented to cripple their efforts. As former U.S. Secretary of State Colin Powell (2001) stated, "For money is the oxygen of terrorism. Without the means to raise and move money around the world, terrorists cannot function." The essential point here is that less money leads to less operational capability for terrorist groups.

The world has collectively focused on terrorist financing as part of a strategic plan to eliminate terrorism altogether or at the very least to have a detrimental impact on terrorists' abilities to plan, coordinate, and conduct operations. Knowing where the money comes from and "'following the money' can go a long way toward disrupting terrorist cells and networks and thereby can help prevent future terrorist attacks" (Greenberg, Wechsler, and Wolosky 2002, 22). This is not always an easy task. For example, oftentimes terrorists use the *hawala* system to transfer money. This cash business "leaves behind few, if any, written or electronic records for use by investigators in following money trails" (Greenberg, Wechsler, and Wolosky 2002, 10). Indeed, the *hawala* money transfer system makes it nearly impossible to locate the source and movement of terrorist transfers.

Although many terrorists obtain their funds illegally, "some terrorist organizations are much more likely to raise their funds legitimately and then use those funds to kill and attack" (O'Connor 2012). Therefore, while some terrorist groups rely on criminal activities like trafficking and counterfeiting, others look to charitable organizations to raise and transfer funds. In this way, terrorists are able to raise financial support "under the cloak of legitimacy" (Greenberg, Wechsler, and Wolosky 2002, 1). By operating in relative obscurity and close-knit networks, terrorists are able to push their agenda in ways that remain concealed from the public. Counterterrorism, therefore, must eradicate this impenetrable haven of terrorist transactions. Although it has been difficult, the United States has enacted a number of policies and procedures in an attempt to combat terrorist financing.

The economic war on terrorism didn't begin after the attacks of 9/11—its roots can be traced to President Ronald Reagan's International Economic Emergency Powers Act, which aimed at freezing any asset that belonged to a state that was suspected of supporting any terrorist action. However, following the events of 9/11, one can see more focused and concerted efforts to eradicate terrorists' sources of revenue. One of the first strikes was Executive Order 13224, which attempts to block assets of organizations associated with terrorism. This executive order allows the United States to block terrorists' financial transactions. Additionally, the United States is able to deny foreign banks access to U.S. markets if they refuse to freeze terrorist resources. Therefore, Executive Order 13224 "expanded U.S. power to target the support structure of terrorist organizations" (O'Connor 2012). In addition, between fiscal year "2001 and FY 2003, funding for homeland security was increased by some 240 percent" (Carafano 2007). These investments were all strategically implemented to fight terror. Moreover, the United States invested heavily in intelligence strategies and law enforcement. For example, groups such as the Financial Crimes Enforcement Network and the Egmont Group were created to analyze and share information on suspicious financial activity (O'Connor 2012). Although investments to fight terrorism are in place, the issue remains that the unintended consequences of counterterrorism may be more costly than the intended consequences.

ADAPTABILITY OF TERRORIST GROUPS

As terrorists adjust their mode of attack, security responses must be modified, and this may impact the economic costs of countering these threats. Terrorists often replace high-risk attacks with softer targets. For example, "in the case of metal detectors, kidnappings increased, in the case of embassy fortification, assassinations became more frequent" (Enders and Sandler 1993, 829). Terrorists react to modifications in security measures by choosing different and often softer targets. In other words, "security responses do not only contribute to the total costs of a past terrorist event but also partly determine the economic repercussions of terrorism in the future" (Schneider, Bruck, and Meirrieks 2010). Since terrorists are likely to attack less protected targets, enhancing the security of one target increases the risk faced by others (Trajtenberg 2006). Investing in security may actually increase the level of risk to certain populated areas. This is because counterterrorist measures actually transfer terrorist attention elsewhere. Therefore, this substitution effect must be taken into account when allocating human and financial capital and resources. Protecting symbols of national importance or those that, if attacked successfully, could cripple our financial system or wreak havoc on a critical infrastructure component raises the economic costs as security is enhanced and expensive technologies are put in place to counter and attempt to disrupt and thwart the ability of individuals to successfully penetrate and attack the protected target (Enders and Sandler 2006, 119). Terrorist group behavior is dynamic rather than static and is adaptable to changes in countermeasures designed to frustrate their objectives. This, in turn, adds to the economic costs as governments and transnational military forces continue to spend money and utilize resources to meet the evolving terrorist threat.

CONCLUSION

Terrorism has affected global economic growth and productivity as well as the stability of international trade and capital flows. Not only have government expenditures for changed security procedures been necessary, but terrorist attacks have completely altered how individuals and organizations conduct business. Yet these security procedures have had a negative impact on global financial activity. While the world responds to an increased need for security, terrorists switch their modus operandi. Ultimately, the war on terror will be more successful if, through global cooperation, terrorists' revenue conduits are disrupted and eventually eliminated.

See also: **Volume 1, Part III:** Identifying and Combating Sources of Terrorist Financing; Multilateral Sanctions against State Sponsors of Terrorism. **Part IV:** Eliminating Terrorist Support Networks; U.S. Legislative Initiatives to Combat Terrorism pre-911; U.S. Legislative Initiatives to Combat Terrorism since 9/11

REFERENCES

Abadie, Alberto, and Sofia Dermisi. "Is Terrorism Eroding Agglomeration Economies in Central Business Districts? Lessons from the Office Real Estate Market in Downtown Chicago." *Journal of Urban Economics* 64, no. 2 (2006): 451–63. http://www.nber.org/papers/w12678.pdf?new_window=1.

Abadie, Alberto, and Javier Gardeazabal. "Terrpros, and the World Economy." *European Economic Review* 52, no. 1 (2008): 1–27.

Blalock, Garrick, Vrinda Kadiyali, and Daniel Simon. "The Impact of Post 9/11 Airport Security Measures on the Demand for Air Travel." *Journal of Law and Economics* 5 (2008): 731.

Carafano, James. "Homeland Security Spending for the Long War." Presentation for the Heritage Foundation, Washington, D.C., February 2, 2007.

Enders, Walter, and Todd Sandler. "The Effectiveness of Antiterrorism Policies: A Vector-Autoregression-Intervention Analysis." *American Political Science Review* 87, no. 4 (1993): 829–45.

Enders, Walter, and Todd Sandler. *The Political Economy of Terrorism.* Cambridge: Cambridge University Press, 2006.

Greenberg, Maurice, William Wechsler, and Lee Wolosky. "Terrorist Financing." Presentation for the Council of Foreign Relations, New York City, 2002.

O'Connor, Tom. "Counterterrorism: Military and Economic Options." Presentation given at Austin Peay State University, Clarksville, TN. Last updated January 2, 2012. http://www.drtomoconnor.com/3400/3400lect08a.htm.

Powell, Colin. "Remarks on Financial Aspects of Terrorism." Presentation to the Financial Crime Enforcement Network, Vienna, VA, November 7, 2001.

Schneider, Friedrich, Tilman Bruck, and Daniel Meirrieks. "The Economics of Terrorism and Counter-terrorism: A Survey." CESifo Working Paper Series. 2010. http://ideas.repec.org/p/ces/ceswps/_3011.html.

Trajtenberg, Manuel. "Defense R&D in the Anti-terrorist Era." *Defence and Peace Economics* 17, no. 3 (2006): 177–99.

Evolution of Global Counterterrorism Initiatives

Cenap Cakmak

Globalization is the sweeping trend of the contemporary world. With the rapid technological advancements, accompanied by the growth of international trade, the world shrank in its physical dimension while transportation and communication became much smoother than they used to be. As a result, today's world is experiencing visible consequences of the globalization process. One such consequence is the rapid rise of transnational organized crime groups and the spread of terrorism without being affected by physical and geographic boundaries.

RISE OF GLOBAL ACTION

The Internet allows individuals to conduct business, communicate with each other, and access information in a matter of seconds. This medium also facilitates criminal activities and interaction between and among members of criminal and terrorist groups. For example, although the growth of international commerce and advances in international banking transactions offer advantages to individuals and help sustain the world economy, they also present many opportunities for criminals and terrorists to hide their illegal activities. It may also be argued that the post–Cold War period created fertile ground for terrorists and other violent nonstate actors.

It is fair to argue that the September 11, 2001, attacks in the United States gave impetus to the emergence and rise of global-scale measures to deal with transnational terrorism. Indeed, the international community responded concertedly and decisively to the September 11 assault in an effort to address this growing and collective threat to global security. Prior to this event such measures were sporadic at best.

The United Nations (UN) was considered the epicenter for global collective action. Regional arrangements were subsequently introduced to supplement UN-sponsored global instruments, and bilateral legislative actions and initiatives were developed to promote cooperation and collaboration between states holding similar views on the urgency of addressing the problem of international terrorism.

EVOLUTION OF UN COUNTERTERRORISM MECHANISMS

The role of the UN in counterterrorism efforts before the September 11 terrorist attacks was relatively insignificant. Negotiations at the General Assembly to create a convention outlawing terrorism had failed despite the partial success in the emergence of 12 international conventions focusing on banning a number of terror-related activities. Yet for the sake of fairness, some successful efforts by the General Assembly need to be cited. Prior to the September 11 attacks the Assembly secured the adoption of three important legal documents on terrorism including the International Convention for the Suppression of Terrorist Bombings (1997), the International Convention for the Suppression of the Financing of Terrorism (1999), and the International Convention for the Suppression of Acts of

Nuclear Terrorism (2005). At the 2005 World Summit, the Assembly was also able to produce a global strategy to counter terrorism. Despite criticisms, the strategy was acclaimed as a major breakthrough given that it established for the first time a truly global counterterrorism framework.

The Security Council, the primary watchdog for international security, reacted several times to terrorist incidents. It could be said that the council's more active role in respect of the notion terrorism in its broadest sense began with the Security Council Summit in 1992 when it, in a final document adopted by consensus, identified terrorism as a threat to international peace and security. This was followed by sanctions against states accused of promoting and sponsoring terrorist activities including Libya, Sudan, and the Taliban regime in Afghanistan. However, prior to 9/11 the permanent members never considered terrorism an imminent threat to international peace and security. As a consequence of this timid and reluctant stance, the UN remained an actor encouraging rather than requiring the members to combat terrorism prior to September 11, 2001.

The UN dramatically changed its position vis-à-vis terrorism after the attacks. In a quick and decisive response, the UN adopted Resolutions 1368 and 1373, establishing the three pillars of the current global counterterrorism system. The first pillar is laid down by Resolution 1368 recalling that states have a right to self-defense when attacked or threatened by terrorist groups. The second pillar refers to the establishment of a universal counterterrorism legal framework. In Resolution 1373, the Security Council requires states to criminalize terrorism, to ratify the 12 international conventions on terrorism, and to amend their counterterrorism legislation accordingly. The third pillar is the Counter-terrorism Committee (CTC), created in accordance with council's adoption of Resolution 1373, along with the Counter-terrorism Executive Directorate (CTED), a specialized agency created in 2004 to assist the CTC's efforts.

The CTC and CTED are subsidiary bodies of the Security Council, meaning that the council is the central player. They were set up to collect and analyze data on the performance of the state to comply with the existing international legal framework on terrorism. The CTC and CTED do not provide technical assistance to the member states. This is a task to be performed by the donor states and intergovernmental organizations. For instance, the International Monetary Fund and the World Bank provide financial and technical assistance, whereas specialized agencies including the Financial Action Task Force, the World Customs Organization, the International Maritime Organization, and the International Civil Aviation Organization set the relevant applicable standards. This implies that the Security Council plays a more strategic than operational role.

The CTC is composed of all 15 members of the Security Council. The council reviews the work of the committee in closed meetings held once every three months. The committee reaches decisions by consensus among members. Three posts of vice-chair were designated to assist the chair and supervise the work of the subcommittees authorized to review the country reports. In consideration of the growing amount of work done by the committee, a revitalization process was launched in 2004 to further institutionalize the CTC's executive body. Following this process its structure has become three-tiered: the Plenary, the Bureau, and the CTED, to be headed by the executive director.

The Plenary is charged with promoting and monitoring the implementation of Resolution 1373 and strengthening contacts and coordination between the CTC and other UN bodies. The Bureau, consisting of the chair and the three vice-chairs, deals with the issues reported to the Plenary for confirmation and harmonizes the work of subcommittees in respect to country reports. The CTED was created to ensure greater compliance by member states with counterterrorism commitments. It provides in-depth analysis of the implementation of Resolution 1373, encourages states in a dialogue through letters, and facilitates capacity building in the area of technical assistance.

Although it was set up by the council acting under Chapter VII of the UN Charter, the CTC has no power to impose sanctions. Moreover, the committee is not authorized to identify terrorists, condemn states accused of sponsoring terrorism, or respond to terrorist acts. Its primary objective is to consolidate the ground required to fight terrorism. Its success therefore depends on cooperation from member states. This forces the committee to avoid acting like a police force and to adopt instead a role of service provider to countries in need of greater counterterrorism capacity.

The UN counterterrorism system has expanded dramatically over the years, now involving more than 70 multilateral institutions. However, these institutions, accompanied by relevant international documents, fail to constitute a properly functioning integrated whole. There are serious flaws in the system including duplication of efforts, overlap between the mandates, and unwillingness to share information and coordinate between the international, regional, and subregional players of the mechanism.

REGIONAL COUNTERTERRORISM MECHANISMS

In December 2005, the Council of the European Union adopted the European Union Counter-terrorism Strategy. Recognizing that the terrorist threat requires both internal and external responses, the strategy covers four strands of work:

"Prevent" refers to the task of preventing people from turning to terrorism in Europe and other parts of the world, and taking the proper measures to achieve this goal.

"Protect" refers to the mission of protecting people and individuals against terrorist threats, reducing Europe's vulnerability to such acts.

"Pursue" considers taking adequate measures vis-à-vis the planning, travel, communications, and funding involved in terrorist acts and bringing the perpetrators to justice.

"Respond" focuses on how to manage and minimize the consequences of terrorist attacks when they occur.

In this setting, the European Council serves as the political supervisor, while the Parliament, the council, and the European commission maintain the high-level political dialogue on counterterrorism through meeting once per presidency to ensure interinstitutional governance. The Committee of Permanent Representatives monitors progress on the strategy with regular follow-up and updates by the counterterrorism coordinator and the commission.

The Council of Europe is also dedicated to combating terrorism on a regional basis. Its efforts in this respect were stepped up in 2001 following the September 11 attacks. Currently, it works to strengthen legal action against terrorism and address its causes. To this end, it set up the Committee of Experts on Terrorism in 2003 to replace the Multidisciplinary Group on International Action against Terrorism to coordinate the implementation of the Council of Europe's action against terrorism. The committee prepares country profiles on counterterrorism capacity, exchanges information on compensation and insurance schemes for victims of terrorism, identifies gaps in international law and action against terrorism, and monitors the implementation of the council's terrorism-related legal mechanisms, particularly the Convention on the Prevention of Terrorism.

BILATERAL ARRANGEMENTS

The September 11 events accelerated the process of cooperation between the United States and the European Union. Transatlantic relations intensified after the terrorist attacks. To this end, the United States and the European Union signed extradition and mutual legal assistance agreements on June 25, 2003. The agreements were made to provide "additional tools to combat terrorism, organized crime, and other serious forms of criminality" (Ashcroft 2003).

U.S. authorities have also been seeking to ensure greater cooperation with the European Police Office (Europol). Europol, the major police organization of the European Union, and the United States signed an agreement on December 20, 2002, allowing both parties to cooperate more fully in combating organized crime and terrorism. This agreement includes the exchange of personal data. A year before this agreement, a strategic cooperation agreement attempting to secure a long-term relationship was signed between the United States and Europol. The strategic agreement was made to ensure "exchanges of strategic information on criminal trend analysis, articulation of best practices for addressing specific crime problems, sharing of training and continuing education programs" (Spinant 2001). The new agreement further enhanced cooperation between the parties. With the agreement in effect, both parties "are now able to fully implement their existing co-operation at a more operational level" (Faull and Soreca 2008, 406).

CONCLUSION

As a consequence of the rapid spread of transnational organized criminal and terrorist activities, it became obvious that domestic measures alone would not be sufficient to effectively address these issues. International cooperation employing state-of-the-art technologies and methods would be required in the struggle against transnational criminal enterprises and terrorism.

See also: **Volume 1, Part I:** Definition and Dimensions of Counterterrorism. **Part III:** Counterterrorism Training; Defensive Measures against Terrorism: Military Preemption and Retaliation; Multilateral Sanctions against State Sponsors of Terrorism; Role of the International Community. **Part IV:** Importance of Mutual Legal Assistance; International Legal Framework to Eliminate Terrorism against Civil Aviation and Maritime Targets; Joint Terrorism Task Forces; United Nations Global Counterterrorism Strategy: Significance and Limitations. **Part VI:** Multilateral Approach to Counterterrorism: Issues, Problems, Responses

REFERENCES

Allen, Brian, ed. *International Process on Global Counter-terrorism Cooperation: A Compilation of Key Documents.* New York: Center on Global Counterterrorism Cooperation, 2008. http://www.globalct.org/images/content/pdf/reports/international_process.pdf.

Ashcroft, John. "Remarks of the Attorney General for the EU/US Extradition and MLA Treaties Signing Ceremonies." June 25, 2003. http://www.justice.gov/archive/ag/speeches/2003/062503eugreekmlattreaty.htm.

Faull, Jonathan, and Luigi Soreca. "EU-US Relations in Justice and Home Affairs." In *Justice, Liberty, Security: New Challenges for EU External Relations,* edited by Bernd Martenczuk and Servaasvan Thiel, 393–420. Institute for European Studies, Vrije Universiteit Brussel. Brussels: VUBPRESS Brussels University Press, 2008.

Nessi, Giuseppe, ed. *International Cooperation in Counter-terrorism: The United Nations and Regional Organizations in the Fight against Terrorism.* Aldershot, UK: Ashgate, 2006.

Romaniuk, Peter. *Global Counterterrorism: How Multilateral Cooperation Works.* London: Routledge, 2009.

Spinant, Daniela. "Agreement Eurpol-US Signed." Euobserver.com. December 6, 2001. http://euobserver.com/9/4458; https://www.europol.europa.eu/

sites/default/files/flags/supplemental_agreement_between_europol_
and_the_usa_on_exchange_of_personal_data_and_related_information.pdf.
Wennerholm, Peter, Erik Brattberg, and Mark Rhinard. *The EU as a Counterterrorism Actor Abroad: Finding Opportunities, Overcoming Constraints.* Brussels:
European Policy Centre, 2010.

Global Arms Trafficking

Małgorzata Zachara

The term *global arms trafficking* refers to the transfer of arms and other military items or technologies that is not authorized by institutions of the states concerned in the transfers or is made in violation of national or international regulations. The arms are transported outside of formal markets, law, and policies from a willing seller to a willing end user. The United Nations (UN) Disarmament Commission defines illicit trafficking more broadly as trade that is contrary to the laws of states and/or international law. Such practices create the possibility that countries, groups, or individuals that have been barred from buying arms through legal channels might acquire weapons. Most often they are subject to UN Security Council sanctions or regional/subregional embargoes, for example, countries involved in wars, terrorists, insurgent groups, or criminal organizations.

BLACK AND GRAY MARKETS

There are two types of illegal and quasilegal arms markets—the black market and the gray market. Black market transfers are conducted in violation of an existing arms embargo, national laws, or other regulations. Gray market transactions are more difficult to classify. They are semilegal or legally questionable transfers made by or with the complicity of national agencies. Arms and military technologies are knowingly trafficked, with the use of front companies or manipulated documentation, to proxies and allies. These kinds of operations, conducted by intelligence services to provide arms to insurgent groups and other types of allies, have been a major source of illicit arms historically. During the Cold War era arms-trade transactions were used as an instrument of the superpowers' foreign policies. Insurgent movements, rebel groups, and dictators involved in conflicts were supported with arms by global superpowers to keep these actors within their sphere of influence.

Such practices have had serious and long-term consequences that are now affecting today's security challenges. For example, a classic boomerang effect appears in Afghanistan, where American forces are threatened by weapons that the Central Intelligence Agency (CIA) provided to Afghan rebels in the 1980s. Among the vast quantity of weapons that later disappeared were several hundred Stinger missiles. Some of these weapons fell into the hands of Taliban forces, while others are believed to have been trafficked to Iran, other countries in the Middle East, and Africa. The end of the Cold War brought significant changes to the structure of the market. The reduction of standing armies throughout the North Atlantic Treaty Organization (NATO) and the Warsaw Pact and the poorly managed liquidation of their arsenals brought about a situation in which a substantial amount of weapons entered into circulation via arms traffickers. The business became highly competitive and increasingly integrated while remaining largely unregulated and becoming even more difficult to control. Since this moment the practice of arms trafficking has been driven primarily by profit, not by strategic or political considerations. The dynamic of globalization processes—especially in the spheres of economics, transportation, communication, and military production—has made arms transfers difficult to control.

ILLEGAL ARMS INDUSTRY

Complex transnational networks have been created for the procurement, financing, and delivery of different prohibited goods. As illegal trade crosses borders, traffickers from many countries are increasingly collaborating with different types of organizations, including front companies, terrorist groups, and corrupt institutions. The globalization of financial markets and communication systems has enabled these actors to easily identify their needs and common interests. The illegal arms business is commonly fueled by profits generated from other sectors of the black market. Many links can be traced on the world's trafficking map between smugglers of diamonds, arms, and technologies; mercenaries; and drug dealers. Sales are organized by a variety of means and through a number of different intermediaries. Taking advantage of more open borders and high-tech communication technologies, arms trafficking is evolving by constantly refining its mechanisms for smuggling and becoming increasingly professional.

The demand for illegal arms has stimulated the development of transnational criminal organizations that in many parts of the world have acquired significant influence through the use of violence or the exploitation of lawless conditions in so-called weak or fragile states. In this context, the trafficking of technologically advanced weapons, nuclear technologies, or radioactive materials has become a problem of dramatically increased importance.

Many attempts to smuggle nuclear, chemical, or missile-based technology to groups or countries governed by unpredictable and dangerous regimes have been reported. In 1995, the Japanese cult Aum Shinrikyo carried out a chemical attack on the Tokyo subway system using sarin gas. Chechen terrorists placed a canister of radiological material in Moscow's Izmailovsky in the same year to prove that they had the necessary materials to stage a nuclear attack within Russia. Many terrorism analysts view a scenario in which terrorists will use nuclear material to create dirty bombs as relatively probable. The acquisition of nuclear, chemical, or biological weapons by rogue states or terrorist organizations will most probably be damaging to national and international security. International arms trafficking also directly affects security by fueling and prolonging conflicts in many parts of the world. Black market arms trading provides the weapons most likely to be used in organized violence, acts of terrorism, and wars. It is also playing an increasingly important role in destabilizing states and endangering civil society. Additionally, it has the potential to fuel conflicts and destroy civil order as well as to empower warlords, organized crime, and brutal regimes. The flow of arms is believed to be among the factors determining the duration and intensity of guerrilla wars and asymmetrical threats in the area of international security. Illegal arms transfers which are financed directly or indirectly by organized criminal and terrorist networks have a huge social, cultural, and political impact. Additionally, the purchase of arms drains the resources needed to improve social conditions. Military expenditure is often substantially greater than public investment in health, education, and infrastructure in many war-torn countries.

CULTURE OF VIOLENCE

The low cost and ready availability of firearms promotes a culture of violence contributing to crime and public insecurity and hampering economic growth by forcing governments to redirect funding from social services and infrastructure to the security domain. The ready accessibility of arms is closely associated with sociopolitical problems within societies, which in turn generate a demand for the means of violence and confrontation. Illegally provided and misused military equipment has become one of the key issues in global human security. In particular, the flow of small arms and light weapons has grown continuously in recent decades, leading to the creation of a worldwide security crisis. These kinds of arms are the most common tool used in conflicts, repression, and crime. Worldwide, small arms are responsible for between 60 and 90 percent of direct conflict deaths (Wille and Krause 2005, 230). It has been estimated that small arms and light weapons cause more than 1,300 deaths every day. The value of the small arms and light weapons circulating internationally has been estimated at roughly $4 billion per year. Of this sum, 10–20 percent comes from the black and gray markets. Small arms are favorites of traffickers due to their widespread availability and portability. These kinds of weapons are very popular with recipients because small arms are inexpensive and easy to obtain, carry, and use, even by poorly trained soldiers. The best example of arms accessibility is the AK-47 assault rifle, coveted for its simplicity and firepower, which can be illegally purchased for $6 in some parts of the world. On the black market it takes as little as a few thousand dollars to acquire a shoulder-fired surface-to-air missile coming from Iraq's arsenals. This price level suggests that these and other kinds of particularly dangerous military devices are within the grasp of almost any organization interested in purchasing them.

INTERNATIONAL CONTROL MEASURES

Addressing this problem is an important part of international efforts to provide security, yet the various systems of arms control are inadequate when faced with the realities of modern arms trafficking. The current system of transfer controls does not provide any consistent, international mechanism to effectively prevent the illegal proliferation of arms, military equipment, and technology.

The growing dynamic of interconnectedness in today's security domain has diminished the effectiveness of traditional means of arms control such as arms embargoes mandated by the UN or other bodies. Instead of restricting the proliferation of arms, they often create preconditions for arms trafficking to thrive.

CONCLUSION

Although the international community is still far from preventing or eradicating arms trafficking, some important steps have been taken in this direction. A range of international responses to this problem include:

- UN Programme of Action to Prevent, Combat, and Eradicate the Illicit Trade in Small Arms and Light Weapons in All Its Aspects (adopted in 2001)
- United Nations Protocol against the Illicit Manufacturing of and Trafficking in Firearms, Their Parts and Components and Ammunition, supplementing the United Nations Convention against Transnational Organized Crime (entered into force in 2005 and was ratified by 40 nations)
- Growing efforts to establish antibrokering legislation at national and international levels, for example, the Inter-American Convention against the Illicit Manufacturing of and Trafficking in Firearms, Ammunition, Explosives, and Other Related Materials (signed by the member states of the Organization of American States in 1997)

See also: **Volume 1, Part III:** Terrorists, Criminals, and Drug Cartels

REFERENCES

Farah, Douglas, and Stephen Braun, S. *Merchant of Death: Money, Guns, Planes, and the Man Who Makes War Possible*. New York: John Wiley, 2007.

Naylor, R. T. "The Structure and Operation of the Modern Arms Black Market." In *Lethal Commerce: The Global Trade in Small Arms and Light Weapons*, edited by Jeffrey Boutwell, Michael T. Klare, and Laura W. Reed, 44–57. Cambridge, MA: American Academy of Arts and Sciences, 1995.

Krause, Keith, David Mutimer, Stephanie Pezard, James Bevan, Aaron Karp, Anna Khakee, Glenn McDonald, Katie Kennedy, Nicolas Florquin, Stephanie Schwandner-Sievers, Silvia Cattaneo, Christina Wille, Robert Muggah, and Eric G. Berman. *Small Arms Survey 2005*. Graduate Institute of International and Development Studies, Geneva, Switzerland. http://www.smallarmssurvey.org/publications/by-type/yearbook/small-arms-survey-2005.html.

Shattered Lives: The Case for Tough International Arms Control. Amnesty International, Oxfam, Control Arms Campaign, London, UK: Amnesty International & Oxfam, 2003. http://controlarms.org/wordpress/wp-content/uploads/2011/02/Shattered-lives-the-case-for-tough-international-arms-control.pdf.

United Nations Office for Disarmament Affairs. (Small Arms) n.d. http://www.un.org/disarmament/convarms/SALW/Html/SALW-PoA-ISS_intro.shtml.

Wille, Christina, and Keith Krause. "Behind the Numbers: Small Arms and Conflict Deaths." In *Small Arms Survey 2005*, edited by Keith Krause et al. Graduate Institute of International and Development Studies, Geneva, Switzerland, July 11, 2005, pp. 229–65. http://www.smallarmssurvey.org/fileadmin/docs/A-Yearbook/2005/en/Small-Arms-Survey-2005-Chapter-09-EN.pdf.

Globalization and Terrorism

Łukasz Kamieński

Globalization and terrorism, very popular and debated concepts of contemporary international relations, remain ambiguous and escape clear-cut definitions. Inevitably, any analysis of their complex interrelationships presents a dilemma. To understand present-day terrorism one must take into account globalization, an interconnective process including economic, cultural, and technological aspects. This phenomenon has had a significant impact on terrorism and its transformation.

POSTMODERN TERRORISM AND GLOBALIZATION

Since the July 1968 hijacking of an Israeli plane by the Palestinians, terrorism, traditionally a local phenomenon, has expanded to become a genuine transnational threat. Globalization has accelerated the rise of a new (postmodern) terrorism, which has become a global problem. The most profound feature of globalization is the widening, deepening, and hastening of global interconnectedness in almost every sphere of life. By destroying, weakening, or bypassing traditional barriers such as distance, time, borders, and technological limitations, globalization not only enables but also encourages transnational flows of goods, services, money, people, and ideas. This usually has positive outcomes for individuals, societies, and states by increasing competitiveness, effectiveness, and profits. However, unrestricted free flows also encourage illicit activities. By undermining old barriers and by weakening states' control globalization profits those actors (mostly terrorists and criminals) who hurt individuals, societies, and states. Thus, globalization can be counterproductive to states' efforts to prevent terrorists from exploiting gaps in the security measures intended to thwart illicit activities. This tendency of disappearing boundaries enables terrorists to be highly mobile, acquire and exchange information, obtain weapons, and smuggle money. A very good example of how globalization is empowering terrorism is the assassins of Afghan warlord Ahmed Shah Masood before the 9/11 attack—Algerians holding Belgian passports with visas to enter Pakistan that were issued in London. Not bound by geographic borders, postmodern terrorists also do not limit themselves in lethality since their axiom is "The more casualties, the better."

Technologies associated with globalization, in particular, products of the information revolution, are eagerly used by terrorists and allow their cells to carry out coordinated attacks on multiple, often remote, locations, thus increasing their operational and lethal capabilities and creating greater psychological effects. This was the case in March 2004 in Madrid (synchronized detonation of 10 bombs on trains) and in November 2008 in Mumbai where four teams simultaneously assaulted different sites. Computers, modems, the Internet, satellite and cell phones, handheld radios, and global positioning systems (GPS) have increased the ability of terrorist organizations to communicate, plan, and coordinate their attacks. The 9/11 assailants, for example, used prepaid phone cards to contact cell leaders. The Lashkar-e-Taiba attackers in Mumbai were receiving instructions and updated information from their accomplices via mobile phones following the live telecast of the rescue operation. Lashkar-e-Taiba is also known for using wireless Internet in its Pakistani camps and utilizing Google Earth to search for targets in Kashmir.

COMMUNICATIONS TECHNOLOGY

Terrorists exploit high-tech devices in various ways, sometimes in a direct or primitive way as during the Madrid bombing when cell phones served as bomb detonators. The miniaturization of electronics adds to terrorists' greater mobility. Portable personal devices enable terrorists, unbounded by state borders, to carry small explosives and weapons to conduct more spectacular and lethal attacks.

Terrorist groups use sophisticated encryption software easily available on the market for security reasons. Communication used to be the weakest point of terrorism due to the vulnerability of being tracked down. Technologies of today, however, enable communication to be highly clandestine and difficult to trace. A good example might be the use of electronic "dead letter mails"—saving messages in shared e-mail accounts without sending them out, so there is nothing that might be intercepted.

The computer and communication technologies of globalization have helped in establishing a new, decentralized network-centered structure of global terrorist groups. Cyberspace became a global blackboard for the subversive exchange of know-how and a worldwide discussion room with, for example, more than 5,000 active militant Islamic discussion sites. A virtual jihadist community has its own cyberspace "academy" with instructive digital videos, guides, scenarios of ambushes, manuals on the manufacture of explosives, and so on. According to some experts, this highly networked transmutation of terrorism takes the form of "al-Qaeda 2.0." In fact, al-Qaeda is not a single organization but a franchising-like agency based on jihadist internationalism whose cells and groups are networked in a global militant movement. It is a "base" of a coalition of extremist Islamist groups (labeled "Holy War Inc." by Peter Bergen) located in different places, including Afghanistan, Algeria, Egypt, Indonesia, Sudan, and Pakistan. What keeps this loose global network going is a religious internationalism whose message has global appeal. Al-Qaeda's strategist, Mustafa Setmariam Nasar, produced a doctrine for a decentralized global jihad spelled out in his Internet-circulated paper "The Call for a Global Islamic Resistance." He advised a reorganization after the group lost its sanctuary in Afghanistan. Nasar called for local, self-sufficient cells acting on their own within a loose network. This strategy of a decentralized war became visible in Casablanca (2003), Madrid (2004), and London (2005).

Globalization encourages networking and cooperation. Sometimes different terrorist groups collaborate as was the case with Irish Republican Army members who were arrested in 2001 in Bogotá for training their counterparts from the Fuerzas Armadas Revolucionarias de Colombia (Revolutionary Armed Forces of Colombia). Also, Lashkar-e-Taiba shares resources and information with al-Qaeda and the Taliban. More urgent than cooperation between various terrorist groups is, however, their closer relationship with organized crime.

TRANSNATIONAL CRIME

Globalization turned organized crime from traditional, local, and clan-based groups such as the Sicilian mafia into truly transnational networks. Criminals make use of global technologies and opportunities, mainly the

Internet, to generate more profit. The shadowy side of globalization, as organized crime is often labeled, has established a symbiosis with certain terrorist entities. In fact, globalization itself has helped to bring these two together. Various groups launched working relationships with Chinese *triads*, Russian and Italian mafias, and so on. Organized crime supplies terrorists with resources, mainly weapons, yet the convergence of terrorism with organized crime is twofold—terrorists are cooperating with criminals (like Hezbollah's nexus with Mexican drug rings), but they also turn to criminal activities themselves (like the Philippine Abu Sayyaf Group, practicing piracy, kidnapping, and gunrunning). Some of them might therefore be referred to as terrorist-criminal groups or hybrids. The Cold War model of state-sponsored terrorism gave way to a pattern whereby many terrorist groups are financing themselves through criminal activities and money laundering. For example, the Taliban generates revenue from both the production of opium and early-stage trafficking of Afghan heroin, while the Fuerzas Armadas Revolucionarias de Colombia have depended on funds generated by taxing coca growers and cocaine exports. The liberalization of money transfers and the rise of global financial markets also serve as a great advantage for self-financing terrorist organizations of the 21st century.

INTERNATIONAL MEDIA

Global terrorism uses Western global media to serve its goals of keeping the "infidel" societies anxious. Casualties are not the ends but the means since the greater, more visible, and more publicized the degree of fatality, the more profound the effect (i.e., intensification of panic and anxiety). The media forcefully and globally magnifies the terrorists' message. According to Bruce Hoffman terrorists exploit and manipulate the media, which serve *them* rather than the state under attack. Globalization and its technologies, mostly the Internet, empower terrorists with range and message sophistication.

Former U.S. Secretary of State Colin Powell was not blunt enough when in April 2001 he observed that "terrorism shows the dark side [of globalization] as it exploits the easing of travel restrictions, the improvements of communications, or the internationalization of banking and finance, making it easier for terrorists to do their work" (Taillon 2002, 173). Postmodern terrorism is one of the products of globalization. For many it is unexpected and unintended, but that is exactly how globalization works: since it began, it has been developing beyond control.

GLOBALIZATION AND EXPLOITATION

Paradoxically, while widely exploiting the products of the globalized world, terrorism denounces globalization as such. When it relies on globalization to reconstruct a Muslim community well beyond national boundaries, it employs the very essence of globalization. The rise of global terrorism can be explained as a response to three aspects of globalization: cultural, religious, and economic. Terrorism becomes a tactic of slowing down the forces of globalization by launching assaults on nations that facilitate globalization. First, Islamist militants use violence as a way of defending and preserving traditions, values, and unique cultural identity against Western materialism, secularism, and decadence, which are aggressively spreading through globalization. Second, globalization encourages religious fundamentalism, which draws on tribalism and the local traditions it wishes to protect. Global jihad might be seen as a reaction to the perceived oppression of Muslims around the world and the spiritual bankruptcy of the West. Third, globalization is not really global; it is an asymmetrical process based on a distinctive mechanism of inclusion and exclusion. Manuel Castells writes about the "variable geometry" of globalization since it creates wealth but also inequalities (Castells 2008, 81). For the excluded it is a tool of constant exploitation of the South, keeping it underdeveloped and dependent—a current form of Western imperialism. The reaction to such uneven economic globalization is violence, which, to get back to Franz Fanon, is to right economic wrongs. Anatol Lieven writes about "the dark side of the global village," whose alienated groups can now hurt their supposed oppressors regardless of the distance (Lieven 2001). To achieve a spectacular effect, terrorism chooses global icons as its targets, be it the World Trade Center in New York City, luxurious hotels in India, or Indonesian tourist spots. However, critics of the economic explanation of global terrorism aptly point out that many of its members, including Osama bin Laden, are well educated and wealthy.

CONCLUSION

Globalization and its technologies produce new risks that proliferate at an exponential rate. Global terrorism, which exploits the anxieties concerning side effects of Western technological advances, is one of them. The risks of the 21st century are more catastrophic than before simply because they have become global. The 21st century will be still witnessing the "clash of globalizations": Western (post)modernity versus the globalization of the reaction against it. Indeed, globalization has changed the character of terrorism but not its very nature.

See also: **Volume 1, Part I:** Global Terrorism Post-9/11; Terrorist Threat in the 21st Century: A Global Security Problem; War on Terror. **Part III:** Identifying and Combating Sources of Terrorist Financing; International Media: Critical Tool in the Battle against Terrorism; Terrorists, Criminals, and Drug Cartels; The United States, Iraq, and the Global Terrorism Problem

REFERENCES

Bergen, Peter L. *Holy War Inc.: Inside the Secret World of Osama bin Laden.* New York: Free Press, 2001.

Bobbitt, Philip. *Terror and Consent: The Wars for the Twenty-First Century.* New York: Anchor Books, 2009.

Castells, Manuel. "The New Public Sphere: Global Civil Society, Communication Networks and Global Governance." *Annals of the American Academy, American Academy of Political and Social Science* 616 (March 2008): 78–93. http://annenberg.usc.edu/Faculty/Communication%20and%20Journalism/~/media/78.ashx.

Cohen, Daniel. *Globalization and Its Enemies.* Cambridge, MA: MIT Press, 2006.

Coker, Christopher. "Globalisation and Insecurity in the Twenty-First Century: NATO and the Management of Risk." Adelphi Paper, no. 345. London: International Institute for Strategic Studies, 2002.

Friedman, Thomas L. *The World Is Flat: A Brief History of the Twenty-First Century.* New York: Farrar, Straus and Giroux, 2005.

Hoffman, Bruce. *Inside Terrorism.* New York: Columbia University Press, 2006.

Kiras, James D. "Terrorism and Globalization." In *The Globalization of World Politics: An Introduction to International Relations,* edited by John Baylis, Steve Smith, and Patricia Owens, 370–85. Oxford: Oxford University Press, 2007.

Lieven, Anatol. "Strategy for Terror." *Prospect Magazine* 67 (October 20, 2001). http://www.prospectmagazine.co.uk/2001/10/strategyforterror/.

Taillon, J. Paul de B. *Hijacking and Hostages: Government Responses to Terrorism.* Westport, CT: Praeger, 2002.

Human and Signal Intelligence: Critical Components in Effective Counterterrorism Strategies

Sean J. McLaughlin

Under perfect circumstances, the well-funded intelligence community of a rich Western country like the United States would closely coordinate the human intelligence (HUMINT) and signals intelligence (SIGINT) sources at its disposal to thwart terrorist attacks before they happen. In practice, however, political decision makers who manage intelligence agencies often have to make difficult decisions that undermine the ideal balance between the two due to budgetary constraints, reliability assessments, and acceptable risks of detection. In the decade leading up to the 9/11 attacks, the Clinton administration chose to scale back American HUMINT capabilities in favor of a major SIGINT expansion. This decision seemed perfectly justifiable at the time with the Cold War over and exponential growth in the use of e-mail and cell phones, but it now appears in hindsight to have left the country more vulnerable to al-Qaeda attacks. The intelligence component of counterterrorism remains an inexact science, however, and there is no perfect catchall strategy. While there have been no successful terrorist attacks against the United States since 9/11, the continued ability of al-Qaeda head Osama bin Laden to elude Washington and its allies almost a decade into the war on terror has demonstrated that a small but determined foe can confound even the world's best-funded, most professional intelligence community.

SIGNAL AND HUMAN INTELLIGENCE

American SIGINT falls under the domain of the National Security Agency (NSA), which serves various branches of the intelligence community, political leaders, and the military. Prior to 9/11 the NSA had succeeded in maintaining a very low public profile, though it has now grown to roughly three times the size of the Central Intelligence Agency (CIA). The NSA is charged with monitoring electronic transmissions emanating from computers, phones, radar, weapons systems, and other sources from hostile powers and individuals in order to provide political and military leaders in Washington with a better sense of enemy intentions. Successful execution of this task requires the NSA to keep abreast of constantly evolving technology and to quickly decipher an enormous volume of signals. As such, SIGINT analysts do not necessarily correspond to popular stereotypes of "spooks" and are most often linguists, mathematicians, engineers, or computer experts.

The chief American HUMINT agencies are the Federal Bureau of Investigation (FBI) and CIA, who work at home and abroad, respectively, and the Defense Intelligence Agency, which requires a constant stream of actionable intelligence to direct military forces in the field. HUMINT is drawn from both open sources and interrogations or interviews of persons who potentially hold unique knowledge of enemy thinking, such as émigrés, refugees, prisoners of war, and legal travelers, but also encompasses the clandestine activities of spies and informants operating in sensitive areas. These assets can provide valuable reconnaissance or information on enemy plans and intentions, weaponry, and so on, but their missions must be undertaken in the utmost secrecy because their discovery would put their sponsor at risk.

SIGINT and HUMINT have very different advantages and vulnerabilities, which means that decision makers are provisioned with the most complete, reliable intelligence when sources from both are mutually reinforcing. SIGINT collectors are capable of providing a nearly instant flow of information that is often highly specific and targeted. That said, they can be evaded through high-grade encryption technology, are sometimes vulnerable to weather conditions, and can be duped by false information sent out for deception purposes. Successful analysis also requires a considerable degree of coordination between fallible human collectors and users of intelligence. The NSA did not detect the failed 1993 attack on the World Trade Center, successful attacks on the American embassies in Kenya and Tanzania in 1998 and the USS *Cole* in Yemen in 2000, and, most important, the 9/11 attacks, because the perpetrators kept electronic transmissions to a minimum. Human assets, by contrast, can be used to penetrate secure areas to obtain hard documentary evidence on enemy plans, new weapons, research, and so on that often eludes SIGINT sources, as well as providing subjective assessments of enemy intentions. There are major downsides to HUMINT, however, most notably unpredictable success rates, the political risk of an agent being discovered or captured, reliability, the possibility human assets will "flip" and become double agents, and a significant time gap between collection and analysis.

There was a huge shift during the Clinton years away from traditional HUMINT in favor of SIGINT. The Clinton administration perceived SIGINT to be a "cleaner" form of intelligence for the post–Cold War era, one that could be acquired without relying on unsavory characters whose criminality or involvement in gross human rights violations had in the past been overlooked in the name of national security. In 1995, the American government placed stricter regulations on the recruitment of human assets to ensure that the CIA operated within the constraints of the law, but this restricted its ability to recruit the type of agent who could penetrate a tightly knit terrorist group like al-Qaeda. By the end of the 1990s the CIA's Directorate of Operations, which oversees most nonmilitary foreign HUMINT operations, had its number of case officers reduced by 25 percent from Cold War levels, while stations in Afghanistan and other sensitive parts of the Arab-Muslim world were closed. Before 9/11, Washington had already set up an interagency unit to hunt down bin Laden, was spending roughly $30 billion a year on intelligence, and had increased direct spending on counterterrorism roughly fourfold over Clinton's second term, but SIGINT had become the dominant source of counterterrorism intelligence for American decision makers.

INTELLIGENCE AND INTERAGENCY COOPERATION

One of the major problems facing the American intelligence community in the wake of 9/11 is the reality that a new generation of terrorists has grown far more cautious about electronic transmissions—often possessing high-grade encryption technology—than in the past. HUMINT assets are thus essential to uncover and thwart plans that terrorists will not run the risk of revealing via electronic transmissions, but they take a considerable amount of time to develop and train. The United States—which has faced chronic shortages of translators familiar with Middle Eastern dialects and able to pass through a vigorous security screening process—simply does not have a large enough pool of loyal, competent, bilingual potential agents with roots in the Arab-Muslim world willing to engage in this sort of high-risk clandestine activity. Building effective HUMINT capabilities in the Middle East continues to be an expensive, time-consuming process.

One of the biggest intelligence reforms after 9/11 was increased cooperation among various agencies. The National Counterterrorism Center was established in McLean, Virginia, in 2005 to coordinate the counterterrorism efforts of the CIA, FBI, NSA, and others. The center sifts through up to 70 terrorist threats to the United States daily, holding thrice-daily conferences seven days a week with the participation of representatives from the Pentagon, the Department of Homeland Security, and the White House. This has been accompanied by the establishment of a formal program to train intelligence officers how to identify potential terrorists and warn other government agencies before terrorists reach American soil. Interagency cooperation has paid dividends; the FBI, CIA, and U.S. military have arrested over 5,000 terrorists worldwide since 9/11 and, most important, have thwarted another major attack. Preventing another 9/11 will require the strengthening of both SIGINT and HUMINT capabilities at all levels—collection, processing, analysis, and dissemination—as well as using each to reinforce the other rather than treating them separately.

The Bush administration's expansion of the NSA's powers to collect electronic transmissions at home was one of the more controversial measures taken during the war on terror. In the early years of the Cold War, the United States partnered with Britain, Canada, Australia, and New Zealand to establish Echelon, a massive global electronic spying network that was hidden from public knowledge until its existence was confirmed by a leak within the Australian government in 1999. Echelon is made up of powerful computers with voice-recognition software that can pick up billions of international phone calls, faxes, e-mails, and radio transmissions anywhere on earth. Listening posts all over the world filter for key words and patterns in messages, with international criminals and terrorists as Echelon's ostensible target. Additionally, a little over a month after the 9/11 attacks, the Bush administration passed the USA PATRIOT Act, which gave law enforcement greater latitude to intercept and analyze a variety of domestic and foreign electronic communications as well as personal and financial records; it also allowed foreign intelligence agencies to gather information within the United States.

In general, these measures undid many restrictions on domestic surveillance imposed by the 1978 Foreign Intelligence Surveillance Act, designed to curb the worst excesses of the intelligence community during the Vietnam War era. It was revealed by the *New York Times* in December 2005 that the Bush administration had secretly authorized the NSA in early 2002 to launch warrantless intercepts of foreign calls and e-mails from thousands of people within the United States—citizens and noncitizens alike—in an attempt to track down al-Qaeda links. The administration defended itself by arguing that the use of Echelon resources on Americans was the only means of gathering actionable, time-sensitive intelligence from the cell phones and computers that were being captured by U.S. forces in Afghanistan and Pakistan. Critics who charged that this was an unconstitutional violation of civil liberties were further incensed upon learning from NSA whistleblower Russell Tice in early 2009 that, as many suspected, the NSA had in fact intercepted all domestic communications, by phone, fax, and computer, not only foreign communications to or from the United States.

CONCLUSION

This intrusive use of SIGINT was an unfortunate price the United States had to pay while it rebuilt its HUMINT capabilities; however controversial the measure, it did save lives. Among its successes were the discovery and thwarting of the plans of a naturalized American citizen, Iyman Faris, to blow up the Brooklyn Bridge in 2003 and the discovery of another al-Qaeda plot to bomb British pubs and train stations in 2004.

See also: **Volume 1, Part III:** Information Security; Information Technologies to Combat Terrorism; Intelligence/Information Sharing between U.S. Government Agencies; Intelligence Sharing and Law Enforcement Cooperation between Nations

REFERENCES

Betts, Richard K. "Fixing Intelligence." *Foreign Affairs* 81(January–February 2002): 43–59.
"'Countdown with Keith Olbermann' for Wednesday, January 21, 2009." *MSNBC,* January 21, 2009. http://www.msnbc.msn.com/id/28794766/.
Kessler, Ronald. "A Journalist's View: The New Spies." *SAIS Review* 28 (Winter–Spring 2008): 147–56.
Kim, Jin, and William M. Allard. "Intelligence Preparation of the Battlespace: A Methodology for Homeland Security Intelligence Analysis." *SAIS Review* 28 (Winter–Spring 2008): 75–87.
Wijk, Rob de. "The Limits of Military Power." *Washington Quarterly* 25 (Winter 2002): 75–92.

Identifying and Combating Sources of Terrorist Financing

Diane Russel Ong Junio

How important is money to a terrorist? An operative of the al-Qaeda network once said, "There are two things that a brother must always have for jihad, the self, and money" (Miniter 2005, 23). Terrorist groups and their operations hinge on the availability of funds and the lifeblood that money brings. Without money, there can be no spectacular attacks, no casualties, and no damages—all of which are considered essential by terrorist groups to draw attention to their cause and advance their objectives.

WHAT IS TERRORIST FINANCING?

The United Nations International Convention for the Suppression of the Financing of Terrorism (1999) provides a comprehensive definition that, in brief, covers any monetary efforts by an individual that lead to an offensive terrorist act or an act that may cause harm to civilians. In addition to more proactive fund-raising efforts, terrorist financing can be seen as *reverse money laundering* as perpetrators use clean money or money from unknown sources for a destructive act. The main difference between terrorist financing and money laundering is essentially that "money laundering cleans dirty money, terrorist financing dirties clean money" and that the illegal act in money laundering occurs at the beginning of the process but the exact opposite is the case in terrorist financing (Waszak 2004, 675).

A number of support and operational activities of terrorist groups require funding, including propaganda, recruitment, procurement, transportation, safe houses, travel, communication, training, initial and final surveillance and reconnaissance activities, rehearsal activities, and the attack itself. Significantly, the cost of carrying out a terrorist attack is relatively cheap considering its enormous and devastating impacts, such as the loss of life, damage to infrastructure, and undermining of specific state and multilateral security measures. It is now widely acknowledged that terrorists' ability to undertake large-scale attacks would be significantly reduced if they were denied access to funds or lacked an adequate financing structure.

INTERNATIONAL INSTANCES OF TERRORISM FINANCING

As terrorist organizations become more sophisticated in nature, new and innovative funding methods are being developed. The money for terrorist operations is derived from both legal and illicit means. Terrorist groups in countries in Southeast Asia and South America have long been documented as carrying out criminal activities—such as extortion, kidnapping, drug trafficking, and fraud—to finance their activities, while terrorist groups in the Middle East are said to get funds from legitimate sources such as businesses and charities. Much of the information about terrorism financing is centered on the so-called jihadi groups. To better illustrate how terrorist groups generate funds, an example would be to look at the funding mechanisms of al-Qaeda and Jemaah Islamiyah.

The funding mechanism of al-Qaeda mainly relied on a network of non-governmental organizations and charities that were established at the height of the Soviet invasion of Afghanistan in the 1980s (Kohlmann 2006, 1). These organizations were used to channel funds, resources, supplies, and recruits to the mujahideen movement. The money for these organizations would usually come from donations and *zakat* (obligatory charity) from Muslims all over the world. Al-Qaeda effectively exploited these nongovernmental organizations and charities for funds and support while using them as fronts or covers for its activities.

During the late 1980s and early 1990s al-Qaeda sought to expand its network in Southeast Asia, where the moderate Muslim population is quite extensive. However, the region takes on a slightly different flavor as most believers are beleaguered by environmental pressures arising from social and economic hardships and thwarted political and developmental expectations. Consequently, many Muslims became disgruntled and angry during this time. Al-Qaeda efficiently manipulated these frustrations to establish its network in Southeast Asia. Additionally, certain locations were selected for having a number of lawless areas that could be used as secure staging areas for attacks and as safe havens for regrouping. More important, the region is deemed vital for al-Qaeda's logistical and financial requirements (Abuza 2003, 5).

Many regional and international terrorism experts and academic studies believe that the influence of the al-Qaeda terrorist network was at its peak in the 1990s when it was expanding across Southeast Asia to Malaysia, Indonesia, Singapore, and the Philippines. Southeast Asian terrorist groups, such as the Abu Sayyaf Group and Moro Islamic Liberation Front in the Philippines and Jemaah Islamiyah in Indonesia, have benefited from the logistical and financial support of al-Qaeda, while the first two are also notorious for engaging in various criminal activities to fund operations. Breaking down the financial structure a bit further, three major local and international sources have been identified: (1) criminal activity, (2) charities or nongovernmental organizations, and (3) front organizations.

The al-Qaeda terrorist network provided Islamic militants, especially members of Jemaah Islamiyah, with financial support and military training. Al-Qaeda's presence in Southeast Asia has resulted in the inclusion of groups such as Jemaah Islamiyah and the Abu Sayyaf Group within the global terrorist network, using their home bases as safe havens where terrorist attacks are planned and launched against the United States and other Western targets.

Since the 1990s, the Jemaah Islamiyah has developed territory-based administrative structures, or *mantiqis,* throughout Southeast Asia. The *mantiqis* are equivalent to regions and are further broken down into *wakalahs,* or districts, which are subdivided into *fiahs,* or cells. *Mantiqi* I, which was based in Malaysia, is said to have provided the economic support for the operations of the Jemaah Islamiyah. The Jemaah Islamiyah has developed a sophisticated structure to handle its funds and to set up front companies and businesses. Its primary sources of funds were identified by Abuza (2003, 9) as:

- Bags of cash or money brought in by cash couriers
- Funds skimmed from Islamic charities
- Front companies and businesses
- *Hawala,* a money remittance system
- Gold and gem smuggling
- *Zakat* (charitable giving) and contributions from Jemaah Islamiyah members and supporters
- Al-Qaeda investments and accounts already established in the region
- Criminal activities

One of the more significant terrorist financing activities by al-Qaeda and Jemaah Islamiyah was a reaction to new government financial policies, especially in Malaysia. From the late 1980s to the mid-1990s, the Malaysian government channeled its efforts toward making the country more viable for businesses. Foreign business investments, trade, and tourism were encouraged. It was also during this time that the country started to emerge as one of the centers for Islamic banking. Setting up front companies and businesses was seen to be the most significant move of Jemaah Islamiyah in Malaysia at that time. These organizations were used as conduits to channel al-Qaeda funds, as well as to procure weapons and explosive materials. According to the Singapore government's white paper on Jemaah Islamiyah, there were also cases wherein members of the group set up legitimate businesses, conducted deals and contracts, and channeled all the earnings back to the organization. It was said that all Jemaah Islamiyah–run businesses and front companies were required to contribute 10 percent of their total earnings to the group. The money was channeled into Jemaah Islamiyah's special fund, *infaq fisbillah,* which means "contributions for the Islamic cause" or in other words the jihad fund.

CONCLUSION

Since the September 11, 2001, terrorist attacks, there have been substantial international efforts to curb terrorist financing activities. Nonetheless, the changing nature of terrorist groups entails that their means of acquiring and moving funds have also evolved. Terrorist groups could now utilize mobile banking, Internet banking, cash couriers, wire transfers, and digital cash for their financing. Furthermore, in countries such as

Indonesia, Malaysia, and the Philippines, *hawala* remains popular. There are no systems in place that would regulate the *hawalas* in these countries, thus rendering it vulnerable for exploitation by nefarious individuals and groups.

The financing of terror networks is a global issue. It is important to realize that what we are dealing with are groups and individuals who are quick to adapt to the measures and safeguards implemented to curtail such activity. Given the fact that there have been countries, especially in Southeast Asia, which have been used as a main base and transit point for terrorist financing, it is important that governments employ all available national and international resources at their disposal to counter the threat. Rather than reinventing the wheel, governments must learn how to benefit from the large pool of regional and international best practices and standards available. Coordination and cooperation of all stakeholders at the local, national, regional, and international levels would strengthen and enhance the security and stability of the global financial system. Vigilance is the key in the strategy to combat terrorist financing and other financial crimes; all governments should make it a top priority to implement measures that will protect their country's financial institutions from these threats.

See also: **Volume 1, Part III:** The Economics of Counterterrorism; Multidisciplinary Approach to Combating Terrorism; Multilateral Sanctions against State Sponsors of Terrorism; Organizational Resilience and Counterterrorism; Role of the International Community; Safe Havens and Weak and Failing States. **Part IV:** Eliminating Terrorist Support Networks; United Nations Global Counterterrorism Strategy: Significance and Limitations. **Part VI:** Weak Link: Identifying and Attacking Terrorists Vulnerabilities

REFERENCES

Abuza, Zachary. "Funding Terrorism in Southeast Asia: The Financial Network of the Al Qaeda and the Jemaah Islamiyah." *NBR Analysis* 14, no. 5 (2003): 1–68.

Kohlmann, Evan. *The Role of Islamic Charities in International Terrorist Recruitment and Financing*. Danish Institute for International Studies (DISS) Working Paper no. 2006/7, 2006.

Miniter, Richard. *Disinformation: 22 Media Myths That Undermine the War on Terror*. Washington, DC: Regnery, 2005.

Schott, P. *Reference Guide to Anti-Money Laundering and Combating the Financing of Terrorism*. 2nd ed. Washington, DC: World Bank/International Monetary Fund, 2006.

Singaporean Ministry of Home Affairs. "The Jemaah Islamiya and the Threat of Terrorism." White Paper, 2003.

Waszak, John. "The Obstacles to Suppressing Radical Islamic Terrorist Financing." *Case Western Reserve Journal of International Law* 36, no. 2/3 (2004): 673.

Ideology That Spawns Islamist Militancy

Nassef M. Adiong

Throughout history Islam has been interpreted in various often discordant and conflicting ways. The debates over the question of authority and legitimacy to speak for and thus define Islam are particularly intense in contemporary times. As a result, confusion and distortion exist among Muslims and non-Muslims alike as to Islam's position on a number of different issues such as human rights, democracy, and international cooperation. An area that has received wide attention is so-called Islamist militancy.

Islam is viewed differently among peoples with diverse cultural and sociological backgrounds, particularly the geographic division of West and East set by traditional orientalist scholars. The West sees Islam as a religion similar to Christianity, although they do not accord it the same level of respect as Christianity or Judaism. They perceive Islam as the "other" and are totally indifferent to their cultural understanding. In contrast, the East regards Islam not only as a religion but as a total way of life that governs every aspect of human existence.

HISTORICAL EVOLUTION OF ISLAMIST MILITANCY

One climatic historical event that caused much discord and the decline of sixth-century Islamic scholarship, and later paved the way for the legalistic interpretation of Islam that eventually spawned the political ideology of Islamism, was the Mongolian invasion of Muslim lands in the early 13th century. Prior to the invasion, there was a blossoming of intellectual competition among scholars from different Islamic schools of thought, disciplines, and sciences. These were the Islamic philosophers, mystics, and jurists competing for intellectual recognition and legitimacy. However, the invasion that massacred Muslims and non-Muslims, committed genocidal acts, and burned Islamic mosques and libraries, especially the "House of Wisdom" in Baghdad during the Abbassid era, resulted in centuries of dark ages characterized by unpleasant and demeaning lives throughout the Muslim world, even though the Mongols eventually converted to Islam later in this period.

Islamic philosophy and mysticism became dormant while Islamic jurisprudence gradually dominated the debates and earned recognition and millions of followers particularly from major groups and sectors of Sunni and Shia. Intensification of the legalistic interpretation intermittently increased and materialized in the post-Nasser era. The Iranian Revolution (1979) and the Soviet invasion of Afghanistan (1979) further strengthened and reinforced this new radical mindset often referred to as political Islam and/or Islamism. The current upheavals in the Arab world, led by youth and other disaffected Arabs clamoring for political change and better socioeconomic conditions and against the tyrannical rule of their dictators, might weaken Islamist militancy, but this remains an open question.

SURVEY OF ISLAMIST THINKERS AND THEIR IDEOLOGIES

An ideology will not take root or proliferate without key thinkers, their intellectual stamina, powers of persuasion, material power, and their supporters and followers. These factors account for the development of the successful implementation and practice of an extremist worldview or ideology. The following are a few prominent Islamist thinkers that have impacted the Muslim world.

Ibn Taymiyya and Puritanism

Taqi ad-Din Ahmad Ibn Taymiyya (1263–1328) is considered to be the father of Islamic Puritanism and fundamentalism. He was a devout follower of Ahmad ibn Hanbal, the founder of the strictest Islamic orthodox school, that is, the Hanbalites, which "is today the law in Saudi Arabia" (Demant 2006, 13). He called for a puritanical way of going back to the original sources of Islam: the Quran and the sunna. He lived during the Mongolian rule and issued a fatwa of jihad against the Muslim convert Mongols for their reluctance to adhere to and employ a strict interpretation of sharia laws. He was the first jurist to consider jihad as an ultimate obligation of every Muslim in their struggle against nonbelievers, infidels, apostates, and even Muslims considered heretics under false leadership (Demant 2006, 102). His idea of a violent jihad against Muslims and non-Muslims greatly influenced the thinking of Islamist militants, who often cite his sources to validate their approach in representing Islam (Sjadzali 1991, 56–63).

Abd al-Wahhab and Wahhabism

Muhammad ibn Abd al-Wahhab (1709–1792) propagated Salafism under Hanbali jurisprudence but questioned the absoluteness and the authoritative legitimacy of the four Sunni orthodox schools of thought, namely, Shafi'i, Hanafi, Maliki, and Hanbali. Since some members of the al- Saud family were his students, he was able to form an alliance with the House of Saud to promote his teachings throughout their territories. This later became the ruling regime in the present Saudi Arabia. He also revived the works of Ibn Taymiyya and advocated for "purification of Islam from what he considered to be heretical and magical accretions" (Zubaida 1993, 10), or the significance of going back to the original principles of Islam in governing human life. Moreover, he implemented the practice of stoning to death for convicted adulterers, gays, infidels, and heretics. He was against innovations and creativity in interpreting Islam. Although Wahhabism is considered an ultraconservative sect within the Salafi movement, it is not considered a potent initiator of the Islamist movement. "Instead, the Wahhabis were simply a part of the broader interactions of many different individuals and groups" (Voll 1997, 233).

Muhammad Abduh and the Contemporary Salafism

Though Salafism can be attributed to the teachings of Ahmad ibn Hanbal, Ibn Taymiyya, and Abd al-Wahhab, it was Muhammad Abduh (1849–1905) who revived the creed of the Salafi movement, along with Jamal al-Din Afghani and Rashid Rida. Abduh's aim was to reform Muslim societies away from the dominant conservative understanding of the religion. His theory was based on the "concept of the pious forefathers, the Salafiyya or the first Muslims" (Sjadzali 1991, 86–87). Abduh rejected the common idea that the entire Quran was divinely inspired. Rather, he ascribed many parts of it to the personal thinking of Muhammad himself. He advocated that the Quran should be understood by the application of reason rather than literally. In addition, he claimed that "the principles of the Qur'an were the only tool by which the human mind truly could understand the difference between right and wrong, indirectly casting doubt on the validity of the Hadiths and the Sunna of Muhammad" (Zubaida 1993, 43–48). He asserted that they represented a rational and practical understanding of society. From that assertion, he claimed that Islam was fully capable of adjusting to modernity. He claimed that *ijtihad*, individual judgment based on case law or past precedent, could still be performed. Abduh's teaching was very much based on the conservative schools of Ibn Taymiyya and Ibn Qaiyim al-Jawziya and the ethics of al-Ghazali (Sjadzali 1991, 83–84).

Hassan al-Banna and the Muslim Brotherhood

Hasan Ahmed Abdel Rahman Muhammed al-Banna (1906–1949) is "frequently characterized as the father of contemporary Islamism" (Euben and Zaman 2009, 49). He wanted to restore an original Islamic order, the same as that theoretically advocated by Ibn Taymiyya, Abd al-Wahhab, and Sayyid Qutb. He aimed to include Islamic education, or madrassa, in all aspects of life for every individual, particularly those who aspire to run for public office. He vehemently rejected alien culture, entertainment, arts, thoughts, and education, especially that coming from West (Europe, Israel, and the United States), which may corrupt the purity and modesty of Islamic civilization. In line with Ibn Taymiyya's thought, he agreed totally that jihad is an obligation that must be imposed in an Islamic state, more so in the *ummah*, or Islamic nation. Furthermore, allegiance to the *ummah* must be by faith alone and not based on origins or cultural or ethnic backgrounds (Euben and Zaman 2009, 54).

Sayyid Qutb and Modern *Jahiliyyah*

Sayyid Qutb (1906–1966) was sentenced to death by the Nasser regime for treason. He declared jihad against the Nasser administration because he believed that Egyptians were living in a state of *jahiliyyah*, or ignorance, and he referred to Nasser as a heretic. He claimed that what propelled people's beliefs and ideas, habits and arts, rules and laws was in opposition to the pure teachings of Islam and thus resembled elements of *jahiliyyah*. He further lamented that the Muslim world had ceased to be and had reverted to pre-Islamic ignorance because of the scarcity in implementation of sharia laws. Consequently, all states of the Muslim world are not Islamic and are thus illegitimate, including his native land Egypt. To restore Islam on earth and free Muslims from "jahili society, jahili concepts, jahili traditions and jahili leadership" (Qutb 2005, 21), he advocated that a vanguard be formed modeling itself after the original Muslims, the Companions of the Prophet Muhammad. The Muslim vanguard (just dictatorship) would successfully vanquish *jahiliyyah*, primarily for two reasons:

1. They will cut themselves off from the *jahiliyyah*; that is, they should ignore the teachings and culture of non-Muslim groups (Greeks, Romans, Persians, Christians, or Jews) and separate themselves from their old non-Muslim friends and family (Qutb 2005, 16 and 20).
2. They must look to the Quran for orders to obey, not for "learning and information" or solutions to problems (Qutb 2005, 17–18).

Ayatollah Khomeini and the *Velayat e-Faqih*

Imam/Ayatollah Ruhollah Musavi Khomeini (1900–1989) was a Shia cleric and *marja* (an authority in Islamic law) and the political leader of the 1979 Islamic Revolution that toppled Mohammad Reza Pahlavi (the shah of Iran). He became the first Supreme Leader of Iran, the highest authority in the leadership of the Islamic Republic, until his death. He adamantly opposed monarchy, arguing that a regime should be ruled only by a leading Islamic jurist who would ensure that sharia law is properly followed through the system of *velayat e-faqih*, or an absolute guardianship of Islamic jurists. He viewed certain elements of Western culture as being inherently decadent and a corrupting influence on the youth. As such, he often advocated the banning of popular Western fashions, music, cinema, and literature. His ultimate vision was for Islamic nations to converge together into a single unified power in order to avoid alignment with either side (West or East), and he believed that this would happen at some point in the near future (Imam Khomeini International University 2009).

OSAMA BIN LADEN AND AL-QAEDA

Now deceased, Osama bin Mohammed bin Awad bin Laden (1957–2011) was the founder of an Islamist extremist group, al-Qaeda, which has been designated as a terrorist organization by most governments and international organizations in the world. He advocated a global jihad against the United States and its allies and those Muslim regimes that tolerate foreign intervention in Muslim lands. He also advocated pan-Islamism or the revitalization of an *ummah* governed by the caliphate system, which is ruled by a pious Muslim and strictly enforces sharia law (Euben and Zaman 2009, 425–59).

CONCLUSION

Historically, Islamist militant ideologies are a by-product of two explicit and parallel circumstances rooted from the "outside" of and "within" the Muslim world. The outside circumstance is the unpleasant experiences of Muslim lands being subjugated by foreign invasions and being subjected to foreign cultural domination. Concomitantly from within come the rejection and avoidance of innovations, creativity, and new thinking or paradigms by certain Muslims who fear these and immediately assume that the acceptance of new ideas might lead to the collapse of the Islamic world. The 9/11 attacks that initiated the U.S.-led war on terror against nonstate groups and their networks and state-sponsored terrorism across the broader Middle Eastern and North African regions to Southeast Asia has led to an intensification of extremism and radical thinking.

See also: **Volume 1, Part I:** Concept of Islamist Jihad; The Terrorist Threat in the 21st Century: A Global Security Problem; War on Terror. **Part II:** Pakistan. **Part III:** Combating Terrorist Recruitment, Propaganda, and Radicalization Campaigns; Organizational Resilience and Counterterrorism. **Part IV:** Central Asia: Emerging Threats; Pakistan's Federally Administered Tribal Areas (FATA); Southeast Asia: Jemaah Islamiyah. **Part VI:** Global Jihad Movement

REFERENCES

Demant, Peter R. *Islam vs. Islamism: The Dilemma of the Muslim World*. Westport, CT: Praeger, 2006.

Euben, Roxanne L., and Muhammad Qasim Zaman. *Princeton Readings in Islamist Thought: Texts and Contexts from al-Banna to Bin Laden*. Princeton, NJ: Princeton University Press, 2009.

Imam Khomeini International University (IKIU). "Imam Khomeini's Biography." 2009. http://www.ikiu.ac.ir/en/page-view.php?pid=438.

Qutb, Sayyid. "Milestones." 2005. http://majalla.org/books/2005/qutb-nilestone. pdf. USA: SIME Journal, 2005.

Sjadzali, H. Munawir. *Islam and Governmental System: Teachings, History, and Reflections.* Jakarta: Indonesia-Netherlands Cooperation in Islamic Studies (INIS), 1991.

Voll, John Obert. "Relations among Islamist Groups." In *Political Islam: Revolution, Radicalism, or Reform?* edited by John L. Esposito, 231–47. Boulder, CO: Lynne Rienner, 1997.

Zubaida, Sami. *Islam, the People and the State: Political Ideas and Movements in the Middle East.* London: I. B. Tauris, 1993.

Information Security

Binoy Kampmark

The emergence of such pervasive technologies as the Internet and the increasing use of computer-generated and computer-operated infrastructure has made states' and private entities' understanding of information security fundamental to public confidence. According to 44 USC 3542(b) (1), the term *information security* means the protection of information and information systems from unauthorized access, use, disclosure, disruption, modification, or destruction in order to provide integrity, confidentiality, and availability. The U.S. Federal Information Security Management Act of 2002 (FISMA, Title III, Public Law 107-347) provides a framework for preventing harm incurred through a breach of information security.

A *national security system*, in turn, is an information system that involves intelligence and cryptological activities relating to national security, command and control of military forces, or equipment integral to weapons systems or is critical to the direct fulfillment of military or intelligence missions (44 USC 3548(b)(2)).

Breaches of information security can take various forms. The acquisition of information from systems can involve fraud, identity theft, the appropriation of authentication passwords, and the compromise of sensitive information due to terrorist and espionage activities. The Information Security Forum, one of the world's leading independent authorities on information security, defines the awareness of information security as "an ongoing process of learning that is meaningful to recipients, and delivers measurable benefits to the organization from lasting behavioural change" (European Network and Information Security Agency [ENISA] 2007, 3).

The risks posed by a compromise of information security are considerable. Global connectivity comes at considerable costs, revealing the vulnerability of network infrastructures and systems to cybercriminals, terrorists, and espionage agencies. In 2004, the presence of malware and viruses cost businesses between $169 and $204 billion. Such instances are also encouraged by an absence of firm limits on the control of information security in cyberspace.

That said, international attempts have been made to develop a regulatory framework for information security. The International Organization for Standardization (ISO) coordinates an international effort involving 157 countries that seeks to develop accepted framework protocols. These involve, among others, ISO-15443, ISO-27002, ISO-20000, and ISO-27001, which respectively deal with information technology security assurance, codes of practice for information security management, service management, and security management systems.

TARGETS

The targets in the context of information security can be significant. Cyberterrorism has emerged as a serious threat to vital infrastructure subject to computer command. Potential targets include electrical power grids, banking systems, and ministry agencies. While the damage inflicted can be immense, the cost expended in carrying out such attacks is minimal. Few operators are needed to stage attacks on network systems. Another feature of such attacks is that the perpetrators are not always clear. Identities are difficult to trace.

Characteristic of such compromises of information security are denial-of-service attacks against websites that alter the nature of the information present on the site. A denial-of-service attack effectively bombards websites with requests for data that paralyze the site's functionality. Hackers tend to use what are termed *botnets,* effectively groups of computers infected with malicious software, to conduct the attacks. The identity behind such attacks is notoriously difficult to determine, as they involve computers across countries. In addition to such "bot" networks are increases in phishing, the use of spam, Trojan horses, and zero-day threats. "Attackers are now refining their methods, so attacks tend to involve multiple attack vectors" (ENISA 2007, 3). The use of indiscriminate Internet worms is now regarded as a thing of the past. Businesses and government organizations are now targets of gathering programs that seek to prise information from organizations (private and public), often proving adept at avoiding detection.

The theft of passwords, the compromise of bank accounts, and the involvement of stolen identities in the context of terrorism are also critical features of the information security landscape. Terrorist financing through phishing attacks, often facilitated through money-laundering operations facilitated through websites, has been documented (Financial Action Task Force [FATF]/Groupe d'action financière 2008).

THE ESTONIAN PRECEDENT

The regularity of cyberattacks has increased, something that the National Intelligence Council (2008, 71) argues "will become more prevalent in conflicts over the next two decades." Countries are regularly engaging in preparations to launch and counter cyberattacks as part of their military policy. These do not merely emanate from state actors but have also been directly attributed to nonstate groups with highly complex cell networks. The most spectacular instance of this was the first recorded instance of cyberwarfare, which took place against Estonia in 2007. The Estonian government sparked considerable controversy when it moved a Soviet-era World War II memorial of a bronze soldier from its original site. Beginning on April 27, 2007, banks, ministry departments, and various arms of government were targeted. The cyberattacks were orchestrated from servers, not merely in Russia but also in Canada, Brazil, and Vietnam (Kirk 2007). However, the Russian sources indicated the use of state servers in mounting the attack. The gravity of the attacks was indicated by the involvement of personnel from the North Atlantic Treaty Organization (NATO). "In the 21st century," explained NATO spokesman James Appathurai, "it's not just about tanks and artillery" ("Estonia Hit" 2007). Estonia's vulnerability was highlighted by its emphasis on a "paperless" government in which e-government practices are implemented from banking to elections.

RESPONSES

Such attacks on the integrity of information security signal a potential redistribution of power from large, sovereign operators to smaller agents. It has been argued that the superpower status of the United States is becoming increasingly questionable in light of technologies that risk undermining its power. Experts warn of the potential that the United States could become a "Third World Country overnight" ("Cyber Attacks Jeopardize" 2010). Various countries have dedicated considerable resources to combating breaches in information security and cybersecurity. The example of the Estonian attack encouraged the European Union to enhance its capabilities to ensure information security in the wake of massive cyberattacks. A report by ENISA, an organization of the European Union Agency, found that organizations "appear to find it very difficult to put effective quantitative metrics in place" (2007, 2).

Little consensus exists on what the most effective ways are to achieve the goals of good information security. One popular way of measuring security for organizations is based on breaches documented by audit reports. The veracity of such reports is taken to be a good indicator in determining the necessary level of security. The number of incidents or breaches and the use of root-cause analysis are taken as a measure. The report found that no one solution necessarily fits all organizations. "[A] balanced set of key performance indicators (KPIs) and metrics can provide real insight into the effectiveness of awareness programs" (ENISA 2007, 2).

Legislative measures and directives exist in some countries to cope with the way data are stored and unlawfully retrieved. This is particularly relevant to private citizens. Breaches by agencies responsible for maintaining information security may result in criminal or civil suits when due diligence is not exercised. Cracking data has been criminalized in various countries, including the United Kingdom's model legislation, the Computer Misuse Act 1990.

Government awareness of the nature of compromises in information security is evidenced by such rehearsed operations as "Silent Horizon" by the U.S. Central Intelligence Agency in 2005. The purpose behind the operation was to unearth who the agents behind a massive cyberattack might be. Perhaps the most significant exercise by American authorities was conducted by the Department of Homeland Security in February 2006. The office concluded that eight cybersecurity enhancement measures should be implemented: "interagency coordination"; "contingency planning, risk assessment" and establishment of "roles and responsibilities"; "correlation of multiple incidents between public and private sectors"; a "training and exercise program"; "coordination between entities of cyberincidents"; "common framework for response and information access"; "strategic communications and public relations plan"; and "improvement of processes, tools, and technology" (Department of Homeland Security 2006, 1–2). The Office of Management and Budget has created a task force to investigate how agencies can better train personnel, respond to incidents, and cope with contingencies.

CONCLUSION

Given the acceleration of global interconnectivity and the increased reliance on e-government and information technology infrastructure, governments are increasingly focused on the threats a compromise in information security might pose. A greater emphasis is now being placed on training personnel about the importance of information integrity and the necessity for readying states in the event of serious cyberconflict and terrorist activities.

See also: **Volume 1, Part III:** Human and Signal Intelligence: Critical Components in Effective Counterterrorism Strategies; Information Technologies to Combat Terrorism; Intelligence/Information Sharing between U.S. Government Agencies; Intelligence Sharing and Law Enforcement Cooperation between Nations

REFERENCES

Barker, William C. *Guideline for Identifying an Information System as a National Security System*. Washington, DC: National Institute of Standards and

Technology, Special Publication 800-59, August 2003. http://csrc.nist.gov/publications/nistpubs/800-59/SP800-59.pdf.

"Cyber Attacks Jeopardize Superpower Status." *CBS News,* April 22, 2010. http://www.cbsnews.com/stories/2010/04/22/eveningnews/main6422768.shtml.

Department of Homeland Security, National Cyber Security Division. *Cyber Storm - Exercise Report.* Washington, DC. 2006. http://www.martinfrost.ws/htmlfiles/sept2006/cyberstorm06.pdf.

"Estonia Hit by 'Moscow Cyber War.'" *BBC News,* May 17, 2007.

European Network and Information Security Agency (ENISA). *Information Security Awareness Initiatives: Current Practice and the Measurement of Success.* July 2007. http://www.enisa.europa.eu/activities/awareness-raising/deliverables/2007/kpi-study/en.

Federal Information Security Management Act 2002 (FISMA), Title III, Public Law 107-347.

Financial Action Task Force (FATF)/Groupe d'action financière. *Terrorist Financing.* Paris, February 29, 2008. http://www.fatf-gafi.org/dataoecd/28/43/40285899.pdf.

Kirk, Jeremy "Estonia Recovers from Massive DDoS Attack." *Computerworld,* May 17, 2007.

National Intelligence Council. *Global Trends 2025: A Transformed World.* November 2008. http://www.dni.gov/nic/PDF_2025/2025_Global_Trends_Final_Report.pdf.

Information Technologies
to Combat Terrorism

Nur Azlin Mohamed Yasin and Gloria Spittel

The protracted combat against Islamist terrorism that began in the early 1990s and in 2010 is well into its second decade clearly needs to transcend the short-term kinetic seek-and-destroy conventional methods of warfare. The rapid spread of the conflict from Algeria in the early 1990s to the United States in 2001 and Pakistan in the late 2000s demonstrates the movement's resiliency. The key to the survival and spread of the struggle is al-Qaeda, vanguard of the violent Islamist movement, and its simple, powerful narrative, which has spread rapidly. The narrative rests on a simple two-part story: Muslims are failing due to the lack of a pure faith, and the West is preventing Muslims from taking their rightful place due to its anti-Muslim positions. Thus Muslims need to follow al-Qaeda and their acolytes if Islam is to succeed. All events, from the Israeli-Palestinian conflict, to the invasion of Iraq, to the burqa debate in France, affirm this narrative.

INTERNET COMMUNICATION

Al-Qaeda's simple but powerful message is easily exported to the wider Muslim world by the extremists through the effective use of the digital communication medium of the Internet. This powerful, nondiscriminatory medium allows the message and audience to escape the constraints of geography to safely tap into this message and the large supporting community. The so-called jihadists are able to disseminate their messages, as well as operational tactics, to a global, anonymous community who can engage in study and conversation from the privacy of their own homes. This can be done from anywhere on the planet in seconds. Because of the convenience, speed, and anonymity it provides, the Internet is an essential networking and communication tool used by sympathizers and terrorist groups to expand their community of supporters worldwide. Sympathizers help disseminate the extremist propaganda in forums and individual blogs. These materials include the expression of grievances vis-à-vis the malevolence of the West, and Islamist content to justify the acts of violence called for to defend what is perceived to be a repressed Muslim community. The terrorist groups can fully develop their cells online, while members who are responsible for recruiting and fund-raising can do so at an unprecedented scale (Hoffman 2008).

Information technology has gone beyond the transfer of information to the creation of operational terrorists. There are increasing cases of self-radicalization, individuals allegedly linking up with Islamist militants on the Internet, reported in the United States, Europe, and Singapore. It appears that the only connection the individuals have with the wider extremist community is through the Internet, and they are using it as their sole source for their preparation to be an Islamist militant gearing up to wage an al-Qaeda–inspired jihad. This is a clear and well-thought-out strategy by extremists to use technology to reach into the homeland of the opponent and take the war to them.

As unsettling as the preceding is, we must realize two things: First, the Internet does not have wider global penetration yet, so the problem is small but has the potential for rapid growth. Second, as we realize that there is a need for more attention and resources to be allocated to this area, we also have to be cognizant of the fact that this time offers an opportunity to develop a strategy as comprehensive as that of the opponent. Measures to curb online radicalization vary from country to country depending on each nation's laws and, most important, assessment of the threat posed. It would be controversial, for instance, for a democracy like Indonesia to control online content and the behavior of Internet users. For Indonesia, however, leaving the Bahasa Indonesian Islamist extremist online activities as they are helps to fuel the continuing radicalization. In the Indonesian context, if the extremists' online activities are allowed to continue, the counterextremist movement, by engaging and interacting with the extremists using the very same information technology used by the latter, can challenge and defeat the distortions and half-truths common on the web.

BEAT THEM AT THEIR OWN GAME

What are the elements of an effective counterstrategy? First is passive monitoring. The extremists are very confident that they are going to win and are desperate to make sure that others believe this as well. Thus, they use the Internet to freely discuss ideological differences, strategic changes, and tactical innovations. This gold mine of information needs to be better examined and understood, as it will allow for a much better counterstrategy to be developed. It is best to use the movement's own weaknesses against them. This is easy to do as the movement is not trying to hide its discussions. Second, one must understand the roots of online radicalization. One key assumption is that online radicalization occurs when an individual innocently desires to seek greater Islamic knowledge but is lured instead to an extremist site. Thus, one step is the creation of more counter-ideological websites (Bergin et al. 2009). The more opportunities there are to find the truth, the better it is for the community. The second assumption is that the attractions of the extremists' sites are not just the message but its presentation. Extremists have learned that music, poetry, dramatic videos, and the use of interactive chat rooms and forums are key hooks in attracting potential recruits. Thus, while creating more countersites is important, if they are dull and static, they will not attract the target audience. This raises the natural question, Who is the target audience? There are in reality two audiences: the general public and the extremists or potential extremists.

One can reach the general public through increasing the number of attractive counterideological sites. Better use of search engines will help in this respect. For this group, the effort is preventative, trying to alert the public before the extremists do. The second group is the radicalized individuals, who once radicalized are unlikely to look for countersites as they have already found their source or sources of information. In this case the counterstrategy has to move from passive to active. The extremists have to be engaged on the very webpage and domain where they can be found—the extremist forums and websites, as well as YouTube postings of extremist materials. Challenging their thinking and interpretations on their "home ground" denies them the safe haven assumed to be offered by the Internet and gives the countercommunity an opportunity to gain an understanding of the opponent—knowledge that can be used against them.

The best people to engage in this part of the effort are clerics and scholars well versed in Islamic studies, prepared to counter the extremist ideology. They are best equipped to infiltrate the forums and engage the extremists. The truth will win, but only those well versed in the truth of Islam can make the arguments that will, at the very least, force people out of the forums and perhaps help those who are only on the fringe to escape before they become radicalized and create additional problems.

A second and effective active element is disruption and contamination of the sites. Disruption is less effective, and closing the sites has no impact. There are more than 5,600 extremist websites, most of which are not producing original content but serving as redundant sites in case of disruption. The best approach is to attack the trust that holds these anonymous sites together. The users assume that all the members of the site are fellow travelers and that the information that is shared is accurate. If one can spread embarrassing, misleading, or false information about the movement on a website, then the users will leave and hopefully lose faith in the struggle. This is difficult and time-consuming but may pay large dividends.

CONCLUSION

Technology has once again assisted the spread of a revolutionary idea. What would take weeks to accomplish in books or letters can now be done in hours or minutes over the Internet. But ultimately it is humans and our ability to distort and manipulate the truth that cause the radicalization, not technology. Thus technology is not the entire answer. People with technological know-how and the truth will ultimately win. The saying "Ye shall know the truth, and the truth shall set you free" has never been truer.

See also: **Volume 1, Part III:** Human and Signal Intelligence: Critical Components in Effective Counterterrorism Strategies; Information Security; Intelligence/ Information Sharing between U.S. Government Agencies; Intelligence Sharing and Law Enforcement Cooperation between Nations

REFERENCES

Arrahmah.Com. http://arrahmah.com/.
Bergin, Anthony, Sulastri Osman, Carl Ungerer, and Nur Azlin Mohamed Yasin. "Countering Internet Radicalisation in Southeast Asia." S. Rajaratnam School of International Studies–Australian Strategic Policy Institute (RSIS-ASPI) Joint Report, March 2009. http://www.aspi.org.au/publica tions/publication_details.aspx?ContentID=202.
Forum Jihad Al-Tawbah. http://al-tawbah.com/f.
Hoffman, Bruce. "The Myth of Grass-Roots Terrorism; Why Osama bin Laden Still Matters." *Foreign Affairs,* May–June 2008. http://www.foreignaffairs.com/ articles/63408/bruce-hoffman/the-myth-of-grass-roots-terrorism.
Ramakrishna, Kumar. "Radical Pathways: Understanding Muslim Radicalisation in Indonesia." Westport, CT: Praeger, 2009.

Intelligence/Information Sharing between U.S. Government Agencies

Justin Lewis Abold

The events of September 11, 2001, highlighted long-standing difficulties in the sharing of intelligence and information between U.S. government agencies. These difficulties stemmed from many sources. Legal and policy impediments—such as the infamous "wall" between law enforcement and intelligence—complicated and then prevented the flow of information from intelligence to law enforcement organizations. Cultural and organizational disincentives—including a "need-to-know" security culture—created a risk-averse approach to sharing intelligence in which the penalty for inadvertent disclosure was greater than the penalty for incomplete dissemination. Gaps in information technology infrastructure made it time-consuming, if not altogether impossible, to physically transmit intelligence and information from the intelligence community to partner organizations in the broader U.S. government. While the difficulty of sharing intelligence and information among U.S. government agencies was a well-known issue, it was not until the events of September 11 that sufficient internal and external pressure arose to generate substantive changes in the previous status quo. Ten years after September 11, changes in intelligence and information sharing are still being implemented, and the impact of these changes has yet to be fully realized.

COLD WAR PRIORITIES FOR INFORMATION SHARING

Prior to September 11, intelligence and information sharing between U.S. government agencies took place within an environment in which there were two legal and cultural priorities—both of which were focused on limiting intelligence and information sharing for what at the time were legitimate concerns. The first priority was to protect classified information and intelligence sources and methods. This arose out of a desire to deny Cold War rivals access to critical information and to limit the risk associated with any one person having broad access to this critical information and then sharing those secrets (i.e., spies). These concerns were well founded—the USSR was very much motivated to penetrate U.S. intelligence organizations, whether technologically or by recruiting spies, such as Robert Hanssen and Aldrich Ames.

The second priority was to prevent the use of intelligence assets and information for political purposes in domestic politics. This priority was focused on safeguarding the rights of U.S. citizens from the extraconstitutional use of governmental power. This priority arose out of well-documented abuses of intelligence resources within the United States to collect information on U.S. persons and organizations in contravention of their constitutional protections (Church and Pike Committees) as well as long-standing American cultural norms that are wary of the use of intelligence and concerned about the establishment of an American gestapo (Kent 1949). Contrary to popular opinion, the limits on intelligence and information sharing that existed leading up to September 11 were not nonsensical products solely of bureaucratic risk aversion and rivalry (though both certainly reinforced the limits in place). Instead, the U.S. government's approach to intelligence and information sharing was grounded in what had previously been logical responses—both to a sophisticated intelligence rival and to historical abuses of government power.

INFORMATION SHARING IN THE 1990S

From the end of the Cold War leading up to September 11 there was already a recognition that greater information and intelligence sharing was needed to deal with the post–Cold War national security environment. Increasing concern with transnational threats—such as illicit narcotics, human trafficking, and terrorism—was leading toward greater partnerships between intelligence and law enforcement and a recognition of the need for sharing information with a larger range of partners within the U.S. government. The greatest focus on improved intelligence and information sharing within the period from 1991 to 2001, however, was on intelligence and information sharing from the intelligence community to the military. This arose out of intelligence and information sharing shortfalls in the first Persian Gulf War, when the intelligence community was unable to provide the enhanced information the military needed to take advantage of its precision munitions. This focus was reinforced by the significant foreign policy issues of the period—the breakup of the former Yugoslav Republic and ensuing conflicts in Bosnia and Serbia.

While intelligence and information sharing from the intelligence community to the military improved dramatically in this period, other forms of intelligence and information sharing lagged behind. Sharing with law enforcement and with less traditional public safety and public health partners was not substantially transformed despite a realization that complex transnational criminal and health issues required broad intelligence and information sharing, synthesis, and analysis. This is likely because these issues simply did not generate enough internal and external pressure to overcome the legacy of the Cold War mindset and break down bureaucratic rigor and rivalries. The events of September 11, 2001, provided this pressure. Those events and the subsequent investigations (9/11 Commission and WMD Commission) exposed in graphic detail the ways in which Cold War cultural and legal norms were creating security vulnerabilities for the United States by inhibiting needed sharing of intelligence and information. The visceral shock to the American people created by a

successful terrorist attack on the U.S. homeland provided the pressure required to make substantive changes in the U.S. government's approach to
information and intelligence sharing.

INFORMATION SHARING AFTER SEPTEMBER 11

There have been four key changes in intelligence and information sharing
in the 10 years since September 11, 2001. First, there has been a significant
reinterpretation of the legality of information sharing by law enforcement
and intelligence organizations—both within their respective communities
and across the infamous law enforcement–intelligence divide. This change
has been facilitated by the USA PATRIOT Act, Section 218, which removed
the wall of separation, and by a rewrite of Executive Order 12333 facilitating greater sharing of intelligence for a wide range of counterterrorism and homeland security missions. Second, a cultural change within the
intelligence community has been initiated that replaces "need to know"
with a "responsibility to provide." This cultural change, emanating from
the director of national intelligence's office, has turned the previous security mindset on its head. Instead of sharing information by exception, the
intelligence community is now expected to withhold information only by
exception (Director of National Intelligence 2008). Third, a host of new organizations have entered the national and homeland security landscape;
these organizations—the Office of the Director of National Intelligence, the
National Counterterrorism Center, the Department of Homeland Security
Office of Intelligence and Analysis, and the Information Sharing Environment Program Manager—are all focused on sharing information with an
ever-increasing number of constituents. These constituents lie far outside
the Cold War boundaries of information and intelligence sharing and include law enforcement and public safety agencies at the state, local (city),
and tribal levels as well as in the private sector. Fourth, investments in information technology have simplified information and intelligence sharing
within the intelligence community and have extended the lines of communication through which intelligence and information are shared with new
partners in the states, localities, tribal areas, and private sector. Through investments by the Department of Homeland Security's Office of Intelligence
and Analysis and the Department of Justice's Federal Bureau of Investigation, nonfederal personnel have classified and unclassified connectivity
with analysts in the intelligence community and with each other. Despite
these changes, critics charge that improvements in intelligence and information sharing remain incomplete.

EVALUATING CHANGES IN INFORMATION SHARING

The *Final Report on the 9/11 Commission Recommendations* (December
2005) gave the U.S. government a D both for "incentives for information

sharing" and for "government-wide information sharing." At that time, the commission highlighted that changes in cultural incentives had been minimally enacted and that work on government-wide information sharing had not progressed beyond the appointment of a program manager (9/11 Public Discourse Project 2005, 3). In the intervening five years, significant changes have been undertaken as discussed in the preceding, and there is a general impression that intelligence and information sharing within the U.S. government has improved. Nonetheless, the Markle Foundation, the leading think tank focused on information sharing, argues that progress is uneven across the U.S. government. Information sharing practices remain outdated, and training and incentives for information sharing are not yet the norm for the U.S. government (Markle Foundation Task Force on National Security in the Information Age 2009, 1–3).

More tellingly, the post–September 11 decade ended with two near misses (the Flight 253 Christmas Bomber in 2009 and the 2010 Times Square attempted SUV bomb) and one tragedy (the Fort Hood Massacre in 2009). In at least two of these, incomplete information sharing contributed to the United States' vulnerability. The difference between these events and September 11, however, appears to be that the shortfalls in information sharing in 2009 were much less a result of "human or systemic resistance to sharing information" (National Commission on Terrorist Attacks upon the United States 2004, 416) and much more a product of failures in recognizing what information to share and successfully placing it in context to create a meaningful understanding of the threat. In these instances, rules designed to positively regulate information sharing failed due to human error and misjudgment.

CONCLUSION

The U.S. government has made improvements in intelligence and information sharing since September 11, 2001, that better align intelligence and information sharing between U.S. government agencies with the current national and homeland security threat environments. Legal and policy impediments have been largely transformed to emphasize appropriate mechanisms to share intelligence. Cultural and organizational incentives have been created to reinforce a "need-to-share" mindset. Organizations such as the Department of Homeland Security, the Office of the Director of National Intelligence, the National Counterterrorism Center, and the Information Sharing Environment Program Manager have been established to take leadership roles in ensuring intelligence and information are shared with a broad set of constituents with roles in national and homeland security. New technological standards—and investments in infrastructure—have extended the information and intelligence sharing architecture into the state, local, and tribal domains. Despite these tangible improvements, an overall evaluation of intelligence and information sharing suggests uneven progress. Ten years after September 11, information sharing has returned as a central issue in national and homeland security because of new failures—Fort Hood and Flight 253. These failures highlight that information sharing is dependent on more than changes in rules, the establishment of new programs, and investments in information technology infrastructure. It is also dependent on the human in the loop, and even the best trained and well-intentioned experts may come to erroneous judgments about when to share information and what all the dots mean.

See also: **Volume 1, Part III:** Human and Signal Intelligence: Critical Components in Effective Counterterrorism Strategies; Information Security; Information Technologies to Combat Terrorism; Intelligence Sharing and Law Enforcement Cooperation between Nations

REFERENCES

Director of National Intelligence. *United States Intelligence Community Information Sharing Strategy.* Washington, DC: Office of the Director of National Intelligence, 2008. http://www.dni.gov/reports/IC_Information_Sharing_Strat egy.pdf.

Kent, Sherman. *Strategic Intelligence for American World Policy.* Princeton, NJ: Princeton University Press, 1949.

Markle Foundation Task Force on National Security in the Information Age. *Meeting the Threat of Terrorism: Culture Change.* Washington, DC: Markle Foundation, 2009. http://www.markle.org/downloadable_assets/20090825_cul turechange.pdf.

National Commission on Terrorist Attacks upon the United States (9/11 Commission). *9/11 Commission Report.* New York: W.W. Norton, 2004. http:// www.9-11commission.gov/report/911Report.pdf.

9/11 Public Discourse Project. *Final Report on 9/11 Commission Recommendations.* Washington, DC: 9/11 Public Discourse Project, 2005. http://www.911pdp. org/press/2005-12-05_report.pdf.

Intelligence Sharing and Law Enforcement Cooperation between Nations

Stéphane Lefebvre

Intelligence sharing and law enforcement cooperation between nations are complex and at times very challenging activities. Because they are generally shrouded in secrecy and have been the cause of harm to individuals, they are now under the increased scrutiny of an array of national, international, and nongovernmental organizations; academics and other experts; the media; and concerned citizens. Yet they are essential if transnational threats and criminal activities are to be effectively countered, prevented, or disrupted.

INTELLIGENCE SHARING

The sharing of intelligence between nations has a long history. During the Cold War, it was done primarily through the formal system of alliances and bilateral arrangements. Post-9/11, its breadth and depth expanded into a multifaceted web of relationships, where even nontraditional allies and traditionally competing nations could recognize the other's comparative advantage and the mutual benefits of working together, albeit very selectively. For example, the United States shared and received some terrorism-related intelligence from countries whose interests are often counter to its own, such as Russia, China, Iran, Syria, and Yemen. Often the benefits of sharing intelligence are very tangible. Used for operational purposes, it can be instrumental in preventing or disrupting a terrorist attack. If not, it may serve as a warning or confirmation of one's intelligence or be used for analytical or investigatory purposes. The sharing of intelligence may also be a quid pro quo, where the recipient and the provider exploit each other's comparative advantage, for example, in providing access to human sources and the use of territory in exchange for the intelligence collected as a result.

The appeal of mutual benefits accruing to each side, such as saving costs, time, and effort, however, is only one of the many reasons justifying the sharing of intelligence. Ulterior, self-centered motives can be discerned as well, where one party engages in sharing activities that would provide for personal enrichment or added personal or organizational power or influence. Sharing may also serve specific national or foreign policy interests, in which case the intelligence itself would be expected to convince the recipient to act in a specific manner or to adopt a particular viewpoint. The gains to be had from sharing, mutual or not, may not be immediately exploitable and are often contingent on future developments whereby reciprocation would be expected. The sharing of intelligence, at heart, is a function of its utility given the associated costs and risks—which suggests that asymmetrical relationships may be as prevalent as symmetrical ones (client-patron relationships, for example, were quite common throughout the Cold War)—and trust is an important ingredient, and a necessary condition, for the broadening and deepening of a sharing arrangement. However, even in cases where there is limited or no trust, and where reputational and monitoring mechanisms are absent, the costs and risks of relying on a particular partner may be exaggerated. In such situations, states may still cooperate while avoiding defection through a dominant state's imposition of a hierarchy on (or direct control of) a subordinate state, whereby the latter, for example, may be made to comply in exchange for a variety of benefits, including shared intelligence, foreign aid, and protection from external threats.

Sharing arrangements come in all shapes and forms; some are permanent, others ad hoc; some are fairly limited in scope, others are more encompassing; some are quite formal (such as executive agreements agreed by heads of states, or simpler memoranda of understanding agreed by heads of services), others very informal (concluded verbally or through the exchange of notes). Most are secret, and a few, generally the large multilateral ones, are widely acknowledged. While sharing arrangements were relatively unidimensional during the Cold War, it is now more common for security intelligence services to have valuable, if limited, sharing arrangements with foreign military and external intelligence services, as well as, incidentally, law enforcement authorities. In fact, several agencies are known to have over 100 sharing arrangements with agencies beyond their borders (for example, Canada's Security Intelligence Service and Russia's Federal Security Service). While bilateral arrangements are preferred to multilateral arrangements—because they are much easier to manage and ensure better control of the intelligence shared—the latter have proliferated since 9/11. Yet secrecy, flexibility, the need to know, and the third-party rule (no sharing with another agency without permission of the originator) are the near-universal hallmarks of sharing arrangements.

The type and scope of the intelligence being shared vary as well, ranging from all-source assessments wherein sources and methods are generally well protected (quite prevalent—sometimes as marketing products—especially at the multinational level), to single-source reporting (such as signals intelligence intercepts or human source information; common between very close allies), to raw product (relatively rare). Some arrangements may cover all types of intelligence, whereas others may be topic specific or constrained by other variables (timeliness, security classification, etc.). Services may also decide to go a step further and share intelligence for the purpose of operational cooperation, which includes activities such as target identification, surveillance, joint agent handling, and the joint use or transfer of technical know-how.

Better and more intelligence is shared through special relationships characterized by a high degree of trust and a strong convergence of interests. The best-known relationships of that kind are those formed in the Anglosphere, for example, the 1948 UKUSA Security Agreement on communications intelligence (with Canada, Australia, and New Zealand as second parties) and the network of counterterrorism fusion centers that each of these five countries set up after 9/11 (Australia's National Threat Assessment Centre, Canada's Integrated Threat Assessment Centre, New Zealand's Combined Threat Assessment Group, the United Kingdom's Joint Terrorism Analysis Centre, and the United States' National Counterterrorism Center). Beyond the strict confines of the Anglosphere, the most intriguing cooperative arrangement to surface post-9/11 was Alliance Base, composed of Australia, Canada, France, Germany, the United Kingdom, and the United States, which was dedicated to counterterrorism operational cooperation. Alliance Base reportedly ceased its activities in 2010 (France never was a fully dedicated member, and it was surmised that successes had been fewer than expected). Regional sharing mechanisms, some quite formal, have increased in size since 9/11. Europe, and the European Union in particular, has a rich and dense set of arrangements, including the Club of Berne (meetings of European heads of intelligence) and counterterrorism and civilian intelligence cells within the European External Action Service's Situation Centre (used for the sharing of intelligence assessments) and Europol. Less integrated and formal arrangements have taken form since 9/11 in Central Asia, Latin America, and Asia.

Sharing intelligence has many benefits, but it also raises many concerns. Major providers of intelligence in multilateral arrangements may feel that the burden sharing is unfair (think of the intelligence arrangements of NATO [the North Atlantic Treaty Organization], which now involves 28 nations) or that their intelligence may end up being used contrary to their preferences. Both providers and recipients, even in highly trusted relationships, know that either party to an arrangement may have been penetrated by a hostile service or deceived by a human source, or may compromise, inadvertently or not, sources and methods and at any time defect. Outsiders have concerns as well, especially when one of the parties to an arrangement is an illiberal or authoritarian state. As domestic and international legal restraints and transparency, as well as oversight and review mechanisms over sharing arrangements, are generally weak or nonexistent, there are risks that the sharing of intelligence (especially when it is erroneous) may lead to human rights abuses, as it in fact has (e.g., extraordinary rendition and associated claims of torture). This is compounded by the fact that most arrangements have no legal force and are not subject to judicial redress in case of breaches. However, in democratic states where redress is generally a possibility, providers are now concerned that the intelligence they have shared may be subject to the recipient's legislative or judicial scrutiny, included in criminal prosecutions, and ultimately compromised. In addition, in cases where international treaties or conventions may have been breached as a result of intelligence being shared (e.g., the Convention against Torture), supranational bodies (such as the European Court of Human Rights), human rights groups, and investigative journalists now launch their own investigations.

LAW ENFORCEMENT COOPERATION

Law enforcement cooperation between nations, the primary approach used against transnational crimes, is primarily conducted through mutual legal assistance agreements (multinational) and treaties (bilateral), which contain specific provisions on the type of offenses covered, the rights of all parties, and the procedures to be followed. In the absence of such instruments, letters of request are issued by a court from the domestic jurisdiction to a foreign court. In both cases, however, an individual under investigation must be suspected of, or have been charged with, a crime in order for cooperation to ensue, and there may be further constraints to effective cooperation. Because of the adversarial process associated with the prosecutions of alleged criminals, this approach is considered more commensurate with democracy, the rule of law, and human rights than the intelligence approach to fighting terrorism. In fact, for that very reason and the differences in culture and the modus operandi, cooperation between intelligence agencies and law enforcement authorities is generally fraught with difficulties. Notwithstanding, Russia, after 9/11, inaugurated a series of annual meetings of heads of special services, security agencies, and law enforcement organizations (54 countries and 76 delegations attended the seventh meeting in 2008) to encourage them to cooperate in the fight against international terrorism.

Law enforcement between nations is more global in scope than intelligence sharing between nations. In 2011, Interpol (the International Criminal Police Organization) had 188 member nations, Europol (the European Law Enforcement Agency) had 27, and the Egmont Group of Financial Intelligence Units, formed in 1995, which helps in the fight against money laundering, terrorist financing, and other financial crimes, had 121 (up from 106 in 2008). While the role and mandate of Europol, which has no supranational authority, in the fight against terrorism is still being debated, Europe has other mechanisms in place to share intelligence and cooperate on law enforcement matters, including the Police Working Group on Terrorism (27 European Union member nations plus Norway and Switzerland), set up in 1979, and the Prüm Convention (Austria, Belgium, France, Germany, Luxembourg, the Netherlands, and Spain) on cross-border cooperation on matters related to terrorism, crimes, and illegal migration, signed in 2005.

CONCLUSION

While face-to-face meetings are often sufficient for intelligence sharing and law enforcement cooperation, it is widely recognized that to be effective (that is, for the right information to reach the right recipient at the right time and under adequate safeguards) both types of activities should be supplemented with a technological capability that is durable, reliable, and secure and that allows the cooperating organizations to work on the basis of standardized protocols and procedures. In this respect, open sources indicate that military organizations have made the most progress, with systems such as NATO's Battlefield Information Collection and

Exploitation System, used by NATO members and partners, and the Combined Enterprise Regional Information Exchange System, which links over 50 countries with the United States and with one another and supports other classified enclaves.

See also: **Volume 1, Part III:** Human and Signal Intelligence: Critical Components in Effective Counterterrorism Strategies; Information Security; Information Technologies to Combat Terrorism; Intelligence/Information Sharing between U.S. Government Agencies

REFERENCES

Aldrich, Richard. "Global Intelligence Co-operation versus Accountability: New Facets to an Old Problem." *Intelligence and National Security* 24 (2009): 26–56.

Born, H., I. Leigh, and A. Willis, eds. *International Intelligence Cooperation and Accountability.* London: Routledge, 2011.

Crawford, Timothy W. "Intelligence Cooperation." In *International Studies Encyclopaedia Online,* edited by Robert Denemark. Singapore: Blackwell, 2010. DOI:10.1111/b.9781444336597.2010.x.

Lander, Sir Stephen. "International Intelligence Cooperation: An Insider Perspective." *Cambridge Review of International Affairs* 17 (2004): 481–93.

Müller-Wille, Björn. "The Effect of International Terrorism on EU Intelligence Cooperation." *Journal of Common Market Studies* 46 (2008): 49–73.

Rudner, Martin. "Hunters and Gatherers: The Intelligence Coalition against Islamic Terrorism." *International Journal of Intelligence and Counterintelligence* 17 (2004): 193–230.

Sepper, Elizabeth. "Democracy, Human Rights, and Intelligence Sharing." *Texas International Law Journal* 46 (2010): 151–207.

Walsh, James Igoe. *The International Politics of Intelligence Sharing.* New York: Columbia University Press, 2010.

International Law, Human Rights, and Counterterrorism

Payam Foroughi and Alexander Sodiqov

The relationship among international law, human rights, and counterterrorism has been organic, still to be fully determined, and heavily influenced by events of the 20th century and the first decade of the 21st century. Among other things, there has yet to be a universal definition for *terrorism,* and though the phrase "one man's terrorist is another man's freedom fighter" applies to today's realpolitik world (Rosand 2003), there is also some amount of agreement among states in recent years. Generally speaking, terrorism is defined as (1) an attack committed against civilians with the intention of causing death or serious bodily injury, (2) hostage taking, or (3) damaging of property (such as an attack on a power plant or even cyberterrorism) with the purpose of inciting terror among the general population, or part of the population, or compelling a government or organization to abstain from a certain act (Universiteit Leiden 2007).

BACKGROUND

International law as related to counterterrorism has been mainly reactive and developed through cycles influenced by historical events. Antiterrorism norms were vague until the 1950s, by which time hijacking, kidnapping of diplomats, and attacking of airports, inter alia, had been outlawed. Exceptions, however, were allowed in such agreements for the next 40 years for those fighting against occupied armies and colonizers. But increased acts of terror such as more sophisticated and deadly car bombings and suicide bombings in the Middle East, and the 9/11 attacks in 2001, led to a new cycle of change and ratification of antiterrorism treaties (Stiles 2009).

The international community's nominal or de jure counterterrorism and human rights norms are reflected in a number of United Nations (UN) guidelines intended to link and balance human rights and combat terrorism, while a number of resolutions adopted by the UN's General Assembly, Security Council, and Commission on Human Rights stress that states are obliged to ensure that counterterrorism measures comply with states' obligations under international law, including compliance with human rights principles (Palti 2004). Both international humanitarian law and human rights law can be applicable to acts of terrorism, but there is no consensus as to the conditions under which they are applicable. There are huge disagreements, for example, on the rules surrounding the taking of life while combating terrorism, the notion of collateral damage, and the controversial issue of detention (Universiteit Leiden 2007). And though torture has been described as "contrary to every relevant international law, including the laws of war" with no "other practice except slavery [being] so universally and unanimously condemned in law and human convention" (Shue 1978, 124), it has also been used on detainees by many states as a counterterrorism tool.

HUMAN RIGHTS

Human rights have had a multi-thousand-year history of evolution. The Persian king Cyrus's Declaration of the Rights of the Nations (538 BCE), the U.S. Bill of Rights (1689 CE), and the French Declaration of the Rights of Man and Citizens (1789 CE) have all given individuals "special and inalienable protections." What has changed as of the latter part of the

20th century has been that human rights have become a legitimate part of international politics and global discourse. The first all-encompassing international document on human rights was the 1948 Universal Declaration of Human Rights, described as a "secularized" formal "agreement across cultures," which intentionally left out details and deeper justifications to individual states. Later on, the signing of two more UN treaties—the International Covenant on Civil and Political Rights and the International Covenant on Economic, Social and Cultural Rights—provided for more precision, benchmarks, and definitions for what constitutes international human rights. In principle, it is agreed that democracies and richer states (especially those with low income disparity) have shown themselves to be far less likely to repress their populations, while economic development on the whole is not necessarily a prerequisite to political freedoms. Still, the global norm changes in favor of human rights remain primarily rhetorical, with neither the norm changes being necessarily nonreversible nor the acquired human rights norms being fully implemented and applied to practice (Schmitz and Sikkink 2002).

COUNTERTERRORISM

In 1934 the king of Yugoslavia, Alexander I, was assassinated in France by a Bulgarian national, resulting in the rebuke of states for not having monitored the extremist organization the assassin belonged to. This act of terrorism, along with others, led the League of Nations to urge states to take coordinated counterterrorism measures. Two collective actions were taken: the 1937 Convention for the Prevention and Punishment of Terrorism and the Convention for the Creation of an International Criminal Court. The 1937 convention, signed by 25 states, defined *terrorism* as "criminal acts directed against a State and intended or calculated to create a state of terror in the minds of particular persons, or a group of persons or the general public" (Stiles 2009, 113).

In the 1960s, acts of air piracy grew, and by 1971, the International Civil Aviation Organization included language in its treaty to penalize member states that did not sufficiently protect international travel. Other acts of violence that many categorized as terrorism had also risen, especially in the colonies of European powers. In 1972, the UN General Assembly commissioned a study on terrorism, though unanimity was missing given the assembly's division (between developing states, the East, and the West). The developing wing, for example, asked that acts "worse than terrorism," such as hegemony, military aggression, use of nuclear bombs, imperialism, colonialism, poverty, and civilian casualties, fall under "state terrorism." Others, such as the nonaligned countries and the Organization of Islamic Cooperation, sought to exempt what would normally be categorized as hostage taking if it applied to "national liberation against colonial rule, racist and foreign regimes, by liberation movements recognized by the United Nations" (Stiles 2009, 117).

Given the perceived political use of the term, by the mid-1970s, a General Assembly resolution (33/14) had been passed only through the removal of the term *terrorism*, while in 1985 the assembly passed another resolution condemning "all acts of terrorism that endangered human lives or fundamental freedoms." By this time, terrorism was still "both condemned and officially tolerated, depending on the motives of the perpetrators and the political interests of states" (Stiles 2009, 118). An attitude shift began to take shape, however, thanks to changes in the Soviet Union and the appearance of Mikhail Gorbachev, and by the latter part of the 1980s, terrorism began to be formally viewed as a crime by the international community. Following the bombings of American and French barracks in Lebanon and deaths of hundreds of young soldiers in 1983, the American National Security Directive 138, under the administration of President Ronald Reagan, sought a more heavy-handed counterterrorism strategy. Later, a reaction to the implication of Libyan involvement in the 1986 discotheque bombing in Berlin, which killed four people, including three U.S. soldiers, led to the 1986 U.S. air strikes on Libya. The events of the era also led to the U.S. Omnibus Diplomatic Security and Antiterrorism Act, whereby counterterrorism became increasingly militarized worldwide (Stiles 2009). President Reagan had described the Central Intelligence Agency (CIA)–funded Nicaraguan contra army, which many in Latin America and the United States called a terrorist entity, as the "moral equivalent" of the U.S. founding fathers (presumably equivalent to Benjamin Franklin, George Washington, and John Adams, inter alia). Reagan also referred to the Afghan mujahideen, another group known for its use of terror, as "freedom fighters." Ironically, among the mujahideen were individuals such as Sheikh Omar Abdel Rahman and Osama bin Laden, individuals later implicated in the planning and implementation of terrorist bombings in the United States in 1993 and 2001, respectively.

POST-9/11 ERA

In the immediate aftermath of the 9/11 terrorist attacks, the United States managed to persuade the international community to support the General Assembly's Resolution 56/1 and Security Council Resolution 1368 (September 12), and "for a brief time, the international community [even] reached consensus on a definition of terrorism—especially its exclusion of any political justifications" (Stiles 2009, 126). Subsequently, Security Council Resolution 1373 (September 27) stood against the financing of terrorism, criminalized any form of abetting by member states and their territories, favored the prosecution of all individuals engaged in terrorism, and aimed to prevent movement of terrorists through international borders. Resolution 1373 also led to the formation of "enforcement structures," chief among them the UN Counter-terrorism Committee (CTC). The resolution asked all UN member states to submit a report to the CTC listing their antiterrorism initiatives. In the years following, nearly one-third of member states stalled in their reporting requirements, however, and thus hindered the CTC's verification system. Hesitation by uncooperating states is thought to have been due to a perception of potential violation of their sovereignty, because of the required CTC verification step in such sensitive areas as money laundering, policing, immigration, and arms control and transfer (Palti 2004).

Despite some convergence among states on reaction to terrorism, 9/11 once again widened the gap between international law, human rights, and counterterrorism. In 2004, the International Court of Justice stated that "in some countries the 'war against terrorism' has given greater legitimacy to long-standing human rights violations carried out in the name of national security" with such consequences as "increasingly militarizing judicial functions" and the transfer of "substantial judicial police powers to the armed forces without any judicial control" (Palti 2004, 27). A common practice in the post-9/11 era has been the use of *extraordinary rendition,* entailing the detention and forced transfer of a suspect to nonjudicial authorities in a manner outside of normal or any treaty and legal processes. Rendition is normally done to expedite arrest and interrogation and to circumvent any constitutional rights that the renditioned individual may have in the location of arrest or under international treaties. The renditioned person often becomes a "ghost detainee" with little, if any, access to legal protection from domestic or international laws (McKenzie Millar 2008). The Bush administration's choice of the phrase "unlawful enemy combatants" is thought to have been a way to ignore both the Geneva Conventions and U.S. civil rights law and to legitimize the use of indefinite "detention without charge and without full due process anywhere in the world" (Stiles 2009, 136).

Despite its widespread use during the immediate post-9/11 years by the United States and its many allies in Western Europe and the Middle East, extraordinary rendition has led to a number of blowback consequences. Aside from serving as excellent propaganda for terrorist organizations such as al-Qaeda, who have been able to refer to such Western tactics and utilize them as a recruiting tool for enraged Muslim youth already frustrated with their own authoritarian governments, renditions have also caused headaches for the security apparatuses of Western states, which at times carried out second-rate operations leaving behind evidence to reveal their direct involvement. In 2009, for example, an Italian court convicted 23 CIA agents and operatives, having found them guilty of kidnapping a Muslim cleric, Osama Moustafa Hassan Nasr (aka Abu Omar), from Milan in 2003 and renditioning him to Egypt for imprisonment, interrogation, and torture by that state's notorious secret police (Donadio 2009).

A more classic case of blowback involving terrorism and human rights violations is that of a suspected al-Qaeda member, Ibn al Sheikh al-Libi, who was captured shortly after 9/11 in Pakistan. Even though al-Libi was initially questioned by the Federal Bureau of Investigation (FBI) using "traditional psychological interrogation methods," and even though the FBI was optimistic of eventually gaining valuable information from him through noncoercive tactics, influential American officials under President Bush's administration, eager to expedite the extraction of information from captured "terrorists," turned al-Libi over to the CIA, which in turn renditioned him to Egypt for interrogation. Among their many torture tricks, the Egyptians threatened to harm al-Libi's family and later used waterboarding on him; it is said that they buried him in a tomblike structure for hours and subsequently severely beat him. Torture used on al-Libi eventually led to his "confession," yet given his supposed training in enduring torture and a chemical engineering background, he was able to convey false but convincing information on the supposed existence of weapons of mass destruction in Saddam Hussein's Iraq, a country and state he had no history of contact with. Al-Libi's torture-extracted false confession was used in the closing argument of American secretary of state General Colin Powell's persuasive 2003 UN speech, which initially justified the subsequent invasion of Iraq (McKenzie Millar 2008). Later, to punish al-Libi for having lied to his Egyptian torturers, he was handed over to his native country of Libya (from which he had presumably been away since the 1980s Cold War jihad against the Soviet Union). Al-Libi was reported to have committed suicide in a Libyan prison in 2009.

HUMAN RIGHTS APPROACH

According to the UN General Assembly, terrorism spreads due to unresolved conflicts, lack of rule of law, human rights violations, ethnic and religious discrimination, political exclusion, socioeconomic marginalization, and lack of good governance. Counterterrorism has throughout the years been approached from a military and law enforcement prism, thus the justification for the use of heavy-handed techniques. That said, a human rights approach in fighting terrorism is at least rhetorically expressed by international bodies. The UN recommendations for countering terrorism were reflected in Secretary-General Kofi Annan's 2005 speech at the International Summit on Democracy, Terrorism, and Security, wherein he articulated the UN's counterterrorism strategy in the form of the "five Ds" of *dissuading* individuals from becoming involved in terrorism as a political tool, *denying* them the means to carry out attacks, *deterring* states from supporting terrorism, *developing* states' capacity for preventing terrorism, and *defending* human rights while fighting terrorism. The five Ds, in turn, fall into four counterterrorism models: military, law enforcement, political, and human rights models. The military model is supported by Article 51 of the UN Charter, while the law enforcement model is reflected in international criminal law and antiterrorism conventions and allows the use of civilian and security personnel to investigate and share critical information to prevent the spread of terrorism (Kielsgard 2006). The political model is that of viewing terrorism as an "armed rebellion to be resolved through negotiation and the political process" (Fenwick 2008, 259), while the human rights model relies on international humanitarian law and human rights conventions (Kielsgard 2006).

The human rights approach is dualistic: both standalone and integrated. The standalone approach provides material, social, and political relief to communities (e.g., infrastructure development, public health, education, etc.) and addresses political grievances while respecting local cultures. The integrated approach establishes human rights norms as an integral or mainstream component in the military, law enforcement, and political counterterrorism models. The human rights approach encourages seeking out the reasons and motivations behind terrorism and attempting to address and alleviate root causes. The mere use of force against individual terrorists "whose children are starving, whose homes are bombed, and who live under the yoke of political or economic tyranny" (Kielsgard 2006, 296), or against individuals who use violence to deter such conditions for others, is from this perspective ineffective in doing away with terrorism and may even exacerbate it. Many believe that without a "counter-terrorism solution grounded in human rights, the cure will result in greater depravation of civil liberties and in a Pandora's Box of atrocities" (Kielsgard 2006, 297).

CONCLUSION

A key challenge to the human rights approach in counterterrorism remains the continuing pull and push between counterterrorism efforts and human rights protection. Former UN high commissioners for human rights Sergio Vieira de Mello and Mary Robinson have urged the CTC to appoint a human rights expert to monitor states' compliance with human rights norms as related to counterterrorism (Rosand 2003), while another high commissioner, Louise Arbour, has been of the opinion that in the long term, "a commitment to uphold respect for human rights and rule of law will be one of the keys to success in countering terrorism—not an impediment" (Kielsgard 2006, 250).

See also: **Volume 1, Part III:** Ideology That Spawns Islamist Militancy; Just War Doctrine; Multidisciplinary Approach to Combating Terrorism; Preemption: Moral and Ethical Considerations. **Part IV:** Ethical and Legal Issues in Democratic Societies: National Security and Civil Liberties; United Nations Global Counterterrorism Strategy: Significance and Limitations. **Part VI:** Multilateral Approach to Counterterrorism: Issues, Problems, Responses; Preemptive Counterterrorism: The Need for a Global Integrated Approach; Public Support and Education Campaigns; Regional Challenges: Promoting Stability through Economic, Social, and Political Reforms

REFERENCES

Donadio, Rachel. "Italy Convicts 23 Americans for C.I.A. Renditions." *New York Times,* November 4, 2009. http://www.nytimes.com/2009/11/05/world/europe/05italy.html.

Fenwick, Helen. "Proactive Counter-terrorist strategies in Conflict with Human Rights." *International Review of Law Computers & Technology* 22, no. 3 (2008): 259–70.

Kielsgard, Mark D. "A Human Rights Approach to Counter Terrorism." *California Western International Law Journal* 36, no. 2 (2006): 250–303. http://www.cwsl.edu/content/journals/Kielagard.pdf

McKenzie Millar, Sangitha. "Extraordinary Rendition, Extraordinary Mistake." ANTI-WAR.com, September 1, 2008. http://www.antiwar.com/orig/millar.php?articleid=3389.

Palti, Leslie. "Combating Terrorism while Protecting Human Rights." *UN Chronicle* 4 (2004): 27–28.

Rosand, Eric. "Security Council Resolution 1373, the Counter-terrorism Committee, and the Fight against Terrorism." *American Journal of International Law* 97, no. 2 (2003): 333–41.

Schmitz, Hans Peter, and Kathryn Sikkink. "International Human Rights." In *The Oxford Handbook of International Relations,* edited by Christian Reus-Smit and Duncan Snidal, 516–37. Oxford: Oxford University Press, 2002.

Shue, Henry. "Torture." *Philosophy and Public Affairs* 7, no. 2 (1978): 124–43.

Stiles, Kendall W. "Terrorism: Reinforcing States' Monopoly on Force." In *International Norms and Cycles of Change,* edited by Wayne Sandholtz and Kendall Stiles, 109–39. New York: Oxford University Press, 2009.

United Nations General Assembly. [Resolution] 60/288. The United Nations Global Counter-Terrorism Strategy. September 20, 2006. http://www.un.org.

Universiteit Leiden. "Counter-terrorism Strategies, Human Rights and International Law: Meeting the Challenges." Final report, Poelgeest Seminar, May 31, 2007.

International Media: A Critical Tool in the Battle against Terrorism

Małgorzata Zachara

One of the main purposes of terrorists is to attract the attention of the public and to influence national, regional, or global public opinion. As a result, a close relationship with the media is considered one of the defining features of modern terrorist activities. As mass media play a determining role in the formation of public views, the scale of coverage strengthens the impact of an act of terror, preserving it in the collective memory. The technological and information revolution has led to global media occupying a more and more prominent role in politics and security. This is reflected in what is called the *CNN effect*—a certain style of news coverage at key moments in foreign crises that can influence the response of the political powers involved. The modern international news media cut across distances, national boundaries, and time differences. This can be demonstrated by the coverage of the September 11, 2001, terrorist attacks on New York and Washington. Media involvement amplified the terrorists' actions by repeating and echoing them in endless variations, while media comments and interpretations heightened the emotions connected with their actions, creating a deeper and more lasting psychological effect. The event proved that the most effective form of terrorist activity involves carefully directing the violent act to make it a spectacular performance aimed at massive casualties as well as maximum media exposure.

MEDIA TERRORISM

The phenomenon of violence carried out with media-centered goals has been called *media terrorism* or *mass-mediated terrorism*. This relationship is twofold, as it is impossible to maintain the democratic responsibilities of the media—designed to provide the public with extensive information—without awarding the terrorists with a worldwide stage for their propaganda. Emerging digital technologies have further expanded their communicative possibilities. Traditional media and cybermedia have been used as conduits for political messages to be delivered to target audiences and to demonstrate the destructive power of the attackers, thereby creating and maintaining a culture of fear in enemy societies. This relationship has a history as long as terrorism itself. Its nature has been expressed in the anarchist concept of "propaganda of the deed." According to certain authors—Carlo Pisacane, Peter Kropotkin, and Mikhail Bakunin, among others—the acts of violence are used more for their visibility and drama than for their military value. They have openly advocated publicizing brutal forms of struggle by saying that anarchic propaganda should be carried out not only by the pen and rallies but also by bombs and pistols.

Analysis suggests that violent acts of terror are often just a tool for communication, a way to send a message and achieve an impact on a wider audience. Providing the mass media with cruel, shocking, and brutal images is part of terrorist tactics, so the media have become indispensable partners in their productions. The broadcasting and reporting of a terrorist attack are seen as an integral part of the event as they provide publicity for the terrorists' cause.

Several kinds of media-centered terrorist objectives have been noted:

1. Publicity and media spectacle: long-lasting terrorist operations that provide the opportunity to create a media spectacle that can be seen to unfold stage by stage. Theatricalization of terror is a growing tendency. The attacks are often condemned in a spectacular way to attract international attention and provide recognition for the terrorists.

2. Channel of communication: the use of media as a communication platform while negotiating, taking responsibility for the violence, and explaining the causes and ideology of the organization. While niche media (e.g., radical Islamic websites, local television stations) or selected ideological stations (Al Jazeera) are used as primary channels of interaction, vital information is repeated on mainstream global networks. In effect, the self-produced propaganda of the terrorists is added to that already existing in the information system.

3. Public relations: the development by major terrorist organizations of their own infrastructure of media production and means for information management. In their efforts they rely mainly on the Internet and on interactive forms of communication (VOIP programs). The jihadist terrorist strategy is inextricably rooted in extensive use of public relations techniques, primarily through new media. The Islamic media publication company Al-Sahab, which is the main information production division of al-Qaeda, may serve as an example of such practices. These practices involve innovative information and communication technology being adapted to maximize the psychological impact of actions through the use of video messages.

4. Recruitment and organization building: use of communication structures and techniques as a tool for extending the membership of terrorist organizations and seeking donors. Interactive communication via cellular or satellite phones and via online media is commonly exploited to connect with current members and recruit new ones. New social media such as YouTube, MySpace, chat rooms, video games, and virtual worlds are increasingly being used to influence a young audience by promoting a certain ideology. The scale of online terrorist fund-raising is growing, and the Internet enables terrorist structures to survive as a loosely connected network.

5. Cyberterrorism: according to some analyses a phenomenon that is not limited to attacks launched on cyber infrastructure and hacking but also includes any use of terrorism on the Internet.

COUNTERING THE THREAT

Technological developments in communication have limited the reach of traditional counterterrorism policies (coercive forms of censorship, denial of access, technical or legal restrictions) regarding the provision of information and the creation of news. However, Western governments constantly take measures to intensify the surveillance of terrorist sites, video channels, and other types of communication tools used to spread violence and the rhetoric of hate. Cybermedia counterterrorism strategies include the establishment of phony terrorist websites and the spreading of disinformation or false intelligence. Media communication makes it possible to reach a large number of individuals in a short space of time, which therefore makes it the simplest way in which ideologies that are used to justify terrorism can be confronted. However, the implementation of these measures is the subject of much discussion in democratic societies. There are serious concerns over civil liberties, the Internet's inherent anonymity, and the basic rights of society to information. The core question in this discussion asks whether reduced attention to terrorism from the side of responsible mass media may have an effect in preventing more attacks. The media goals of speed and sensational content stand in direct confrontation with security needs for accuracy, responsibility, and balanced reporting. For example, the practice of interviewing terrorists creates a setting in which they are treated as legitimate political actors. There have been many examples of attempts to create a terrorist television or press drama instead of strictly transmitting the facts objectively and with respect to crisis security limitations. Given the centrality of the media in most aspects of contemporary terrorism and counterterrorism, their representatives hold a responsibility to exercise their influence carefully.

The development of modern communication tools has obviously created new pressing challenges as well as opportunities for counterterrorism. Although global media pluralism negates much of the effectiveness of propaganda and makes the efficient control of the flow of information impossible, modern public communication management has become an indispensable element in the international effort against terrorism.

An effective media strategy has become a major determinant in the strengthening of the public understanding of terrorism and the building of a moral base to fight against terrorism. In the battle against terrorism, the safety of societies can be secured by direct counterterrorism measures as well as by improving their understanding of the challenges in combating terrorism. The media is a critical tool in building—and in some cases rebuilding—trust and a sense of community. Public communication is used to raise awareness and educate society in order to diminish the scale of anxiety connected with the threat of terrorism.

The importance of a transparent information policy as part of a counterterrorism effort has been recognized at many levels involving the strategic management of states and alliances. North Atlantic Treaty Organization (NATO) structures maintain close cooperation with the media in carrying out information operations, psychological operations, and public affairs. They form part of the strategic communication that conveys information to selected audiences (governments, organizations, and individuals) to affect their worldview and behavior. Influencing the "will," "capability," and "understanding" of key international decision makers and societies, as well as keeping the public fully informed, is seen as a vital part of counterterrorism activities. The American-led war on terror also reinforces the idea of a deliberate media strategy employed with the purpose of securing public support and "winning hearts and minds" in the Islamic world.

CONCLUSION

The capacity of modern media networks to gather and transmit information globally is used by governments wishing to create an information context for their security policies and actions. To build an effective public communication frame, a close relationship between the media and the counterterrorist and security services has to be created. International social media represent the most effective platform to educate and mobilize societies and to undermine the ideologies that drive extremism. Responsible international discourse—which should eliminate black-and-white terms or generalizations that lead to discrimination against certain religions, nationalities, and ethnic groups—cannot be created without global media involvement.

See also: **Volume 1, Part III:** Combating Terrorist Recruitment, Propaganda, and Radicalization Campaigns

REFERENCES

Centre of Excellence Defence against Terrorism. *The Media: The Terrorists' Battlefield.* Amsterdam: IOS Press, 2007.
Jackson, Richard. *Writing the War on Terrorism: Language, Politics and Counterterrorism.* Manchester, UK: Manchester University Press, 2005.
Nacos, Brigitte L. *Mass-Mediated Terrorism: The Central Role of the Media in Terrorism and Counterterrorism.* New York: Rowman & Littlefield, 2007.

Just War Doctrine

M. George Eichenberg

Just war is a doctrine of military ethics originating in ancient Rome (Childress 1978; Arendt 1963b). The modern conception of just war doctrine, however, dates from the immediate post–World War I era when the horrors of industrialized warfare were still being assimilated into the collective consciousness of the Western world (Childress 1978). Modern just war doctrine is the belief that war can and should conform to specific criteria of moral and social justice. As articulated since the 1930s, just war doctrine is generally recognized as comprised of three components, *jus ad bellum*, just cause for going to war; *jus in bella*, just conduct during war; and *jus post bellum*, just conduct after war or just peace.

DEVELOPMENT

Just war doctrine originated as the concept of *justifiable war*. Livy, a Roman historian, famously wrote, "The war that is necessary is just" (Arendt 1963b, 13). Livy regarded as necessary wars of conquest or expansion (colonialism) as well as wars for the preservation of national power or prestige (honor) or for revenge. Cicero, a Roman philosopher and political theorist often referred to as the "father" of just war doctrine, regarded such wars as justifiable provided the goal was peace for Rome.

Augustine (1984), an early church father writing near the end of the Roman Empire, sought to reconcile the pacifism of Christian teaching with the Christian Roman state's need to survive invasions by pagan Germanic tribes. Church doctrine caused him to shift the concept from wars that are justifiable to wars meant to bring justice, such a shift being more in keeping with church teaching. Augustine concluded that just war is waged to create or preserve a just social order, the prerequisite for a community at peace.

Thomas Aquinas (1987), as a papal advisor, found Augustine's parameters for just war inadequate to ensure protection of basic church doctrines. Writing from Augustine's recognition of war as a moral challenge for Christians, Aquinas developed a just war doctrine he believed would provide more cogent guidance to Christian sovereigns than did the writings of Augustine. According to Aquinas there were three points to be addressed in waging just war. First, the decision to make war must be that of the legal ruler of the state; as such, revolutions or civil wars were by definition unjust, as was any war waged by a private entity or religious group apart from a lawful government. Second, there must be a just cause for the war, specifically, self-defense or the defense of a nonaggressive allied state. This excluded wars of conquest or colonization as well as wars of revenge or national honor. Finally, the war must without exception be waged in an uncompromisingly moral manner with the sole intention of restoring a just civil order. Thus, there could be no compromise of the rules of war nor could a Christian state ally itself with non-Christian state.

Hugo Grotius, a Dutch legal scholar credited by many as laying the foundation to modern international law, wrote an exhaustive treatise on just war doctrine in his three-volume *De Jure Belli ac Pacis* (*On the Law of War and Peace*; Grotius 1625). In volume 1 he developed the idea of just cause for war (*jus ad bellum*), concluding that nations may go to war in self-defense, for reparation of injury, and as punishment for those who violate international law. In volume 2 he further defined and explained the three just causes for war. In the third volume he discussed just conduct of war (*jus in bello*). Grotius added little to the ideas of Aquinas; his genius lay in his explication and systematization of theory and its application to the development of an international law of war.

MODERN JUST WAR DOCTRINE

Jus ad Bellum

Modern theorists of just war have retained much of Aquinas and Grotius (Childress 1978; Brough, Lango, and van der Linden 2007). As currently articulated by most secular just war philosophers, *jus ad bellum* is limited to six main points. First, only a lawfully constituted government may make war. Second, a nation may make war only in self-defense (this includes preemptive attacks) or defense of nonaggressive allies (referred to as *interventionism*). Third, war must be the last resort in defending the nation or its allies. Fourth, the decision to go to war must be purely to achieve the goal of defense. Fifth, there must be a reasonable probability war will actually accomplish the ostensible defensive goals of the nation. The final requirement of *jus ad bellum* is proportionality; is the goal sought proportional to the potential destructiveness of the means employed? More simply, this calls for a cost-benefit analysis; which alternative, war or perhaps an unjust peace, will be least harmful to society?

The *Catechism of the Catholic Church* states these points somewhat differently while not straying from the essential meaning. The catechism states,

- The damage inflicted by the aggressor on the nation or community of nations must be lasting, grave, and certain.
- All other means of putting an end to it must have been shown to be impractical or ineffective.
- There must be serious prospects of success.
- The use of arms must not produce evils and disorders graver than the evil to be eliminated. The power of modern means of destruction weighs very heavily in evaluating this condition (Catholic Answers [Documents] n.d., paragraph 2309).

Jus in Bello

Just conduct during war must address principles of discrimination, proportionality, and necessity (Childress 1978). *Discrimination* refers to who or what may be a legitimate target of force. Just war doctrine requires that discrimination be made between enemy combatants, noncombatants, and civilian populations. Noncombatants, such as wounded soldiers or prisoners of war, and civilians must not be the deliberate targets of military actions. *Proportionality* refers to how much force may be morally applied in given circumstances. Specifically, will the military advantage gained be proportional to the probable amount of harm done to civilians and the local ecology as well as to one's own forces and civilians? *Necessity* requires that the force used be the least harmful means to accomplish a particular, legitimate military objective.

Additionally, *jus in bello* prohibits the use of weapons banned by the recognized rules of war: poison gas, for example, or biological weapons. Actions such as rape campaigns and reprisals against civilians and noncombatants are forbidden, as are genocide and certain forms of deception. Finally, prisoners of war must be given certain rights including "benevolent quarantine," that is, incarceration out of harm's way.

Jus Post Bellum

Jus post bellum refers to bringing a war to a just ending and transitioning warring nations to a just peace (Iasiello 2004). The peace must be just and based on publicly agreed-to terms by the lawful authorities of all nations involved. Treaties may not be used to exact revenge or lay a basis of grievances leading to another war. Peace agreements must address and resolve the issues that actually caused the war and do so in a manner proportional to those issues as well as any issues of justice that developed during the course of the war. Military and civilian leaders may be treated differently from soldiers and soldiers differently from civilians based on actual conduct during the war and culpability for the war itself. Those who engaged in war crimes must be given fair, public trials and proportionate punishment depending on individual responsibility. Rogue regimes must be rehabilitated in a manner consistent with national self-determination and international law.

CONCLUSION

The use of terrorist tactics by governments (terror from above) violates several tenets of modern just war doctrine, perhaps most notably the deliberate targeting of civilians and symbolic targets of limited or no military value. Terror campaigns waged by revolutionaries, special interest groups, or religious extremists also violate these basic points of just war doctrine as well as the requirement that only a lawful government can wage war. Nongovernmental actors also violate the prohibition against the deliberate targeting of civilians as well as attacking targets of limited or no military value. These factors relegate terrorists, of whatever ilk, to the status of criminals rather than soldiers in a just cause.

REFERENCES

Aquinas, St. Thomas. *Politics and Ethics*. New York: W. W. Norton, 1987.
Arendt, Hannah. *Eichmann in Jerusalem: A Report on the Banality of Evil*. New York: Viking Press, 1963a.

Arendt, Hannah. *On Revolution*. New York, Viking Press, 1963b.

Augustine, St. *City of God*. New York: Penguin Group, 1984.

Brough, Michael W., John W. Lango, and Harry van der Linden. *Rethinking the Just War Tradition*. New York, State University of New York Press, 2007.

Catholic Answers [Documents]. "Just War Doctrine." n.d. http://www.catholic.com/library/Just_War_Doctrine_1.asp.

Childress, J. "Just-War Theories: The Bases, Interrelations, Priorities, and Functions of Their Criteria." *Theological Studies* 39 (1978): 427–45.

Fotion, N. *War and Ethics*. New York: Continuum, 2007.

Grotius, H. *On the Law of War and Peace (De iure belli ac pacis)*. The Laws of Nature and Nature's God, 1625. http://lonang.com/exlibris/grotius/index.html.

Iasiello, L. "Jus Post Bellum: Moral Obligations of the Victors of War." *Naval War College Review* 57, no. 3/4 (2004): 33–52. http://www.usnwc.edu/getattachment/022caef3-60c8-4caa-9153-bd08f28387d5/Jus-Post-Bellum—The-Moral-Responsibilities-of-Vic.

Ramsey, P. *The Just War*. New York: Scribners, 1969.

Reed, C., and D. Ryall. *The Price of Peace: Just War in the Twenty-First Century*. Cambridge: Cambridge University Press, 2007.

Limitations of Technology

Roxana Georgiana Radu

Terrorism, a phenomenon dating back to antiquity, has acquired an unprecedented importance due to the recent advancements in information and communication technology (ICT). Terrorist groups have historically been among the first to embrace and seize the potential of the newest technologies, from the invention of dynamite in 1866 to the satellite television expansion, World Wide Web boom, and cell phone diffusion in the early 1990s. Along with military innovations in asymmetrical conflicts, the modern ICT tools have become indispensable components of terrorist operations worldwide. Homegrown and transnational groups engaged in terrorist activities at local, regional, national, or international levels, especially those established after the 1980s and 1990s, tend to adopt a networked form of organization and thus coordinate their communication via ICT means. This major shift has added to the transformation of terrorism from a nuisance to be managed within national borders to a challenge requiring global changes (Nye 2004, 207).

POWER OF TECHNOLOGY

In anticipating and preempting different types of terrorist attacks, the counterterrorist thrust ultimately relies on the power of technology for working much faster with massive amounts of structured or unstructured data, sharing information across borders more quickly, and conducting more accurate analyses in order to inform policymaking processes at different stages. The end of the Cold War was partially attributed to the effectiveness of ballistic missiles and satellite surveillance systems (Popp et al. 2004, 38), but possessing these no longer secures against major infrastructure disruptions or information attacks, or against the loss of civilian lives in the pursuit of terrorist objectives. Nowadays, counterterrorism is thoroughly supported by key information technologies such as pattern analysis, predictive modeling tools, analysis tools and decision aids, and foreign-language translation tools, which are designed to facilitate and improve the understanding of the complex phenomena backing terrorist preparations and activities. Among the information technologies considered important for counterterrorism, the following categories of systems are included: biometrics, categorization and clustering, database processing, event detection and notification, geospatial information exploitation, information management and filtering, knowledge management and context development, publishing, searching, semantic consistency, video processing, visualization, and workflow management.

The features that make the global ICT-mediated channels so valuable to contemporary societies—primarily ubiquitous and instant delivery of information—represent, at the same time, the crucial vulnerabilities to be exploited in any terror-inflicting activity. Two ICT-related developments have made terrorism more difficult to contain: the integration of science and technology advancements in all aspects of day-to-day life, and the high reliance on infrastructure for the functioning of all basic systems. This progress has reduced the costs and the entry barriers for potential information disruptions at different levels, making it possible for medium-trained individuals to take part in large-scale operations coordinated by perpetrator groups. This is what Nye (2004, 207) refers to as the "democratization of technology," by which access to information as a precondition for enabling civic empowerment entails, concomitantly, that terrorist organizations are able to misuse this same information for their own nefarious purposes. The control over information, its distribution, and timely responses in particular settings have become of such vital importance that knowledge itself has come to constitute the key target of attacks. For offensive activities conducted in the online environment (cyberterrorism), computer network tools are employed in order to "shut down critical national infrastructures (such as energy, transportation, government operations) or to coerce or intimidate a government or civilian population" (Lewis 2002, 2).

TERROR IN CYBERSPACE

While the advancements in cyberspace have made possible a series of strategic and tactical moves intended to counter today's threats, there are considerable limitations inherent to the use of technology for anti- and counterterrorism measures. To begin with, the built-in character of ubiquity reduces the possibility of following all transnational communications between terrorist groups and does not allow for enough preparation time for countermeasures. The Internet facilitates the retrieval of valuable information by offering a disproportionate advantage to the planning of the operations rather than to the tracking down and attribution of them to those who stand behind these operations. Moreover, the mobilization and recruitment potential of the terror groups is strengthened by the easy access to like-minded websites and individuals (Nacos 2010, 270–78). As a large number of websites appear instantly in different parts of the world and can be replicated incessantly, other means for obstructing the recruitment and mobilization of terrorists are required. Encrypted action-oriented messages and fragmented messages placed on "sport sites, chat rooms, pornographic bulletin boards and other web sites" (Kelley 2001) facilitate the transmission of propaganda and strengthen the fund-raising mechanisms, as well as the sources of support. In this sense, the global media have an amplifier effect in inflicting panic and fear following terrorist events, especially after the 9/11 attacks.

The pace at which technology evolves is not reflected in the adoption of adequate policies for protection against terrorist threats. One reason for that is the use of ICT in creative ways, which gives the attacker competitive advantage and more time for a strategic strike. On the other hand, the policymaking process following traditional deliberation cycles is not equipped for responding immediately through effective regulation. A series of regulatory measures taken after the 9/11 attacks led to increased concerns over the restrictions imposed on freedom, privacy, and free movement of individuals. Following the introduction of the USA PATRIOT Act and similar legislation for information control in European states, access to Internet records, retrieval of email databases, Internet surveillance of financial transactions, and similar privacy infringements became important components of transnational counterterrorism strategies at the expense of limitations on personal freedoms. These regulations have been accompanied by self-restraint on the side of the day-to-day beneficiaries of different services put at risk by terrorist incidents, such as exercising self-limitation in the use of online communication or in boarding a transatlantic flight. The specific legislation triggered by counterterrorist strategies had unintended consequences as well. The globally interconnected information network spread fear and insecurity to other parts of the world and thus created new targets by making public the newly formed alliances to combat terrorism. The 2001 attacks on the World Trade Center in New York showed the potential of using technology in innovative ways, such as airplanes-turned-missiles, and of seizing all opportunities for expanding devastation. Terrorist operations conducted by networks of loosely organized people, whose identities and locations are not fixed, remain difficult to detect, as the war on terror demonstrated.

Moreover, the ICT developments have not altered considerably the capacities of counterterror groups to identify the locations where perpetrators are hiding. To carry on with ideologically, religiously, and politically motivated attacks, terrorist organizations still need popular support. Without it, their acts lack legitimacy and cause identification problems in the targeted public audience. While access to information in the online realm might have influenced the perception of the general audience in different parts of the world, the appeal that terrorist groups have within different populations has been complemented by a more focused recruitment strategy that targets youth and other vulnerable individuals. In the words of Arquilla, Ronfeldt, and Zanini (1999, 100–101), "the likelihood that young recruits will be familiar with information technology implies that terrorist groups will be increasingly networked and more computer-friendly in the future than they are today."

CONCLUSION

As this article has shown, the growth of loosely connected organizations involved in terrorist operations cannot be disconnected from the expansion of global communications. Relocating operations from one geographic area to another relies heavily on the rapid exchange of information. The inherent features of ICT that shape its indispensable use limit the potential and the effectiveness of counterterrorism measures by creating additional difficulties in combining information and monitoring terrorist activities. In the global security paradigm, the limitations of technology are yet to be overcome.

See also: **Volume 1, Part I:** The Terrorist Threat in the 21st Century: A Global Security Problem; War on Terror. **Part III:** Globalization and Terrorism; Information Security; Information Technologies to Combat Terrorism; International Media: Critical Tool in the Battle against Terrorism; Threat, Vulnerability, and Criticality Assessments. **Part VI:** Counterterrorism Research: Current Efforts and Future Challenges

REFERENCES

Arquilla, John, David Ronfeldt, and Michele Zanini. "Networks, Netwar, and Information-Age Terrorism." In *Strategic Appraisal: The Changing Role of Information in Warfare,* edited by Zalmay Khalilzad, John P. White, and Andrew Marshall, 75–111. Santa Monica, CA: RAND, 1999.

Kelley, Jack. "Terror Groups Hide behind Web Encryption." *USA Today,* February 5, 2001. http://www.usatoday.com/tech/news/2001-02-05-binladen.htm.

Lewis, James. "Assessing the Risks of Cyber Terrorism, Cyber War and Other Cyber Threats." Center for Strategic and International Studies, Washington

DC, December 2002. http://csis.org/files/media/csis/pubs/021101_risks_of_cyberterror.pdf.

Nacos, Brigitte. *Terrorism and Counterterrorism.* 3rd ed. New York: Penguin Academics, 2010.

Nye, Joseph S., Jr., ed. "Terrorism." In *Power in the Global Information Age: From Realism to Globalization,* 206–13. New York: Routledge, 2004.

Popp, Robert, Thomas Armour, Tom Senator, and Kristen Numrych. "Countering Terrorism through Information Technology." *Communications of the ACM 47,* no. 3 (March 2004): 36–43. http://portal.acm.org/citation.cfm?id=971642.

Military Force: Effective against Terrorists?

Marcus Schulzke

Over the past 40 years, small groups of military counterterrorist specialists have performed successful hostage rescues and captured suspected terrorists, but since the declaration of the war on terror, counterterrorist operations have expanded to become a primary function of the armed forces. The effectiveness of military force against terrorists remains an open and highly controversial question. At present, the majority opinion seems to be that conventional military force can only be partially successful against terrorists, unless it is linked to a broader political and social strategy designed to address the causes of terrorism. Although counterterrorist operations abroad are, for most countries, the military's responsibility, few have managed to make the transition between conventional and unconventional operations that this role requires. They have also encountered problems in regulating their use of force. Successful use of military force against terrorists is largely a struggle of adapting to a new role, bringing terrorists to battle on terms that favor conventional forces, and using the military in conjunction with other programs.

ASYMMETRICAL WARFARE

A central problem with using military force against terrorists is that of retraining soldiers to use a different level of force than they would in conventional operations. Regular infantry units and many special operations forces are primarily trained to fight against enemy soldiers in pitched battles or to strike against rear echelon targets. Success in these types of missions depends on surprise and overwhelming firepower. The same tactics are often counterproductive when used against terrorists. Discrimination and proportionality, central tenets of just war theory, become even more important considerations in asymmetrical conflicts. Terrorists routinely hide in religious buildings, hospitals, and schools, where they can be attacked only with caution.

Militaries are always at a moral disadvantage compared with terrorists. Terrorists can use their opponents' accidental violence against civilians and destruction of property to mobilize popular support. Yet they can appeal to numerical inferiority and victimization to excuse their own deliberate targeting of civilians. This deficit is a major obstacle that forces the military to either act carefully, with the aim of minimizing accidental damage, or suffer the consequences of losing the moral battle. It also demands a high level of cultural sensitivity and programs to delegitimize terrorists' actions in the eyes of their host population. It may even require militaries to avoid conflict. Surprise raids or assassinations can create hostility that may be more damaging to the operation's objectives than allowing low-priority targets to escape. There is always a tradeoff between achieving military objectives and cultivating support among the terrorists' potential supporters.

COUNTERTERRORIST OPERATIONS

The different constraints on use of force, and the necessity of operating in civilian areas, mean that soldiers must be retrained for counterterrorism or employed only selectively. A prime example of the danger of using soldiers in police actions, especially elite units trained to fight against a larger enemy, is the 1972 Bloody Sunday incident in Northern Ireland. The British First Parachute Regiment had trouble adapting to a context that demanded restraint, and the result was unwarranted violence against protestors. In the following years, Special Air Service operatives fared better when they attacked specific targets, or ambushed terrorists in rural areas, than when they had to act as police forces. The same lesson has been borne out in other contexts. Coalition forces in Afghanistan and Iraq often successfully attack terrorists in rural areas using conventional tactics but have had to learn new tactics to fight in urban areas and around mosques.

The coalition attack on al-Qaeda in Afghanistan in 2001 was a test of the effectiveness of technologically sophisticated militaries operating against terrorists. The concern over collateral damage to civilians was reduced because many bases were in remote, mountainous regions. The attack had some measure of success, as many terrorist-training centers were eliminated and some key leaders were captured or killed. However, many members of al-Qaeda survived the attack and were able to relocate to Pakistan. Coalition forces also failed to capture or kill Osama bin Laden, the attack's primary target. Thus, although there may be contexts in which conventional forces can operate in their traditional role, doing so provides only a partial victory. It succeeds in killing or capturing some terrorists and eliminating their bases, but it falls short of decisive victory.

Airpower has the potential to give militaries a greater advantage by allowing them to secretly monitor terrorists from the sky and attack without warning. One strategy, developed by the U.S. Air Force and Central Intelligence Agency (CIA), is using unmanned drones to monitor and attack terrorists. These, and manned gunships like the AC-130, are capable of finding specific targets and engaging them without inflicting as much collateral damage as other kinds of aerial attack. However, no matter how precise, these weapons are bound by the same limitations as other kinds of military force. Most notably, they provoke a great deal of popular indignation, especially given the drone pilots' distance from the battlefield and perceived detachment from the battle. This perception has been encouraged by American drone attacks on terrorists in Pakistan. Airpower is also limited by its dependence on intelligence drawn from local sources or soldiers on the ground.

A recurrent problem in counterterrorist operations is that terrorists rarely fight when they are at a disadvantage. Terrorists' favored tactics—bombings, hijackings, and ambushes—limit their exposure to counterterrorist forces. Terrorists are consistently able to surprise opponents and attack without exposing themselves to counterattack. They do not have to defend territory or capture objectives. Their ability to break contact quickly and disappear makes it difficult to engage terrorists on favorable terms. At the same time, the predictability of military forces makes them vulnerable. In many instances, terrorists have used bombs to inflict large casualties against weak military targets. The bombing of the Marine barracks in Beirut, the attack on the USS *Cole*, and the attacks on coalition convoys in Iraq and Afghanistan show how readily terrorists can find and attack soft military targets without being drawn into a battle.

GROUND REALITIES

Terrorists are most vulnerable wherever they present a fixed target. Weapons caches, headquarters, and training facilities have been successfully attacked on many occasions. In 1998, the United States used cruise missiles to strike targets in Afghanistan and Sudan, and while this failed to achieve the objectives, the attacks did show the power of Western militaries to strike at terrorist bases from a distance. Ground forces can take the same approach, as the Special Air Service's (SAS) practice of setting up ambushes near weapons caches illustrates. Terrorists are also at a disadvantage when taking hostages. In a few well-publicized cases like the 1972 attack in Munich, terrorists have managed to take hostages and escape. Yet this was an exceptional case, and only partially successful. Hostage rescue specialists learned from this experience and have generally performed well since. Hostage takers are usually killed, whether or not they achieve their objectives, because they are easily surrounded and counterattacked by superior forces.

With military effectiveness depending so heavily on the terrorists' freedom of movement, national borders are one of the most significant impediments to militaries bringing terrorists to battle. The Turkish army's fight against the Partiya Karkareni Kurdistan (Kurdistan Workers' Party) has been defined by the latter's ability to persistently avoid major confrontations by retreating from Turkey and into Kurdish territory. The same is true of al-Qaeda's move into Pakistan and Hezbollah's attacks into Israel from Lebanon. In each of these cases, terrorists' power to cross borders has allowed them to avoid conflict with well-armed opponents whose operations are limited by territorial boundaries. Boundaries are not always respected—counterterrorist forces routinely cross borders without authorization—but by doing so they risk diplomatic crises and increasing popular discontent.

CONCLUSION

Although the war on terror has expanded the role of many conventional militaries, the most important counterterrorist operations are still delegated to small groups of specially trained, elite soldiers. For example, U.S. Navy SEAL Team 6 and CIA operatives were responsible for the May 1, 2011, killing of Osama bin Laden in Abbottabad, Pakistan. These units are often more effective than conventional forces because of their experience with using force in sensitive areas, like hostage rescue missions, and an organizational culture that permits flexible responses to unpredictable opponents. These forces usually react to terrorist attacks, instead of finding terrorists before they are able to strike. There are many instances of counterterrorist forces intervening in ongoing crises or capturing those who have already attacked, but far fewer cases of them finding and attacking terrorists preparing to attack. This may be an insurmountable difficulty, given the challenge of predicting attacks, but it raises the matter of more proactive countermeasures.

The limited effectiveness of conventional forces and the reactive character of most special units support the growing consensus that counterterrorism and counterinsurgency are best seen as operations that require political solutions. This puts the military in a support role, one that requires greater restraint, and may demand a shift toward small-unit actions, policing, and humanitarian work.

REFERENCES

Banks, William C., Mitchel B. Wallerstein, and Renée de Nevers. *Combating Terrorism, Strategies and Approaches.* Washington, DC: CQ Press, 2007.

Bolz, Frank, Kenneth J. Dudonis, and David P. Schulz. *The Counterterrorism Handbook: Tactics, Procedures, and Techniques.* Boca Raton, FL: CRC Press, 2005.

Cronin, Audrey Kurth, and James M. Ludes, eds. *Attacking Terrorism: Elements of a Grand Strategy.* Washington, DC: Georgetown University Press, 2004.

Ganor, Boaz. *The Counter-terrorism Puzzle: A Guide for Decision Makers.* New Brunswick, NJ: Transaction, 2007.

Ochmanek, David A. *Military Operations against Terrorist Groups Abroad: Implications for the United States Air Force.* Arlington, VA: RAND, 2003.

Multidisciplinary Approach to Combating Terrorism

Kathryn H. Floyd

Contemporary policymakers are increasingly faced with a complex counterterrorism environment that blends lessons from the 1998 East Africa bombings, copious kidnappings in South America, suicide bombers throughout the Middle East, 9/11, and hundreds of other attacks, plots, and near misses that keep the brains and brawn of national defense constantly in motion. As terrorists' tactics and procedures to hit attractive or strategic targets evolve, nations are responding with multidisciplinary approaches that are reactive, corrective, and preventive. In particular, this demands a coordinated program of action that integrates various military and nonmilitary means at the disposal of the state.

MILITARY MEANS: SECURITY SECTOR

In crafting a strategy to combat terrorism, the military or "hard" component is often at the forefront owing to its ultimate ability to enforce security and restore stability to an affected area. Using the military has a number of distinct advantages, provided it is supplemented by other disciplines. When the military leads the counterterrorism effort, as the French did in Algeria from 1954 to 1962 and as the Sri Lankans did against the Tamil Tigers for more than two decades, its force guards against disorder as a professional instrument of state policy. With this civilian oversight, the military launches a counterterrorism operation to establish or reinstate security and sovereignty, often enhancing intelligence operations. Above all, an armed force is oriented toward violence and, when specialized units like commandos or the paramilitary are used, entertains the calculated likelihood that lethal force will be a primary option. There was no question that lethal force would be used when the Israeli Defense Forces stormed a plane hijacked by Palestinians with Israeli citizens onboard in Operation Entebbe in Uganda on July 4, 1976. Military actions alone, without the support of other counterstrategies risks alienating the global community and increasing the level of violence on both sides of the conflict. They can also confuse the mission and lack an exit strategy against what is essentially a tactic, terrorism. However, using the military may be the exact approach a government wishes to take as it portrays its opponent in a negative light, thereby receiving wide public support.

NONMILITARY MEASURES: JUDICIAL PROCEEDINGS AND LAW ENFORCEMENT

International and state legislation help to codify a collective understanding of what acts of terrorism entail and how to legally counter any violations. Above all, legislation can delegitimize the terrorist as a common criminal rather than a soldier dying for his cause. On the international level, states have been incredibly slow to define what terrorism is, owing to many differing opinions, but have made progress in other areas. Aviation security has been the easiest area for nations to reach a consensus. This is evidenced by the number of international instruments that have been ratified, including the 1971 Convention for the Suppression of Unlawful Acts against the Safety of Civil Aviation (Montreal Convention). In more recent history, there has been the 1999 International Convention for the Suppression of the Financing of Terrorism and the 2005 International Convention for the Suppression of Acts of Nuclear Terrorism. Regional bodies—like the Organization for American States, African Union, and Organization of the Islamic Conference—also enact similar statutes.

On the state level, a government can pass legislation to define more narrowly actions and penalties affiliated with terrorism, especially homegrown extremism. Whether operating under common law like the United States or civil law like France, the judge or jury examines the facts to prove a case or find the truth regarding a specific terrorist incident. In the case of Mas Selamat Kastari, the alleged leader of terrorist group Jemaah Islamiyah, who is suspected of planning to bomb Changi Airport in 2002, he has been detained without trial under Singapore's Internal Security Act but has not been formally charged in a court of law. Additionally, emergency or special legislation, like the USA PATRIOT Act, helps address pressing concerns associated with counterterrorism but could skirt existing laws that are applicable or even move the incident out of the law's reach.

Law enforcement personnel, operating under the umbrella of civilian control, blend military and nonmilitary approaches while observing these state or national laws. Trained to use the minimum force possible, officers are primarily concerned with arresting a suspect and enforcing the law, not killing a suspected terrorist. In the case of Faisal Shahzad, the alleged American terrorist who planted a car bomb in New York City's Times Square in May 2010, the New York Police Department was the first on the scene to handle the situation, not a special weapons and tactics (SWAT) military unit. Furthermore, by using the police to randomly patrol neighborhoods and be an integrated part of the wider community, the nation ensures that its counterterrorism approach is partially led by a civilian force that is concerned primarily with enforcing existing laws and protecting the population, as well as hardening attractive targets. As both a reactive and preventive measure, terrorist rehabilitation programs can be led by the police, as is the case in Indonesia, and help reintegrate the person back into society. In all of these situations, counterterrorism takes a measured and disciplined approach.

BLENDING MILITARY AND NONMILITARY MEANS: THE INTELLIGENCE COMMUNITY

Through espionage, communication interception, cryptanalysis, and cooperation with other institutions, the intelligence community is able to assist counterterrorism efforts in a number of critical ways. Intelligence informs policy, supports national objectives, and ultimately helps keep the nation safe by alerting the government to a pending attack or suspicious patterns of behavior. Intelligence becomes most useful to military and civilian leaders when it is of strategic importance, involves an actionable recommendation, and fits into a larger tactical plan. When six young jihadists aimed to "kill as many soldiers as possible" at Fort Dix, New Jersey, in a terrorism plot, actionable intelligence by the U.S. Federal Bureau of Investigation led to their swift arrests in May 2007. The advantages of using intelligence for counterterrorism are fairly self-evident: it enhances knowledge, is of a clandestine nature, ideally allows preemptive action, and enables cooperation between different bureaucracies. However, it also walks the fine line between the legal and the illegal regarding certain collection methods, can be considered morally questionable, often leads to a militaristic "we must act now" response, and possibly curtails the civil liberties of those being monitored. The controversy in the United States over the wiretapping that was revealed during the George W. Bush administration led to heated debates on whether the nation's security required listening in on citizens' phone calls without a warrant. The central question is whether the threat justifies using any means possible to prevent an attack. Overall, good intelligence in any number of its many forms is critical to inform counterterrorism operations.

SOFTER, ASYMMETRICAL APPROACHES

Combating violent extremism with a bullet risks compromising long-term security with short-term stability if the underlying situation that gave rise to the terrorist or organization is not corrected. In addition to the more kinetic elements described thus far, a multidisciplinary approach must blend social, economic, and psychological "soft" measures. First, a vigilant population helps to balance societal values and the threat at hand, as Israel has quite successfully done. Under the policy of the government, society must prepare, communicate, educate, and build a population that informs the trusted law enforcement officer when there is suspicious activity, rather than quietly returning home to lock the door. When preventing terrorism that may be a result of immigration, the nation's infrastructure should support this difficult transition and seek to connect that person to the wider community in as many ways as possible. In areas, whether a country or neighborhood, where terrorism breeds owing to a lack of opportunity in a failing state or rampant instability in a failed nation like Somalia, one integrated strategy would include economic and developmental assistance. There is also the propaganda element in any multidisciplinary strategy; effective communication through a credible information and public education campaign can educate a vulnerable population by pointing out the inconsistencies inherent in the terrorist mindset. This strategy may deny the insurgent a critical source of support and also serve to enhance population support for a government's plan of action.

CONCLUSION

Based on the severity of the terrorism plot or attack, the leader of the affected nation will decide whether it is the military or another branch that takes the lead. Considering the strengths and weaknesses of each approach, it is imperative that any multifaceted approach combine a plethora of elements to not only stop the direct threat but also eradicate underlying causes and rally the population behind legally acceptable norms of behavior. Although it is a constant game of cat and mouse, counterterrorism must stay one step ahead in order to prevent another 9/11 or attack like those in London in 2005 and in Mumbai in 2008.

See also: **Volume 1, Part III:** Combating Terrorist Recruitment, Propaganda, and Radicalization Campaigns; International Media: Critical Tool in the Battle against Terrorism; Multilateral Sanctions against State Sponsors of Terrorism; Role of the International Community. **Part VI:** Psychological Profiling of Terrorists; Regional Challenges: Promoting Stability through Economic, Social, and Political Reforms; Rehabilitation of Extremists: Methods and Practice; Root Cause Analysis and Counterterrorism

REFERENCES

Ganor, Boaz. *The Counter-terrorism Puzzle: A Guide for Decision Makers.* New Brunswick, NJ: Transaction, 2005.
Lesser, Ian O., Bruce Hoffman, John Arquilla, Ronald Ronfeldt, and Michele Zanini. *Countering the New Terrorism.* Santa Monica, CA: RAND, 1999. http://www.rand.org/pubs/monograph_reports/2009/MR989.pdf.

Quiggin, Thomas. *Seeing the Invisible: National Security Intelligence in an Uncertain Age*. Singapore: Nanyang Technological University, 2007.

Wardlaw, Grant. *Political Terrorism*. Cambridge: Cambridge University Press, 1989.

Wilkinson, Paul. *Terrorism versus Democracy: The Liberation State Response*. London: Frank Cass, 2001.

Multilateral Sanctions against State Sponsors of Terrorism

Sean J. McLaughlin

Targeting states that have sponsored or supported terrorist groups has understandably become one of the major aims of American foreign policy since 9/11, but the noose cannot be effectively tightened on these regimes through unilateral means alone short of using military force. Winning United Nations (UN) approval for multilateral sanctions against a state sponsor of terrorism adds legitimacy to American policy, usually ensures global compliance, and has been proven to be a serious-enough measure to induce behavior change in certain instances. That said, securing agreement on which acts should be punished by multilateral sanctions, and how severely, can be a long, difficult process, one that has to date allowed serial offenders like Iran and Syria to largely evade international penalties for their actions.

STATE-SPONSORED TERRORISM

The United States and Russia have developed a shared interest in curbing terrorism in the post–Cold War period, during which time Washington has been fairly effective in rallying multilateral action against state sponsors of terrorism. The threat from al-Qaeda that emerged in the 1990s was much bigger and better funded than that of other terrorist groups targeting various Western countries, and it was well known that certain governments allowed al-Qaeda members to operate freely on their territory. In 1995, Aum Shinrikyo, a Japanese religious cult, released a deadly gas (sarin) inside the Tokyo subway system. This attack stoked fears that terrorist groups would use weapons of mass destruction (WMDs) on civilian targets. Subsequently many countries rallied around American efforts to crack down on state-sponsored terrorism. Numerous successes were chalked up in the 1990s. For example, in March 1992 the UN Security Council placed mandatory economic sanctions on Libya in response to its involvement in the bombings of two flights in 1988 and 1989, following suit in Sudan in 1996 and Afghanistan in 1999 when both countries were accused of harboring Osama bin Laden and his collaborators. These sanctions did not stomp out terrorism, but they did make it extremely expensive for states to sponsor terrorists and brought positive results in both Libya and Sudan.

On September 28, 2001, the Security Council passed the U.S.-sponsored Resolution 1373, which required all UN members to criminalize terrorist acts and their financing, deny safe haven to terrorists, and prevent open support for them, as well as cooperate with other states on counterterrorism measures. Additionally, the Security Council established the Counterterrorism Committee (CTC) to help further Resolution 1373. Almost all UN members have been eager to comply, but there has been some confusion over definitions (e.g., what sort of terrorist funds are open for freezing: the proceeds from illegal activities alone or money drawn from legal sources?), a lack of resources and funding, diverging views as to which states are sponsors of terrorism, and questions over who will ensure compliance. Nevertheless, never before has the international community been as equipped, both legally and organizationally, to clamp down on state sponsorship of terrorism as it is today.

The U.S. State Department maintains a list of state sponsors of terrorism, countries that are accused of providing logistics, funding, weapons, or safe havens for terrorists. As of the summer of 2010, only four countries retain this designation: Cuba, Iran, Sudan, and Syria. During the Bush years Iraq was removed 18 months after the March 2003 invasion that toppled Saddam Hussein's regime, Libya followed in 2007 after Muammar al-Gadhafi's 2003 decision to renounce his country's WMD program, while North Korea—once named by Bush as part of the so-called axis of evil—was also dropped in October 2008 as a reward for complying with international nuclear inspections. Of the remaining countries on the State Department list, Iran, Syria, and Sudan have faced only limited or unrelated UN sanctions, while Cuba continues to languish under a crippling U.S. trade embargo established in the waning days of the Eisenhower administration.

During the Cold War, the Cuban government provided safe haven to left-wing terrorists from various corners of the Spanish-speaking world— men who many Communists would have viewed as revolutionary freedom fighters—in addition to a small number of fugitives from American justice. Then president Fidel Castro renounced his government's support of foreign insurgents as part of Cuban foreign policy in 1992, a move that was confirmed by American intelligence six years later, and few security experts believe Cuba currently poses any serious risk to the United States. Cuba remains on the State Department's list of terrorism sponsors because it has maintained close relations with Iran and Syria, as well as failing to shore up its counterterrorism measures to Washington's satisfaction after 9/11. Not only is there no interest from the international community in imposing multilateral sanctions on Cuba, but the UN General Assembly has voted repeatedly in recent years to condemn the American embargo by a margin of 180 or more members to 3 or 4, with the only support for Washington coming from Israel and some small Pacific Island nations.

Syria, Iran, and, to a lesser extent, Sudan are singled out as state sponsors of terrorism for their support of Islamic terrorists that target Israel. Washington has proven unable to convince the UN to impose far-reaching multilateral sanctions on the first two countries for their role in terrorist activities due to widespread sympathy and support in the Arab-Muslim world for the relatively limited, regional aims of well-known Islamist groups operating in Lebanon and Palestine.

Sudan is an odd case, though one in which most of the international community's terrorism concerns were resolved through the application of multilateral sanctions. UN sanctions were imposed in April 1996 to limit the travel of government officials after Khartoum refused to extradite three suspects in a failed assassination attempt on Egyptian president Hosni Mubarak. The sanctions prompted the government to expel some terrorists (including bin Laden), but sanctions were left in place, and an air embargo was put on the country in August 1996 when the United States convinced the Security Council that al-Qaeda members were still using Sudan as a safe haven. These sanctions were relatively limited—the Security Council wanted to avoid setting off an even worse humanitarian crisis in a country with a long-running civil war between the Muslim government and non-Muslims in the oil-rich South—and designed to set a precedent for action by the international community against state sponsors of terrorism. Sanctions were lifted in September 2001 when Sudan promised full support for the U.S.-led war on terror. Khartoum is currently under an UN arms embargo and other limited sanctions for engaging in genocide in Darfur and major abuses in the Christian and animist South, but it has cooperated with Washington on counterterrorism to the point that the State Department has described it as a "strong partner." It retains the label of state sponsor of terrorism solely for allowing the Palestinian group Hamas to maintain a political presence on Sudanese soil.

SANCTIONS AND CHALLENGES

Libya is the one unqualified success story for multilateral sanctions. Blending Islamic nationalism and revolutionary Socialism, the al-Gadhafi regime brought international condemnation and isolation for this oil-rich country of 6.2 million people in the 1980s by orchestrating increasingly brazen terrorist attacks against the West. In 1984, an unidentified shooter in the Libyan embassy murdered a London policewoman responsible for crowd control at an anti-Gadhafi demonstration; in 1986, Libyan agents bombed a popular Berlin discotheque, killing two American servicemen and a Turkish woman; and, finally, Libyan agents were responsible for the worst terrorist attack in British history, the 1988 bombing of Pan Am Flight 103 that killed 270 people (including 189 Americans) over Lockerbie, Scotland. The collapse of the Soviet Union removed Libya's only friend on the Security Council, which imposed strict multilateral sanctions in 1992 that hobbled the country's once-lucrative oil industry. Over the next 11 years, the Libyan government responded to the sanctions by cutting off its support of various terrorist groups, handing over the two suspects in the Pam Am bombing to the UN for trial in the Netherlands in 1999, and renouncing its WMD programs in 2003. Nonetheless, the 2011 Arab Spring uprisings in Tunisia and Egypt spawned the February 2011 uprising in Libya by oppositional forces to the dictatorial rule of Colonel Muammar Gaddafi. This revolution led to a civil war involving NATO air strikes. In October 2011 Colonel Gaddafi and his loyalists, who had been on the run, were defeated at Sirte. Gaddafi was killed during this battle.

Syria and Iran pose far greater challenges. Syria has a secular government led by Dr. Bashar al-Assad, a British-trained ophthalmologist, but it has long provided backing to anti-Israel Islamist groups such as Hamas and Palestinian Islamic Jihad—which are headquartered in Damascus—as well as the Lebanon-based Hezbollah. It has continuously interfered in Lebanese politics, and Syrian agents are widely suspected of orchestrating the assassination of popular Lebanese prime minister Rafik Hariri in 2005. The State Department believes that Damascus has not been directly involved in terrorist acts since 2006 and has been careful to ensure that terrorist groups based on its soil do not attack Westerners, though it has been accused of taking a lax policy in regards to Iraq-bound insurgents passing through its territory. The Syrian government is currently under sanctions from Washington but will retain a considerable amount of diplomatic leverage so long as the international community believes it can bring its proxies to heel as part of a comprehensive peace settlement with Israel.

Iran is widely assumed to be the most active remaining state sponsor of terrorism, but this is often overlooked for the greater threat posed by its ongoing nuclear weapons program. Tehran's Islamic Revolutionary Guard Corps and Ministry of Intelligence and Security have long planned and supported terrorist acts, in addition to providing encouragement, training, and weaponry for various terrorist groups, such as Hezbollah, Hamas, Palestinian Islamic Jihad, and the al-Aqsa Martyrs Brigade. After the American invasion of Iraq in March 2003, Iran has been accused of arming Shia militants fighting coalition forces, most notably training them to build improvised explosive devices, used to devastating effect. Iran, currently facing an UN arms embargo and a ban on the trade of materials or technology that could further its nuclear program, remains defiant. Tehran understands that the United States and its allies will have a great deal of difficulty passing more stringent multilateral sanctions so long as it enjoys sympathy from Turkey and Brazil for its nuclear ambitions. Iran's greatest trump card is China's growing dependence on Middle Eastern oil, a challenge that has so far led Beijing to run the risk of angering the West by using its veto power in the Security Council to postpone and weaken sanctions directed at Tehran.

CONCLUSION

In the short term, it appears highly unlikely that the international community will devise a solution to end Iranian and Syrian state-sponsored terrorism before Israel and its neighbors begin serious negotiations for a comprehensive peace settlement.

REFERENCES

Byman, Daniel. "Confronting Syrian-Backed Terrorism." *Washington Quarterly* 28 (Summer 2005): 99–113.

Hovi, Jon, Robert Huseby, and Detlef F. Sprinz. "When Do (Imposed) Economic Sanctions Work?" *World Politics* 57 (July 2005): 479–99.

Nincic, Miroslav. "Getting What You Want: Positive Inducements in International Relations." *International Security* 35 (Summer 2010): 138–83.

O'Sullivan, Meghan L. *Shrewd Sanctions: Statecraft and State Sponsors of Terrorism.* Washington, DC: Brookings Institution, 2003.

Rosand, Eric. "Security Council Resolution 1373, the Counter-terrorism Committee, and the Fight against Terrorism." *American Journal of International Law* 97 (April 2003): 333–41.

Schwartz, Jonathan B. "Dealing with a 'Rogue State': The Libya Precedent." *American Journal of International Law* 101 (July 2007): 553–80.

Organizational Resilience and Counterterrorism

Layla Branicki and Bridgette Sullivan-Taylor

Despite extensive post-9/11 state efforts, terrorist organizations continue to not only exist but also grow in both numbers and reach (Hoffman 2004). While no definition is universally supported and many are controversial, for the purpose of this section *terrorism* signifies non–state-sanctioned actors who direct attacks at defenseless targets (Townshend 2002, 8). The focus is on global terrorism, and in particular the contemporary face of international terrorism, as exemplified by the al-Qaeda terrorist network, as opposed to more local, that is, domestic, terrorist action.

ADAPTABILITY

On May 1, 2011, Osama bin Laden, leader of al-Qaeda and thought to be the key orchestrator of the 9/11 attacks, was shot dead by U.S. forces in Pakistan. Yet like the multiheaded Hydra of myth, the targeting of one terrorist leader or cell may not be enough to destroy or undermine a movement or ideology. We argue that a terrorist group's organizational capability incorporates and indeed has demonstrated a capacity for resilience and therefore is a key concern to those involved in the formulation and implementation of counterterrorist policies and operations. Resilience can be understood as the ability to bounce back in the face of extreme challenge (Wildavsky 1988) and is often associated with characteristics of flexibility and rapid response (Weick and Sutcliffe 2001). To quote Hoffman, "Al Qaeda has clearly shown itself to be a nimble, flexible and adaptive entity" (2004, 551) and in this view possesses characteristics associated with organizational resilience. Based on the work of Stohl and Stohl (2007) and Schoeneborn, Haack, and Scherer (2009) it is proposed that these characteristics emerge in part from the loose network structure associated with contemporary international terrorist organizations and the manner in which these are joined up through a common ideology as opposed to hierarchical chains of command.

TERRORIST ORGANIZING: HIERARCHY, NETWORK, OR OTHER?

Defining the boundaries of a terrorist organization, such as al-Qaeda, is a complex analytical task. First, the determination of boundaries may be an intensely political activity for both governments and other actors (Stohl and Stohl 2007). Researchers have observed the conflation of different terrorist groups for political purposes (e.g., securing budget and support; Stohl and Stohl 2007), while groups themselves often reject the terrorist label attributed to them or membership in a particular group (Townshend 2002).

Second, these are not necessarily organizations in the traditional sense. Al-Qaeda is thought to comprise a mixture of both hierarchical organizations and networks of disparate individuals and groups that operate with varying levels of autonomy and distinctiveness across a number of country contexts (Hoffman 2004). This creates a very complex picture that makes a counterterrorist response incredibly challenging. For example, it has been highlighted that the leadership of al-Qaeda neither fully selects nor controls its membership (Stohl and Stohl 2007). This moves away from a conception of terrorism predicated purely on traditional (or mechanistic) forms of organization, and this in itself critiques the often-accepted wisdom of the terrorist mastermind (Stohl and Stohl 2007, 100). This critique has key implications for counterterrorist responses as structural assumptions about the organizing of al-Qaeda may not play out in reality. A more fluid and loosely connected set of individuals and groups is a very different proposition than a clear hierarchical organization predicated on command and control and identifiable through clear boundaries. Designing counterterrorist interventions when linkages, boundaries, and locations are unclear is arguably much more problematic.

Some (although not all) aspects of a terrorist organization may therefore be understood to take the form of a network. This form is commonly associated with organizing across spatial boundaries and as having properties that are dynamic, emergent, and flexible (Stohl and Stohl 2007). These properties are associated with organizational resiliency. U.S. counterterrorism policy has taken into account this networked form of terrorist organizing, and yet critics have argued that a misunderstanding of networks has led to some flaws in the articulated policy and operational response (Stohl and Stohl 2007). The theory of networks formulated by the U.S. government is thought to be predicated on too strong a sense of traditional organizing, such as hierarchy and information cascades, leading to a continuing belief that the best way to undermine a terrorist network is to destroy essential parts of it or linkages within it (Stohl and Stohl 2007). Collapsing one key link of a network, however, does not necessarily nullify other linkages, as new connections may also emerge over time. The structure of a network therefore may evolve as opposed to being planned. An alternative conceptualization of network may therefore be more useful here, whereby this form of organizational structure can be understood as a set of loose connections united by a shared ideology as opposed to a clear and bounded organization (Hoffman 2004, 552; Stohl and Stohl 2007).

COMMUNICATION AND THE DIFFUSION OF IDEOLOGY

The act of terrorism can be understood as "propaganda by deed" (Townshend 2002, 13), and the violence, targeting, and location of an event may lead to communication about it at not only the local but also the national and international levels. In this understanding the event in part becomes a symbolic communication act. With the advent of 24/7 news coverage, and the increasing use of social-networking technologies, these events can unfold in real time and be watched by millions around the globe. This is significant as it has been argued that communication about terrorism can in itself lead to the proliferation of extremist ideologies and as a result to the extension of an existing terrorist network or the creation of affiliated groups (Schoeneborn, Haack, and Scherer 2009). In this context the spread of extremist perspectives, and ultimately in some cases actions, can be seen as complex, dynamic, and potentially emergent (e.g., without necessary recourse to the formal structures usually associated with organizing).

The impact on terrorist organizing of this diffusion of ideological communications has been written about with reference to the theory of "communication constituting organizations" (see Schoeneborn, Haack, and Scherer 2009), which highlights the potential for individuals to become connected (or organized) by a shared set of communication acts (in this case beliefs) as opposed to either physical or virtual direct linkages. This approach is one way of understanding why these loose networks might have characteristics that make them resilient against attempts to undermine their structure. The structure, in part, may be unknown to both the other members of the loose network and even its leaders, and in this sense its anonymity might guard it against intervention. As a terrorist organization receives media attention or commits a terrorist act, the communication may also lead to the emergent creation of new parts of the network. In effect, if a terrorist network is in part ideologically constituted rather than structurally connected (Schoeneborn, Haack, and Scherer 2009; Stohl and Stohl 2007), there may not be clear lines of control, lines of dependence, or the need for terrorist masterminds to distribute and implement plans (other than perhaps a communicative role as a figurehead).

CONCLUSION

The weakness, and independence, of the network ties may therefore be the very thing that enables what appears to be a terrorist organization to continue in the face of challenge. Individuals and groups may be able to operate in the name of an ideology despite having no, or limited, direct links, and while working in isolation they may associate themselves with or be viewed as part of the same terrorist organization. As these networks, at least in part, are arguably created, bound, and sustained by an ideology (Schoeneborn, Haack, and Scherer 2009), each news story covered by the global media creates the possibility for new ideological communication acts to occur and subsequently the potential for an expanded terrorist network. Counterterrorism is constituted by organizations that function using traditional organizational forms, and counterterrorist measures seem to reflect some implicit assumptions about organizing (Stohl and Stohl 2007). To undermine al-Qaeda's apparent capacity for resilience, counterterrorist measures may need to consider how to undermine not just the organization but the organizing of contemporary terrorism. It remains to be seen how the death of al-Qaeda's leader, Osama bin Laden, will impact the "core" organization and its networked affiliates and associates.

See also: **Volume 1, Part I:** Concept of Islamist Jihad; Global Terrorism: Post-9/11; Insurgent Terrorism; The Terrorist Threat in the 21st Century: A Global Security Problem. **Part III:** Intelligence/Information Sharing between U.S. Government Agencies; Intelligence Sharing and Law Enforcement Cooperation between Nations; Psychological Operations; Role of the International Community; Safe Havens and Weak and Failing States. **Part IV:** Eliminating Terrorist Support Networks. **Part VI:** Sun Tzu's *Art of War:* Lessons for 21st-Century Counterterrorism Practitioners; Weak Link: Identifying and Attacking Terrorists Vulnerabilities

NOTE

The basis for this entry is a research project funded by the Engineering and Physical Sciences Research Council (EPSRC) in the United Kingdom entitled Game Theory and Adaptive Networks for Smart Evacuations (EP/I005765/1). The authors would like to thank the EPSRC for their support.

REFERENCES

Engineering and Physical Sciences Research Council (EPSRC). "Game Theory and Adaptive Networks for Smart Evacuations." Research Project EP/ I005765/1, Cass School of Education, University of East London, United Kingdom, October 1, 2010–September 30, 2012. http://www.orau.gov/ dhssummit/presentations/March%2031/Day2A/Preston_Panel7.pdf.

Hoffman, Bruce. "The Changing Face of Al Qaeda and the Global War on Terrorism." *Studies in Conflict and Terrorism* 27 (2004): 549–60.

Schoeneborn, Dennis, Patrick Haack, and Andreas Georg Scherer. "How Terrorist Organizations Transcend Their Inherent Improbability: A Communication Perspective on the Organizational Dimension of Terrorism." Presented at the European Group for Organizational Studies (EGOS) Colloquium, Barcelona, 2009.

Stohl, Cynthia, and Michael Stohl. "Networks of Terror: Theoretical Assumptions and Pragmatic Consequences." *Communication Theory* 17 (2007): 93–124. http://ceps.anu.edu.au/publications/pdfs/stohl_pubs/stohl_and_stohl-networks_of_terror.pdf.

Townshend, Charles. *Terrorism: A Very Short Introduction.* Oxford: Oxford University Press, 2002.

Weick, Karl E., and Kathleen, M. Sutcliffe. *Managing the Unexpected—Assuring High Performance in an Age of Complexity.* San Francisco: Jossey-Bass, 2001.

Wildavsky, Aaron. *Searching for Safety.* New Brunswick, NJ: Transaction, 1988.

Preemption: Moral and Ethical Considerations

George Eichenberg

Preemptive war is a concept of military and political theory justifying a nation in making a preemptive, or first, strike against a belligerent nation or group believed to constitute a threat to national security (Dershowitz 2006). In effect, the defender becomes the aggressor, seeking to achieve a strategic or tactical advantage in what is regarded as an inevitable conflict. Preemptive war is closely related to the natural law concept of self-defense and the just war doctrine of military ethics (Childress 1978; Grotius 1625; Ramsey 1969). International law permits preemptive warfare under narrowly tailored criteria, as do many ethicists and theologians (Dershowitz 2006; Rouillard 2004).

PREEMPTIVE WAR DOCTRINE

In many respects, preemptive warfare is an application to nations of the natural law doctrine of self-defense (Dershowitz 2006; Grotius 1625; Rouillard 2004). Natural law assumes that nonaggressors may defend themselves, by force if necessary. The defender need not have suffered direct physical attack, but moral and legal doctrine demand the defender be in fear of imminent attack. The usual standard is whether a reasonable person would have believed themselves in immediate danger (Dershowitz 2006). Additionally, the amount of force used must be proportional to the threat; that is, no more force may be used than is needed to prevent or stop an attack. Under this doctrine one may go to the defense of an innocent third party as well.

One recent scholar has distinguished between preemptive war and preventive war, writing that the term *preemptive warfare* refers to striking first in the face of an imminent threat, while *preventive war* refers to attacking a possible future aggressor before that aggressor is fully prepared to attack or perhaps to even wage war (Beres 1991. Rouillard (2004) refers to preventive war as "anticipatory self defense." For example, in June 1967, Israel made preemptive attacks against Egyptian and Syrian targets in the face of their major military buildups along her borders and after several incidents that constituted casus belli, or cause for war, under international law. Israel was roundly applauded for this. Additionally, in 1981, Israel made preventive strikes against targets in Iraq for which the Israelis allegedly had hard intelligence on facilities built for the development of nuclear weapons, probably to be used against, or at least used to threaten, Israel. Israel was not so roundly applauded for this.

The reaction to Israel's actions in 1967 and in 1981 may be seen as based in international law and the accepted morality of international relations. Preemptive strikes in the face of imminent aggression are generally recognized as both morally and legally based on a long history of ethical theory and international jurisprudence (Rouillard 2004). However, preventive strikes are not entirely accepted as either legal or moral. The major problem with the acceptance of preventive war as justifiable lies in the high probability of "false positives" and their consequences; that is, the inherent inability of national leaders to infallibly predict the future conduct of nations will result in unnecessary wars and attendant human suffering. For example, in some cultures rhetoric outpaces action as a matter of course; this could be highly problematic as nations where such a culture predominates could be punished through preventive attacks for posturing, though largely empty words, rather than for a serious threat or actual aggression.

DEVELOPMENT

The Talmud, a collection of rabbinic commentary on the Mosaic law written between roughly 200 CE and 500 CE derived the concept of both pure self-defense and preemptive self-defense from Deuteronomy 22:26, concluding that "If someone is coming to kill you, rise against him and kill him first" (Epstein 2004). The Talmudists extended this doctrine to defending innocent third parties, actually obligating one with the means to kill a potential murderer to do so to save an innocent victim.

Augustine (1984), writing within the same general era as the Talmudists, believed the Gospel of Christ prohibited Christians from injuring or killing in defense of one's self, thus concluding self-defense was a sin. Using a complex theological argument, however, he was able to conclude that a Christian may righteously injure or kill non-Christians if done in defense of a Christian state, such as Rome during Augustine's lifetime. Therefore, a Christian who went to war in defense of a Christian state incurred no mortal sin for killing. Augustine did not explicitly permit preemptive war, nor did he explicitly condemn it.

Aquinas (1988) wrote that wars fought in national defense or defense of a nonaggressive ally were just wars and thus permissible under church doctrine. Aquinas believed that an imminent threat of enemy aggression (invasion) was a sufficient cause to go to war. He did not clearly articulate that preemptive strikes were morally justifiable per se, merely that imminent threat was sufficient justification to go to war. Thus, Aquinas's acceptance of preemptive war must be regarded as implicit rather than explicit. Some 300 years after Aquinas, Sir Thomas More, an English jurist and philosopher later canonized a saint by the Catholic Church, stated that attacking a massing enemy on the enemy's side of the border was both common and morally preferable to exposing one's own people to the destruction of an invading army (Childress 1978).

Machiavelli, the well-known political realist, believed waging preemptive war was less morally objectionable than awaiting attack (Rouillard 2004). He regarded delay as advantageous only to one's enemy, thus causing more loss and suffering to one's own populace. His ideas ran directly counter to those of contemporary Catholic doctrine that viewed war as a last resort. Hugo Grotius (1625) in his exhaustive study of the international law of war concluded that preemptive attacks were both legal and moral in the face of imminent aggression.

MODERN VIEW

Article 51 of the United Nations (UN) Charter applied the classical view of self-defense to the defense of nations; self-defense is justified only in response to actual armed attack (United Nations 1945; Rouillard 2004). This would seem to condemn both preemptive and preventive war, but

Article 51 does not explicitly define when an armed attack has actually occurred. Rouillard states that it has been argued that the charter's failure to clearly proscribe preemption should be interpreted as consent. That is, if the authors had wanted to prohibit preemption they would have unequivocally done so. He also cites a counterargument that in French, the language in which the charter was originally drafted, the term *agression armée* is the literal English equivalent of "armed attack," thus implying prohibition on any warfare not purely in response to an actual armed attack.

Most scholars of the law and ethics of war and international relations accept both the legality and morality of preemption and prevention (Rouillard 2004). The arguments in favor of preemption have several centuries of legal, ethical, and theological debate in their support. The arguments in favor of preventive war have a more recent basis and tend to cite an obscure 1837 incident known as the *Caroline* affair. The *Caroline* was a steamboat being used by a group of Canadian revolutionaries to transport arms and personnel across the Niagara River from the United States to their headquarters on Canadian Navy Island. This was being done in advance of a series of planned attacks designed to free parts of Canada from British rule. In the early morning hours of December 29, 1837, a small force of Royal Marines invaded the United States, started a rather sharp firefight, and burned the *Caroline*, touching off an international incident that took several years to settle. The British claimed this was an act of preventive self-defense and permissible under international law. This defense was widely accepted in Europe (though less so in the United States) and served as a major argument to widen the doctrine of preemption to include prevention in international law.

Despite the doctrines resulting from the *Caroline* affair, and many claims made since, prevention, as opposed to preemption, is still not an entirely settled legal or moral doctrine. However, after carefully weighing the evidence, Rouillard (2004) concluded, "There is no reason to change the criterion established more than a century and a half ago. They remain absolutely valid. The existence of a right to anticipatory self-defence can be established and there certainly are clear and imminent dangers that must be pre-emptively addressed. But they must be so addressed within the strict and narrow confines of the exhaustion of all alternative means, the necessity of its actions being established by the immediacy of the danger, and must be proportional to the threat." He added that such cases are exceedingly rare and that, in his belief, no such cases had occurred since World War II. So while both preemptive and preventive war may be regarded as established legal and moral doctrine, preparing a case to justify a preventive war would be quite difficult.

In an attempt to articulate clear justification for preventive attacks, Sofaer (2003) required that four criteria be met. First, the nature and magnitude of the threat must be severe enough to justify a casus belli, or cause for war, under international law; second, there must be a very high degree of certainty the threat would be realized unless immediate action was taken; third, all alternative responses must have failed to mitigate the threat; and, finally, the use of preemption must be consistent with Article 51 of the UN Charter and other international law. Amstutz (2008) added that prior to taking preemptive action it must be clear that one's enemy is intending to cause injury; that one's enemy is actively making preparations for war, military or otherwise, that increase the level of danger; and that immediate action is required because of the heightened level of danger that thus exists.

CONCLUSION

President Bush, in a speech at West Point in 2002, stated, "We cannot defend America and our friends by hoping for the best. We cannot put our faith in the word of tyrants, who solemnly sign non-proliferation treaties, and then systemically break them. If we wait for threats to fully materialize, we will have waited too long." These words marked a departure from long-standing U.S. foreign policy, one of questionable legality and morality. While preemptive action to forestall an immediate threat of war or to gain a strategic or tactical advantage in the face of an immediate threat are settled matters of international law, prevention is not. However, prevention has become an increasingly legitimized means of waging war as may be seen by the increasing reliance on drone attacks against terrorist leaders, which are a form of preventive warfare.

Walzer (2004) suggested that preventive war may in fact be a self-defeating doctrine. He believed that one may be attacked because of the heightened fear in others of an imminent preventive attack. That is, if a nation makes preventive attacks a centerpiece of foreign policy (as in the Bush Doctrine) it runs the risk that other nations may consider that policy a cause for war and make preemptive attacks of their own. Given the concerns of the war on terror it is doubtful this issue will be settled in terms of morality or legality in the foreseeable future.

REFERENCES

Amstutz, M. *International Ethics: Concepts, Theories, and Cases in Global Politics.* Lanham, MD: Rowman & Littlefield, 2008.

Aquinas, St. Thomas. *Politics and Ethics.* New York: W. W. Norton, 1988.

Augustine, St. *City of God.* New York: Penguin, 1984.

Beres, Louis Rene. "On Assassination as Anticipatory Self-Defense: The Case of Israel." *Hofstra Law Review* 20 (Winter 1991): 321–40. http://heinonlinebackup.com/hol-cgi-bin/get_pdf.cgi?handle=hein.journals/hoflr20&section=16.

Bush, G. Remarks by the President at 2002 Graduation Exercise of the United States Military Academy, West Point, New York, June 1, 2002. http://ics.leeds.ac.uk/papers/vp01.cfm?outfit=pmt&folder=339&paper=380.

Childress, J. "Just-War Theories: The Bases, Interrelations, Priorities, and Functions of Their Criteria." *Theological Studies* 39 (1978): 427–45.

Dershowitz, A. *Preemption: A Knife That Cuts Both Ways.* New York: W.W. Norton, 2006.

Epstein, I., ed. *Hebrew-English Edition of the Babylonian Talmud: Sanhedrin, folio 72a.* Brooklyn, NY: Soncino Press, 2004.

Grotius, H. *On the Law of War and Peace (De iure belli ac pacis libri tres).* 1625 http://lonang.com/exlibris/grotius/index.html.

Ramsey, P. *The Just War.* New York: Scribners, 1969.

Rouillard, L.-P. "The Caroline Case: Anticipatory Self-Defence in Contemporary International Law." *Miskolc Journal of International Law* 1, no. 2 (2004): 104–20. http://www.uni-miskolc.hu/~wwwdrint/20042rouillard1.htm; http://epa.oszk.hu/00200/00294/00002/20042rouillard1.htm.

Sofaer, A. "On the Necessity of Pre-emption." *European Journal of International Law* 14, no. 2 (2003): 220.

United Nations. "Action with Respect to Threats to the Peace, Breaches of the Peace and Acts of Aggression." In *Charter of the United Nations,* chap. 7. June 26, 1945. http://www.un-documents.net/ch-07.htm.

Walzer, M. *Arguing about War.* New Haven, CT: Yale University Press, 2004.

Psychological Operations

Chamila S. Liyanage

War is a complex phenomenon comprising underlying ideologies, attitudes, behaviors, and personalities. The human factor of war, with its many dimensions and numerous characteristics, has made psychological operations (PSYOP) a significant factor in the history of warfare. Psychological warfare can be traced back to the earliest conflicts in human history. Sun Tzu, the notable ancient Chinese strategist, implies the importance of psychological warfare in his famous dictum "For to win one hundred victories in one hundred battles is not the acme of skill. To subdue the enemy without fighting is the acme of skill" (Griffith 1963, 77). In other words, to subdue the enemy without the use of force requires persuasion to convince and lessen the enemy's will to fight. It is the realm of alternative strategies and tactics, which provides substitutes to coercive force.

DEFINING PSYCHOLOGICAL OPERATIONS

Several broad and concise definitions cover the scope and define the objectives of psychological operations. According to Paul Linebarger (1955, 25), "Psychological warfare applies the elements of psychology to the conduct of war. It also uses propaganda against the enemy together with other military and operational measures." Psychological operations are also defined as "planned political, economic, military and ideological activities directed toward foreign countries, organizations, or individuals in order to create emotions, attitudes, understandings, beliefs, or behavior favorable to the achievement of U.S. political and military objectives" (Curtis 1989, 1). The Doctrine for Joint Psychological Operations issued by the U.S. Department of Defense has defined psychological operations as "planned operations to convey selected information and indicators to foreign audiences to influence the emotions, motives, objective reasoning, and ultimately the behavior of foreign governments, organizations, groups, and individuals" (Department of Defense, Joint Chiefs of Staff 2003, ix).

Psychological warfare comes under the broader heading of special warfare. It can also be categorized as an important element of strategic influence. The sole aim of strategic influence is direct or indirect persuasion. Psychological operations are generally a classified and secret approach in military strategy and tactics. As a critical component of modern-day warfare, psychological operations add an important element to the theory and practice of warfare and have as their ultimate purpose a direct negative impact on enemy objectives.

The scope of psychological operations is extensive. It consists of a set of specific goals and defines calculated measures to achieve these objectives. In its broader connotation, psychological operations employ strategies and tactics that are designed to influence and persuade specific targets to comply with the intended objectives. The term even suggests the entire efforts a nation can put forward to achieve its national interests by persuading numerous actors at home and abroad. Psychological operations may have general objectives and also ad hoc dynamic or specific objectives. Ideally, intensive work with allied nations should be paramount in this endeavor as multilateral efforts could achieve common objectives.

PSYCHOLOGICAL WARFARE AND INFORMATION

Information plays a central role in psychological operations; this consists primarily of gathering, assessing, selecting, manipulating, and delivering controlled information in a way that impacts the selected target. Information can be negative or positive depending on the predefined specific objectives. The information employed in psychological operations can be broken down into three distinct categories: white, gray, and black. This color code signifies the source of the information and the characteristics of the psychological operation. White information used in psychological operations is overt and identifiable in relation to its source or origin. Additionally, since this type of information is not concealed, it can be more credible and thus more influential. Gray information is controlled through disguised or camouflaged sources. This type of information can appear to come from a completely unrelated source and is designed to mislead and misdirect the target's perceptions and expectations. Finally, black psychological operations can be extremely hostile. These types of operations are clandestine, usually delivered via secret channels, and are designed to create a devastating impact on the selected target.

In addition to foreign adversaries, enemies, or audiences, psychological operations can also target domestic or friendly audiences and the general public to create perceptions and impressions designed to facilitate an environment conducive for specific actions or planned intentions about to be carried out. In other words, its objective is to encourage, create, and maintain certain perceptions that create a favorable atmosphere to achieve specific political, military, economic, and ideological objectives. Through the targeted delivery of persuasive information, psychological operations can be utilized to achieve wider national interests or specific ad hoc objectives in peacetime and war.

Psychological operations can be employed to destabilize the underlying justifications of conflicts, thereby destroying the enemy's credibility. Furthermore, successful psychological operations can target specific ideological elements of conflicts, which is critical to winning the hearts and minds of indigenous populations. It can further extend to target critical emotions related to human behavior and reasoning in order to manipulate the outcome of conflicts. It is important to note that the human mind is the battleground of psychological operations. Contemporary psychological operations advance knowledge in theory and practice. They employ many interrelated disciplines, concepts, and working areas, which use similar practices to achieve particular goals in various fields. The notable few, neocortical warfare, perception management, and public diplomacy involve psychological operations at various levels. The networked world in the current information age produces many innovative working realms for psychological operations and related disciplines.

In past conflicts, propaganda campaigns played an integral part of psychological operations. During World War II, psychological operations used mass leaflet droppings dubbed as "paper bullets." More than 60 million leaflets were dropped targeting Japanese forces based in the Philippine Islands alone (White 1948, 68). The goal was persuasion. Nevertheless, the advancement of global technological and information capabilities limited the use of propaganda. Widespread access to information made propaganda extinct as a credible method of persuasion. Propaganda often denotes a meaning associated with fabrication, but even credible information can be used for propaganda purposes. However, Cull, Culbert, and Welch (2003, xv) note that "the word 'propaganda' continues to imply something sinister; synonyms for propaganda frequently include 'lies', 'deceit' and 'brainwashing.'"

Contemporary psychological operations have developed into a more technical and operational concept than mere propaganda campaigns.

Psychological operations, as a classified means of special operations, still imply negative perceptions in the public mind. Nevertheless, as an alternative to coercive force, psychological operations contribute significantly in the conduct of 21st-century warfare. Ideally, psychological operations will break the enemy's will to fight before the commencement of war, thus avoiding lengthy and costly battles. They can also serve to weaken the contributing factors that could eventually lead to potential conflicts.

Globalization and advances in information technology that began at the end of the Cold War provide both challenges and innovative opportunities for conducting successful psychological operations. As a consequence of globalization, civil society started to acquire increasingly global perspectives. Advances in communications technology provide wider access to information and create globally connected individuals, communities, and nations. This global networking expands the boundaries of many subjects. Many areas of inquiry and knowledge, particularly those connected to the study of international relations, have expanded as a result of evolving and forward-moving advances in communication technology. This presents a challenge to psychological operations but an innovative prospect to explore beyond its present-day boundaries. Thus, the evolving field of psychological operations in international affairs is at a critical juncture of growth and innovation. As Whitley (2000, iii) noted, "A revolution in psychological operations (PSYOP) will occur in the near future." Indeed, advances in information technology will expand the scope and capabilities of psychological operations throughout the global theater (Whitley 2000).

CONCLUSION

Psychological operations will continue to be a critical component of strategic planning in both peace and war. Current international realities and challenges make it extremely difficult to rely solely on the use of military force as the primary strategic asset in national security policy. Innovative methods that are designed to achieve specific objectives while reducing the use of coercive force are a critical component in the conduct of successful international relations. As evidenced by events in the Middle East and North Africa, empowered masses augmenting their global presence provide immense opportunities for successful psychological operations. That said, psychological campaigns demand an adequate understanding of foreign cultures, underlying value systems, and mindsets. A clear recognition and comprehension of the vast differences inherent in other cultures will provide the necessary framework to minimize the use of force in international affairs.

See also: **Volume 1, Part I:** Concept of Islamist Jihad; Global Terrorism: Post-9/11; Insurgent Terrorism; The Terrorist Threat in the 21st Century: A Global Security Problem; War on Terror. **Part III:** Combating Terrorist Recruitment, Propaganda, and Radicalization Campaigns; Information Technologies to Combat Terrorism. **Part IV:** Combating Religiously Based Terrorism. **Part VI:** Psychological Profiling of Terrorists; Sun Tzu's *Art of War:* Lessons for 21st-Century Counterterrorism Practitioners; Understanding Foreign Cultures; Weak Link: Identifying and Attacking Terrorists' Vulnerabilities

REFERENCES

Cull, Nicholas John, David Holbrook Culbert, and David Welch. *Propaganda and Mass Persuasion: A Historical Encyclopedia, 1500 to the Present.* Santa Barbara, CA: ABC CLIO, 2003.

Curtis, Glenn. *An Overview of Psychological Operations.* Washington, DC: Library of Congress, 1989. http://www.dtic.mil/cgi-bin/GetTRDoc?AD=ADA302389&Location=U2&doc=GetTRDoc.pdf.

Department of Defense, Joint Chiefs of Staff. *Doctrine for Joint Psychological Operations.* Joint Publication 3-53, Washington, DC, September 5, 2003. http://www.iwar.org.uk/psyops/resources/doctrine/psyop-jp-3-53.pdf.

Griffith, Samuel B., trans. *Sun Tzu: The Art of War.* Oxford: Oxford University Press, 1963.

Linebarger, Paul. *Psychological Warfare.* Washington, DC: Combat Forces Press, 1955.

White, David M. "Shakespeare and Psychological Warfare." *Public Opinion Quarterly* 12 (1948): 68–72.

Whitley, Gary L. *PSYOP Operations in the 21st Century.* Carlisle, PA: U.S. Army War College, 2000. http://www.iwar.org.uk/psyops/resources/21st-century/psyop.pdf.

Role of the International Community

Ross Prizzia

The role of the international community in meeting the challenge of domestic and international terrorism depends significantly on the political will and ability of each member state and organization in this community to effectively coordinate and integrate their respective material and human resources. Countries vary widely in their approaches to policies on when and how to assist or become involved in the event of man-made and natural disasters. Some countries adopt a reactive approach and confine themselves to offering assistance with search and rescue after the disaster has occurred. By contrast, other countries assist in forming intergovernmental institutions and programs whose major goals are to reduce the incidence of disasters and to increase the capacity of poor countries to respond to emergencies. Some institutions representing the international community have created new common mechanisms for collaboration and have developed a global capacity against terrorism and transnational crime, such as the International Criminal Police Organization (Interpol), the World Customs Organization, and the Financial Action Task Force (Kirchsteiger, Christou, and Papadakis 1998; Winer 2003). Also, several U.S. federal police agencies are involved in combating international terrorism, including the Federal Bureau of Investigation, the Drug Enforcement Administration, and various other U.S. law enforcement agencies that have distinctly international roles (Deflem 2002).

COLLABORATION OF UNITED NATIONS AND REGIONAL LAW ENFORCEMENT ORGANIZATIONS

The United Nations (UN) has been instrumental in securing, monitoring, and enhancing global participation in sanctions against terrorist financiers. In 2006, the UN Global Counter-terrorism Strategy was adopted, representing a unique global instrument to support national, regional, and international efforts to counter terrorism (A/RES/60/288; Council of Europe n.d.). This was the first time that all member states agreed to a common strategic approach to fight terrorism and to take practical actions individually and collectively to prevent and combat domestic and international terrorism. These actions included a variety of strategies, tactics, and measures ranging from strengthening state capacity to better coordination of UN systems to counter terrorist threats and activities. Since the terrorist attacks in the United States on September 11, 2001, the UN has been instrumental in developing and implementing antiterrorism measures throughout the world, especially in the area of creating new strategies to combat terrorist finance. In September 2001, the UN Security Council created the Counterterrorism Committee (CTC), which established procedures and criteria to monitor and stimulate action on a national basis against terrorist finance (Kirchsteiger, Christou, and Papadakis 1998). The CTC adapted the criteria previously developed by the Financial Action Task Force and used by the International Monetary Fund and World Bank. By March 2003, more than 100 countries were identified as needing assistance in the drafting, passing, and enforcement of antiterrorism, banking, and financial laws and regulations related to the financing of terrorism (Kirchsteiger, Christou, and Papadakis 1998). The CTC also assisted these countries needing help with the application of best practices and developed a comprehensive online *Directory of Counter-terrorism Information and Sources of Assistance.* A Technical Assistance Team was also created to address counterterrorism assistance. Moreover, an Action Assistance Plan was created to facilitate self-help and work to strengthen the capacity of regional organizations to assist states (Kirchsteiger, Christou, and Papadakis 1998). The CTC also facilitates the flow of information between states and potential providers, such as the International Monetary Fund, World Bank, and Council of Europe (Winer 2003; Kirchsteiger, Christou, and Papadakis 1998).

The UN, Financial Action Task Force, World Customs Organization, Interpol, and regional law enforcement institutions are also addressing the cross-border gap with resources to improve standards, training, and strategies to combat terrorism (Kirchsteiger, Christou, and Papadakis 1998). In 2002 the UN General Assembly approved an expanded program of activities for the UN Office on Drugs and Crime Terrorism Prevention Branch, which focuses on assisting states, upon request, in the legal aspects of counterterrorism, especially ratifying and implementing the international legal instruments against terrorism. Other antiterrorism efforts followed, which included the UN-sponsored World Summit Outcome in 2005, the UN Global Counter-terrorism Strategy in 2006, relevant elements of the UN's Strategic Framework for the period 2010–2011, and the UN Office on Drugs and Crime Strategy for the period 2008–2011.

COORDINATION OF EUROPEAN AND ASIA-PACIFIC CIVIL AND NATIONAL SECURITY ORGANIZATIONS

There are also regional organizations such as the European Commission–operated Monitoring and Information Center and the Joint Research Center's Institute for the Protection and Security of the Citizen (IPSC), which provides overall assessments to the Monitoring and Information Center and to all civil protection agencies in Europe. The official mission of the IPSC is "to provide research results and to support EU policies-makers in their effort towards global security and towards protection of European citizens from accidents, deliberate attacks, fraud and illegal actions against EU policies" (European Commission 2012). By sharing assessment techniques and methods, international antiterrorist experts contribute to the effectiveness of joint operations (Winer 2003).

Closely supported by the Joint Research Center (JRC) and the IPSC, the Monitoring and Information Center is the operational heart of the Community Mechanism for Civil Protection. It serves as a communications hub for emergency relief operations, disseminates information on civil protection preparedness, and supports coordination, thus providing European emergency assistance through the Community Mechanism for Civil Protection (Winer 2003).

Further, IPSC uses scientific and technical crisis management tools, including the Global Disaster Alert and Coordination System, which provides a platform for stakeholders in international disaster response to exchange disaster-related information and automated analysis of satellite images for the processing, interpretation, and evaluation of geospatial data, which help to quantify damages following conflicts or man-made and natural disasters (Winer 2003; Kirchsteiger, Christou, and Papadakis 1998). The United States has seven mutual defense treaties with Asia-Pacific nations in that region, where the world's six largest militaries operate.

Other than the UN and regional organizations such as the Association of Southeast Asian Nations's Regional Forum, there are no regional institutions to reconcile conflicts. Therefore, cooperation and collaboration through existing institutions and organizations are essential to the stability and security of the Asia-Pacific region in meeting the challenge of domestic and international terrorism. This common challenge of terrorism and the mutual concern to develop and implement strategies to respond to changing terrorist tactics bind the United States to other Asia-Pacific nations, requiring a commitment for the long term (Plummer 2009). The U.S. concerns with national security in the Asia-Pacific region have increased requiring monitoring of the threats of terrorism and the proliferation of weapons of mass destruction and missile technology (Prizzia 2008). Coordination through programs such as the Container Security Initiative and alliances such as the Custom-Trade Partnership against Terrorism play an important role in addressing vulnerabilities in the shipping industry. The Container Security Initiative authorizes exchanges of customs inspectors between the United States and participating nations and allows the United States to place inspectors in 26 international ports including Singapore, Hong Kong, and Malaysia. The initiative enables custom officers to safely and efficiently screen for contraband, including weapons of mass destruction, by using large-scale gamma ray and X-ray imaging systems (Prizzia 2006). Other technologies such as electronic seals and container-tracking devices provide additional protection against container tampering and help to secure ports and ships from possible attack. These precautions are critical to the Asia-Pacific region, which has some of the largest container ports in the world; one-third of the world's shipping and half of its oil pass through the straits of Southeast Asia (U.S. Department of State 2004).

The North Atlantic Treaty Organization (NATO) declared at the Riga Summit in 2006 that "terrorism, together with the spread of weapons of mass destruction, are likely to be the principal threat to the Alliance over the next 10 to 15 years" (NATO 2010). Since antiterrorism has been identified as essential to the alliance's work, NATO has established regular dialogue on terrorism and related issues among its members, as well as with nonmember countries and other international organizations, and has developed an extensive network of cooperative relationships and partnerships to meet the threat of domestic and international terrorism (NATO 2010). Since August 2003, NATO has been leading the International Security Assistance Force in assisting the government of Afghanistan, and NATO allied forces have been involved in Operation Enduring Freedom, the ongoing U.S.-led military counterterrorism operation (NATO 2010). Combating terrorism was a primary objective in the creation of the

NATO-Russia Council in May 2002. Antiterrorism remains a primary objective of NATO's dialogue with Russia and a focus of the NATO-Russia Council's cooperation activities.

CONCLUSION

NATO's Center of Excellence Defense against Terrorism provides a location and a forum for international dialogue for antiterrorism (NATO 2010). The center has developed links with over 50 countries and 40 organizations providing subject-matter experts on terrorism. NATO has also strengthened relations with the European Union, the Organization for Security and Cooperation in Europe, and the UN in collaborative efforts in fighting terrorism. In its effort to cooperate with the UN, NATO works with affiliated bodies such as the UN CTC, its Executive Directorate, and the Security Council Committee and has established contacts with the UN on its Global Counter-terrorism Strategy in responding to international disasters (NATO 2010).

See also: **Volume 1, Part III:** Evolution of Global Counterterrorism Initiatives; International Law, Human Rights, and Counterterrorism; Multilateral Sanctions against State Sponsors of Terrorism; Threat Perception and Multinational Cooperation. **Part IV:** Ethical and Legal Issues in Democratic Societies: National Security and Civil Liberties; Importance of Mutual Legal Assistance; International Legal Framework to Eliminate Terrorism against Civil Aviation and Maritime Targets; United Nations Global Counterterrorism Strategy: Significance and Limitations. **Part VI:** Multilateral Approach to Counterterrorism: Issues, Problems, Responses; Regional Challenges: Promoting Stability through Economic, Social, and Political Reforms

REFERENCES

Deflem, Mathieu. *Policing World Society: Historical Foundations of International Police Cooperation.* Oxford: Oxford University Press, 2002.

European Commission. "Mission Statement." Joint Research Centre, Institute for the Protection and Security of the Citizen. Last updated December 3, 2012. http://ipsc.jrc.ec.europa.eu/index.php/Mission/29/0/.

Kirchsteiger, Christian, Michalis Christou, and Georgios Papadakis. "Risk Assessment and Management in the Context of the Seveso II Directive." Amsterdam: Elsevier Science, 1998.

North Atlantic Treaty Organization (NATO). "NATO and the Fight against Terrorism." 2010. http://www.nato.int/cps/en/natolive/topics_48801.htm.

Plummer, M. G. "The Global Economic Crisis and Its Implications for Asian Economic Cooperation." *Policy Studies* 55, Honolulu: East-West Center, no. 10 (2009): 32–45. http://www.eastwestcenter.org/sites/default/files/private/ps055.pdf.

Prizzia, Ross. "Coordinating Disaster Prevention and Management in Hawaii." *Disaster Prevention and Management* 15, no. 2 (2006): 275–85.

Prizzia, Ross. "The Role of Coordination in Disaster Management." Chapter 5, Section I. In *The Disaster Management Handbook,* edited by Jack Pinkowski, 75–100. Florida, Taylor and Francis, 2008.

United Nations. "United Nations General Assembly Adopts Global Counter-Terrorism Strategy A/RES/60/288." UN Action to Counter Terrorism (Resolution and Plan of Action), September 8, 2006. http://www.un.org/terrorism/strategy-counter-terrorism.shtml.

U.S. Department of State. "Terrorism Requires Global Response." International Information Programs, Washington File, November 15, 2004.

Winer, Jonathan M. "Building Global Jurisdiction, Systems and Capacity to Build Global Security—or Even a Superpower Needs Friends." Council on Foreign Relations/American Society of International Law, March 4, 2003. http://www.cfr.org/world/building-global-jurisdiction-systems-capacity-build-global-security-even-superpower-needs-friends/p5655.

Safe Havens and Weak and Failing States

James D. Perry

In post-1945 warfare, insurgents or terrorists attacking a particular nation often seek, or create, safe havens across the border in another nation. These havens are exempt from attack and thus serve as refuges within which the insurgents can safely rest, arm, train, and receive support from external powers. Safe havens can emerge as a result of political restraint or through the weakness of national governments. Safe havens can exist within a sufficiently weak nation, usually as the result of complex terrain, such as jungles, swamps, deserts, or mountains, where government forces are unwilling or unable to go. Safe havens not only shield insurgent forces from attack but also provide an advantageous place from which they can attack the enemy.

INSURGENTS AND TERRORISTS

Safe havens have existed in traditional warfare; China was a haven during the Korean War. However, safe havens are particularly essential for the conduct of terrorism and insurgency, because insurgents and terrorists are by definition much weaker than the government forces they oppose. Insurgents and terrorists often establish safe havens in failed states, or in uncontrolled areas within weak states, and attack their target government from these havens. These safe havens are effective when target nations and their allies refuse to incur the military burden and political costs of retaliation against groups located on the territory of a supposedly neutral state. In some cases, states deliberately provide sanctuary to insurgents and terrorists on their soil and periodically unleash them on neighboring enemies as a form of proxy warfare. For example, India and Pakistan have both supported insurgents and terrorists against each other, as have Iraq and Iran. Motives for doing so include weakening or overthrowing an enemy regime, supporting co-religionists or co-ethnics, and advancing an ideology. In these cases, the target nation is deterred from retaliating directly because this would entail open warfare with a neighbor and its allies.

In safe havens, insurgents organize, recruit, train, plan, and stockpile weapons and materiel. Insurgents often receive foreign support in a safe haven rather than in the target nation itself. Insurgents launch operations from safe havens and recuperate in them afterwards. Safe havens permit insurgent groups to control the pace of operations and may allow insurgent units to escape annihilation at the hands of pursuing government forces. Examples abound of insurgencies and terrorist groups that have made highly effective use of safe havens: Algerian guerrillas in Tunisia in the 1950s, Vietnamese Communists in Laos and Cambodia from 1959 to 1975, the Palestine Liberation Organization (PLO) and Hezbollah in Lebanon, the Irish Republican Army in the Irish Republic, Afghan mujahideen in Pakistan in the 1980s, the anti-Sandinista contras in Honduras and Costa Rica in the 1980s, and Islamic militants seeking to "liberate" Kashmir from India, who enjoyed a safe haven in Pakistan after 1989. On the other hand, the lack of a safe haven often contributed significantly to the defeat of an insurgency. For example, in the 1940s and 1950s, the Huks in the Philippines, Communist guerrillas in Malaya, Tibetans opposing Chinese occupation, and the Mau Maus in Kenya all lacked external safe havens and were defeated. The Greek Civil War ended after Yugoslavia no longer provided a safe haven to Greek Communist insurgents. Lack of a safe haven does not always ensure defeat. The success of Fidel Castro's 26th of July Movement in overthrowing Fulgencio Batista is a notable example of an insurgency that lacked an external safe haven but was nevertheless victorious. After Nepalese Maoists lost their safe haven in India in 2001, they still won the Nepalese Civil War that ended in 2006.

Iran provided a safe haven for insurgents in Afghanistan and Iraq after the United States occupied these countries in 2001 and 2003. To support the insurgents in Iraq, the Iranian Republican Guards Corps provided the insurgents with funding, training on Iranian soil, advanced explosive munitions, arms and ammunition, intelligence, and advice. Reportedly, the Iranians assisted every faction fighting the United States in Iraq—not just the Shiite militias but also Sunni insurgents and al-Qaeda. In Afghanistan, Iran provided arms, explosives, and advanced roadside bombs to Taliban fighters, and some argue that the Taliban and al-Qaeda train in eastern Iran. During the war in Iraq Syria provided a haven for foreign militants, who received funding, training, weapons, and false papers before entering that country. The border provinces in Pakistan remain a sanctuary from which al-Qaeda and the Taliban launch attacks into Afghanistan; the insurgents reportedly receive assistance from some elements of Pakistan's Directorate for Inter-Services Intelligence. The May 1, 2011, attack (Operation Neptune Spear) on a compound in Abbottabad, Pakistan, conducted by U.S. Navy SEALs and Central Intelligence Agency (CIA) paramilitary personnel has raised new questions in this regard. Ironically, the insurgents use much of the same infrastructure, including a vast network of caves that the Afghan resistance used when Pakistan was a safe haven from the Soviets in the 1980s. The United States remains concerned that al-Qaeda, having been driven from Iraq, might establish safe havens in weak or failed states such as Yemen and Somalia.

OPERATIONAL AND STRATEGIC SANCTUARIES

Safe havens in neutral countries might be termed *strategic* sanctuaries, but insurgents can also obtain *operational* sanctuaries—areas where insurgent forces can operate with relative safety—within the nation they are attacking. A basic goal of any insurgency is to establish such areas. In an operational safe haven, insurgents can control the pace of operations and engage the enemy on favorable terms. On the offensive, insurgents have freedom of action to prosecute attacks while remaining insulated from effective counterattack. On the defensive, insurgents can conserve their forces until a favorable moment arises to commit them to combat. Operational safe havens generally leverage complex terrain such as forests, jungles, cities, and underground shelters, but insurgents also create safe havens in areas government forces decide to place legally or politically "off limits" to attack.

Mountains have frequently provided safe havens to insurgents. Rugged, high-altitude terrain limits the effectiveness of mechanized forces, artillery, and aviation and enables small, autonomous infantry units with superior knowledge of the country to hold vital points, ambush superior forces, and refuse combat when desired. During Operation Allied Force, heavily forested mountain terrain masked the Yugoslav Army from airborne sensors such as Joint Surveillance Target Attack Radar System. Mountain safe havens enabled the Serbians to retain the tactical initiative, since they could determine when and where to reposition themselves for ethnic cleansing operations. Mujahideen in Afghanistan, Chechens in the Caucasus, the Fuerzas Armadas Revolucionarias de Colombia (Revolutionary Armed Forces of Colombia), and the Sendero Luminoso in Peru have all successfully exploited this type of sanctuary.

Jungles and dense forests are excellent safe havens because thick foliage limits the effectiveness of overhead reconnaissance, aerial attack, and the operation of heavy ground forces. During the Vietnam War, the

North Vietnamese constructed an entire system of roads, truck parks, and storage areas under the jungle canopy in the Laotian panhandle. This network allowed thousands of trucks and hundreds of tanks to travel hundreds of miles with little chance of detection by American intelligence. In jungles, poor visibility hinders the application of direct-fire weapons, artillery, and aviation. Limited mobility and lack of open terrain mean that fewer conventional attacks occur in jungles relative to ambushes, raids, and meeting engagements. Defensive positions are easily camouflaged, and booby traps difficult to detect. Jungles are perfect terrain for insurgencies, because the terrain facilitates guerrilla tactics of infiltration, surprise attack, and engagement at extremely close ranges to nullify enemy firepower. Historically, insurgencies have flourished in the jungles of the Philippines, Southeast Asia, Indonesia, Latin America, and sub-Saharan Africa.

Cities have long provided formidable advantages to the defender. Cities can negate technological superiority and impose high costs in time, money, materiel, and manpower on the attacker. Urban terrain limits visibility and mobility, degrades communications, isolates and separates units, and renders vehicles vulnerable to ambush. Artillery and airpower are difficult to employ in cities, even when the rules of engagement do not prohibit their use, and the resulting rubble often provides better protection for the defenders than undamaged buildings. Highly restrictive rules of engagement, and the requirement to minimize civilian casualties and collateral damage, increase the value of the city as a safe haven for insurgents and terrorists. Interestingly, the historical record of insurgent use of cities is mixed, with urban insurgencies often being more easily defeated than their rural counterparts. Government forces are typically concentrated in cities, and insurgents cannot easily assemble, train, rehearse, and operate without the government observing and crushing them. These difficulties are not insurmountable—insurgents in Chechnya made good use of urban terrain against the Russians in the 1990s, and insurgents in Iraq quickly learned how to operate in urban environments after Operation Iraqi Freedom began. The likelihood of urban insurgency is expected to increase as a result of rapid population growth and increasing urbanization in the Third World.

Insurgencies and terrorist groups can develop quite extensive safe havens underground. According to the U.S. Army Corps of Engineers, Viet Cong underground complexes "contained armories, hospitals, mess halls, manufacturing centers, and storage facilities. Some complexes ranged up to 40 miles long; the Cu Chi tunnel complex contained 130 miles of passageways." Al-Qaeda and the Taliban have significant underground complexes in Afghanistan and Pakistan. One site in eastern Afghanistan included over 70 interconnected tunnels containing tanks, artillery, antiaircraft guns, and millions of pounds of explosives and ammunition. In the 2000s, Hezbollah built an extensive bunker complex, including concrete bunkers 130 feet (40 meters) underground, near the southern Lebanon border.

CONCLUSION

Many safe havens emerge from self-imposed political and legal inhibitions. In these cases, political leaders restrain government forces from attacking insurgents in safe havens because politicians consider the costs and risks excessive, despite the critical importance that the denial of safe havens has for the success of any counterinsurgency effort. Unfortunately, lack of political will is probably not amenable to a technological solution. However, some technologies—such as unmanned systems and precision weapons—can reduce the costs and risks associated with employing military power, and this may lift inhibitions and thus reduce or eliminate safe havens.

See also: **Volume 1, Part III:** Terrorists, Criminals, and Drug Cartels; **Part IV:** Eliminating Terrorist Support Networks; **Part VI:** Global Jihad Movement; Threat Convergence; Weak Link: Identifying and Attacking Terrorists' Vulnerabilities

REFERENCES

Byman, Daniel, Peter Chalk, Bruce Hoffman, William Rosenau, and David Brannan. *Trends in Outside Support for Insurgent Movements.* Santa Monica, CA: RAND, 2001. http://www.rand.org/pubs/monograph_reports/2007/MR1405.pdf.
Taw, Jennifer, and Bruce Hoffman. *The Urbanization of Insurgency.* Santa Monica, CA: RAND, 1994.
Vick, Alan. *Aerospace Operations against Elusive Ground Targets.* Santa Monica, CA: RAND, 2001.

Target Hardening

Hank Prunckun

Target hardening is one of a number of strategies that comprise a sound approach to counterterrorism management. Not to be confused with the related strategy of *target removal,* target hardening is based on the premise that acts of terrorism can be controlled without having to address the root cause. In this context, target hardening is a defensive strategy that has much in common with deterrence theory. However, unlike deterrence theory, which reasons that there will be swift retaliatory action that is greater than any possible benefit that could be derived from an attack, target-hardening theory reasons that a terrorist attack can be prevented by changing the environment to remove the opportunities for an attack, or it removes the likelihood that an attack would be successful should it be carried out.

TARGET HARDENING AS PREVENTION

The origin of the term *target hardening* is not known, but it is likely that it was derived from the military. For instance, during the early years of the Cold War the U.S. Air Force hardened its strategic missile silos against enemy attack. In the early 1970s the term then found application in one of the concepts of crime prevention—situational crime prevention. Situational crime prevention is the foundation on which *crime prevention through environmental design* (CEPTED, pronounced *cep-ted*) is based. CEPTED aims to change the environment in three important ways: (1) increase the likelihood that a terrorist will be detected (e.g., landscapes that aid natural surveillance), (2) increase the effort (e.g., time, energy, resources, and/or funding) required to carry out an attack, and (3) reduce the potential impact of an attack. Target hardening is one of the tenets for achieving this CEPTED outcome.

With regard to terrorist attacks, which are a specific form of crime (i.e., acts prohibited by law), target hardening is a supporting strategy that guides the principles of counterterrorism policy—prevention. Prevention along with the other three principles—preparation, response, and recovery (often abbreviated simply as PPRR)—has its genesis in emergency management, where strategists first try to prevent the impact of a hazard and then prepare for the consequences should this fail. This is followed by considering an effective response and immediately followed by a plan for recovery. Therefore, the prevention phase of a PPRR policy should be seen as part of a systematic approach to counterterrorism policy development.

STRENGTHS AND LIMITATIONS

Although on the surface target hardening has strengths, it also has limitations. In the main its strengths come from its time-tested results; that is, it is not an emerging science. Target hardening has the added benefit that it reduces fear of terrorism/crime, and it can be used in relation to a number of crime types, for instance, from preventing local bank robberies to protecting embassies abroad. Its chief limitation is that it can simply displace acts of terrorism from sites employing target hardening to those that do not. This is known as displacement theory.

Another limitation is what has been termed *tactical displacement*. That is, terrorists may look for ways to circumvent target-hardening strategies.

Moreover, there is also the issue that employees and customers of firms employing these strategies, as well as other users of target hardened facilities, will become annoyed with the countermeasures and avoid using the facilities or use them less often. If this happens, it can become a public relations problem, and if this occurs in the private sector, such adverse reactions could affect the firm's cash flow and its financial bottom line. The most serious of the limitations regarding target hardening is that terrorists may increase the level of violence in order to overcome the countermeasures. For instance, a terrorist may use a larger truck-borne improvised explosive device to breach barriers that have been erected in front of, say, a building rather than a smaller car-borne device that would have carried only a fraction of the destructive power had the protective obstacle not been constructed.

In practice, implementing a target-hardening program entails a three-step process: vulnerability analysis, risk analysis, and selection of the appropriate target-hardening strategy. Vulnerability analysis assesses all potential targets for susceptibility to attack. This list may comprise primary, secondary, and tertiary targets, as well as soft targets. Once a list of potential targets have been identified, strategists assess the likelihood and consequences of a terrorist attack on these targets, which in turn leads to devising a set of options to harden the targets.

The key to implementing a target-hardening program begins with giving consideration to how the strategy will be integrated with other counterterrorist strategies and, once implemented, publishing the countermeasure. Although this latter action might seem counterintuitive as many counterterrorist strategies, and how they are put into practice, are classified, the theory underscoring target-hardening reasons that the environmental change removes the opportunity to commit the attack or removes the likelihood of success. If it is not made public, it may lose some of its effectiveness.

However, this strength underscores many of the limitations cited— knowing that there are countermeasures can deter terrorists, but it can also allow them time to devise ways to get around the obstacle (tactical displacement) or increase the level of violence in order to neutralize the protective effects of the strategy. Or terrorists can simply wait until staff or customers become alienated by the countermeasure and fail to use it and then, when this happens, launch their attack.

This is why the second step in implementing a target-hardening strategy involves a risk analysis. In this phase of target-hardening planning process strategists will typically conduct a cost-benefit analysis. This analysis examines the monetary costs of implementing the countermeasure and weighs them against the benefit that might be gained. For example, a water pipeline that supplies a city might be assessed as being vulnerable, but the cost of securing the entire pipeline might be disproportionately expensive. This result suggests alternate target-hardening strategies. In this instance, strategists might suggest to policymakers that they implement a response that relies on repairing the pipeline within a small number of hours rather than protecting the entire pipeline, which would, in effect, achieve the same result but at a fraction of the cost.

To increase the protection and further aid in cost reduction, target hardening has also borrowed the military tactic of *defense in depth*. Defense in depth relies on a number of "rings" of protection that surround the facility considered vulnerable. By adding a number of protective layers, the three tenets of CEPTED are more likely to be achieved.

CONCLUSION

Target hardening is a key strategy in counterterrorist policy. Although it cannot afford a perfect protective shield, it has the potential to deter attacks and to mitigate any effects if an attack is carried out.

REFERENCES

Bullock, Jane, George Haddow, Damon Coppola, and Sarp Yeletaysi. *Introduction to Homeland Security: Principles of All-Hazards Response*. 3rd ed. Boston: Butterworth-Heinemann, 2009.

Crowe, Timothy. *Crime Prevention through Environmental Design*. 2nd ed. Boston: Butterworth-Heinemann, 2000.

Levi, Barbara, Mark Sakitt, and Art Hobson, eds. *The Future of Land-Based Strategic Missiles*. New York: American Institute of Physics, 1989.

Prunckun, Hank. *Handbook of Scientific Methods of Inquiry for Intelligence Analysis*. Lanham, MD: Scarecrow, 2010.

Terrorism, Counterterrorism, and the Internet

Joshua Sinai

The Internet has become one of the dominant instruments used by terrorist groups and their supporters to publicize their cause, radicalize and recruit new members, and raise funds; they even use cyberspace for operational command and control. Understanding the spectrum of dimensions in which terrorists exploit the Internet also provides government counterterrorism agencies a multilevel capability to counter such activities, whether by closely monitoring them to pick up trends in their thinking and agendas, and possible clues about imminent operations, or by identifying and apprehending participants who engage in illegal activities, such as threatening physical violence against their adversaries.

HOW TERRORISTS EXPLOIT THE INTERNET

The Internet provides terrorists with a myriad of benefits. First, it provides them with a relatively secure means from anywhere a computer can be used to spread their extremist propaganda, radicalize supporters, recruit new members, train members, communicate, and even conduct operational planning and execution of attacks. Many of these websites may be run from regions where terrorist operatives have found safe haven, such as, in the case of al-Qaeda and its affiliates, in Pakistan and Yemen. In other regions, such as Western societies, militants have moved their activities online into cyberspace, because physical meeting places, such as extremist religious houses of worship or community centers, are likely to be monitored by law enforcement agencies (Sageman 2008, 116).

A second benefit to a terrorist group is the relatively low cost of maintaining websites and the relative ease with which webmasters can register their websites and deploy new ones if they are removed by Internet service providers, for instance, by using proxy servers that hide the user's identity. Third, cyberspace also provides terrorist groups with the capability to penetrate a targeted country's geographic borders, thereby bypassing border checkpoints and other security-manned entry points, such as at airports. Finally, terrorist groups and their supporters turn to the Internet because of its "ease of use, the unprecedented reach of the technology, the difficulty to monitor, censor, or control online communications, as well as its vast potential to empower the disenfranchised and the ability to belittle real and imagined enemies" (Sageman 2008, 116).

Terrorist and extremist sites online span the range ideologically, from religiously extremist to radical animal or environmental groups, neo-Nazi white supremacists, antiabortion groups, and so on. In such a way, the Internet has come to replace—although not necessarily supplant—the traditional terrorist modus operandi on the ground, making it easier to recruit homegrown terrorists or communicate with sleeper cells in the country. It may never substitute for physical field training, but, like flight simulation software, it can approximate situations on how to train for a spectrum of attacks.

Two basic types of terrorist websites exist on the Internet: static, or "passive," ones and those that are "active." As discussed by Marc Sageman, the online presence of terrorists and extremists goes beyond static websites and includes discussion groups in chat rooms and forums, blogs, videos, and podcasts (2008, 113–14). Some offer a public face for the terrorist group and its associated movements, while others have operational components. These websites are further differentiated according to two types of interaction: passive and active (Sageman 2008, 113–16). The passive interaction consists of websites that provide information to their users, just like conventional media such as books, newspapers, radio, and television. Such websites perform an educational role by spreading and reinforcing radical beliefs, such as, in the case of radical Islamists, getting radical figures to issue religious justifications for jihad, with their fatwas (religious rulings) posted on these sites.

These religious rulings are then reinforced by horrific images and videos of conflict environments or "heroic" operations by terrorist operatives. In the case of religious extremists, the constant repetition of grievances that supposedly portray their adversaries' disrespect for their coreligionists, especially the alleged "humiliation" of their brethren, "serve as an emotional spur that leads to calls to avenge the disrespect shown by the enemy" (Simon Wiesenthal Center n.d., 11). It is through this process that such "calls for revenge go far beyond the theoretical and directly into the practice of terrorism" (Sageman 2008, 115).

These websites also provide relevant operational information to would-be operatives, such as instructions on building improvised explosive devices. Despite these sites' promotion of violence, they are still passive because, as Sageman (2008, 117) explains, individuals "access those sites but passively absorb the information provided."

In the active interaction, however, the Internet's e-mails, Listservs, and, especially, forums and chat rooms enable the participants, while maintaining their anonymity, to communicate and form bonds with one another via "computer-mediated technology" (Sageman 2008, 121). There are also two types of forums: open and closed (Sageman 2008, 118). The open forums act as a gateway into the radicalized world and welcome new visitors by providing them an easy registration process. These closed forums also enable their members to remain anonymous and secure, so they create tougher barriers to entry by making participation "by invitation only" and password protected. It is often through closed forums that terrorist groups first broadcast their messages and videos. As Sageman (2008, 119) explains, "Closed forums also receive material from al Qaida Central for distribution to the greater audience."

As individuals, whether as groups of friends or loners, become increasingly radicalized through interactivity in both types of forums, some small-scale terrorist networks have been created by such cyber meeting places. As Sageman (2008, 116) explains, "The interactivity among a 'bunch of guys' act[s] as an echo chamber, which progressively radicaliz[es] them collectively to the point where they [are] ready to collectively join a terrorist organization."

COUNTERING TERRORISTS' INTERNET ACTIVITIES

Different types of terrorist activities on the Internet require appropriately differentiated responses. First, according to Yaacov Lappin, author of *Virtual Caliphate,* governments' strategies must recognize that the battle against the online terrorist presence is part of their physical war against these adversaries. Just as counterterrorist strike forces are deployed to counter them in physical space, comparable counterterrorist cyberspace forces are required to fight Internet terrorists (Lappin 2010, 129).

Second, as outlined by Gabriel Weimann, a leading expert on terrorists' use of the Internet, such governmental responses must be based on what he terms a "MUD" approach, that is, monitoring, using, and disrupting (Sinai, October 8, 2006). Such a strategy consists of three components:

1. Terrorist websites need to be *monitored* to learn about terrorists' mindsets, motives, persuasive buzzwords, audiences, operational plans, and potential targets for attack. These sites will also reveal whom they consider to be their political and religious authorities, as well as which moderate religious clerics they regard as particularly threatening. Monitoring also reveals their inner debates and disputes.

2. Counterterrorism organizations need to *use* the terrorist websites to identify and locate their propagandists, chat room discussion moderators, Internet service provider (ISP) hosts, operatives, and participating members.

3. Terrorist websites need to be *disrupted* through negative and positive means. In a negative-influence campaign, sites can be infected with viruses and worms to destroy them or kept alive while flooding them with false technical information about weapons systems, circulating rumors to create doubt about the reputation and credibility of terrorist leaders, or inserting conflicting messages into discussion forums to confuse operatives and their supporters. In a more positive approach, alternative narratives can be inserted into these websites to demonstrate the negative results of terrorism or, to potential suicide bombers, to suggest the benefits of the "value of life" versus the self-destructiveness of the "culture of death and martyrdom."

An effective MUD approach, Weimann explains, depends on several conditions. It must be interdisciplinary, involving experts in communications and rhetoric, psychologists who understand the impact of influence campaigns on their targeted audiences' cognitive and behavioral responses, graphic designers who understand the type of graphic interface and layout that would appeal to such potential audiences, and civil liberty attorneys to ensure such influence campaigns do not infringe on constitutional rights of free speech and expression.

Third, international cooperation is required to implement and coordinate global campaigns. As advocated by Maria Alvanou, a Greek counterterrorism expert, a new international legal regime is required to counter such entities that exist in a virtual sphere (Lappin 2010, 130–31). This was also echoed by the Eilat workshop, which added that under such an international institutional framework, joint governmental and independent nongovernmental organization (NGO) campaigns would be driven by coordinated official and unofficial international monitoring entities that would form a so-called Web site Interpol. Guidelines would be issued to define "red lines" in terrorist supporters' websites that, when crossed, would trigger measures to end their presence on the Internet.

This is a dynamic arena of continuous feedback loops in which our actions must ceaselessly anticipate and respond to the reactions of the targeted terrorist websites. For instance, when a website is brought down, it usually reemerges in a different configuration elsewhere.

Such influence campaigns must be led by moderate political and religious leaders within the affected communities to formulate alternative messages and narratives to the extremist religious ideologies. It is important to prioritize the audiences to be targeted by such influence campaigns. For example, devoted activists may be considered a lost cause, while potential recruits who have not yet been activated into terrorism represent new opportunities for influence operations.

It is also crucial that whatever is being offered to counter terrorism on the Internet must be as authentically true to that religion and close to the ground truth as possible. It is here that the root causes underlying the problems that the religious extremists are exploiting for their own purposes must be resolved. In addition, as Weimann (2006, 140) explains, an "alternative online stage" needs to be created that would rival the terrorists' message by providing "a voice of peace, an alternative to death and suicide."

CONCLUSION

Finally, as Lappin (2010, 132–35) notes, robust multilingual search technologies are required to monitor the Internet for online terrorist activity in order to identify the connections among extremist websites, uncover their camouflaged communications (especially those that are related to potential plots), and detect the identities and locations of their participants. Cumulatively, success in countering terrorists' exploitation of the Internet requires effective government programs and capable partners, such as other government allies or international and regional organizations, as well as nonstate organizations, including private sector companies that develop technologies that can aid in such counteraction. Above all, this must be done while protecting the free flow of information and freedom of expression by responsible parties.

See also: **Volume 1, Part III:** Information Security; Information Technologies to Combat Terrorism

REFERENCES

Lappin, Yaacov. *Virtual Caliphate: Exposing the Islamist State on the Internet.* Washington, DC: Potomac Books, 2010.

Sageman, Marc. *Leaderless Jihad: Terror Networks in the Twenty-First Century.* Philadelphia: University of Pennsylvania Press, 2008.

Simon Wiesenthal Center. "Online Terror and Hate: The First Decade." Snider So-
    cial Action Institute, iReport. Los Angeles, CA: Simon Wiesenthal Center,
    n.d. http://www.friendsofsimonwiesenthalcenter.com/downloads/ire
    port.pdf.
Sinai, Joshua. "Defeating Internet Terrorists." *Washington Times,* October 8, 2006.
Weimann, Gabriel. *Terror on the Internet: The New Arena, the New Challenges.* Wash-
    ington, DC: Potomac Books, 2006.

Terrorist Recruitment in Correctional Institutions

Ami Angell

Today, an estimated 2.3 million people are serving time in American correctional facilities. An estimated one-third of them claim some form of religious affiliation (Dammer 2002). Research suggests that many of these
prisoners began their incarceration with little or no religious calling
but adopted a faith during their imprisonment (Clear and Sumter 2002;
Thomas and Zaitzow 2004). That number has been shown to significantly
increase among individuals incarcerated on foreign soil. Some individuals argue this is most probably because the Muslim world is responding
faster than the West. Radical Muslim clerics feed on the vulnerability of inmates, encouraging them to participate and contribute to radical dialogue
in exchange for security, higher purpose, and kinship within prison walls.

BREEDING GROUNDS FOR VIOLENCE

Given that many individuals are unable to cope with the harsh reality of
prison life, along with the fact that prisons have traditionally been breeding grounds for some of the world's most violent and organized criminal
organizations, anyone might see the predicament at hand. Prison environments often inspire the creation of well-organized gangs and networks
that thrive behind prison walls. In the United States alone, organized
gangs such as the Black Guerilla Family, Aryan Brotherhood, and Mexican Mafia have formed in an effort to promote ethnic and racial solidarity
and compete for power and influence inside and outside the penal system. In many cases, these networks are comprised of effective leadership
councils, chains of command, and strict codes of conduct for members.
Members of prison gangs are forced to join, and gangs often include psychologically vulnerable inmates seeking the physical protection that gang
members appear to provide. Often, these individuals are indoctrinated in
what they perceive as a worthy cause or one that provides them a sense
of belonging.

Likewise, a number of prominent Islamist radicals, including Ayman al-Zawahiri and Abu Musab al-Zarqawi, spent years in Egyptian and Jordanian prisons. The Egyptian and Jordanian prison systems are known to have harsh conditions that include systematic abuse and torture (Zamelis 2006). It can therefore be assumed that these experiences contributed to their radicalization. These two al-Qaeda leaders were notorious in both Afghanistan and Iraq. Similarly, in Spain, José Emilio Suárez Trashorras, a Spanish mineworker, was jailed in 2001 for a drug offense. Trashorras was incarcerated with Jamal Ahmidan, who was also convicted of a petty crime. Both Trashorras's and Ahmidan's initial crimes were not religiously or politically motivated; it was while in custody that they embraced radical Islamic fundamentalist beliefs and were recruited into an al-Qaeda–linked Moroccan terrorist group. This group was responsible for the Madrid train bombings in Spain, which influenced the 2004 Spanish presidential elections (Cuthbertson 2004). Muktar Ibrahim, leader of the 21 July cell that attempted to bomb the London Underground in a follow-up to the July 7, 2005, attacks (a series of coordinated attacks on London's public transport systems during the morning rush hour), found religious Islam at a British institution for young offenders (Fox 2005). The attempted bombings on July 21, 2005, disrupted part of London's public transport system for two weeks. Richard Reid, the al-Qaeda "shoe bomber" who attempted to blow up an American Airlines flight between Paris and Miami in 2001, converted to Islam at the same institution ("Who Is Richard Reid?" 2001).

The London-based Quilliam Foundation, a counterextremism think tank, reported that Muslim cleric Abu Qatada—once described as Osama bin Laden's ambassador in Europe—managed to smuggle extremist propaganda out from a British prison with the help of visitors, who then spread his message through the Internet. It also stated that another radical preacher, Abu Hamza al-Masri—the one-eyed, hook-handed cleric whose extradition is being sought by the United States—was able to hold sermons through the pipes that link cells. Meanwhile, another inmate used his allotted phone calls to speak to an Islamic television station. Interestingly, the report suggested that most prison staff lack the training to recognize or tackle Islamist extremists—sometimes treating them as representatives of all Muslim prisoners and even allowing them to lead Friday prayers.

According to Mark Hamm of the Quilliam Foundation, "Although some religious conversions are motivated by personal crisis and others by need for protection, the primary motivation for conversion appears to be spiritual searching—seeking religious meaning to interpret and resolve discontent" (2009, 673). While "searching" in and of itself does not condemn a person to a path of terrorism, arguably without religious scholars to lead mainstream services, in addition to a lack of rehabilitation programs, this can easily be the fate of some. The design of a facility can also contribute to an individual being indoctrinated; the larger the population, the easier it is for extremists to thrive among them. Through the absence of any kind of rehabilitative program, in addition to a large violent population, the situation is ripe for a correctional facility to become a fertile breeding ground for extremism and violence. Take, for example, Folsom Prison in California, a prison known to house some of the "worst of the worst." The prison is grossly overcrowded with an acute absence of any kind of rehabilitative programs; inmates spend their days "pacing the sun-baked yard, pumping pig iron and bangin' Crip, Blood, Mexican Mafia, Aryan Brotherhood, Nazi Low Rider" (Hamm 2009, 682). Thus, unsurprisingly, 7 out of 10 inmates released from the Folsom Prison system return—one of the highest recidivism rates in the United States.

COUNTERING INDOCTRINATION

Multiple studies have been conducted on the necessity of countering recruitment in correctional institutions through the introduction of rehabilitation programs, yet little has been done in actual implementation. And yet, for those that offer programs, the result is a significant decrease in violence over facilities that do not have any. A study conducted by the Developing Justice Coalition, published as the report "Current Strategies for Reducing Recidivism," found that correction programs with rehabilitative and treatment services have a lower recidivism rate than those that do not offer any services (McKean and Ransford 2004). It has been determined that if we want to change an inmate's thought and behavior characteristics to a favorable outcome, we first need to address physical aspects that could be impeding the change.

All detention facilities facilitate recruitment by their very nature, as individuals are separated from mainstream society, as well as being forced to follow rules that they would prefer not to. Therefore, Muslims living, or confined, within the United States subsequently become targets for recruiting and radicalization. Likewise, transferring violent Islamist detainees into a U.S. system or elsewhere will provide an avenue for the radical movement to firmly establish and strengthen a presence within that new location. This is why it is increasingly relevant to be familiar with and understand the variables involved in countering violent Islamists in a detention and prison setting.

To best counter indoctrination in a correctional setting, not only is the introduction of rehabilitative programs compulsory, but the guards must also engage positively with the detained population. When guards treat the detained population well and actively listen to their needs, the inmates are better able to come to terms with incarceration and react positively to the many compromises it requires. Further, they become more willing to trust that the guards are there for their safety; cooperation and trust are a natural by-product. However, to effectively do this, it is necessary that underlying grievances are addressed, no matter how difficult they might be to consider. In addition, active engagement with the population might require the flexibility to change the "way things have always been" to better match the way things are now or should be. Unfortunately, this is often met with a lot of resistance from within policymaking and enforcing bodies, so it takes a strong leader to encourage and enforce new procedures.

By involving and encouraging detained populations through the provision of programs, intelligence and information gathering can be enhanced. Detained individuals who have opportunities to participate in programs—that they for various reasons might never have otherwise had—are far more likely to ensure that nothing comes between them and those opportunities. So if a cell mate is acting out—that is, planning an escape, preaching radical teachings, or causing violence—the cooperative detained person will want to do whatever he or she can to remain uninvolved in that person's actions. Likewise, the chances of him or her informing the guards of the actions are increased. Correctional facilities often become a place of self-survival. If given the opportunity, detained persons will take care of themselves foremost, before they take care of anyone else.

SUBCULTURES WITHIN PRISONS

Radicalization continues in the secretive underground of inmate subcultures through prison gangs and extremist interpretations of religious doctrines that inspire ideologies of intolerance, hatred, and violence. As resources are expended in the search for prison outsiders, the root causes of radicalization—overcrowded maximum-security prisons with few rehabilitation programs and a shortage of religious scholars to provide guidance to spiritual searchers—are ignored. Only a small percentage of converts to Islam—primarily fresh converts, the newly pious, with an abundance of emotion and feeling—turn their radical beliefs into terrorist action (Stern 2003). And yet it takes only one radicalized individual to potentially cause the deaths of thousands of people.

CONCLUSION

Correctional facilities are now a matter of international and national security. And unless radicalization within prisons is addressed through the provision of rehabilitation programs and mainstream religious scholars, individuals like Trashorras, Ahmidan, Ibrahim, and even Reid will most assuredly be replaced by a new and more dangerous prototype.

See also: **Volume 1, Part III:** Combating Terrorist Recruitment, Propaganda, and Radicalization Campaigns. **Part IV:** Detention, Interrogation, and Torture of Terrorist Suspects. **Part VI:** Rehabilitation of Extremists: Methods and Practice

REFERENCES

Brandon, James. *Unlocking Al-Qaeda: Islamist Extremism in British Prisons.* London: Quilliam, 2009. http://www.quilliamfoundation.org/images/stories/pdfs/unlocking_al_qaeda.pdf.

Clear, T. R., and M. T. Sumter. "Prisoners, Prison, and Religion: Religion and Adjustment to Prison." *Journal of Offender Rehabilitation* 35 (2002): 125–60.

Cuthbertson, I. "Prisons and the Education of Terrorists." *World Policy Journal* 21 (2004): 15–22.

Dammer, H. "The Reasons for Religious Involvement in the Correctional Environment." *Journal of Offender Rehabilitation* 35 (2002): 35–58.

Fox, U. "Captive Converts." *Times (of London) Online,* August 11, 2005.

Hamm, Mark S. "Prison Islam in the Age of Sacred Terror." *British Journal of Criminology* 49 (2009): 667–85.

McKean, Lisa, and Charles Ransford. "Current Strategies for Reducing Recidivism." Chicago: Center for Impact Research, 2004. http://www.Impact research.org/documents/recidivismfullreport.pdf.

Stern, Jessica. *Terror in the Name of God: Why Religious Militants Kill.* New York: Ecco, 2003.

Thomas, J., and B. H. Zaitzow. "'Conning or Conversion?' The Role of Religion in Prison Coping." *Prison Journal* 86 (2004): 242–59.

"Who Is Richard Reid?" *BBC News,* December 28, 2001. http://www.bbc.co.uk.

Zamelis, Chris. "Radical Networks in Middle East Prisons." *Terrorism Monitor* 4 (2006). http://www.jamestown.org/programs/gta/single/?tx_ttnews%5Btt_news%5D=761&tx_ttnews%5BbackPid%5D=181&no_cache=1.

Terrorists, Criminals, and Drug Cartels

Ming Hwa Ting

Prior to the September 2001 attacks, government agencies perceived problems associated with terrorist organizations and drug cartels as distinct and separate law enforcement issues. Granted that they are both criminal groups, their objectives were different. Yet there is evidence of a growing convergence in the way both groups raise funds and in the tactics they use to achieve their objectives. This overlap in activities has proved to be both a boon and a bane to law enforcement agencies. If a terrorist organization could be linked to the trafficking of illicit narcotics, law enforcement agencies could use the resources of the military and intelligence services, previously unavailable, to deal with it. However, countries have different definitions of what constitutes terrorism. Hence, international cooperation might be difficult to achieve. This nexus between terrorist networks and drug cartels has therefore presented both opportunities and challenges, which is why this issue has gained international attention.

TERRORISM AND DRUG TRAFFICKING: CONVERGENCE AND OVERLAP

Unlike drug cartels, which are motivated by financial gains, terrorist groups seek to achieve social or political change. A close examination of these two criminal groups shows a convergence in the means both groups use to achieve their ends, for example, drug trafficking and counterfeiting to raise money and laundering of their proceeds to use the money legitimately. Additionally, both groups undermine political stability in the countries they operate in.

The term *narco-terrorism* was coined by Peruvian president Belaunde Terry to describe the Sendero Luminoso's (Shining Path) attacks on antidrug agencies in 1983. The Drug Enforcement Administration (DEA) has defined narco-terrorism as "an organized group that is complicit in the activities of drug trafficking in order to further, or fund, premeditated, politically motivated violence perpetrated against noncombatant targets with the intention to influence (that is, influence a government or group of people)" (Casteel 2003, 48).

In February 2004, Afghan president Hamid Karzai stated that drug money was fueling terrorism in his country (United Nations Office on Drugs and Crime 2004, 29), an alarming situation that is not confined to terrorist groups operating there. The drug activities of Turkey's Partiya Karkareni Kurdistan (PKK; Kurdish Workers' Party) also support Karzai's somber assessment. The PKK was founded in 1974 with the aim of establishing an independent Kurdish state in southeastern Turkey. Often through violence, the group has sought to compel the Turkish government to give in to its demands. For example, between 1988 and 1998, the organization killed more than 25,000 Turks in a number of brazen urban bombing campaigns. To fund its terrorist activities, the PKK has turned to drug trafficking and has attracted the attention of various law enforcement agencies such as the U.S. DEA, the United Nations International Drug Control Programme, Interpol, and the French Observatoire Géopolitique des Drogues.

The link between terrorism and drug trafficking, therefore, is not new. During the late 1990s, the Fuerzas Armadas Revolucionarias de Colombia (FARC; Revolutionary Armed Forces of Colombia) started a clandestine effort with the Tijuana-based Arellano Felix Organization to smuggle firearms and narcotics. In March 2002, FARC's 16th Front Commander Tomas Molina-Caracas and his Brazilian and Colombian criminal associates were arrested and later indicted in the District of Columbia on charges of drug-related activities. In June 2002, DEA fugitive Carlos Bolas, a FARC member who was named in the March indictment, was arrested in Suriname. The results of Operation Titan, a collaborative effort between the United States and Colombia in October 2008, also confirm the link between some terrorist groups and drug cartels. Over the course of the two-year investigation over 130 people were arrested on money-laundering and drug trafficking charges; part of the proceeds from these illegal activities were used to fund the activities of Hezbollah in Lebanon.

The alarming convergence between terrorist groups and drug cartels was again explicitly demonstrated by the arrest of al-Qaeda's operatives Oumar Issa, Harouna Touré, and Idriss Abelrahman in Ghana by the DEA in 2009. Earlier, Taliban operative Khan Mohammad was arrested in Afghanistan and subsequently convicted and sentenced in a U.S. federal court in 2008. Additionally, Haji Juma Khan, with known ties to the Taliban, was arrested in October 2008 and charged in October 2009 with drug trafficking and supporting terrorism (U.S. Attorney Southern District of New York 2009). The activities of al-Qaeda in the Islamic Maghreb (AQIM) lend further credence to the growing symbiosis between terrorists and drug cartels. Based in North Africa, AQIM has added drug trafficking to its other criminal activities such as smuggling and counterfeiting. In December 2009, three Malians were arrested in Ghana on charges of trafficking narcotics from North Africa to Europe for AQIM and FARC.

The nexus between terrorists and drug cartels is also present in the Indian subcontinent. Dawood Ibrahim's D Company, with its rumored headquarters in Karachi, was listed as a "specially designated global terrorist" by the U.S. Department of the Treasury in October 2003, and in June 2006 he was cited by former president George Bush as a "significant foreign narcotics trafficker" (Rollins and Wyler 2010, 14–15). The blurring of the distinction between terrorist groups and drug cartels is also evident in the Tri-Border Area of Argentina, Paraguay, and Brazil, where terrorist groups such as Al-Gama'a al-Islamiyya, Al Jihad, Hezbollah, and Hamas have been known to be involved with the drug trade, with part of the proceeds funding their terrorist activities. This link is fast becoming ubiquitous as there is strong evidence that Jemaah Islamiyah, a terrorist organization based in Southeast Asia, has also turned to drug trafficking as well as armed robberies to fund their terror activities (Schliebs 2011).

Speaking in August 2010, Mexican president Felipe Calderón summed up the political instability wrought by drug cartels in his country. He said that drug trafficking has "become an activity that defies the government, and even seeks to replace the government" ("Mexico" 2010). The promotion of instability is precisely the objective of terrorists as well as drug traffickers. Hence, while these two criminal groups have different motivations, their pursuit of revenue through the illegal drug trade provides a logical argument for narco-terrorism. Moreover, the drug activities of the Autodefensas Unidas de Colombia (AUC; United Self-Defense Forces of Colombia) strongly support this argument. In 2001, the U.S. Department of State designated the group as a foreign terrorist organization. It has remained on the list of foreign terrorist organizations since then, and the United States has arrested some of its members on drug-trafficking charges, such as the AUC political leader Carlos Castano-Gil.

DRUG CARTELS AS TERRORISTS

Just as terrorists are increasingly involved in the international drug trade, drug cartels are also increasingly adopting terror tactics such as kidnapping, beheading, and using car bombs to intimidate both the public and law enforcement agencies. The use of car bombs by drug cartels does not differentiate between lawful combatants and noncombatants, which is arguably one of the defining traits of terrorists, and further erases the distinction between the two groups.

One key similarity between terrorists and drug cartels is their diffused and cellular networks, which makes efforts to eradicate them very difficult. Such an organizational approach is common to terrorist networks. Hence, despite the deaths and detentions of senior al-Qaeda operatives such as Abu Musab al-Zarqawi, Khalid Sheikh Mohammed, Mustafa Ahmed al-Hawsawi, Abdul Rahman al-Muhajir, and Abu Bakr al-Suri, the organization still poses a very credible threat. The development of a horizontal network, as opposed to a vertical hierarchy, was expedited by increased law enforcement pressure after the September 2001 attacks, and this form of operational diffusion may well be applied to drug cartels. Likewise, despite the success of the American and Colombian authorities at targeting the leaders of the Medellín and Cali cocaine cartels, Mexican drug cartels such as Gulf, Sinaloa, and Juárez have stepped into the void, and the trafficking problem remains.

Another commonality between these two groups is that both entities have also turned to other criminal activities, such as counterfeiting, to raise funds; it is less risky and is commonly regarded as a victimless crime. Hence, engaging in these activities is less likely to draw the attention of law enforcement agencies, and even if one is caught, the sentences are comparatively lighter than those imposed for drug-related crimes. According to the latest Organisation for Economic Co-operation and Development (OECD 2009, 3) figures, from 2007, global counterfeiting is estimated to be worth $250 billion, a figure that is likely to be even higher today.

OPPORTUNITIES AND CHALLENGES

Ironically, the terrorist-criminal nexus has provided law enforcement agencies with more options to combat terrorism. Jacobson and Levitt note that labeling terrorists as criminals impinges on their reputation as freedom fighters with principles and a clear political ideology, thereby hindering their ability to recruit members or raise funds (Jacobson and Levitt 2010, 121). Likewise, engaging in more diverse criminal acts increases their exposure to law enforcement agencies, thereby increasing the probability of prosecuting them. Conversely, just as redefining terrorists as criminals undermines their reputation, ironically it might prove to be useful at other times to redefine criminals as terrorists. For instance, this change in term might make additional resources available to law enforcement agencies, such as those of the military or the intelligence services, thereby making law enforcement more effective.

However, there are some limitations associated with this latter approach. The old adage that a terrorist to one is a freedom fighter to another still holds true today. This difference of opinion therefore renders it difficult for states to cooperate in joint counterterrorism operations. For instance, even though the United States and the United Kingdom have a special relationship dating back to World War II, it does not mean that these two close allies see eye to eye on all matters. The United States regards the entire Hezbollah group as a terrorist organization; the United Kingdom regards only the organization's military wing as a terrorist organization. Yet if attention were turned to the issue of law enforcement, this pragmatic shift would lead to fewer obstacles to cooperation between them because it would be easier to prosecute Hezbollah's members for their criminal activities that breach either domestic or international laws. Furthermore, the burden of proof in criminal cases is also arguably lower than in terror cases, which means that prosecution is more likely to succeed. From a law enforcement perspective, it is therefore logical to exercise flexibility in affixing labels to these criminal groups.

CONCLUSION

In conclusion, the modus operandi of these two groups has converged even though their objectives are quite different. Terrorists seek to undermine and change the political status quo. However, because of greater scrutiny of their financial activities, raising funds through conventional means is becoming more difficult for terrorist organizations, hence creating a need to engage in criminal activities to generate operational revenue. On the one hand, drug cartels are motivated by profit and usually do not wish to draw attention to their activities. Yet their very actions can create political instability that dovetails neatly with the goals of terrorists. Furthermore, terrorist groups and drug cartels have also moved from a vertical hierarchy to a horizontal network of diffused cells, which shows that they learn from one another. Terrorist networks turn to drug trafficking to raise money, and drug cartels are involved in this illegal trade because it is profitable, and they do not shy away from using terror tactics to protect their financial interests. This linkage between these two groups has presented law enforcement agencies with unique opportunities to disrupt and dismantle their operations. Undertaking more diverse criminal activities increases terrorists' exposure to law enforcement agencies. Moreover, if evidence exists that terrorist groups are engaged in drug trafficking, it becomes possible for law enforcement agencies to call on the expertise of the military and intelligence services. In 1971, Richard Nixon initiated the war on drugs; in 2001, George W. Bush initiated the war on terror. As of this writing it appears that in some instances these two problems have converged.

See also: **Volume 1, Part II:** Colombia. **Part III:** Identifying and Combating Sources of Terrorist Financing; Safe Havens and Weak and Failing States. **Part IV:** Eliminating Terrorist Support Networks. **Part VI:** Narco-terrorism: How Real Is the Threat?; Threat Convergence

REFERENCES

Casteel, S. W. *Narco-terrorism: International Drug Trafficking and Terrorism—a Dangerous Mix.* Statement and Testimony before the U.S. Senate, Committee on the Judiciary, Washington, DC, May 20, 2003, pp. 7–10, 18–26. http://www.au.af.mil/au/awc/awcgate/congress/narco_terror_20may03.pdf.

Jacobson, Michael, and Matthew Levitt. "Tracking Narco-terrorist Networks: The Money Trail." *Fletcher Forum* 34, no. 1 (2010): 117–24.

"Mexico: Cartels Move beyond Drugs, Seek Domination." *ABC News,* August 4, 2010. http://abcnews.go.com/International/wireStory?id=11326758.

Organisation for Economic Co-operation and Development (OECD). "Magnitude of Counterfeiting and Piracy of Tangible Products: An Update." 2009. http://www.oecd.org/dataoecd/57/27/44088872.pdf.

Rollins, John, and Liana Sun Wyler. *International Terrorism and Transnational Crime: Security Threats, U.S. Policy, and Considerations for Congress.* Washington, DC: Congressional Research Service, 2010. http://www.fas.org/sgp/crs/terror/R41004.pdf.

Schliebs, Mark. "Indonesian Terror Cells Turn to Drug Trade." *The Australian,* January 26, 2011.

United Nations Office on Drugs and Crime. *International Counter Narcotics Conference on Afghanistan.* Kabul: United Nations Office on Drugs and Crime, February 8–9, 2004. http://www.unodc.org/pdf/afg/afg_intl_counter_narcotics_conf_2004.pdf.

U.S. Attorney Southern District of New York. *Afghan Drug Kingpin Charged with Terrorist Financing for Funding Taliban Insurgency,* Department of Justice. Washington, DC: Department of Justice, 2009. http://www.justice.gov/dea/pubs/pressrel/pr102408.html.

Threat Perception and Multinational Cooperation

Roger Peace

The history of counterterrorism from the Cold War to the present offers cautionary lessons with regard to national governments unilaterally defining and acting against terrorism. Without an international set of agreements that define terrorist activity and an international agency to coordinate counterterrorist operations, national governments will continue to frame "terrorism" according to their self-interest and conduct operations that secure their advantage.

DEFINING AND ACTING AGAINST TERRORISM REQUIRES INTERNATIONAL AGREEMENT AND LEADERSHIP

The United States employed the term *terrorist* to define its enemies long before its so-called war on terror began in 2001. In March 1947, President Harry S. Truman framed America's new Cold War containment policy as a struggle against terrorism and totalitarianism. The Greek state, he said, was "threatened by the terrorist activities of several thousand armed men, led by communists." With U.S. assistance, the Greek royalist government won its civil war and proceeded to implement police state measures. The United States ignored the repression and continued to support the Greek government, including a military dictatorship between 1967 and 1974. This left a legacy of resentment, such that when President Bill Clinton visited Greece in November 1999 to secure a bilateral treaty enabling closer cooperation between the Federal Bureau of Investigation and the Greek antiterrorist police, he was met in Athens by some 10,000 protesters ("Huge March" 1999).

An expansive definition of the "Communist threat" during the Cold War provided cover for a wide variety of actions designed to secure U.S. national and economic interests. To a large degree, the U.S. containment policy consisted of U.S. military and economic aid to dictatorial and right-wing military regimes. The "free world," as such, became a euphemism for U.S.-allied governments; "terrorists" were those who rebelled against these governments. In practice, U.S. client states were often the practitioners of state terrorism. In the aftermath of the civil wars in El Salvador and Guatemala, international truth commissions determined that the massive violence against civilians that took place was largely attributable to military and police forces on the government side. In Nicaragua, where leftist Sandinista revolutionaries overthrew the U.S.-backed Somoza government in 1979, the Reagan administration organized, armed, and directed a guerrilla army of "contras" who systematically murdered civilians and attacked communities. Former Central Intelligence Agency director Stansfield Turner, testifying before a congressional committee in April 1985, declared, "Rightly or wrongly, there are many of us today who see the actions of the contras as being beneath the ethical standards we would like the United States to employ. And specifically, I believe it is irrefutable that a number of the contras' actions have to be characterized as terrorism, as state-supported terrorism" ("Statement" 1985, 4).

During the 1980s, America's definition of terrorism broadened to include non-Communist states such as Libya and Iran. This move away from the Communist identification heralded the post–Cold War shift to Muslim terrorist groups and their state backers as the primary national security concerns. Concerted efforts are surely needed by the international community to prevent terrorist acts and to disrupt terrorist organizations. Yet it is doubtful, even after the horrific 9/11 terrorist attacks on the United States, that the primary concern of the U.S. war on terror is fighting terrorism as opposed to maintaining its global interests.

While the United States clearly wants to rid the world of al-Qaeda, the Bush Doctrine of 2002 and the U.S. mission in Iraq in 2003 reflect other motives, motives formerly rationalized under the Cold War anti-Communist mission. The Bush Doctrine, as international relations scholar Patrick Hayden has written, "declares that the U.S. will proceed to consolidate with relative impunity its position as the world's only military superpower, and reserve for itself the right to strike preemptively at any perceived threat with or without UN endorsement and irrespective of international legal prohibitions" (2009, 66). This is not a blueprint for fighting terrorism but for enhancing U.S. global power and prerogatives.

In Afghanistan, the United States has extended the label of *terrorist* from a proven terrorist group, al-Qaeda, to a political faction, the Taliban, who provided it with safe haven. This linkage was reasonable enough for the North Atlantic Treaty Organization (NATO) to join U.S. forces in ousting the Taliban from power, but it nonetheless begs for clarification, particularly in terms of appropriate responses. Could the United States have negotiated with the Taliban instead of issuing an ultimatum? With Taliban forces now in neighboring Pakistan, does the United States have the right to open a new war front in Pakistan, an allied country, as it has with its Predator attacks on perceived Taliban strongholds? Does the populace's cooperation with Taliban forces constitute support for terrorism and thus justify attack by the United States?

Surely the definition of terrorism cannot be abstracted from policy implications. Before the 9/11 attacks, the "terrorist states" on the U.S. State Department's list were not deemed so threatening as to impel overt U.S. military action. In the current war on terrorism, however, the impetus to action appears much greater. A U.S. attack on Iran is not out of the question. As for nonstate actors, the Bush Doctrine has established the "right" of the United States to attack any individual or group anywhere in the world with missiles launched from bases in the United States. In constituting itself as prosecutor, jury, judge, and executioner of alleged terrorists, the United States has usurped the authority of the international community.

CONCLUSION

The international community must come together through the United Nations or other agencies to develop agreements on what constitutes terrorism, what groups are conducting terrorist activities, what agencies should be used or created to respond to terrorist activities, and what means should be used to prevent terrorism. This is a huge task, no less daunting than reaching agreements on global warming and use of natural resources, but there is really no other viable choice. The United States has little credibility as the leader of an international struggle against terrorism. It has molded this struggle to fit its foreign policy agenda, skewed the struggle toward military action, defined itself as the leader that others must follow, and caused more civilian casualties in Afghanistan and Iraq than resulted from the 9/11 attacks.

REFERENCES

Hayden, Patrick. "The War on Terror and the Just Use of Military Force." In *America's War on Terror,* edited by Tom Lansford, Robert P. Watson, and Jack Covarrubias, 49–72. Burlington, VT: Ashgate, 2009.

"Huge March in Athens Protests Visit by Clinton." *New York Times,* November 18, 1999, p. A10.

"Statement of Adm. Stansfield Turner, Former Director of Central Intelligence." April 16, 1985. In *U.S. Support for the Contras, Hearing before the Subcommittee on Western Hemisphere Affairs of the Committee on Foreign Affairs, House of Representatives, Ninety-Ninth Congress, First Session, April 16, 17 and 18, 1985.* Washington, DC: U.S. Government Printing Office, 1985.

Truman, Harry S. "Address of the President of the United States: Recommendation for Assistance to Greece and Turkey, March 12, 1947." Truman Presidential Museum and Library, http://www.trumanlibrary.org.

Threat, Vulnerability, and Criticality Assessments

Bentley Nettles

The terrorist threat to targets in America's homeland is dynamic and fluid. The porous nature of our borders; the destructive power of weapons now within the reach of states, groups, and individuals who desire to endanger our way of life; and the personal security of our fellow Americans are all factors causing the threat of terrorism to be greater today than ever before in history (U.S. Executive Office of the President 2000). The U.S. Constitution provides that it is the government's responsibility to "provide for the common defense" (Carafano 2008).

COUNTERTERRORISM RISK MANAGEMENT

Assessing vulnerability, determining the best risk-mitigation means, and managing and providing the resources to reduce vulnerability are largely the responsibility of the entity that owns and operates infrastructure—whether that is the public, in the case of government-owned infrastructure, or private enterprise. Most often, the consumers and users of the infrastructure and the services it provides bear the fiscal responsibility for implementing measures to reduce vulnerability. These measures should be reasonable. Vulnerability reduction is an "economy of force" measure, an additional and supplementary line of defense designed to supplement, not supplant, addressing threats and criticality. Overemphasis on vulnerability reductions threatens the competitiveness of private sector activity, which in turn could represent a far greater threat to the resiliency of the American economy than any terrorist threat (Carafano 2008).

THREAT IDENTIFICATION

Counterterrorism risk management includes three primary elements: a threat assessment, a vulnerability assessment, and a criticality assessment (U.S. General Accounting Office 2001, 2). The first of these, a threat assessment, serves the purpose of identifying and evaluating potential threats based on various factors, including an identified threats capability as well as the potential lethality of an attack (U.S. General Accounting Office 2001, 3). This assessment focuses on analyzing what the adversary can accomplish and the degree of lethality (Carafano 2008). When conducting a threat assessment, the assessment team evaluates the probability of a terrorist attack against a specific target. A threat assessment identifies and evaluates each threat on the basis of various factors, including capability, intention, and lethality of an attack (U.S. General Accounting Office 2001, 3). Threat assessments serve as decision-support tools that assist organizations in the decision-making process of security program planning and identification and focus on critical elements of the security program.

VULNERABILITY ASSESSMENT

A vulnerability assessment looks at our susceptibilities and how they can be mitigated, including weaknesses in structures (both physical and cyber) and other systems/processes that could be exploited by a terrorist. It then asks what options there are to reduce the vulnerabilities identified or, if feasible, to eliminate them (Carafano 2008). Through the vulnerability assessment, the decision maker can establish and prioritize security requirements, plans, and resource allocations. An analysis from the other side of the security equation involves a vulnerability assessment. A vulnerability assessment attempts to identify weaknesses within the security program that are capable of being exploited by terrorists and identifies potential options that will eliminate or mitigate those weaknesses (U.S. General Accounting Office 2001, 3). A vulnerability assessment could reveal weaknesses in the security system an organization relies on to protect key infrastructure, or unprotected key infrastructure, such as water supplies, bridges, and tunnels. In general, these assessments are conducted by teams of experts skilled in such areas as engineering, intelligence, security, information systems, finance, and other disciplines (U.S. General Accounting Office 2001, 4). With information on both vulnerabilities and threats, planners and decision makers are in a better position to manage the risk of a terrorist attack by more effectively allocating resources. However, risk and vulnerability assessments need to be bolstered by a criticality assessment, the final major element of the risk management approach (U.S. General Accounting Office 2001, 4).

CRITICALITY ASSESSMENT

A different type of assessment—equally important to counterterrorism risk management—is a criticality assessment. This analysis evaluates an organization's assets based on their importance or function in accomplishing the organization's mission. By systematically evaluating the significance of a structure, or the group of people at risk if successfully attacked, the organization can identify those structures and processes critical to its organizational resiliency. Based on the results of a criticality assessment, an organization can begin prioritizing which assets, processes, and structures should receive greater attention and protection when developing their security program and defending against a terrorist attack (U.S. General Accounting Office 2001, 4). The systematic process of a criticality assessment is designed to identify and evaluate important assets and infrastructure. Depending on the mission and significance of the target, nuclear power plants, key bridges, and major computer networks might be identified as critical in terms of their importance to overall national security, economic activity within a particular area, and public safety. It is important to remember that these critical assets might be critical at certain times but not others (U.S. General Accounting Office 2001, 5). By evaluating the effect that will be achieved if the adversary accomplishes his goals, a criticality assessment examines physical consequences, social and economic disruption, and psychological effects (Carafano 2008). Obviously, not all consequences and effects of terrorist activity can be prevented; a criticality analysis will help identify the value of various assets to the mission of the entity, helping to prioritize protection based on assets' overall significance.

Criticality assessment is an activity that must be conducted jointly by the public and private sectors (Carafano 2008). They share equal responsibility for determining which structures and processes are most vital to protect the public good. There is no practical alternative to this shared obligation. Most national infrastructure is in private hands. The private sector understands best how systems function and impact the economy. On the other hand, only the national government can offer the national perspective of prioritizing needs and obligations in times of national emergency. Thus, criticality can be determined only by sharing information and conducting joint assessments made in trust and confidence between the public and private sectors.

CONCLUSION

While it is understandable that it is a fundamental responsibility of governments to identify and reduce the risk of transnational terrorist threats, it is not only the responsibility of the government but also an essential component to any risk management in the security operating environment.

REFERENCES

Carafano, James, Sub-Committee on Transportation Security and Infrastructure Protection, Committee on Homeland Security, U.S. House of Representatives. *Risk and Resiliency: Developing the Right Homeland Security Public Policies for the Post-Bush Era.* Washington, DC: Heritage Foundation, 2008. http://chsdemocrats.house.gov/SiteDocuments/20080625151302-26534.pdf.

U.S. Executive Office of the President. *A National Security Strategy for a Global Age.* Washington DC: Government Accounting Office, 2000.

U.S. General Accounting Office. "Statement of Raymond J. Decker, Director Defense Capabilities and Management." In *Homeland Security: Key Elements of a Risk Management Approach,* 2. Washington, DC: U.S. General Accounting Office, 2001. http://www.gao.gov/new.items/d02150t.pdf.

U.S. Immigration Policies: Impact on Moderate Muslims

Kathryn H. Floyd

Muslims have been immigrating to the United States for hundreds of years but have only recently exploded into public debate. In the land of the free and home of the brave, Muslims are encountering everything from a friendly neighborhood face to deportation, owing to the direct effects of U.S. immigration policies and the subsequent ripple that is felt throughout American society. When looking at subsets of the Muslim population, a picture of integration and eagerness emerges as immigration rates from Middle Eastern nations recover from the dramatic decline after September 11. As with all new communities, Muslims experience changes and challenges when building their new lives in America. Quite predictably, they bring their own beliefs on a variety of issues, politics, and religion. Immigrants further undergo varying levels of social integration as the family assimilates and moderate elements are affected by state decisions.

THE 1990 IMMIGRATION ACT, 2001 USA PATRIOT ACT, AND VISA REGULATIONS

Although America has been limiting who can make a life on its soil since the country was founded, it was not until the 1990 Immigration Act that barring entry on ideological grounds was outlawed. Ironically, this happened at roughly the same time that radical Islamic teachings were spawning extremist groups around the world. In the aftermath of September 11, 2001, isolated sectors of the American population began to call for exclusion of Muslims or even people with Arab-sounding names, much to the unease of civil liberties organizations and recent Pakistani arrivals, among many other nationalities. By October 26, 2001, the USA PATRIOT Act had been signed into law to help protect against terrorism, although it has had consequences for Muslims and other newcomers alike. Among its many provisions, the USA PATRIOT Act has an impact on immigration policies, as it allows for indefinite detention without charge of aliens whom the federal government believes to be affiliated with terrorism. Another clause prohibits material support of terrorism and has impacted American Muslims donating to overseas charities or assisting family members (see also Section IX, International and Regional Instruments: USA PATRIOT Act, 2001). Although this is also considered controversial, congressional bill HR 1127 was signed into law on March 20, 2009, by President Barack Obama. It loosens some of the visa regulations for nonminister special immigrant religious workers, who have the potential to grow the moderate Muslim community and enhance America's religious diversity.

ASSIMILATION PRESSURES

Muslims in the United States are generally considered to be well off, earning a respectable salary and receiving a generally good education when compared to society at large. That said, immigration policies have both positive and negative effects on moderate Muslims. First, there is the suspicion across media and society that additional Muslim immigrants could mean more homegrown terrorist attacks. There is, however, also the recognition that larger communities naturally guard against more extreme elements and seek to collectively advance their futures. Based on social theory, competition for democratic recognition and resources could explain why otherwise mainstream adolescents or young adults are driven toward the adoption of an extreme Islamic ideology and so form the Virginia Jihad Network or Lackawanna Six, for example. To further illustrate social disintegration, an imbalance between an individual's minority needs and state interests can occur. This could cause the person to be unable or unwilling to participate in elections or other institutional traditions. This may also shed light on the statistics that about half of these immigrants think of themselves first as Muslims and second as American (Pew Research Center 2007). If U.S. immigration policies are seen to be exclusive or the Muslims are seen to be an undesirable group for admittance into America, then there is the risk that the middle-class Muslims will become alienated and unable to help fringe elements join the new culture.

SWINGING ELECTORATE AND REPRESENTATION

In addition to mosques, community centers, charities, and Islamic schools, nationwide organizations like the Council on American-Islamic Relations have been established to represent the larger population as well as its politics. In the 2008 presidential election, states with concentrations of Muslim voters all went for Barack Obama with the exception of Texas. That said, the Muslim vote is hardly tied to an ideology, as they voted strongly for George W. Bush in 2000. However, the increasingly unpopular wars in Iraq and Afghanistan likely affected this swing in the traditionally conservative Muslim bloc. This growing minority is engaging in the American political arena to have their needs and voice heard, like the African Americans and Hispanics before them, but is willing to vote for the person, regardless of party affiliation, who will best look after their interests. It was not until 2006 that the first Muslim, Keith Maurice Ellison, was elected to the U.S. Congress, representing Minnesota's 5th Congressional District in the House of Representatives. Slowly, more Muslims have been running in and winning local, state, and nationwide elections, giving a voice to the needs of their community—and their concerns over immigration—in the nation's capital.

CONCLUSION

Ten years after September 11, 2001, moderate Muslims in America seem to be faring well under immigration policies as they adjust to a slightly different United States, vote in Congress, and welcome newcomers to their homeland. However, regardless of whether immigration policies are having a direct—positive or negative—impact on moderate Muslims, it matters how they perceive their surroundings and modify their behavior to reflect that vision. Generally speaking, Muslims in America have found it slightly more difficult to embrace their culture in a nation that listens for an Arabic-sounding name every time the news breaks a story on a terrorist incident. Stereotyping and ignorance must be combated across society to prevent hateful discrimination against Muslims who seek to follow in the footsteps of the American patriots Thomas Jefferson and John Adams. While protecting against the infusion of Islamic extremism, most

Americans are striving to be open armed, but the government's policies must guide and reinforce inclusive immigration policies that allow legitimate candidates to start their lives anew in the United States.

REFERENCES

Berry, J. W. "Acculturative Stress." In *Psychology and Culture,* edited by W. J. Lonner and R. S. Maplass, 211–15. Needham Heights, MA: Allyn and Bacon, 1994.
Council on American-Islamic Relations. "American Muslim Voters and the 2008 Election: A Demographic Profile and Survey of Attitudes." January 30, 2008. http://www.cair.com/portals/0/pdf/american_muslim_voter_sur vey_2008.pdf.
Heitmeyer, Wilhelm, and Sandra Legge, eds. "Youth, Violence, and Social Disintegration." *New Directions for Youth Development* 2008, no. 119 (Fall 2008).
Pew Research Center. *Muslim Americans: Middle Class and Mostly Mainstream.* Washington, DC: Pew Research Center, 2007.
Ramakrishnan, S. *Democracy in Immigrant America: Changing Demographics and Political Participation.* Palo Alto, CA: Stanford University Press, 2005.
Sinno, Abdulkader H. "Muslim Underrepresentation in American Politics." In *Muslims in Western Politics,* edited by Abdulkader Sinno, 69–95. Bloomington: Indiana University Press, 2009.

The United States, Iraq, and the Global Terrorism Problem

Cord Scott

When a militarily superior country engages in war with a much weaker nation, some segments of the local population often rise up to counter the foreign threat. These irregular armies (unofficial, with little training or formal structure) become freedom fighters, often employing terrorist tactics to achieve their objectives. These groups often attack and terrorize local populations in order to coerce and intimidate them for the purpose of controlling their actions and preventing collaboration with the invading enemy. The invasion of Iraq in 2003 has served as a recruiting tool for many extremist groups. Technologies such as the Internet have expanded the reach and the message of those seeking recruits and support for the cause. At their core, however, insurgencies are aimed at gaining sympathy for the cause. Radical Islamic elements have used this sympathy to expand their training and recruitment of individuals for martyrdom operations in order to increase their level of violence, thereby taking actions that they hope will achieve their goals.

BACKGROUND

Traditionally the 20th century saw the United States supporting regimes (e.g., Shah Reza Pahlavi in Iran and the government of Israel) in the Middle East that were not viewed well among the local populations. The U.S. backing of Shah Reza Pahlavi of Iran from the 1950s through 1979, and then of President Saddam Hussein of Iraq during the Iran-Iraq War (1980–1988), was curious, as it often placed the two dictators directly against each other. From the American standpoint these alliances exemplified the Arabic proverb, "An enemy of an enemy is my friend." Many minority groups within these two countries considered the actions of the American government hypocritical. To that end, when the opportunity presented itself to strike back at the United States, it was often taken by those who wished to promote their own form of government and/or express their grievances through acts of violence.

The American government was often depicted as an enemy to Islam because of its continued backing of the Israeli government and its furtherance of policies that encroached on Palestinian lands set aside by United Nations mandates. While many governments in the region often turned a blind eye to Arab incursions or attacks against Israelis or other Western targets, the United States was often seen as a power-wielding villain intent on imposing its will on local populations. American support of Israel was often viewed as a direct contradiction to any U.S.-sponsored peace initiatives. Following the First Gulf War (1991) and the Oslo Accords (1993), some thought that perhaps the United States was trying to serve as an honest broker. However, some extremist groups, such as al-Qaeda, viewed these actions on the part of the United States as interference in Middle Eastern affairs for its own nefarious purposes and followed up with a series of devastating terrorist attacks, such as the 1998 African embassy bombings, the 1993 World Trade Center attack, the 2000 attack on the USS *Cole*, and the devastating attacks on the U.S. homeland on September 11, 2001. This catastrophic event triggered the invasion of Afghanistan. Although many in the Islamic world viewed the U.S. response as appropriate, the subsequent U.S. invasion of Iraq was not viewed in the same way.

OPERATION IRAQI FREEDOM
AND THE IRAQI RESPONSE

Saddam Hussein often used his position as president to rally support for his cause from other Arab states and groups. When elements of the U.S. armed forces pushed into Iraq at the end of March 2003, Saddam Hussein's sons, Qusay and Uday, were recruiting fedayeen fighters to defend their country. These warriors are willing to inflict damage on their enemy through any possible means, even if it means using civilians as shields or cover for their own actions. Their unwillingness to surrender and their willingness to die (through the promise of entering Paradise as a martyr) makes this type of enemy very dangerous to whatever force they face.

Various martyrs' brigades, international terrorists, and other extremists view Iraq as a unique training ground. Entry into Iraq, through the desert expanses of an occasionally porous border, was simple especially in the early months of occupation. Upon entering the country terrorists could blend in with the local population with relative ease, carry out attacks against various targets of choice, and, if they chose, return home. If they wanted, they could even fight and then return home. This was noted when several terrorists were searched following the U.S. Marines' push into the Fallujah area. When searched, the terrorists carried Syrian passports that noted jihad as their reason for entering Iraq.

The religious Shiite population, which resides mostly in the southern part of Iraq, also allowed terrorist groups training for "real-world" scenarios. Cleric Moqtada al Sadr often called for volunteers to fight a holy war against the foreign invaders from the West (America) as part of his Mahdi Army. The name is significant as it refers to the Shiite Messiah (Mahdi), who they believe will return to earth to judge humankind. The name also harkens back to the Immortal battalions that were used during the Iran-Iraq War. That particular war was another part of the U.S. effort to combat radical Shiite Islam in the Middle East. It was believed that the United States openly equipped the Iraqi army with material support and intelligence while secretly working with the Iranian government to trade spare parts and equipment for U.S. hostages that were taken and held in Lebanon during the 1980s.

By 2007 it was reported through various intelligence agencies and interrogations of captured insurgents by U.S. military sources that al-Qaeda in Iraq was using fighters recruited from other countries. Many of the new fighters entered through Syria, but they came from various countries throughout the Islamic world. Most came from Saudi Arabia to the south, but significant numbers came from Yemen, Algeria, and Morocco. It was commonly reported that al-Qaeda chose younger men who came from large families, were isolated to various degrees (either through social ostracization or a need to fulfill various desires), and wanted to make a contribution to the Islamic cause for past and present injustices to Islam, real or perceived. Many also seemed to have limited education and were heavily encouraged to become martyrs for the cause by becoming human bombs. The U.S. Department of Defense noted that up to 90 percent of terrorist suicide bombings were carried out by individuals who were not Iraqi.

One of the ways in which the insurgency in Iraq has impacted other conflicts is that the tactics favored by al-Qaeda in Iraq—specifically, the use of improvised explosive devises—are now being incorporated with deadly effect in Afghanistan and Pakistan. The use of this type of weapon is designed to demoralize the enemy and upset any sort of alliance or truce worked out between the North Atlantic Treaty Organization/International Security Assistance Force (NATO/ISAF) and regional factions or groups. The United States has even taken the approach of paying off local groups such as Taliban warlords. This system has had mixed success but, more important, is often tied to the perception expressed by religious groups that the United States is immoral and simply tries to buy its success.

SHIFTS IN COALITION STRATEGY

The U.S. military and its coalition partners have tried various strategies and tactics to counter the rise in extremist activity in Iraq. One concept proposed in 2008 was the Iraq Awakening Council. It was formed primarily by Sunnis in Iraq to counter the more zealous elements within the country who wished to see the sectarian violence continue. The members of the council are used to patrol the areas and prevent any sort of weapons planting by groups. They were also paid US$300 a month. This gave the members of the council employment as well. For the United States, the councils are used as a way to lessen U.S. troop commitments in Iraq and then shift those troops to Afghanistan to fight the Taliban and al-Qaeda there.

The fear of coalition forces is that the various terrorist groups could use Iraq as a jihadist training ground and return to their countries of origin to foment further violence. The fact that various groups in Iraq have broadcast their attacks on military and civilian targets on the Internet provides them with a direct and real-time public venue to continue drawing attention to their demands. Many of these attacks are planned so that the videographer can gain the most dramatic camera angle. When interspliced with patriotic music as well as images of helpless victims, the recruiting aspect succeeds in bringing more disgruntled and alienated individuals over to their cause and portraying the United States as an occupying nation whose sole purpose is the imposition of its will on the Iraqi people and the exploitation of its resources.

CONCLUSION

By the spring of 2010, U.S. military officials in Iraq had noted publicly that they had either captured or killed most of the 42 known leaders of al-Qaeda in Iraq. While this no doubt has an effect on al-Qaeda's long-term objectives in Iraq, it may not curtail the group's activities in other countries such as Pakistan or Afghanistan. With the exit of U.S. combat forces from Iraq the biggest issue is how the Iraqis will provide for their own security without the assistance of U.S. combat forces, especially in volatile areas such as Anbar Province. Time will tell whether the U.S. strategy in Iraq was, in the long run, successful.

See also: **Volume 1, Part I:** Global Terrorism: Post-9/11; The Terrorist Threat in the 21st Century: A Global Security Problem; War on Terror. **Part III:** Defensive Measures against Terrorism: Military Preemption and Retaliation; Military Force: Effective against Terrorists?; Preemption: Moral and Ethical Considerations. **Part IV:** Lessons of Afghanistan and Iraq

REFERENCES

Hudson, Rex. *Who Becomes a Terrorist and Why: The 1999 Government Report on Profiling Terrorists.* Guilford, CT: Lyons, 1999.

Lubold, Gordon. "New Look at Foreign Fighters in Iraq." *Christian Science Monitor,* January 7, 2008. http://www.csmonitor.com/2007/1026/p01s01-wome. html/(page)/1.

Selby, William. "Detained Terrorists Reveal Al Qaeda Recruiting Process." U.S. Department of Defense. March 18, 2008. http://www.defense.gov/news/newsarticle.aspx?id=49310.

Stout, Mark, Jessica M. Huckabey, John Schindler, and Jim Lacey. *The Terrorist Perspectives Project.* Annapolis, MD: Naval Institute Press, 2008.

U.S. Government. 2007. *The United States Army/Marine Corps Counterinsurgency Field Manual.* Chicago, IL: University of Chicago Press.

IV

Post-9/11 Global Counterterrorism Campaign

Assassination: Targeted Killing of Terrorists

Hank Prunckun

The word *assassin* comes from the Arabic *hashasin,* a collective name for the 11th-century hashish eaters of Persia. Crusaders who clashed with the Persians not only faced death on the battlefields of the Middle East but also found themselves the victims of another kind of killing—*assassination* at the hands of the hashish eaters. Over the years the phenomenon of assassination has evolved, arguably, to become the most powerful form of individual violence in both the military and political arenas. This is because its victims are often people who can influence the destinies of nations. When an assassin strikes, the consequences can send shock waves flowing down through history, changing the course of politics forever.

TACTIC OF GOVERNMENTS AND TERRORISTS

Assassination is a common tactic used by terrorists. It is used against citizens as well as military and political leaders and is well documented in the press and news media. The use of assassination by nations as a means of dealing with terrorists is also well known, though in most cases denied by the country employing it. In the parlance of secret intelligence this is referred to as *plausible denial.* One reason for invoking plausible denial is that assassination as an instrument of national security carries grave consequences—both legal and political.

However, it is not necessarily the legal issues that attract the most concern but rather the political impact. In the main, this is because the issues involving terrorist causes are tied closely to religious, political, historical, or other emotionally charged issues. Terrorists often argue that they are freedom fighters fighting a *war* of oppression, and nation-states argue that they are waging a war against them.

Under various international conventions to war (known as the *Laws of Armed Conflict*), assassination is acceptable when a member (or members) of an armed force is tasked to kill a person deemed to be a combatant. And targeted assassination has been employed as a tactic in war, whether during conventional warfare, with its genesis during the Crusades, or unconventional warfare, in particular terrorist campaigns. The consummate example of assassination in war is Operation Vengeance—the targeting of Japanese admiral Isoroku Yamamoto during World War II. On April 18, 1943, the U.S. Army Air Force carried out an "aerial ambush" to kill Admiral Yamamoto, the commander of the Imperial Japanese Navy, and a combatant. The raid was successful.

In contrast, if a law enforcement paradigm is adopted, targeted assassination can be viewed as *extralegal* or *extrajudicial*—that is, operating outside the law and the normal legal processes, hence making it illegal. However, there is some ambiguity as to whether terrorists are combatants or criminals. Many countries have passed legislation that makes terrorist activity illegal, including membership in terrorist organizations and the possession of particular information or materials, as well as the possession and use of arms and explosives. In other words, by passing legislation nation-states have deemed them criminals, not combatants in a war.

However, it would be unreasonable to tie a nation-state to one or the other determination—that is, defining terrorists as criminals or as combatants in an unconventional war. There is enough support in the subject literature to show that it is practical to classify terrorists as either or both, but such a classification would be contingent on the terrorist group, the particular event, and the vector of the threat or attack.

It would therefore seem a prudent self-defense option that nation-states do not rule out the use of targeted assassination of terrorists in formulating their national security policies (note the focus on *terrorists* and not enemy *heads of state*). Even if the policy is never implemented, its currency could stand as a form of prevention under deterrence theory. An example of deterrence theory in use is the 1986 air raid on Libyan leader Muammar al-Gadhafi. The United States targeted Gadhafi, but although he was not killed in the raid, a quantitative evaluation later found that there was a clear deterrent effect resulting in a statistically significant reduction in terrorist attacks on U.S. interests overseas after that period.

However, if such a policy is enacted, or retained, then several factors are worthy of consideration. The first is that assassination should be employed only when more moderate means fail or there is no hope of success. Nation-states are by definition politically sophisticated—they share a common goal regarding the betterment of their citizens. This usually means adhering to democratic and humanitarian principles. So any approach that could resolve a conflict with terrorists, or subdue the terrorist threat, should therefore be explored. Only after all avenues of redress have been exhausted should assassination be contemplated.

When the targeted killing of terrorists is considered, the decision to carry out the operation ought to be made by the state's highest level of civilian control—the head of state. In most cases, this is likely to be the country's president or prime minister. This is because the head of state has to balance many issues and weigh not only the country's counterterrorist policy but also the social, economic, and political issues affecting the nation's well-being and its global interstate relations. Such was the case when U.S. President Barack Obama issued orders to launch Operation Geronimo, a successful mission that killed al-Qaeda leader Osama bin Laden in Abbottabad, Pakistan, on May 1, 2011.

All of the previously mentioned issues could be adversely affected if a targeted assassination was carried out. This underscores the point made earlier about assassination having both legal and political consequences. The political consequences, which encompass social, economic, and commercial trade ramifications, are likely to weigh heavily in the decision-making process. Military leaders are not likely to have these same issues at the fore of their thinking, though this does not suggest that they are not mindful or sensitive to such considerations. Heads of state carry the ultimate responsibility for all decisions, including military ones.

Above all, assassination must be used judiciously because, if not, it could be interpreted that the political, military, and/or law enforcement leadership of the country responsible has lost control of the situation. Therefore, this tactic should be used only as a means of last resort. If it becomes part of a state's standard operating procedures, the policy should be reappraised.

CONCLUSION

Although the Crusaders and the Persian hashish eaters have long since vanished into the pages of history books, assassinations remain. Whether the tactic of altering the outcome of conflicts using this approach resides in the hands of terrorists alone, or is employed judiciously and as a matter of last resort by heads of state, will be a matter for continued consideration and debate.

See also: **Volume 1, Part I:** Definition and Dimensions of Counterterrorism; Concept of Islamist Jihad; War on Terror. **Volume 1, Part III:** Defensive Measures against Terrorism: Military Preemption and Retaliation

REFERENCES

Davis, Donald. *Lightning Strike: The Secret Mission to Kill Admiral Yamamoto and Avenge Pearl Harbor.* New York: St Martin's, 2005.

Hosmer, Stephen. *Operations against Enemy Leaders*. Santa Monica, CA: Rand, 2001.
Office of the Judge Advocate General. *Law of Armed Conflict at Operational and Tactical Levels*. Ottawa, Ontario, Canada: National Defence, 2001.
Prunckun, H. *Shadow of Death: An Analytic Bibliography on Political Violence, Terrorism, and Low-Intensity Conflict*. Lanham, MD: Scarecrow Press, 1995.
Prunckun, H., and Philip B. Mohr. "Military Deterrence of International Terrorism: An Evaluation of Operation El Dorado Canyon." *Studies in Conflict and Terrorism* 20, no. 3 (1997): 267–80.

Aviation Security since 9/11

Sarah Eastlake-Smith

The 9/11 attacks had a global impact and triggered a two-wave response to improving aviation security. The first wave was characterized by the immediate response of the United States, which began exploring measures to further enhance aviation security. This response and subsequent responses have affected physical and watch-list elements of passenger screening and the carry-on, checked, and cargo elements of baggage screening. The subsequent responses constitute the second wave, characterized by the changing risks and threats posed to U.S. aviation security.

9/11 AND AVIATION SECURITY

While the events of 9/11 have affected international airports around the world, changes in security protocols are not universal due to each country's aviation history, alliance with the United States, national motivations, airport enforcement agencies, and ability to meet the minimum security standards of the International Civil Aviation Organisation (ICAO). The minimum ICAO training standards have also been updated, and given " 'that terrorists are still watching and looking for weaknesses that can be abused' in the aviation system" (Levine 2004), there is still a great need for all elements of aviation security to cooperate.

TRANSPORTATION SECURITY ADMINISTRATION

Prior to the 9/11 attacks, airlines employed private companies to provide checkpoint screening; however, poor-quality training and pay rates resulted in a workforce providing only a mirage of protection. This mirage was highlighted in May 2000 when Argenbright Holdings Ltd. pleaded guilty to fraud after hiring 1,300 untrained security guards, many of whom had criminal records. Argenbright, while still on probation, acknowledged

it screened passengers on two of the hijacked planes. In an immediate response to the attacks, the Federal Aviation Administration banned knives
and other metal and plastic cutting implements of any size from commercial planes and airport terminals, restaurants, and concession stands.
Curbside check-in was eliminated, and passenger planes stopped carrying cargo and mail. Jetliners were searched by security before passengers
boarded, and unattended cars within 300 feet of a terminal were towed
away. The Air Transport Association suggested the Federal Aviation Administration should nationalize passenger screening and revive the sky
marshals program introduced and disbanded in the 1970s. On November 19, 2001, President Bush signed the Aviation and Transportation Security Act to create the Transportation Security Administration (TSA) to
oversee a new federalized workforce of screeners and 100 percent of
baggage screening. The federalized screener workforce aimed to raise the
standard of security at all U.S. airports, but some people with criminal
records were hired due to background check problems, and covert tests
found that some knives and fake bombs were missed by screeners. In
2004, airports had the option of switching back to private security screeners operating under federal supervision to allow more flexibility in how
airports run security while meeting federal standards. The screener workforce is responsible for screening passengers and baggage.

PASSENGER SCREENING

Passenger screening consists of physical and watch-list screening, both
of which have increased since 9/11. Physical screening involves passengers removing their shoes and walking through metal detectors; however,
the detectors cannot spot most nonmetallic materials such as plastic explosives. In 2003, a TSA lab director stirred controversy by recommending
the use of X-ray technology to reveal weapons or explosives hidden under
clothing. However, after privacy concerns were noted, full-body scanners that safely screen passengers for metallic and nonmetallic threats,
including weapons, explosives, and other objects hidden under clothing, without physical contact were introduced in 2010. In addition to the
no-physical-contact policy, privacy is promoted through the inability of
scanners to save images and through remote placement of the security
personnel viewing the images. Use of scanners may reduce the need to
frisk some passengers, as was controversially authorized in 2004. Watch-
list screening is conducted by the TSA, which compares flight manifests
provided by airlines with names on a watch list using computer-assisted
passenger prescreening. But civil liberties groups have argued that this is
problematic as watch lists are not well maintained and flight manifests
should not be shared; therefore, the TSA developed the Secure Flight and
Registered Traveller Programs. The former involves government officials
checking flight manifests against lists of known or suspected terrorists,

while the latter involves passengers voluntarily providing background information and biometric identifiers.

BAGGAGE SCREENING

Baggage screening involves inspecting carry-on baggage, checked baggage, and cargo. Carry-on baggage is scanned, but as terrorists can no longer access locked cockpits, the threat of bringing explosives aboard is very real, hence the recent prohibition of carrying on liquids and gels in quantities greater than three ounces (100 ml). All checked baggage is scanned for bombs and passed through explosive-detection systems, but the large scanning machines are creating congestion problems in some airports due to their size and location at check-in counters. Even if carry-on and checked baggage scanning was airtight, the focus on passenger screening has left holes in cargo security. Most U.S. passenger planes carry some mail and cargo, but only a fraction of it is manually checked and X-rayed due to costs, technology, and an emphasis on quick shipping. The current system involves random screening and relies on a database of "known shippers"; the TSA, however, is starting to test explosive-detection machines and to screen all high-risk freight. The TSA has aimed to screen 100 percent of baggage; however, this has so far been unsuccessful as the current system is unreliable, as evidenced by a man in 2003 who flew in a cargo crate that went unchecked because it bore the name of a known shipper. Moreover, freight companies do not want 100 percent checking as "it would kill air cargo." An alternative approach to preventing explosions is to make cargo holds blast-proof, but this would add weight to planes, thus impacting on costs by increasing fuel usage or requiring planes to carry fewer passengers and less cargo. In addition to increased passenger and baggage screening, a heightened police presence, increased cooperation between airlines and security, and expansion of the air marshals program have provided additional layers of security to raise the standard of airport security.

INTERNATIONAL AIRPORTS

While the United States has embarked on a mission to improve aviation security for its own airports, not all international airports have followed suit for numerous reasons. First, some countries including France, Canada, Israel, and India all experienced notable aviation security breaches before 9/11 and thus had already implemented improved security arrangements. Second, in countries allied with the United States that have yet to experience an aviation breach, including the United Kingdom and Australia, aviation security required improvement, regardless of the actual threat terrorists pose to allied countries. The United Kingdom rushed through the introduction of full-body scanners in early 2010 after a scare on Christmas Day 2009, and Australia announced a complete restructuring of aviation security systems in 2008 in spite of only experiencing hijackings committed by mentally ill people acting alone. Third, for countries without previous breaches or an alliance with the United States, there is little motivation to improve aviation security as a direct result of the 9/11 attacks. Finally, the inconsistency also stems from the airport security enforcement agencies of each country. Some counties have one key national agency that handles airport security, as in Australia, while security is provided at the state or local level in countries such as the United States. Depending on how the agencies work together, the security arrangements may be consistent within each country but may fail to meet the minimum security standards set out by the ICAO. These standards may not be met due to economics, politics, history, or national security interests, and the agency may subsequently fail to establish a consistent level of protection at both departure and arrival points. This means that even if foreign airports screen 100 percent of baggage as required by the ICAO, other countries may be using inferior technology, as evidenced by a U.S. student who boarded a plane in Argentina with explosive powder and dynamite in his checked baggage in 2006. Moreover, despite the wealth and technological advancement of the United States, the Tel Aviv airport, Ben Gurion, is considered the safest in the world. Airport security personnel interview every single passenger using the same techniques that are being tested in the United States. However, some of the techniques involve racial profiling, which prevents their full implementation in the United States due to objections by civil liberties groups.

At an ICAO training symposium in 2006, it was noted that implementing technical measures to prevent aviation breaches required financial investment and personnel training. The ICAO also noted that countries faced problems relating to performance standards. The ICAO determined this was due to an inconsistent and nonuniform implementation of ICAO standards and recommended practices, and it identified three indicators to support this hypothesis. The first is the steady rate of recorded aviation security breaches as most perpetrators used weapons that should have been identified and confiscated by security personnel prior to the person boarding the aircraft. The second is the lack of national aviation security and international airport security programs that meet ICAO standards and recommended practices, as evidenced by screening personnel lacking knowledge of how to properly screen and search passengers and by fully functional equipment being improperly or inadequately used. Finally, operating procedures to establish security performance standards are either absent or inadequately implemented.

CONCLUSION

After evaluating a country's ability to implement standards and recommended practices, the ICAO determined that there are three reasons for ineffective implementation. First, the importance of aviation security training is underappreciated, resulting in insufficient training and inability to produce local or national training programs. Second, the current training standards are inadequate, and, finally, the existing ICAO training centers are not being used. Similar to the security performance standards, there is also an absence of or failure to implement realistic recruitment criteria and provide sufficient supervision and staffing at checkpoints. Consequently, the ICAO has developed an updated training program that considers the diverse characteristics of each country. This will impact the training received by all levels of airport security personnel, and hopefully this effort to improve the training received by security officials will enhance global aviation security.

REFERENCES

Antonini, D. *ICAO Aviation Security Training Programme Training Symposium.* Montreal, Quebec, Canada: ICAO, n.d. http://legacy.icao.int/tcb/trainair/meetings/gtc9/Panel%2002%20-%20Dominique%20Antonini.pdf.

Australian Federal Police. "AFP Role at Airports Enhanced." December 18, 2009. http://www.afp.gov.au/media-centre/news/afp/2009/december/afp-role-at-airports-enhanced.aspx.

Barber, N. "TSA Installs Full-Body Scanners to Screen Air Travellers." *PC World,* March 6, 2010. http://www.pcworld.com/article/190939/tsa_installs_full body_scanners_to_screen_air_travelers.html.

Crouthamel, J. "Woman Accuses Airport Security of Ogling." *Travel,* March 25, 2010. http://travel.ninemsn.com.au/Blog.aspx?blogentryid=625989&show comments=true.

Department of Infrastructure, Transport, Regional Development and Local Government. *Aviation Security Screening Review—Consultation Paper: Overview of Issues July 2008.* Canberra: Australian Government, 2008. http://www.infrastructure.gov.au/transport/security/aviation/screening/files/Con sultation_Paper.pdf.

Kaplan, E. "Targets for Terrorists; Post 9/11 Aviation Security." Council on Foreign Relations, September 7, 2006. http://www.cfr.org/publication/11397/targets_for_terrorists.html#.

Levine, S. "Toward Safer Skies: Aviation Security Has Improved since 9/11 but Not by Enough." *U.S. News & World Report,* September 19, 2004. http://www.usnews.com/usnews/news/articles/040927/27aviation.htm.Transportation Security Administration. "Prohibited Item for Travelers." Ca. 2010. http://www.tsa.gov/travelers/airtravel/prohibited/permitted-pro hibited-items.shtm.

Williams, C. "Aviation Security: Weighing Up the Costs." *The Drum Opinion,* February 12, 2010. http://www.abc.net.au/unleashed/stories/s2817037.htm.

Zielbauer, P., and J. Sullivan. "After the Attacks; Airport Security; FAA Announces Stricter Rules; Knives No Longer Allowed." *New York Times,* September 13, 2001. http://www.nytimes.com/2001/09/13/us/after-attacks-airport-sec urity-faa-announces-stricter-rules-knives-no-longer.html.

Central Asia: Emerging Threats

Payam Foroughi and Alexander Sodiqov

The turbulent region of Central Asia has various geographic and political definitions. For most purposes, the area consists of Afghanistan, China's Xinjiang Uighur Autonomous Province, and the five Central Asian states that emerged from the breakup of the Soviet Union: Kazakhstan, Kyrgyzstan, Tajikistan, Turkmenistan, and Uzbekistan. Based on this geographic designation, Central Asia encompasses a massive land area—estimated at 2.4 million square miles (6.3 million square kilometers)—consisting of six states and a large province of another state, for a total population of over 100 million. Given the region's problematic political climate—where instability and various degrees of dictatorial and authoritarian rule have been the norm; where potentially extremist Islamist groups, at least one major secessionist movement, and drug-trafficking networks have gotten footholds; where a widening intra- and interstate income gap has emerged; and where natural resources (of water, petroleum, natural gas, cotton, gold, silver, and other minerals) are increasingly becoming sources of interest for rich consuming nations and factors of interstate contention—threats of violence and terrorism also loom. There are at least four different general categories that can be identified as emerging and evolving terrorism and related threats in Central Asia. They are global, regional-local, nationalist-secessionist, and narco-terrorist.

GLOBAL

The main global terror alert vis-à-vis Central Asia remains the often phantom-like al-Qaeda Islamist terror group. While the post-Soviet states of Central Asia did not experience religious terrorism prior to the early 1990s, modern Afghanistan was home to militant Islamist insurgent groups as early as the late 1970s. Following the Communist coup in 1978 and the subsequent Soviet invasion in 1979, thousands of volunteers from Muslim countries, with financial and technical support from the United States and Saudi Arabia and logistical assistance from Pakistan, joined the mujahideen, the Afghan umbrella popular resistance movement that opposed the Moscow-backed Communist regime in Kabul, Afghanistan's capital (Rashid 2003). Then, the little-known Osama bin Laden, himself among the Arab mujahideen, or "holy warriors," ran a clearinghouse that recruited, financed, and trained thousands of foreign Muslim fighters for the jihad, or "holy war," against the "godless" Soviet army in Afghanistan. Around 1988, bin Laden formed al-Qaeda.

The withdrawal of Soviet forces from Afghanistan in 1989 was prompted mainly by the intense resistance that targeted both military personnel and facilities and also civilian Afghans believed to be collaborating with the Soviet army. As the Communist regime in Kabul collapsed in April 1992, the country disintegrated into regional factions and tribal leaders engaging in an increasingly ethnic struggle for political power and control over the lucrative drug trade. This struggle led to the rise of the Pakistan-backed Taliban militia led by Mullah Muhammed Omar, which established control over most of Afghanistan, including Kabul. In addition to imposing radical Islamic rule, the Taliban regime also made Afghanistan a haven for terrorists and their training camps—many of these were the remaining "freedom fighters" who had never left Afghanistan after the Soviet withdrawal. Aside from the Arabs, an estimated 80,000–100,000 mostly Pashtun Pakistani militants had also trained and fought for the Taliban in Afghanistan during 1994–2001 (Crews and Tarzi 2008). Al-Qaeda, due to U.S. pressure on Sudan, had returned to Afghanistan in 1996 and was subsequently granted safe haven by the ruling Taliban regime.

Following the U.S.-led invasion that toppled the Taliban in 2001, an interim government led by Hamid Karzai was formed in Afghanistan. Escaping the invasion, al-Qaeda's leadership is believed to be hiding in Pakistan's Waziristan region along the Afghan border. Although the U.S.-led coalition maintains a strong presence in the country and is building and training a growing national army and police force, insurgent attacks against the coalition and the government security forces continue, and the Taliban appears to be regaining influence in much of Afghanistan. Due to their proximity and resilience, the al-Qaeda network represents a formidable challenge to other Central Asian states as well. Al-Qaeda's transformation from a hierarchical organization into a transnational ideological movement and its strong ties with homegrown Islamic extremists continue to threaten regional and international security.

REGIONAL-LOCAL

The independence of the five post-Soviet Central Asian states in 1991 potentially opened them to international Islamist extremists, who were operating mostly from or through Afghanistan, who inter alia had set a goal of replacing the governments in these predominantly Muslim countries with Islamist regimes. The civil war in Tajikistan in 1992–1997, which pitted the Soviet-era Communist elite against an Islamist-led opposition, served as an entry point for extremist preachers and recruits. The densely populated Fergana Valley spanning the borders of Kyrgyzstan, Tajikistan, and Uzbekistan, with its ethnically diverse communities and strong Islamic tradition, became the focus of radical Islamist groups. Though very likely not al-Qaeda related, the still-unresolved bombing in Tashkent in February 1999 (which the government blames on the Islamic Movement of Uzbekistan [IMU]), followed by the IMU's 1999 and 2000 incursions into Kyrgyzstan and Uzbekistan, became post-Soviet Central Asia's first experiences with terrorism. The IMU remains the main regional-local terror threat in the Central Asian states of Tajikistan, Uzbekistan, and Kyrgyzstan.

The IMU was formed in summer of 1998 in Afghanistan, though its ideological origin dates back to the early 1990s in Namangan, Uzbekistan. Having been declared a terrorist organization by the United States in 2000, the IMU, which had most of its then few hundred fighters stationed in Afghanistan, fought against the U.S.-led coalition on the side of the Taliban after September 11, 2001. The IMU's leader, Jumanboy Khojaev (nom de guerre: Juma Namangani) was killed in northern Afghanistan as a result of the U.S.-led invasion in 2001. His deputy, Tahir Yuldashev, who took over the leadership, was in turn killed in August 2009 by bomb from an American Predator drone in Pakistan. As of summer 2010, the IMU is said to be led by Usman Odil (aka Abu Usman), who is thought to be based with possibly a few thousand fighters in Pakistan's Waziristan region (Pannier 2010).

Hizb ut-Tahrir (HT; Freedom Party) is another regional-local threat to Central Asian security. HT is a nonviolent but politically extreme transnational movement with substantial support among young Muslims in Western Europe and Southeast Asia as well as a large organizational base in London (International Crisis Group [ICG] 2002). HT and its members have been banned by all the Central Asian states. HT was founded in 1953 by Taqiuddin an-Nabhani, an Islamic scholar and judge in the sharia appeal court in East Jerusalem; its original members were mostly Palestinians from Jordan and Syria. HT's belief system and ideology, which are known to provide simple answers to difficult questions, are attractive to a potential base of the politically and/or economically marginalized segment of the region's population (Chaudet 2006). HT's global and pan-Islamist utopian vision, in which poverty and corruption are to be "banished by the application of Islamic law" (ICG 2002, 6) and the establishment of the caliphate, is another source of attraction to its adherents, many of whom are frustrated over economic and social problems facing their communities. HT's metastate political-religious vision is also a cause for annoyance to the Central Asian nation-states, which in the process of ongoing nation-building have limited their ideological and political reach to their borders. HT is thus considered by the region's governments as anticonstitutional and extremist (Horseman 2005) and thus as posing a potential existential threat to the ruling regimes. The Central Asian governments have been quite hostile toward Islamist activism, and thousands of Islamists, including HT members and sympathizers (but also others, such as alleged members of Salafiya and Jamoati Tabligh and even some pacifist Muslims, such as the Nurcus), have been arrested and have received brutal treatment at the hands of the security services and penitentiaries of the region. This often happened with tacit approval of Western democracies eager to fight terrorism. This could lead to either HT itself or a potential disillusioned offshoot denouncing their still-nonviolent ways, leading to "a dynamic" that can "boomerang and further destabilize" Central Asia over time" (ICG 2002, 1).

Central Asian states' reactions to the threat of terrorism (whether religious or other) have been "proactive, aggressive and highly ideological," translating into repressive measures of dealing with real and imaginary threats and representing individual states' "genuine sense of insecurity" (Horseman 2005, 209), which comes both from threats of terrorism and also often from legitimate sources of dissent that question the economic and political status quo. The mere banning of violent or extremist groups and the long prison terms imposed on their alleged members often give the "appearance of an effective policy, but probably advance the Islamist cause" instead (ICG 2009). The roots of extremism and organized non-state violence in the region are found in a combination of factors, including ubiquitous corruption, high unemployment, low wages, increasing disparity between the rich and the poor, a significant lowering of the post-Soviet quality of education, insufficient access to social services, deteriorating environmental conditions, conflict over natural resources, and infiltration of fundamentalist ideologies. Ironically, imprisoning Islamist proselytizers often provides them an opportunity to extend their influence among imprisoned convicts who may well then become extremists—if not they were not already—due to harsh prison conditions and the detention itself serving as an opportunity for learning about extremist ideologies. Detention conditions in Uzbekistan, Turkmenistan, and Tajikistan are thought to be far worse than in the semiliberal Kazakhstan and Kyrgyzstan (ICG 2009). Conditions in China and Afghanistan are no better, though given the massive international presence in Afghanistan, the judiciary and penitentiary systems are beginning to take some steps to correspond to international standards. The International Committee of the Red Cross, for example, has access to most detention facilities in Kazakhstan, Kyrgyzstan, and Afghanistan and nearly no access to detention facilities in the other Central Asian states.

NATIONALIST-SECESSIONIST

Separatist aspirations, frequently fueled by ineffective or repressive ethnic policies, are among the factors contributing to terrorist activity in Central Asia. Although there are several areas in the region where ethnic groups have sporadically resorted to violence in pursuit of secession, China's westernmost Xinjiang province remains the region's major hot spot. There have been many attempts to create an independent state in Xinjiang province (during the invasion of the Qing Empire up through the present day). Emboldened by the independence of five post-Soviet Central Asia states in 1991, the Uighurs, a predominantly Muslim community that accounts for about 45 percent of Xinjiang's population, have increasingly called for greater autonomy of the province or its complete independence from China and the creation of the independent state of East Turkestan (Tang and He 2010). Besides purely ideological and political motives, the Uighurs' separatist aspirations have been prompted by social and economic hardships, political repression, and repressive cultural policies.

Although the Uighur pro-independence groups have mostly been nonviolent, several clandestine militant groups have repeatedly used terror to pursue their political objectives and are believed to have developed ties to international terrorist networks. The Chinese government has claimed that 162 people have been killed and more than 440 injured in numerous terror attacks by Uighur separatist militants between 1990 and 2001, and it has designated several pro-independence groups in Xinjiang as terrorist organizations (Millward 2004). In addition, China has reported that it has raided al-Qaeda–linked Uighur terrorist training camps on the border with Afghanistan and Pakistan, foiled numerous suicide attacks and plane hijacking plots by Uighur militants, and prevented a series of sophisticated attacks to disrupt the 2008 Olympic Games in Beijing (Wayne 2008).

NARCO-TERRORIST

Trafficking in illicit drugs in Central Asia is mainly a one-way route for much of the opiates generated in and trafficked from Afghanistan through the five post-Soviet Central Asian states. According to the United Nations Office of Drugs and Crime, a total of 6,900 tons of opium was produced by and mostly exported from Afghanistan during 2009, with about one-third passing through Central Asia on its way to lucrative markets in Russia and Western Europe. Of the drugs that pass through Central Asia, no more than an estimated 6 percent are interdicted by the regions' security services. Much of that traffic is via Tajikistan due to its long border with Afghanistan (850 miles). This highly porous and mountainous border is difficult to police and has a large presence of ethnic Tajiks, Pamiris, and Uzbeks, groups that also exist in Afghanistan. Moreover, Tajikistan has a relatively high poverty rate, which entices drug couriers to work at lower prices.

Drug trafficking has also been linked to violence and terror in Central Asia. In 2001, for example, the assassination of Tajikistan's deputy minister of internal affairs, Habib Sanginov, is thought to have been linked to drug traffickers upset over increased scrutiny of their activities. Border incursions by traffickers have also become more intense and deadly, whereby the engagement of the border guards in running gun battles has become an intermittent occurrence resulting in casualties on both sides. Afghan drug traffickers have also turned to the occasional taking of hostages from Tajikistan, normally as a means to secure overdue payment for past drug deliveries. More critical, there has been a marriage of drug trafficking and Islamist terrorism, with the IMU being quintessential, as the movement is known to fund its terrorist activities largely through the Afghan drug trade. In spring 2009, the Tajik government's security forces engaged in an operation in the eastern Gharm Valley, resulting in the death of 13 suspected extremists and drug traffickers. Among those killed was a former commander of the United Tajik Opposition, Mirzo Ziyoev, who was killed under mysterious circumstances; allegations that he was involved in drug trafficking had surfaced for a number of years. The Tajik government, in turn, suggested that Ziyoev and his associates had been engaged in drug trafficking and channeled the profits to the IMU, a fact that the then IMU leader, Yuldashev, rejected (Economist Intelligence Unit 2009). More recently, a 2010 suicide car bombing at the regional police headquarters for countering organized crime in northern Tajikistan and major skirmishes in Tajikistan's eastern Rashd Valley, where over 60 government soldiers and security personnel were killed by unknown gunmen, may well have been the work of narco-traffickers or the IMU.

CONCLUSION

Though profits from drug trafficking constitute a large, but unspecified, portion of the gross domestic product (GDP) of Central Asia, the overall effects and threats of drug trafficking for the region's countries are negative and often deadly. Continuing drug trafficking can lead to increased corruption, increased rates of addiction and an HIV/AIDS epidemic, heightened violence that at times is linked to terrorist groups such as the IMU, economic insecurity, and political instability in Central Asia.

See also: **Volume 1, Part I:** The Terrorist Threat in the 21st Century: A Global Security Problem; War on Terror. **Part III:** Ideology That Spawns Islamist Militancy; Safe Havens and Weak and Failing States; Terrorists, Criminals, and Drug Cartels. **Part IV:** Combating Religiously Based Terrorism; Eliminating Terrorist Support Networks; Lessons of Afghanistan and Iraq

REFERENCES

Chaudet, Didier. "Hizb ut-Tahrir: An Islamist Threat to Central Asia?" *Journal of Muslim Minority Affairs* 26, no. 1 (2006): 113–25.

Cornell, Svante E. "The Narcotics Threat in Greater Central Asia: From Crime-Terror Nexus to State Infiltration?" *China and Eurasia Forum Quarterly* 4, no. 1 (2006): 37–67.

Crews, Robert D., and Amin Tarzi, eds. *The Taliban and the Crisis of Afghanistan.* Cambridge, MA: Harvard University Press, 2008.

Economist Intelligence Unit (EIU). *Tajikistan: Country Report.* London: Economist Intelligence Unit, 2009.

Horseman, Stuart. "Themes in Official Discourses on Terrorism in Central Asia." *Third World Quarterly* 26, no. 1 (2005): 199–213.

International Crisis Group (ICG). "Central Asia: The IMU and the Hizb-ut-Tahrir: Implications of the Afghanistan Campaign." *Central Asia Briefing*, January 30, 2002.

International Crisis Group (ICG). "Central Asia: Islamists in Prison." *Asia Briefing*, no. 97 (December 15, 2009).

Millward, James. "Violent Separatism in Xinjiang: A Critical Assessment." *Policy Studies 5,* East-West Center, Honolulu, HI: East-West Center, 2004. http://www.eastwestcenter.org/fileadmin/stored/pdfs/PS006.pdf.

Omelicheva, Mariya Y. "The Ethnic Dimension of Religious Extremism and Terrorism in Central Asia." *International Political Science Review* 31, no. 2 (2010): 167–86.

Pannier, Bruce. "IMU Announces Longtime Leader Dead, Names Successor." *Radio Free Europe*, August 17, 2010. http://www.rferl.org/content/IMU_Announces_Longtime_Leader_Dead_Names_Successor/2130382.html.

Rashid, Ahmed. *Jihad: The Rise of Militant Islam in Central Asia.* New Haven, CT: Yale University Press, 2003.

Tang, Wenfang, and Gaochao He. "Separate but Loyal: Ethnicity and Nationalism in China." *Policy Studies 56.* Honolulu, HI: East-West Center, 2010. http://www.eastwestcenter.org/sites/default/files/private/ps056.pdf.

United Nations Office on Drugs and Crime (UNODC). *Annual Report: Promoting Health Security and Justice: Cutting the Threads of Drugs, Crime and Terrorism.* Geneva, Switzerland: United Nations, 2010.

Wayne, Martin I. *China's War on Terrorism: Counter-insurgency, Politics and Internal Security.* New York: Routledge, 2008.

China's Xinjiang Province

Rohan Kumar Gunaratna

The Turkistan Islamic Party (TIP) and its militant wing, the Eastern Turkistan Islamic Movement (ETIM), exploited the recent violence in Urumqi in China on July 5, 2009, by issuing an inflammatory statement on July 9, 2009. Accusing China of genocide of the Uighur Muslims, ETIM propaganda claimed that the Chinese government had killed "more than 1000," wounded a "number that exceeded 2000," and "dumped in prison more than 2000" (The Search for International Terrorist Entities [SITE], July 17, 2009). Furthermore, Seyfullah, TIP's military commander, threatened the Chinese by saying, "Know that this Muslim people have men who will take revenge for them. Soon, the horsemen of Allah will attack you, Allah willing. So lie in wait; indeed, we lie in wait with you."

CONTEXT

Mounting ethnic clashes between local Uighur Muslims and Han Chinese settlers in the capital of western China's Xinjiang Uighur Autonomous Region on Sunday, July 5, 2009, killed a total of 197 people and injured 1,700 (Wong and Ansfield 2010). Although three-quarters of the dead were Han Chinese, propaganda by ETIM and other Uighur separatist groups including the Washington, D.C.–based World Uighur Congress attacked Beijing for discrimination against the Uighurs. Most Turkic-speaking Uighurs, nine million of whom live in Xinjiang, live in harmony with the dominant Han ethnic group, but the riots damaged the social fabric of Xinjiang. A minority of the politicized Uighurs accuse Beijing of repressing their faith, language, and culture and discriminating against them by reserving all the best jobs for the migrant Han (Foreman and Wong 2009).

The riot in Xinjiang, the worst in China since 1949, is likely to remain a continuing source of instability. Although China's Communist mindset precludes the country from reviewing and changing its policies toward the Tibetans, Uighurs, and other minorities, China understands the complex challenge it faces in managing its minorities. When the riots broke out, the Chinese president, Hu Jintao, who was overseas attending the G8 Summit in Italy, grasped its seriousness and returned home on July 8 to personally take charge of the situation. Ethnic and religious violence, especially terrorism, will be the biggest national challenge to China in the coming years. As Wu Shimin, the vice-minister of China's State Ethnic Affairs Commission, says, the protesters who caused the violence in Urumqi were not motivated by economic factors. Very rightly, Wu says the riot was perpetrated by what Beijing calls the "three forces of evil"—extremism, terrorism, and separatism (Ho 2009).

The troubled province of Xinjiang, which experiences sporadic terrorist attacks, is 45 percent indigenous Uighur and 40 percent Han settlers. Of the 47 ethnic groups in Xinjiang, Uighurs are the largest group, but in Urumqi, Han make up more than 70 percent of the 2.3 million residents (Jacobs 2009). Uighurs resent the Han settlements by the government, which have made the Uighurs a minority in some areas of their traditional home. China's 55 recognized minorities account for about 8 percent of China's 1.3 billion people. The other 92 percent are Han, including those who dominate the central government.

Like Tibet, Xinjiang is an autonomous region in China. Among other irritants, Beijing's policy of settling Han Chinese in Xinjiang has been a source of tension between the native Uighur community and the government for years. The Uighur claim that the Han moved into Xinjiang to exploit its oil, natural gas, and agricultural resources as part of Beijing's policy to "develop the West." However, there is concern and fear that the Uighurs will soon be marginalized in their native territory. Even though China is developing Xinjiang into one of the most productive regions of the country, a minority of the Uighurs resent Beijing's assimilation and integration policy. The Uighurs' support and sympathy for the separatist movement in Xinjiang have grown significantly during the last decade. The Chinese authorities periodically detain Uighurs who support separatism. In the lead-up to the Olympics, the authorities arrested and tried more than 1,100 people in Xinjiang during a campaign against what they called "religious extremists and separatists" (Jacobs 2009). Shortly after the arrests, Wang Lequan, the region's Communist Party secretary, described the crackdown as a "life and death" struggle. The majority of the Uighur Muslims are moderate and tolerate, but both the influences from neighboring Pakistan and the developments in Afghanistan continue to radicalize a segment of the Uighurs.

Ethnically akin to Central Asians, the Uighurs voice concerns regarding discrimination, a charge denied by the government. Beijing claims that minorities have greater benefits than the Han, such as permission to have more than one child. Also, there are 23,000 mosques to practice Islam, and just over half the civil servants come from minorities (Ho 2009). Nonetheless, the government places restrictions on the practice of Islam and bans practicing Muslims from most government jobs. Most Han employees in Xinjiang prefer not to employ Uighurs: they consider them "trouble" (interview with Chinese government official, July 31, 2009). Even outside Xinjiang, the Han regard Uighurs as untrustworthy, aggressive, and inclined toward crime (Leow and Fairclough 2009). Increasingly, the Han believe that Uighurs are linked to international terrorism (interview with Chinese government official, July 31, 2009). Although neither is true, the perception is creating a gulf between these two communities and damaging the prospect of future peace.

The propaganda by both violent and nonviolent Uighur separatist groups (including the TIP and its militant wing, ETIM, which is associated with al-Qaeda) is driving the hatred and fueling the anger. ETIM was responsible for a series of bombings both in Xinjiang and elsewhere in China in the lead-up to the Beijing Olympics. To create an environment of insecurity, Seyfullah, the military commander of TIP, said, "Bomb the Chinese government buildings, military barracks, airplanes, airports, railways, foreigner hotels, entertainment venues, tourist spots and similar places! Set on fire! You are even permitted to use biological weapons this time" (SITE, June 27, 2008).

The ETIM leadership, located in Waziristan on the Afghanistan-Pakistan border, is out of China's reach. Having received training, weapons, and financing from al-Qaeda, and absorbed its ideology, ETIM's members been have transformed. They not only attack China but also fight both the Pakistani security forces in tribal Pakistan and the Afghan security forces in Afghanistan. Al-Qaeda–trained ETIM suicide bombers present a growing threat both to coalition forces in Afghanistan and to China's stability and security. Al-Qaeda ideologues have argued that after the defeat of the existing superpower, the U.S. forces in Iraq and Afghanistan, the next enemy of the Muslims will be the multiheaded dragon, a reference to China, the emerging superpower. In addition to ETIM, a dozen Uighur separatist groups in the United States, Canada, and Europe are radicalizing the Uighur communities in China. Some groups with terrorist links have been able to influence the U.S. and other Western governments to release the Uighur detainees held in Guantánamo Bay.

THE FUTURE

Xinjiang is China's new flashpoint. In terms of containment and restoring stability, Xinjiang will present a greater challenge than Tibet. Bordering Afghanistan, Pakistan, India, Russia, Kazakhstan, and Kyrgyzstan, Xinjiang is a crucial region in both geopolitical and geostrategic terms. As threats are increasingly transnational, Beijing will have to take extra care to secure Xinjiang and build counterterrorism partnerships with its neighbors.

The United States politicized the global fight against terrorism when it refused the Chinese government's request to extradite the Uighur terrorists in U.S. custody. The Uighur terrorists, captured in Pakistan and Afghanistan in 2001–2002, were operating with both the Taliban and al-Qaeda. Citing human rights abuses in China, the United States has released the Uighur detainees to other countries. Instead of remaining divided, the United States and China should build a partnership to fight the global threat of terrorism and extremism. The United States should invite the Chinese to contribute their forces to Iraq and Afghanistan to restore stability and security in these two defining conflict zones.

Although Beijing's military might is capable of countering the threats from the neighborhood, it has limitations in countering the virulent ideologies affecting its citizens. Beijing's existing capabilities are not suitable to restoring long-term stability in Xinjiang. To meet the challenge of Xinjiang after the July 2009 violence, Beijing will need to invest even more in developing Xinjiang economically and empowering the mainstream Uighur community. In addition to repairing the broken bridges and building new ones, Beijing will need to win over the Uighurs who resent the Han settlers. Beijing and its representatives in Xinjiang also must work with Xinjiang's community and religious leaders to build social resilience. The Chinese government needs to build a norm and an ethic in the communities of Xinjiang against extremism and its vicious by-product of violence.

Today, 70–80 percent of all the world's conflicts are ethnopolitical or politico-religious. The ethnic and religious conflict zones produce human suffering, virulent ideologies, internal displacement, refugee flows, and terrorists and extremists. China needs to study how other countries have most successfully managed, or failed to manage, ethnic and religious tensions. China needs to craft a long-term policy to manage and mitigate the emerging and existing drivers of separatism.

Violence in Xinjiang, ETIM, and the Uighur separatist movement will remain at the top of the Chinese agenda in the coming months and years. Despite efforts by Beijing to restore peace, the episodic violence between ETIM and the government, and between Uighur and Han communities, is likely to spread beyond Xinjiang. Unfortunately, the Chinese hard-line approach toward Uighur separatists fails to differentiate between terrorists, supporters, and sympathizers. Instead of investing in community engagement initiatives, to build broken bridges between Uighurs and the Han, the Chinese government has detained several thousand protestors, thus creating a tit-for-tat mentality.

CONCLUSION

Today, China suffers from unrest in both Tibet and Xinjiang. Its policies to manage these sensitive areas have been unsuccessful. Ongoing unrest in Tibet and Xinjiang will be an irritant to China's steady progress. There is no evidence to suggest that the situation in Tibet sparked the violence in Xinjiang. Despite the overbearing attitude of Beijing toward Tibet, the Tibetan movement for autonomy remains untainted with violence and confined to nonviolent protests. As such, there is no direct connection between the protests in Tibet and the violence in Xinjiang. Nonetheless, it is very likely that one may continue to influence the other in the future.

If there is greater radicalization of the Uighur communities both in China and overseas, the Uighur and Tibetan communities may work together, starting outside China. Like the Tibetan exile groups, the Uighur exile groups are becoming better organized. Although the Dalai Lama personally is unlikely to encourage such a union, his successors may decide on joint protests and even joint action. Beijing's short-term approach of being unwilling to speak to mainstream leaders such as the Dalai Lama reflects its lack of understanding of managing ethnic and religious communities.

For China, the July 2009 riot is a major loss to its reputation and prestige. At a strategic level, the riot demonstrated that China's approach to managing minorities has been a failure. Despite efforts to recognize and empower minorities economically, China's approach has not dampened the cry for cultural and religious freedoms. Interactions between Han Chinese and the Tibetans and Uighurs living on the country's western frontier can be especially fraught. The government, in an attempt to quell resentment among Uighurs and Tibetans, has poured development money into the West to create jobs and economic growth.

Although most officials are unwilling to revisit China's failed policy on managing minorities, China will have to rethink its approach to minorities. Both Tibet before the Beijing Olympics and now Xinjiang have suffered riots reflecting a general failure on the part of the Chinese to manage ethnic politics. A few understand it, but only very few are willing to talk about it openly. Wang Yang, Guangdong's powerful Communist Party leader, who is close to President Hu Jintao, said, "We have to adjust to the actual situation. China is a multi-ethnic society. If adjustments are not made promptly, there will be some problems" ("Beijing to Rethink" 2009).

See also: **Volume 1, Part I:** The Terrorist Threat in the 21st Century: A Global Security Problem; War on Terror. **Part II:** China. **Part III:** Ideology That Spawns Islamist Militancy. **Part IV:** Combating Religiously Based Terrorism; Eliminating Terrorist Support Networks; Lessons of Afghanistan and Iraq

REFERENCES

"Beijing to Rethink Ethnic Policies." *Reuters,* July 31, 2009.
Foreman, William, and Gillian Wong. "Death Toll from China's Ethnic Riots Hits 184." Associated Press, Urumqi, China, July 10, 2009.
Ho, Stephanie. "China Blames Separatists for Deadly Xinjiang Riots." Beijing: Voice of America (VOA), July 21, 2009.
"Islamic Party of Turkistan—Our Blessed Jihad in Yunnan." International Centre for Political Violence and Terrorism Research (ICPVTR) translation of the video, July 23, 2008. http://de.youtube.com/watch?v=E6DLGShOnEg. Jacobs, Andrew. "Countering Riots, China Rounds Up Hundreds." *New York Times,* July 19, 2009.
Leow, Jason, and Gordon Fairclough. "Clash at Factory Employing Uighurs Triggered Riot." *Wall Street Journal,* July 8, 2009.
The Search for International Terrorist Entities (SITE). "TIP Leader Threatens China over Urumqi Violence." The Search for International Terrorist Entities (SITE), July 17, 2009.
Wong, Edward, and Jonathan Ansfield. "China Replaces Leader of the Restive Xinjiang Province." *New York Times,* April 25, 2010, p. A12.
Ye, Yuan, and Xia Wenhui. "After Horrible Riot, Xinjiang People Hope to Mend Tainted Relations of Ethnic Groups." Xinhua News Agency, July 11, 2009. http://news.xinhuanet.com/english/2009-07/11/content_11693738.htm.

Combating Religiously Based Terrorism

Ramazan Hakki Oztan

Perhaps the most striking characteristic of modernity is the interconnectedness in all categories of life. The boundaries dividing religion, politics, culture, and social conduct are so indistinct that it is rather problematic to employ a particular terminology such as *religiously based terrorism* that favors one category of analysis over others. With all due attention to such definitional problems, for the purpose of this article the term *religiously based terrorism* means terrorism that uses religious beliefs, symbols, and slogans to justify and draw support for its violent activities in the targeted population. Terrorism enmeshed in religious symbolism is also functional for purposes of personal and group identification. Religiously based extremism is also tied to politics and culture, and this multifaceted discourse makes it difficult to combat. Discourse set aside, how does a government counter violent activities that attempt to restore a religion to its once-cherished place?

TERRORISM AND RELIGION

Religiously based terrorism is not purely religious; the objectives of these group's are often political and expressed in religious terminology. Needless to say, acts of terrorism wrapped in a religious discourse cannot be purely reduced to a single religion. The broad literature on religion and terrorism is rather successful in listing the terrorist activities that reference Judaism and Christianity. However, while terrorism is not a method of struggle that dominates the everyday political life in Muslim countries, many terrorists are Muslims. This very irony here is suggestive of the fact that there is no such thing as a monolithic Islam but that the religion differs from region to region, country to country, and continent to continent. While this multidimensionality is extant both in the Islamic past and in the present, it is the recent claim to a pure Islam—to be precise, that attempts to organize life along the lines of an *imagined* Islamic community. It is this phenomenon that scholars refer to as *political Islam* that certain groups employ the tactics of terror to bring about their own view of the world. While sharing similar goals some political Islamists may either reject the option of terror outright or lose their radical elements over time. In the end, it is possible to find textual evidence in the wide body of Islamic literature that either prohibits or validates the use of terrorist violence against the innocent.

Such differentiation obviously suggests a preference for the groups that are willing to work within the system over the ones that threaten the system through the use of terror, that is, a categorization that is clearly reflective of our "liberal bias." Clear categorizations and a universal consensus regarding the definitional problem are two important aspects of any counterterrorism mission. For counterterrorism missions with a military dimension, particularly when positioned as an offensive, a plain articulation defining the enemy is relevant to the success of the mission. The lack of a clear articulation of the objectives to be accomplished and the lack of sensitivity on the part of some Westerners on the ground in Iraq and Afghanistan are part of the reason why Muslim public support for the fight against terrorism began to erode. Thus, in 2009 President Barack Obama believed it was important to announce a new beginning by declaring that the United States was not at war with Islam because this is what many people in the Middle East had come to perceive as the U.S. role across the region.

Particularly relevant here is the length of counterterrorism missions. Arguments are often put forward, with some significant grounding, that the lengthy presence of U.S. military forces is one factor explaining why religiously based terrorist groups recruit more local members to their ranks, which naturally translates into an increase in terrorist attacks. While the length of counterterrorism operations as a category does not emerge as a major concern in domestic counterterrorism operations, the lack of a clear articulation of the objectives and the need for popular support for the action do clearly apply to counterterrorism operations conducted on foreign soil.

Finally, from a legal and legislative perspective the USA PATRIOT Act of 2001, a legislative instrument in U.S. counterterrorism strategy, is often criticized on the grounds that it not only endangers civil liberties but also, perhaps more important, does not differentiate terrorists from ordinary citizens. Such unilateral approaches on the domestic front, as exemplified in various legislative initiatives, also characterize the American-initiated global war on terrorism. Compared to European countries, which have also suffered from religiously based terrorist attacks in the post-9/11 period, the U.S. approach seems to lack nuance, a clear articulation of the objectives to be achieved, and stated reasons for why particular actions will be or have been taken.

CONCLUSION

While the European mindset regarding counterterrorism preferred peacekeeping, development projects, and diplomatic maneuvers, the U.S. strategy was to declare and conduct a global war on terrorism. In hindsight, terrorism is a tactic that is elusive in nature, fueled partially by political frustration. Therefore, to effectively combat it requires international cooperation and a clear articulation of the policies being implemented. The United States needs to do more in these areas.

See also: **Volume 1, Part I:** Concept of Islamist Jihad; War on Terror. **Part II:** United States. **Part III:** Ideology That Spawns Islamist Militancy; U.S. Immigration Policies: Impact on Moderate Muslims; The United States, Iraq, and the Global Terrorism Problem. **Part IV:** Lessons of Afghanistan and Iraq

REFERENCES

Al-Khattar, Aref M. *Religion and Terrorism: An Interfaith Perspective.* Westport, CT: Praeger, 2003.
Blakesley, Christopher L. *Terrorism and Anti-terrorism: A Normative and Practical Assessment.* New York: Transnational Publications, 2006.
Owens, John E., and John W. Dumbrell, eds. *America's "War on Terrorism": New Dimensions in U.S. Government and National Security.* Lanham, MD: Lexington Books, 2008.

Rees, Wyn, and Richard J. Aldrich. "Contending Cultures of Counterterrorism: Transatlantic Divergence or Convergence?" *International Affairs (Royal Institute of International Affairs)* 81, no. 5 (2005): 905–23.

Counterterrorism in Germany: Post-9/11

Pavan Kumar Malreddy

The counterterrorism laws, policies, and procedures observed by the German state after 9/11 have complex historical and political genealogies. Following World War II, the state security, policing, and intelligence services have been carefully reengineered to disavow the Nazi legacy of Hitler's centralized police force—the Gestapo. However, it was not until the terrorist attacks at the 1972 Olympics in Munich that Germany's weakness in combating terrorism was exposed. Yet the reunification of Germany in 1990 posed a serious threat to the state's internal security; the socialist tradition of intelligence, particularly East Germany's secret police—the Staatssicherheit—needed to be fully disintegrated. After 9/11, however, 3 of the 11 hijackers (Mohamed Atta, Marwan al-Shehhi, and Ramzi Binalshibh), known as the Hamburg Cell, were found to have been trained by a secret al-Qaeda group operating on German soil (Safferling 2006; Glaessner 2010).

FEDERAL COUNTERTERRORISM POLICY

The counterterrorism policy in Germany is administered through a complex network of law enforcement bodies. Under the federal system, the 16 German states control their own police forces, each headed by its own State Office for Criminal Investigations (Bensinger n.d., 2). At the federal level, the federal minister of the interior oversees the internal security of the state, including the counterterrorism policy. The federal police force consists of two major security wings, the Federal Criminal Police Office, known as the Bundeskriminalamt, or BKA, and the Federal Police, known as the Bundespolizei, or BPOL (formerly Bundesgrenzschutz [BGS]). The elite commando unit Grenzschutzgruppe 9 (GSG 9), which was created after the 1972 terrorist attacks in Munich, is an extension of the BPOL. Within the federal control, the Federal Intelligence Service (Bundesnachrichtendienst, or BND) operates under the direct control of the Chancellor's Office—a German equivalent of the U.S. Central Intelligence Agency. Domestic intelligence matters are handled by the Federal Office for the Protection of the Constitution, known as the Bundesamt für Verfassungsschutz, or BfV (Bensinger n.d., 2). The BfV reports to another federal wing, the Office of the Directorate General Police, which consists of the Directorate of Police Affairs and the Directorate for Counter-terrorism.

It is primarily the BKA that is responsible for the investigation of criminal activities related to border security, extremism (neo-Nazis), espionage, and financial crimes (Bensinger n.d., 1). The BND, on the other hand, collects intelligence related to money laundering, terrorist financing, immigration, and asylum, among other external threats. After 9/11, a specialized though unnamed division within the BND was created to fight terrorism and organized crime (Glaessner 2010). In October 2001, Zentralstelle für Verdachtsmeldungen (financial intelligence unit) was established within the BKA to serve as Germany's central registration office overseeing money laundering and terrorist financing (Miko and Froehlich, 2004 p.7). In late 2001, Germany introduced new police competencies and powers for the BGS in order to allow them to "stage house searches of buildings belonging to religious organizations" (den Boer, 2003 p.17). Intelligence units were given the authority to intercept telecommunications and e-mails in a preventive manner. On June 4, 2008, a draft legislation approved by the German government elevated the BKA to a "superpolice" by endowing it all the necessary tools that it requires for preventing threats arising from international terrorism. In accordance, the BKA may now use secret investigative methods that were generally reserved for the BND and the Federal Defense Force—Bundeswehr. On the ground level, however, it is the federal commando units of BPOL, Grenzschutzgruppe 9, and the state and municipal police units known as the Schutzpolizei and Kriminalpolizei (detectives) who conduct raids, security operations, and data mining on suspected terrorist activities.

ACTIONS AND OBJECTIVES

The counterterrorism policies in Germany after 9/11 are deployed as a combination of emergency measures, amendments to the existing laws, the establishment of new legislation and new organizations, and allocation of funds. Taken together, the central objectives of Germany's counterterrorism policies have been (1) to disable terrorist structures and groups within Germany; (2) to prevent terrorism by banning organizations and by controlling immigration and the borders; (3) to increase data mining operations and surveillance of immigrants; (4) to protect sensitive infrastructure; and, finally, (5) to provide reconstruction aid and foster international peace and stability by addressing the root causes of the problem (Albrecht n.d., 37–38; Neve et al. 2006).

On September 12, 2001, the German government invoked Article V of the North Atlantic Treaty Organization (NATO) to mobilize military support for the United States (Miko and Froehlich 2004, 1). Under Chancellor Schroeder's leadership, the Parliament approved the deployment of 1,000 troops in Afghanistan, joining Operation Enduring Freedom led by the United States. This was increased to 3,500 troops in 2004, and 4,500 in 2005

(Miko and Froehlich 2004, 9–10). Currently, there are at least 7,700 German troops abroad. Since January 2002, the German troops have served in the International Security Air Force and the Provincial Reconstruction Team missions in Afghanistan.

Shortly after the 9/11 attacks, German police authorities conducted more than 200 raids on an emergency scale (Bensinger n.d.) and banned three radical Islamic organizations—Kalifatstaat, al-Aqsa Martyrs Brigade, and Hizb ut-Tahrir—that were operating in Germany. To that effect, both the BKA and the BGS (which became BPOL in 2005) are given a free hand in protecting sensitive infrastructure, such as nuclear sites, government buildings, especially U.S. and Israeli properties. The BGS was also given extended powers to stop, interrogate, and identify people and to conduct searches and engage in computer-aided profiling. The new government provisions mandated that all students of Muslim origin at universities be screened and that the data from their student files be retrieved for security checks. In October 2001, Germany became the first country to adopt the recommendations of the European Union's Financial Action Task Force on Money Laundering (FATF). As of December 2001, nearly 214 bank accounts had been seized under the guidelines of the task force (CDI Terrorism Project n.d.). In late 2001, the Customs Criminal Investigation Office—Zollkriminalamt—also set up a special unit to support counterterrorism and to ensure that relevant information is forwarded to national and international law enforcement authorities (Albrecht n.d, 19).

In November 2001, Germany introduced the First Counter-terrorism Package with a budget of €1.4 billion, followed by a Second Counter-terrorism Package in September 2002 with an additional budget of €1.5 billion (Paffenholz and Brede 2004). In 2005, and again in 2007, a supplement to the two packages was added without a further increase in funds.

Up until 9/11, Article 129a of the German Criminal Code served as a legislative guideline for both defining and responding to terrorism, which is strictly—albeit narrowly—viewed as a domestic and regional problem (e.g., the Irish Republican Army, Rote Armee Fraktion, and Euskadi Ta Askatasuna). After 9/11, a supplement (129b) was added to extend the legal definition of terrorism to foreign organizations (Albrecht n.d., 7–8). This supplement was part and parcel of the Constitutional and Criminal Code amendments undertaken by the so-called Suppression/Prevention of Terrorism Act enacted during the 1980s. After 9/11, the act focused mainly on organizations operating outside of Germany but that posed a considerable threat to the German state. In August 2002, Germany used the Suppression/Prevention of Terrorism Act to ban a Palestinian-based organization known as al-Aqsa Martyrs Brigade.

Apart from this, the First Counter-terrorism Package introduced new legislation on immigration (especially for those traveling from Arab countries), data mining, policing, and intelligence on suspected terrorist movements within and outside of Germany. The first package also allocated funds for the purchase of special weapons and new communications equipment for the federal police. The most significant outcomes of the first package have been deportations, the banning of religious privilege, the prevention of money laundering, the outlawing of religious organizations that are considered dangerous, the induction of the 129b code, and the expansion of the definition of terrorism(Albrecht n.d., 38–39). In addition, airport security and intelligence staff were increased, and the military and federal intelligence were brought to use a common platform to intensify border security operations (Albrecht n.d., 38–39). A database known as the Aliens Central Record was created, while fingerprinting in visas was also introduced under the first package. Currently, the use of biometric data on immigration documents has been made mandatory (Albrecht n.d., 38–39).

ORGANIZATIONAL CHANGES

The Second Counter-terrorism Package, also known as the International Counterterrorism Act (Gesetz zur Bekämpfung des internationalen Terrorismus), was designed to amend existing legislation and to create cooperation between the police, intelligence, and security units. Given that "German law requires complete organizational separation of executive agencies" (Miko and Froechlich 2004, 8) such as the BKA, BfV, and BPOL, and given the intricate nature of the decentralized institutions, in December 2003 the Terrorism Information and Analysis Center was founded. The center brought "11 government departments and agencies together for the purpose of exchanging information in real time, analyzing threats, and organizing a timely response" (Bensinger n.d., 4). Subsequently, in 2004, the federal and state ministers of the interior introduced some key organizational changes, including "a central database that will now collect and store all available information on Muslim radicals" and "a joint coordination center consisting of the BKA, BND, BfV, and German Military Intelligence" (Miko and Froechlich 2004, 7).Within the second package, a number of new laws were introduced. The Act on the Protection of the Constitution mandated that the federal authorities track information from bank accounts, postal services, airlines, and telecommunications. Similarly, the Federal Bureau of Criminal Investigation Act allowed the BKA to prosecute cybercrimes, with certain bureaucratic hazards being removed. The Federal Border Guard Act and the Aliens Act provided the BSG and federal authorities with resources to establish the security of identification, visa requirements, and the immigration process. These measures were expanded by the Asylum Procedure Act, Alien Central Registry Act, Act on Security Clearance, and Passport Act—all of which dealt with the issues of identification, fingerprinting, and biometric data concerning immigrants and asylum seekers (Glaessner 2010). Among others, the Air Traffic Act permitted the use of guns by German authorities on civilian aircraft. Additionally, in 2005, the German Parliament passed the Air Security Act with the aim of increasing security screenings at airports.

CONCLUSION

Admittedly, although Germany's counterterrorism policies are rather comprehensive, they are not necessarily effective. There is no centralized institution or person that oversees the policies and law enforcement units. Hence, they remain only symbolic in value, ambitious in scope, and elusive in practice.

REFERENCES

Albrecht, Hans-Jörg. "Country Report on Germany." Max Planck-Institute for Foreign and International Criminal Law, n.d. http://wodc.nl/images/Werkdocument%201%20Germany_tcm44-59194.pdf.

Bensinger, Gad J. "Law Enforcement and Counterterrorism in Post-9/11 Germany." *Crime & Justice International.* n.d. http://www.cjimagazine.com/content/blogcategory/259/548/.

CDI Terrorism Project. "The Financial War against Terrorism." Center for Defense Information. n.d. http://www.cdi.org/terrorism/financial-pr.cfm.

den Boer, Monica. "9/11 and the Europeanisation of Anti-terrorism Policy: A Critical Assessment." Notre Europe, Policy Papers No. 6. Paris, France: Notre Europe, 2003. http://www.notre-europe.eu/uploads/tx_publication/Policypaper6_01.pdf.

Glaessner, Gert-Joachim. "Internal Security and the New Anti-terrorism Act." *German Politics* 12, no. 1 (2010): 43–58.

Miko, Francis T., and Christian Froehlich. *Germany's Role in Fighting Terrorism: Implications for U.S. Policy.* Washington, DC: Congressional Research Service, 2004.

Neve, R., Lisette Vervoorn, Frans Leeuw, and Stefan Bogaerts. *First Inventory of Policy on Counterterrorism.* The Hague: Dutch Ministry of Justice, 2006.

Paffenholz, Thania, and Dunja Brede. *Possibilities and Limits of Development Cooperation for Crisis Prevention and Peace Building in the Context of Countries at Risk from Terrorism.* Eschborn, Germany: Federal Ministry of Economic Cooperation and Development, 2004.

Safferling, Christoph J.M. "Terror and Law: German Response to 9/11." *Journal of International Criminal Justice* 4 (2006): 1152–65.

Counterterrorism in India

Scott S. Mischka

India has been the target of terrorist attacks since it gained its independence from Great Britain in 1947. During the late 1970s and 1980s terrorism intensified, and it remains a critical challenge for the Indian government at the national and regional levels. Terrorist movements and organizations in India reflect the numerous religious, class, and ethnic differences that challenge modern India. India is ranked fourth in the world for terrorist attacks behind Iraq, Afghanistan, and Pakistan. Counterterrorism agencies and their initiatives are often frustrated by logistical and political problems. The Indian government oversees the world's largest security force, including 1.2 million police and 1 million paramilitary troops. Government officials maintain that these resources are insufficient in a country with an ethnically, religiously, and economically diverse population of 1.2 billion. The political implications of a direct military response to domestic terrorism often restrict politicians, who want to avoid accusations of human rights abuses from political opposition parties and the international community. These factors have severely limited the Indian government's response to terrorism. Many Indian and foreign observers charge that the Indian government has consistently failed to produce an effective counterterrorism strategy to combat one of the most critical terrorism situations in the world.

India has a number of low-intensity regional conflicts that are perpetuated by terrorist organizations representing various religious or class-based movements. The majority of terrorist attacks in India have been conducted by religious terrorist groups. Secular, class-based terrorist groups have not been as prominent or high profile as the religion-based terrorist groups in their attacks but still remain a critical challenge to the Indian government. Religion-based groups have perpetrated the most violent terrorist acts against civilians and regularly include the use of improvised explosive devices (IEDs), the blowing up of aircraft, kidnappings, and suicide bombers. The low-intensity conflicts that produce the majority of terrorist acts in India can be categorized regionally, and although the individual terrorist movements and organizations are based on broader religious or class-based ideologies, they are generally associated with particular regions.

Since 1947, the Jammu and Kashmir state has been the object of a territorial dispute between India, Pakistan, China, and the Kashmiri people. During the 1970s and 1980s India and Pakistan waged a series of military confrontations over each nation's claim to the region. The cessation of state-level military conflicts and the occupation by India of 47 percent of the region and by Pakistan of 37 percent of the region resulted in an insurgency movement that India claims is supported by Pakistan. Nearly two-thirds of all terrorist attacks in India occur in Jammu and Kashmir and are perpetrated primarily by militant Islamist groups. These groups share ideological principles but often have divergent objectives for the region, which include either complete independence for the state or a merger with Pakistan. The Lashkar-e-Taiba (LeT), or "Army of the Pure," is one of the most high-profile Islamist terrorist groups. The LeT has suspected but unconfirmed ties to al-Qaeda. Their primary objective is the independence of Jammu and Kashmir, and their secondary objective is the spread of Islamic rule throughout India. The group was believed to be funded by Pakistani intelligence organizations. In 2001, the U.S. State Department designated it a foreign terrorist organization, and the Pakistani government subsequently froze all of LeT's financial assets in Pakistan. On July 11, 2006, the LeT claimed responsibility for one of the most high-profile terrorist attacks in recent history when they bombed the Mumbai commuter rail, an attack that killed 209 and injured over 700 people. In 2000, the Jaish-e-Mohammed (JeM), or "Army of Muhammad," was founded with the purpose of eliminating Indian control of the region and transferring power to Pakistan. The Jaish-e-Mohammed operates from Pakistan and has been blamed for a significant number of high-level terrorist attacks. In 1980, the Harakat ul-Jihad-I-Islami (HUJI) emerged as an insurgent group to fight the Soviet occupation of Afghanistan. Following the Soviet withdrawal from Afghanistan the group shifted its focus to gaining independence for Jammu and Kashmir from India. The Harakat ul-Jihad-I-Islami operates from Pakistan and Kashmir, and the majority of its attacks are against Indian military targets in the region. The Harakat ul-Mujahideen (HuM), or "Islamic Freedom Fighters' Group," was also founded to fight the Soviet occupation of Afghanistan and currently operates as a terrorist group to eliminate Indian rule in Jammu and Kashmir.

The state of Andhra Pradesh along the Bay of Bengal coast has been the site of many terrorist attacks stemming primarily from economic causes. The issues of land reform, high rural unemployment, and the economic exploitation of laborers by the landowning class gave rise to several Marxist and Maoist revolutionary-terrorist groups. In 1967, the Naxalite Marxist-revolutionary group was formed in the town of Naxalbari. Not all Naxalites advocate violent revolution, but an estimated 10,000-strong armed Naxalite militia conducts a low-intensity insurgency that claims hundreds of lives. In addition to Andhra Pradesh, the states of Bihar, West Bengal, Jharkhand, Orissa, and Chhattisgarh have been the site of intense Naxalite violence. The Naxalites regularly convene trials for individuals they describe as "class enemies" or "caste oppressors," and convictions often result in executions. In 2004, a Maoist group called the Communist Party of India emerged from the ranks of the Naxalite group. The group's primary objective is the establishment of a "revolutionary zone" from the border of Nepal to southern Andhra Pradesh that would achieve independence from India.

The Indian government has established counterterrorism measures that include intelligence agencies, the military, and numerous national and local police organizations. The Ministry of Home Affairs has oversight over all internal counterterrorism efforts and is organizationally equivalent to the U.S. Department of Homeland Security. Indian intelligence agencies that monitor terrorist groups include the Research and Analysis Wing for external intelligence gathering. The Intelligence Bureau gathers internal intelligence and operates an interagency counterterrorism agency.

The Joint Intelligence Committee analyzes intelligence data from the Research and Analysis Wing and Intelligence Bureau and provides the appropriate ministries with tactical information and analysis. The Ministry of External Affairs contains a counterterrorism division responsible for the analysis of terrorism intelligence and the sharing of information with counterparts in other countries.

In 2002, passage of the Prevention of Terrorism Act broadened the state's ability to combat terrorism by allowing police to hold suspected terrorists in custody without trial and increasing prosecutors' powers to investigate terrorist organizations. In 2004, the act was repealed after continuous allegations that police investigators and prosecutors were abusing their expanded powers. The terrorist attacks in the Mumbai hotel district on November 26, 2008, caused widespread demands for new counterterrorist legislation. The Unlawful Activities (Prevention Act) Amendment Act (2008) was passed and included many of the measures previously included in the Prevention of Terrorism Act. Indian state legislatures have also passed antiterrorism legislation to increase their power to investigate and prosecute terrorists. In Karnataka the Karnataka Control of Organized Crime Act and in Maharashtra the Maharashtra Control of Organized Crime Act facilitate the prosecution of suspected terrorists. Antiterrorist legislation is also under way in other states such as Rajasthan, Andhra Pradesh, and Uttar Pradesh.

Special security forces such as the Central Industrial Security Force are designated to guard transportation and infrastructure centers. The National Security Guards is a specially trained paramilitary force designated to terminate terrorist situations including hijackings and kidnappings. The Border Security Force patrols the borders and provides counterterrorism support for local police. The Central Reserve Force has 165,000 personnel and is a key component of the counterterrorism efforts in Kashmir. The Indian Army does not participate regularly or on a large scale in internal counterterrorism activities. Exceptions were Operation Bluestar and Operation Woodrose, which were large-scale military counterterrorism campaigns to fight Sikh terrorists in the 1980s. More recent Indian Army participation in counterterrorism campaigns has consistently occurred in Jammu and Kashmir.

The Indian government maintains that its counterterrorism programs implement a number of tactics and techniques that are used at the national and state levels. These tactics and techniques include the use of human and technological prevention, detection, and monitoring systems to address terrorist threats. These systems incorporate village- and community-based grievance-detection networks to prevent unaddressed social and economic problems. Objective and balanced threat analysis is also incorporated to limit the possibility of overreaction to potential problems. The government consistently attempts to avoid the spread of terrorist movements that might stem from overzealous suppression of political grievances. These measures reflect the government's attempt to achieve a political balance that will not further aggravate political and religious tensions.

CONCLUSION

The attempt to achieve a balance between effectively eliminating terrorism and not alienating the populace has resulted in mixed results in India's fight against terrorism. Domestic and foreign analysts state that the Indian government has failed to develop and implement a consistent and effective counterterrorism strategy. The government's responses to terrorist attacks have been episodic and largely reactive and have demonstrated an inability or unwillingness to make political decisions that might alienate diverse constituencies. Critics also charge that police and intelligence agencies lack organizational cohesion and are unwilling to share information with rival bureaucracies. These problems present a consistent challenge to the Indian government and are the subject of a continued national and state-level debate over the most effective methods to address terrorism in the future.

See also: **Volume 1, Part II:** India. **Volume 2, Part I:** National Security Guard (India); Para Commandos (India). **Part II:** Golden Temple, Amritsar, India (1984); Air India Flight 182 (1985); Mumbai, India, Attacks (2008)

REFERENCES

Marwah, Ved. *Uncivil Wars: Pathology of Terrorism in India.* Dehli: South Asia Books, 1996.
Marwah, Ved. *India in Turmoil: Jammu & Kashmir, the Northeast and Left Extremism.* Dehli: Rupa, 2009.
Mohan, Raja C. *Crossing the Rubicon: The Shaping of India's New Foreign Policy.* New Dehli: Viking, Penguin Books, India, 2003.

Counterterrorism Policy in France

James McIntyre

Since the 1960s, France has been forced by events to develop a set of policies to respond to the threats of both international and domestic terrorism. These policies have evolved drastically over the course of the past 30 years in response to two distinct waves of terrorist activity the country witnessed, first in the 1980s and then in the 1990s. This article examines French counterterrorism policy as it currently exists and describes the institutions that the French government utilizes to enact such policies and the mode in which they function.

TERRORISM AND RESPONSES

To discuss the various policies France has adopted in response to the dangers posed to the nation by various terrorist threats, it is first necessary to disclose the nature of the threats the country has faced These fall into three general categories. The first was that posed by radical leftist groups in the 1980s and 1990s. These organizations sought to overturn the capitalist system. The second threat appeared in the form of regional separatist groups within the country. The third, and currently most significant, threat is from international terror groups, most often with some connection to the Middle East, either as a state-sponsored network or in the form of a nonstate actor.

Over the course of the past 50 years French counterterrorism policy developed through four distinct phases following the war in Algeria. The first response of the French government to the challenge of terrorism was essentially one of complete neutrality to the extent of essentially offering safe haven to terrorist groups. This phase has been referred to by some commentators as the sanctuary phase. Despite its moral implications for the government, it was successful, for a time, at reducing terrorist attacks on French soil. This approach was abandoned as the result of a series of attacks that wracked France in the mid-1980s.

The successor policy to neutrality was accommodation. This was marked by what appeared to be a series of secret agreements between France and the various state sponsors of terrorist activities, which in turn led to their cessation. This policy, which the French government has never publicly admitted to practicing, did succeed in drastically reducing terrorist attacks on France for a time and stood as the initial French policy to thwart terrorism on its soil. This effort was followed by policies enacted by former president François Mitterand (1981–1995) when he and his Socialist Party came to power. President Mitterand did not trust the traditional agencies entrusted with defending France against terrorist attacks and therefore resorted to his own organization, which he created within the presidential palace. The ad hoc arrangement proved highly ineffective. Accommodation stood as a short-lived policy as public outcry drove the government to resort to a more aggressive stance.

The third French response to terrorism was suppression. This response to terrorism, as the name implies, encompassed a more aggressive approach to the challenge posed by terror groups. This phase of French policy came about in 1986, as a result of public outcry over perceived government weakness in regards to terrorist activity. Public furor resulted in the passage of a set of legislation that greatly enhanced and centralized the

French legal apparatus for responding to the threat of terrorism. The laws constituted the beginning of the policy of suppressing terrorist activities in France. The laws vastly expanded the authority of existing counterterrorist agencies in the government and added some new bureaus. The suppression strategy generated an interest by many in French counterterrorism circles in assailing the assets of various groups known to be plotting activities against France.

The focus on the logistics of various groups, in turn, spawned a more robust response in the form of prevention, the fourth and current policy response of the French government toward terrorist groups. At the same time, this redirection received further impetus from a 1996 French law that declares conspiracy to commit an act of terrorism itself a crime. The current French counterterrorism policy is seen by many commentators as one of the most vigorous in the world. It is extremely successful at detecting and interdicting threats to the French state and its citizens as well as providing high-quality intelligence to other nations.

COMITÉ INTERMINISTÉRIAL DE LUTTE ANTI-TERRORISTE

The success of French counterterrorism policy comes as the result of the coordination of various organizations within the French government to counter threats posed by various national and international groups. The overarching authority in France in matters of counterterrorism is the Comité Interministérial de Lutte Anti-Terroriste (Interministerial Liaison Committee against Terrorism). This committee, which includes the prime minister, as well as the ministers of defense, foreign affairs, the interior, and justice, is charged with the development and direction of counterterrorism policy. France's Ministry of the Interior is a defense and law enforcement department. The key figures in this arrangement are the counterterrorist investigative magistrates, better known as the *juges d'instruction*.

This office was created in 1986 in response to the first wave of terrorist attacks launched against the French state. These officials are judges who possess extraordinary powers to investigate individuals, interdict their activities, and assign punishments when the perpetrators are apprehended and subsequently found guilty. In addition, they can direct the various police elements within France to counter terrorist activities, including the intelligence section of the French national police. The powers of the judges include the ability to (1) detain suspected terrorists for up to four days without leveling charges against them, (2) deny access to lawyers for terrorism suspects in confinement for the first three days they are held in custody, (3) issue warrants and conduct searches of suspects' dwellings at night, (4) request that suspects be given a nonjury trial to prevent possible threats to jurors by other terrorists, and (5) round up potential terrorists prior to their engaging in any illegal actions in order to prevent their perceived plot. The judges therefore combine in a single figure the powers of prevention, deterrence, and punishment. The concentration of so much power in a single position has made these people extremely effective in rooting out terrorist conspiracies and punishing the conspirators. Over time, many of the investigative judges have developed a profound expertise in various forms of terrorism. Their expertise has allowed them to become very effective at taking preventive measures upon the discovery of new terrorist cells.

At the same time, the concentration of so much power in individual hands has drawn criticism from some portions of the French political spectrum. The principal issues that generate criticism are the powers judges possess to launch preventive roundups of terrorism suspects, as well as their ability to hold suspects for extended periods on the mere suspicion of their involvement in terrorist activity. Furthermore, some human rights groups have criticized the 1996 law making conspiracy to commit terrorism itself a crime for providing law enforcement agencies with dangerously broad powers to intervene into the personal lives of French residents.

DIRECTION DE LA SURVEILLANCE DU TERRITOIRE AND GROUP D'INTERVENTION DE LA GENDARMERIE NATIONAL

Another counterterrorism agency that possesses a great deal of power to intrude on the lives of French citizens is the Direction de la Surveillance du Territoire (Directorate of Territorial Surveillance). While it does not have the same amount of individual power as the *juges* described in the preceding, the agency still has broad powers to intervene in the daily lives of the French people and often works closely with the *juges*. The group that tends to attract the most attention out of all of the various counterterrorism organizations in France is the Group d'Intervention de la Gendarmerie National (GIGN; National Police Intervention Group). This is a small and very elite national counterterrorism police force. Below this group in the hierarchy of policing agencies is the National Police. The latter performs various policing tasks in cities throughout France.

In addition to the National Police, which falls under the direction of the Ministry of the Interior, there is another agency, which is under the control of the Ministry of Defense. This agency is known as the Direction Générale de Gendarmerie Nationale (National Gendarmerie). The role of the National Gendarmerie consists in the direction of law enforcement in rural areas, including small towns.

CONCLUSION

When it is considered that the initial response of the French government to the threat of terrorism was essentially passive, it becomes all the more remarkable that their current policy is so aggressive. Certainly, France experienced a painful transition through the various policies, from sanctuary to accommodation to suppression. Likewise, it passed through these stages haltingly. In addition, it is worth noting that the shifts in French policy toward terrorism have often been driven by events within the country. In the end, even with the criticisms of some aspects of their policies, the French have achieved a level of organization that has made them quite capable of meeting current terrorist threats to their state, to the extent that they are often held up as a highly successful strategy for counterterrorism.

See also: **Volume 1, Part II:** France. **Volume 2, Part I:** Groupe d'Intervention de la Gendarmerie Nationale (GIGN) (France); Groupes d'Intervention de la Police Nationale (GIPN) (France). **Part II:** Air France Flight 8969 (1994)

REFERENCES

Bourret, Jean Claude. *GIGN, Vingt Ans d'Actions: 1974–1994.* Paris: M. Lafon, 1995.
Gerecht, Marc Reuel, and Gary Schmitt. "France: Europe's Counterterrorism Powerhouse." *American Enterprise Institute for Public Policy Research* 3 (November 2007): 1–6.
Shapiro, Jeremy, and Bénédicte Suzan. "The French Experience of Counterterrorism." *Survival* 45, no. 1 (Spring 2003): 67–98.
Van de Linde, Erik J.G., Kevin A. O'Brien, Gustav Lindstrom, Stephan De Spiegeleire, and Han Vayrynen de Vries. *Quick Scan of Post 9/11 National Counter-terrorism Policymaking and Implementation in Selected European Countries: Research Project for the Netherlands Ministry of Justice.* Santa Monica, CA: RAND Europe, 2002. http://www.rand.org/pubs/monograph_re ports/2005/MR1590.pdf.

Counterterrorism Policy in the United Kingdom

Orla Lynch

Terrorism as we know it has been recognized as such since the 1950s and has existed in a more general sense internationally for as long as historical records allow an insight. However, what was once a marginal issue has since 9/11 become the dominant security concern for a number of countries, particularly in the West. Terrorism, if considered in a body-count mentality, kills fewer people each year than car accidents, cancer, heart disease, obesity, or smoking, yet it seems to have become lodged in the consciousness of Western governments as one of the most destructive threats to the human condition (Sprang 2003).

NEW TERRORISM

Since the 1990s, and 9/11 in particular, the phrase *new terrorism* (Kegley 2008) has been used by government officials and security experts to convey the sense of an arguably heightened risk from violent, politically motivated activity that liberal democratic states face. Given the hysteria that at times surrounds the phenomenon, it has become difficult, if not impossible, to deconstruct the notion of terrorism in a public arena as terrorism has become, among other things, a political tool in the aftermath of the 9/11 attacks on the United States.

The emergence of terrorism as the dominant perceived security threat has led to some worrying developments in Western countries with regards to counterterrorism legislation, immigration policy, departures from certain human rights set out in international human rights treaties, and extra-legal measures such as extraordinary rendition and designations such as enemy combatants. For example, the British government has in just seven years introduced four major pieces of counterterrorist legislation. Many provisions of these laws created new offenses, extended police powers, and gave the home secretary the power of indefinite detention (Walker 2001).

The speed and timing of the publication of recent terrorism legislation demonstrate the reactionary nature of counterterrorism policy. As a reactionary output counterterrorism policy is an at best inevitable and at worst deliberate attempt to enact a predetermined social, political, and bureaucratic system. However, regardless of the motivations surrounding the development of extranormal criminal justice measures to counter terrorism, the impact of these measures on a number of communities is immeasurable. Despite the fact that the threat of terrorism is marginal and that many believe that the criminal justice system should be more than capable of addressing the problem (Hillyard 2005), we have over the past 10 years witnessed the introduction of vast amounts of counterterrorism legislation written for very specific and local threats.

COUNTERTERRORISM LEGISLATION

The reactionary nature of the criminal justice measures used to tackle terrorism has been a feature of UK law since the reemergence of the Provisional Irish Republican Army campaign in Northern Ireland in the early 1970s. The impact of these measures was seen among the Catholic communities in Northern Ireland, and today we can witness the same circumstances among a very different community. Evidence from a study conducted by Hillyard (1993) in the 1980s with individuals who experienced the reality of counterterrorism legislation firsthand documented the physical, social, emotional, political, and financial impacts of being the target of police and military operations. Also mentioned was the subsequent lack of confidence in the law and the police and a profound sense of victimization and injustice. The treatment of Irish Catholic communities in Northern Ireland and the United Kingdom using counterterrorism legislation in the 1970s and 1980s served not to reduce the terrorist threat but to construct a suspect community. Today, under very different circumstances we have a new suspect community (Hillyard 1993) that is experiencing the same victimization—this community is the varied British Muslim population.

History dictates that counterterrorism measures have the ability to impact on a far wider population than is necessary to combat the violent threat; an example is the internment in Northern Ireland (Hillyard 2005). More modern times have revealed similar consequences under a different guise: stop-and-search legislation (Police National Legal Database and Staniforth 2009). In the United Kingdom these measures have been seen to impact disproportionately on the country's Muslim, African, and Middle and Far Eastern populations (Bowling and Philips 2007). With full awareness of the need to balance the rights of direct victims with acknowledgment of and attention to the rights of suspects and offenders, there is a key issue here that needs to be debated. Terrorism research is in many cases increasingly based on the worst-case scenario rather than empirical research; this is particularly true with regard to attacks using weapons of mass destruction. This sensationalist approach to the phenomenon is propagating the belief in the need for "special measures"; especially worrying are the executive (nonjudicial) measures being enacted to deal with the "unprecedented threat" (Home Office 2008). A worrying effect of this inclination to exaggeration is the real impact of such an assumption on another category of victim, a group that is equally important in this balance of rights: the "suspect community" (Hillyard 1993).

BRITAIN'S MUSLIM POPULATION

In the United Kingdom there is one group that is very much part of the political debate around terrorism and synonymous with the so-called new terrorism; that group is Britain's Muslim communities. Although a diverse population these people have been relabeled and reimagined as a coherent, denationalized, and unified community associated with terrorism in its many forms, both terrorism against the civilian population of the United Kingdom and terrorism against its military targets in theaters of war. The reality for the vast majority of British Muslims is that they are experiencing the negative aspects of counterterrorism on a number of levels, their identity has been challenged and renegotiated in the public sphere, their faith has been stigmatized, and they are held responsible for the actions of a few and are the victims of popular suspicion. For British Muslims, terrorism and counterterrorism each have their own impact.

In the case of Britain's diverse Muslim communities, the literal interpretation of counterterrorism legislation does not discriminate between individuals based on their ethnic, social, or religious backgrounds; however, the operationalization of counterterrorism legislation has shaped the experiences, attitudes, and identities of young British Muslims (Mythen and Khan 2009). Following on from the 9/11 terrorist attacks and July 7, 2005, Underground bombings (7/7), the practices, habits, and political values of young Muslims have been subjected to intense speculation among security experts, politicians, policymakers, youth workers, and media professionals.

The suspect community exists in all substate terrorist campaigns and consists of those the state deems to be involved in, actively supportive of, silently supportive of, or related to (individuals involved in) terrorism. Some obvious examples are the Catholic community in Northern Ireland and Irish Catholics in London at the height of the Provisional Irish Republican Army campaign, the Basque diaspora living on Spanish territory, Kurds living in Turkey, Arabs in Israel, and most recently Muslims living in the United Kingdom. However, the impact of counterterrorism goes beyond those in a suspect community. For example, Irish Protestants living in the United Kingdom and Sikhs mistaken for British Muslims have experienced similar issues. Interestingly, in the weeks and months following the 7/7 attacks, "Mistaken Identity" posters and social network pages (http://www.facebook.com/group.php?gid=6890621759) were posted in the United Kingdom stating "Sikhs are not Muslims, Sikhs are not terrorists." While perhaps seen as an attempt to protect a community from harm, they actually highlight the association between Muslims and terrorists predominant after the terrorist attacks.

Of particular note for Britain's Muslims and their experience with counterterrorism legislation is the government's stop-and-search powers (Lambert and Spalek 2010). British Muslims found that police within their community overly exercised these laws. It is of interest that, like many of the measures for prevention of terrorism (re)enacted after 9/11 and 7/7, stop-and-search powers based on suspicion and not a specific reason existed in the 1980s (Terrill 1989). Commonly known as *sus laws* these stop-and-search laws were retracted because they were believed to be responsible for race riots due to enforcement efforts that primarily targeted minority communities (Walker 2001). Additionally, these laws were thought to have contributed to the race riots in London in 1981. Regardless, stop-and-search legislation is alive and well and is being used inordinately within the minority and in particular Muslim communities. Corinna Ferguson, a lawyer for the human rights group Liberty, said, "A threefold increase in anti-terror stop and search is the clearest signal that these powers are being misused. Only 6 in 10,000 people stopped were arrested for terrorism, let alone charged or convicted. And the disproportionate impact on ethic minorities is even greater than in previous years" (Verkaik 2009).

According to Dodd (2005), after 7/7 there was a sevenfold increase in the number of Asian people stopped and searched by British Transport

Police. The effect of such powers has not gone unnoticed, even within police circles. For example, in evidence to a Home Affairs Committee in 2004, a representative from the Metropolitan Police recognized that the stop-and-search measures have created deeper racial and ethnic tensions against the police, trampled on the basic human rights of too many Londoners, cut off valuable sources of community information and intelligence, exacerbated community divisions, and weakened social cohesion. Despite these reservations, stop-and-search powers remain in effect.

CONCLUSION

Terrorism is a complex and multidimensional social and political problem that has existed in many forms over thousands of years. This brief note has suggested some of the issues that exist for minority communities at the center of counterterrorism campaigns. As has been witnessed in the past, reactions to terrorism are often political and rooted in the need for action rather than the need to tackle the realities of the violence. This can lead to well-meaning but poorly thought-out policy and legislation, which serves not to prevent terrorism but in fact to sustain and extend it (Hillyard 2005).

See also: **Volume 1, Part II:** United Kingdom. **Volume 2, Part I:** Counter Terrorism Command (United Kingdom); Special Air Service (United Kingdom); Special Boat Service (United Kingdom); **Part II:** Operation NIMROD (1980); London Subway Attack (2005)

REFERENCES

Bowling, B. *Violent Racism, Victimization, Policing, and Social Context.* Oxford: Clarendon, 1998.
Bowling, B., and C. Philips. "Disproportionate and Discriminatory: Reviewing the Evidence on Police Stop and Search." *Modern Law Review* 70, no. 6 (2007): 936–61.
Brown, C., and C. Morris. "Race-Hate Crimes Surge after Bombs." *The Independent,* August 4, 2005. http://news.independent.co.uk/uk/crime/article 303276.ece.
Dodd, J. "Asian Men Targeted in Stop and Search." *The Guardian,* August 17, 2005.
Hillyard, P. *Suspect Community: People's Experience of the Prevention of Terrorism Acts in Britain.* London: Pluto, 1993.
Hillyard, P. "Suspect Communities: The Real 'War on Terror' in Europe." [Conference Report] International Conference held at London Metropolitan University, Proceedings of the Conference, May 21, 2005, 7–13. http://www.eldh.eu/ . . . /Suspect%20Communitites%20Conference%20Report.pdf.
Home Office. 2008. "National Archives." http://www.homeoffice.gov.uk/about-us/news/counter-terrorism-bill-08.
Islamic Human Rights Watch. *The Hidden Victims of September 11: The Backlash Against Muslims in the UK.* London: Islamic Human Rights Commission, 2002.

Kegley, Charles W. *World Politics: Trends and Transformation*. Beverly, MA: Wadsworth Publishing, 2008.

Lambert, Robert, and Basia Spalek. "Policing within a Counter-Terrorism Context Post 7/7: The Importance of Partnership, Dialogue and Support when Engaging with Muslim Communities." In *The "New" Extremism in 21st Century Britain*, edited by Roger Eatwell and Matthew J. Goodwin, 103–22. London: Routledge, 2010.

"Muslims Have 'Victim Mentality.'" *BBC News*, September 17, 2008. http://news.bbc.co.uk/1/hi/uk/7619642.stm.

Mythen, Gabe, and Fatima Khan. "Futurity, Governance and the Terrorist Risk: Exploring the Impacts of Pre-emptive Modes of Regulation on Young Muslims in the UK." Paper presented at Beijing Normal University, Peoples Republic of China, April 15–17, 2009. http://www.kent.ac.uk/scarr/events/beijingpapers/Mythenppr.pdf.

Police National Legal Database and A. Staniforth. *Blackstones's Counter Terrorism Handbook*. Oxford: Oxford University Press, 2009.

Sprang, G. "The Psychological Impact of Isolated Acts of Terrorism." In *Terrorists, Victims and Society: Psychological Perspectives on Terrorism and Its Consequences*, edited by A. Silke, 133–60. London: Wiley, 2003.

Terrill, R. J. "The Psychological Impact of Isolated Acts of Terrorism." *American Journal of Comparative Law* 37, no. 3 (1989): 429–56.

Verkaik, R. "Muslims Hit by Trebling in Stop and Search. Police Used Antiterror laws to Screen More than 120,000 Individuals." *The Independent*, May 1, 2009. http://www.independent.co.uk/news/uk/crime/muslims-hit-by-trebling-in-stop-and-search-1677107.html.

Walker, C. *Blackstone's Guide to the Anti-terrorism Legislation*. Oxford: Oxford University Press, 2001.

Detention, Interrogation, and Torture of Terrorist Suspects

K. B. Usha

Following the September 11, 2001, terrorist attacks on the United States, the United Nations (UN) Security Council passed Resolution 1368 supporting military action and Resolution 1373, which globalized counterterrorism efforts; obligating all member states to take effective domestic legislative and regulatory actions to prevent future terrorist attacks from al-Qaeda and other groups. Resolution 1368 also recognized the right of states to individual and collective self-defense in accordance with Article 51 of the UN Charter.

The U.S.-led war on terror was launched in Afghanistan on October 7, 2001 (Operation Enduring Freedom) and later in Iraq (Operation

Iraqi Freedom) on March 19, 2003. The United States rightly feared the al-Qaeda terrorist network and considered this group and other like-minded organizations a direct threat to U.S. and global security. In the context of two ongoing wars the detention, treatment, and legal status of "enemy combatants" would become an issue of international concern and debate.

INTERNATIONAL LAWS AND CONVENTIONS REGARDING DETENTION, INTERROGATION, AND TORTURE

The existing international instruments with respect to the detention, interrogation, and torture of terrorist suspects are those specifying the international laws of war such as the Geneva Conventions and Protocols; the UN Universal Declaration of Human Rights; the UN Convention against Torture and Other Cruel, Inhuman or Degrading Treatment or Punishment; the International Covenant on Civil and Political Rights; the UN Body of Principles for the Protection of All Persons under any Form of Detention or Imprisonment; the UN Standard Minimum Rules for the Treatment of Prisoners; the European Convention for the Protection of Human Rights and Fundamental Freedoms; and the International Criminal Tribunal for the Former Yugoslavia. These instruments prohibit torture of war detainees. The war laws provide captured combatants and civilians in times of war with the status of prisoners of war and call for their humane treatment.

U.S. DETENTION AND INTERROGATION OF "ENEMY COMBATANTS": LEGAL BACKGROUND

The war on terror included a highly secretive component for dealing with terrorist suspects as a preventive strategy against future attacks or as part of an investigation. However, as international law is binding for all UN member states, any practice regarding detention, interrogation, and torture should be in compliance with the international and domestic legal framework.

U.S. detention and interrogation policies evolved through congressional legislation that authorized new legal measures. Resolutions enacted by the U.S. Senate and House of Representatives authorized President Bush to use all necessary and appropriate force against those responsible for the terrorist attacks on September 11, 2001 ("Joint Resolution" 2004).

In October 2001, the Congress passed the USA PATRIOT Act (officially the Uniting and Strengthening America by Providing Appropriate Tools Required to Intercept and Obstruct Terrorism Act) in the context of September 11. The act provides broader powers to federal officials to monitor suspected terrorist activity and gather and share information. It also gave the secretary of the treasury regulatory powers to combat corruption of U.S. financial institutions especially in the area of foreign money laundering. The act seeks to further close U.S. borders to foreign terrorists and to detain and remove those within U.S. borders. In the words of Doyle (2002, 1), it "creates new crimes, new penalties, and new procedural efficiencies for use against domestic and international terrorists."

On November 13, 2001, Military Order—Detention, Treatment, and Trial of Certain Non-citizens in the War against Terrorism was issued by the president. This order gives the secretary of defense expanded powers regarding individuals considered threats to U.S. national security. This order also spells out the conditions under which such individuals will be detained and tried by military tribunal rather than a civil proceeding in a U.S. federal court, which would offer detainees certain rights and privileges under the American system of jurisprudence (Bush 2001). Furthermore, on February 7, 2002, the president of the United States issued a memorandum declaring that the "common article 3 of Geneva does not apply to either Al-Qaeda or Taliban detainees" and that "Taliban detainees are unlawful combatants and, therefore, do not qualify as prisoners of war under article 4 of Geneva."

In October 2002, the U.S. Congress passed a "Joint Resolution to Authorize the Use of the United States Armed Forces against Iraq" and launched Operation Iraqi Freedom in March 2003. The Homeland Security Act of November 2002, the 2005 Detainee Treatment Act, and the 2006 Military Commissions Act granted the executive sweeping powers to detain, interrogate, and prosecute alleged terror suspects and collaborators (including U.S. citizens) and imprison them indefinitely in military prisons without proof of guilt.

CENTRAL INTELLIGENCE AGENCY INTERROGATION TECHNIQUES AND TORTURE

The Central Intelligence Agency (CIA) has been empowered to detain, interrogate, and torture terrorist suspects. On September 17, 2001, President Bush issued a secret directive authorizing the CIA to set up detention facilities known as "black sites" outside the United States and employ "an alternative set of interrogation procedures" on suspected terrorist leaders taken into custody (Fletcher and Stover 2009). According to the UN Human Rights Council, the CIA runs several offshore secret prisons in over 66 countries worldwide for dissidents and alleged terrorists (Lendman 2010). The United States imprisoned those it suspected of terrorism at Guantánamo Bay, Cuba; in Abu Ghraib, Iraq; at Bagram Air Base in Afghanistan (and other sites in that country); and in the so-called CIA black sites, reportedly at the Stare Kiejkuty base in Poland and the Mihail Kogalniceanu Air Base in Romania as well as sites in Thailand and Jordan. The United States may have detained suspected terrorists in other American military bases around the world and off base in other countries (McDonnell 2010, 48).

Based on the September 18, 2001, joint U.S. House and Senate Authorization for the Use of Military Force, the Bush administration held "high-value" al-Qaeda and Taliban detainees and brought them to secret detention facilities. The high-value detainees in U.S. custody were subjected to severe and torturous "enhanced interrogation" methods and techniques. Former detainees describe nightmarish treatment, including waterboarding, sleep deprivation, beatings, and other procedures designed to obtain information from those reluctant to provide it (Fletcher and Stover 2009).

The Bush administration's argument for authorization of harsh interrogation techniques was a legal memorandum written by assistant attorney general Jay S. Bybee and deputy assistant John Yoo in August 2002 stating that abuse does not rise to the level of torture under U.S. law unless such abuse inflicts pain "equivalent in intensity to the pain accompanying serious physical injury, such as organ failure, impairment of bodily function, or even death." *Mental torture* required "suffering not just at the moment of infliction but it also requires lasting psychological harm, such as seen in mental disorders like posttraumatic stress disorder." To qualify as torture, the infliction of pain had to be the "precise objective" of the abuse (Fletcher and Stover 2009). According to this author these arguments understate physical abuse and mental torture and are intended to justify torture.

CONCLUSION

The U.S. treatment of detainees, especially in the Guantánamo Bay and Abu Ghraib prisons, unleashed criticism of its policies for noncompliance with international legal norms, humanitarian laws, and U.S. laws. Due to the worldwide criticism of Bush administration policies, President Obama decided to review the detention and interrogation policies and follow a new approach on counterterrorism policy. His first act on assuming office was his order to close down the Guantánamo Bay prison within a year. This was not achieved. The Obama administration appears to have determined that the rendition program was one component of the Bush administration's war on terrorism that it could not afford to discard.

See also: **Volume 1, Part VI:** Interrogation: A Multidisciplinary Approach; Rehabilitation of Extremists: Methods and Practice

REFERENCES

Doyle, Charles. "The USA PATRIOT Act: A Sketch." CRS Report for Congress, Order Code RS21203, April 18, 2002. Federation of American Scientists. http://www.fas.org/irp/crs/RS21203.pdf.

Federal Register. "Detention, Treatment, and Trial of Certain Non-Citizens in the War Against Terrorism." [Presidential Documents] Military Order of November 13, 2001, vol. 66, no. 222, November 16, 2001. http://www.gpo.gov/fdsys/pkg/FR-2001-11-16/pdf/01-28904.pdf.

Fletcher, Laurel E., and Eric Stover. *Guantánamo Effect: Exposing the Consequences of U.S. Detention and Interrogation Practices*. Berkeley: University of California Press, 2009.

"Joint Resolution 64: To authorize the use of United States Armed Forces against those responsible for the recent attacks launched against the United States," September 18, 2001, *Congressional Record*, September 14, 2004, p. H5638. Federation of American Scientists. http://www.fas.org/irp/threat/useofforce.htm.

Lendman, Stephen. "America's Secret Prisons." Thepeoplesvoice.org, March 16, 2010. http://www.thepeoplesvoice.org/TPV3/Voices.php/2010/03/16/america-s-secret-prisons.

McDonnell, Thomas Michael. *The United States, International Law and the Struggle against Terrorism*. London: Routledge, 2010.

Watson, Steve. "Terror Memos Reveal Total Destruction of U.S. Constitutional Freedoms." *Infowars.net*, March 3, 2009. http://www.infowars.com/terror-memos-reveal-total-destruction-of-us-constitutional-freedoms/.

Eliminating Terrorist Support Networks

Chris J. Kirkpatrick

In a post–Cold War world, many terrorist groups exist and operate outside the confines of the modern nation-state. The transnational nature of modern terrorism presents new challenges for the international community. States and transnational organizations must focus their efforts across a wide spectrum to eliminate the support networks that enable terrorists to perpetrate attacks. Hence, a multifaceted approach must consider several relevant factors. First, the organizational models used by terrorist actors and hierarchies must be understood. Second, states and organizations must understand the mechanics of how to eliminate or interdict these networks, including modern technological challenges. Finally, states must understand how national and international law impacts efforts to eliminate terrorist networks.

ORGANIZATIONAL MODELS

Terrorist networks must be modeled before they can be interdicted or eliminated. There are numerous theories on how networks operate, but the essential question is one of motivation. Three general models are used:

a strict hierarchical model, a flat network model, and a social network model. The strict hierarchical model assumes a chain of command and a vertical understanding of links between plans, finance, support, and operations. The entire hierarchy is understood to be united by ideology. This model provided a basic understanding of al-Qaeda before 2001 and is still preferred due to its simplicity (Eilstrup-Sangiovanni 2010, 366–69). The flat network model focuses more on horizontal connections, treating al-Qaeda as an umbrella franchise organization that distributes resources. This type of model is flexible and allows for a multitude of divergent motivations between leaders and operatives; including the possibility of a profit motive in the middle ranks of organizations (Shapiro and Siegel 2007, 410–13). The social network model assumes that one of the primary motives for participation in terrorist groups is the promise of social reward (Sageman 2008, 16–20; Abrahms 2010, 186–95).

The labeling of a terrorist support network requires a brief discussion of support. The most obvious—and most commonly targeted—element is financial support. However, support could also include other forms such as communications, propaganda, or transit conduits. The importance of all these forms of support is highlighted across the entire spectrum of attacks. For example, the September 11, 2001, attacks in the United States and the female suicide bomber who traveled from Belgium to Iraq in 2005 to conduct her attack used the same basic network of support. The attacks were far different in complexity and numbers of casualties but equally enabled by their respective support network (Brimley 2006, 30–31). It is important to understand these considerations in order to legally prosecute supporters of terrorist networks. Depending on the state or supranational organization, the definition of support is crucial to the successful prosecution of an action as a crime or an act of war. Furthermore, the inclination of Western states is to prosecute violations of law on an individual basis. Often, the collusion intrinsic to terrorist support networks is beyond reach due to a reluctance to pursue and prosecute groups as entities (Giraldo and Trinkhunas 2007, 1–3, 260–67).

ELIMINATING TERRORIST FINANCES

In the post–Cold War world, states have attempted several strategies to eliminate terrorist groups, but regardless of the model employed the most common strategies have been tactical and focused on lethality and financial interdiction. Rarely have states or supranational organizations used a model to create an operational or strategic policy of interdicting based on motive and method at all levels of a terrorist organization. For example, few states demonstrate a sophisticated understanding of possible profit motives at the "middle-management level" of terrorist support networks. Rather than use the motives internal to terrorist groups as tactics to disrupt and dissolve the organization, states have preferred a scorched-earth policy of trying to eliminate funding altogether (Shapiro and Siegel 2007, 410–13, 426–27).

Modern terrorists are often paradoxical in rhetoric and action. While groups such as al-Qaeda reject Western innovations and some aspects of modernity, they simultaneously harness globalization and the ubiquity of the Internet to perpetrate attacks, maintain communications, and raise operating funds (Brown et al. 2010, 34–37). In both the physical world and cyberspace, support nodes are crucial for continuing terrorist operations. A diverse system of funding, for example, may draw from robbery, drug trafficking, and kidnapping operations to provide financial support to a larger support network. Collected funds are then redistributed efficiently to maximize the tempo and concentration of attacks in a specific time and space (Giraldo and Trinkhunas 2007, 22–26). These types of operations were once considered impossible to sustain without state support. However, al-Qaeda and various franchised groups have demonstrated a capacity to sustain pace and tempo without a definitive hierarchy (Sageman 2008, 40–45). All of this coordination is done over a wide technological spectrum; part of the communications are via the Internet using sophisticated but widely available encryption technology, but other forms include cell phones, handwritten notes delivered by courier, or perhaps face-to-face meetings. (Brimley 2006, 34–36).

In the face of a robust and varied support network, the international community has focused on a primarily two-dimensional response. While some have characterized financial interdiction after September 11 as the most successful counterterrorism operation to date, the continuing proliferation of attacks indicates otherwise. Most states have signed the International Convention for the Suppression of the Financing of Terrorism or other similar agreements. These agreements focus on digital interdiction of financing (Giraldo and Trinkhunas 2007, 282–85). Most states also actively participate in international agreements on the use of force and interdiction to directly observe and prosecute individual supporters of terrorism. However, this focus on digital technology and the use of force and legal authority on individuals does not yield a strategic solution to the network of support outlined in the preceding. At best, it provides a tactical resolution for isolated incidents (Cronin 2010, 47–56).

CONCLUSION

To interdict the entirety of support networks requires an international approach that all interested states are willing to participate in; however, such an endeavor would also require a uniform definition of terrorism that has thus far eluded the international community.

See also: **Volume 1, Part III:** Identifying and Combating Sources of Terrorist Financing; Safe Havens and Weak and Failing States. **Part IV:** Pakistan's Federally Administered Tribal Areas (FATA)

REFERENCES

Abrahms, Max. "What Terrorists Really Want: Terrorist Motives and Counterterrorism Strategy." In *Contending with Terrorism: Roots, Strategies, and Responses*, edited by Michael E. Brown, Owen R. Coté Jr., Sean M. Lynn-Jones, and Steven E. Miller, 171–98. Cambridge, MA: MIT Press, 2010.

Brimley, Shawn. "Tentacles of Jihad: Targeting Transnational Support Networks." *Parameters* (Summer 2006): 30–46.

Brown, Michael E., Owen R. Coté, Jr., Sean M. Lynn-Jones, and Steven E. Miller. *Contending with Terrorism: Roots, Strategies, and Responses*. Cambridge, MA: MIT Press, 2010.

Cronin, Audrey Kurth. "Behind the Curve: Organization and International Terrorism." In *Contending with Terrorism: Roots, Strategies, and Responses*, edited by Michael E. Brown, Owen R. Coté Jr., Sean M. Lynn-Jones, and Steven E. Miller, 28–56. Cambridge, MA: MIT Press, 2010.

Eilstrup-Sangiovanni, Mette. "Assessing the Dangers of Illicit Networks: Why al-Qaida May Be Less Threatening Than Many Think." In *Contending with Terrorism: Roots, Strategies, and Responses*, edited by Michael E. Brown, Owen R. Coté Jr., Sean M. Lynn-Jones, and Steven E. Miller, 336–76. Cambridge, MA: MIT Press, 2010.

Giraldo, Jeanne K., and Harold A. Trinkhunas. *Terrorism Financing and State Responses: A Comparative Perspective*. Stanford, CA: Stanford University Press, 2007.

Sageman, Marc. *Leaderless Jihad: Terror Networks in the Twenty-First Century*. Philadelphia: University of Pennsylvania Press, 2008.

Shapiro, Jacob N., and David A. Siegel. "Underfunding in Terrorist Organizations." *International Studies Quarterly* 51 (2007): 405–29.

Ethical and Legal Issues in Democratic Societies: National Security and Civil Liberties

Alejandro Vélez

Liberty and security are the most important pillars that sustain democratic societies. Both political principles have been in constant evolution, but they have always been inevitably linked like the two sides of a coin. However, if human beings are given a choice between security and liberty, many would choose security. This is because "raw" security is intimately linked to human survival and the fear of death. Social contract theorists understood this fact and articulated the hypothetical trade by which we gave up our sovereignty and the monopoly on violence to a monarch or a government in exchange for their maintenance of a secure social order. In a nutshell, security was paid for by a reduction in civil liberties.

POST-9/11 SECURITY

After 9/11, at least for Western middle- and upper-level social classes, death seemed closer than ever, as if a fifth Apocalypse Rider was hidden inside the gray dust cloud that originated at Ground Zero after the twin towers collapsed. Suddenly, there was a new enemy on the geopolitical horizon: international Islamic fundamentalists with the al-Qaeda trademark, and it was more elusive, irrational, and unpredictable than the "evil empire" during the fateful years of the Cold War. According to the Bush administration this was a new type of enemy, "a new kind of evil" in Bush's words, that had just attacked Western civilization because they hated its civil liberties and technological accomplishments. That is why, in order to face this new enemy and avoid another 9/11 type of attack, the Bush administration and its allies thought it was necessary to elevate security to the top of the Olympus of political principles, above liberty, justice, and the pursuit of happiness.

However, a different type of security was needed after 9/11. The Cold War concept of national security that revolved around military power, especially nuclear power, was still useful, but it needed to consider new threat variables such as ecological crises, financial crises, scarce natural resources, global criminal networks, international drug dealing, immigration, and, since 9/11, global terrorism. As a direct result of the attacks on the U.S. homeland, the U.S. Congress, six weeks after 9/11, drafted the USA PATRIOT Act, and the Department of Homeland Security was created. The creation of this new cabinet-level department is important because the last creation of a ministerial structure for security purposes in the United States took place in 1947 when the Pentagon was created. Now, the Department of Homeland Security was given the monumental task of bringing together 22 agencies and federal programs specializing in a multitude of various issues and structuring them in a way that would improve the information-sharing process. Several democratic countries like the United Kingdom, Canada, Australia, and New Zealand rushed to adopt some of the features of the U.S. homeland security model because they thought bringing together departments and agencies under the same roof was the best way to prevent future terrorist attacks.

Even though the states just cited were the only countries that embraced the homeland security model, a report issued by Pen International, a worldwide association of writers created in 1921 to promote literature and defend freedom of expression, notes that more than 35 states have passed some type of counterterrorism law as a response to the events of 9/11 (Gordillo 2008, 86). This legislative tendency is a direct consequence of United Nations (UN) Security Council Resolution 1373, by which the UN called on all states to incorporate the crime of terrorism into their law codes; prevent, suppress, and criminalize the financing of terrorist acts; freeze the funds, financial assets, or economic resources of alleged terrorists; refrain from providing any form of support to entities or persons involved in terrorist acts; afford one another the greatest measure of assistance in connection with criminal investigations relating to the financing or support of terrorist acts; and prevent the movement of terrorists by effective border controls and limitations on the issuance of identity papers and travel documents (UN Security Council 2001).

According to Hans-Jörg Albrecht of the Max Planck Institute, most of the counterterrorist measures adopted after 9/11 were not new pieces of legislation; instead, they were laws inspired by European and international counterterrorist treaties from the 1960s, 1970s, and 1980s, when several European states faced the threat of leftist or nationalist terrorist groups (Albrecht 2006, 1142). At the core of the counterterrorist effort we can find tougher and more restrictive immigration and asylum laws, money-laundering controls, interstate cooperation treaties to fight international crime, new police powers, new secret service attributions, approval of intensive surveillance, and the insertion of the crime of terrorism into national law codes.

Some of these laws have nothing to do with the prevention of terrorism. For example, the tougher immigration and asylum laws do not have any effect on preventing terrorist attacks because there has never been a direct correlation between immigrant or refugee populations and terrorist attacks. As a matter of fact, English citizens were the ones who carried out the attacks in London on July 7, 2005, even though the mainstream media usually chose to refer to them as "second-generation immigrants." In another example, the suspects accused of hijacking the planes on 9/11 were either tourists or legal immigrants, so even with tougher immigration controls, the attacks would more than likely still have occurred. These types of laws should be classified as *symbolic criminal law,* a term used by several German experts in criminal law (e.g., Winfried Hassemer of Frankfurt University) to describe laws that are issued just to have a symbolic impact on society with little effective means of protecting the population (Diéz Ripolles 2001). In fact, this type of legislation does little to counter the terrorist threat.

PREEMPTIVE MEASURES

Several post-9/11 counterterrorist laws can also be read through the optics of the legal trend known as *enemy criminal law.* This legal concept was devised by German legal scholar Günther Jakobs and refers to a criminal law that deals with the offenders not as citizens but as possible enemies. In this type of juridical ordination, the sentences imposed are used as security measures because they are created to isolate the more "dangerous" members of society, either by shutting them inside prisons with disproportionate and excessive sentences or by expelling them from the country (Cancio Meliá 2002). The United Kingdom has an impressive array of laws that fit under Jakobs's enemy criminal law concept because they carry an unnecessary punitive burden. Some of these measures, such as precharge detention, control orders, stop-and-search procedures, punishment for glorification of terrorism, and penalties for withholding information are preemptive actions that punish an individual before he or she commits a crime.

A great tool in preemption has been surveillance methods. We cannot entirely blame the 9/11 attacks for the rise in surveillance methods, but according to David Lyon, director of the Surveillance Studies Centre at Queens University, it is unquestionable that the attacks have brought to the surface a number of surveillance trends that had been developing quietly for the previous decade, and it also granted the opportunity to develop new ideas and technologies and transform them into policies (Lyon 2003, 4–5). Democratic countries have employed surveillance as a way to deliver security and deter future terrorist attacks. Most of these changes have started in the United States, and even if the United States is not a representative sample of the world, it establishes a precedent. Since 9/11 several democratic countries have increased the use of closed circuit television, biometrics, and intelligent IDs, regardless of their implications for privacy, freedom of speech, and freedom of movement.

Many provisions of these national and international counterterrorism treaties and laws clash with human rights and fundamental liberties in democratic societies, but most governments have decided to underestimate these "ethical bottlenecks" in order to protect their citizens and institutions from the consequences of terrorism. With the decision to curtail some fundamental liberties and trample on some human rights for the sake of security, several democratic countries have created a kind of "state of exception" justified under the global war on terror. Some of the measures states have used to address terrorism are depriving prisoners of habeas corpus, kidnapping terrorism suspects wherever they are, obtaining intelligence information by torture, and/or spying illegally on innocent citizens.

The justification for these emergency measures is an overly broad definition of terrorism. In fact there is no universally acceptable definition of terrorism from the UN or the International Criminal Court that every state is obliged to recognize. Instead, there are many definitions of terrorism that have been applied depending on the circumstances and the country, government body, or agency providing the definition. Before being classified as terrorists, some members of al-Qaeda who fought Soviet forces in Afghanistan during the 1980s were described as "freedom fighters." Additionally, the African National Congress that brought down apartheid in South Africa was considered a terrorist organization by the United States in the 1980s but is presently a major political party and a universal example of a successful civil rights movement.

CONCLUSION

It is this author's opinion that if the societies of democratic countries do not impress on their representatives in government the need to stop the unnecessary trade-off between security and civil liberties, we could soon face a scenario where civil demonstrations like strikes could be criminalized under the guise of national security.

See also: **Volume 1, Part III:** Just War Doctrine; Multidisciplinary Approach to Combating Terrorism; Preemption: Moral and Ethical Considerations. **Part IV:** Prosecuting Terrorists in a Democratic Society. **Part VI:** Psychological Profiling of Terrorists; Understanding Foreign Cultures

REFERENCES

Albrecht, Hans-Jörg. "Respuestas legislativas al 11 de septiembre. 'Un análisis comparado de la legislación antiterrorista.' " In *Derecho penal y criminología como fundamento de la política criminal. Estudios en homenaje al profesor Alfonso Serrano Gómez,* edited by Alfonso Serrano Malló, Francisco Bueno Aruz, and Jose Guzmán Dálbora. Madrid: Dykinson, 2006.

Cancio Meliá, Manuel. "Derecho penal del enemigo y delitos de terrorismo. Algunas consideraciones sobre la regulación de las infracciones en materia de terrorismo en el Código penal español después de la LO 7/2000." *Jueces para la Democracia,* no. 44 (July 2002): 19–26.

Diéz Ripolles, José Luis. "El derecho penal simbólico y los efectos de la pena." *Actualidad Penal,* no. 1 (January 2001): 1–22. http://www.juridicas.unam.mx/publica/rev/boletin/cont/103/art/art3.htm.

Gordillo, José Luís. *Nostalgia de otro futuro. La lucha por la paz en la posguerra fría.* Madrid: Trotta, 2008.

Lyon, David. *Surveillance after September 11.* Cambridge: Polity, 2003.

United Nations Security Council. Resolution 1373 (S/RES/1373 2001). September 28, 2001.

Global Initiative to Combat Nuclear Terrorism

Jamie Walsh

On July 15, 2006, in St. Petersburg, Russian Federation president Vladamir Putin and U.S. president George W. Bush launched The Global Initiative to Combat Nuclear Terrorism (GICNT). The aim of the initiative is to "improve accounting, control, and physical protection" of nuclear materials and radioactive substances, counter illicit trafficking in nuclear materials, respond to and mitigate the consequences of nuclear terrorism, ensure cooperation and capacity building among states in this regard, and strengthen national legal frameworks to ensure effective prosecution and certainty of punishment for those who facilitate terrorist acts (U.S. Department of State 2009).

COMBATING NUCLEAR TERRORISM

In October 2006 the 13 founding GICNT states met in Rabat, Morocco, and agreed on a statement of principles to combat nuclear terrorism and a set of procedures for evaluating progress. The statement of principles and the "terms of reference for implementation and assessment" are designed to provide assistance to states in their implementation of the GICNT (U.S. Department of State 2009). The principles commit participating states "to combat nuclear terrorism on a determined and systematic basis, consistent with national legal authorities and obligations they have under relevant international legal frameworks, notably the Convention for the Suppression of Acts of Nuclear Terrorism, the Convention on the Physical Protection of Nuclear Material and its 2005 Amendment, and United Nations Security Council Resolution 1540" (U.S. Department of State 2009).

The initiative is a voluntary one, in the sense that there are no formal legal commitments. However, states are expected to make a meaningful effort to become engaged in joint exercises and meetings, as well as ensuring that national measures and legislation live up to best practice. An Implementation and Assessment Group was also established to assist states in implementation and to engage in outreach.

Initiative participants are expected to:

- "Develop, if necessary, and improve accounting, control, and physical protection systems for nuclear and other radioactive materials and substances;
- Enhance security of civilian nuclear facilities;
- Improve the ability to detect nuclear and other radioactive materials and substances in order to prevent illicit trafficking in such materials and substances, to include cooperation in the research and development of national detection capabilities that would be interoperable;
- Improve capabilities of participants to search for, confiscate, and establish safe control over unlawfully held nuclear or other radioactive materials and substances or devices using them;
- Prevent the provision of safe haven to terrorists and financial or economic resources to terrorists seeking to acquire or use nuclear and other radioactive materials and substances;
- Ensure adequate respective national legal and regulatory frameworks sufficient to provide for the implementation of appropriate criminal and, if applicable, civil liability for terrorists and those who facilitate acts of nuclear terrorism;

- Improve capabilities of participants for response, mitigation, and investigation, in cases of terrorist attacks involving the use of nuclear and other radioactive materials and substances, including the development of technical means to identify nuclear and other radioactive materials and substances that are, or may be, involved in the incident; and

- Promote information sharing pertaining to the suppression of acts of nuclear terrorism and their facilitation, taking appropriate measures consistent with their national law and international obligations to protect the confidentiality of any information which they exchange in confidence." (U.S. Department of State 2009)

GICNT participants have met in Rabat (Morocco) on October 30–31, 2006; Ankara (Turkey) on February 12–13, 2007; Astana (Kazakhstan) on June 1–12, 2007; Madrid (Spain) on June 17, 2008; the Hague (Netherlands) on June 16–17, 2009, and Abu Dhabi (United Arab Emirates) on June 29, 2010. To date, partner nations have completed 35 activities aimed at building capacity to prevent, detect, deter, and respond to acts of nuclear terrorism.

PARTNER NATION COOPERATION

At the third GICNT meeting in Astana, Kazakhstan, in June 2007, partner nations endorsed a U.S. plan of work activity proposal to create an information portal that would provide partners the opportunity to share information regarding GICNT activities and collaborative tools to facilitate interaction among partners. The charter of the Global Initiative Information Portal is to implement GICNT Principle 8, which calls on states to "promote information sharing pertaining to the suppression of acts of nuclear terrorism and their facilitation, taking appropriate measures consistent with their national law and international obligations to protect the confidentiality of any information which they exchange in confidence" (U.S. Department of State 2009). The portal is a secure means to communicate controlled and publicly releasable, unclassified information in a shared portal across the GICNT partnership via the Internet.

The most recent GICNT Plenary Meeting in Abu Dhabi in June 2010 agreed on several items aimed at enhancing implementation of partner nations' voluntary commitments. These items included "adoption of a revised Terms of Reference" (not yet publicly available) that "more clearly defines participant roles and responsibilities and establishes concrete mechanisms for GICNT implementation; endorsement of the Russian Federation and the United States to continue to serve as GICNT Co-chairs"; and the selection of Spain as the first coordinator of the Implementation and Assessment Group (U.S. Department of State 2010). Significantly, delegates at the plenary identified nuclear detection and nuclear forensics as priority functional areas for the GICNT to focus on in the future.

Despite the generally positive reception of the initiative by states, non-governmental organizations, and academics, structural flaws such as the absence of any evaluation mechanism and the exclusion of military-related nuclear materials and sites are likely to make the impact of the GICNT far less global than expected (Alcaro 2009).

While there are significant geographic gaps in the GICNT's list of participating states (particularly in the Middle East), it has succeeded in bringing on board states such as China, India, Pakistan, which are traditionally wary of committing to international arrangements that could infringe on their internal affairs. As of June 2010, 82 countries have signed on to the GICNT, and it seems likely that membership will continue to grow. The International Atomic Energy Agency, the European Union, and the International Criminal Police Organization (Interpol) also serve as official observers.

CONCLUSION

A priority of the Obama administration is to secure all vulnerable nuclear material around the world within four years; in his Prague speech in April 2009, the president spoke of turning efforts such as the GICNT and the Proliferation Security Initiative into durable international institutions. The importance of the GICNT was also reiterated at the Washington Nuclear Security Summit in April 2010, where participating governments characterized nuclear terrorism as "one of the most challenging threats to international security" (Nuclear Security Summit 2010). The number of partner nations has increased steadily, as has the scope of activity, and given the political engagement there seems little doubt about the initiative's survival, though its shape and structure remain somewhat unwieldy.

REFERENCES

Alcaro, Riccardo. "The Global Initiative to Combat Nuclear Terrorism: Big Potential, Limited Impact?" *International Spectator* 44, no. 1 (March 2009): 99–112.

Nuclear Security Summit 2010. "Communique of the Washington Nuclear Security Summit." Washington, DC, April 13, 2010. http://photos.state.gov/libraries/libya/19452/public/NSS%20-%20Communique%20With%20Logo%20040710.pdf.

U.S. Department of State. "Statement of Principles." Bureau of International Security and Nonproliferation. Washington, DC: U.S. Department of State, 2009. http://www.state.gov/t/isn/rls/other/126995.htm.

U.S. Department of State. "Joint Co-Chair Statement Regarding the 2010 Global Initiative to Combat Nuclear Terrorism Plenary Meeting." June 29, 2010. http://www.state.gov/r/pa/prs/ps/2010/06/143754.htm.

Importance of Mutual Legal Assistance

Simeon P. Sungi

Mutual legal assistance refers to treaties, bilateral or multilateral, between two or more states, that permit international legal cooperation in private and public sources for use in official investigations and prosecutions. It also allows access to documents and witnesses and other legal and judicial assistance in the member states (Association of Certified Anti-Money Laundering Specialists [ACAMS] 2005, 88). This practice can be traced back to Hugo Grotius's *aut dedere aut judicare* doctrine, which has been adopted as a general principle of international law: the duty to "prosecute or extradite" individuals who are accused of offences that violate international law, such as war crimes and terrorism, to mention just a few (Bassiouni 2008, 194).

MUTUAL LEGAL ASSISTANCE TREATIES

States have concluded mutual legal assistance treaties (MLAT) to assist them in sharing information and evidence relating to criminal investigations and prosecutions in drug trafficking and narcotics-related money laundering. For example, Article 1 of the MLAT between the United States of America and Ireland (2001) provides for the scope of assistance. It states: "The parties shall provide mutual assistance, in accordance with the provisions of this Treaty, in connection with the investigation, prosecution, and prevention of offenses and in proceedings related to criminal matters" (U.S.–EU Mutual Legal Assistance Agreement [Ireland] 2005, 4).

The article continues to explain the areas of assistance under subarticle 2: (a) taking the testimony or statements of persons; (b) providing documents, records, and articles of evidence; (c) locating or identifying persons; (d) serving documents; (e) search and seizure request (f) transferring persons in custody for testimony or other purposes; and (g) identifying, tracing, freezing, seizing, and forfeiting the proceeds and instrumentalities of crime and assistance in related proceedings (U.S.–EU Mutual Legal Assistance Agreement [Ireland] 2005, 4).

The events of 9/11 changed the whole scope of MLATs where states have collectively determined to fight terrorism by putting in place agreements that provide more stringent legal frameworks to tackle this problem. Core to MLATs is the cooperation of security forces to track, arrest, and extradite alleged terrorists on a request by a member state. Hand in hand with these provisions is that of restraining and forfeiture proceeds procured for the purposes of funding terrorism activities, sharing of banking information on suspects, and creation of joint investigative teams (e.g., in the MLAT between the European Union and the United States in 2003).

As this essay illustrates, the importance of MLATs in the age of fighting terrorism cannot be overemphasized. It is essential that MLATs include the following areas in their provisions: (i) cooperation in judicial efforts in investigation, which include letters rogatory, service of writs and judicial verdicts, and the appearance of witnesses, experts, and prosecuted persons; (ii) provisions on seizure and forfeiture—that is, confiscation of criminal proceeds as mandated by United Nations Security Council Resolution 1373; (iii) the recognition of foreign penal judgments and the transfer of criminal proceedings; and (iv) the transfer of sentenced persons or persons convicted of terrorism. While all these areas are significant in fighting terrorism, MLATs should ensure that authorities track the finances of terrorist suspects. Other tracking measures, such as body scanners, should not jeopardize the health or privacy of individuals and/or violate their fundamental human rights.

IMPORTANT AREAS FOR MUTUAL LEGAL ASSISTANCE

The crime of terrorism provides numerous challenges if the counterterrorism measures lack crucial international cooperation. First, ambiguous provisions in MLATs that provide for cooperation in judicial efforts in investigations may hinder counterterrorism efforts. Article 1(2) of the European Convention on Mutual Assistance in Criminal Matters (1959), for example, prohibits cooperation in arrests, the enforcement of verdicts, or offenses under military law, which are not considered crimes under ordinary criminal law. This distinction between military law and ordinary criminal law becomes a problem when this provision is applied to the crime of terrorism because ordinarily military laws do not proscribe crimes of international terrorism but leave it to civilian criminal legislation and courts to address the problem (Federal Register 2001, 57831–36).

Second, it is essential that MLATs have provisions that deal with seizures and forfeitures of proceeds that provide material and financial support for terrorist groups and activities. Security Council Resolution 1373 directed member states to criminalize terrorist financing and to adopt regulatory regimes intended to detect, deter, and freeze the funds of terrorists. Paragraph 1(b) of Resolution 1373 mandates that all member states "criminalize the willful provision or collection, by any means, directly or indirectly, of funds by their nationals or in their territories with the intention that the funds should be used, or in the knowledge that they are to be used, in order to carry out terrorist acts" and "freeze without delay funds and other financial assets or economic resources of persons who commit, or attempt to commit, terrorist acts or participate in or facilitate the commission of terrorist acts; of entities owned or controlled directly or indirectly by such persons; and of persons and entities acting on behalf of, or at the direction of such persons and entities, including funds derived or generated from property owned or controlled directly or indirectly by such persons and associated persons and entities" (United Nations 2001). An MLAT should incorporate such provisions if the objective is to restrict funding sources for terrorist entities. Intergovernmental bodies, such as the Financial Action Task Force, whose purpose is the development and promotion of policies, at both the national and international levels, to combat money laundering and terrorist financing, are important forums that can generate political will to harmonize national legislation in individual member states and in MLATs.

Third, MLATs should contain provisions that foster an integrated system of cooperation among states in recognizing foreign judgments and the transfer of criminal proceedings. An example of such cooperation is found in the Council of Europe, through the European Convention on the International Validity of Criminal Judgments of 1970. This agreement embodies provisions that recognize foreign criminal judgments among member states of the Council of Europe. The problem that these states face is the lack of a universally accepted definition of terrorism and what constitutes a terrorist act. For example, one state may refuse to recognize a judgment of another state on crimes that the latter views as terrorism. The same applies to the transfer of criminal proceedings. Since the alleged perpetrators of terrorism may be subject to diverse jurisdictions, their prosecution may raise double-jeopardy questions. MLATs need to provide remedies where there is a conflict of jurisdiction because states need to agree on which state assumes jurisdiction in a case involving a terrorist action.

CONCLUSION

MLATs should provide provisions that allow states to dismantle terrorists' cash flows, seize assets that support terrorism, and provide the necessary technical assistance to support states that do not have the technical nor training abilities to prevent terror attacks. Additionally, these critical measures need to uphold basic standards of human rights, avoid arbitrary arrests or detentions, and operate within the principles of democracy and the rule of law.

REFERENCES

Association of Certified Anti-Money Laundering Specialists (ACAMS). *International Glossary of Key Terms and Acronyms*, Miami, FL, 2005. http://www.acams.org/Home/; http://www.assetrecovery.org/kc/node/786c5ae2-5c7c-11dd-8c6a-7bd68e2d933e.html.

Bassiouni, M. Cherif. "Legal Control of International Terrorism: A Policy-Oriented Assessment." *Harvard International Law Journal* 43 (2002): 83–103.Bowles, William. "Big Brother is Acting." Centre for Research on Globalisation. October 12, 2004. http://www.globalresearch.ca/articles/BOW410A.html.

Bassiouni, M. Cherif. "International Crimes: The Ratione Materiae of International Criminal Law." In *International Criminal Law: Multilateral and Bilateral Enforcement Mechanisms*, edited by M. Cherif Bassiouni, 129–204, 3rd ed., vol. 2. Leiden, The Netherlands: Martinus Nijhoff Publishers, 2008.

Federal Register. [Presidential Documents] "Military Order of November 13, 2001: Detention, Treatment, and Trial of Certain Non-Citizens in the War Against Terrorism." Vol. 66, No. 222, November 16, 2001, 57831–36. http://www.fas.org/irp/offdocs/eo/mo-111301.htm.

Kanter, James. "E.U. Tries to Balance Terror War and Privacy." *New York Times*, June 16, 2010. http://www.nytimes.com/2010/06/16/world/europe/16swift.html.

Lehmkuhler, S. "Countering Terrorist Financing: We Need a Long-Term Prioritizing Strategy." *Journal of Homeland Security* (April 2003). http://paneir.blogspot.com/2011/11/countering-terrorist-financing-we-need.html.

Maged, Adel. "International Legal Cooperation: An Essential Tool in the War against Terrorism." In *Terrorism and the Military: International Legal Implications*, edited by Wybo P. Heere, 157–80. The Hague: T.M.C., Asser Press, 2003.

Shane, Scott, and Eric Schmitt. "Norway Announces Three Arrests in Terrorist Plot." *New York Times*, July 9, 2010, p. A4.

Terwillinger, George J., III, Theodore Cooperstein, Shawn Gunnarson, Daniel Blumenthal, and Robert Parker. "The War on Terrorism: Law Enforcement or National Security?" National Security White Papers, February 15, 2005. http://www.fed-soc.org/publications/detail/the-war-on-terrorism-law-enforcement-or-national-security. .

United Nations. Security Council Resolution 1373 of 21 December 2001. United Nations Document S/2001/1237.

U.S.–EU Mutual Legal Assistance Agreement [Ireland]. 2005. http://www.statewatch.org/news/2005/aug/ireland-usa-mlat.pdf.

International Legal Framework to Eliminate Terrorism against Civil Aviation and Maritime Targets

Barbara Janusz-Pawletta

There is no universal and legally binding definition of terrorism. Indeed, the definition of terrorism varies among nations, governmental agencies, federal and state law enforcement, the military services, and ordinary citizens. Today's antiterrorist legislation was developed primarily by the efforts of the United Nations (UN) after World War II. The UN

Security Council (Resolution 1368, 2001; Resolution 1373, 2001), the UN General Assembly (Resolution 60/288, 2006), and regional bodies such as the Council of Europe (Warsaw Convention 2005) and European Union (European Union Counter-terrorism Strategy, 2005) have condemned terrorism but do not define it. Neither is there a binding legal concept of terrorism against civil aviation and maritime targets.

DEFINING TERRORISM

The problem of reaching a universally acceptable definition of terrorism is of immense legal significance. Labeling an act as "terrorist" delineates its legal assessment, the scope of provisions to be applied to it, and, finally, an adequate punishment according to provisions and statutes of international law. Much disagreement exists among states regarding the term *terrorism* and what constitutes a terrorist act. Despite years of efforts (the United Nations Ad Hoc Committee on International Terrorism has been drafting a comprehensive convention on international terrorism since 2000) the international community has not been able to reach a universally acceptable international treaty on terrorism. Moreover, there is no political consensus regarding some terrorism-related issues, for example, state terrorism and violence perpetrated during wars of national liberation. The lack of a universally acceptable definition of terrorism raises some important issues such as a specific act's criminal liability and prosecution and may also negatively affect multilateral cooperation in combating it.

Present-day international antiterrorism conventions condemn acts popularly referred to as *terroristic* but do not explicitly use the term *terrorism* to describe them. These treaties are not comprehensive in scope in that they address specific acts such as offenses against internationally protected persons, the taking of hostages, the protection and trafficking of dangerous materials (e.g., nuclear and plastic explosives), nuclear terrorism, and acts against civil aviation. However, these antiterrorism conventions are not universally binding, nor do they constitute mandatory legal custom, which can be derived only from individual state legislative bodies (Symonides 2001). Nevertheless, the UN conventions have cited relevant characteristics of terrorism such as unlawful violence, political motivations, actions targeting innocent victims, and certain tactics.

Regarding the legal consequences of acts of terrorism, it seems that a state's inherent right to self-defense enshrined in the UN Charter (Article 51) cannot justify a state's unilateral actions in responding militarily to such acts (Franck 2001). Terrorist attacks do not equate to an "armed attack" as defined in the UN Charter, nor should they trigger an armed conflict. Hence, a terrorist attack by a nonstate entity, organized group, or individual should not serve as a basis for state military action against another sovereign state. Terrorist attacks do not constitute war in the legal sense; therefore, the phrase *war on terrorism* is void of any lawful meaning.

The only exception allowed under Article 51 of the UN Charter is in the case of a terrorist act attributable to a state (International Court of Justice 2005, 168; International Court of Justice 1984, 392). Article 51 of the UN Charter appears to be a sound international instrument for addressing state use of military force. Moreover, it is this author's opinion that acts of terrorism should be addressed by domestic criminal law provisions and statutes.

TERRORISM AGAINST CIVIL AVIATION: INTERNATIONAL INSTRUMENTS

Acts of terrorism against civil aviation are part of the terrorism phenomenon and are directed against and threaten the safety of international aviation (Galicki 1981, 34). Civil aviation was first covered by a special set of sectoral international rules on combating terrorism. For example, the provisions of the Chicago Convention of December 7, 1944, established one general rule for protecting aircraft against such acts: obliging states to adopt measures to ensure that every aircraft flying over or maneuvering within its territory and every aircraft carrying its nationality mark, wherever such aircraft may be, shall comply with the rules and regulations relating to the flight and maneuver of aircraft there in force (Article 12). Only in the 1960s and 1970s, after a series of aircraft hijackings, did the issue of air transport safety become a major international concern. This concern led to the adoption of four international treaties signed under the auspices of the International Civil Aviation Organization.

The Aircraft Convention (United Nations 1963) is applicable with respect to offenses "against penal law" (Article 1.1a) as well as acts that, whether or not they are offenses, may or do endanger "the safety of the aircraft or of persons or property therein or which jeopardize good order and discipline on board" (Article 1.1b). This excludes aircraft used by "military, customs or police services" (Article 1.4). This convention applies to "offences committed or acts done by a person onboard . . . while that aircraft is in flight or on the surface of the high seas or of any other area outside the territory of any State" (Article 1.2). The jurisdiction over such offenses and acts is to be exercised by the "State of Registration of the aircraft" (Article 3.1). Additionally, another state "may not interfere with an aircraft in flight" except when the offense impacts on another state's territory, permanent resident, or the "security of such State" (Article 4c).

The Unlawful Seizure Convention of 1970 limited and specified the scope of offenses committed against air transport. It makes it unlawful to forcibly seize, or exercise control of, an aircraft, as well as to threaten, attempt, or be an accomplice in such acts. "The Convention does not exclude any criminal jurisdiction exercised in accordance with national law" (Article 4, 3).

Therefore, the treaty gives greater assurance that a perpetrator will not escape punishment. However, it simultaneously complicates the dispensation of justice by according jurisdictional competences to a number of states (United Nations 1973).

The Civil Aviation Convention of 1971 forbids unlawful and intentional acts of violence (including attempts or support for these acts) that are likely to endanger a flight's safety and that are performed against a person onboard an aircraft in flight or an aircraft in service causing damage that renders it incapable of flight or that place on an aircraft in service a device that is likely to destroy that aircraft or to cause damage that renders it incapable of flight. This convention also applies to air navigation facilities and covers communications that the perpetrator knows to be false, thereby endangering the safety of an aircraft in flight (United Nations 1971). The Airport Protocol of 1988 extended the catalog of offenses against air transport to include unlawful acts performed in airports (United Nations 1988).

In 1991, the international community adopted the Plastic Explosives Convention as a result of a series of attacks on aircrafts that utilized such materials. The goal of this treaty was not to penalize new forms of terrorism but rather to strengthen the protection against these acts in all life spheres, not only in aviation (United Nations 1991).

TERRORISM AND MARITIME TARGETS

Despite some similarities there are differences between terrorism and piracy. While both of these acts threaten the safety of ships and the security of people, the legal ban on piracy was introduced in antiquity while terrorism against maritime targets is a rather new phenomenon. Piracy, as defined in the UN Law of the Sea Convention of 1982 (Article 101), differs from acts of terrorism mainly by the fact that it is committed for personal or private ends, while terrorist acts are perpetrated primarily for political or social reasons. A major impetus for adopting international maritime regulations against terrorist acts on the high seas was the hijacking by Palestinian terrorists of the Italian cruise ship *Achille Lauro* in October 1986. As a result of this incident the UN Convention for the Suppression of Unlawful Acts of Violence against the Safety of Maritime Navigation (1988) was adopted under the auspices of the International Maritime Organization and entered into force on March 1, 1992.

The main goal of the convention is to ensure that appropriate action is taken against persons committing intentionally unlawful acts against maritime targets. These include seizing or exercising control over maritime vessels by force, acts of violence against persons on board these vessels, destroying or damaging ships or maritime navigational facilities, and deliberately communicating false information, thereby endangering the safe navigation of a ship. The broad scope of offenses mandated by the convention covers terrorist acts, as well as attempts and threats, and also applies to those who render assistance or encourage such acts. The convention does not apply to warships and other government vessels operated for noncommercial purposes. However, the convention does obligate states to either extradite or prosecute persons who have committed such acts (United Nations 1992).

The Fixed Platform Protocol also entered into force on March 1, 1992, and extends the requirements of the convention to offenses committed onboard or against fixed platforms located on the continental shelf. The shortcoming of this protocol is a rather limited understanding regarding the conception of a "fixed platform." It is defined as an artificial island, installation, or structure permanently attached to the seabed for the purpose of exploration or exploitation of resources or for other economic purposes. Restrictive application of the law's protection to platforms that serve economic interests disregards protection of similar constructions, for example, platforms constructed for scientific purposes. Any act of terrorism against platforms located in territorial waters falls under the jurisdiction and protection of the coastal state (United Nations 1992).

CONCLUSION

A more comprehensive and universally binding antiterrorism law is warranted. It is important to note that such legislation cannot infringe on basic human rights and freedoms; nor can it serve as an excuse for a state to limit these rights (UN General Assembly Resolutions 50/186 (1995) and 62/159 (2007); Council of Europe Resolution 1400 (2004); *Takhayeva and Others v. Russia*). Limitations imposed on human rights and freedoms must not be rooted in current political necessities but in existing law. This assumption was strengthened by the judgments of the constitutional courts of Germany (Bund für vereinfachte Rechtschreibung 357/05, 2006, para. 1–156) and Poland (Dziennik Ustaw 1095, 2008, No. 177). They overruled an empowerment allowing the state authorities to use force in the case of a "renegade flight." Their reasoning was that the right to life cannot be measured and weighed out in law. There is a customary law, binding on all states and repeated in the 1944 Chicago Convention (Article 3 bis), preventing states from resorting to the use of weapons against civil aircraft, thereby endangering airline passengers. However, some states try to override existing legal regulations in favor of their own interpretation of convention provisions, which is often based on their own unique security concerns. The international community needs to collectively engage in meaningful dialogue to assess whether the legal measures cited in the preceding have enhanced air and maritime safety.

See also: **Volume 1, Part III:** Threat Perception and Multinational Cooperation. **Part IV:** United Nations Global Counterterrorism Strategy: Significance and

Limitations. **Part VI:** Multilateral Approach to Counterterrorism: Issues, Problems, Responses; Preemptive Counterterrorism: The Need for a Global Integrated Approach

REFERENCES

Additional Protocol to the Geneva Conventions of 12 August 1949, and relating to the Protection of Victims of International Armed Conflicts (Protocol I) from 1977.

Additional Protocol to the Geneva Conventions of 12 August 1949, and relating to the Protection of Victims of Non-international Armed Conflicts (Protocol II) from 1977.

Arab Convention on the Suppression of Terrorism of 22 April 1998.

Bund für vereinfachte Rechtschreibung, 1 BvR 357/05 of 15 February 2006, para. 1–156.

Convention of the Organization of the Islamic Conference on Combating International Terrorism of 1 July 1999.

Council of Europe. Recommendation no. R (82) 1 of the Committee of Ministers to member states concerning international co-operation in the prosecution and punishment of acts of terrorism of 15 January 1982.

Council of Europe. *Human Rights and the Fight against Terrorism—The Guidelines of the Council of Europe.* 2002 and 2005. http://www.coe.int/t/e/human_rights/Guidelines%20compendium%20ENG.pdf.

Council of Europe. Parliamentary Assembly Resolution 1400 (2004) and Recommendation 1677 (2004) on the Challenge of Terrorism in Council of Europe Member States.

Council of Europe Convention on the Prevention of Terrorism of May 16, 2005, European Treaty Series No. 196.

Council of the European Union. "Council Common Position of 27 December 2001 on Combating Terrorism 2001/930/CFSP." Official Journal of the European Communities, Aberdeen, UK: Millstream Associates, December 28, 2001. http://eur-lex.europa.eu/LexUriServ/LexUriServ.do?uri=OJ:L:2001:344:0090:0092:EN:PDF.

Council of the European Union. "Council Framework Decision of 13 June 2002 on Combating Terrorism 2002/475/JHA." Official Journal of the European Communities, Aberdeen, UK: Millstream Associates, June 22, 2002. http://eur-lex.europa.eu/LexUriServ/LexUriServ.do?uri=OJ:L:2002:164:0003:0003:EN:PDF.

Council of the European Union. "European Union Counter-Terrorism Strategy." 14469/4/05 REV4, Brussels, Belgium: Council of the European Union, November 30, 2005. http://register.consilium.eu.int/pdf/en/05/st14/st14469-re04.en05.pdf.

Dziennik Ustaw Official Journal of the Laws of 7 November 2008, no. 177, item 1095.

European Court of Human Rights. *Takhayeva and Others v. Russia,* Judgement of the European Court of Human Rights of 18 September 2008. Strasbourg, France. http://www.echr.coe.int/ECHR/Homepage_EN.

Franck, T. "Terrorism and the Right of Self-Defence." *American Journal of International Law* 95 (2001): 839.

Galicki, Zdzislaw. *Air Terrorism in international law.* Warsaw, Poland: University of Warsaw, 1981.

Geneva Convention (I) for the Amelioration of the Condition of the Wounded and Sick in Armed Forces in the Field, 1949.

Geneva Convention (II) for the Amelioration of the Condition of Wounded, Sick and Shipwrecked Members of Armed Forces at Sea, 1949.

Geneva Convention (III) relative to the Treatment of Prisoners of War, 1949.

Geneva Convention (IV) relative to the Protection of Civilian Persons in Time of War, 1949.

International Court of Justice. Military and Paramilitary Activities in and against Nicaragua (*Nicaragua v. United States of America*), Jurisdiction and Admissibility, Judgment. International Court of Justice Reports (1984): 392.

International Court of Justice. Legal Consequences of the Construction of a Wall in the Occupied Palestinian Territory, Advisory Opinion. International Court of Justice Reports (2004): 219–34, separate opinion of Judge Kooijmans. http://www.icj-cij.org/docket/files/131/1683.pdf.

International Criminal Tribunal for the Former Yugoslavia. *Prosecutor v. Dusko Tadic aka "Dule"* (Decision on the Defence Motion for Interlocutory Appeal on Jurisdiction), IT-94-1, International Criminal Tribunal for the Former Yugoslavia (ICTY), of 2 October 1995. http://www.icty.org/.

Organization of African Union Convention on the Prevention and Combating of Terrorism of 14 July 1999 and the Protocol to that Convention, of July 2004.

Organization of American States, Convention to Prevent and Punish Acts of Terrorism Taking the Form of Crimes against Persons and Related Extortion that are of International Significance of 2 February 1971.

South Asian Association for Regional Cooperation Regional Convention on Suppression of Terrorism of 4 November 1987.

Symonides, J. "International Legal Aspects of Combating Terrorism." *Sprawy Międzynarodowe* 4 (2001): 26.

Treaty on Cooperation among States Members of the Commonwealth of Independent States in Combating Terrorism, of June 1999.

United Nations. Aircraft Convention—Convention on Offences and Certain Other Acts Committed on Board Aircraft from 1963. United Nations Treaty Series, no. 10106 (1969): 220.

United Nations. Unlawful Seizure Convention—Convention for the Suppression of Unlawful Seizure of Aircraft from 1970. United Nations Treaty Series, no. 12325 (1973): 106.

United Nations. Civil Aviation Convention—Convention for the Suppression of Unlawful Acts against the Safety of Civil Aviation from 1971. United Nations Treaty Series, vol. 974, no. 14118 (1975): 178.

United Nations. Protection of Diplomats Convention—Convention on the Prevention and Punishment of Crimes against Internationally Protected Persons, including Diplomatic Agents of 1973. United Nations Treaty Series, vol. 1035, no. 15410 (1977): 168.

United Nations. Convention on the Law of the Sea. Ocean and Law of the Sea, Division for Ocean Affairs and the Law of the Sea, December 10, 1982. http://www.un.org/depts/los/convention_agreements/convention_overview_convention.htm.

United Nations. Hostages Convention—International Convention against the Taking of Hostages from 1979. United Nations Treaty Series, vol. 1316, no. 21931 (1983): 206.

United Nations. Nuclear Materials Convention—Convention on the Physical Protection of Nuclear Material from 1979. United Nations Treaty Series, vol. 1589, no. 24631 (1987): 125.

United Nations. Airport Protocol—Protocol for the Suppression of Unlawful Acts of Violence at Airports Serving International Civil Aviation, supplementary to the Convention for the Suppression of Unlawful Acts against the Safety of Civil Aviation from 1988. United Nations Treaty Series, vol. 1035, no. 14118 (1990): 474.

United Nations. Convention on the Marking of Plastic Explosives for the Purpose of Detection, 1991. http://treaties.un.org/doc/db/Terrorism/Conv10-english.pdf.

United Nations. Convention for the Suppression of Unlawful Acts against the Safety of Maritime Navigation (1988). United Nations Treaty Series, vol. 1678, no. 29004 (1992): 222. (And Additional Protocol, 2005.)

United Nations. Protocol for the Suppression of Unlawful Acts against the Safety of Fixed Platforms Located on the Continental Shelf. United Nations Treaty Series, vol. 1678, no. 29004 (1992): 304. (And Protocol to the Protocol, 2005.)

United Nations General Assembly. "Human Rights and Terrorism," A/RES/50/186, 99th plenary meeting, December 22, 1995. http://www.un.org/documents/ga/res/50/a50r186.htm.

United Nations. Terrorism Financing Convention—International Convention for the Suppression of the Financing of Terrorism, 1999. http://treaties.un.org/doc/db/Terrorism/english-18-11.pdf.

United Nations. Terrorist Bombing Convention—International Convention for the Suppression of Terrorist Bombing.1997. http://treaties.un.org/doc/db/Terrorism/english-18-9.pdf.

United Nations. International Convention for the Suppression of Acts of Nuclear Terrorism, 2005. http://treaties.un.org/doc/db/Terrorism/english-18-15.pdf.

United Nations General Assembly. "Protection of Human Rights and Fundamental Freedoms while Countering Terrorism." A/RES/62/159, 76th plenary meeting, December 18, 2007. http://daccess-dds-ny.un.org/doc/UNDOC/GEN/N07/473/31/PDF/N0747331.pdf?OpenElement.

United Nations Ad Hoc Committee established by General Assembly Resolution 51/210 of 17 December 1996. Report from Fourteenth Session (12–16 April 2010), General Assembly Official Records, Sixty-fifth Session, Supplement no. 37.

Joint Terrorism Task Forces

Mathieu Deflem

Joint terrorism task forces (JTTFs) are cooperative counterterrorism forces consisting of officers drawn from multiple police and security agencies.

They constitute the most central law enforcement means by which terrorist activities are investigated in the United States. JTTFs are organized and managed by the Federal Bureau of Investigation (FBI), the primary U.S. law enforcement organization responsible for counterterrorism cases, but they are comprised of officers from many different law enforcement agencies, including other federal police and security agencies (such as the U.S. Coast Guard, Immigration and Customs Enforcement, and Customs and Border Protection), regional law enforcement agencies (including state and municipal police agencies), and other first-responder organizations.

COUNTERTERRORISM MISSION

JTTFs engage in all aspects of a counterterrorism investigation, including following up on information and leads, gathering evidence, collecting intelligence, and making arrests. JTTFs thus seek to fulfill reactive objectives to respond to and investigate terrorist cases as well as to be proactively engaged in counterterrorism efforts by seeking to deter and prevent terrorist activity. Additionally, JTTFs provide security at special events, such as mass sports gatherings, and organize counterterrorism training for law enforcement personnel. Presently, about 100 JTTFs are operating across the territory of the United States, with at least one task force in each FBI field office. These various JTTFs are locally organized and coordinate their respective efforts through a National Joint Terrorism Task Force that is located at the FBI headquarters in Washington, D.C. In total, almost 4,000 officers are working in JTTFs, with a little over half of those coming from the FBI itself.

JTTFs exemplify the centrality that is accorded to interagency cooperation in the organization of counterterrorism police work in the United States. At the governmental level, the emphasis on cooperation is demonstrated by the creation of the Department of Homeland Security, which brings together a multitude of counterterrorism and security agencies. At the level of police, cooperation is articulated in various interagency partnerships, such as the Border Enforcement Security Task Forces under the direction of U.S. Immigration and Customs Enforcement, the Integrated Border Enforcement Teams under the supervision of U.S. Customs and Border Protection, and the FBI-run JTTFs. The first JTTF was set up in New York City in 1980 in response to domestic terrorism coming from ethnonationalist groups. This first, small task force consisted of some 11 FBI special agents and 11 detectives from the New York City Police Department. In the wake of the terrorist attacks of September 11, 2001, the strategy of employing JTTFs was considerably expanded. No less than 65 (out of 100) task forces have been created after the events of September 11.

FORCE MULTIPLIER

The main advantage of the JTTF, from the viewpoint of the FBI, is that it serves as a so-called force multiplier because many of the agents in a JTTF are recruited from other agencies, yet they work to serve FBI objectives. Thus, the FBI has been able to alleviate some of the budgetary and personnel pressures that had been placed on the bureau by the massive reassignment of its special agents to terrorism cases after the events of September 11. The JTTF is for the FBI primarily a cost-efficient structure of cooperation. From an operational viewpoint, moreover, JTTFs can facilitate communication exchange among various agencies, and they provide integrated enforcement of terrorism investigations. Among police officials, these advantages are conceived of in terms of an objective of "fusion," whereby counterterrorist intelligence can be shared vertically from the FBI's central headquarters to the various local JTTFs as well as horizontally across all participating agencies. It is to be noted that interagency police partnerships such as JTTFs are practical arrangements that are created independently by law enforcement agencies outside the context of legal regulations and irrespective of any political considerations.

It affects the success of JTTF activities that the centrality of cooperation is not always evenly recognized across law enforcement agencies, especially not among local police organizations, which may emphasize other concerns besides terrorism. Most striking in this respect has been the decision to withdraw the local police from participation in a JTTF that had been set up in Portland, Oregon, in the wake of September 11. Among certain community groups in the city, concerns had been raised about the purported overly broad surveillance powers that would be accorded to municipal police officers through participation in the FBI-managed JTTF. Furthermore, it was alleged that local officials would not be able to overlook the activities of the city police agents when they were cooperating with the FBI. These concerns were amplified after FBI agents arrested seven Muslim Americans in the Portland area in October 2002 and April 2003. The arrests, now known as the case of the Portland Seven, not only angered Islamic leaders in the local Oregon community but also fueled anxieties about the potential of counterterrorism law enforcement efforts potentially violating civil rights and relying on problematic surveillance methods, such as racial profiling tactics.

CONCLUSION

In 2005, then newly elected mayor Tom Potter eventually led a successful effort to withdraw the Portland Police Bureau from participation in the JTTF. Despite such occasional criticisms and obstacles, however, JTTFs remains the primary structure through which U.S. police investigate terrorist activity in the United States.

See also: **Volume 1, Part I:** Definition and Dimensions of Counterterrorism. **Part III:** Border, Port, and Transportation Security; Countering Weapons of Mass Destruction (WMD); Counterterrorism Training; Crisis Management: The Public Health System. **Part IV:** U.S. Legislative Initiatives to Combat Terrorism pre-911; U.S. Legislative Initiatives to Combat Terrorism since 9/11. **Volume 2, Part I:** Hostage Rescue Team (United States); NYPD Counter Terrorism Division (United States)

REFERENCES

Deflem, Mathieu. *The Policing of Terrorism: Organizational and Global Perspectives.* New York: Routledge, 2010.

Erickson, Kris, John Carr, and Steve Herbert. "The Scales of Justice: Federal-Local Tensions in the War on Terror." In *Uniform Behavior: Police Localism and National Politics,* edited by S. K. McGoldrick and A. McArdle, 231–53. New York: Palgrave-Macmillan, 2006.

Herman, Susan N. "Collapsing Spheres: Joint Terrorism Task Forces, Federalism, and the War on Terror." *Willamette Law Review* 41 (2005): 941–69.

Murphy, Gerard R., and Martha R. Plotkin. *Protecting Your Community from Terrorism: Strategies for Local Law Enforcement,* The Strategies for Local Law Enforcement Series, Vol. 1, Local-Federal Partnerships. Washington, DC: Police Executive Research Forum, 2003. http://www.au.af.mil/au/awc/awcgate/doj/prot_cmty_fm_terr_1a.pdf.

Lessons of Afghanistan and Iraq

Chamila S. Liyanage

The attacks in New York and Washington on September 11, 2001, changed the strategic threat outlook of the post–Cold War era and marked a new phase of international conflicts ranging from threats produced by failed states to dispersed networks of terror cells. The new strategic threat outlook pressured the Bush administration to act on foreseeable security challenges, which led to the invasion of Afghanistan in October 2001 and of Iraq in March 2003. In the aftermath of the interventions, the United States and its allies found themselves facing a difficult challenge confronting the deep-rooted social, economic, and political issues of two Muslim countries.

BACKGROUND

"We are content with discord, we are content with alarms, we are content with blood . . . but we will never be content with a master" (Macintyre 2008). This cliché of an old man in Afghanistan describes quite succinctly Afghanistan's age-old mindset. Afghanistan has been a country caught up in external power rivalries. Internally, it has experienced sustained struggles between various warring factions competing for power and land. Afghanistan was at the center of the Cold War power struggles, which substantially defined its post–Cold War development. While the post–Cold War world started to experience a relative paradigm shift on the political, economic, social, and ideological fronts with the growing influence of globalization, Afghanistan submerged into religious medievalism under the Taliban. The Afghan Taliban, who first appeared as saviors of rural Afghan interests, were by the late 1990s in control of most of the country and had established a fanatic theocracy, which impacted regional as well as global security. In a very real sense, Afghanistan under the Taliban created the preconditions that eventually led to the American invasion in October 2001.

In Iraq, the authoritarian regime of Saddam Hussein maintained a divisive power base crushing rival political dissent. Hussein's famous dictum exemplifies his political outlook: "Keep your eyes on your enemy and be faster than him" (Hussein 2002; Borisov 2002). Hussein's government was responsible for many atrocities against Shiite and Kurdish populations in Iraq. The Ba'ath Party, a Socialist movement influenced by pan-Arab nationalism, was a powerful rallying ground, but at the same time Iraq was riddled with clashing sectarian divisions, regional disputes, and mounting tensions with the Western world prior to the American invasion in March 2003.

Domestic support for the invasions of both Afghanistan and Iraq gathered momentum because of the changing threat scenario and somewhat clouded judgments in the wake of the unprovoked September 11 attacks on the U.S. homeland. It became a convincing argument that unless the threats beyond our borders were addressed, it would not be possible to be safe at home. Therefore, the events of September 11, growing religious extremism, and the belief that Hussein's regime had acquired and was in the process of developing weapons of mass destruction (WMD) all contributed to the invasions of Afghanistan and Iraq. Following the invasion of both countries, the consequences and implications of these actions revealed the complexity of the challenges undertaken more clearly than had the initial plans.

LESSONS OF IRAQ

A crucial lesson of the Iraq invasion is the importance of verified facts, credible intelligence, and cutting-edge threat assessments. Most important, a careful assessment and analysis of intelligence needs to be carried out before it is presented to those responsible for implementing plans of action. Additionally, an awareness of various trigger factors that can misrepresent information and obscure sound judgment is equally important.

The Iraq invasion did not receive much support from key European allies except the United Kingdom. It is worth assessing the importance of consent building to maintain agreement among allies. Collective will is not impossible to achieve if key allies can be convinced through credible and verifiable facts that a threat does indeed exist. It is important to be aware of different perspectives and approaches and their impact on dynamic situations. As U.S. Navy admiral and former chairman of the joint chiefs of staff Mike Mullen (2010) once stated, "The importance of understanding challenges from someone else's perspective becomes more and more evident to me with each passing day." Slight differences of perception can lead to major drifts and intractable conflicts.

Awareness of the consequences of using coercion as a main strategic arm of foreign policy is another critical lesson that needs to be examined. The state of Iraq collapsed as a result of the 2003 invasion. One of the most important challenges in the postinvasion era is the rebuilding of sustainable state machinery capable of integrating sectarian divisions. If the state does not integrate divisions though consent building and power sharing, the infighting and the subsequent possibility of a civil war in Iraq will create more national challenges and ultimately have adverse repercussions on regional and global security.

The long-held American enthusiasm for nation building is another lesson that needs to be reevaluated. Western views of nation building are not always compatible with the ground realities and the deep-rooted structural and cultural factors in countries such as Iraq. State building is a more pragmatic option in this case. State building through the strengthening of democratic institutions can be viable only if the new state political apparatus is established on the principle of inclusion rather than divisiveness. The state's ability to include opposing factions indicates at least the beginning stages of a workable democracy. Similarly, it is necessary to develop an outlook that defines Iraq's present-day ground realities. Political reconstruction in Iraq will not be achieved through shortcuts or halfhearted measures. It has to find ways to address and accommodate the factors that fragmented the society and the polity. The dilemma of integration in Iraq arises from a fragmented structure that long sustained a political culture of sectarian hostility. It is not a superficial fragmentation but rather a historically rooted, politically maintained, and socially established practice of power politics. The Iraq government needs to gain public support and establish trust in domestic politics in order to become a viable democracy. It is about acknowledging, implementing, and facilitating policies that promote unity among rival factions in order to ease the deep-rooted and historically divisive tensions among various groups.

It is also important to consider how far the United States and its allies can commit manpower, time, and national treasure to deal with the prolonged and difficult task of postwar reconstruction and, perhaps more important, the critical task of facilitating a democracy within a long-practiced autocracy. It should have been a preinvasion issue to consider the monumental task of transforming a polity that is founded on sectarian hostility into a viable democracy. Factors such as religious and cultural divisions can continue to tear at the social fabric thereby presenting greater challenges to pluralist integration.

It is necessary to have a realistic assessment of the resources and capacity needed to facilitate the potentially prolonged and challenging task of Iraq reconstruction. It is also important to focus on strengthening democratic ideals and values. Democratic institutions need an underlying set of values to create the social contract between the government and the governed. Democratic mobilization at the grassroots level can best support the transformation process. If not, the discrepancy between implanted democratic institutions and the preexisting authoritarian ideals can continue to create complications.

Massachusetts Senator John Kerry (2005) stated, "History will judge the invasion of Iraq as one of the greatest foreign policy misadventures of all time." Even if this statement is based on facts, transforming Iraq into at least a functioning democracy is a responsibility and an obligation that was acquired when the former regime was toppled in 2003. Perhaps the most profound lesson of Iraq was the lack of a carefully thought-out plan for the country during the postinvasion phase and the depth of commitment any outside force can face in trying to establish a viable democracy. Sophisticated threat analysis and consequence assessments that are based on sound intelligence are vital factors when decisions involving regime change are being assessed. Contemporary events have shown that these changes are best accomplished internally. In Iraq, it is necessary to build on and maximize favorable ground factors while simultaneously containing and managing numerous threats and challenges to allied forces as well as the new Iraqi government. Postwar political changes are often a prolonged and difficult process requiring an inordinate amount of work and the cooperation of civil society. When the institutions, economy, and civil society need to be rebuilt to facilitate a democratic polity, the task can be long-lasting and more complex than anticipated.

LESSONS OF AFGHANISTAN

Afghanistan has been viewed by many as a justifiable war and therefore received wide national and international support. Many members of the international community have shared the responsibility for reconstruction and developmental assistance in this war-ravaged and impoverished state. There has never been a substantial space for a modern democratic upspring in Afghanistan. Moreover, political turmoil has prevented the country from achieving sustainable social, political, and economic advancement. Thus, Afghanistan is one of the world's least developed countries. For the past several decades Afghanistan has been continuously under the grip of warring factions, sectarian power struggles, and foreign power politics. Some of the many challenges facing reconstruction are antigovernment factions, the drug trade, and the corruption of public officials at all levels of government. Therefore, periodic threat, risk, and feasibility assessments are necessary to ensure that preestablished goals are effectively realized.

Reconstruction and the establishment of a stable government in Afghanistan are a multifaceted undertaking. This process is not only peace building; it is about building a country from scratch. Initially, Afghanistan needs to build a sustainable economy and a political system that can meet the demands and daily necessities of the Afghan people. It needs to build its civil society, the space that is continuously crushed by foreign and internal actors. Economic development and its challenges are at the center of Afghanistan's reconstruction efforts. However, this cannot occur without a modicum of security and domestic stability. Afghanistan's future depends on how it "responds to the challenge of globalisation and constructs a viable economic system" (Riphenburg 2006, 507). Transforming a country that has survived on opium cultivation, the illegal smuggling of licit consumer products, and corruption is a major challenge. It is equally important to find ways to promote pluralism, a distant idea in Afghanistan, and democratic values within a theocratic sociocultural legacy.

State building has, thus far, been relatively successful even though antidemocratic practices and corruption are widespread. Nation building is the dilemma in Afghanistan. The society is deeply fragmented along sectarian allegiances. Power struggles among different factions and allegiances, which often shift, have defined the country and its history. Therefore, it is imperative that the current national government promote a political process of inclusion, eliminate regional power vacuums, and establish the rule of law that applies to all citizens of Afghanistan.

Current issues in Afghanistan cannot be effectively addressed without controlling various extremist factions, warlords, and the war economy of narcotics. The British-supported scheme to distribute wheat seeds in Helmand province as an alternative to poppy growing was a strong grassroots intervention. Afghanistan needs multipronged interventions in many identified domestic issue areas. Assistance in areas such as crop substitution, alternative livelihood strategies, and the provision of basic services can help strengthen the process of reconstruction. Other important considerations arise from the regional context. Regional interests play a vital role in the stability of Afghanistan and its ultimate success in becoming a self-sustaining state. Undercurrents of regional interests have the potential to destabilize current developments while strengthening extremist factions inside and outside the country. Matt Waldman's 2010 discussion paper portrays a clear view of the regional political dynamics that can weaken the ongoing process of transformation in Afghanistan.

Another difficult task is containing domestic and Pakistan-based terrorism and religious extremism and its negative impact on the Afghan society, governance, and economy.

CONCLUSION

Regional interests, fractured domestic institutions, government corruption, and globally affiliated networks of extremist groups all create conditions that can cause the reconstruction process in Afghanistan to deteriorate. That said, notable progress has been made on the political, economic, and social fronts since 2001. However, the present and future challenges facing Afghanistan and the international community remain enormous.

See also: **Volume 1, Part I:** Insurgent Terrorism; War on Terror. **Part III:** Ideology That Spawns Islamist Militancy; Just War Doctrine; Military Force: Effective against Terrorists?; Organizational Resilience and Counterterrorism; Psychological Operations; Safe Havens and Weak and Failing States; Terrorists, Criminals, and Drug Cartels; The United States, Iraq, and the Global Terrorism Problem. **Part IV:** Central Asia: Emerging Threats; Combating Religiously Based Terrorism; Eliminating Terrorist Support Networks; Pakistan's Federally Administered Tribal Areas (FATA). **Part VI:** Afghanistan: Present and Future Challenges; Global Jihad Movement; Multilateral Approach to Counterterrorism: Issues, Problems, Responses; Regional Challenges: Promoting Stability through Economic, Social, and Political Reforms; Understanding Foreign Cultures

REFERENCES

Borisov, Sergey. "Saddam Hussein's Book of Wisdom." *Pravda.ru*, December 18, 2002. http://english.pravda.ru/world/ussr/18-12-2002/1665-iraq-0/.

Hussein, Saddam. *Great Lessons, Commandments to Strugglers, the Patient and Holy Warriors.* Baghdad, Iraq: Iraq Information Ministry, 2002.

Kerry, John. "Senator John Kerry Lays Out Path Forward in Iraq." *Global Security*, October 26, 2005. http://www.globalsecurity.org/wmd/library/news/iraq/2005/10/051026-kerry01.htm.

Macintyre, Ben. "The Harsh Lesson of Afghanistan: Little Has Changed in 200 Years." *The Times*, November 13, 2008. http://www.timesonline.co.uk/tol/comment/columnists/ben_macintyre/article5141513.ece.

Mullen, Mike. "Objective Analysis, Leadership Needed in Today's World, Adm. Mike Mullen Says." *RAND Corporation.* June 17, 2010. http://www.rand.org/news/press/2010/06/17.html.

Riphenburg, Carolos J. "Afghanistan: Out of the Globalisation Mainstream." *Third World Quarterly* 27, no. 3 (2006): 507–24.

Waldman, Matt. "The Sun in the Sky: The Relationship between Pakistan's ISI and Afghan Insurgents." *Foreign Policy.* 2010. http://www.foreignpolicy.com/files/fp_uploaded_documents/100613_20106138531279734lse-isi-taliban.pdf.

Pakistan's Federally Administered
Tribal Areas (FATA)

Matthew H. Wahlert

The Federally Administered Tribal Areas (FATA) of Pakistan make up 10,510 square miles (27,220 square kilometers) and include a 370-mile (600-kilometer) border with Afghanistan. The FATA are home to approximately 3.17 million inhabitants, primarily of Pashtun origin, and border the Pakistan Northwest Frontier Province. After the U.S. attacks on al-Qaeda and Taliban strongholds in Afghanistan beginning in October 2001, the FATA quickly emerged as a new front for the war on terrorism. In 2002, the FATA became a safe haven for Islamist militants from al-Qaeda and the Taliban and a base for homegrown Pakistani militants.

UNGOVERNED TRIBAL AREAS

The FATA includes seven administrative agencies:

Bajour (500 square miles [1,290 square kilometers], with a population of 595,000)

Khyber (995 square miles [2,576 square kilometers], population 547,000)

Kurram (995 square miles [2,576 square kilometers], population 450,000)

Mohmand (886 square miles [2,296 square kilometers], population 334,000)

Orakzai (594 square miles [1,538 square kilometers], population 225,000)

South Waziristan (2,556 square miles [6,620 square kilometers], population 430,000)

North Waziristan (1,817 square miles [4,707 square kilometers], population 361,000)

Life in the FATA follows Pashtun tribal traditions that date back hundreds of years. *Pashtunwali,* the behavioral code, guides conduct, which includes *nanawati* (hospitality cannot be denied) and *badal* (the right of revenge).

The colonial legal system, dating to 1901, employs a bureaucratic model of governance. Specifically, FATA bureaucrats report to the Pakistani president, and enforcement is managed through the Frontier Crimes Regulations. These regulations give no Pakistani constitutional or political rights to the tribesmen in the FATA. Journalists, political parties, and nongovernmental agencies are not permitted in the region. Moreover, the historical lack of political parties allows mullahs to exercise undue political influence. Traditionally, the FATA have served as a historic buffer with Afghanistan. During the Cold War, the Central Intelligence Agency weapons pipeline to Afghanistan went through the FATA—effectively giving Pakistan plausible deniability. In the 1990s, Pakistan was pressured by both India and the United States to close terror training camps in Kashmir but quickly relocated them to the FATA and Afghanistan. Later, the FATA were a key link to Pakistan's material support of the Taliban regime in Afghanistan. Generally, the lack of a defined international border between Pakistan and Afghanistan and the remote geographic position of the region mean that international law does not apply and gives Pakistan a free hand in using the tribes of the FATA to manipulate Afghan affairs.

MILITANT BREEDING GROUND

Pakistani political analyst Ahmed Rashid claims that the FATA became a center for terrorism in December 2001 when Osama bin Laden and his al-Qaeda protectors, followed by the Afghan Taliban, sought sanctuary in the region. In addition, evidence suggests that the former Taliban official Jalaluddin Haqqani hired Wazir and Mahsud tribes to lead al-Qaeda fighters safely out of the Tora Bora region and into the agencies of North and South Waziristan. South Waziristan, due to the influence of al-Qaeda and the Taliban, soon gained the moniker the Islamic Emirate of Waziristan. As a result, Islamic militants from Central Asia, Chechnya, Africa, China, and Kashmir also fled to the FATA. Ultimately, the FATA evolved into a central planning venue for terrorist plots aimed at London, Madrid, Bali, Islamabad, Germany, and Denmark. U.S. Secretary of State Hillary Clinton spoke of the significance of Pakistan when she categorized it as "a mortal threat to the security and safety of our country and the world" ("Clinton" 2009), and U.S. security officials identified the tribal regions of Pakistan as a key variable in the fight against terrorism.

The initial Pakistani base for al-Qaeda and Taliban fighters centered in the town of Angur Adda in South Waziristan where the Taliban and al-Qaeda created their own government based on their Afghan model. Militants quickly targeted and eliminated elders supportive of the United States and Afghanistan. Meanwhile, the Pakistani Inter-Services Agency (ISA) supported Talibanization in order to pressure Afghanistan and the United States. In 2002, al-Qaeda forces would launch attacks on Shikin and Lawara—both U.S. bases in Afghanistan. Often, after a military operation, the al-Qaeda fighters would return to South Waziristan under the protection of cover fire from the Pakistani Frontier Corps (FC). By January 2003, the United States, under the direction of Lieutenant General Dan McNeil, threatened to cross into Pakistan to pursue attackers. Later that year, two assassination attempts aimed at Pervez Musharraf and threats from the al-Qaeda leader Ayman al-Zawahiri led Islamabad to undergo a change of heart regarding the presence of militant groups in the FATA. Pakistan committed to take action against the growing militant threat in South Waziristan.

By 2004, Pakistani officials also faced enormous external pressures to confront the militancy in South Waziristan. Secretary of State Colin Powell issued an ultimatum to Islamabad that Pakistan should act or the United States would. On March 16, 2004, the Pakistani FC attacked a compound in the village of Kalosha. Evidently, al-Qaeda and the Islamic Movement of Uzbekistan had advance warning and waited in ambush. The FC retreated into mosques and individual homes while others were killed and taken hostage. As a result, an estimated 8,000 regular Pakistani troops responded and engaged in two weeks of combat. By the end of the fighting, the FC stood morally defeated, and Waziri militants were the victors. The Pakistani government negotiated and signed an agreement with the Waziri militants on April 24, 2004. Militant leaders were pardoned and foreign fighters allowed to remain as long as they registered with the appropriate authorities. Quickly, the agreement fell apart, and Pakistan redeployed approximately 80,000 FC and military to South Waziristan.

As Pakistan drained the terror swamp in South Waziristan, militants quickly found another willing host in North Waziristan. Violence peaked in September 2004 when Pakistani army units killed 80 in an attack on a madrassa. Ultimately, the Pakistani government settled and paid $200,000 in compensation to the militants. In late 2005, Musharraf replaced the traditional political agents with military officers—effectively cutting the connection between the tribes and the Pakistani government. Taliban forces followed with increased terror in North and South Waziristan. Finally, Pakistani officials reached an agreement with seven Pakistani Taliban leaders on September 5, 2006. Basically, the militants agreed to stop the attacks on U.S., Afghan, and Pakistani military forces. In return, Pakistani officials would remove checkpoints, release equipment, and pay tribesmen for financial losses. In effect, the agreement merely acted to strengthen the Taliban hold in North Waziristan. Specifically, Pakistan would have no enforcement mechanism should Taliban officials violate the agreement. The end result was that attacks on Pakistani forces slowed to a standstill while those on Afghan and U.S. forces increased.

CONCLUSION

The FATA have historically been a significant instrument of Pakistani policy implementation. As of the time of this writing, the FATA promise to continue to hold a primary position in both the U.S. war on terror and internal Pakistani politics.

See also: **Volume 1, Part I:** Concept of Islamist Jihad; Insurgent Terrorism; War on Terror. **Part II:** Pakistan. **Part IV:** Combating Religiously Based Terrorism. **Part VI:** Global Jihad Movement. **Volume 2, Part I:** Special Service Group (Pakistan). **Part II:** Islamabad's Red Mosque (2007); Lahore (2009)

REFERENCES

Baxter, Craig, Yogendra K. Malik, Charles H. Kennedy, and Robert C. Oberst. *Government and Politics in South Asia.* 5th ed. Boulder, CO: Westview, 2002.

Bose, Sugata, and Ayesha Jalal. *Modern South Asia: History, Culture, and Political Economy.* London: Routledge, 1998.

"Clinton: Pakistan 'Mortal Threat' to World." *United Press International,* April 22, 2009. http://www.upi.com/Top_News/2009/04/22/Clinton-Pakistan-mortal-threat-to-world/UPI-34481240421045/.

Haider, Ziad. *The Ideological Struggle for Pakistan.* Stanford, CA: Hoover Institution Press, 2010.

International Crisis Group. *Pakistan's Tribal Areas: Appeasing the Militants.* Asia Report no. 125, December 11, 2006.

Rashid, Ahmed. *Descent into Chaos.* New York: Viking, 2008.

Shaikh, Farzana. *Making Sense of Pakistan.* New York: Colombia University Press, 2009.

Proliferation Security Initiative

Jamie Walsh

The Proliferation Security Initiative (PSI), launched by President George W. Bush on May 31, 2003, is a U.S.-led multinational counterproliferation effort that aims to improve the interdiction of third-party shipments (by land, sea, or air) of biological, chemical, and nuclear weapons, as well as missiles and goods that could be used to deliver or produce such weapons, to terrorists and countries suspected of trying to acquire weapons of mass destruction (WMD). The initiative arose in the post-9/11 security environment and stems from the U.S. National Strategy to Combat Weapons of Mass Destruction issued in December 2002. That strategy recognized the need for more robust tools to stop the proliferation of WMD around the world and specifically identified interdiction as an area where greater focus was needed.

Ten states originally joined the United States at the inception of the PSI in 2003, namely, Australia, France, Germany, Italy, Japan, the Netherlands, Poland, Portugal, Spain, and the United Kingdom. Since then, the number of PSI participants has grown steadily. As of June 2010 the number of PSI participants stands at 97.

STRUCTURE

Like the Global Initiative to Combat Nuclear Terrorism, the PSI is not a formal international organization. The initiative does not have a governing treaty, formal structure, or set of procedures for applying for membership. Nor does the PSI have a distinct funding program or secretariat to coordinate activities.

The initiative is an informal arrangement among states that voluntarily agree to endorse the PSI "Statement of Interdiction Principles," to strengthen and enforce their own nonproliferation laws, and to participate in training activities and interdiction operations. An informal coordinating structure for the PSI has developed through the Operational Experts Group (OEG), which discusses proliferation challenges and plans future exercises. The OEG is cross-disciplinary in nature and is composed of military, law enforcement, intelligence, legal, and diplomatic experts from 20 PSI states. The 20 members of the OEG are Argentina, Australia, Canada, Denmark, France, Germany, Greece, Italy, Japan, the Netherlands, New Zealand, Norway, Poland, Portugal, Russia, Singapore, Spain, Turkey, the United Kingdom, and the United States.

"STATEMENT OF INTERDICTION PRINCIPLES"

The "Statement of Interdiction Principles" calls on participating states to:

1. Undertake effective measures, either alone or in concert with other states, for interdicting the transfer or transport of WMD, their delivery systems, and related materials to and from states and nonstate actors of proliferation concern. "States or non-state actors of proliferation concern" generally refers to those countries or entities that the PSI participants involved establish should be subject to interdiction activities because they are engaged in proliferation through (1) efforts to develop or acquire chemical, biological, or nuclear weapons and associated delivery systems or (2) transfers (either selling, receiving, or facilitating transfers) of WMD, their delivery systems, or related materials.

2. Adopt streamlined procedures for rapid exchange of relevant information concerning suspected proliferation activity, protect the confidential character of classified information provided by other states as part of this initiative, dedicate appropriate resources and efforts to interdiction operations and capabilities, and maximize coordination among participants in interdiction efforts.

3. Review and work to strengthen their relevant national legal authorities where necessary to accomplish these objectives and work to strengthen when necessary relevant international law and frameworks in appropriate ways to support these commitments.

4. Take specific actions in support of interdiction efforts regarding cargoes of WMD, their delivery systems, or related materials, to the extent their national legal authorities permit and consistent with their obligations under international law and frameworks, to include:

   a. Not to transport or assist in the transport of any such cargoes to or from states or nonstate actors of proliferation concern, and not to allow any persons subject to their jurisdiction to do so.

b. At their own initiative, or at the request and good cause shown by another state, to take action to board and search any vessel flying their flag in their internal waters or territorial seas, or areas beyond the territorial seas of any other state, that is reasonably suspected of transporting such cargoes to or from states or nonstate actors of proliferation concern, and to seize such cargoes that are identified.

c. To seriously consider providing consent under the appropriate circumstances to the boarding and searching of its own flag vessels by other states, and to the seizure of such WMD-related cargoes in such vessels that may be identified by such states.

d. To take appropriate actions to (1) stop and/or search in their internal waters, territorial seas, or contiguous zones (when declared) vessels that are reasonably suspected of carrying such cargoes to or from states or nonstate actors of proliferation concern and to seize such cargoes that are identified; and (2) to enforce conditions on vessels entering or leaving their ports, internal waters, or territorial seas that are reasonably suspected of carrying such cargoes, such as requiring that such vessels be subject to boarding, search, and seizure of such cargoes prior to entry.

e. At their own initiative or upon the request and good cause shown by another state, to (a) require aircraft that are reasonably suspected of carrying such cargoes to or from states or nonstate actors of proliferation concern and that are transiting their airspace to land for inspection and seize any such cargoes that are identified; and/or (b) deny aircraft reasonably suspected of carrying such cargoes transit rights through their airspace in advance of such flights.

f. If their ports, airfields, or other facilities are used as transshipment points for shipment of such cargoes to or from states or nonstate actors of proliferation concern, to inspect vessels, aircraft, or other modes of transport reasonably suspected of carrying such cargoes and to seize such cargoes that are identified (U.S. Department of State 2003).

LEGAL CONTEXT

It is important to note that the PSI operates under preexisting legal frameworks and does not grant participating governments any new legal authority. Interdictions in international waters or airspace are confined to what is currently permissible under international law. Maritime law generally allows for the free passage of ships in international waters. To get by this, PSI nations are often forced to resort to the so-called broken taillight scenario, in which officials exploit all possible legal means for stopping and searching a ship. To expand their legal authority to interdict shipments, some PSI participants have signed bilateral boarding agreements to secure expedited processes or preapproval for stopping and searching ships at sea. However, in effect, participating states are politically, not legally, bound to the PSI "Statement of Interdiction Principles."

A significant legal boost for the PSI came in the form of United Nations (UN) Security Council Resolution 1540 in April 2004. This legally binding resolution commits all UN member states to "refrain from providing any form of support to non-State actors that attempt to develop, acquire, manufacture, possess, transport, transfer or use nuclear, chemical or biological weapons and their means of delivery."

While UN Security Council Resolution 1540 does not codify PSI operations (despite the efforts of the United States during the negotiations), its directive for states to craft laws prohibiting transfers and transportation of WMD and related materials increases the likelihood that governments will put in place national laws authorizing PSI-related actions within their sovereign jurisdiction (Holmes and Winner 2009, 146). Resolution 1540 also likely helped to increase the number of participating states as it became a way for governments to demonstrate their compliance with their obligations under the resolution.

Nevertheless, key states with large shipping industries, such as China and India, as well as states in important regions like the Arabian Peninsula, remain outside the PSI. This is due in part to misgivings about the legality of PSI operations and mistrust about what the PSI might hypothetically develop into in the future. The origins of the PSI as an initiative that was started by a like-minded group of Western nations rather than as a cooperative multilateral effort feed into this mistrust. The fact that PSI operations and exercises are shrouded in secrecy does little to assuage these concerns.

CONCLUSION

The Obama administration has stated that it would like to "institutionalize PSI" as part of its nonproliferation agenda. Indeed, the May 2010 "U.S. National Security Strategy" commits the United States to turn the PSI into a "durable international effort" (White House 2010), though details on how this is to be achieved have not yet been announced. Such high-level political support suggests the future of the PSI is secure, at least in the short to medium term. However, its future growth and success may depend on participating states widening their circle to include less like-minded states and their willingness to increase transparency.

REFERENCES

Holmes, James R., and Andrew C. Winner. "The Proliferation Security Initiative." In *Combating Weapons of Mass Destruction: The Future of International Non-Proliferation Policy*, edited by Nathan E. Busch and Daniel H. Joiner, 139–55. Athens, GA: University of Georgia Press, 2009.

Nikitin, Mary Beth. "Proliferation Security Initiative." Congressional Research Service. Washington, DC: CRS, 2011.http://www.fas.org/sgp/crs/nuke/RL34327.pdf.

U.S. Department of State. "Proliferation Security Initiative: Statement of Interdiction Principles ." 2003. http://www.state.gov/t/isn/c27726.htm.

U.S. Department of State. "Proliferation Security Initiative Participants." 2010. http://www.state.gov/t/isn/c27732.htm.

The White House. "U.S. National Security Strategy" May 2010. http://www. whitehouse.gov/sites/default/files/rss_viewer/national_security_strat egy.pdf.

Prosecuting Terrorists in a Democratic Society

Linda S. Watts

The judicial processes employed within a democratic society help convey the nation's core values concerning such matters as human rights, civil liberties, and due process. That remains the case regardless of the identity of the defendants or the charges against them. When prosecuting suspected terrorists, a democracy's commitment to equitable treatment under the law may be tested. Democracies struggle to balance the competing claims of national security and personal freedom. In the instance of the United States, a constitutional democracy, that balance must include compliance with both the Constitution and the Bill of Rights. In prosecuting terrorists, a society holds in tension the need to uphold its democratic ideals while simultaneously ensuring the safety of the nation and its people.

PROCEDURAL ISSUES AND PROBLEMS

One key factor complicating the prosecution of suspected terrorists is the distinctive nature of the offense. A terrorist attack is not merely a criminal act but also a political one. Persons engaged in terrorism undertake their actions not simply to damage their targets but also to communicate a message. Those who engage in acts of political violence typically seek to change societies, not merely to imperil them. They call attention to problems citizens in a democracy otherwise might fail to notice, often because they are complicit in those conditions. Because terrorism represents a special category of criminal activity, debates persist surrounding how best to prosecute accused terrorists. In particular, stakeholders' views diverge widely concerning the most appropriate practices related to the detention, interrogation, and trial of suspected terrorists.

First of all, there is not a consensus about the legal status of persons charged with terrorism. Some observers consider them to be criminal defendants, subject to the federal criminal justice system. Others regard such individuals as unlawful enemy combatants, arguing that they should be accorded that status before military commissions. Still others contend that a third option should be configured for prosecution of terrorists, such as a national security court. Depending on the status accorded to those charged with terrorism, they will appear in a different trial venue, such as the civil court system, a military commission, or a specially designed prosecutorial forum.

Prior to the 9/11 attacks in 2001, U.S. law enforcement agencies typically employed the federal criminal justice system to prosecute alleged terrorists. This process was used for such cases as the 1993 World Trade Center bombing and the 1995 Oklahoma City bombing. Following 9/11, though, the United States became more inclined to consider military options for detaining, interrogating, and trying suspected terrorists. Many perceived the federal criminal justice system as ill suited for the purpose. Trying terrorists in open criminal courts raised concerns regarding such matters as the disclosure of classified information (most notably in instances where suspects opt to serve as their own legal counsel, as was the case for Zacarias Moussaoui, a 9/11 defendant tried in U.S. district court), the availability of witnesses when subjects were apprehended in combat and/or abroad, and the prospect of a fair trial for high-profile suspects.

Some observers also deemed criminal courts unduly restrictive in terms of rules of evidence, suggesting that alleged terrorists instead should be subject to the rules of armed conflict, which may abridge peacetime justice rights for insurgents or terrorists. Not simply for the purposes of prosecution but also for the sake of preventing further acts of terrorism, government officials argued that contested interrogation methods such as waterboarding were permissible means of eliciting information from detainees. They made these claims on the basis that military prosecution rendered such suspects subject to different rules of evidence and procedural safeguards than would be in place within the civilian criminal justice system. Confessions or other statements by suspected terrorists might be found inadmissible in civilian courts, rejected as the products of coercive tactics. Prosecutors also favored latitude in charging suspected terrorists, accomplished in some instances through broad interpretation of existing laws, such as the Antiterrorism and Effective Death Penalty Act of 1996, which made it a criminal offense to provide material support to any terrorist organization. In addition, subsequent legislation, such as the Uniting and Strengthening America by Providing Appropriate Tools Required to Intercept and Obstruct Terrorism Act of 2001 (better known as the USA PATRIOT Act), expanded the definition of conduct that might constitute material support.

USA PATRIOT ACT

Also at issue when prosecuting terrorists are the proper conditions under which to detain suspects. Once again, the events of 9/11 proved pivotal. For instance, the PATRIOT Act's provisions loosened restrictions on surveillance and records review while increasing law enforcement's discretion regarding detention of foreign terrorist suspects. The PATRIOT Act, passed shortly after the 9/11 attacks, occasioned considerable controversy. Detractors questioned whether there had been sufficient examination of the specific stipulations and implications of the legislation, particularly the authority granted to detain individuals indefinitely without charging them. Indeed, if regarded as unlawful enemy combatants, they might be held in this way until the end of military conflict. For example, the Bush administration contended that detainees at Guantánamo Bay, a U.S. naval facility located in Cuba, were not subject to the Geneva Conventions because they were held in military rather than criminal custody. With the Military Commissions Act of 2006, Congress ruled that only alien unlawful enemy combatants fall under the jurisdiction of military commissions. U.S. citizens or lawful combatants may not be tried before military commissions. The distinction between lawful and unlawful combatants is not delineated clearly in international treaties and conventions and so remains ambiguous in implementation.

In the face of terrorist threats, especially since 9/11, some democracies have granted extraordinary powers to law enforcement in the area of counterterrorism. These expanded capacities, designed to facilitate detection of terrorist plots, may have both benefits and unintended consequences. That is, emergency powers may enhance the intelligence capabilities of a democracy, yet they may also antagonize those who believe that democratic practice has been compromised.

CONCLUSION

The prosecution of terrorists remains both a legal and a civic challenge within democratic societies. Disputes persist regarding the best procedures for identifying, detaining, interrogating, and trying suspected terrorists in a democracy. It is important that citizens of a democracy be assured that the treatment of terror suspects is consistent with both national ideals and international standards of justice. At the same time, the prosecution of suspected terrorists must protect the safety of a democracy's citizens, for a citizen's rights to life and liberty hinge on some measure of national security.

See also: **Volume 1, Part I:** Defining Terrorism: Issues and Problems; Definition and Dimensions of Counterterrorism. **Part II:** United States. **Part III:** Countering Terrorism: Law Enforcement or Military Problem; International Law, Human Rights, and Counterterrorism. **Part IV:** Detention, Interrogation, and Torture of Terrorist Suspects; Ethical and Legal Issues in Democratic Societies: National Security and Civil Liberties; U.S. Legislative Initiatives to Combat Terrorism pre-9/11; U.S. Legislative Initiatives to Combat Terrorism since 9/11. **Part VI:** Interrogation: A Multidisciplinary Approach. **Volume 2, Part II:** Oklahoma City Bombing (1995). **Part III:** Uniting and Strengthening America by Providing Appropriate Tools Required to Intercept and Obstruct Terrorism Act (USA PATRIOT Act) of 2001

REFERENCES

Chesney, Robert, and Jack Goldsmith. "Terrorism and the Convergence of Military and Criminal Detention Models." *Stanford Law Review* 60, no. 4 (February 2008): 1079–133.

McCarthy, Andrew C., and Alykhan Velshi. "We Need a National Security Court." Working paper, American Enterprise Institute, 2006. http://www.defend democracy.org/images/stories/national%20security%20court.pdf.

Wittes, Benjamin. *Law and the Long War: The Future of Justice in the Age of Terror.* New York: Penguin, 2008.

Wittes, Benjamin, ed. *Legislating the War on Terror: An Agenda for Reform.* Washington, DC: Brookings Institution Press, 2009.

Zabel, Richard B., and James J. Benjamin. *In Pursuit of Justice: Prosecuting Terrorism Cases in the Federal Courts.* New York: Human Rights First, 2008.

Russian Counterterrorism Efforts

Hans Brun

In the former Soviet Union political violence carried out by nonstate actors was rather unusual. On a few occasions, Soviet diplomats were targeted internationally—for example, in Beirut during the early 1980s. The Soviet security services responded to these incidents swiftly, and this usually deterred terrorist organizations from attacking any targets linked to the Soviet Union. This changed, however, after the collapse of the Soviet empire in 1989–1990 (Bolt et al. 2008, 23).

CHECHEN SEPARATISTS

The Chechen Republic of Ichkeria sought political independence from the Russian Federation in the early 1990s. The Russian government opposed this request, leading to the First Chechen War, which lasted from December 1994 to August 1996. The Russian military used indiscriminate firepower and killed a large number of civilians, including both ethnic Russians and ethnic Chechens. The brutality of the Russian forces galvanized and radicalized the Chechens (Lieven 1998).

One of the leading Chechen separatists, Shamil Basayev, together with about 200 Chechen fighters, planned and executed an attack against a hospital in Budennovsk in June 1995. Approximately 1,500 staff and patients were taken hostage, and a number of male hostages were executed immediately to demonstrate the Chechens' resolve to the Russian authorities. Basayev and his soldiers demanded an end to the war in Chechnya. The Chechens were able to repel several attacks from Russian security forces, and they eventually received a promise from the Russian authorities that the military operations in Chechnya would end. More than 100 hostages were killed in firefights between the Chechens and Russian security forces, and a large number of buildings were completely destroyed during the fighting (Soldatov and Borogan 2010, 138–40).

Political violence continued to haunt Chechnya during the rest of the 1990s. In May 1998, President Yeltsin's personal representative in Chechnya, Valentin Vlasov, was kidnapped and held hostage for six months. Later the same year, four engineers from Great Britain and New Zealand were kidnapped and executed. In March 1999, Moscow's envoy to Chechnya, General Shpigun, was kidnapped and murdered (Bolt, Changhe, and Cross 2008, 23).

ATTACKS IN RUSSIA

In September 1999, a number of apartment buildings were bombed in Moscow, Volgodonsk, and Buinaksk, killing a total of approximately 300 people. The perpetrators were never identified; nevertheless, the Russian government blamed Chechen separatists and resumed military operations in Chechnya. The Chechens never claimed responsibility for these attacks as they usually do, and it has been argued that an unidentified Russian security agency orchestrated the bombings to create support for renewed military actions in Chechnya. As a result of the apartment bombings, the second war in Chechnya started in October 1999 (Satter 2003).

In mid-September 2002, several teams of Chechens traveled to Moscow by bus from the republic of Dagestan and gathered at several apartments. On October 19, 2002, the group planned to detonate two car bombs in order to distract the Russian authorities. One car bomb exploded outside a McDonald's restaurant, killing one person and injuring eight others. The other car bomb failed to explode. The team attacked their main target, a theater, on the evening of October 23, taking 920 people hostage. Once again, the Chechens demanded that Russia end the war in Chechnya. Russian security forces stormed the theater early in the morning of October 26, using an anesthetic gas known as fentanyl to subdue the terrorists before entering the building. Unfortunately, the rescue attempt was poorly planned, and approximately 130 hostages died. Most of them died of suffocation due to the inhalation of fentanyl. Five hostages appeared to have been killed by the terrorists (Soldatov and Borogan 2010, 135–51).

SUICIDE ATTACKS

The Chechen separatists started to use suicide bombers in Chechnya near the end of 2002, killing a large number of people in several spectacular attacks. In December, a suicide bomber attacked Russian government offices in the Chechen capital, Grozny, killing 80 people. In May 2003, another suicide bomber killed more than 50 people in northern Chechnya. The separatists also carried out several suicide attacks against airliners and the Moscow subway system. At least 41 people were killed in the Moscow subway by a suicide bomber on February 6, 2004, and another bomber killed 10 people in the subway on August 31, 2004. On August 24, 2004, two civilian airliners—Volga-AviaExpress Flight 1303 and Siberia Airline Flight 1047—left from Moscow; both airliners exploded in midair, killing all 89 passengers and crew. It is widely believed that two female suicide bombers were responsible ("Many Dead" 2004; Associated Press 2004; Arvedlund and Kishkovsky 2004; Bolt, Changhe, and Cross 2008, 23–24). It is believed that the terrorist attacks in August 2004 intended to create a diversion from a far more serious attack.

BESLAN INCIDENT

On September 1, 2004, more than 40 heavily armed Chechens and Ingush attacked a school in Beslan, North Ossetia. More than 1,100 people were taken hostage, including some 770 children. More than a dozen adult males were executed during the first hours of the hostage crisis, and their bodies were thrown out the windows of the school. Russian security forces, including elite units from the Federal Security Service (FSB, the successor of the KGB), established a loose cordon around the school, and the Russian authorities established contact with the terrorists. On September 3, several of the security force teams left Beslan to rehearse an eventual rescue attempt on a building similar to the school, 19 miles (30 kilometers) away. The remaining security forces apparently did not expect any trouble or major operations. Without warning, two bombs exploded inside the school, partly destroying the walls of the school's gymnasium, where most of the hostages were gathered. A number of children tried to escape, only to be gunned down by the terrorists. Members of the security forces tried to save the escaping children but to no avail. They were totally unprepared; in their efforts to save as many of the hostages as possible, they did not even don their flak jackets before assaulting the school. Ten members of the FSB were killed immediately, marking the largest loss in the FSB's history. The Russian security forces continued their ad hoc rescue attempt, with disastrous results. A firefight with heavy weapons broke out and lasted for several hours; it ended when the Russian authorities used tank fire to destroy the terrorists' last stronghold. When the conflict ended, 334 hostages had been killed, including 186 schoolchildren (Soldatov and Borogan 2010, 158–60; Phillips 2008).

A number of the Chechen separatists changed their ideology in 2007, under the leadership of Doku K. Umarov; they began to establish a sharia-based state independent of Russia. This led to a revival of suicide bombing, organized in a formation known as Riyadus-Salikhin (the Garden of Martyrs). In this formation, separatists conducted a double suicide bombing on the Moscow subway system on March 29, 2010, killing 39 people. Since then, the Garden of Martyrs has been responsible for at least 17 suicide bombings against targets in southern Russia ("Doku K. Umarov" 2010).

CONCLUSION

In November 1995, unidentified Chechens contacted a Russian television station, claiming to have the capacity to build a dirty bomb. The caller also claimed to have buried radioactive materials in a Moscow park; a container containing cesium was later found at that location by Russian authorities. This is the first known case of radioactive terrorism. The source of the cesium was never identified. Three years later, in December 1998, a container filled with radioactive materials attached to a mine was discovered 10 miles east of Grozny. The dirty bomb was most likely placed by Basayev, who was known to be operating in the area at the time. Additionally, in September 1999, several individuals tried to steal radioactive materials from a chemical factory in Grozny. One of them died almost immediately due to exposure to radioactivity. The others were hospitalized in critical condition (Krock and Deusser 2003). Incidents involving dirty bombs and the theft of radioactive materials are a unique feature of the terrorism problem in Russia.

See also: **Volume 1, Part II:** Russia. **Volume 2, Part I:** Alpha Units (Russia); Spetsnaz (Russia); Vega Group (Russia). **Part II:** Nord-Ost Siege (2002); Beslan Massacre (2004); Moscow Metro Attacks (2004 and 2010)

REFERENCES

Arvedlund, Erin E., and Sophia Kishkovsky. "After a Spate of Bombings, Moscow's Full of Foreboding." *New York Times,* September 2, 2004. http://query.nytimes.com/gst/fullpage.html?res=980DE1DE1231F931A3575AC 0A9629C8B63&scp=1&sq=After%20a%20Spate%20of%20Bombings,%20 Moscow%27s%20Full%20of%20Foreboding&st=cse.

Associated Press. "Russia Plane Crashes Caused by Explosives." *MSNBC.com,* August 30, 2004. http://www.msnbc.msn.com/id/5810127.

Bolt, Paul J., Su Changhe, Robin L. Bowman, and David H. Sacko, eds. "Chinese, American and Russian Security Policies: The Response to Terrorism." In *The United States, Russia, and China: Confronting Global Terrorism and Security Challenges in the 21st Century,* edited by Paul J. Bolt, Su Changhe, and Sharyl Cross, 8–30. Westport, CT: Praeger, 2008.

"Doku K. Umarov." *New York Times,* April 1, 2010. http://topics.nytimes.com/ top/reference/timestopics/people/u/doku_k_umarov/index.html? scp=1&sq=moscow%20subway%20bombing&st=cse.

Krock, Lexi, and Rebecca Deusser. "Dirty Bomb." *Nova,* February 2003. Public Broadcasting Service. http://www.pbs.org/wgbh/nova/dirtybomb/ch rono.html.

Lieven, Anatol. *Chechnya: Tombstone of Russian Power.* New Haven, CT: Yale University Press, 1998.

"Many Dead in Moscow Metro Blast." *BBC News,* February 6, 2004. http://news.bbc.co.uk/2/hi/europe/3464545.stm.

Phillips, Timothy. *Beslan: The Tragedy of School No. 1.* London: Granta, 2008.

Satter, David. *Darkness at Dawn: The Rise of the Russian Criminal State.* New Haven, CT: Yale University Press, 2003.

Soldatov, Andrei, and Irina Borogan. *The New Nobility: The Restoration of Russia's Security State and the Enduring Legacy of the KGB.* New York: Public Affairs, 2010.

Southeast Asia: Jemaah Islamiyah

Jolene Jerard

Jemaah Islamiyah (JI) is a Southeast Asian terrorist group that has its roots in Darul Islam (DI), an organization that has existed since the 1940s. DI was an anticolonial movement that later became a political opponent of the Indonesian government after the colonial period. The prominent founders of JI are Abu Bakar Ba'asyir and the late Abdullah Sungkar, both of whom became members of DI in 1976 (Asi 2005). They were members of DI for 17 years until 1993 when they broke away to form JI. As a formal organization, JI came into being on January 1, 1993. On October 25, 2002, JI was added to the United Nations 1267 Committee's list of terrorist organizations linked to al-Qaeda. The Indonesian government has not designated the group as a terrorist organization.

TERROR IN SOUTHEAST ASIA

The group JI has been involved in a string of terrorist incidents in Southeast Asia. These include the devastating attacks in Bali in 2002 and 2005, the 2004 attack on the Australian embassy in Jakarta, the 2003 attack on the JW Marriott Hotel, and the 2009 attack of the JW Marriott and Ritz Carlton Jakarta. Collectively these are the most devastating attacks in Southeast Asia to date. JI has chosen targets based on their symbolic value, such as military bases, embassies, government establishments, police headquarters, train stations, airports, businesses (both foreign and domestic, including nightclubs, hotels, banks, and shopping malls), and places of religious worship.

Ba'asyir, an Indonesian Muslim cleric of Hadrami ancestry, was the leader of JI. After Ba'asyir's arrest in 2002, JI appointed temporary emirs, who would take over the vacuum left by Ba'asyir. The temporary emirs included Abu Rusdan, Ustadz Adung, and Yusron Mahmudi Zarkas (aka

Zarkasih). Presently, it is unclear who leads JI today. Albeit some factions believe that Zarkasih continues to sign off on key decisions, others speculate that a Semarang-based religious teacher leads the organization. JI has been affiliated with a multitude of groups including Majelis Muhjahideen Indonesia, the Action Committee for Crisis Response, al-Qaeda, the Moro Islamic Liberation Front, the Anti-Apostasy Movement Forum, Jamaah Ansharut Tauhid, Tauhid wal Jihad, and the Islamic Defenders Front, among others.

JI has as its primary objective the establishment of an Islamic caliphate in Southeast Asia (Daulah Islamiyah Nusantara). This caliphate would include Indonesia, Malaysia, Singapore, Brunei, and even part of Australia. JI's ideology is enshrined in a book titled *General Guidelines for the Jemaah Islamiyah Struggle (PUPJI)*. According to this text, JI is an organizing platform that would empower its members to rise against oppressive states and regimes. JI points to the lack of a central Muslim leadership in the world. According to the group's leadership this has led to the degradation of Islam and Islamic values. JI "has placed 5 principles at its foundation: *belief* (iman), hijrah (emigration), *I'dad* (preparation to struggle in the way of God), *jihad* (struggle in the way of Allah) and *al wala' wal bara'* (principle of loyalty and disloyalty)" (Bin Ali n.d.). The final principle provides not only the necessary religious justification but also the necessary parameter for the creation of a secret organization excluding anyone whose beliefs were not similar to those of JI and who would therefore be regarded as an apostate. This exclusion extended to Muslims who did not adhere to the values professed by JI. The five principles set out by the *PUPJI* were mirrored on the various stages that the Prophet Muhammad had to undertake to bring people to Islam. JI members as such see themselves as part of this higher calling to expedite the establishment of a world governed by the principles of God. JI preaches the need to practice Islam in its totality.

JI interprets jihad as war, which they believe is an obligation to be undertaken by each individual. The endgame will be the establishment of Daulah Islamiyah, or pan-Islamic caliphate. According to JI, to attain this goal, armed conflict will have to be waged against the enemies of Islam and anyone who supports them. Ideologues that have influenced JI's key leaders include the Spanish-Syrian cleric Abu Musab al-Suri, the Iraq-based Abu Musab al-Zarqawi (now deceased), and the Jordanian radical scholar Abu Muhammad al-Maqdisi.

All of JI's top leaders and many of the men involved in JI bombings have undergone training in terrorist training camps in Afghanistan over the 10-year period 1985–1995. The war in Afghanistan provided them with the necessary terrorist and guerrilla training skills and had a huge influence in shaping their worldview and reinforcing their commitment to jihad. JI today is not a monolithic organization. The JI faction that was led by Noordin Mohammad Top prior to his death provided a glimpse into the factionalized structure of the group. One of the key differences that had surfaced among JI members was its choice of targets and the lack of a coordinated and accepted strategy to achieve their ultimate objectives. In the Australian embassy bombings in 2004, nine Indonesians were killed. Several factions within JI were not pleased with the number of local Indonesians killed. On the other hand, the JI faction led by Top was interested in focusing on a broader anti-Western agenda similar to al-Qaeda's aspirations and in effecting change in the short term. Still other members of JI preferred a long-term strategy that would involve proselytizing and a continual recruitment effort to build and expand the organization, until such time as the group would be strong enough to engage in battle.

COUNTERING JI

In the aftermath of recent counterterrorism operations against JI in Indonesia, the capabilities of the organization have been severely crippled. In September 2009 Top was killed. In March 2010, Dulmatin, another key JI leader, was also killed. The string of counterterrorism operations that followed in the aftermath of the attacks on the JW Marriot and Ritz Carlton in Jakarta led to the discovery of a training facility in Aceh and the subsequent arrest of close to 100 JI militants. In February 2010, another militant training facility was discovered near Banda Aceh in Indonesia (Rondonuwu 2010). This training facility was formed by a cross-organizational network of groups headed by the Islamist militant Dulmatin. Since its formation in 1993, JI has successfully managed to stay resilient in the face of counterterrorism operations against it. On August 9, 2010, Ba'asyir was arrested for his role in establishing and providing direct support to a terrorist training facility in Aceh (Sarangih 2010).

CONCLUSION

In light of recent counterterrorism operations by Indonesia's elite counterterrorism task force, Detachment 88, JI is now placing increased emphasis on proselytization and the production and distribution of extremist literature. Unfortunately, it appears that JI will continue to remain a prominent transnational threat in the Southeast Asian region. The group's ability to recover and rebuild itself has been confirmed by its successful efforts at building a new generation of leaders.

See also: **Volume 1, Part II:** Indonesia. **Part V:** South Asian Association for Regional Cooperation. **Volume 2, Part II:** Bali, Indonesia (2002)

REFERENCES

Asi, Rohaiza. "Darul Islam: A Fertile Ground for Jemaah Islamiyah's Recruitment?" Institute of Defence and Strategic Studies (IDDS), Nanyang Technological

University, Singapore, IDSS Commentaries, July 5, 2005. http://www.rsis. edu.sg/publications/Perspective/IDSS412005.pdf.

Bin Ali, Mohamed. "Identifying Key Concerns of Jemaah Islamiyah: The Singapore Context." Institute of Defence and Strategic Studies (IDDS), Nanyang Technological University, Singapore, n.d. http://www.pvtr.org/pdf/Ideol ogy%20Response/Identifying%20key%20concerns%20of%20JI.pdf.

Rondonuwu, Olivia. "Indonesia Police Link Aceh Training Camp to Hotel Bombings." *Reuters*, April 30, 2010. http://www.reuters.com/article/idUS TRE63T2F820100430.

Sarangih, Bagus. "Ba'asyir Mastermind behind Aceh Terrorist Camps: National Police." *Jakarta Post*, August 9, 2010. http://www.thejakartapost.com/news/ 2010/08/09/ba039asyir-masterminds-aceh-militarystyle-training-camp. html.

Spain's Counterterrorism Measures

Hans Brun

Spain has been haunted by various forms of state, domestic, and international terrorism since the Spanish Civil War (Jiménez 1993). The fascist dictator Francisco Franco came to power in 1939 at the end of the Spanish Civil War (Thomas 2003; Beever 2001). During the Franco years, the Spanish military was steeped in the notion of a culturally homogeneous and indivisible Spain and were entrusted to see through the mission to protect the country from both external and internal enemies. The belief in a culturally homogeneous nation was one of the main reasons behind the harsh repression of Basque nationalism and a policy to eradicate the Basque culture, which, of course, radicalized parts of Basque society.

BASQUE HOMELAND AND FREEDOM

In consequence, the Euskadi ta Askatasuna (ETA or, in English, Basque Homeland and Freedom) was created by a group of university students in 1959 with the strategic goal of turning the Basque area of Spain and France into a unified and monolingual state. Initially, the ETA focused its efforts primarily on spreading propaganda and committing vandalism. However, in 1968, the ETA picked up arms and began to ambush police and military units. As a result, the Spanish army was deployed to the Basque region. The Spanish authorities also created special antiterrorism legislation that applied in this region and also addressed extrajudicial violence in various forms (e.g., state-sponsored unofficial paramilitary death squads) against known and suspected ETA members. Such units had been used by the Franco regime for a long time to track down and eliminate political opponents. During the 1940s and 1950s, such units were used to kill Republicans (so-called *huídos*) who refused to accept Franco's regime, as well as Spanish citizens (*maquis*) who had been active in the French Resistance during World War II and had returned to Spain with the ambition to oust Franco from power. Some of these paramilitary units were later used to fight the ETA, and in 1975, a number of them were recruited to a unit known as Battallón Vasco-Español (BVE) that mainly carried out operations in parts of France that served as sanctuaries for ETA members. Just like its predecessor, the BVE became known for its use of indiscriminate violence and torture. This campaign against the ETA, which was sometimes referred to as the "first dirty war," was phased out in the early 1980s (Encarnación 2007, 958–61; Woodworth 2004, 172).

SPAIN'S COUNTERTERRORISM POLICY POST-1975

The death of Franco in 1975 caused a significant shift in Spanish counterterrorism policies. A transition process from dictatorship toward democracy was initiated, and free elections were held in June 1977. A new constitution was drafted and approved in a national referendum. The Spanish authorities started to use a two-pronged strategy against the ETA. On the one side, the government initiated a process of decentralization and increased political rights for the Basques and the Basque region. The Basque language, Euskera, was recognized as an official language, and the Basque Autonomous Community was established in 1979. The Spanish authorities granted amnesty to nearly 900 ETA members who were either imprisoned in Spain or lived abroad in exile. The amnesty program was combined with the legalizing of political symbols that that had been forbidden during the Franco years (e.g., the Basque flag, the *ikurriña*). At the time, the ETA had split into two major factions, and some of the ETA members recognized the opportunities and importance of the political reforms and development in Spain. Thus, a number of ETA members were perceived as being willing to give up arms, and the Spanish government introduced several new counterterrorism measures to encourage this development. One vital part of this new strategy was social reintegration, a policy that was based on the success of Italian authorities in the struggle against the Red Brigades. Initially, individual pardons were granted to imprisoned ETA members in exchange for their willingness to renounce violence; later, such pardons were extended to active ETA members. Since 1989, the policy of social reintegration has been combined with penitentiary provisions (i.e., the authorities tried to disperse imprisoned members of the ETA to penitentiaries across Spain, instead of concentrating them in just a few prisons, as had been the practice up until 1989). This policy was aimed at weakening group cohesiveness and, by doing so, making it easier for individual ETA members to defect and accept the reintegration policy (Reinares and Alonso 2007, 107, 110–11; Soria 2004, 526–29).

EXTRAJUDICIAL VIOLENCE

The Spanish authorities resorted to extrajudicial violence once again and launched a "second dirty war" against the ETA in 1983. A unit called Grupos Antiterroristas de Liberación (GAL) was created specifically for this purpose, drawing on the experience and expertise of BVE and sometimes recruiting former members from that unit. Up until 1987, the GAL carried out dozens of operations in both Spain and France. At least 27 people were killed by means of targeted killings, car bombs, and random gun and grenade attacks against bars frequented by ETA members and sympathizers. At least 10 of the victims had no ties at all to the ETA. The GAL also frequently resorted to kidnappings and torture in order to gain intelligence. The existence of the GAL and its activities became public in the late 1990s, creating a major political scandal, and a number of politicians were prosecuted (Woodworth 2004, 172; Encarnación 2007, 951; Soria 2004, 520–21). Within this context, it must be mentioned that the Spanish authorities and law enforcement and security agencies have been reformed and became much more effective and discriminating after 1988. Not one illegal killing in actions against the ETA has been recorded since that year (Reinares and Alonso 2007, 125).

More than 800 individuals have been killed over the years during the struggle between the ETA and the Spanish authorities, most of them during the 1980s and 1990s (Brotóns and Espósito 2002, 174–75). The Spanish authorities have, up until 2005, engaged in serious negotiations with the leadership of ETA on at least two occasions. The first round of talks was held as early as 1981, and a second round was held in 1989. A third meeting was held in 1999, but unlike the other negotiations, it seemed to have been a tactical move by the ETA (Reinares and Alonso 2007, 113). During the last 10 years, few fatal attacks have been carried out by the ETA. However, the ETA has bombed a number of targets during this period, usually alerting the authorities in advance in order to avoid casualties. Support for armed actions has decreased among ETA supporters, and there are indications that the ETA and Spanish authorities are involved in serious negotiations.

POST-9/11

Immediately after 9/11, Spain extended the definition and scope of crimes linked to terrorism. Various indirect forms of support of terrorist acts were criminalized, and the use of intercept evidence and search powers was extended and broadened. Spain also introduced rather unique legislation regarding the Internet in June 2002. This legislation requires that website operators and owners must notify the authorities if they receive any income from the website. The legislation also allows for the collection and storage of communication data (e.g., e-mails) for later analysis if such information is believed to be of use in a criminal investigation (Beckman 2007, 119–20; Soria 2004, 544).

The Spanish legislation and counterterrorism policies were also reformed on several occasions after 9/11. One example is a ban on political parties that encourage "hatred, violence and social confrontation" or promote "a culture of civil confrontation." This legislation was used to ban the political branch of the ETA, known as the Batasuna, and to prohibit membership in the organization. This ban also made it possible for the Spanish authorities to arrest and incarcerate many individuals who were unwilling to sever their ties with the ETA. In February 2003, *Euskaldumn Egunkanin*, the only newspaper published solely in the Basque language, was closed down by the Spanish authorities, who claimed that it was used to launder money and provide financial support to the ETA (Beckman 2007, 116–17; Soria 2004, 545–46).

Spain openly supported the U.S. invasion of Iraq in 2003 and deployed 1,300 Spanish soldiers to that country. Spain also allowed the United States and its allies to use Spanish military bases for forces involved in military operations in Afghanistan. As a consequence of this decision, a major terrorist attack was carried out by an al-Qaeda affiliate on March 11, 2004, when several commuter trains in Madrid were blown up, resulting in the deaths of nearly 200 commuters (Beckman 2007, 113; Soria 2004, 555–56). The domestic political reaction to this attack forced Spain to recall its troops from Iraq.

CONCLUSION

Spain did not introduce new counterterrorism legislation after the Madrid bombings. This is a rather unusual response, since most countries that have become victims of serious terrorist attacks are usually quick to introduce new legislation and policies in accordance with a phenomenon that is sometimes referred to as the counterterrorism spiral (Donohue 2008, 11–16; Beckman 2007, 118).

See also: **Volume 1, Part II:** Spain. **Volume 2, Part II:** Madrid Train Bombing (2004)

REFERENCES

Alexander, Yonah, ed. *Combating Terrorism. Strategies of Ten Countries.* Ann Arbor: University of Michigan Press, 2002.

Art, Robert J., and Louise Richardson, eds. *Democracy and Counterterrorism: Lessons from the Past.* Washington, DC: United States Institute of Peace Press, 2007.

Beckman, James. *Comparative Legal Approaches to Homeland Security and Anti-terrorism*. Burlington, VT: Ashgate, 2007.

Beever, Anthony. *The Battle for Spain: The Spanish Civil War 1936–1939*. New York: Penguin Books, 2001.

Brotóns, Antonio Remiro, and Espósito, Carlos. "Spain." In *Combating Terrorism: Strategies of Ten Countries*, edited by Yonah Alexander, 163–86. Ann Arbor: University of Michigan Press, 2002.

Crelinsten, Ronald D., and Alex P. Schmid, eds. *Western Responses to Terrorism*. London: Frank Cass, 1993.

Donohue, Laura K. *The Cost of Counterterrorism: Power, Politics, and Liberty*. New York: Cambridge University Press, 2008.

Encarnación, Omar G. "Democracy and Dirty Wars in Spain." *Human Rights Quarterly* 29, no. 4 (2007): 950–72.

Jiménez, Fernando. "Spain: The Terrorist Challenge and the Government's Response." In *Western Responses to Terrorism*, edited by Ronald D. Crelinsten and Alex P. Schmid, 110–30. London: Frank Cass, 1993.

Reinares, Fernando, and Alonso, Rogelio. "Confronting Ethnonationalist Terrorism in Spain: Political and Coercive Measures against ETA." In *Democracy and Counterterrorism: Lessons from the Past*, edited by Robert J. Art and Louise Richardson, 105–32. Washington, DC: U.S. Institute of Peace Press, 2007.

Soria, José Martínez. "Country Report on Spain." In *Terrorism as a Challenge for National and International Law: Security versus Liberty?* edited by Christian Walter, Silja Vöneky, Silja Röben, and Frank Schorkopf, 517–56. Heidelberg, Germany: Springer, 2004.

Thomas, Hugh. *The Spanish Civil War*. London: Penguin Books, 2003.

Walter, Christian, Silja Vöneky, Silja Röben, and Frank Schorkopf, eds. *Terrorism as a Challenge for National and International Law: Security versus Liberty?* Heidelberg, Germany: Springer, 2003.

Woodworth, Paddy. "The War against Terrorism: The Spanish Experience from ETA to al-Qaeda." *International Journal of Iberian Studies* 17, no. 3 (2004): 169–82.

Terrorism, War, and Revolution in the Middle East: Problems for U.S. Foreign Policy

Itai Nartzizenfield Sneh

U.S. foreign policy is predicated on protecting national security and fostering friendships while advancing national and commercial goals. Specific objectives pertain to individual states, where conflicts of interest often ensue. Contemporary threats include terrorism, oil scarcity, and ambitions for weapons of mass destruction. Counterterrorism strategy, an important aspect of U.S. foreign policy in the Middle East, is complicated by continuous regional instability, religious fervor, sectarian conflicts, weak civil societies, robust demographics, precious commodities, and crucial trade routes. This article highlights some of the events and policies that have made foreign policy in this region of the world particularly difficult for the United States and other Western nations.

STATECRAFT

Statecraft strategies create, maintain, and help allies while encouraging incremental reforms in authoritarian partners and providing relief to refugees. Policy is framed by politicians, and warriors frame the goals of specific operations. Domestic factors include partisan congressional scrutiny; isolationism; opposing actions and programs abroad; ethnic, ideological, and religious issues; pro-Israeli or pro-Arab advocacy groups; and the pro-oil and armament lobbies. Failing states such as Lebanon and Sudan generate transnational problems by incubating, enabling, or serving as catalysts to acts of genocide; by harboring terrorists; and by exporting radicalized refugees. Indignities endured in poor or dysfunctional countries such as Egypt, Syria, and Yemen facilitate negative attitudes toward a prosperous and free America.

American foreign policy seeks to maximize opportunities without compromising principles and to balance pragmatism and idealism. It has supported local, regional, and international initiatives, including humanitarian interventions mandated, authorized, or cosponsored by, or blessed by a multilateral partnership with, the United Nations Security Council, the North Atlantic Treaty Organization (NATO), the Arab League, the African Union, the Gulf Cooperation Council, and the European Union. Presidents vociferously promote human rights policies such as political freedoms, multiparty democracy, pluralism, religious tolerance, the rule of law, respect for individual and collective dignity, protection of minorities, social justice, equal opportunities, and a market economy. Besides monetary assistance and security guarantees, the United States embraces "soft" or "smart" powers to counter oppression and fundamentalism that foster violent extremism. Strategies have included providing training that heightens transparency and accountability by respectfully engaging independent political, social, and economic groups opposed to authoritarian elites; avoiding moral judgments to facilitate robust media; empowering academic institutions; supporting consensual democratic governance as well as better schools and economic opportunities; and strengthening the positive, civic-minded capabilities of the judiciary, police, and security services.

Nevertheless, U.S. weariness of nongovernmental organizations has often led to unilateral actions. In some cases America has favored corrupt, authoritarian allies who crush independent political, social, and religious institutions and has carried out or supported long-term occupation of foreign lands. Thus, competing agendas sometimes contradict human rights values of social justice and civic liberties.

TERRORISM PROBLEM

While there is no universally accepted definition of terrorism, it involves organized violence for a social, political, or religious cause by disaffected national, ethnic, ideological, or religious groups against established states or communal powers. Terrorists have attacked economic targets (such as oil fields), logistical targets, civilians in crowded markets or places of worship, symbols such as the World Trade Center, military bases and recruitment stations of enemy forces, and political, religious, and civic leaders. States such as Saddam Hussein's Iraq (1968–2003), Muammar al-Gadhafi's Libya (1969–2011), and Bashar al-Assad's dynasty in Syria (since 1970) repeatedly justify, glorify, and fund acts of terrorism as an appropriate counterbalance to colonialism, occupation, and exploitation.

Continuous dilemmas include collaborating with unpopular regimes such as the shah's Iran (1941–1979) and Saudi Arabia (since 1944). Other problems encountered in this region are ideological and religious foes such as the Ayatollah Khomeini (1902–1989) and al-Qaeda (since the 1990s) and the need to be proactive against terrorist havens in a diverse region with multiple ethnicities and religions. Engaging these actors risks open-ended commitments such as Iraq. Additionally, engaging adversaries to turn them into assets and monitoring and destroying sworn enemies often embolden suicide bombers, as has been experienced in Afghanistan, Pakistan, and Iraq. Moreover, the U.S. military, financial, and diplomatic support for Israel, a reliable counterterrorism ally, is resented by many Arabs and Muslims and viewed as an unbalanced policy.

The September 11, 2001, attacks prompted President George W. Bush to wage a global war on terrorism to deter potential perpetrators but also to promote free and fair elections in Iraq and Palestine. In 2011, the Jasmine Revolution toppled Egyptian, Tunisian, and Libyan rulers. Local activism endangered conservative Bahraini and Saudi monarchs, indicating that U.S. support of oppressive stability can only precariously deny popular demands for human rights. Compromising moral legitimacy may culminate in losing allies.

WORLD WAR II AND THE COLD WAR

In 1941, the World War II allies the United States, Britain, and the Soviet Union installed Mohammad Reza Shah in Iran, replacing his pro-German father, Reza Shah, to maintain legitimate leadership in a traditional society. After World War II, replacing traditional Europeans, mostly the British and the French, as the leader in the West, the United States confronted Communist subversion against allies in the Middle East in key states such as oil-rich Saudi Arabia. In 1947, the Truman Doctrine supported Turkey and Iran, which were confronting Soviet threats. The Fifth Fleet cruised in the Red Sea and the Persian Gulf. The Sixth Fleet sailed the Mediterranean.

America monitored naval and land activities alike, securing trade, especially the oil supply, and providing allies with commitment and comfort. Some internationally based terrorists exploited this Middle Eastern omnipresence to target U.S. institutions, civilians, and symbols of its military and economic power.

In 1952, Central Intelligence Agency operatives, frustrated by the corrupt, incompetent Egyptian regime of King Farouk (1920–1965) and concerned about a potential Communist takeover, helped the progressive, anticolonial, Arab nationalist Free Officers Movement, led by Gamal Abdel Nasser (1918–1970), to execute a military coup. In 1953, bruised by attacks perpetrated by Egyptian-backed fedayeen, Israel recruited Egyptian Jews to bomb American and British institutions, hoping that Arabs would be blamed, thus triggering conflict between nonaligned Egypt and the West. In 1954, this attempt backfired as Egyptians caught and publicly prosecuted Israeli agents.

In 1953, fearing hostile leadership, the Central Intelligence Agency's Kermit Roosevelt (1916–2000) helped orchestrate the toppling of the democratically elected Iranian prime minister Mohammad Mossadegh (1882–1967), who nationalized the Western-controlled oil industry. Iran also served as a forward base for American monitoring of Soviet activities and a conduit for commercial routes in the Persian Gulf.

Emulating NATO's success as a bulwark against Communism in Europe, America facilitated the creation of the Central Treaty Organization (Baghdad Pact) in 1955 to cement military cooperation with Iran, Iraq, Pakistan, and Turkey. Nevertheless, in 1956, the United States took a stance against a colonialism-like conspiracy of its closest allies and collaborated with the Soviets during the Suez Crisis to oust British, French, and Israeli troops from Egyptian territory. In 1958, a wave of pan-Arabic riots encouraged by Nasser's increasingly pro-Soviet stance toppled pro-Western rulers in Iraq and Syria. The Eisenhower Doctrine committed the United States to secure and protect the territorial integrity and political independence of allies threatened by Communism through consistent economic and military support. Indeed, 14,000 U.S. Marines salvaged the Lebanese regime.

Alienation from Nasser and his followers led to regular American collaboration with moderate Arab regimes such as Jordan, Morocco, Tunisia, Saudi Arabia, Bahrain, Kuwait, and the United Arab Emirates. This cooperation extended into counterterrorism efforts against the growing Islamist threat and Palestinian groups funded, in part, by Iraq's president Saddam Hussein. Over the years Israel has become a staunch, reliable U.S. ally. Its effective intelligence units, especially Mossad, have provided consistent operational counterterrorism information and logistical support locally, regionally, and internationally, especially against Palestinian and Muslim perpetrators. Israel, moreover, secretly furnished America with Soviet leader Nikita Khrushchev's (1894–1971) February 1956 speech "On the Cult of Personality and Its Consequences," given at a closed session of the 20th Communist Party Congress. This speech denounced Stalin's atrocities, including purges and anti-Semitism, helping legitimize the U.S. global agenda in the Cold War. Israeli operatives also helped the United States and Iran sustain a Kurdish uprising against pro-Soviet Iraq into the 1970s.

Israel, however, has been at war with most of its Arab neighbors. Specifically, the plight of Palestinian refugees causes ongoing global resentment against the Jewish state. Israel needed armament supplies in 1973 when Egypt and Syria waged war against it. In 1974, this complication caused Joint Chief of Staff George S. Brown (1918–1978) to castigate Israel. He resented burdensome equipment requests, alleging that continued military aid was due to Jewish influence on America's banks, newspapers, and elected officials.

PALESTINE LIBERATION ORGANIZATION

In 1964, Nasser sponsored the establishment of the Palestine Liberation Organization (PLO). The PLO was subsequently sponsored by the Soviets. The PLO's first act of terrorism was against an Israeli water carrier on January 1, 1965. Escalating tensions following PLO attacks and Israeli retaliations culminated in the June 1967 Six-Day War. In that brief conflict Israel defeated three Arab countries. Unlike Jordan, the other two, Egypt and Syria, were Soviet clients.

Following continuous PLO assaults on its citizens, Israeli troops launched a land operation against PLO bases on March 21, 1968. Israel targeted refugee camps in Karameh, Jordan. Casualties, infrastructure destruction, and increasing Jordanian opposition limited the PLO's ground capacity, causing some units' relocation to southern Lebanon, bordering Israel. Four months later the Popular Front for the Liberation of Palestine (PFLP), a PLO faction, pioneered plane hijackings to gain global attention for the Palestinian struggle. PFLP members forced a Rome-Tel Aviv flight of Israel's El Al airline to fly to Algeria. After 40 days of negotiations, Israel had to exchange its citizens for Palestinian militants.

During the War of Attrition (1969–1970) waged by Egypt and Syria against Israel, Soviet military advisers and pilots helped Arab forces, which included training and arming PLO fighters. U.S. president Richard Nixon (1913–1994) responded by supplying Israel with sophisticated weaponry, especially planes and tanks. The secretary of state, William Rogers (1913–2001), helped negotiate a cease-fire. He then offered, unsuccessfully, the "Rogers Plan" to broker peace between Israel and its neighbors.

In September, 1970, PFLP terrorist squads simultaneously hijacked three Western airliners, forcing them to land in Jordan. Over 400 passengers were held hostage but subsequently released in exchange for terrorists held in Germany, Switzerland, and Britain. Jordan's King Hussein seemed to lose power as the PLO controlled bases, using them to launch attacks against Israel. In response Hussein deployed his army to crush the PLO. The Palestinians called their defeat "Black September." The Nixon administration facilitated, through Israeli ambassador Yitzhak Rabin (1924–1995), tacit Israeli support for Hussein during a short-lived Syrian invasion in support of the PLO.

In 1970, upon Nasser's death, Anwar el-Sadat (1921–1981) succeeded him. Sadat turned toward America, expelling Soviet military advisers in 1972 and lessening support for the PLO. The PLO, seeking revenge for their defeat in Jordan, launched an attack against the Israeli delegation during the Munich Summer Olympics in September 1972. Eight PLO Black September terrorists murdered 11 Israeli athletes. Communist East Germany was likely used as the exit base for this unit. In March of the following year eight PLO Black September members attacked the Saudi embassy in Khartoum, Sudan, taking 10 people hostage. The terrorists murdered three Western hostages, including U.S. ambassador Cleo A. Noel and the deputy chief of mission, Curtis G. Moore. The terrorists eventually released the remaining hostages and surrendered to Sudanese authorities. Sudan tried the terrorists for murder but released them to Egypt. In protest, the United States withdrew its ambassador for five months. By 1976, relations with the United States had normalized after Sudanese officials negotiated the release of 10 American hostages held by Eritrean rebels in Ethiopia.

In June 1982, Israel invaded PLO bases and Syria-occupied Lebanon following PLO attacks, specifically an assassination attempt on Israel's ambassador in London. In September 1982, Western troops, including Americans, were stationed in Beirut to serve as a buffer between Israelis and Palestinians following massacres perpetrated by Israel's Christian allies in Beirut's Palestinian refugee camps. In October 1983, Lebanese Shiite Hezbollah terrorists supported by Iran and Syria killed 241 American soldiers based in Beirut. While the United States retaliated, its troops left Lebanon within months.

MUAMMAR GADHAFI

In Libya in 1969 Muammar Gadhafi (1942–2011), a junior military officer from western Libya, overthrew the pro-Western king Mohammad Idris al Senussi (1890–1983) of Eastern Libya. Positioning himself as a radical global leader, Gadhafi granted bases and weapons to PLO factions and European terrorist groups including the Irish Republican Army, the German Red Army Faction (Baader-Meinhof Group), and the Italian Red Brigades.

Conflict with Gadhafi's Libya was violent. In 1981, American planes shot down Libyan jets for menacing gestures over the Gulf of Sidra, which was unilaterally claimed by Libya. On April 5, 1986, Libyan agents, likely helped by East Germany, bombed La Belle Discotheque, frequented by U.S. soldiers in West Berlin. Three people, including two U.S. servicemen, were killed; 230 people, including 79 Americans, were injured. On April 15

President Ronald Reagan retaliated with air strikes that targeted Gadhafi's residence, killing 30 people, including his adopted daughter. Seeking revenge, Gadhafi authorized the December 1988 bombing of a Pan Am plane over Lockerbie, killing 270 people.

At this writing the civil war in Libya, which began in February 2011 with peaceful protests, has succeeded in toppling Gadhafi and his regime, with members of his family and top aides fleeing the country. Gadhafi, who had vowed to fight until death, was killed by rebel forces during a gun battle in Sirte on October 20, 2011.

RADICAL ISLAM

By 1979, radical Islam was spreading. In Iran, the Shiite Ayatollah Khomeini led the Iranian Revolution, and in early November the Revolutionary Guards took control of the U.S. embassy, capturing 52 American hostages and detaining them for 14 months. In late November, Sunni terrorists seized Mecca's Grand Mosque. Echoing Khomeini, they protested corruption and Westernization. This crisis lasted for two weeks and ended only after Saudi clergy permitted counterterrorism in Islam's holiest area. In December, fearing an Islamist victory over its allies there, Soviet troops invaded Afghanistan. The United States and other countries, through Pakistan's Inter-Services Intelligence Agency, supplied Afghan resistance forces with weapons and other logistical support throughout the 1980s. The defeated Soviet forces withdrew in 1989. Fundamentalist warriors such as Osama bin Laden gradually turned from American clients into sworn enemies.

In 1980, Iraq invaded the postrevolutionary, militarily weaker Iran. American clients Kuwait and Saudi Arabia feared fundamentalist Shiites. In 1985, however, American operatives secretly provided weapons to Iran, hoping to regain access and secure the release of American hostages held by Hezbollah; they used the proceeds to fund the Nicaraguan contras without congressional approval. In 1988, the Iran-Iraq War ended in a stalemate. Further violence ensued in 1990 when Iraq invaded Kuwait, refusing to pay war debts and claiming Kuwait as ancestral territory. American troops subsequently established bases in Saudi Arabia, and then, in a multilateral action with secular Arab regimes, such as Egypt and Syria, waged Desert Storm, ousting Iraq from Kuwait. The United States then established a no-fly zone in southern and northern Iraq to protect the Shiite and Kurd populations.

In 1992, the departing U.S. president George H. Bush intervened in Somalia to stop famine amid a devastating civil war. America, however, had oil interests and chose sides in the internal conflict. Suspecting the United States of hegemonic aspirations, fundamentalist warriors and possibly bin Laden orchestrated the October 1993 attacks known as Black Hawk Down. This operation left 19 U.S. servicemen dead.

Another country of concern to U.S. counterterrorism officials is Yemen. Yemen is polyethnic and multicultural with competing versions of Islam. Ali Abdullah Saleh's military regime failed to force unity onto potent secessionists. Saleh supported Hussein's invasion of Kuwait; he was anti-Saudi and friendly with Iran. In 2000, suicide bombers from al-Qaeda in the Arabian Peninsula, aided by Sudan, attacked the USS *Cole*, docked in Aden. Seventeen U.S. Navy personnel were killed, and another 39 were injured. Nevertheless, as Wikileaks confirmed in 2010, fears of Islamic fundamentalists in bin Laden's paternal homeland facilitated U.S. collaboration with Yemen on counterterrorism, including port visits and clandestine human and drone operations.

After September 11, President George W. Bush ordered attacks against Taliban and al-Qaeda bases in Afghanistan when the Taliban refused to surrender bin Laden. NATO troops joined this armed conflict, now in its 10th year. The Bush Doctrine demanded the accountability of terrorists and host countries alike. To stop future attacks President Bush advocated a preemptive strike against Iraq, for harboring terrorists and potentially possessing weapons of mass destruction. Simultaneously, American public diplomacy advocated a "freedom agenda" to spread democracy through civil institutions and free elections as an alternative to the repression and fear advocated by Muslim fundamentalism. In June 2005 in Cairo, Secretary of State Condoleezza Rice admitted that the United States preferred stability over democracy, often securing neither. Pressuring the secular PLO for such elections resulted in a January 2006 electoral victory for Hamas, the Palestinian ally of Egypt's Muslim Brotherhood. In June 2007, Hamas manipulated this victory to oust the PLO from the Gaza Strip. Hamas and other Palestinian groups use Gaza as a base for ground and missile attacks against Israel.

CONCLUSION

In the 1990s, the United States helped Muslims in the Balkans against Serb aggression, including armed attacks to help Kosovo in 1999. Following a relatively speedy victory over Saddam Hussein's regime in 2003, U.S. interests faced ongoing terrorist attacks from various local groups and cross-border mercenaries. The prolonged occupation of Arab and Muslim lands and the documented tale of torture in prisons such as Abu Ghraib, diminished American moral stature. Simultaneously, fundamentalist Iran's advanced nuclear program caused understandable fear among U.S. allies such as Israel and Saudi Arabia. Consistent Israeli sabotage increased regional tensions. America, by contrast, helped Iran following its 2004 earthquake.

The Tunisian, Egyptian, and Libyan revolutions coupled with political unrest throughout the Middle East and North Africa in 2011 are politically reshaping the region, realigning bilateral and international relationships. It remains unclear what direction these states will take regarding their domestic and international policies. Thus, the future role the United States will play as events unfold in this region is uncertain.

See also: **Volume 1, Part I:** Global Terrorism: Post-9/11; The Terrorist Threat in the 21st Century: A Global Security Problem; War on Terror. **Part II:** Egypt; Israel; Jordan; Saudi Arabia; United States; Yemen. **Part III:** Military Force: Effective against Terrorists?; Safe Havens and Weak and Failing States. **Part IV:** Combating Religiously Based Terrorism. **Part VI:** Global Jihad Movement; Regional Challenges: Promoting Stability through Economic, Social, and Political Reforms. **Volume 2, Appendix:** Al-Awlaki, Anwar

REFERENCES

Ben-Zvi, Abraham. *Me' Truman ad Obama: Alyiatm ve Shekiatam shel Yahasei Arzot Habrit-Israel* [From Truman to Obama: The Rise and Early Decline of American-Israeli Relations]. Tel Aviv: Yediot Books, 2011. [In Hebrew.]

Crenshaw, Martha. *Terrorism in Context.* University Park: Pennsylvania State University Press, 2004.

Kinzer, Stephen, *All the Shah's Men: An American Coup and the Roots of Middle East Terror.* Hoboken, NJ: John Wiley, 2003.

Leffler, Melvyn P., and Jeff Legro, eds. *In Uncertain Times: U.S. Foreign Policy after the Berlin Wall and 9/11.* Ithaca, NY: Cornell University Press, 2011.

Ninkovich, Frank. *The Wilsonian Century: U.S. Foreign Policy since 1900.* Chicago: University of Chicago Press, 1999.

Painter, David. *The Cold War: An International History.* London: Routledge, 2000.

Pillar, Paul R. *Terrorism and U.S. Foreign Policy.* Washington, DC: Brookings Institution Press, 2003.

Rose, Gideon, and Jonathan Tapperman, eds. *The U.S. vs. Al Qaeda: A History of the War on Terror.* New York: Council on Foreign Relations, 2011.

Wright, Lawrence. *The Looming Tower: Al-Qaeda and the Road to 9/11.* New York: Knopf, 2006.

United Nations Global Counterterrorism Strategy: Significance and Limitations

Sherrow Pinder

Many states struggled with terrorism prior to the 9/11 attacks in the United States in 2001. As early as 1934 the issue of developing a global framework for counterterrorism to address the issue of terrorist activities was presented to the League of Nations, the precursor of the United Nations (UN), which was founded in 1919. Terrorism, especially after 9/11, has provoked highly heated debates among many governments and intergovernmental bodies about how to develop and implement effective strategies to deal with the terrorism threat locally, nationally, and internationally. The UN General Assembly, one of the principal arms of the UN and the only one in which all of its 192 member states have equal representation, unanimously agreed to a global strategy to counter terrorism, both real and perceived. Framed around a broad range of issues pertaining to terrorist threats, on September 8, 2006, the UN Global Counterterrorism Strategy (UNGCS) was adopted.

MAIN OBJECTIVES

The main objectives of the UNGCS include addressing conditions that are contributing to the spread of terrorism; developing measures to prevent and combat terrorism by taking into account essential social, economic, and political conditions; building states' counterterrorism capacities; strengthening the responsibility of the UN in providing and facilitating support for regions that face grave challenges in the implementation of counterterrorism strategies; and counteracting terrorist threats, ensuring that human rights and civil liberties are not violated. Each UN member state is responsible for implementing the UNGCS. This article briefly outlines some of the significance and limitations of the UNGCS.

SIGNIFICANCE

Following the events of 9/11, the UN Security Council was charged with upholding international peace and security and defining the UN's post-9/11 response. A significant aspect of the UNGCS is its shift away from the approach led by the UN Security Council, whose main emphasis was on law enforcement and additional security measures. Another key component of the UNGCS is that it reflects the views of the member states in taking a more holistic approach to addressing the complexities and multifaceted nature of terrorist threats both nationally and globally. Given that the threat of terrorism varies in different regions of the world such as Africa, Latin America, Central America, and the Caribbean, "regional and subregional bodies are potentially better suited to develop approaches that can take into account cultural and other contextual issues and undertake specific, geographically-focused initiatives or other actions that complement and can build upon strategic objectives" (Rosand 2008, 8).

Additionally, the UNGCS, while focusing on efforts to persuade state governments to implement law enforcement and other security measures, is making important efforts to combat real terrorist threats to member nation states. Finally, with the help of the Counterterrorism Task Force and its working groups, many of the UN member states have taken steps to implement counterterrorism strategies. Bearing in mind the objectives of the UNGCS, some important steps are being taking into account by many state governments as well as intergovernmental organizations to incorporate provisions of the UNGCS into their counterterrorism strategies.

LIMITATIONS

In spite of the significance of the UNGCS in addressing terrorist threats, there are several limitations. First, the UNGCS adds very little to the pre-existing UN counterterrorism resolutions, norms, and procedures. Second, poverty, corruption, internal conflicts, and major health issues that present themselves in many countries located in regions such as Africa, Latin America, Central America, and the Caribbean pose many challenges for the effective implementation of the UNGCS. In fact, a great concern is whether terrorism in its existing form and manifestations represents a severe threat to these regions "on the same scale as poverty, the health crisis and internal conflicts" (Ewi and Aning 2006, 33), for example. Given the prevailing state of affairs in these regions, it is clear that counterterrorism strategy is not a priority for many state governments in these areas.

Third, while the UNGCS is fundamental for combating terrorist threats, in the face of human rights violations and lack of respect for fundamental rights and liberties, freedom, the rule of law, and religious and ethnic discrimination, there is not a clear and binding definition of terrorism and what constitutes a terrorist act, nationally and globally. Clearly, the lack of such a definition is an impediment to the development of uniform laws for combating terrorist attacks across the international system. In part, this lack of definitional consensus has prevented many governments from developing the proper framework for the enforcement of the UNGCS objectives. In fact, until now, some countries continue to lack counterterrorism legislation.

Fourth, for the UNGCS to have any meaningful and sustained impact on global counterterrorism efforts, the UN member states must convert the objectives of the UNGCS into action, as the chief of the UN's Terrorism Prevention Branch, Jean-Paul Laborde, noted in an unofficial statement to the General Assembly (Rosand 2008, 2). However, in some regions, it is difficult for many state governments to get cooperation from relevant regional bodies, civil society, and international organizations. The African Union, the forerunner of the Organization of African Unity, is a case in point. In fact, terrorism represents "the first global challenge" for the African Union (Ewi and Aning 2006, 33), and in spite of its own shortcomings in terms of building financial and human resource capacities, the African Union is a vital component in the various African states' ability to combat terrorism (Ewi and Aning 2006, 34). Finally, the implementation and effective distribution of the UNGCS pose grave challenges to nation-states that lack the needed technologies, infrastructure, and training capabilities for law enforcement officials and that have limited labor power.

CONCLUSION

In an effort to combat and thwart terrorist threats there are many important roles that other UN agencies, international organizations, governments, and nongovernmental organizations can play in enhancing the overall success of the UNGCS, most important, in regions that present grave challenges.

REFERENCES

Center on Global Counterterrorism Cooperation. "Implementing the UN Global-Counter Terrorism Strategy in the Americas." n.d. http://www.globalct.org/images/content/pdf/discussion/americas.pdf.

Ewi, Martin, and Kwesi Aning. "Assessing the Role of the African Region in Preventing and Combating Terrorism in Africa." *African Security Review* 15, no. 3 (2006): 33–46.

Rosand, Eric. "Implementation of the UN Global-Counter Terrorism Strategy in Africa: Opportunities and Challenges." Center on Global Counterterrorism Cooperation. 2008. http://www.globalct.org/resources_publications.php.

United Nations Security Council Resolution 1540

Jamie Walsh

In the wake of the September 11, 2001, attacks on the United States and subsequent international acts of terrorism that followed, it became clear that terrorist networks were determined to carry out, and capable of, large-scale operations on a level not previously considered. Information gathered in the aftermath of these attacks about the ambitions of terrorists and terrorist organizations to acquire and use nuclear, biological, or chemical weapons forced the international community to address the paucity of measures to deal with this security risk. Furthermore, revelations about the proliferation of nuclear weapons technology by a global network headed by Pakistan's Dr. A. Q. Khan pointed to the shortcomings of existing nonproliferation treaties and demonstrated that nonstate actors were active in both receiving and supplying weapons of mass destruction (WMD) capabilities.

CONTROLLING WMD PROLIFERATION

In response, on April 28, 2004, after months of intensive negotiations, the United Nations (UN) Security Council unanimously adopted Resolution

1540 (UNSCR 1540) under Chapter VII of the UN Charter. The resolution legally obliges states, in accordance with their national procedures, to adopt and enforce appropriate and effective laws that prohibit any non-state actor to manufacture, acquire, possess, develop, transport, transfer, or use nuclear, chemical, or biological weapons and their means of delivery, in particular for terrorist purposes, as well as to attempt to engage in any of the foregoing activities, participate in them as an accomplice, or assist or finance them.

The resolution also requires states to take and enforce effective measures to establish domestic controls to prevent the proliferation of nuclear, chemical, or biological weapons and their means of delivery, including by establishing appropriate controls over related materials in the areas of accounting/securing, physical protection, border and law enforcement, export, and transshipment.

Accordingly, states must:

(a) Develop and maintain appropriate effective measures to account for and secure such items in production, use, storage or transport;

(b) Develop and maintain appropriate effective physical protection measures;

(c) Develop and maintain appropriate effective border controls and law enforcement efforts to detect, deter, prevent and combat, including through international cooperation when necessary, the illicit trafficking and brokering in such items in accordance with their national legal authorities and legislation and consistent with international law;

(d) Establish, develop, review and maintain appropriate effective national export and trans-shipment controls over such items, including appropriate laws and regulations to control export, transit, trans-shipment and re-export and controls on providing funds and services related to such export and trans-shipment such as financing, and transporting that would contribute to proliferation, as well as establishing end-user controls; and establishing and enforcing appropriate criminal or civil penalties for violations of such export control laws and regulations. (United Nations Security Council 2004)

UNSCR 1540 represents a new component of the nonproliferation regime and a new role for the Security Council in the prevention of WMD proliferation. It is important to note that the resolution does not focus narrowly on terrorists but uses the rather broader concept of a nonstate actor, which it defines as an "individual or entity, not acting under the lawful authority of any State in conducting activities, which come within the scope of the resolution." This in itself is a departure from the traditional approach of nonproliferation arrangements that target the activities of states.

Significantly, by adopting the resolution entirely under Chapter VII of the UN Charter, which addresses "threats to the peace, breaches of the peace, and acts of aggression," the resolution is not only legally binding but also enforceable through the punitive measures available to the

Security Council. Furthermore, decisions adopted under Chapter VII are binding on all member states and override other international obligations. Thus, UNSCR 1540 attempts to fill the gaps in voluntary multilateral non-proliferation instruments such as the Biological Weapons Convention, the Chemical Weapons Convention, and the Nuclear Non-Proliferation Treaty.

This universal approach has significant potential to tackle some of the most pressing proliferation threats faced by the international community. However, the resolution requires complex implementation measures and mechanisms that stretch the capacity of a number of states, regardless of whether or not they support the objectives of the resolution. This raises questions regarding the feasibility of universal state adherence to its numerous obligations. As of June 2010, 27 states have yet to submit a national report on implementation of the resolution. Many states that have submitted national reports cite their membership in the WMD treaties mentioned earlier as proof of adherence to the resolution without providing any indication of domestic legal measures taken to address nonstate actors. Indeed, a serious challenge to implementation of the resolution is the lack of clarity about what it means for a state to be legally in compliance or noncompliance with the resolution's obligations.

1540 COMMITTEE

Paragraph 4 of UNSCR 1540 established a subcommittee of the Security Council to function as the repository of the national reports on the implementation of the resolution; this committee initially had a mandate of two years. However, given the slow progress of implementation, the Security Council extended the mandate of the 1540 Committee for a further two years with the adoption of Resolution 1673 on April 27, 2006. This resolution reiterated the objectives of Resolution 1540, expressed the interest of the Security Council in intensifying its efforts to promote full implementation of the resolution, and obliged the 1540 Committee to report again by April 2008.

The Security Council extended the mandate of the 1540 Committee again in 2008 with the adoption of Resolution 1810, this time for a period of three years, until April 25, 2011. Like UNSCR 1673, the resolution reaffirms the objectives of UNSCR 1540 and urges the 1540 Committee to continue strengthening its role in facilitating technical assistance to states, including by engaging actively in matching offers and requests for assistance. Through Resolution 1810, the Security Council also requested the 1540 Committee to consider a comprehensive review of the status of implementation of Resolution 1540.

The scope of activities of the 1540 Committee is derived from these resolutions and the Programmes of Work submitted to the president of the Security Council by the chair of the 1540 Committee. In the Ninth Programme of Work, which covers the period from January 2010 to January 31, 2011, the committee established working groups in the following areas:

(i) Monitoring and national implementation;

(ii) Assistance;

(iii) Cooperation with international organisations, including the Security Council Committees established pursuant to resolutions 1267 (1999) and 1373 (2001); and,

(iv) Transparency and media outreach.(United Nations Security Council 2010)

CONCLUSION

The 1540 Committee released its first report on implementation of the resolution to the UN Security Council in April 2006. The second one was presented in July 2008. A third report is expected by April 24, 2011.

REFERENCES

Crail, Peter. "Implementing UN Security Council Resolution 1540: A Risk Based Approach." Monterey Institute of International Studies, Center for Nonproliferation Studies. *Nonproliferation Review* 13, no. 2 (2006): 355–99. http://cns.miis.edu/npr/pdfs/132crail.pdf.

Nuclear Threat Initiative. UN Security Council Resolution 1540 Database. n.d. http://www.nti.org/db/1540/.

United Nations Security Council. "Programme of Work of the Security Council Committee Established Pursuant to Resolution 1540 (2004) from 1 February 2010 to 31 January 2011." S/2010/112, Annex. March 2, 2010, p. 11. http://daccess-dds-ny.un.org/doc/UNDOC/GEN/N10/255/57/PDF/N1025557.pdf?OpenElement.

United Nations Security Council. "United Nations Security Council Resolution 1540." 1540 Committee. 2004. http://www.un.org/sc/1540/index.shtml.

U.S. Antiterrorism Assistance Program

Michael B. Kraft

International cooperation is a critical component to countering terrorism, and the U.S. State Department's Antiterrorism Assistance (ATA) program is the U.S. government's premier foreign assistance program to bolster cooperation and strengthen the capabilities of friendly countries' civilian officials to counter terrorist threats. The ATA program was approved by Congress and launched in 1983 in the wake of a series of aircraft hijackings and other terrorist attacks overseas. In particular, it helped fill the gap left by post-Vietnam legislation that prohibited the Department of Defense from providing any assistance to the civilian security forces (especially the police) of other countries. The State Department and Congress realized that there was a need to strengthen the counterterrorism capabilities of civilian officials in friendly countries.

ANTITERRORISM TRAINING ASSISTANCE

From an American viewpoint, the devastating attacks by Hezbollah on the U.S. embassy and the Marine barracks in Beirut in 1983 underscored the reality that although some steps can be taken to protect American installations and personnel overseas, the basic security responsibility lies with the host country. Repeated terrorist attacks undermine the safety and stability of friendly countries.

From the outset, the ATA's legislative mandate has been to enhance the antiterrorism skills of friendly countries by providing counterterrorism training and equipment to civilian law enforcement officials; to improve bilateral ties with partner nations by offering assistance; and to increase respect for human rights by sharing modern, humane, and effective antiterrorism techniques with foreign civilian authorities (Public Law 98-151, 1983).

A broad array of training courses are offered, ranging from courses on the training of dogs to sniff out explosives and other explosives countermeasures to courses on airport and border security and crisis management seminars for senior officials. According to the State Department Office of the Coordinator for Counterterrorism, specific goals of ATA program include the following:

- "Protect national borders
- Protect critical infrastructure
- Protect the national leadership
- Respond to and resolve terrorist incidents
- Investigate and prosecute those responsible for terrorist acts
- Respond to weapons of mass destruction attacks
- Manage kidnapping for ransom crimes
- Respond to terrorist incidents resulting in mass casualties or fatalities"

In addition to teaching critical skills in a variety of security disciplines, the ATA program also helps develop international networks among U.S. and foreign counterterrorism experts and law enforcement officers at the national and local levels. State Department officials say the network of contacts and exchanges of information have been instrumental in foiling various international terror plots. In many countries, they have testified, ATA-trained officials have played key roles in local, regional, and global counterterrorism efforts. ATA alumni have also served as the lead investigators of a number of recent terrorist attacks and have utilized their training to arrest many of the perpetrators (Pope 2005).

The program also indirectly protects American interests overseas and indirectly helps protect Americans traveling or living abroad, as host countries are responsible for protecting persons on their soil. The 2009 ATA report stated that the director of the Colombian National Police training facility credited ATA for much of the country's success in reducing by almost 90 percent the high number of kidnappings for ransom that plagued the country (U.S. Department of State 2010a).

Since the ATA program was first authorized in fiscal year 1983 at a cost of $5 million, about 67,000 persons from 159 countries have taken part in ATA training events, according to the State Department report. In fiscal year 2009, 6,015 persons from 75 countries took part in training events, such as courses that can last from one to five weeks or seminars and workshops. The administration's fiscal year 2012 budget request submitted to Congress was $192.7 million, a reduction of about $13 million from the previous year, but the Obama administration also requested $17 million to help train foreign officials in countering terrorism financing. Depending on their funding and scheduling, the ATA programs typically provide about 350 training courses and events annually, for officials from 60 countries (U.S. Department of State 2010b).

The State Department's ATA program is a cooperative effort between the Office of the Coordinator for Counterterrorism and the Bureau of Diplomatic Security. The Office of the Coordinator for Counterterrorism, which is charged with coordinating U.S. overseas counterterrorism policies, provides policy guidance to the ATA program. It determines, for example, the priorities for which countries are authorized to participate in the program. The Bureau of Diplomatic Security's Office of Anti-terrorism Assistance implements and manages program operations. Congress divided the functions in 1985, with members and staff saying that the regional security officers in each embassy, assigned by the Diplomatic Security Bureau, are the U.S. officials who usually have the most direct contact with local security forces. In managing the program, the Office of Anti-terrorism Assistance draws on the training expertise of not only State Department officials but also the staff of a variety of other federal agencies, such as the Justice Department, Transportation Security Administration, and local officials, for example, in training hostage negotiators.

Before training is initiated within a specific country, assessment teams from the U.S. government meet with the host country officials. The approval process includes not only the Office of the Coordinator for Counterterrorism and the Bureau of Diplomatic Security but also the regional bureaus, the local embassy, and State Department human rights officials. When the program first started in the 1980s, Congress required that the courses be taught within the United States, reflecting concerns that some programs in previous years, such as the old Public Safety Program, had trained local officials who later violated human rights. Human rights issues are woven into the training programs, and as Congress became more comfortable with the program, it agreed to the State Department's request to lift the ban. It is generally less costly and more efficient to send a small number of trainers overseas than to bring a class of 20 or 40 persons to the United States. Currently, about 90 percent of the courses are taught overseas, either in the host country or in regional centers.

The program has evolved over the past decades, both to meet changing terrorist threats and to improve crisis coordination capabilities as well as technical skills. Pakistan, for example, is a high priority, with programs offered at the federal and provincial levels. The ATA program also provides follow-up training where necessary, for example, after a few years when those who originally received training, such as airport officials, move on to other jobs or retire. There has, therefore, been an increasing emphasis on "training the trainers." As part of the effort to monitor and evaluate performance, the Office of Anti-terrorism Assistance conducts regular assessments of the country programs.

CONCLUSION

In the 2009 assessments, the programs for some countries were refocused, and Colombia had entered the sustainment phase. Colombia, Turkey, and Jordan have progressed through bilateral and independent efforts to the point that they can not only train many of their new officers but also provide training assistance to officials from neighboring countries. This is a major development for a program where the demand for U.S.-led courses often exceeds the supply of funds and manpower available.

See also: **Volume 1, Part III:** Counterterrorism Training. **Part IV:** U.S. Legislative Initiatives to Combat Terrorism pre-911; U.S. Legislative Initiatives to Combat Terrorism since 9/11. **Part VI:** Counterterrorism Research: Current Efforts and Future Challenges

REFERENCES

Kraft, Michael B. "Helping Other Countries Counter Terrorism." *Journal of Counterterrorism & Homeland Security International* 14, no. 2 (Summer 2008): 30–34.
Kraft, Michael B., and Celina Realuyo. "U.S. Interagency Efforts to Combat International Terrorism through Foreign Capacity Building Programs." In *Project on National Security Reform: Case Studies*. Vol. 2. Carlisle, PA: Strategic Studies Institute of the U.S. Army War College, 2011. Summary available at http://www.pnsr.org/web/page/707/sectionid/579/pagelevel/3/parentid/590/interior.asp.
Pope, William P. "Eliminating Terrorist Sanctuaries: The Role of Security Assistance." Prepared testimony before the U.S. House of Representatives International Relations Committee, Subcommittee on International Terrorism and Nonproliferation, Washington, DC, March 10, 2005. http://merln.ndu.edu/archivepdf/terrorism/state/43702.pdf.

Public Law 98-151, "Joint Resolution: Making Further Continuing Appropriations for the Fiscal Year 1984." Antiterrorism Assistance Program, November 14, 1983, 22 U.S.C. §§ 2349aa 2349aa-1. http://codes.lp.findlaw.com/uscode/22/32/II/VIII/2349aa-1; http://history.nih.gov/research/downloads/PL98-151.pdf.

U.S. Department of State. "Executive Budget Summary: Function 150 and Other International Programs." FY 2012. 2011, 105–6 and 163. http://www.state.gov/documents/organization/156214.pdf.

U.S. Department of State, Bureau of Diplomatic Security. "Antiterrorism Assistance Program." 2010a. http://www.state.gov/m/ds/terrorism/c8583.htm.

U.S. Department of State, Bureau of Diplomatic Security. "ATA report for FY 2009." 2010b. http://www.state.gov/documents/organization/143139.pdf.

U.S. Department of State, Office of the Coordinator for Counterterrorism. "Antiterrorism Assistance Program (ATA)." n.d.

U.S. Counterterrorism Policy: Impact on International Relations

Peter Rainow

U.S. counterterrorism policy involves the selection, distribution, and application of all resources and means available to prevent and/or eradicate global terrorism and its support networks. U.S. counterterrorism policy impacts the whole pattern of American relations with a number of international actors (U.S. allies, neutral countries, states supporting terrorism, and nonstate actors). A successful counterterrorism policy must target the vital dimensions of terrorism; address its current and prospective trends; reflect its rapidly changing nature, complexity, and flexibility; and employ a wide array of military, political, economic, social, ideological, cultural, law enforcement, and other means in often intermingled offensive and defensive efforts.

EXPANSION AND LETHALITY OF INTERNATIONAL TERRORISM

Terrorist activity, especially from Islamic extremists based in Asia and the Middle East, has in recent years demonstrated significantly increasing diversity and complexity. There is a wide range of participants with a diverse set of motivations, goals, structures, and strategies. Despite the destruction of the al-Qaeda sanctuaries in Afghanistan after the September 11, 2001, terror attacks, this global terrorist clearinghouse network continues to operate and, utilizing global information technology, continues to recruit and train supporters, share experiences, coordinate the activities of various widely dispersed terrorist cells, and advance its ideological and strategic goals. These include the eradication of U.S. and Western influence and presence in the region and the overthrow of existing regimes that cooperate with the West.

The successful expansion of transnational terrorism owes much to the emergence of so-called failed states such as Afghanistan or Somalia, where such terrorism was able to prosper, virtually unchecked, due to a combination of political and social disintegration, fierce civil strife, and a lack of interest and support from the international community. Accordingly, transnational terrorists use the paramount anarchy in the failed states as well as weak governmental control over some portions of territory to obtain safe haven and to set up their training camps and communication centers, exploiting the remains of local infrastructure. In the late 1990s al-Qaeda managed to secure a close alliance with the Taliban in Afghanistan. The Taliban, after being driven from power in Afghanistan in 2001, has managed to reestablish itself in certain areas, including the remote Afghanistan-Pakistan border.

An effective U.S. counterterrorism policy must also take into account new developments in the strategy and tactics of terrorist actors. Terrorists have consistently tried to acquire more lethal weapons. This is particularly true with respect to weapons of mass destruction. Until 2001 al-Qaeda, using sanctuaries in Afghanistan, planned to launch chemical or biological attacks on U.S. and European targets. In addition to the continuous pursuit of more deadly weapons, the terrorists persistently employ suicide bombings to increase the lethality of their attacks.

Terrorist leaders have also demonstrated their ability to adjust to changing conditions. The decentralized, loose organizational structure of al-Qaeda allowed it to continue to operate even after the loss of Afghanistan in 2001. This has been amply demonstrated in terrorist attacks perpetrated in Yemen, Tunisia, Saudi Arabia, Jordan, and Kuwait as well as in Istanbul, Madrid, and London. The U.S. government had argued that al-Qaeda operated a network that recruited and operated in the Muslim communities of Britain, France, Germany, Italy, Spain, the Netherlands, and Belgium. Current thinking, however, sees al-Qaeda more as an inspiration to and clearinghouse for local groups that are autonomous from the al-Qaeda "core." Through active participation in the Iraqi insurgency since 2003, terrorist networks have acquired experience in urban warfare and enhanced their skills in ambush tactics, assassinations, and kidnappings.

The profound transformation in both the scale and the complexity of the operations that terrorists can undertake allows powerful, well-organized, and devoted groups and associations as well as smaller ones to evade state powers and to obtain global-reach capability. These terrorists are able to profoundly endanger international security.

TRANSNATIONAL STRUGGLE

Because the terrorist challenge amounts to a new form of warfare, successful counterterrorism policy must constantly realign itself with the developments in the threats. The experience of American strategic allies is important in this respect. Conventional military force has played a strong role in the struggle against alleged terrorism, as the long history of Israeli military campaigns against the Palestine Liberation Organization, the Israeli-Hezbollah War of 2006, and the Gaza War of 2009 demonstrate. At the same time, Israel's strategy of heavy punishment of a neighboring state for permitting and/or abetting terrorism, while inflicting disproportionate loss of life and property damage, does not seem to have ended terrorist activity, which its proponents regard as rightful and necessary resistance, and has led to serious criticism of the Jewish state, even from its traditional allies.

Special operations forces play an important role in the struggle against terrorism. While capable of global reach, military operations against terrorists need to be pinpointed and limited in scale to avoid harm to civilians and collateral damage. This is particularly important because of particular government's inability or reluctance to attack terrorist leadership and cells directly. Special operations transcend national boundaries and reflect the transnational character of the struggle against terrorism. The Israeli experience with deep-penetration commando raids and targeted assassinations of terrorist leaders reveals the ability of special operations to undermine the morale and disrupt the activities of terrorist organizations and to violate state sovereignty as well as the terms of truces concluded with the enemy, although there are limits to what special operations can accomplish. Primarily, these special operations have angered local populations, making the resistance, or terrorism, that much more difficult to uproot.

Conventional military approaches retain their importance in dealing with state-sponsored terrorism, namely, to wage wars against nations and achieve regime change, surely denying safe haven for terrorists and their allies. At the same time, as the U.S.-led campaigns in Afghanistan after 2001 and Iraq after 2003 have demonstrated, even victorious conventional campaigns can be complicated by ensuing insurgencies, which demand much greater flexibility on the part of the military. Here again, special operations come into play.

While the achievement of a decisive military victory remains elusive because of the dispersed and decentralized organizational structure of modern terrorism and while the use of military means resembles an endless war of attrition, the readiness to apply overwhelming and destructive military force can work to some extent. As recent changes in the policies of the Palestinian National Authority and Libya suggest, providing government bodies with enticements to stop terrorist activities can also work to curb terrorist activity. These include economic, territorial, and governing incentives.

Diplomacy is another essential tool in counterterrorism policy. International cooperation is vital in collecting information on terrorist cells, which includes the tracking and disruption of terrorists' financial transactions, recruitment, and propaganda activities. It is also of paramount importance in seeking to isolate regimes that sponsor terrorism.

Intelligence gathering is likewise essential in any successful counterterrorist policy. Simply gathering the information is not sufficient; it must be properly disseminated and coordinated within government agencies. The failure of the U.S. intelligence community to provide early warning about the September 11 terrorist attacks demonstrates this all too clearly.

Defensive efforts within the framework of counterterrorism policy focus predominantly on homeland security and encompass enhanced border security. This includes monitoring and protecting likely terrorist targets (transportation, communication systems, and other critical infrastructure as well as high-profile targets and places where there is a significant concentration of people) using intelligence, law enforcement, and military means. The importance of the task is underlined by the reality that despite large-scale domestic security improvements since September 11, 2001, the United States and European countries still remain vulnerable to terrorist attacks because of porous borders and/or the ability of the Islamic terrorists to strike from inside, mobilizing militants from the Muslim diaspora, particularly in Western Europe.

CONCLUSION

Comprehensive and multifaceted counterterrorism policy must also involve political efforts to mobilize domestic support, social and cultural efforts to resist extremist propaganda, and a determination to resolve problems and issues that terrorists often use for their own advantage. This is perhaps the most challenging aspect of any successful counterterrorism policy. It should include the resolution of regional disputes, especially the Israeli-Palestinian issue; the advancement of economic development; progress in addressing economic inequality and poverty; the promotion of democracy; high-quality governance; and the rule of law.

See also: **Volume 1, Part III:** Defensive Measures against Terrorism: Military Preemption and Retaliation; Intelligence Sharing and Law Enforcement Cooperation between Nations; International Law, Human Rights, and Counterterrorism; U.S. Immigration Policies: Impact on Moderate Muslims. **Part IV:** Terrorism, War, and Revolution in the Middle East: Problems for U.S. Foreign Policy; U.S. Antiterrorism Assistance Program; U.S. Legislative Initiatives to Combat Terrorism since 9/11. **Part VI:** Counterterrorism Research: Current Efforts and Future Challenges

REFERENCES

Berntsen, Garry. *Human Intelligence, Counterterrorism, and National Leadership: A Practical Guide.* Washington, DC: Potomac Books, 2008.

Forrest, James J.F. *Countering Terrorism and Insurgency in the 21st Century.* 3 vols. Westport, CT: Praeger Security International, 2007.

Freedman, George. *America's Secret War: Inside the Worldwide Struggle between America and Its Enemies.* New York: Broadway Books, 2004.

Guiora, Amos N. *Global Perspectives on Counterterrorism.* New York: Aspen, 2007.

U.S. Legislative Initiatives to Combat Terrorism pre-9/11

Michael B. Kraft

Long before the 9/11 attacks and disputes over the use of civilian courts versus military tribunals for trying major terrorist suspects, the U.S. government had already been using a variety of laws and regulations as major tools against terrorism. The wide-ranging pre-9/11 U.S. legal measures against terrorists and their supporters include international counterterrorism treaties and their implementing legislation, sanctions against exports to or imports from state sponsors of terrorism, denial of visas to persons involved in terrorist activities, and prohibitions on providing funding or other material support for terrorist acts and organizations. By way of illustration of the many laws, aviation security statutes authorize the president to ban air service to countries that harbor terrorists who threaten aviation. Other laws control biological, chemical, and nuclear materials that could be used for weapons of mass destruction. Legislation also allows private U.S. citizens to file civil suits against foreign governments that support international terrorism and terrorist groups.

LEGISLATION TO COMBAT TERRORISM

Beginning in the 1970s, U.S. legislative counterterrorism efforts focused on sanctions against countries that supported terrorism. This caused some terrorist groups to begin developing their own funding sources. The United States reacted by enacting specific counterterrorism measures aimed at nonstate actors to bolster existing criminal laws covering murder and other acts that are crimes regardless of the motive.

Apparently forgotten by many who criticize the use of criminal laws instead of military courts and actions against terrorists, President Ronald Reagan's administration emphasized that terrorists are criminals and should be treated as such. "We must attack the problem of terrorism as a crime against the international community whenever and wherever possible," President Reagan told Congress in 1984 while seeking additional counterterrorism legislation (Reagan 1984). Following a series of major terrorist attacks, the Reagan administration developed a public diplomacy program to counter the notion overseas that the terrorists were romantic "freedom fighters" (Reagan 1986).

In strengthening the rule of law against terrorists, the United States promoted additional international counterterrorism treaties covering terrorist attacks such as bombings of buildings and attacks on civilian shipping. A common feature of the 13 international United Nations conventions is a requirement that the signatory countries prosecute or extradite culprits found on their territory. Congress usually passed the necessary implementing legislation as part of broader bills. For example the Comprehensive Crime Control Act of 1984 included implementing legislation for the conventions on hostage taking (18 U.S.C. 1203) and the Montreal Convention on Aircraft Sabotage (18 U.S.C. 32).

ECONOMIC SANCTIONS

Economic sanctions were among the first major legal counterterrorism tools used against terrorists and governments that support them. In 1976, Congress authorized the president to cut off foreign aid to "any government which aids or abets, by providing sanctuary from prosecution, to any group or individual which has committed an act of international terrorism" (International Security Assistance and Arms Export Control Act 1976). Three years later, Congress enacted a broader major counterterrorism law that is still a pillar of sanctions legislation after more than three decades: the so-called terrorism list legislation. The Export Administration Act of 1979, Section 6 (j), required the executive branch to notify Congress 30 days in advance before issuing export licenses for dual-use goods and services (that can be used for military or terrorism purposes as well as civilian use) to countries that the secretary of state has determined have "repeatedly provided support for acts of international terrorism" (U.S. Congress 1979).

The U.S. House of Representatives Foreign Affairs Committee members initiated the legislation after learning that midlevel Commerce and State Department officials approved licenses for exporting to Libya 400 heavy-duty trucks used for tank transport and exporting to Syria six C-130 cargo planes. Both countries were involved in terrorism activities. I was a legislative aide to one of the co-authors at the time and remember that committee members felt that such sales had foreign policy implications. Therefore, they contended, such sales should first be approved at high levels in the executive branch, followed by a notification to Congress with enough time for members to take action if they so chose (Alexander and

Kraft 2008, 12–17). Additional sanctions enacted later cut off foreign or military assistance and denied tax credits for income earned in countries on the terrorist list. Other provisions prohibited financial transactions, a measure also intended to discourage business dealings as well as travel. The United States is also required to oppose loans to the terrorist countries by international banking institutions.

In the mid-1990s, as some terrorist states began reducing their active support, the legislative focus shifted to pressuring terrorist groups that were increasingly independent from rogue states. Some secular terrorist groups, such as the Abu Nidal Organization, began using front companies and organizations to obtain and transfer funds rather than depending on state sponsors. Extremist fundamentalist groups such as al-Qaeda and Hamas were emerging and raising large sums of money through so-called charities, used as front organizations. I was the U.S. State Department Counterterrorism Office legislative officer at the time and worked with State Department and Justice Department lawyers to draft comprehensive legislation that was intended to take the offensive against terrorists by curbing money flows and other forms of material support to reduce their ability to attack. A significant impetus was a series of major terrorist attacks in the Middle East in 1994.

In January 1995, the Clinton administration's major counterterrorism legislation was introduced in Congress. In April 1996, after numerous hearings and some congressional revisions, President Clinton signed the Antiterrorism and Effective Death Penalty Act (AEDPA) of 1996 (P.L. 104-132, 110 Stat; Doyle 1996). The many counterterrorism sections include two material support provisions. One makes it a criminal offense for American citizens, residents, or organizations to knowingly provide funds and other material forms of support, such as weapons, safe houses, training, communications equipment, and financial services, to groups formally designated as foreign terrorist organizations by the secretary of state with the concurrence of the attorney general and secretary of the treasury. As of November, 2010, 47 groups were on the foreign terrorist organization list, which changes as groups are added or removed, based on analysis by State Department and intelligence officials (U.S. Department of State 2011).

A second material support provision, strengthening an earlier version in the 1994 Crime Bill, criminalizes material support for specific acts, whether perpetrated by individuals or previously unknown groups. The material support provisions have been a major tool in the fight against terrorists. More than 190 persons have been charged with violations under one or both of the material support provisions, of whom more than 112 have been convicted or pled guilty.

Another useful legal tool is the so-called long-arm statute, enacted following the 1985 series of aircraft hijackings and the capture of the *Achille Lauro*, an Italian cruise liner, by Palestinian terrorists who tossed overboard an American passenger in his wheelchair, Leon Klinghoffer. Enacted as part of the Omnibus Diplomatic Security and Antiterrorism Act of 1986, the long-arm statute makes a terrorist's murder of an American citizen overseas a crime punishable in U.S. courts. The attorney general first has to make a determination that the event was terrorist related (U.S. Department of Justice 1986).

The new statute enabled the Federal Bureau of Investigation to station legal attaches (Legats) at many U.S. embassies to conduct investigations of terrorist attacks against Americans and assist the host governments. Currently, there are 60 Legat offices worldwide with another 15 suboffices. In another expansion of U.S. law, sought by the families of victims of Pan Am Flight 103, section 221 of the Antiterrorism and Effective Death Penalty Act of 1996 amended the Foreign Sovereign Immunities Act to allow U.S. nationals to bring civil actions against terrorist actions supported by governments on the secretary of state's terrorism list (Title 28 U.S.C. Section 1605(a) (7)). After 9/11, the civil-suit approach was broadened to permit civil suits to also be brought against individuals, foreign nongovernmental organizations, and domestic organizations. In some instances courts have awarded large damages. But collection has been very difficult (Elsea 2007).

In addition to laws relating to crime and punishment, Congress enacted legislation authorizing specific programs to counter terrorism. For example, in 1983, Congress authorized the Antiterrorism Assistance (ATA) training program to help the law enforcement personnel of foreign countries improve their ability to deter terrorist attacks, and in 1984 Congress enacted the Reagan administration's legislation to establish the U.S. Department of State's Rewards for Justice Program (i.e., paying rewards for information leading to the effective prosecution of persons committing terrorism against American targets or information leading to the prevention of an act of terrorism). The largest reward ever offered was $25 million, for Osama bin Laden. In 1986, Congress authorized the Technical Support Working Group, an interagency counterterrorism research and development program within the U.S. Department of Defense.

CONCLUSION

The laws cited in the preceding, by no means a comprehensive list, indicate the large platform of underlying laws used to support the counterterrorism efforts of the U.S. government. They provide a base for post-9/11 laws such as the USA PATRIOT Act. For more than four decades, specific laws aimed at deterring and prosecuting terrorists have been a major feature of America's counterterrorism effort. Justice Department officials expect they will continue to evolve and be fine-tuned.

See also: **Volume 1, Part III:** Counterterrorism Training. **Part IV:** U.S. Antiterrorism Assistance Program; U.S. Legislative Initiatives to Combat Terrorism since 9/11. **Part VI:** Counterterrorism Research: Current Efforts and Future Challenges

REFERENCES

Abrams, Norman. *Anti-terrorism and Criminal Enforcement.* 3rd abridged ed. St. Paul, MN: Thompson/West, 2008.

Alexander, Yonah, and Michael Kraft, eds. *The Evolution of U.S. Counterterrorism Policy.* Vol. 1. Westport, CT: Greenwood/Praeger, 2008.

Chesney, Robert. "The Sleeper Scenario: Terrorism-Support Laws and the Demands of Prevention." *Harvard Journal on Legislation* 42, no. 1, (2005): 1–89. http://papers.ssrn.com/sol3/papers.cfm?abstract_id=587442.

Doyle, Charles. "Antiterrorism and Effective Death Penalty Act of 1996: A Summary." American Law Division, Congressional Research Service, June 3, 1996. http://www.fas.org/irp/crs/96-499.htm.

Elsea, Jennifer K. "Suits against Terrorist States by Victims of Terrorism." Congressional Research Service, December 17, 2007.

International Security Assistance and Arms Export Control Act of 1976, Section 303, modified in P.L. 107-115: Stat. 3147, 2153, 2155, in 2002. Cornell University Law School. http://www.law.cornell.edu/uscode/html/uscode50a/usc_sec_50a_00002405-

Levitt, Matthew. *Targeting Terror: U.S. Policy toward Middle Eastern State Sponsors and Terrorist Organizations, Post September 11.* Washington, DC: Washington Institute for Near East Policy, 2003.

McCormack, Wayne. *Legal Responses to Terrorism.* 2nd ed. San Francisco: Lexis-Nexis, Mathew Bender, 2008.

Reagan, Ronald. "Message to the Congress, International Terrorism Legislation." April 26, 1984. http://www.gwu.edu/~nsarchiv/NSAEBB/NSAEBB55/nsdd138stmt.pdf

Reagan, Ronald. "Radio Address to the Nation." May 31, 1986. http://www.reagan.utexas.edu/archives/speeches/1986/53186a.htm.

United States Code. Title 18 U.S.C. 1203. Cornell University Law School. http://www.law.cornell.edu/uscode/uscode18/usc_sec_18_00001203—000-.html.

United States Code . Title 18 U.S.C. 32. Cornell University Law School. http://www.law.cornell.edu/uscode/uscode18/usc_sec_18_00000032—000-.html.

United States Code . Title 28 U.S.C., section 1605(a) (7), Cornell University Law School. http://www.law.cornell.edu/uscode/28/usc_sec_28_00001605—A000-.html

United States Code. Title 50 U.S.C. 2405, subsection j as modified. Cornell University Law School. http://www.law.cornell.edu/uscode/html/uscode50a/usc_sec_50a_00002405—000-.html.

U.S. Congress. Export Administration Act (EAA) of 1979 (P.L. 96-72) Section 6 (j), 1979.

U.S. Congress Omnibus Diplomatic Security and Anti-Terrorism Act of 1986, P.L.99-399 and later modified as 18 USC 2332, Section 1202 in U.S.

Department of Justice. Criminal Resource Manual 12, n.d. http://www.usdoj.gov/usao/eousa/foia_reading_room/usam/title9/crm00012.htm.

U.S. Department of Defense, Combating Terrorism Technical Support Office. "About TSWG Technical Support Working Group." n.d. http://www.tswg.gov/about.html; http://www.tswg.gov/.

U.S. Department of Justice. Legal Attache Offices, Federal Bureau of Investigation (FBI), International Operations. n.d. http://www2.fbi.gov/contact/legat/legat.htm.

U.S. Department of State. "Rewards for Justice Program." http://www.rewardsforjustice.net/.

U.S. Department of State, Office of the Coordinator for Counterterrorism. "Antiterrorism Assistance Program." n.d. http://www.state.gov/m/ds/terrorism/c8583.htm.

U.S. Department of State, Office of the Coordinator for Counterterrorism. "Foreign Terrorist Organizations." August 18, 2011. http://www.state.gov/j/ct/rls/crt/2010/170264.htm.

U.S. Legislative Initiatives to Combat Terrorism since 9/11

Katherine E. Ellison

When terrorists attacked the World Trade Center and Pentagon on 9/11 in 2001, effectively using commercial passenger jets as missiles, it was not the first time that terrorism had struck the United States at home. Prior to 9/11, terrorists had attacked the United States a number of times; the most notable attacks included the 1993 bombing of the World Trade Center and the bombing of the Murrah Federal Building in Oklahoma City in 1995. However, these previous attacks did not garner the immediate and overwhelming response of the American people that the 9/11 attacks did. In the wake of these attacks, the George W. Bush administration in conjunction with the 107th Congress began work on a series of legislative reforms designed to counter the terrorist threat and strengthen national security.

FEDERAL LEGISLATION AND U.S. NATIONAL SECURITY

These legislative initiatives set in place sweeping security reforms not seen since President Harry Truman's creation of the National Security State in 1947. Additionally, as a result of the subsequent war on terror, much of this legislation was renewed and improved on in the years following 9/11.

In the first few days after the 9/11 attacks, Congress looked to the immediate problems with the air transportation industry that allowed the 9/11 hijackers to board and gain control of American Airlines Flights 11 and 77 and United Airlines Flights 175 and 93. This inquiry resulted in the 2001 Air Transportation Safety and System Stabilization Act and Aviation and Transportation Security Act. The first of these acts simply sought to save the airline industry from almost certain financial collapse due to victim compensation and lost revenue, retaining air transportation as an option for future travelers. The Aviation and Transportation Security Act amended this first act just two months later, adding an improved element of security to the recovering aviation industry.

The Aviation and Transportation Security Act largely sought to increase security measures via the establishment of two new regulatory bodies, the Transportation Security Administration (TSA) and the Transportation Security Oversight Board, within the Department of Transportation. The TSA provided airport screening of passengers and property and placed federal air marshals on any flights that required increased security. The board oversaw the actions of the TSA and coordinated federal transportation-related intelligence, security, and law enforcement activities. The remainder of the Aviation and Transportation Security Act sought other increased safety measures such as strengthening cockpit doors on airplanes, prohibiting aliens from certain pilot training programs, and increasing civil and criminal penalties for those interfering with airport security.

After Congress dealt with the airlines, they turned to other threats, renewed by the unforeseen nature of the 9/11 attacks. Along these lines, Congress passed the Bioterrorism Preparedness Act and the Financial Anti-terrorism Act of 2001. The former enlarged the responsibilities of the secretary of health and human services and the Centers for Disease Control while increasing the available supply of vaccines and medical supplies in the event of a bioterrorist attack. This act also sought to better coordinate states and the federal government in the event of a biological disaster as well as to protect agriculture and the food supply. As part of the Bioterrorism Preparedness Act, Congress provided block grants to U.S. states and territories to improve their internal bioterrorism response and coordination procedures.

TERRORIST FUNDING

The Financial Anti-terrorism Act dealt with what was believed to be at the heart of all terrorist activity: funding. The largest problem with terrorists, as opposed to a traditional enemy, was their transient and transnational nature. To successfully execute their plots, terrorist groups needed funding for training, living expenses, and necessary materials. The U.S. government believed that al-Qaeda and other terrorist groups filtered much of this funding through American financial institutions to evade detection and avoid alerting authorities to the suspicious nature of the recipients. As a result, the Financial Anti-terrorism Act sought stricter regulation of currency and domestic and international money-laundering activities, as well as increased cooperation between the government and private financial institutions that might first recognize questionable activities.

USA PATRIOT ACT

While the legislation already mentioned was necessary and addressed many security-related shortcomings, the keystone of post-9/11 counterterrorism legislation was the Uniting and Strengthening America by Providing Appropriate Tools Required to Intercept and Obstruct Terrorism Act of 2001, better known by its acronym, the USA PATRIOT Act, or simply the PATRIOT Act. Despite the initial controversy over it, the PATRIOT Act did not differ dramatically from preexisting legislation in allowing government designation of groups as terrorist organizations, permitting the use of secret evidence in terrorist cases, and criminalizing the provision of material or expert support to terrorist groups. The 107th Congress took these key provisions from the earlier Anti-terrorism and Effective Death Penalty Act of 1996, put into effect after the Oklahoma City bombing.

The PATRIOT Act also incorporated earlier security measures passed by Congress. Strengthening of the U.S. borders, surveillance, and criminal laws against terrorism, combating of cyberterrorism, and better detection of money laundering used to fund terrorist groups were all individual efforts brought together in the PATRIOT Act. The original act also included provisions on using spies to infiltrate terrorist groups. However, the real backbone to the PATRIOT Act was its removal of legal barriers between law enforcement and judicial agencies. The former separation between agencies had prevented law enforcement and intelligence officials from sharing information between different investigations. Congress and the Bush administration cited this disconnection as the reason why the 9/11 attacks had happened despite some warnings across agencies. Additionally, under the PATRIOT Act, law enforcement officials were given greater leeway with administering search warrants. One warrant now covered any and all locations where suspected terrorist activity was taking place, instead of officials needing multiple warrants for multiple locations.

While the PATRIOT Act became law on October 26, 2001, the original document neglected many necessary checks and balances on the extensive authority granted the government and law enforcement. The law did have a "sunset" provision that required Congress to renew certain parts on a periodic basis prior to their expiration. The first of these renewals came up in 2005 after the PATRIOT Act had taken full effect. Concerns over the abuse of surveillance techniques, such as the roving wiretap, caused the public, media, and Congress to question the act's infringement on civil rights. Despite this initial disagreement over renewal, Congress finally passed the renewal with some minor revisions. Congress continues to extend the PATRIOT Act despite its faults.

HOMELAND SECURITY

The other major congressional initiative designed to counter terrorism in the post-9/11 period was the Homeland Security Act of 2002. The Homeland Security Act served to bring together the various institutions that dealt with issues of terror detection and prevention in more than 20 federal departments and agencies under one Department of Homeland Security. Homeland Security brought members of border security, cyberterrorism forces, and emergency response teams, along with those agencies dealing with countermeasures for chemical, biological, nuclear, and radiological weapons, together under one chain of command so that they could theoretically be as effective as possible. Additionally, the Homeland Security Act shifted antiterrorism-related prevention and emergency management offices within other departments into the Department of Homeland Security.

Subsequent acts during the George W. Bush administration further synchronized the intelligence community and expanded their terrorist-hunting capabilities. The Intelligence Reform and Terrorism Prevention Act of 2004, passed after Bush's reelection in November 2004, actually amended Truman's National Security Act of 1947. The act further restructured the intelligence community and provided additional measures to improve the U.S. response to terrorist threats. Among other things, this act created a president-appointed director of national intelligence to head and coordinate all agencies that comprise the intelligence community, serve as a liaison between the Federal Bureau of Investigation and Central Intelligence Agency, and advise the president on all intelligence matters. Additionally, a National Counterterrorism Center became part of the Office of the Intelligence Director.

One aspect of the Intelligence Reform and Terrorism Prevention Act that was especially controversial was known as the "Lone Wolf" Amendment. This provision allowed the government to track foreign individuals involved in terrorist activity who were not agents of a foreign government or terrorist organization. In the final version of this provision, the act designated any individual terrorists to be assumed agents of a foreign power. This aspect brought into question the definition of both "terrorist activity" and "agent of a foreign power." Opponents of the Lone Wolf Amendment argued that this provision violated citizens' civil rights by giving the government free-range surveillance capabilities over anyone of foreign nationality.

The Intelligence Reform and Terrorism Prevention Act additionally included several suggestions from the National Commission on Terrorist

Attacks upon the United States, sometimes known as the 9/11 Commission. Better security regarding driver's licenses, birth certificates, social security cards, and passports was part of these recommendations. These features were intended to serve as a deterrence to terrorist travel by making the forging of documents more difficult. A more advanced method of tracking immigration through biometric entry was also instituted through the 9/11 Commission's recommendations.

CONCLUSION

Despite the needed overhaul of the intelligence community in the post-9/11 period, many of the U.S. legislative initiatives to counter terrorism have been challenged on their constitutionality. Federal judges have deemed provisions of the PATRIOT Act unconstitutional due to the violation of civil liberties and Fourth Amendment search and seizure processes. Other counterterrorism laws continue to be scrutinized in the courts.

REFERENCES

Alexander, Yonah, and Michael B. Kraft, eds. *Evolution of U.S. Counterterrorism Policy.* 3 vols. Westport, CT: Praeger Security International, 2008.

Bazan, Elizabeth B. "Intelligence Reform and Terrorism Prevention Act of 2004: 'Lone Wolf' Amendment to the Foreign Intelligence Surveillance Act." Congressional Research Services, December 29, 2004.

Cavanagh, Susan. "The Oklahoma City Bombing Investigation: A Chronology." Congressional Research Services, June 5, 1998.

U.S. Congress. Uniting and Strengthening America by Providing Appropriate Tools Required to Intercept and Obstruct Terrorism (USA PATRIOT Act) Act of 2001. Public Law 107-56. 107th Cong., 1st sess. (October 26, 2001).

U.S. Congress. *Congressional Record.* 107th Cong., 1st sess., 2001. Vol. 147. http://www.gpoaccess.gov/crecord/index.html.

U.S. Congress. House. Committee on the Judiciary. Homeland Security Act of 2002. 107th Cong., 2nd sess., June 26, 2002.

U.S. Congress. House. Intelligence Reform and Terrorism Prevention Act of 2004. 108th Cong., 2nd sess., 2004. H. Rpt. 108-796.

U.S. Congress. Senate. Nuclear Security Act of 2002. 107th Cong., 2nd sess., 2002. S. Rpt. 107-335.

U.S. Congress. Senate. Committee on the Judiciary. Foreign Terrorists in America: Five Years after the World Trade Center. 105th Cong., 2nd sess., February 24, 1998.

V

Counterterrorism Efforts by Regional Organizations

African Union

Simeon P. Sungi

A number of authors have questioned whether the threat of terrorism or the threat of conflicts, civil war, poverty, diseases, and hunger is the most serious for the African peoples (Sturman 2002; Ewi and Aning 2006). This school of thought argues that poverty, hunger, and diseases such as malaria, HIV/AIDS, and tuberculosis are major threats, that is, real terrorists that kill Africans in mass, unlike the terrorism that emerged after the 9/11 attacks on the United States in 2001 or the twin U.S. embassy bombings in Dar-es-Salaam, Tanzania, and Nairobi, Kenya, in 1998.

COMBATING TERRORISM IN AFRICA

The purpose of this essay is to critically assess the steps that the African Union (AU) has taken to combat the threat of terrorism in Africa. In particular, this article provides a brief discussion of the following instruments: the Organization of African Unity (OAU) Convention on the Prevention and Combating of Terrorism, 1999 (the Algiers Convention); the United Nations Security Council (UNSC) Resolution 1373 of 2001, which mandated that members of the United Nations adopt wide-ranging measures to suppress the financing of terrorism and improving international cooperation; and the Protocol to the OAU Convention on the Prevention and Combating of Terrorism, 2004.

The definition of terrorism or what constitutes a terrorist act has slowly evolved in Africa. During the fight for independence, some activities conducted by independence fighters were labeled as terrorist acts by the colonial powers (Efrat 1976). The Algiers Convention of 1999 made a clear distinction between terrorism and acts motivated by the struggle for self-determination, as stated in its Preamble: "REAFFIRMING the legitimate right of peoples for self-determination and independence pursuant to the principles of international law and the provisions of the Charters of the Organization of African Unity and the United Nations as well as the African Charter on Human and Peoples' Rights."

By the same token, the preamble to the Plan of Action of the African Union for the Prevention and Combating of Terrorism of September 14, 2002 (hereinafter the Action Plan) recognizes that "terrorism is a violent form of transnational crime that exploits the limits of the territorial juris-diction of States, differences in governance systems and judicial proce-dures, porous borders, and the existence of informal and illegal trade and financing networks." The Action Plan further states:

Eradicating terrorism requires a firm commitment by Member States to pursue common objectives. These include: exchange of information . . . mutual legal as-sistance, exchange of research and expertise, and the mobilization of technical assistance and co-operation, both within Africa and internationally, to upgrade the scientific, technical and operational capacity of Member States. Joint ac-tion . . . at intergovernmental level . . . includes: coordinating border surveil-lance . . . developing and strengthening border control-points; and combating the illicit import, export and stockpiling of arms, ammunition and explosives. . . . Few African governments are in a position, on their own, to marshal the requisite re-sources to combat this threat. Pooling resources, therefore, is essential.

ALGIERS CONVENTION

The Algiers Convention has been ratified by 40 African states. Core to the Algiers Convention is Article 2, which mandates that state parties un-dertake a review of their national laws and establish criminal offenses for terrorist acts as defined in the convention and make such acts punishable by appropriate penalties that take into account the grave nature of such offenses. However, this provision lacked teeth as it did not contain an en-forcement mechanism such as monitoring or compliance protocols. It is the Constitutive Act of the African Union, 2000, that provided for moni-toring and compliance mechanisms. Article 23(2) of the act provides for sanctions against a member state that "fails to comply with the decisions and policies of the Union." The Plan of Action through the Protocol Relat-ing to the Establishment of the Peace and Security Council of the African Union, concluded in Durban in 2002 (the Durban Protocol), also provides for the monitoring and enforcement of the Algiers Convention. It tasks the Peace and Security Council to ensure the implementation of it and other relevant international, regional, and subregional instruments for counter-terrorism. Article 7 (i) provides: "Ensure the implementation of the OAU

Convention on the Prevention and Combating of Terrorism and other relevant international, continental and regional conventions and instruments and harmonize and coordinate efforts at regional and continental levels to combat international terrorism."

ADDITIONAL PROTOCOL

The Protocol to the OAU Convention on the Prevention and Combating of Terrorism, concluded in 2004, came as a response to the events of 9/11 and served as a clear signal of solidarity with the United States in the fight against global terrorism. The Algiers Convention was viewed as insufficient and lacking the necessary monitoring and implementation mechanisms; hence the additional protocol was implemented to fill this void. Serious debates followed on the importance of the additional protocol. Some member states argued that the Algiers Convention should be operationalized rather than obscured with a new protocol. They further argued that UNSC Resolution 1373 had already mandated that member states of the United Nations report actions they had taken to implement it. Therefore, this protocol would in effect be duplicating UNSC Resolution 1373 (Sturman 2002, 107).

CONCLUSION

The AU has demonstrated through the Algiers Convention that it is a serious party in the fight against global terrorism. The convention has been able to stay away from the politicized debate on the definition of terrorism while ensuring nonviolation of human rights principles. The fact that the Algiers Convention was concluded prior to both Resolution 1373 and the 9/11 attacks is evidence that Africa's fight against terrorism is not dictated by powerful nations. On the contrary it is Africa's genuine commitment to fight against threats to her own internal security.

See also: **Volume 1, Part V:** Asia-Pacific Economic Cooperation Forum; Council of Europe; European Union; Organization of American States: Inter-American Committee against Terrorism; Organization of the Islamic Conference; Organization for Security and Cooperation in Europe; South Asian Association for Regional Cooperation

REFERENCES

Efrat, E. S. "Terrorism in South Africa." In *International Terrorism: National, Regional and Global Perspectives,* edited by Y. Alexander, 194–208. New York: Praeger, 1976.

Ewi, M., and K. Aning. "Assessing the Role of the African Union in Preventing and Combating Terrorism in Africa." *African Security Review* 15 (2006): 32–46. http://www.issafrica.org/pgcontent.php?UID=407.

Makinda, S. "Terrorism, Counter-terrorism and Norms in Africa." *African Security Review* 15, no. 3 (2006): 19–31. http://www.issafrica.org/pgcontent.php?UID=405.

Sturman, K. "The AU Plan on Terrorism: Joining the Global War or Leading an African Battle?" *African Security Review* 11, no. 4 (2002): 102–8. http://www.iss.co.za/pubs/ASR/11No4/Sturman.html.

Weigend, T. "The Universal Terrorist: The International Community Grappling with a Definition." *Journal of International Criminal Justice* 4 (2006): 912–32.

Asia-Pacific Economic Cooperation Forum

Edy Parsons

In the late 1980s, Australia, Japan, and the United States proposed to have closer regional economic cooperation respectively. In 1989, Bob Hawke, former prime minister of Australia, proposed to hold a meeting of ministers from the Asia-Pacific region. In November 1989, ministers from 12 nations in the region met in Canberra, Australia. These 12 nations became the founding members when the Asia-Pacific Economic Cooperation Forum (APEC) was formed in 1989. These countries include Australia, Brunei Darussalam, Canada, Indonesia, Japan, Korea, Malaysia, New Zealand, the Philippines, Singapore, Thailand, and the United States.

REGIONAL COOPERATION

The idea behind APEC was to build nonbinding regional cooperation. APEC was formed as an economic organization. The major objectives of APEC were to promote trade liberalization and investment in the region. In 1991, China, Hong Kong, and Taiwan joined APEC. Mexico and New Guinea became members in 1993. Chile became an APEC member in 1994. In 1998, Peru, Russia, and Vietnam joined the organization. APEC connects Northeast and Southeast Asia with Central and South America, North America, Australia, and New Zealand. APEC members have different levels of economic development, from industrialized economies to developing economies. Free trade can affect these members in various ways.

In 1992 APEC established its secretariat in Singapore and prior to 1993 met only informally. Dialogue was on a senior official and ministerial level. In 1993 U.S. president Bill Clinton proposed and established an annual APEC Economic Leaders' Meeting to be held by one of the 21 members each year. Member states fund APEC activities. Since China, Japan, and the United States are APEC members, this makes the organization more influential in the international arena. In 1994 APEC members agreed to set up free and open trade in the Asia-Pacific region for industrialized economies by 2010 and for developing economies by 2020. Major terror attacks would be a big blow to APEC economies since they represent 60 percent of the world's gross domestic product and almost half of global trade.

APEC AND COUNTERTERRORISM AFTER SEPTEMBER 11

Following the terror attacks in New York on September 11, 2001, APEC issued the APEC Leaders Statement on Counter-terrorism. In this statement, APEC members committed to fight terrorism individually and cooperatively. On October 12, 2002, there was a terrorist bombing in Bali, Indonesia. After the attack, APEC issued the Leaders' Statement on Fighting Terrorism and Promoting Growth. APEC condemned the attack and made it clear that terrorism was a threat to regional stability and challenged the economies of member nations. APEC leaders believed that it was important to strengthen international cooperation in this vital area. APEC also considers the United Nations' (UN) previously adopted resolutions on terrorism instrumental in combating this growing threat. The 2002 statement also revealed that APEC members signed and either had ratified or were in the process of ratifying the International UN Convention for the Suppression of the Financing of Terrorism, adopted in 1999. Since some APEC members were also members of the Financial Action Task Force on Money Laundering, APEC also supported this task force, which was formed in 1989. In October 2001, the task force issued the eight special recommendations on how to deal with terrorist financing and money laundering. These recommendations received APEC support in 2002. Based on the 2002 statement, APEC established the Counter-terrorism Task Force (CTTF) in 2003, implementing the Leaders' Statement on Fighting Terrorism and Promoting Growth. The main objectives of the CTTF included helping members identify and cooperate with organizations charged with fighting terrorism. Based on this idea, APEC developed Counter Terrorism Action Plans that helped its members combat terrorism. APEC also initiated Secure Trade in the APEC Region (STAR). Since 2003, APEC holds a STAR conference annually. The aim of this program is to enhance secure trade throughout the region; businesses and government officials work together to identify ways to trade more efficiently while maintaining security.

In 2006 the APEC Hanoi Summit put a lot of emphasis on counterterrorism, with various proposals being discussed. The proposals were not only about how to prevent terrorism in the region but also about how to recover economically after a successful terrorist attack was launched. APEC's counterterrorism emphasis was significant because it went beyond promoting open and free trade in the region. APEC members looked at terrorism as a direct challenge to the trade liberalization that all members valued and shared. In 2007, APEC developed the Trade Recovery Program, and in 2009, APEC held a Trade Recovery Program Pilot Exercise. Seven member countries participated in this exercise, which provided the participants an opportunity to see how they could handle trade recovery after a terrorist event.

APEC also initiated a number of workshops related to counterterrorism and security. In 2008, APEC workshops included the seminar "Protection of Cyberspace from Terrorist Use and Attacks," the seminar "Securing Remittance and Cross Border Payments from Terrorist Use," the workshop "Effective Public Private Partnerships in Counter-Terrorism and Secure Trade," and a workshop on the Trade Recovery Program.

CONCLUSION

In 2009 and 2010, APEC also held a series of workshops targeting methods and trends in terrorism financing and money laundering (e.g., the workshop "Improving Regulation of the Non-profit Organization Sector," which focused on counterterrorism financing, and the workshop "Optimizing the Use of Audits and Investigation to Strengthen Aviation Security"). Since terror attacks could have a big impact on APEC's goals of free trade and regional growth and stability, the organization needs to commit to strengthening and promoting policies and initiatives to combat terrorism.

See also: **Volume 1, Part V:** African Union; Council of Europe; European Union; Organization of American States: Inter-American Committee against Terrorism; Organization of the Islamic Conference; Organization for Security and Cooperation in Europe; South Asian Association for Regional Cooperation

REFERENCES

Asia-Pacific Economic Cooperation. "Counter Terrorism." n.d. http://www.apec.org/.

Beeson, Mark. *Institutions of the Asia-Pacific : ASEAN, APEC, and Beyond.* New York: Routledge, 2009.

Shelton, Dinah. *Commitment and Compliance: The Role of Non-binding Norms in the International Legal System.* New York: Oxford University Press, 2000.

Wesley, Michael. *The Regional Organizations of the Asia Pacific: Exploring Institutional Change.* New York: Palgrave Macmillan, 2003.

Wilson, John Sullivan. *Asia-Pacific Economic Cooperation Forum (APEC).* Atlanta: Georgia Tech Center for International Business Education and Research, School of Management, Georgia Institute of Technology, 1995.

Council of Europe

Andrew Orr

Created by the signing of the Treaty of London on May 5, 1949, the Council of Europe (COE) has grown from its original 10 members to include 47 European states (Albania, Andorra, Armenia, Austria, Azerbaijan, Belgium, Bosnia and Herzegovina, Bulgaria, Croatia, Cyprus, Czech Republic, Denmark, Estonia, Finland, France, Georgia, Germany, Greece, Hungary, Iceland, Ireland, Italy, Latvia, Liechtenstein, Lithuania, Luxembourg, the Former Yugoslav Republic of Macedonia, Malta, Moldova, Monaco, Montenegro, the Netherlands, Norway, Poland, Portugal, Romania, Russia, San Marino, Serbia, Slovakia, Slovenia, Spain, Sweden, Switzerland, Turkey, Ukraine, and the United Kingdom). The council also grants observer status to Canada, the United States, Mexico, and Japan. The COE's antiterrorism policies have operated principally through the Committee of Ministers, the European Court of Human Rights (ECHR), and the Parliamentary Assembly of the Council of Europe. The council has sought to build democracy and protect human rights through the rule of law within the territory of its members.

CRIMINAL ACTS

Dating back to the 1970s, the COE has sought to channel antiterrorism efforts into the civilian judicial system. The Committee of Ministers' 1974 Resolution (74) 3, titled "On International Terrorism," recognized the particular danger of terrorist acts that created a "collective danger to human life" and that endangered civilians who were "innocent persons foreign to the motives behind" the terrorist acts. The ministers urged member governments to apply extradition agreements and to treat terrorist attacks in other countries as serious criminal acts under domestic law. The ministers' concerns contributed to the signing of the 1977 European Convention on the Suppression of Terrorism, which urged states to cooperate against terrorist violence, apply extradition agreements, and maintain strong legal guarantees for suspects (Directorate General of Human Rights 2005, 3–16, 165–82, 219–20).

ACTION AND HUMAN RIGHTS
AFTER SEPTEMBER 11

In the wake of the September 11, 2001, attacks, the Committee of Ministers reinforced the council's preexisting antiterrorism work. On July 15,

2002, it recognized the fundamental human right of all people to be free from terrorism as part of its *Guidelines on Human Rights and the Fight against Terrorism*. Building on the 1977 European Convention on the Suppression of Terrorism, the committee laid out a governmental duty to prevent terrorist acts, protect the privacy rights of victims and suspects alike, and guarantee that suspects would not face torture or capital punishment (Directorate General of Human Rights 2005, 295–330). The council's advice produced controversy in the United States, because it suggested that if European troops in Afghanistan captured al-Qaeda leaders linked to the September 11 attacks, they could be extradited only if the United States provided binding promises not to implement the death penalty. In 2005, the Committee of Ministers produced supplementary guidelines emphasizing the rights of victims of terrorism to receive emergency and continuing assistance with the medical, mental, social, and economic impact of terrorist attacks (Directorate General of Human Rights 2005, 331–58).

Sitting in Strasbourg, the ECHR is the council's judicial arm. The court can be directly accessed by individuals, organizations, and governments, and its decisions are enforced by the Committee of Ministers. The Committee of Ministers cannot implement a decision, but it does have an array of sanctions, including suspending a member's voting rights in the Committee of Ministers if it fails to comply with a court ruling (Keller and Sweet 2008, 2–10; Jordon 2003, 662–64). ECHR rulings have emphasized protecting the individual human rights of accused terrorists. Rulings have curtailed pretrial detentions and sanctioned many European governments for cooperating with the United States' extraordinary rendition policy. Repeated rulings have condemned the Russian government's counterinsurgency campaign in Chechnya following the second Russian invasion of Chechnya in 1999. ECHR rulings have held the Russian government responsible for human rights abuses including extrajudicial killings, forced disappearances, and widespread torture of captured fighters and civilians. The Russian government has denied responsibility for the abuses identified by the court and has frequently ignored its rulings, but the ECHR's verdicts have led to compensation for some victims and have focused international attention on the human effects of Russia's counterinsurgency strategy (Nussberger 2008).

The Parliamentary Assembly of the Council of Europe has encouraged an integrated law enforcement response to the danger of terrorist attacks throughout Europe. The assembly has also campaigned to restrain perceived government abuses of human rights. On June 12, 2006, Assembly Member Dick Marty released a seminal report that exposed cooperation between the U.S. Central Intelligence Agency (CIA) and 14 European countries in the illegal arrest, detention, and transfer of prisoners (Hakami 2007, 442; Siddiqui 2008, 47–48). The report documented examples of European states, including Britain, Italy, and Germany, allowing the CIA to use their airspace to carry out renditions. It also condemned Poland and Romania for allowing the CIA to operate secret detention facilities within their territory. The assembly called on member states to investigate and prosecute those responsible and to rehabilitate and compensate the program's targets. As part of the council's investigation, the European Commission for Democracy through Law (the Venice Commission) continued the investigation and determined that European governments had breached the European Convention on Human Rights by supporting the American program (Hakami 2007, 444–47).

Since 2003, the Council of Europe's Committee of Experts on Terrorism (CODEXTER) has assessed the antiterrorism capabilities and policies of member states. CODEXTER's reports aim to improve the quality of counterterrorism policies while encouraging member states to respect the values of democracy through law and individual rights. CODEXTER replaced the Multidisciplinary Group on International Action against Terrorism, which had been created after the September 11 attacks. CODEXTER provides a permanent structure to coordinate the council's antiterrorism efforts, pool antiterrorism expertise, and create European-wide standards of best practices in the investigation of terrorist acts and the treatment of suspects and victims (Council of Europe n.d.).

CONCLUSION

When the Council of Europe Convention for the Prevention of Terrorism came into force in January 2007, it required all members to legislate to expand antiterrorism laws to include the crimes of public provocation to commit a terrorist offense, solicitation to commit a terrorist offense, and provision of training for a terrorist offense. The convention built on previous agreements and declarations as well as the work of CODEXTER to lay out a structure of laws to allow European security services to use the civilian criminal justice system to root out the support system for terrorist attacks without impinging on the human rights of suspects or innocent members of the public (Directorate General of Human Rights 2005, 165–82).

REFERENCES

Council of Europe. "Action Against Terrorism." n.d. http://www.coe.int/gmt.
Directorate General of Human Rights. *Guidelines on Human Rights and the Fight against Terrorism* 3rd ed. Strasbourg: Council of Europe, Committee of Ministers, 2002. http://www1.umn.edu/humanrts/instree/HR%20and%20 the%20fight%20against%20terrorism.pdf.
Hakami, Minica. "The Council of Europe Addresses CIA Rendition and Detention Program." *American Journal of International Law* 101 (2007): 442–52.
Jordon, Pamela A. "Does Membership Have Its Privileges?: Entrance into the Council of Europe and Compliance with Human Rights Norms." *Human Rights Quarterly* 25 (2003): 660–88.

Keller, Helen, and Alec Stone Sweet. "The Reception of the ECHR in National Legal Systems." In *A Europe of Rights: The Impact of the ECHR on National Legal Systems*, edited by Helen Keller and Alec Stone Sweet, 3–30. Oxford: Oxford University Press, 2008.

Nussberger, Angelika. "Reception Process in Russia and Ukraine." In *A Europe of Rights: The Impact of the ECHR on National Legal Systems*, edited by Helen Keller and Alec Stone Sweet, 603–76. Oxford: Oxford University Press, 2008.

Siddiqui, Niloufer. "Of Note: Extraordinary Rendition and Transatlantic Intelligence Cooperation." *SAIS Review* 28 (2008): 47–49.

European Union

Kimberly A. DeTardo-Bora

The European Union (EU) is a joint economic and political partnership of 27 European countries. Currently, the mission of the EU is to provide peace, freedom, and security to these unified nations while at the same time balancing economic and social development. The institutions that comprise the EU include the European Parliament, the Council of Ministers, and the European Commission. The majority of counterterrorism efforts have been put into place by the European Commission and the Council of Ministers as well as the Justice and Home Affairs division.

FORMATION OF THE EU

Unlike other regional efforts to combat terrorism, the EU was not firmly established until November 1, 1993, under the Maastricht Treaty. Thus, more concerted counterterrorism efforts were not attributed to the EU until much later. However, the foundational organization to the EU, known as the European Coal and Steel Community, called for the political and economic unification of the region to maintain peace after World War II. And there is evidence that some of the early states coordinated efforts in the late 1970s and throughout the 1980s to address terrorist activity brought on by the Irish Republican Army (Keohane 2005, 17). Shortly after the EU was established, the Treaty of Amsterdam was signed in 1997 to address not only the challenges of globalization and the economy but also terrorism.

Prior to the formation of the EU, Europol, or the European Police Office, was created on February 7, 1992 (Deflem 2006, 341). Specifically, Europol began operations in 1994, and by 1998 a formally mandated policy had been created to address terrorism. While each country has its own police force, Europol facilitates cross-border cooperative efforts between the law enforcement entities of EU nations such as the police, gendarmerie, and customs from its headquarters at the Hague. Europol acts as a hub for disseminating information, sharing intelligence, and creating threat assessment reports (known as an Organized Crime Threat Assessment) and EU Terrorism Situation and Trend Reports (Europol 2011). Because much of Europe is democratic and has open borders, the EU has put into place mechanisms for border security and tackling crimes that often coincide with terrorist activity. These activities include drug trafficking, illegal immigration networks, human trafficking, child pornography, counterfeiting (the Euro), money laundering, organized crime, and cybercrime.

RESPONSE TO 9/11

While it can be argued that national terrorism had been addressed by the EU for many years, 9/11 signified that Islamist terrorism (particularly al-Qaeda) was no longer confined to a single country and presented a threat to the security of all European countries. In essence, 9/11 was the catalyst for the EU and the European Council to create a set of preventive and protective strategies that would make Europe a safe place to live while at the same time respecting human rights (Deflem 2006, 344). In addition, the Counter-terrorism Task Force began operations on November 15, 2001, at the Europol center (Deflem 2006, 344). Immediately after the attacks on the United States, the EU responded with an Action Plan against Terrorism. This action plan was later modified in 2004 and again in 2005. From this plan, four main pillars were established: prevent, protect, pursue, and respond. Within each of these pillars or strategy areas, objectives were put forth, some of which include exchanging information with and accessing information from other EU states and the United States, preventing violent radical terrorist acts, seizing terrorist financing sources and freezing funds, protecting victims, providing compensation to victims, improving aviation security, extending the power of arrest and the issuing of warrants, extraditing terrorists between member states, coordinating emergency responses, and creating and strengthening the power of EU counterterrorism agencies such as Eurojust and Europol (EUROPA).

As collaborative efforts with the United States took hold, EU states were encouraged to address terrorism and counterterrorism by adopting several frameworks and policy directives. For example, in 2002, the Council of Ministers established a definition of terrorist offenses and established the protocol for a European arrest warrant (EAW). In regards to the former, the definition of terrorism includes any serious offense against a person, causing bodily injury, kidnapping, taking hostages, or seizing aircrafts, and so on. In addition, the definition refers to acts that are "intentionally committed with a specific terrorism aim" (European Commission 2003, 19). As for the EAW, in the event that a person has committed a serious offense or alleged offense in one country and resides in or has fled to another country, the EAW depoliticizes the process and allows one EU member state to essentially surrender their procedures to another.

Another important institution called the European Judicial Cooperation Unit, or Eurojust, was formed on February 28, 2002, by the Justice and Home Affairs Council. Eurojust is comprised of prosecutors, magistrates, and judges who handle transnational events and cross-border legal matters at the Hague. These senior officials and legal counsel serve as advisers to member states to support the investigation and prosecution of organized criminals with the goal of combating and ending criminal operations (EUROPA 2012).

Additional EU efforts and policies were initiated after the terrorist attacks in Madrid (on March 11, 2004) and London (on July 7, 2005), namely, the Declaration on Combating Terrorism. Furthermore, the Hague Programme was voted on by the Justice and Home Affairs Council on November 4, 2004, and was implemented from 2005 to 2010. As part of this program, an action plan that outlines 10 priority areas to combat terrorism was created. The council also set forth the EU Counterterrorism Strategy on November 30, 2005 (EUROPA 2012).

CONCLUSION

In sum, the EU as an international organization has responded to terrorism by creating a multifaceted approach, increasing many circles of defense, increasing international cooperation, and heightening border security and intelligence sharing among the EU member states. After the 9/11 attacks on the United States in 2001, many of the numerous counterterrorism initiatives of the EU exist in the form of policies, treaties, and the creation of cross-border cooperative institutions. The fight against terror also includes preventing access to weapons of mass destruction, bringing together a variety of law enforcement practices across Europe, and ensuring that counterterrorism initiatives and policies are fully enforced and implemented by member states.

REFERENCES

Deflem, Mathieu. "Europol and the Policing of International Terrorism: Counterterrorism in a Global Perspective." *Justice Quarterly* 23 (2006): 336–59.
EUROPA. "Justice, Freedom, and Security." Justice and Home Affairs. Last updated February 3, 2012. http://europa.eu/pol/justice/index_en.htm.
European Commission. "Freedom, Security and Justice for All: Justice and Home Affairs in the European Union." European Union: Direcorate-General for Press and Communication, 2003, 1–21.
Europol. "EU Situation and Trends Report." The Hague, The Netherlands: Europol, 2011. https://www.europol.europa.eu/sites/default/files/publications/te-sat2011.pdf.
Keohane, Daniel. *The EU and Counter-terrorism.* London: Centre for European Reform (CER), 2005.

Organization for Security and Cooperation in Europe

Payam Foroughi and Kristian Alexander

Formed during the Cold War, the Organization for Security and Coopera-tion in Europe (OSCE; known until 1995 as the Conference for Security and Cooperation in Europe, or CSCE) is an international security institu-tion with a set of norms and commitments stipulating the internal behav-ior of its 56 participating states and cooperation among them. The origins of the OSCE are found in a series of forums between the Soviet-led com-munist block and the U.S.-led West, which ultimately brought about a key agreement signed in August 1975, referred to as the Helsinki Final Act. The OSCE functions on the concept of "comprehensive security," where national and regional security is considered to be dependent on three di-mensions: the politico-military, economic-environmental, and human. Counterterrorism efforts fall primarily under the OSCE's first and third dimensions. By the mid-2000s, the OSCE had an annual budget of around US$250 million and a worldwide staff of 3,500, with its headquarters in Vienna, its institutional arms in various European cities, and 18 field of-fices, all in the former communist states. The closure of two field offices in Russia (Chechnya, 2002) and Georgia (2009) was primarily due to a deci-sion by Russia, given that the organization functions based on the princi-pal of consensus.

EVOLVING EFFORTS TO COMBAT TERRORISM

The Helsinki Final Act contains a reference to countering or opposing terrorism with the participating states encouraged to "refrain from direct or indirect assistance to terrorist activities, or to subversive or other ac-tivities directed towards the violent overthrow of the regime of another" participating state. The OSCE is recognized as a "regional arrangement" under Chapter VIII of the United Nations (UN) Charter, and thus it rec-ognizes the UN conventions and protocols, considers the UN Security Council resolutions as the "legal framework for combating terrorism," and recognizes that the Counter-terrorism Committee of the UN Security Council plays a coordinating role in global counterterrorism activities (Wycoff 2007). The OSCE has not had a consensual definition of terror-ism, but global events affecting influential OSCE participating states have been instrumental in forming the OSCE's overall antiterrorism strategies. The U.S. experience, for example, of its diplomats having been taken hostage for 444 days in Iran (1979–1980) influenced the OSCE's 1983 Madrid Concluding Document, wherein countering terrorism was referred to as a subject requiring international cooperation. The 1980s saw more acts of terror against both East and West Cold War players, including the kidnapping and murder of U.S. and Russian diplomats in Lebanon; the bombings of U.S. and French barracks, resulting in the deaths of 299 soldiers, also in Lebanon; and the 1988 bombing of Pan Am Flight 103 (aka Lockerbie bombing) resulting in the death of 270 civilians (Steinacker 2004).

The OSCE's role underwent a makeover with the imminent collapse of communism, and in November 1990, most of its participating states signed the Charter of Paris for a New Europe, an ambitious and historic document establishing the post–Cold War role of the OSCE and setting the stage for much of the organization's existing institutional arms, with not only a Vienna-based Secretariat being formed but also the entities of the Parliamentary Assembly (in Copenhagen), the Conflict Prevention Centre (in Vienna), and the Office for Free Elections (in Warsaw; later becoming the Office for Democratic Institutions and Human Rights [ODIHR]) being established by the mid-1990s. Soon after the September 2001 attacks, the OSCE put together its Bucharest Plan of Action for Combating Terrorism, adopted at its Ninth Ministerial Council in December 2001, wherein participating states pledged to strive to "become parties to all twelve UN conventions and protocols relating to terrorism." The Bucharest Plan also talked about the necessity for cooperation on combating terrorism through both international legal obligations and political commitments, under both the UN aegis and the OSCE's comprehensive security approach and field experience in such areas as police training, legislative support, and border monitoring. Both the OSCE Secretariat—where the agency's Action against Terrorism Unit (ATU, established in May 2002) is based—and ODIHR are tasked to assist participating states in the ratification and implementation of the UN antiterrorist conventions in cooperation with the UN Office for Drugs and Crime.

NEED FOR SAFEGUARDS

According to a former ODIHR director, Gerard Stoudmann, the OSCE's participating states must be cautious not to "condone terrorism by the very measures that terrorists themselves resort to: Striking fear at innocent citizens, persecuting those who hold different religious beliefs" and are of different ethnicities, "denying the right to express freely different views or to associate with those who have different opinions" (Zaagman 2002). And yet the OSCE can be criticized for at times having done exactly so, that is, condoned terror tactics by a number of its participating states in the name of antiterrorism—especially after September 11, 2001. Aside from the United States, which in its war on terror and use of torture, by means of waterboarding and other coercive methods, is known to have violated its OSCE commitments and the UN Convention against Torture and Other Cruel, Inhuman or Degrading Treatment or Punishment, other liberal Western participating states have also winked at—and at times actively cooperated with—such tactics when practiced by the United States and some repressive OSCE participating states. The Central Asian republics, for example, have been regular recipients of OSCE largess for police and security services training, reform, and technical assistance in counterterrorism.

Here the danger lies in a self-fulfilling prophecy, in which thousands of real and imaginary Islamic extremists and potential terrorists have in recent years been arrested, often tortured, and sentenced to long prison terms by the same institutions receiving OSCE assistance. And if they were not already, those detained may well become hardened fundamentalists and extremists who may potentially engage in acts of terror upon their eventual release. The OSCE and its participating states appear not to have a concrete program in place to prevent the arrest and conviction of innocent suspects, to avoid the use of torture and other cruel treatments during investigation and interrogation, and, in the case of those convicted and detained, to provide any significant and systematic rehabilitation programs. This is likely due largely to a lack of precision and consensus among participating states as to the proper means of fighting extremism and potential terrorism and also to the OSCE field offices' insufficient monitoring and lack of criticism of the modus operandi of security and justice systems in violating participating states.

CONCLUSION

Those favoring realpolitik would argue that, as an institution, the OSCE's avowed commitments to fighting terrorism while abiding by human rights principles, in coordination and concert with other participating states, are never achievable since states regularly break the rules of the game, including the use of terror to fight terror or to gain material goods and territory in their favor. Like most wars, countering terrorism, they would argue, is never pretty and will involve violations of liberal human rights principles including the use of terror tactics. Still (aside from the U.S. experience under George W. Bush's administration), overall violations of rights by individual OSCE participating states fighting terrorism appear to be far more acute the farther a given state lies to the east of Vienna . As opposed to the situation in Central Asia, in Southeast European OSCE participating states, for example, which are looking ahead to European Union membership, liberal standards are, to a large extent, in place to ensure respect for human rights while countering terrorism. That said, as it stands, the OSCE's counterterrorism efforts remain largely symbolic and in the realm of ideas and ideals, with much room for maneuvering and fine-tuning in the coming years.

See also: **Volume 1, Part V:** African Union; Asia-Pacific Economic Cooperation Forum; Council of Europe; European Union; Organization of American States: Inter-American Committee against Terrorism; Organization of the Islamic Conference; South Asian Association for Regional Cooperation

REFERENCES

Mearsheimer, John J. "The False Promise of International Institutions." *International Security* 19, no. 3 (1994–1995): 5–49.

Steinacker, Gudrun. "The Role of the OSCE as a Regional Security Organization in Combating International Terrorism." In *OSCE Yearbook 2003*, edited by Centre for OSCE Research (CORE), the Institute for Peace Research and Security Policy at the University of Hamburg, 89–93. Baden Baden, Germany: Nomos, 2004.

Wycoff, Karl E. "Overview of the OSCE's Work in Support of the Global Effort against Terrorism." In *OSCE Yearbook 2006*, edited by Centre for OSCE Research (CORE), the Institute for Peace Research and Security Policy at the University of Hamburg, 331–41. Baden Baden, Germany: Nomos, 2007.

Zaagman, Rob. "Terrorism and the OSCE: An Overview." *Helsinki Monitor* 3 (2002): 204–15.

Organization of American States: Inter-American Committee against Terrorism

Andrew Orr

The Inter-American Committee against Terrorism (Comité Interamericano Contra el Terrorismo [CICTE]) was created by the Organization of American States (OAS; Organización de los Estados Americanos) in October 1999. During the 1990s major terrorist attacks by transnational organizations, including the 1992 and 1994 Buenos Aires bombings and the 1993 World Trade Center bombing in New York City, heightened concern about terrorism in the Americas. The 1992 suicide bombing of the Israeli embassy in Buenos Aires killed 29 and wounded 242, and the 1994 car bombing of the Asociación Mutual Israelita Argentina killed 85 people and wounded over 300. These attacks and a series of other bombings, including the destruction of Alas Chiricanas Flight 00901 by a presumed suicide bomber days after the attack on the Asociación Mutual Israelita Argentina, increased concern about terrorist organizations operating in Latin America.

COUNTERTERRORISM IN THE AMERICAS

The Islamic Jihad Organization, which has been linked to Hezbollah, claimed responsibility for the 1992 bombing, and security services quickly focused on Hezbollah as the presumed culprit of both Buenos Aires bombings. The Buenos Aires bombings, combined with domestic terrorist attacks in the United States, such as the 1995 Oklahoma City bombing, and residual violence by leftist guerrillas in South America, eventually convinced the United States and Latin American countries to use the OAS framework to coordinate antiterrorism efforts in North and South America (Harab and Leenders 2005, 176).

A series of intergovernmental meetings, including the First and Second Summit of the Americas (1994, 1998), the First and Second Specialized Conferences on Terrorism (1996, 1998), and the 1997 First Meeting of Ministers of Justice or of Ministers or Attorneys General of the Americas (REMJA), led to the creation of CICTE within the OAS in October 1999 (Warner 2006, 389). After its creation CICTE developed slowly until the September 11, 2001, attacks led the U.S. government to focus its resources on antiterrorism efforts (Ribando 2005, 5). On September 21, 2001, the OAS's foreign ministers adopted a declaration calling on all OAS members to coordinate a hemisphere-wide fight against terrorism. The ministers followed the September 21 declaration with a second one that recognized the September 11 attacks as an attack against all OAS members under the Inter-American Treaty of Reciprocal Assistance. The ministers endorsed using CICTE to coordinate these efforts within the OAS, and the United States soon increased funding to CICTE. In October 2002, OAS secretary general César Gaviria reorganized the OAS's administration, and although CICTE retained some autonomy, it was transformed into an executive secretariat within the OAS Secretariat General's Department of Multidimensional Security (Ribando 2005, 2).

CICTE's efforts helped ensure the adoption of the Inter-American Convention against Terrorism in June 2002. The convention committed its signatories to implement the United Nations Security Council Resolution 1373 on suppressing terrorism, enforce the provisions of the United Nations Convention on Transnational Organized Crime, enact the recommendations of the Financial Action Task Force, and coordinate their general antiterrorism efforts. Following the 2001 attacks CICTE began holding yearly general meetings to coordinate antiterrorism initiatives among OAS members. CICTE's annual conferences highlighted specific issues, such as terrorist financing (2009—Ninth Regular Session), cybersecurity (2008—Eighth Regular Session), and the protection of critical infrastructure (2007—Seventh Regular Session). CICTE has emphasized the need to develop financial controls, strengthen the procedures and competence of law enforcement and regulative bodies throughout the OAS, strengthen border security, and share intelligence on national, regional, and global terrorist groups (Ribando 2005, 6).

CICTE organized intergovernmental conferences on counterterrorism and jointly sponsored the April 2009 Conference on Terrorism and Cyber Security with the Council of Europe. The joint conference highlighted the danger of terrorist groups mounting cyberattacks alone or as part of a larger nuclear or conventional attack against key physical infrastructure

(Council of Europe 2009). In March 2010, the Tenth Regular Session of CICTE adopted a declaration encouraging member states to expand the role of civil society groups and public-private partnerships in fighting terrorism in order to better target terrorist funding and support networks (Organization of American States 2010).

COMPREHENSIVE ANTITERRORISM STRATEGY

Although CICTE is not itself a police, intelligence, or military organization, it has moved beyond politics and policy advice to provide direct training to national law enforcement, regulatory, and border security agencies throughout Latin America. CICTE's workshops cover a wide range of topics including aviation cargo screening, crisis management, cybersecurity, customs searches, border security, and bioterrorism response. Workshops have been aimed at policymakers, administrators, investigators, doctors, emergency responders, and screeners (Organization of American States n.d.).

In addition to its independent activities, CICTE has worked with other parts of the OAS to build a multidimensional antiterrorism strategy. CICTE's partners include the Inter-American Drug Abuse and Control Commission (CICAD) and the Department of Public Security. CICTE and CICAD have collaborated on projects aimed at controlling the illicit movement of money and arms across borders through informal networks. Their intelligence-sharing projects have highlighted the link between violence and drug trafficking. With the escalation of drug cartel–related violence in northern Mexico during 2008, CICTE and CICAD both focused more attention on supporting the Mexican government's efforts by targeting the transnational networks that the Mexican cartels used to obtain arms and launder money.

CICTE and the OAS have also coordinated their efforts with the European Union, Council of Europe, United Nations, and other international antiterrorism bodies. CICTE has collaborated with the United Nations Security Council's Counter-terrorism Committee in implementing Resolution 1373 (2001) on combating terrorism. In particular, the two organizations have supported the exchange of information and expertise between the two groups and countries in the region through workshops and country visits by the committees.

CONCLUSION

Critics of CICTE including Venezuelan president Hugo Chávez have claimed that it is U.S. dominated and functions largely to further U.S. interests in Latin America. They have attributed the relatively low level of Latin American financial support for CICTE to claims that the organization targets anticapitalist groups opposed to U.S. foreign and economic policy in Latin America. The U.S. government showed a special interest in CICTE's development and provided much of the organization's early funding, including all but $43,000 of CICTE's budget of $1,043,000 in 2003. CICTE's efforts to isolate the Fuerzas Armadas Revolucionarias de Colombia (FARC; Revolutionary Armed Forces of Columbia) further fueled claims by Chávez and others that CICTE functioned as an extension of U.S. foreign policy (Daudelin 2003, 655).

REFERENCES

Council of Europe. "CoE- OAS/CICTE Conference on Terrorism and Cyber Security—Conclusions." 2009. http://www.coe.int/t/dlapil/codexter/Source/Working_Documents/Conclusions%20CoE%20OAS-CICTE%20Conference.pdf.
Daudelin, Jean. "Foreign Policy at the Fringe: Canada and Latin America." *International Journal* 58 (2003): 637–66.
Harab, Mona, and Reinoud Leenders. "Know Thy Enemy: Hizbullah 'Terrorism' and the Politics of Perception." *Third World Quarterly* 26 (2005): 173–97.
Organization of American States. "Inter-American Committee against Terrorism—Tenth Regular Session." March 17–19, 2010. http://www.cicte.oas.org/Rev/EN/Meetings/Sessions/10/.
Organization of American States. "Inter-American Committee against Terrorism—Events." n.d. http://www.cicte.oas.org/Rev/En.
Ribando, Clare. *Organization of American States: A Primer.* Washington, DC: Congressional Research Service, 2005.
Warner, David. "Law Enforcement Cooperation in the Organization of American States: A Focus on REMJA." *University of Miami Inter-American Law Review* 37 (2006): 387–419.

Organization of the Islamic Conference

Andrew J. Waskey

The Organization of the Islamic Conference (OIC; http://www.oic-oci.org/) is an international Muslim organization that seeks to be a collective voice for Muslims and to protect Muslim interests around the world while promoting international peace and harmony among all other people in the world. Its current membership of 57 countries from the Middle East, Africa, Central Asia, the Caucasus, the Balkans, South and Southeast Asia, and South America (Guyana and Suriname) makes it the second-largest international organization in the world after the United Nations. It is also an accredited organization to the United Nations. In 2008, President George W. Bush appointed a special envoy to the OIC. President Obama has continued the practice. The OIC has an Islamic Summit every three years at which heads of state meet. It has an annual Islamic Conference of Foreign Ministers every year. And its Permanent Secretariat is based in Jidda, Saudi Arabia.

FORMATION OF THE OIC

The OIC was formed following a notorious arson attack on the Al-Aqsa Mosque in Jerusalem on August 21, 1969. The arson was committed by a Protestant Australian tourist, Dennis Michael Rohan (1941–), who had been influenced by the teachings of Herbert W. Armstrong, leader of the Worldwide Church of God. Armstrong broadcast a television program, *The World Tomorrow,* and published a religious magazine, *Plain Truth.* Armstrong's eschatological teachings are premillennial and include the belief that Christ will return after the Temple of Solomon is rebuilt and temple sacrifices are restored. Armstrong had sent Rohan literature on his teachings in reply to Rohan's request, as had also done with millions of other inquirers; that was the extent of his association with Rohan. However the London *Daily Telegraph* published a picture showing Rohan with a copy of *Plain Truth* in his coat pocket.

Rohan was tried in an Israeli court, where he testified that he had acted as a divine agent who would open the way for the Jews to restore Solomon's temple. The rebuilding of the temple would fulfill a prophecy in the Book of Zechariah and bring Christ's Second Coming. He was convicted of arson but deported as an undesirable lunatic.

The Al-Aqsa Mosque is sacred to Moslems because it is opposite the Temple Mount, which has a marking that looks like a horse's hoofprint. Surah 16 (Surah al Baqarah) of the Quran teaches that Muhammad had a night vision in which he was transported to the Temple Mount and there got on a winged horse, El-Buraq, which left its hoofprint as it mounted up to heaven with Muhammad on its back.

Muslim critics from the beginning of the fire blamed Israelis for the attack. Muslim worshippers attacked Israeli firefighters in the streets who were attempting to put out the fire. Their immediate charge, which was never abandoned, was that the Jews had deliberately set the fire. The charges that Rohan was actually Jewish, that he was a Zionist, that the Jews set the fire deliberately, that it was only one of a number of attacks on Muslim sacred sites and other similar charges have continued to be accepted by Muslims as facts ever since. In fact, attacks by Hamas on Israel in 2003 were justified with the charge that the Israelis had deliberately started the fire. Yassir Arafat, head of the Palestine Liberation Organization (PLO), repeatedly cited the fire as a reason for the PLO to attack Israel. Other PLO spokesmen have declared it to be a reason for their jihad.

On August 28, 1969, 24 Muslim countries, led by Jordan, filed a complaint with the United Nations Security Council about the fire. Israel was again accused of profaning a sacred site. On September 25, 1969, Muslim countries met in response to the fire at Rabat, Morocco, and formed the OIC. In 1970, the organization held the first Islamic Conference of Foreign Ministers in

Jidda, Saudi Arabia. The Jidda Conference also established a permanent secretariat that would be headed by the OIC's secretary-general. In 2004, Ekmeleddin Ihsanoglu of Turkey was chosen as the ninth secretary-general.

In 1990, the OIC adopted the Cairo Declaration of Human Rights in Islam, which was viewed by many as an Islamic response to the 1948 United Nations Declaration of Human Rights. The major difference is that human rights according to the Cairo Declaration are subject to sharia. In 1999, the OIC adopted its own Convention on Combating International Terrorism. Its definition of terrorism in Article I has been criticized as extremely vague. In essence, the definition is aimed at defining terrorism in such a way that Israel will be marked as a terrorist state. In contrast, the OIC has been criticized for failing to define as terrorist violence that its member states practice or approve of. The impasse has blocked attempts to reach a common definition with the United Nations.

In 2002, the OIC rejected attempts to define violence practiced against Israel by Palestinians or others as terrorism. The intifada was blessed as a virtuous effort of a subjected people to establish an independent state. During the 2003 meeting of the OIC, the prime minister of Malaysia engaged in harsh anti-Semitic rhetoric against the Jews and Israel in particular. His anti-Semitism was enthusiastically received by the delegates although denounced in international circles. In 2007, the OIC defined *Islamophobia* as the worst form of terrorism. The term is used by the OIC and its members as an ideological weapon against critics.

REFERENCES

Moinuddin, Hasan. *The Charter of the Islamic Conference*. New York: Oxford University Press, 1987.

Organisation of the Islamic Conference: Organisation of the Islamic Conference. New York: General Books, 2010.

Organization of Islamic Conference Handbook. Washington, DC: International Business Publications, 2005.

Sheikh, Naveed S. *The New Politics of Islam: Pan-Islamic Foreign Policy in a World of States*. New York: Routledge Curzon, 2003.

South Asian Association for Regional Cooperation

Edy Parsons

In May 1980, President Ziaur Rahman of Bangladesh sent letters to the heads of Bhutan, India, Maldives, Nepal, Pakistan, and Sri Lanka proposing to hold a summit to discuss regional security and development issues.

Subsequently, on December 7–8, 1985, the leaders of these seven South Asian nations met at Dhaka. At this summit, the leaders discussed regional cooperation and issues including drugs, terrorism, and the situation of South Asia in the General Agreement on Tariffs and Trade. At this first summit the South Asian Association for Regional Cooperation (SAARC) was formally established with the adoption of the SAARC Charter.

SAARC EXPANSION AND INTERNATIONAL RECOGNITION

SAARC members include Bangladesh, Bhutan, India, Maldives, Nepal, Pakistan, and Sri Lanka. In 2007, SAARC accepted Afghanistan as its eighth member. In 2005, SAARC granted China and Japan observer status. During that year, SAARC also secured United Nations (UN) observer status and signed a memorandum of understanding with various UN agencies such as the UN Conference on Trade and Development, the UN International Drug Control Program, and the UN Development Program. The following year, SAARC granted observer status to South Korea, the European Union, and the United States. These moves marked the expansion of SAARC as a regional organization and enhanced its global clout and international stature. Additionally, observer status has been granted to Iran (2007), Mauritius (2007), and Australia and Myanmar (2010). As of 2010, SAARC had nine observer states.

The heads of state of the member countries serve in a council, which represents the highest authority in SAARC. The members of this council generally meet once a year. Under this council, there is the Council of Ministers, which meets twice a year to help establish SAARC policy and addresses other issues of significance to member states. Under the Council of Ministers, there is a standing committee comprised of member states' foreign secretaries. The members of this committee review and approve projects, such as those that address energy, the environment, social development, and poverty alleviation, and then arrange financing for these various programs. This committee also tracks the progress of approved projects and identifies new areas of cooperation. SAARC also has technical committees that implement specific programs and projects, such as agricultural and rural development and projects that require ongoing scientific and technological cooperation. After the 1986 Bangalore Summit, SAARC established a permanent secretariat at Kathmandu, Nepal. The secretariat consists of the secretary-general, who works under a standing committee. Initially, there were four directors working under the secretary-general. By 1989, each member country appointed one director.

SAARC provides its members an opportunity to have informal discussions designed to lessen political tension, address economic issues, and foster regional cooperation. SAARC members believe that economic cooperation may eventually lead to regional stability and development.

Although SAARC was not formed as a security-oriented organization, security was still an important concern since terrorist attacks were increasing throughout the region. For example, the Tamil Tigers were conducting terrorist activities in Sri Lanka. A number of states (e.g., India, Canada, the European Union, the United Kingdom, and the United States) have designated the Tamil Tigers as a terrorist organization. SAARC members believe that the threat of terrorism in the region could affect current and future investments and economic growth. They also believe that a level of stability in the region would benefit the countries of South Asia.

REGIONAL TERRORISM

At the 1986 Bangalore Summit, SAARC members discussed the problem of regional terrorism. All members agreed that it was important to combat and mitigate terrorism as it was affecting economic and political stability as well as the lives of average people residing in the region. At the 1987 Kathmandu Summit in Nepal, SAARC members agreed that the convention should accept the principles adopted in UN Resolution 2625 on October 24, 1970. Under this resolution, states should not assist or participate in any terrorist or other subversive activities or armed factions within its borders and should not organize such activities in other countries. At this summit all SAARC members signed the Regional Convention on the Suppression of Terrorism. In 1988, this accord came into force following its ratification by all member nations. Under this accord, member countries would combat terrorism within their individual legal frameworks and cooperate with each other in combating terrorism. In 2004, this convention was strengthened by a protocol aimed at stopping the financing of terrorism and allowing the confiscation of funds used to aid or promulgate terrorist activities.

After the terrorist attacks in the United States on September 11, 2001, the threat of terrorism also increased in South Asia. Consequently, South Asian government officials were interested in putting more efforts into combating terrorism. However, implementation of its programs and agreements has been a problem for SAARC. Although SAARC members had heightened concerns regarding the threat of terrorism and security, they did not have detailed policies in place to organize security cooperation. Since the SAARC Charter states that all decisions within the organization have to be unanimous, it is a slow process when critical issues need to be addressed and decisions made. At the 2004 Islamabad Summit, SAARC members supported security cooperation in South Asia; however, no comprehensive plan was developed.

At the Colombo Summit in August 2008, SAARC members agreed that combating terrorism was their first priority. Hence, all members signed the Convention on Mutual Legal Assistance in Criminal Matters. This action condemned terrorist violence and encouraged SAARC members to cooperate and exchange information on terrorism and organized crime. However, they did not initiate a firm counterterrorism plan of action. Muslim terrorists from Pakistan launched the Mumbai attacks beginning on November 26, 2008. These attacks wounded or killed close to 500 people and involved bombing and shooting incidents against targets in Mumbai, India. Even after these horrendous attacks, SAARC members still could not agree on a counterterrorism strategy that every member country would be willing to approve. At the SAARC Terrorist Offences Monitoring Desk meeting on June 23, 2010, SAARC members exchanged lists of banned organizations that were linked to terrorism.

CONCLUSION

On June 26, 2010, the SAARC interior ministers' conference held in Islamabad discussed how to strengthen police cooperation in the fight against regional terrorism. However, there was no mechanism in place for police cooperation since the conference failed to approve proposals from Bangladesh and Sri Lanka. Bangladesh proposed to set up a SAARC Anti-terrorism Task Force, while Sri Lanka proposed to form the SAARC Police to fight terrorism and transnational crimes. Due to political differences among member countries, SAARC still does not have a common strategy in place to combat terrorism.

See also: **Volume 1, Part V:** African Union; Asia-Pacific Economic Cooperation Forum; Council of Europe; European Union; Organization of American States: Inter-American Committee against Terrorism; Organization of the Islamic Conference; Organization for Security and Cooperation in Europe

REFERENCES

Dash, Kishore C. *Regionalism in South Asia: Negotiating Cooperation, Institutional Structures.* New York: Routledge, 2008.
Khan, Rashid Ahmad. "Terrorism and SAARC." [Comment] *Daily Times,* July 7, 2010. http://dailytimes.com.pk/default.asp?page=2010%5C07%5C07%5C story_7-7-2010_pg3_4.
Maloney. Clarence. *SAARC: The Nations of South Asia Begin to Cooperate.* Indianapolis, IN: Universities Field Staff International, 1989.
Mendis, Vernon L. B. *SAARC: Origins, Organisation, and Prospects.* Perth, Australia: Indian Ocean Centre for Peace Studies, 1991.
Waterman, Daniel F. *SAARC: A New Framework for Regional Cooperation.* Honolulu, HI: East-West Center, 1986.

VI

Research Agenda and Future Counterterrorism Challenges

Afghanistan: Present and Future Challenges

Ferhat Pirincci

After the September 11 attacks the United States shifted its foreign policy from a defensive to an offensive approach and started the war on terror. Considering the causes and possible consequences, there is no doubt that the most important part of this new policy is still staged in Afghanistan. The war in Afghanistan began on October 7, 2001, and in 2003, there were 8,000 U.S. troops deployed in Afghanistan. In July 2010, seven years later, that number increased to about 80,000 U.S. servicemen and -women. Moreover, some of the objectives established by the International Security Assistance Force (ISAF) for the postconflict stage have not been realized because of ongoing military operations.

There are a lot of lessons to be learned from the previous developments in Afghanistan, but it would be better to focus on current realities and future prospects. It is obvious that in Afghanistan there are some challenges that have the potential to bear either positive or negative consequences for the future of the country. Regarding its historical, ethnic, religious, and geopolitical location, Afghanistan has unique and somewhat challenging characteristics that need to be considered. Thus, the challenges that led to the enduring war of attrition or the desperate war on terror for the United States are the consequences not only of Afghanistan's sui generis nature but also of a combination of the factors including the perceptions, mistakes, and attitudes of the United States itself; the will and attitudes of its partners; and the geostrategic landscape of the region. Additionally, some challenges born long before 2001 are likely to remain in the near future.

Those present and prospective challenges are all interrelated within a complex structure.

CHALLENGES ON THE GROUND:
DETERMINANTS OF A PROLONGED WAR

At the outset, there were some challenges stemming from Afghanistan's unique structure that would affect the fate of the operation as well as the efforts for the global war on terror. From an inside view, one of the challenges is the transformation of the Afghan people from hospitality to hostility. The present Afghan perception of and expectation from the United States is different from what they felt in 2001. While most of the people who had suffered for decades were ready to sacrifice and thus gave support to the coalition to achieve peace and establish security, their hopes became more desperate as each year passed. Civilian casualties in the aerial bombardments, nighttime house searches, and arbitrary arrests made it difficult for the majority of the people to support the U.S.-led operation. As a consequence, the hospitality showed by the local Afghans at the initiation of the war gradually turned to hostility toward the West. The former commander of U.S. forces in Afghanistan, General Stanley McChrystal, pointed out the situation in a Senate Hearing on June 2, 2009: "I believe the perception caused by civilian casualties is one of the most dangerous enemies we face . . . loss of popular support will be strategically decisive" (Ackerman 2009). The United States and its partners are losing the hearts and minds of the people, and these events have also globalized the Afghans. As one observer noted, before 2001, very few Afghan citizens had heard of Palestine, but in the late 2000s it became common for the Afghans to link their fate with that of Palestinians, Iraqis, and Kashmiris, seeing themselves as part of the global Muslim community that is being attacked by the West (Clark 2009, 50–51; Schmeidl 2009, 153–54).

Another domestic and interrelated challenge in Afghanistan is literacy. The literacy rate in Afghanistan remained under 5 percent throughout the 20th century, and according to an optimistic United Nations (UN) estimate, 90 percent of women and 63 percent of men in rural areas of Afghanistan are still illiterate (United Nations News Center 2009). This challenge is so tragic because, as one high-level ISAF official indicated, speaking on condition of anonymity (pers. comm., April 28, 2010), "some of the innocent civilians were shot just because they could not read the warnings and got close to the checkpoints."

Opium poppy cultivation and drug trafficking are among the biggest challenges that the ISAF is still facing in Afghanistan. Although opium cultivation was prominent before the fall of the Taliban, in the first half of this decade the cultivation rate exceeded past levels, and today Afghanistan is the source of 90 percent of the world's illicit opium. Opium poppy is also one of the funding sources of the Taliban and other extremist factions. Indications show that neither the counternarcotics efforts of the United States nor those of its partners or the Afghan government are sufficient. President Obama's special envoy for Afghanistan and Pakistan, Richard Holbrooke, described the counternarcotics efforts as "the most wasteful and ineffective program I have seen in forty years" (Farmer 2009). Nevertheless, income from poppy cultivation is also an important source of revenue for the farmers and their families in rural areas. Hence, pursuing direct aggressive or oppressive policies toward the producers in order to suppress one challenge would yield additional challenges.

Afghanistan's ethnic structure and lack of a substantial national identity are other challenges. This, combined with complex tribal and local relations, makes it difficult to build a strong Afghan national identity. Political power is usually used at the expense of other ethnic groups or factions and causes additional troubles in building a national identity as well as in creating a stable state structure. One of the major domestic challenges concerns the legitimacy of the current government in the eyes of many Afghans. Former alleged war criminals and local militias are forming the new government's security apparatus, and for the presidency, being a member of Afghanistan's most populous group (Pashtun) is not a sufficient criterion for legitimacy. As a president who was elected in an insecure environment, with a low turnout and widespread ballet box stuffing, Karzai is seen as an instrument manipulated by outsiders rather than an Afghan nation founder. Karzai is not viewed favorably by some U.S. officials as well. In a leaked classified cable from the U.S. ambassador Karl W. Eikenberry in Kabul to Washington, Karzai was described as "not an adequate strategic partner" and as a leader who "continues to shun responsibility for any sovereign burden" (Schmitt 2010).

Another challenge, one that is interrelated with the already mentioned issues, is the weak state structure and lack of an effective judicial system. Corruption, which is at an unprecedented level, has become an unavoidable characteristic of the Afghan political system, and without the deterrent of a judicial system, it undermines all efforts to prevent terrorism and drug trafficking and to create a stable political structure in a secure and developed environment (U.S. Agency for International Development 2009, 1–2). Thus, while some live in the populous cities in luxury and enjoy the benefits of the corrupt economic and political system, the vast majority of people in Afghanistan suffer. This links with another challenge: the difference in perceptions between the urban and rural areas.

OPTIMISM IN PURSUIT OF PESSIMISM

One of the biggest challenges faced since the start of the war is the illusion that ousting the Taliban would mean their defeat. Even if a central government is established in Kabul, the Taliban are a viable force especially in the rural areas. Considering the prolonged war and the current situation, it can be argued that installing weak allies to achieve tactical goals does not bear strategic gains.

Actually drawing a line between some of the Taliban members and al-Qaeda is vital. Most Taliban supporters perceive the insurgency as defending their homeland against non-Muslim invaders, while al-Qaeda sees Afghanistan as just one of the battlegrounds in their global jihad wherein they can take revenge on the West, especially the United States. Through separating those two factions (Taliban and al-Qaeda), some nonaggressive high-level Taliban members and their sympathizers could be included in future peace negotiations. In the current situation Taliban supporters in Afghanistan continue to perceive the ISAF as invaders and the Kabul government as a puppet, and this perception makes it difficult to cut the ideological ties and defeat al-Qaeda and its associated networks.

However, the objective is to regain the hearts and minds of ordinary Afghans. Showing more respect for the sovereignty of Afghanistan may help to overcome this challenge. Since symbols are very important for the Muslim community especially for the Afghan people, some legal or statutory arrangements and constraints may be implemented. Furthermore, the UN may play a more active role in state-building and development projects, and other Muslim countries may be willing to participate in civilian operations in order to gain more public support. Also, the Kabul government needs to shoulder more responsibility for its internal situation. Without a major input by the central government in providing security and a means of making a living for the Afghan people, especially in the rural areas, a strong and stable state structure cannot be created and the prolonged conflict could continue for decades.

Apart from the civilian casualties, the rising casualties sustained by the North Atlantic Treaty Organization (NATO)/ISAF forces are becoming a major problem for coalition partner nations. During the first seven years of the war, only 295 soldiers died in Operation Enduring Freedom, while 953 were killed in the period 2009–2010 (iCasualties n.d.). These casualties make support for the operation difficult, especially for some European countries. Needless to say, today the solidarity with and public support for the United States are not as the same as in 2001 and are gradually declining.

Allocation of inadequate resources to Afghanistan is another challenge that must be dealt with. While Afghanistan has received less assistance from donors compared with Bosnia, Kosovo, East Timor, and Lebanon, inefficiency and corruption in the dispersal of those funds create additional negative consequences as well (Spanta 2007, 4–5). Finally, a failure in Afghanistan may spawn unavoidable challenges in the region. In this context political instability in Afghanistan and Pakistan comes to the fore. A destabilized Pakistan might create challenges that could possibly ignite a nuclear war.

CONCLUSION

The future of Afghanistan is predicated on many unknowns. A successful outcome would not only eliminate existing terrorist networks but also encourage and strengthen counterterrorism efforts in the global context. Terrorist organizations would learn that the global community will fight against terrorism whatever it costs. However, considering the challenges cited here, one can argue that there are more reasons to be pessimistic. A failure not only means chaos in Afghanistan and possibly political turmoil in neighboring countries but could also empower militant groups to expand the insurgency beyond Afghanistan's borders. Operation Neptune Spear, which killed al-Qaeda leader Osama bin Laden in Pakistan, and other initiatives launched under President Obama's new strategy aimed at disrupting, dismantling, and defeating al-Qaeda in Afghanistan and Pakistan have yielded some successes. However, the full implementation of this new strategy will take longer than planned. In this context, it should be noted that the most important factor that needs to be addressed to overcome the unique challenges in both Afghanistan and Pakistan is strong and viable leadership in both countries and the support of ordinary Afghans and Pakistanis.

REFERENCES

Ackerman, Spencer. "McChrystal on Civilian Casualties." *The Washington Independent*, June 2, 2009. http://washingtonindependent.com/45299/mcchrystal-on-civilian-casualties.

Clark, Kate. "How the Guests Became an Enemy: Afghan Attitudes towards Westerners." In *Viewpoints Special Edition, Afghanistan, 1979–2009: In the Grip of Conflict*, 50–52. Washington, DC: Middle East Institute, 2009, 50–52.http://www.scribd.com/doc/23570326/Afghanistan-1979-2009-In-the-Grip-of-Conflict.

Farmer, Ben. "Afghanistan Opium Crackdown Doing Little, Says US Envoy." *Daily Telegraph*, April 22, 2009. http://www.telegraph.co.uk/news/world news/asia/afghanistan/5032711/Afghanistan-opium-crackdown-doing-little-says-US-envoy.html.

iCasualties. "Operation Enduring Freedom." n.d. http://icasualties.org/OEF/index.aspx.

"Rumsfeld Declares Major Combat Over in Afghanistan." *Fox News*, May 1, 2003. http://www.foxnews.com/story/0,2933,85688,00.html.

Schmeidl, Susanne. "Who Guards the Guardians? The Protection of Civilians in Afghanistan." In *Viewpoints Special Edition, Afghanistan, 1979–2009: In the Grip of Conflict*, 152–55. Washington, DC: Middle East Institute, 2009.

Schmitt, Eric. "U.S. Declares Major Combat in Afghanistan to Be Over." *New York Times*, May 2, 2003. http://www.nytimes.com/2003/05/02/world/afteref fects-kabul-us-declares-major-combat-in-afghanistan-to-be-over.html.

Schmitt, Eric. "U.S. Envoy's Cables Show Worries on Afghan Plans." *New York Times*, January 25, 2010, A1.

Spanta, Rangin D. "Future Challenges for Afghanistan." *Chatham House,* February 1, 2007. http://www.chathamhouse.org.uk/files/8145_010207spanta.pdf.
United Nations News Center. "UN Agencies Launch Much Needed Literacy Programmes across Afghanistan." April 20, 2009. http://www.un.org/apps/news/story.asp?NewsID=30527&Cr=education+for+all&Cr1=.
U.S. Agency for International Development. *Assessment of Corruption in Afghanistan,* January 15, 2009–March 1, 2009. http://pdf.usaid.gov/pdf_docs/PNADO248.pdf.
U.S. Department of Defense. "News Transcript." May 1, 2003, http://www.defense.gov/transcripts/transcript.aspx?transcriptid=2562.

Airpower and Counterterrorism

James Perry

Airpower is a formidable force multiplier that is integral to modern war. Advanced nations have used aircraft in their efforts to suppress insurgencies and strike at terrorists, with varying degrees of success. In general, aircraft provide counterinsurgency forces with surveillance, mobility, and strike capabilities and can counter the typical insurgent tactic of trying to surprise isolated government units. Counterinsurgency is extremely frustrating for air forces that, like the U.S. Air Force, are culturally and historically oriented toward air superiority and strategic bombing missions; insurgent groups have no air force with which to contest control of the air, and no major military or industrial targets to bomb. Simple aircraft that fly low and slow are best suited for counterinsurgency, but advanced air forces prefer to buy complex, fast jets best suited for conventional wars. Since 2001, the U.S. government has employed unmanned air vehicles (UAVs) with great success against insurgents and terrorists. UAVs can remain airborne for much longer than manned aircraft, and this "persistence" greatly enhances their utility as surveillance, strike, and communications relay platforms.

AIRPOWER IN WARFARE

In the aftermath of World War II, the French attempted to hold their colonies in Indochina and Algeria against guerrillas who sought independence. French airpower in Indochina consisted largely of propeller-driven fighters and transports that supported the ground troops and transported paratroops to reinforce beleaguered garrisons under Viet Minh attack. Due to the heavy jungle and Viet Minh camouflage, French aerial reconnaissance proved quite ineffective at detecting enemy troop movements

and bases. After 1949, the United States provided the French with sur-
plus World War II aircraft; some flew from French carriers in the Gulf of
Tonkin. In 1950, the Viet Minh began methodically attacking French fortified outposts. French aircraft bombed the attacking forces and dropped
paratroops to reinforce their outposts. In 1953, the French established a
fortified outpost at Dien Bien Phu, thinking to lure the enemy into battle.
Air transports inserted and sustained French troops at the outpost, which
could not be reached overland. The Viet Minh assembled a massive force
of artillery and antiaircraft guns that shut down French airfields and severely restricted aerial resupply and reinforcement. In due course, the Viet
Minh forced the French garrison to surrender, and the French government
decided to withdraw from Indochina. French airpower inflicted significant casualties during this war but never broke the enemy's determination
to gain independence.

The French regarded Algeria as part of France and fought desperately to
retain it from 1954 to 1962. Against the Algerian guerrillas, the French employed helicopter transports and gunships, as well as propeller-powered
T-6, P-47, F4U, and F6F fighters, B-26 bombers, and C-47 transports. As
in Indochina, French air transports rushed elite troops to reinforce threatened garrisons and to conduct search-and-destroy missions. A large force
of armed reconnaissance aircraft looked for enemy movements in rural
areas and provided rapid fire support to ground troops. Airpower was
critical to the very effective effort to prevent the guerrillas from infiltrating
into Algeria from their sanctuaries in Morocco and Tunisia. Ultimately, the
French defeated the insurgents militarily, but French president Charles de
Gaulle nevertheless granted independence to Algeria in 1962.

From 1948 to 1960, the British sought to prevent Communist guerrillas from seizing control of Malaya. To support this effort, the Royal Air
Force initially used propeller-driven Lincoln heavy bombers and Spitfire
and Tempest fighters but later employed jet-powered Canberra bombers
and Vampire and Venom fighters. Many participants considered the jets
less useful than the propeller-driven aircraft. Most direct air strikes on the
enemy were ineffective, because Malaya, like Indochina, was covered in
thick jungle that made observation of enemy infantry very difficult. However, air transport and resupply operations proved highly effective. The
British began using helicopters to move and supply troops in 1950, particularly to support long-range Special Air Service patrols. After 12 years,
the British had isolated and defeated the communist guerrillas and declared the counterinsurgency effort at an end.

American airpower had many roles in Indochina from 1954 to 1975.
American airmen trained and equipped the South Vietnamese Air Force,
supported U.S. troops in South Vietnam, hunted infiltrators on the Ho
Chi Minh Trail in Laos and Cambodia, supported the invasions of Laos
and Cambodia, and attempted to bomb North Vietnam into submission.
The U.S. air effort suffered from lack of clear thinking about the role of

airpower in counterinsurgency, itself a reflection of the U.S. Air Force's preoccupation with air superiority and strategic bombardment. After U.S. ground troops intervened, airpower in South Vietnam focused on close air support, reconnaissance, tactical airlift and resupply, and interdiction of enemy troop movements. Many different aircraft fought in South Vietnam, including propeller-driven A-1 attack planes and AC-130 gunships, F-4 and F-105 supersonic jet fighters, and B-52 bombers. In addition, the U.S. Army deployed thousands of helicopter transports and gunships. Over time, the original Viet Cong insurgents were largely defeated, but North Vietnamese Army troops began infiltrating South Vietnam, ultimately mounting powerful conventional mechanized assaults. The Americans inflicted enormous casualties on the Vietnamese Communists but never broke their will to unite Vietnam under their rule.

In March 1999, the North Atlantic Treaty Organization (NATO) launched an air campaign to force the Yugoslavian government to halt ethnic cleansing in the province of Kosovo. NATO forces included about 1,055 U.S. and Allied aircraft, which flew 38,000 sorties over 78 days. Notable events included the first combat use of the B-2 bomber, employment of Predator and Hunter UAVs to spot targets, and the loss of an F-117 stealth fighter. NATO labored under considerable self-imposed disadvantages, such as highly restrictive rules of engagement to minimize enemy civilian casualties and the requirement to fly above 15,000 feet to avoid enemy air defenses. Further, the task of finding dispersed enemy infantry in forested, mountainous terrain was inherently difficult. Airpower inflicted relatively few casualties on the Yugoslav Army and paramilitary forces, who were not defeated on the ground. The Yugoslav decision to capitulate to NATO demands likely resulted from attacks on infrastructure in Serbia and the prospect of a NATO ground assault.

The U.S. war in Afghanistan (after 2001) and Iraq (after 2003) featured a relatively short conventional phase followed by a prolonged effort to suppress insurgents and terrorists. The enemy in Afghanistan and Iraq (after the initial invasion) consists primarily of guerrillas who attack targets of opportunity. Consequently, the principal role for airpower is surveillance, close air support, and airlift. Operations in Afghanistan require extensive aerial refueling operations due to the great distance from regional airbases (and aircraft carriers) to the theater of war. Despite the employment of precision weapons, air strikes in Iraq and Afghanistan have caused enough civilian casualties to generate controversy and cause some to question whether airpower does more harm than good. The most notable innovation in the use of airpower in these wars is "time-sensitive targeting"— persistent surveillance platforms, like Global Hawk and Predator UAVs, are linked to strike platforms and troops on the ground to permit an extremely rapid response to any call for close air support.

In 2006, Israel fought a 34-day war against Hezbollah in southern Lebanon. The immediate cause was Hezbollah missile attacks on southern

Israel and a Hezbollah cross-border raid that killed three Israeli soldiers and captured two more. Over the next month, Israel launched over 10,000 F-15 and F-16 sorties and 2,000 attack helicopter sorties, as well as 2,500 transport and reconnaissance missions, to strike Hezbollah. Israel allegedly killed over 600 Hezbollah fighters while losing 118 soldiers. Israel also struck roads, bridges, airports, and other infrastructure in Lebanon. However, a primary objective—to stop Hezbollah rocket fire—was not achieved, as Hezbollah fired some 4,000 rockets into Israel during the conflict. Israeli ground forces invaded southern Lebanon and were shocked to discover a well-prepared Hezbollah defense in depth that included extensive underground bunker complexes and bases intentionally located in densely populated areas. Hezbollah conducted a skillful guerrilla campaign, featuring many ambushes and booby traps, as well as antitank missile fire from inside civilian houses. The conflict ended after the combatants accepted a United Nations Security Council cease-fire resolution. Both sides declared victory, but from a strategic perspective, Hezbollah remains in control of southern Lebanon. There, Hezbollah has stockpiled tens of thousands of rockets and periodically fires them into Israel.

AIRPOWER AGAINST TERRORIST TARGETS

Airpower is useful not merely to support a protracted counterinsurgency but also to conduct punitive raids on terrorist targets. Examples of punitive air raids conducted in response to terrorist attacks include Operation Wooden Leg in October 1985, when eight Israeli F-15s attacked the Palestine Liberation Organization headquarters in Tunisia. In April 1986, the United States launched Operation El Dorado Canyon, in which 18 U.S. Air Force and 27 U.S. Navy aircraft struck Libya. Operation Infinite Reach consisted of U.S. cruise missile attacks on a pharmaceutical factory in Sudan and al-Qaeda training camps in Afghanistan in August 1998.

The United States and Israel use airpower for targeted killings of terrorists who are beyond the reach of capture and who represent an imminent threat of future attacks. These attacks use precision weapons and seek to minimize collateral damage and civilian casualties. Israeli Apache helicopters, F-16 jets, and drones have killed a number of Palestinians (mainly members of Hamas) who led the terrorist bombing campaign that began in September 2000. In 2002, U.S. Predator drones used Hellfire missiles to kill an al-Qaeda leader in Yemen. In 2006, U.S. F-16s killed Abu Musab al-Zarqawi, the leader of al-Qaeda in Iraq.

CONCLUSION

Since 2004, the United States has conducted over 100 Predator strikes in the ongoing campaign against al-Qaeda leaders hiding in Pakistan. These strikes have killed at least nine important al-Qaeda leaders and some 800 to 1,200 other people. These attacks have generated controversy over the infringement of Pakistani sovereignty and over whether the majority of the casualties were militants or civilians. The Predator attacks are likely to continue, however, because the U.S. government believes it has no other option.

See also: **Volume 1, Part III:** Defensive Measures against Terrorism: Military Preemption and Retaliation; Military Force: Effective against Terrorists?

REFERENCES

Arkin, William M. *Divining Victory: Airpower in the 2006 Israel-Hezbollah War.* Maxwell Air Force Base, AL: Air University Press, 2007.
Corum, James S., and Wray R. Johnson. *Airpower in Small Wars.* Lawrence, KS: University Press of Kansas, 2003.
Lambeth, Benjamin S. *NATO's Air War for Kosovo.* Santa Monica, CA: RAND, 2001.
Lambeth, Benjamin S. *Airpower against Terror: America's Conduct of Operation Enduring Freedom.* Santa Monica, CA: RAND, 2006.
Tilford, Earl H. *Setup: What the Air Force Did in Vietnam and Why.* Maxwell Air Force Base, AL: Air University Press, 1991.

Biometrics Technology

Arpad Palfy

In their purest form, *biometrics* are the measurements of individual characteristics differentiating one person from another, such as body size and shape or eye, hair, and skin color. On a microlevel, these can also include fingerprints and vascular and retinal details. In short, biometrics equate to the sum of what makes us who we are.

BACKGROUND

In the 19th century, Alphonse Bertillon developed a scientific process known as anthropometry as a means of accurately measuring, and thereby identifying, criminals and individuals of interest. Anthropometrics involved the manual measurement and cataloging of bodily dimensions, such as hand, arm, leg, and foot sizes or lengths, as well as notable bodily identifiers, such as birthmarks, scars, and tattoos. His efforts resulted in the development of the first set of fundamental biometric measurements and identification criteria (Wayman et al. 2005, 2–3; Raina 2003, 26).

Overall, the traits used by biometric systems in identifying or verifying the identity of an individual must generally be *robust* and *distinctive*. The robustness of a particular trait refers to its repetitive consistency in terms of biometric measurement. Thus, regardless of how many times that trait is measured or presented to a biometric system, its robustness ensures that the measurement is always the same. Similarly, the distinctiveness of a trait refers to both the differences between that trait in several individuals, such as fingerprints, and to the measurable distinctions between the traits themselves. In other words, a biometric trait must be different enough to tell one person from another, and the differences leading to such individual distinctions should be measurable (Wayman et al. 2005, 3–4).

CHARACTERISTICS

Biometric characteristics are broken down into three areas: genetic, phenotypic, and behavioral. Genetic traits, such as eye color and face structure, are inherited and relatively hard, though not impossible, to change. Phenotypic traits are those that are individually distinctive and emerge during early (embryonic) stages of development, such as vascular networks and iris patterns. Iris patterns, for instance, are considered to be the most robust and therefore most consistent biometric over time. Lastly, behavioral traits are learned behaviors related to repetitive usage patterns, such as an individual's handwriting or voice. Behavioral traits are also those that tend to be the least consistent, therefore least robust, because they change the most over time (Raina 2003, 28–29).

While the types of biometric systems used to measure these traits may vary, the underlying internal measurement processes used are relatively similar. Initially, biometric systems begin with a data collection, or an enrollment, process. During this stage a genetic, phenotypic, or behavioral sample is collected by the biometric system as an identification template for a given individual. These stored templates or pieces of biometric information are then used as the means to identify or verify individual identities at a later time (Went 2007, 102).

Consequently, it becomes possible to distinguish the types of biometric systems through the number of comparisons a given system computes in relation to the originally stored template. For instance, a *verification* process or system denotes a confirmatory process relating to a single claimed identity. This therefore results in a one-to-one (1:1) verification by the biometric system, in that it compares the biometric information of a single individual it is presented with to the information already held on the stored template. Conversely, an *identification* process denotes a profile comparative process, where captured information is compared to countless other individuals or templates. This results in a one-to-many (1:N) attempted identification by the system (Went 2007, 102; Smith 2003, 8).

In either case, because no two biometric profiles are completely identical, even if collected with the same biometric scanner for the same individual, biometric systems must necessarily integrate a decision process resulting in a yes-no or pass-fail outcome. Therefore, all biometric systems must include a predefined acceptance threshold that dictates the level of accuracy required to attain a "pass" or "yes" when verifying or identifying an individual in relation to a stored template (Stapleton 2003, 167–68; Went et al. 2007, 102).

COUNTERTERRORISM APPLICATION

Of the two types of biometric comparisons, identification remains the most difficult decision process for a biometric system for several reasons. First, as the size of a given biometric database grows, the number of records searched at each attempt increases proportionally. Hence, the number of potential matches also increases. Consequently, biometric systems produce ordered lists of potential matches leaving the user to draw the ultimate conclusion. This process is referred to as *negative identification* or *negative matching* (Raina 2003, 34–36).

Finally, the accuracy of a biometric system as a whole is measured by the amount and type of errors it produces. Specifically, a false rejection rate, also known as a false nonmatch rate or type I error, denotes the number of occurrences when an individual who *should* have been identified by a biometric system was not. Conversely, a false acceptance rate, also known as a false match rate or type II error, denotes the number of occurrences when an individual is positively identified who should *not* have been. The intersection between the rates of these two types of errors when plotted on a graph equates to the rating given to a biometric system. Therefore, the lower the error rate, the higher the rating of the biometric system (Raina 2003, 34–36).

In a counterterrorism context, biometric technologies, particularly if combined with data-mining systems, represent a valuable and sought-after tool for governments and law enforcement agencies alike. Similarly, and with increasing frequency, these same tools are also being adopted by areas of the private sector where security remains paramount, such as airports and air carriers, as well as the banking and gaming industries (Woodward et al. 2003, 286–95, 330–37).

CONCLUSION

As beneficial as biometric systems may be from a security perspective, they are not infallible (Went 2007, 105–8), and their use and continued spread often leads to challenges related to information exchange, ownership, protection, and privacy (Woodward et al. 2003, 200–15). For instance, several large-scale data collection programs in the United States, including

Total Information Awareness (TIA), Multi-state Anti-terrorism Information Exchange (MATRIX), and the Analysis, Dissemination, Visualization, Insight, and Semantic Enhancement (ADVISE) programs, some of which included biometric subcomponents such as the TIA's Human Identification at a Distance (HumanID) project, were ultimately cancelled due to privacy concerns.

See also: **Volume 1, Part III:** Information Technologies to Combat Terrorism. **Part VI:** Counterterrorism Research: Current Efforts and Future Challenges; Data Mining; Psychological Profiling of Terrorists

REFERENCES

Chen, H., R.T. Santanam, R. Ramesh, A. Vinze, and D. Zeng, eds. *Handbooks in Information Systems: National Security.* Vol. 2. Amsterdam: Elsevier, 2007.

Libicki, Martin."Biometrics and the Feasibility of a National ID Card." In *Biometrics,* edited by D.J. Woodward, N.M. Orlans, and P.T. Higgins, 353–80. Berkeley, CA: McGraw-Hill, 2003.

Raina, Kapil. "How Biometrics Work." In *Biometrics,* edited by D.J. Woodward, N.M. Orlans, and P.T. Higgins, 25–44. Berkeley, CA: McGraw-Hill, 2003.

Smith, Richard E. "How Authentication Technologies Work." In *Biometrics,* edited by D.J. Woodward, N.M. Orlans, and P.T. Higgins, 3–24. Berkeley, CA: McGraw-Hill, 2003.

Stapleton, Jeff. "Biometric Standards." In *Biometrics,* edited by D.J. Woodward, N.M. Orlans, and P.T. Higgins, 167–82. Berkeley, CA: McGraw-Hill, 2003Valencia, Valorie. "Biometric Liveness Testing." In *Biometrics,* edited by D.J. Woodward, N.M. Orlans, and P.T. Higgins, 139–50. Berkeley, CA: McGraw-Hill, 2003.

Wayman, J., A. Jain, D. Maltoni, and D. Maio, eds. *Biometric Systems: Technology Design and Performance Evaluation.* London: Springer, 2005.

Went, P.C. "The Necessity of Funny Logic for Identity Matching." In *Handbooks in Information Systems: National Security,* edited by H. Chen, R.T. Santanam, R. Ramesh, A. Vinze, and D. Zeng, 101–32. Vol. 2. Amsterdam: Elsevier, 2007

Woodward, D.J., N.M. Orlans, and P.T. Higgins, eds. *Biometrics.* Berkeley, CA: McGraw-Hill, 2003.

Combating Terrorism: A New Way Forward

James Fitzgerald

Since its popular inception during the early 1970s, the development of terrorism studies has greatly contributed to an increased understanding of the phenomenon of terrorism. Despite the ever-increasing interest and activity in terrorism studies, however, many associated scholars have lamented deep-seated problems within the discipline, including the lack of an accepted definition, inherent disagreement over the causes of terrorism, and the classification of terrorist groups in terms of an old-versus-new dichotomy, as well as much scholarly confusion on the operational nature and ideological aims of groups such as al-Qaeda (Ranstorp 2007). In addition to these issues, the emerging field of critical terrorism studies has gained momentum in challenging the orthodox basis of terrorism studies itself, thereby challenging the theoretical and methodological foundations on which much of the popular scholarship on terrorism that has entered the public realm is based (Jackson, Breen Smyth, and Gunning 2009). Whether the consumers of terrorism scholarship find themselves gravitating toward a more dogmatic subscription to the output of "orthodox" or "critical" terrorism studies, or simply find themselves implementing a more pragmatic approach to the wide range of available scholarship on terrorism, a central issue traverses all considerations—how one combats terrorism depends precisely on how one understands it.

TERRORISM AS COMMUNICATION

Despite the many schisms within the literature, few would argue against the fact that terrorism has always existed as a communicative act; terrorists want a lot of people watching, whether or not one believes that they want a lot of people dead. The synchronicity between physical action and communicative meaning therefore forms an essential basis from which to understand terrorist groups. Embedded examples of this are replete across the literature; citations from Osama bin Laden's 1996 "Declaration of Jihad" are popularly used to exemplify core aspects of the al-Qaeda ideology, while the deeper symbolism of attacks such as the 1972 Munich Olympics massacre is used to convey a deeper meaning to terrorist acts than simply murder, which would otherwise fall into the sole classification of crime.

With the proliferation of an increasingly facilitative infrastructure across the Internet, however, terrorist communication is becoming more direct and more dynamic; bin Laden's statements can be broadcast from increasingly sophisticated media outlets such as as-Sahab, while lectures by the Muslim cleric Anwar al-Awlaki are easily accessible across open mediums such as YouTube. Indicative of an overall trend, we are now seeing more terrorist propaganda than ever before, which is widely available to both Arabic- and English-speaking audiences (Ryan 2010, 673). With an increasingly open network from which terror groups and related ideologues can release their public discourse, the state's traditional status as a relative gatekeeper in the context of terrorist propaganda is steadily eroding (Ryan 2010, 673). Indeed, the relative standing of state authority in the context of proliferating digital networks yields further problems in the context of user-generated videos from within the ranks of the state army. From gunship recordings that appear to show the killing of innocent civilians to impromptu Lady GaGa parodies (Cohen 2010), the traditional hierarchical control exerted by states over their primary apparatus of force can be challenged by digital depictions ranging from the tragic to the ridiculous. The classic tension between terrorism and civil liberties thus remains; if we are to accept the central dichotomy between states and substate groups in the formulation of terrorism, then how can states seek to combat terrorism in an age of digital multitude without negatively impacting on core formulations of liberty that have so often been exalted as defining the positive character of states in opposition to the terrorist "other"?

TOWARD AN UNDERSTANDING OF TERRORISM

The fundamental question of how to combat terrorism does not have an easy answer, yet I return, for a moment, to the formulation submitted earlier: how one combats terrorism depends precisely on how one understands it. In a survey of the post-9/11 literature in terrorism studies, Andrew Silke noted a distinct dearth of pioneering scholarship such that barely 20 percent of articles "provided substantially new knowledge that was previously unavailable to the field" (2007, 80). I would argue that this need not be the case. If we embrace the power of communication at the heart of our depiction of terrorism, then in the context of the masses of data constantly becoming available online, scholars within the terrorism community can avoid a stagnation in innovative research as highlighted by Silke. Applications of techniques such as discourse analysis and network analysis to the study of terrorism are extremely encouraging in this respect, as are the applications of more "critical" techniques to the study of terrorism. In a temporal environment of constantly flowing data and identities, I would argue that a de facto understanding of terrorism can never be achieved: the conundrum of combating terror in the context of protecting civil liberties is arguably as taxing today as it was during the 1970s and 1980s—indeed, if not more so. Similarly, we still have not "discovered" the causes of terrorism, agreed on a definition of terrorism, or resolved the new-versus-old terrorism debate, all in the midst of the increasing relevance of critical terrorism studies, which eschews many of the philosophical foundations on which such endeavors are based.

CONCLUSION

It should not be the job of the terrorism researcher to uncover encompassing generalities that provide a final coherent understanding of a phenomenon as diverse as terrorism; rather, the job of the terrorism researcher is to try and keep ahead of the curve insofar as possible and to monitor the discourses that contingently define the terrorists and the fields within which terrorism operates. We need to reexamine the generalities that buttress our understanding of terrorism—for it is only through the proliferation of discourses seeking to *understand* terrorism that we can hope to combat the proliferating discourses that constitute the continuing essence of terrorism itself.

See also: **Volume 1, Part VI:** Counterterrorism and the Forensic Sciences; Counterterrorism Research: Current Efforts and Future Challenges; Multilateral Approach to Counterterrorism: Issues, Problems, Responses; Preemptive Counterterrorism: The Need for a Global Integrated Approach; Rehabilitation of Extremists: Methods and Practice; Root Cause Analysis and Counterterrorism; Sun Tzu's *Art of War:* Lessons for 21st-Century Counterterrorism Practitioners Understanding Foreign Cultures

REFERENCES

Cohen, N. "Through Soldiers' Eyes, 'The First YouTube War.'" *New York Times,* May 23, 2010. http://www.nytimes.com/2010/05/24/business/media/24link.html?fta=y.

Jackson, R., M. Breen Smyth, and J. Gunning, eds. *Critical Terrorism Studies: A New Research Agenda.* London: Routledge, 2009.

Ranstorp, M., ed. *Mapping Terrorism Research: State of the Art, Gaps and Future Direction.* London: Routledge, 2007.

Ryan, J. "The Internet, the Perpetual Beta, and the State: The Long View of the New Medium." *Studies in Conflict and Terrorism* 33, no. 8 (2010): 673–81.

Silke, A. "The Impact of 9/11 on Research on Terrorism." In *Mapping Terrorism Research,* edited by M. Ranstorp, 76–93. London: Routledge, 2007.

Connecting the Dots: Fort Hood Massacre and Northwest Airlines Flight 253

Justin Lewis Abold

Mass killings like the one at Fort Hood invariably prompt the question, Could it have been prevented? Seen through a rearview mirror, the clues appear tantalizingly obvious—if only we had been able to connect the dots. That famous phrase sometimes seduces us into overestimating what is reasonably knowable. While I await the government's own inquiry, in this case I remain skeptical. (Jenkins 2009, 3)

"Connecting the dots" became a mainstay of American political and policy discourse following the events of September 11, 2001. It is shorthand for the 9/11 Commission findings that shortfalls in information

sharing—as well as a "lack of imagination"—contributed to the terrorists' ability to successfully attack the continental United States. The emphasis immediately after September 11, 2001, and in the first half of the
following decade was on improving information sharing—ensuring that
all those who needed the "dots" were able to access them. This emphasis
on information sharing was instantiated in legislation, such as the Homeland Security Act of 2002, which created the Department of Homeland
Security, and in a variety of executive branch policies, to include the National Information Sharing Strategy. Events in the latter half of the decade
after September 11, 2001, including the Fort Hood Massacre (November 5,
2009) and the attempt on Northwest Airlines Flight 253 (aka the Christmas
Bomber, December 25, 2009), have shifted the emphasis toward a recognition that connecting the dots requires both *sharing* them and also accurately *connecting* them. In these events, the resulting security shortfall was
less a product of specific and easily rectifiable legal or bureaucratic information-sharing barriers. Instead, the events at Fort Hood and on Flight
253 appear to be the product of a mélange of factors that facilitated errors in human judgment. These errors resulted in failures to synthesize
available information and create an accurate, timely understanding of the
threat.

FORT HOOD MASSACRE

On November 5, 2009, Major Nidal Malik Hasan, an army psychiatrist due to be deployed to Afghanistan, entered the Soldier Readiness
Center at Fort Hood, Texas, and opened fire in the open-workplan office
space, where between 300 and 400 people were at work. Before being apprehended by two police officers responding to a 911 call reporting the
shooting, Major Hasan killed 12 Army soldiers and 1 civilian and injured
at least 30 others. After the fact, investigations suggest there may have
been sufficient information to place Major Hasan under increased monitoring—if this information had been more broadly available and the dots
had been connected.

In 2008 and 2009, the Federal Bureau of Investigation (FBI), as part of
its investigation into Anwar al-Awlaki (the Yemeni-based radical Muslim
cleric), intercepted several e-mails between Major Hasan and al-Awlaki.
The e-mails were reviewed by a joint terrorism task force (JTTF). Task
force members assessed that the content was consistent with research
Major Hasan was conducting under the auspices of his training at Walter
Reed. The existence of the e-mails was not shared outside the JTTF due to
routine information dissemination restrictions that prohibited sharing
information outside the JTTF without a specific reason (FBI 2009).

From 2003 to 2009, Major Hasan was in training at Walter Reed. During his training at Walter Reed, he was apparently the subject of considerable discussion and review, both due to his performance issues and due

to concern about his mental health. He apparently espoused extremist views, attempted to convert patients to Islam, and gave a presentation titled "The Koranic World View as It Relates to Muslims in the U.S. Military" (Saslow et al. 2009, graphic) in lieu of a report on a medical topic. His supervisors at Walter Reed discussed his performance and reportedly had concerns that he was unstable and could be at risk for disclosing classified information and potentially even engaging in fratricide. They reportedly concluded they were not certain enough in their judgment to engage in the lengthy and bureaucratic process of removal, were concerned they were potentially discriminating against him because of his religious views, and believed that the support of his colleagues in future assignments, especially at Fort Hood, would provide sufficient support—and monitoring—for Major Hasan (Zwerdling 2009).

Neither the JTTF nor the military staff of Walter Reed was aware of the information the other possessed, and neither had enough information on their own to make the decision that there was a justification to share their information with another party. There was no specific legal, bureaucratic, or even cultural barrier preventing the information from being shared. Instead, typical rules protecting classified information (in the FBI) and personal information (in the Department of Defense) facilitated erroneous human judgments about when to share—judgments based on incomplete information, inaccurate analysis, and everyday human uncertainty that resulted in incomplete information sharing and a failure to connect the dots.

NORTHWEST AIRLINES FLIGHT 253

On December 24, 2009, Umar Farouk Abdulmutallab boarded a plan from Lagos, Nigeria, to Detroit, Michigan, via Amsterdam. He checked in with only minimal carry-on baggage and no checked baggage. He successfully passed through security screening in Lagos and Amsterdam. On December 25, 2009, on the Amsterdam-to-Detroit leg of the flight, Abdulmutallab attempted to detonate explosives he had sewn into his underwear. Passengers heard a loud "pop" and saw smoke. They apprehended him and prevented him from taking further actions. The explosives sewn into his underwear burned him severely but did not achieve their intended purpose of bringing down the flight, which landed safely. Postevent reviews within the U.S. government show a possibility that there was sufficient information within the National Counterterrorism Center to correctly risk-assess Abdulmutallab and place him on the no-fly list. However, this information was not accurately synthesized by analysts: they did not connect information about Abdulmutallab with information about a threat emanating from Yemen and a threat connected to a Nigerian (Leiter 2010, 1–3).

In 2009, the intelligence community had had strategic warning of an attack by al-Qaeda in Yemen. Over time, the intelligence community became aware that the attack was directed at U.S. interests and that the threat might possibly emanate from Yemen rather than taking place against U.S. interests in Yemen. The National Counterterrorism Center remained focused on the al-Qaeda threats on the Arabian Peninsula, however, rather than the potential for an attack on U.S. interests elsewhere, including the United States itself (Senate Select Committee on Intelligence 2010). In the Central Intelligence Agency (CIA), additional information about Abdulmutallab had been collected but was not disseminated until after the Christmas Bombing (Lipton, Schmitt, and Mazzetti 2010). In part, this was because it was waiting for a photo (Lipton, Schmitt, and Mazzetti 2010) and in part because it was viewed as of low importance due to its sourcing (Milton 2009). In November 2009, Abdulmutallab's father visited the U.S. embassy in Nigeria to inform the State Department that he was concerned his son was involved with Yemeni-based extremists. The embassy officials checked to determine if Abdulmutallab had a U.S. visa, but because they misspelled his name, they did not find out that he did indeed have a current U.S. visa. A message from the embassy was sent to the intelligence community and law enforcement entities through normal channels and included the information on Abdulmutallab.

Analysts in the intelligence community in theory had access to all of the preceding information (except the report held within the CIA) but did not successfully connect the dots. In some cases, the technological limitations of searching databases—and simple spelling errors—inhibited the retrieval of information. This prevented an FBI analyst from accessing available information and contributed to the State Department's overlooking of Abdulmutallab's visa record. In other cases, rules designed to prevent abuse or inefficient use of the watchlists had created standards of analytic rigor that may have made it too difficult to place names on the watchlist where there was reasonable suspicion. Yet it is again human judgment that erred—errors as simple as misspellings, as routine as waiting to send out a report until it was complete with a photo, and as complex as a failure to recognize a lesser-known threat in part due to a preoccupation with a more well-known threat.

CONCLUSION

While the circumstances of the failures in the Fort Hood Massacre and Northwest Airlines Flight 253 differ—the first a failure to adequately synthesize information about Major Hasan's contacts with the Yemeni-American cleric Anwar-al Awlaki with information contained in his military performance evaluations; the second a failure to make the connection between a threat from a Nigerian in Yemen and a father's complaint about his son's potential radicalization—both share a common failure in information synthesis and analysis. They illustrate that connecting the dots is more than a logistical challenge of moving information from one place to another and instead requires the ability to connect and contextualize often seemingly disparate pieces of information. Even when there are no specific barriers to sharing the dots, human decisions about when it makes sense to share information—and human decisions about how to synthesize information—are still subject to error.

The reports and reviews after the fact recommend improved training for individuals to help them identify what information is critical and deserves additional attention; improved technological tools to help individuals make connections between disparate but linked pieces of information; improved accountability, clear ownership, and better coordination for analysis; and improved physical and personnel security (of various types). These recommendations highlight—though leave largely untouched—the aspects of connecting the dots that complicate bureaucratic solutions: the hidden, mental aspects of synthesizing and analyzing large amounts of information and constructing an accurate representation of the threat in a timely manner. Until there is a huge technological step forward in knowledge technology or artificial intelligence, connecting the dots remains dependent on the human in the loop to recognize what information is important enough to receive additional attention and the context within which that piece of information reveals something previously unknown.

See also: **Volume 1, Part III:** Ideology That Spawns Islamist Militancy. **Part VI:** Psychological Profiling of Terrorists; Public Support and Education Campaigns

REFERENCES

Federal Bureau of Investigation. "Investigation Continues into Fort Hood Shooting" [Press release]. Washington, DC: FBI National Press Office, 2009. http://www.fbi.gov/pressrel/pressrel09/forthood111109.htm.

Jenkins, Brian M. "Going Jihad: The Fort Hood Slayings and Home-Grown Terrorism." Testimony, Senate Homeland Security and Governmental Affairs Committee, November 19, 2009. http://www.rand.org/pubs/testimonies/2009/RAND_CT336.pdf.

Leiter, Michael E. "Flight 253: Learning Lessons from an Averted Tragedy." Statement for the Record, House Homeland Security Committee, January 27, 2010. http://homeland.house.gov/SiteDocuments/20100127100923-82356.pdf.

Lipton, Eric, Eric Schmitt, and Mark Mazzetti. "Review of Jet Bomb Plot Shows More Missed Clues." *New York Times*, January 17, 2010. http://www.nytimes.com/2010/01/18/us/18intel.html.

Milton, Pat. "CIA's Abdulmutallab Info Not High Priority." *CBS News*, December 30, 2009. http://www.cbsnews.com/stories/2009/12/30/cbsnews_investigates/main6038832.shtml.

Saslow, E., P. Rucker, W. Wan, and M.P. Flaherty. "In Aftermath of Fort Hood, Community Haunted by Clues That Went Unheeded." *Washington Post,* December 31, 2009. http://www.washingtonpost.com/wp-dyn/content/story/2009/12/30/ST2009123002982.html?sid=ST2009123002982.

Senate Select Committee on Intelligence. *Attempted Terrorist Attack on Northwest Airlines Flight 253.* Washington, DC: U.S. Government Printing Office, 2010.

Zwerdling, Daniel. "Walter Reed Officials Asked: Was Hasan Psychotic?" *National Public Radio,* November 11, 2009. http://www.npr.org/templates/story/story.php?storyId=120313570.

Countering Agroenvironmental Terrorism

Heather M. Hilliard

Defending the national food supply and delicate ecosystem that supports the national way of life has gained increasing importance in the last decade. Many nations are formally documenting the need for specific terrorism-protection programs for natural resources. Within the United States, Homeland Security Presidential Directive 9 (HSPD 9) specifically addresses the defense requirements of our agriculture and food, investments in the protection of key agroenviro critical infrastructure, and vulnerability mitigation for production and processing (U.S. Department of Homeland Security 2004). A subcomponent of Homeland Security Presidential Directive 10 (HSPD 10) also stresses the need for agricultural defense against biological contamination (U.S. Department of Homeland Security 2004). Further, recent events such as the industrial catastrophe from the British Petroleum Macondo Prospect failures in the Gulf of Mexico are recognized not only by environmental advocates as debilitating but also by political pundits like James Carville, who presented a comparison with the flow of oil that could have feasibly been the result of a terrorist attack for which the nation is still unprepared (Davis 2010, 19). Protecting ourselves from biological and chemical attack or industrial sabotage through agricultural and environmental preparedness is essential in the years ahead as technological advances along with flexibility enhance the posture of adversaries.

AIR AND WATER POLLUTANTS

In May 2010, the *New York Times* reported that the U.S. Environmental Protection Agency (EPA) had admitted that it was at least a decade behind on issuing pollutant guidelines for a host of toxic air pollutants (Torbati 2010). The EPA issued a written response to address the delay, explaining that "air toxics support has been cut over 70 percent since FY 2001" (U.S. Environmental Protection Agency, Office of the Inspector General 2010). The U.S. General Accounting Office is cited in the Torbati article as stating that in the past the low priority of the air toxics program and limited funding had been found to be partly to blame for the ongoing delay; however, they are not the sole reasons. While HSPD 9 specifically calls for "the development of current and new countermeasures against the intentional introduction or natural occurrence of catastrophic" destruction of the food supply (U.S. Department of Homeland Security 2004), without the appropriate classification of toxicity (as in this given example of air pollutants), it is difficult to combat an infiltrating chemical or biological agent that may indeed already have effective counterterrorism methods available. Focus has traditionally been directed toward rapid detection and identification of agents with diagnostic techniques (National Research Council of the National Academies 2003) rather than tactical identification of agroenvironmental targets and mitigation of intentional introduction.

The expanding environmental exposures and measurements of toxicity for additives or contaminants in the water supply also highlight the outdated methods for measuring chemical constituents and their safe levels in drinking water. The Safe Drinking Water Act was passed in 1974 and contained basic thresholds for a few dozen chemicals that were permitted to be present at certain levels in drinking water in the United States. The last significant update to this law was in the 1980s, to include 91 contaminants; however, the EPA estimates that over 60,000 chemicals are currently used in the United States (Duhigg 2009). While the EPA announced in March 2010 that the drinking water regulations would be reviewed and updated, as of this writing, the standards for environmental exposure and human health effects continue to be those last modified by the EPA in 2000.

The preceding illustrates air and water contamination within the United States, both of which can significantly contribute to soil pollution as well. The biodiversity and national significance of the coastal ecosystems have prudently been identified—and ironically just prior to the recent chemical incident in the Gulf of Mexico from the Macondo Prospect, termed the Deepwater Horizon Incident, or Mississippi Canyon 252 Event. In March 2010, the Restoration Working Group (which focuses on restoring economic and ecological soundness to the Gulf region) issued a statement in their "Roadmap" report drawing attention to the importance of the "marine and terrestrial environment, national commerce, the maritime industry, energy security, fisheries, and the rich cultural legacy" of the very area now polluted with oil and dispersants (White House, Louisiana-Mississippi Gulf Coast Ecosystem Restoration Working Group 2010, 22). While the research on the effects of Hurricanes Katrina and Rita is forever changed and expanded as of April 22, 2010 (the date the rig collapsed to the floor of the Gulf), the sustainability and social vulnerability of our entire nation are already reflected in certain food costs within just the first 90 days of the oil spill—the reduction in availability of various types of seafood as well as increased delivery costs.

Regulatory efforts are in place for industries, but the key to success as a mitigation tool is the enforcement of these safety measures. For example, Senator Jim Webb (D-VA) pointed out that the "National Regulatory Commission requires that nuclear reactors be able to withstand plan crashes" (CNN Wire Staff 2010). However, there are no such requirements for oil rigs or similar critical infrastructure resources for hydrocarbon refinement although these sites are typically much more susceptible to external attack. These rigs' geographic isolation (by hundreds of miles of water), logistical self-sufficiency (for periods of 30 days or greater), and obvious fallacies in the beliefs held internationally on big corporations' safety and response capabilities to handle all aspects of operations create a nest of immature preparedness in the private sector as well as governmental support. The regulations (mitigation) and preparedness requirements merely generalize the necessity of response rather than providing for the protection of the asset.

FOOD SYSTEM VULNERABILITY

While the nation may have some adaptive capacity to respond to a variety of threats, such as toxins that eliminate food production or harvesting ability or impair economic independence, it is recognized internationally that the United States is environmentally vulnerable. Our environmental openness—one of the prides of the nation—and our rapid development of biotechnology actually increase our vulnerabilities in the area of food system security (Environmental Vulnerability Index 2005). The coping strategies typically employed during times of climate strain (drought, flooding) are short-term temporary responses to specific events that are limited in scope and duration (Vásquez-León, West, and Finan 2003, 161). These mechanisms, or buffers, utilize technology adjustments or social policy to spread the risk across greater geographic regions or economic industries and attempt to build resilience into the food system. Federal disaster programs, for instance, may reimburse ranchers for supplemental feed during a drought (Vásquez-León, West, and Finan 2003, 167), or the U.S. National Flood Insurance Program may offset the cost of rebuilding appropriate structures for individuals when floodwaters inundate their residences.

But how, then, do these generally weather-oriented lessons apply to terrorist events that threaten not only the safety of the food supply but also the self-imposed veil of safety in which hundreds of millions of people function—now that they are not self-sustaining family farmers but contributors to a larger, more synergistic society? A fresh vulnerability assessment of one of the weakest areas of defense for any nation is required. While agricultural assets are not typically considered at the top of the critical infrastructure lists, the components that contribute significantly to the production of food supplies—arable land availability and water purity, just two aspects—and distribution mechanisms (such as highway, railway, or river systems) are significant infrastructure components. Damage to these key resources could adversely impact global food supplies and the ongoing sustainability of defensive campaigns against agroenvironmental terrorism.

CARVER

The CARVER offensive prioritization tool developed by the U.S. military during the Vietnam War for identification of targets is one method of analysis that could be more widely adapted for vulnerability and criticality analysis. The six attributes represented by the acronym CARVER are *criticality* (the target's value, such as public health and economic impacts), *accessibility* (infiltration of and egress from a target), *recuperability* (time to recover), *vulnerability* (ease of accomplishing as well as construction of target), *effect* (direct loss by measuring production), and *recognizability* (ease in identifying target) (U.S. Army 1991). In recent years, a seventh attribute, *shock,* has been added to the original six features to assess the combined health, economic, and psychological impacts of an attack *specifically on the food industry*—primarily from the defensive perspective (U.S. Food and Drug Administration 2010). In CARVER+Shock, a numeric score is developed for each attribute on a scale of 1 to 10 (with 10 being the most attractive for an offensive maneuver). All assets are considered equally, though each attribute is weighted differently. For instance, targeting the leader of a country could rate the same as eliminating a significant transportation corridor. However, falling into different attributes, they would be weighted differently.

Utilization of the CARVER+Shock method—not only by federal agencies but also by local government officials involved in homeland security and emergency availability (stockpiles)—would provide critical information to develop mitigation steps and appropriate resource preparedness for HSPD 9 compliance. This is primarily to address domestic safety but also to mitigate against devastation of the global food sourcing of imports and exports. Preparedness personnel identifying risks and developing mitigation steps for critical infrastructure typically employ another version of CARVER, called CARVER2, which ranks the importance of the infrastructure relative to a limited number of other potential targets in a given attack scenario (Peimer 2006). However, assessment with CARVER—in any of its variations—lacks a social context or cultural impact aspect.

MSHARRPP APPROACH

When one is assessing the appropriate defense posture from the attacker's viewpoint, the MSHARRPP model can be used to complete a vulnerability assessment of national resources as it is more closely aligned with the needs and tactics of antiterrorism units (U.S. Joint Chiefs of Staff 2004). The U.S. Department of Defense and some state-level divisions of government utilize the MSHARRPP approach: mission, symbolism, history, accessibility, recognizability, recoverability, population, and proximity of primary/secondary targets (Peimer 2006; note that the second *R* is a more recent military addition, not listed in Peimer's work; further, *V* for vulnerability is sometimes used in recent years.). Each attribute in MSHARRPP has subcategories for consideration, providing a more detailed review of each variable in the analysis (U.S. Joint Chiefs of Staff 2004). This analytical approach also includes the critical factor of target "emotional investment" in the selection of viable targets, primarily under the attributes of symbolism and history. It also evaluates personnel vulnerabilities. The importance of the target to a society as well as a society's attachment to the ideological representation of the location may greatly enhance target value and should be considered in the analysis.

MSHARRPP will allow inclusive consideration not only of the biophysical context of geographic considerations but also of socioeconomic and political influences. Performing this assessment of the risk of a specific threat/target versus a generalized vulnerability assessment develops insights for local decision makers and response plans through the expertise of the immediate local first responder. This also addresses the more recent HSPD 18, which requires planning for the vision of integrated holistic biopreparedness for chemical, biological, radiological, and nuclear integrated consequence management (U.S. Department of Homeland Security 2007). There are other threat assessment tools familiar to law enforcement entities—such as SIPREEDD, which utilizes compartmentalized assessment criteria (suspect, offense, weapons, site, time) to produce an overall risk rating (Macdonald 1999). However, these types of evaluations are more easily applied when a known group or assailant is identified with a particular target site. In addition, there are other vulnerability assessments used by the U.S. Marine Corps and other U.S. Department of Defense branches (such as the Critical Asset Prioritization Methodology), though they have not typically been applied in nonmilitary or commercial settings.

AGROENVIRONMENTAL RESPONSE

The architecture of agroenvironmental response, in line with the National Incident Management System, is that all response is local and should thus be managed at the local level. This allows for the recognition of cultural prowess and tactical synergies that preexist in local first responders' relationships and knowledge of geography—both literal and political. Consider the case example of a toxin release in a water supply that irrigates 100,000 acres of farmland. As a result of ongoing trainings and exercises, the first responders—law enforcement officers as well as public health epidemiological investigators—approach the incident site as a unified local team. Health precautions are issued by the health officials, whereas criminal evidence preservation and logistics safety are under the purview of the law enforcement official. Together, applying the principles utilized during the hazard analysis and risk assessment, the likely agent and aggressor can be identified. See Tables 3 and 4 for the CARVER-Shock/MSHARRPP and SIPREEDD assessments and the subsequent basic investigation activity that could be reasonably expected for this scenario.

Table 3
Crosswalk of CARVER+Shock, MSHARRPP, and SIPREEDD Assessments

	CARVER+Shock	MSHARRPP	SIPREEDD*
Ability to tactically review subsystems	1 (one score per item on each CARVER variable/letter)	0.5	1 (score per each variable listed; yields aggregate item score)
Criteria based on known importance to infrastructure (historical weaknesses)	1	1	0
Evaluation of emotional impact of attack (based on location or personnel targeted)	0	1	0
Ability to be performed in abstract (without identified aggressor)	1	1	0
Ability to extract key details about aggressors/preferred tactics	0	0.5	1
Research required for validated scoring	0.5	1	1

(Continued)

Table 3 *(Continued)*

	CARVER+Shock	MSHARRPP	SIPREEDD*
Operations focused	1	1	0.5
Tactics focused	0	0	1
Target reconnaissance advised for scoring	1	0.5	1
Score/numeric results	1	1	1
Supports operational resources required	0.5	1	1
Specific agricultural or environmental component	1	0	0
Yields or suggests best protection (based on highest weakness)	0.5	0.5	NA
Signature of authoritative person required	1	0	1
Vulnerable if . . . ?	High score	High score	NA
Action recommended?	Yes, on high-score items	Summary statement	Yes, above 25 points

Note: "1" means fully considered; "0.5" means partially able to analyze; "0" means not integrated into matrix assessment tool.
Source: Macdonald (1999).

Table 4
Joint Investigative Considerations for Agroenvironmental Event by Suspected Aggressor(s)

Joint Investigation	Additional Considerations
• **Interactions and discussions together for source detection (joint efforts between public health and law enforcement)**	• Consider joint questionnaires that reflect law enforcement as well as public health questions; the order of the questions may help/hinder responses
• **Team composition: law enforcement or public health as lead (situational dependence for task force leadership)**	• Review of occupational and recreational activities for exposure and/or ability to obtain agent/delivery method in question

(Continued)

Table 4   (*Continued*)

Joint Investigation	Additional Considerations
• **Consideration and review of appropriate applicable privacy laws (such as Healthcare Information Portability and Privacy Act)**	• Translation services may be necessary (friends/family not typically appropriate interpreters)
• **Interaction with health care facility (hospital) administration**	• Identify laboratory personnel that can provide follow-up expertise
• **Discussions with health personnel before direct contact with the patient/person of interest/ victim (note all three categories may apply)**	• Review of other seemingly nonrelated health-aggregate and patient-specific data may present trends or triggers from the public health perspective

Intrinsic in even non-CARVER+Shock/MSHARRPP analytics, however, is still the very pertinent and timely identification of the human enemy. As a systemic attack on farm-to-fork (terminology used for food system supply chain) is generally speaking prohibitive, as a result of the geographic expansiveness of the agricultural business (among other variables), the categories of adversary depicted in the initial Food and Drug Administration publication addressing the needs of HSPD 9 still hold true. Aggressors attack from outside the system and exploit existing weaknesses or create new opportunities for entry. Insiders—which may truly be categorized as outsiders exploiting an identified opportunity—may also utilize these methods to destroy the supply or the ability to regenerate/sustain supplies. Agents utilized for weapons remain in the same categories— biological, chemical, radiation, and physical (pieces of plastic or other foreign objects, for instance).

While it may not be apparent in all regions of a nation that a risk to the agricultural production/harvest or environmental mechanism(s) is an immediate or likely occurrence, the ramifications to public health if even one episode is experienced—multiple injuries, panic instigation, or future vulnerability—are overwhelmingly sufficient to give credence and resources to these issues. Heightened surveillance, increased screenings/ tracking of workers, and other monitoring processes are beginning to be implemented at the production/distribution facets of the supply chain. While general preventive public health behaviors are routinely encouraged—such as good hygiene or safe food-handling practices—these efforts reduce the introduction of additional contaminants at the "fork" end of the supply chain rather than the "farm" side. Additional farm and processing resources need enhancement, while federal and local agencies—as well as industry—work simultaneously on closing other existing vulnerabilities in the chain. Additional manufacturing and production inspections by the Food and Drug Administration as well as the U.S. Department of Agriculture show increased diligence and continue to pull unsafe products off the market before consumption or mass distribution has occurred.

CONCLUSION

Worldwide agroenvironmental terrorist situations are high consequence and low probability events, but this only serves to increase the need to be appropriately prepared to respond efficiently through all-hazard local operations. Many of the current tools used at the local government level as well as national military law enforcement techniques should be applied in new ways—retraining personnel and repurposing tools to fight new technological battles to counter terrorism. As first responders are deployed from local areas to investigate and contain or mitigate impacts, expertise from other fields—such as petrochemical and technological—already encompasses many skills, tools, medications, and processes to handle events that threaten agriculture and the environment. However, without cooperation and cross-training, the response time of state-level and national experts will exacerbate the damage caused by these types of terrorist catastrophes. The impacts in a globally interdependent economy will have a ripple effect through many facets of the farm-to-fork chain. Intelligence sharing—on both threats and solutions—is needed in all fields to perpetuate learning and effective responses.

See also: **Volume 1, Part III:** Crisis Management: The Public Health System; Target Hardening; Threat, Vulnerability, and Criticality Assessments. **Part VI:** Protecting Critical Infrastructure: Government/Private Sector Alliance; Public Support and Education Campaigns

NOTE

All material in this section is in the public domain. The views expressed in this section are those of the author and do not necessarily represent the official policy or position of the Parish of Jefferson, State of Louisiana, the Centers for Disease Control and Prevention, the U.S. Department of Health and Human Services, or the U.S. Department of Homeland Security.

REFERENCES

CNN Wire Staff. "Senator Warns of Terrorist Threat to Oil Rigs." *CNN*, July 13, 2010. http://www.cnn.com/2010/US/07/13/offshore.rigs.security/.

Davis, Matt. "Beyond Rogue—An Interview with James Carville." *Gambit*, June 29, 2010, 17–19.

Duhigg, Charles. "That Tap Water Is Legal but May Be Unhealthy." *New York Times*, December 16, 2009. http://www.nytimes.com/2009/12/17/us/17water. html?scp=3&sq=drinking%20water&st=cse.

Environmental Vulnerability Index. "EVI Indicators Report." 2005. http://www. vulnerabilityindex.net/EVI_Background.htm.

Macdonald, Fred G., III. *High Risk Event Planning System, SIPREEDD Threat Assessment Risk Analysis*, 1999.

National Research Council of the National Academies. *Countering Agricultural Bioterrorism*. Washington, DC: National Academies Press, 2003.

Peimer, Ron. "Target Analysis." *Government Technology's Emergency Management*, November 27, 2006.http://www.ni2cie.org/targetanalysis.php.htm.

Torbati, Yeganeh June. "E.P.A. Lags on Setting Some Air Standards, Report Finds." *New York Times*, June 26, 2010. http://www.nytimes.com/2010/06/27/ science/earth/27epa.html?_r=1&scp=8&sq=torbati&st=cse.

U.S. Army. *Field Manual 34–36: Special Operations Forces Intelligence and Electronics Warfare Operations; Appendix D—Target Analysis Process*. September 30, 1991. http://www.enlisted.info/field-manuals/fm-34–36-special-operations-forces-intelligence-and-electronic-warfare-operations.shtml.

U.S. Department of Homeland Security. "Homeland Security Presidential Directive 9: Defense of Unites States Agriculture and Food." January 30, 2004. http://www.dhs.gov/xabout/laws/gc_1217449547663.stml.

U.S. Department of Homeland Security. "Homeland Security Presidential Directive 18: Medical Countermeasures against Weapons of Mass Destruction." January 31, 2007. http://www.fas.org/irp/offdocs/nspd/hspd-18.html.

U.S. Environmental Protection Agency, Office of the Inspector General. "Evaluation Report: Key Activities in EPA's Integrated Urban Air Toxics Strategy Remain Unimplemented." June 23, 2010. http://www.epa.gov/oig/ reports/2010/20100623-10-P-0154.pdf.

U.S. Food and Drug Administration. "CARVER Software 2.0 Release Details." 2010. http://www.fda.gov/Food/FoodDefense/CARVER/default.html; http://www.fda.gov/Food/FoodDefense/ToolsResources/ucm295900. htm.

U.S. Food and Drug Administration and U.S. Department of Health and Human Services. "Food Safety and Security: Operational Risk Management Systems Approach." November 21, 2001. http://www.cdph.ca.gov/pubsforms/ Guidelines/Documents/fdb%20ORM%202001.pdf.

U.S. Joint Chiefs of Staff. "Joint Tactics, Techniques, and Procedures for Antiterrorism (Unclassified)." 2nd draft, December 8, 2004. http://www.bits.de/ NRANEU/others/jp-doctrine/jp3_07_2rsd.pdf.

Vásquez-León, Marcela, Colin Thor West, and Timothy J. Finan. "A Comparative Assessment of Climate Vulnerability: Agriculture and Ranching on Both Sides of the US-Mexico Border." *Global Environmental Change* 13 (2003): 159–73.

The White House, Louisiana-Mississippi Gulf Coast Ecosystem Restoration Working Group. "Roadmap for Restoring Ecosystem Resiliency and Sustainability." March 2010. http://www.whitehouse.gov/sites/default/ files/microsites/ceq/100303-gulf-coast-roadmap.pdf.

Counterterrorism and the Forensic Sciences

John P. Sullivan

Criminalistics and forensic science are important tools for counterterrorism. Not only can they aid postevent investigations, but they can help shape ongoing incident response by providing essential forensic intelligence support. Typically, forensic science and crime scene investigation are seen as tools for building a case for court, that is, establishing the perpetrators of the crime. Yet recent practice has shown that forensic efforts are not effective only in postincident prosecution but also in preincident deterrence.

FORENSICS AND COUNTERTERRORISM

A wide range of forensic techniques and instrumentation are germane to terrorism cases. These include DNA analysis, trace organic chemical analysis, toxicology, explosives, fingerprinting, drug and materials analysis, database development, anthropology, microbial forensics, and field instrumentation. Forensic science measures facilitate understanding the situation, tactics, techniques, and procedures employed, as well as the attribution (or identification) of the terrorist actors involved, both individuals and groups.

Forensic technologies can assist in preventing terrorism and identifying perpetrators of terrorist acts. Specifically, both crime scene investigators and forensic laboratories have key roles to play. This includes detecting and identifying explosives; detecting and identifying chemical, biological, and nuclear/radiological materials; assessing the cause and source of arson; and medicolegal identification of persons killed in terrorist attacks.

The proper collection, preservation, and forensic analysis of evidence are important elements of counterterrorism response—both in civil settings and on the battlefield. Forensic analysis is frequently the only means to provide conclusive information to a jury to assist them in their determination of guilt or innocence. It is also valuable in establishing intelligence to identify the signatures of key terrorist operatives and cells. This is widely appreciated in explosives investigations. Understanding the mechanism of injury can lead to establishing the seat of an explosion or incendiary device, which in turn can lead to collection of evidence in the field that identifies the type of device constructed, the source of its components, and the hallmarks of a specific bomb maker. All of these can support intelligence analysis that leads to identifying supply chains and cells supporting attacks. These can then be targeted to disrupt the terrorist enterprise.

For example, forensic analysis by the Federal Bureau of Investigation was essential in assembling the evidence used to identify those responsible for, as well as the supporters of, several key terrorist attacks including Pan Am Flight 103, the 1993 World Trade Center bombing, the 1995 Oklahoma City Federal Building bombing, the bombing of two U.S. embassies in East Africa, the attack against the USS *Cole*, and the 9/11 attacks on the World Trade Center and the Pentagon.

Forensic science is also a key element in understanding cyberattacks. The growth of Internet communications technologies has made cyberspace a forum for a range of terrorist enterprises. Terrorists are increasingly exploiting these technologies, including encryption, to facilitate their operations by gathering digital intelligence, transferring funds, and potentially using cyber means to attack Internet communications infrastructure.

LAW ENFORCEMENT SUPPORT

Medicolegal investigations are important elements in establishing the cause of death in civil settings. Since terrorism frequently results in deaths, this element of forensic investigation is applicable. Typically death investigations include the accumulation and analysis of ante- and postmortum evidence. This provides an opportunity to disclose signs of torture and the use of chemical, biological, or radiological weapons. Applicable scientific disciplines include pathology, radiology, anthropology, archaeology, and odontology. Evidence is collected and its location of recovery documented in the field through notes, photos, and laser imaging. The evidence is then documented, and its movement through the process tracked to maintain a chain of evidence, preserving the integrity of the collected artifacts for presentation as exhibits in court.

At the scene of a terrorist attack, criminalists are also important providers of response safety information by assessing on-scene hazards (chemical, biological, or nuclear/radiological) in order to provide force protection advice (or forensic intelligence) to on-scene responders. Field interventions are supported by definitive laboratory analysis. Increasingly, digital links between field criminalists, their sensors and instrumenation, and off-site laboratories are used to provide "virtual reachback" to on-scene responders. In this manner, distributed real-time (or near real-time) analysis of hazards and evidence is possible, facilitating rapid response.

Crime scene investigations of terrorism are now increasingly an element of battlefield practice for counterinsurgency—battlefield forensics. Consider the case of Aafia Siddiqui, a Pakistani national captured in Afghanistan in August 2008. She had been on the radar of U.S. intelligence since late 2003/early 2004. Her behavior and links to al-Qaeda, combined with an extensive education in biology and the neurosciences, fueled concerns that she had the ability to produce weapons of mass destruction.

It has been reported in open sources that forensic samples (hair, saliva, and fingernail scrapings) were allegedly employed to ascertain if she had been in recent proximity to substances used in the production of weapons of mass destruction.

According to Neil Livingstone (2008), forensic tools developed by law enforcement agencies are informing practice by a new breed of specialists using modern combat forensic techniques. These combat criminalists rapidly process battlefield evidence in situ to support judicial, tactical, and strategic operations. This information includes latent fingerprints recovered from explosive devices and safe houses, hair and blood samples, firearms (for clues as to their origin and use), and papers, identity cards, software, and computer data captured in engagements with terrorists or seized from their bases and safe houses. These skills were pioneered by the 203rd Military Intelligence Battalion, which became known as CSI Baghdad.

CONCLUSION

The benefits of forensic analysis are especially germane in the case of potential nuclear terrorism. An exploded nuclear device could yield information about the nuclear material in the device as well as information regarding other materials that went into its construction. Such postblast analysis for attribution will be a significant element in stabilizing the situation. On the biological front, a network of high-throughput labs will play important roles in determining the nature of bacteria and viruses used in potential biological terrorist attacks on people, agriculture, and food supplies. It can be expected that the contributions of the forensic sciences and crime scene investigation will increasingly become key elements of counterterrorism efforts, supporting intelligence, response, and investigations prior to, during, and after attacks.

See also: **Volume 1, Part VI:** Biometrics Technology; Data Mining; Psychological Profiling of Terrorists

REFERENCES

Fahey, A. J., C. J. Zeissler, D. E. Newbury, J. Davis, and R. M. Lindstrom. "Postdetonation Nuclear Debris for Attribution." *Proceedings of the National Academy of Sciences,* November 8, 2010.

Fisher, Barry A.J. *Techniques of Crime Scene Investigation.* 6th ed. Boca Raton, FL: CRC Press, 2000.

Layne, Scott P., Tony J. Beugelsdijk, and C. Kumar N. Patel, eds. *Firepower in the Lab: Automation in the Fight against Infectious Diseases and Bioterrorism.* Washington, DC: Joseph Henry Press, 2001.

Livingstone, Neil C. "Battlefield Forensics: Rebirth of an Ancient Science." *Domestic Preparedness Journal* 4, no.8 (August 13, 2008): 17. http://www.domestic preparedness.com/pub/docs/DPJournalAug08.pdf.

Rohde, David. "Medico-Legal Investigations of War Crimes." In *Crimes of War 2.0: What the Public Should Know,* edited by Roy Gutman, David Rieff, Anthony Dworkin, and Sheryl Mendez (contributor), 245–47. Rev. exp. ed. New York: W. W. Norton, 2007.

Counterterrorism Research: Current Efforts and Future Challenges

Michael B. Kraft

Research and development (R&D) of specialized equipment and techniques is a major tool to counter terrorism, along with intelligence gathering, diplomacy, the arrest and prosecution of terrorists, rewards for information, sanctions, and programs that train security officials and hinder terrorism financing.

RESEARCH, DEVELOPMENT, AND EVALUATION

Apart from airport scanning equipment, most of the fruits of the U.S government's R&D programs are seldom noticed by the general public, such as monitoring devices in buildings to detect biological, chemical, or radioactive agents. The large airport scanners are just the bulky tip of a huge international effort to harness technology and science to save lives by helping to prevent terrorist attacks or minimizing the damage if they do occur.

Nearly all federal departments and agencies and subagencies—about 100 in all—are involved in one aspect or another of counterterrorism research, development, and evaluation. The R&D effort has grown from about $10 million in the mid-1980s for the major interagency R&D program, the Technical Support Working Group (TSWG), to more than $5 billion appropriated to a variety of agencies five years after 9/11. The R&D programs continue to evolve. Early research concentrated on aircraft hijacking and hostage rescue. As the terrorist threat has changed, research efforts have been directed toward detecting improvised explosives and biological weapons, as well as improving older systems, such as airport scanners and lightweight masks for protection against biological or chemical agents.

The organizational framework has also changed, most markedly since the creation of the Department of Homeland Security (DHS) in 2003. As noted in Kraft and Marks (2012, 106), there are basically three types of organizational frameworks for the U.S. government's counterterrorism R&D programs:

1. Projects coordinated and funded primarily but not exclusively through the TSWG, an interagency coordinating body established three decades ago
2. Projects under the auspices of DHS, which has become a hub for selecting and funding research projects that were previously approved and conducted by some of the previously independent agencies
3. Individual agencies conducting specialized research, such as the Departments of Agriculture, Energy, and Defense and the Justice Department's National Institutes of Justice (NIJ)

TSWG

TSWG is a stand-alone interagency working group established in 1982. Its mission is to identify, prioritize, and coordinate R&D requirements for combating terrorism. It brings together representatives of a dozen major agencies, such as the Department of State (DOS), Department of Defense (DOD), DHS, Department of Health and Human Services, Department of Energy (DOE), Department of Justice, Federal Bureau of Investigation (FBI) and the intelligence community, and the various subgroups of these agencies.

Its goals include reducing duplication of research among the agencies and funding worthwhile research projects that are needed but not conducted by any of the agencies because they fall into the gaps between their missions and jurisdictions. A report issued by the now-dismantled Office of Technology Assessment, titled "Technology against Terrorism: The Federal Effort," provided the first assessment of the U.S. government's growing counterterrorism reach and development. Similar descriptions were used by the counterterrorism officers of the DOS and DOD, including the author, in preparing talking points for Congress.

TSWG typically focuses on short-term projects, emphasizing rapid R&D, testing, and evaluation. After the initial development stage, projects often transition to a specific agency that may have the most immediate potential use for the final project. Internationally, TSWG has conducted joint cooperative research projects with the United Kingdom, Canada, and Israel since the early 1990s. Australia and Singapore joined in 2006. On average, about 10 percent of the TSWG annual budget helps fund projects with other countries, which in turn provide matching funds.

TSWG operates under the policy guidance of the DOS's Office of the Coordinator for Counterterrorism and with the management and technical oversight of the DOD, centered in the Office of the Assistant Secretary for Special Operations and Low Intensity Conflict. The members of its Executive Committee are from the DOS, DOD, DOE, and the FBI.

Specialized subgroups of experts from the relevant agencies develop priorities, evaluate project proposals, and implement approved R&D projects. TSWG officials say the requirements for a research project come from practitioners such as local police departments or security specialists, not from the top down. TSWG officials note that designing with affordability in mind is essential when developing equipment for state and local governments. The TSWG subgroups and their chairs or subchairs sometimes change, but as described in the 2011 TSWG annual report, they are:

- Advanced Analytic Capabilities, DOD
- Chemical, Biological, Radiological, and Nuclear Countermeasures, DOD and DOS
- Explosives Detection, DHS Transportation Security Administration (TSA)
- Improvised Device Defeat, FBI, DHS
- Investigative Support and Forensics, U.S. Army Criminal Investigation
- Laboratory (USACIL)
- Personnel Protection, Department of Energy, DOS
- Physical Security, ATF/DOE, Office of Provost Marshal General
- Surveillance, Collection, and Operations Support; intelligence community
- Tactical Operations Support, DOD, DOE
- Training Technology Development DOD

To illustrate the size of the interagency program, the budget from the Pentagon for fiscal year (FY) 2010 was $117.153 million with supplemental funding, and approximately another $90 million was provided by other agencies as part of TSWG's leveraging effort. The baseline DOD request for the TSWG program for FY 2012 is $85.148 million, and the total figure was about the same in FY 2010. The DOS baseline request for the TSWG program remained at $3.1 million. These figures are provided to illustrate the size of the program. The impact of appropriations cut on the DOD and other department budgets is uncertain.

About 500 projects are currently under way. The cost of an individual project typically runs between $0.5 million and $1 million. The TSWG outreach program to the private sector uses websites and conferences to advertise its requirements. An estimated 40 percent of the research is conducted by small businesses. The TSWG program funds a wide range of projects, for example, a dual-energy X-ray system to detect bulk explosives that may be concealed in cars or trucks, which can drive past the sensors at five miles per hour; improved mass transit surveillance and early warning systems; and wireless emergency vehicle kits that can be carried on a plane and allow law enforcement officials to quickly mobilize any vehicle for emergency use, complete with sirens, lights, and other equipment.

DHS

In addition to the TSWG interagency group in which they are represented, many individual agencies also have their own counterterrorism R&D programs. The largest is centered in DHS's Science and Technology Directorate, the primary R&D arm for that large agency. Its goals include developing and deploying state-of-the art, high-performance, low-operating-cost systems to prevent, detect, and mitigate the consequences of chemical, biological, radiological, nuclear, and explosive attacks as well as developing equipment, protocols, and training procedures for response to and recovery from chemical, biological, radiological, nuclear, and explosive attacks.

The research effort is organized into the following major categories and is somewhat similar to TSWG: borders and maritime security; chemical and biological; command, control, and interoperability; explosives; human factors/behavioral sciences; infrastructure and geophysical; and radiological and nuclear. The directorate's budget funds R&D projects on counterterrorism as well as all types of catastrophic threats. For example, some equipment can be used for both countering terrorist attacks and addressing a dangerous chemical spill. Thus, the directorate's $1.027 billion budget request for FY 2012 is not solely for counterterrorism R&D. It funds about 200 projects a year.

Following recent reorganizations within DHS, some research previously conducted by the Transportation Security Administration (TSA) is now conducted under the S Science and Technology Directorate although TSA takes the lead on specialized projects. The Coast Guard, also under the DHS tent since the agency was formed in 2003, also conducts its own specialized research.

As part of DHS's outreach efforts, the Homeland Security Advanced Research Projects Agency works with the private sector and academia in innovative R&D and rapid prototyping and technology transfer to meet operational needs. Proposals for projects and suggestions for equipment improvement often come up from the field, from local and state governments, police and fire departments, or DHS officials involved with emergency preparedness duties. As with TSWG's R&D projects, there is an incentive to develop products that are affordable and can be maintained by state and local governments. DHS's R&D efforts include developing training modules, simulators, videos, and other tools to help train personnel in the use of equipment, coordination techniques, and other crisis responses.

R&D AT INDIVIDUAL AGENCIES

Space limitations prohibit describing or even mentioning all the agencies involved in counterterrorism R&D; however, to help illustrate the variety of research, the following brief outlines are provided for the Department of Agriculture, the DOE, and the NIJ. The Agriculture Department's relatively little-known counterterrorism R&D efforts are a result of concerns that terrorists might try to attack the food supply, perhaps through poisoning or contaminating crops, animals, poultry, and processed food before their distribution to market. Some of the key programs include expanding the Food Emergency Response Network and research on automated diagnostic methods for rapidly detecting and identifying pathogens and chemical contaminants and modeling food security incident scenarios.

The DOE is involved in programs to protect nuclear facilities, detect toxic agents, and develop genomic sequencing and microfabrication techniques. DOE also has been developing virtual reality–type software to provide more realism for exercises in protecting nuclear facilities or other buildings from potential attackers. DOE protects some 30 buildings, including nuclear reactors.

The NIJ is the DOJ's R&D and evaluation arm. It seeks to improve the effectiveness of the criminal justice system through scientific research. It conducts research in the social sciences as well as in physical sciences and technology. Research areas include nonlethal weapons, critical incident prevention and response, interoperable communications, sensors and surveillance (including long-range detection of weapons), information sharing, electronic crime detection, personnel protection, DNA forensics (including identification of terrorists through DNA analysis), and general forensics. In its efforts to improve communications interoperability among local governments, NIJ collaborates closely with DHS. NIJ also develops performance standards to assist state and local governments in evaluating commercially available equipment, working with the National Institutes of Standards and Technology.

CHALLENGES AND ISSUES

Effective counterterrorism R&D faces numerous challenges. Scientific problems, such as the development of reliable devices that can quickly detect explosives from a distance in a vehicle in a pollution-heavy environment, are one such challenge. "The laws of physics are quite inconvenient at times," remarked John Reingruber, a retired TSWG deputy, during an interview with the author.

Fully understanding and anticipating future needs, which often evolve as terrorists modify their techniques, is not easy. As the United States develops countermeasures against some threats such as improvised explosive devices, the bomb makers come up with new methods that may be more difficult to defeat until new countermeasures are developed.

R&D does not always produce speedy results and sometimes lines of research do not pan out. Furthermore, when budgets are tight, the budget officials in the White House and Congress tend to put more priority on short-term issues, so funding for longer-term R&D often suffers. During an interview and later e-mail exchanges, Mr. Reingruber noted that finding and retaining good managers for the vast number of projects is not always easy.

CONCLUSION

Coordinating research programs to avoid duplication, while at the same time meeting evolving threats, is an ongoing challenge. There are, however, various contact points between agencies, some bilateral and others interagency. Working relationships between midlevel career government officials from different agencies are extremely important. Several of these professionals, from different agencies, have commented in interviews that they have often worked together for years and serve on overlapping committees or working groups. They further noted that this has been an important element in preventing duplication and saving potentially good projects from falling between the cracks. As experienced experts retire, as is occurring in greater numbers, or change jobs, the challenges are likely to become more difficult (Interviews with DOD and DOS officials, not for attribution, August and September 2010).

See also: **Volume 1, Part VI:** Combating Terrorism: A New Way Forward; Counterterrorism and the Forensic Sciences; Multilateral Approach to Counterterrorism: Issues, Problems, Responses; Need for Empirical Research on the Effectiveness of Counterterrorism Strategies; Preemptive Counterterrorism: The Need for a Global Integrated Approach; Understanding Foreign Cultures

REFERENCES

Knezo, Genevieve J. "Homeland Security Research and Development Funding, Organization, and Oversight." Congressional Research Service, August 23, 2006. http://www.fas.org/sgp/crs/homesec/RS21270.pdf.

Kraft, Michael B., and Edward Marks. *U.S. Government Counterterrorism: A Guide to Who Does What.* Boca Raton, FL: CRC Press, 2012.

Morgan, John S., National Institute of Justice Assistant Director for Science & Technology. Testimony before the U.S. House of Representatives Committee on Homeland Security, Subcommittee on Emergency Preparedness, Science and Technology, April 25, 2006. http://hsc.house.gov/files/Testimony Morgan.pdf.

Office of Technology Assessment. "Technology against Terrorism: The Federal Effort." Washington, DC: U.S. Government Printing Office, 1991.

Technical Support Working Group (TSWG). http://www.tswg.gov/.

"2011 Review: Countering Terrorism Technical Support Office." Program review
    book 2011. http://www.tswg.gov/reviewbook/CTTSOReviewBook2011_
    ALL.pdf; see also 2010 Review: Countering Terrorism Technical Support
    Office.

U.S. Department of Homeland Security. "Budget in Brief, Science and Technol-
    ogy for Fiscal 2011." pp.151–59 February 14, 2011. http://www.dhs.gov/
    xlibrary/assets/budget-bib-fy2012.pdf.

U.S. Department of Homeland Security. Science and Technology Resources (ref-
    erence website for state/local governments and businesses). http://www.
    dhs.gov/files/scitech.shtm.

U.S. Department of Justice, Office of Justice Programs, National Institute of Justice.
    "NIJ's Role in Terrorism Research." Modified April 4, 2011. http://www.
    ojp.usdoj.gov/nij/topics/crime/terrorism/terrorism-research.htm.

U.S. Government Accountability Office. "Transportation Security R&D: TSA and
    DHS are Researching and Developing Technologies, but Need to Improve
    R&D Management." September 2004. http://www.gao.gov/products/
    GAO-04-890.

Data Mining

Arpad Palfy

From a counterterrorism perspective, data mining is a process that attempts to make sense of structured or unstructured data found within data
sets, and in some cases entire databases, so as to provide a more contextualized foundation for further processing and analysis (McCue 2007, 25).
As part of a broader information discovery process it focuses on turning
raw data into useful information and intelligence via automated methods.
Data mining is more specifically defined as an algorithm-based computer-
executed process that aims to extract or discover relevant patterns from a
given data set (DeRosa 2004, 3). Though sometimes considered as separate,
data mining can also be viewed as an automated data analysis method
within the larger body of information discovery processes, in that it helps
draw meaningful baseline inferences or contextualized structure from information based on subject- or pattern-based queries (DeRosa 2004, 3).
Data-mining systems and processes can also be used in conjuncture with
biometric scanners, devices, and databases.

EXAMINING RELATIONSHIPS AND
BEHAVIORAL PATTERNS

Subject-based queries are searches originating from a known subject
or entity-based data point, such as a person, event, or organization, or

even a report, account, or personal item. The purpose of subject-based queries is to determine what other entities the given subject is linked to in an effort to identify, analyze, and ultimately draw meaning and conclusions from known or suspected interrelationships. Most often represented graphically in the form of a link diagram, it is important to note that the diagrams themselves are not representative of what data mining is per se, even though the underlying data points may have been gathered as a result of data-mining processes. As an example of a subject-based query system, the Non-Obvious Relationship Analysis (NORA) software was developed to enhance security for the Las Vegas gaming industry. This particular system is capable of conducting subject-based queries across multiple data layers and sources in order to identify possible relationships between individuals on a defined watch list (McCue 2007, 37; DeRosa 2004, 4).

Conversely, pattern-based queries are related to finding a model or pattern of actions, behaviors (or inactions and the absence of behaviors), or anomalies within a given dataset, which analysts or parallel systems could use as indicators of future behavior based on behavior frequency, sequence, type, or contexts, such as time, location, or type of event.

Therefore, the difference between subject- and pattern-based queries lies in the *purpose* of the queries themselves. Specifically, the former seeks to find, establish, and understand interentity relationships and their meanings, potentially leading to a clearer view of hierarchical and command relationships, linkages between events and their perpetrators, or relationships between organizations and their various members. The latter, on the other hand, seeks to find discernable patterns of activity or behavior so as to identify the type, frequency, sequence, location, and ultimately likelihood of a potential (re)occurrence of similar activity in an attempt to exploit, deter, preempt, or defend against such activity. Regardless of the query type, it should be emphasized that the actual purpose of data mining is not to replace or automate analytic processes entirely nor to retrieve lost, corrupted, or misfiled entries and information from databases. Instead, its purpose is to increase analyst's processing capacity by finding and assembling hidden pieces of data spread throughout potentially segregated databases, or unrelated pieces of information, in order to better focus analytic efforts and help guide further knowledge discovery.

FACTORS IMPACTING THE PROCESS

In both subject- and pattern-based queries, the criteria for data-mining success are largely dependent on three factors. First, the size of the dataset being mined must be representative of the overall database from which it is drawn. Should the dataset be disproportionate, the results will likely be representative of only the mined dataset rather than the database within which they are contained, thereby leading to incorrect or suboptimal analyses, inferences, and decisions. For instance, data-mining processes would prove ineffective at discovering relevant patterns if those patterns were present only beyond a given data sample size or threshold. Conversely, patterns appearing in smaller data sets may be relatively insignificant when compared to the larger picture.

Second, it is critical that the accuracy and integrity of the mined data be known prior to the initiation of the data-mining process. In all instances, corrupted, missing, or incomplete data will likely result in irrelevant, incorrect, and/or unusable results, thereby negating the very benefits that data-mining tools and processes are intended to provide. Finally, the expected outcome of the data-mining process must be clarified before it is initiated, to ensure that the relevancy of the results can be understood and adequately contextualized.

It should also be added that while data mining provides analysts and decision makers with an extra means of correlating very large volumes of information in a relatively short time for further analysis, there is always the potential that the data and information being mined are wrong. While it is possible that incorrect mined data may nevertheless result in making "data sense," it is unlikely that such results would adequately reflect reality or be applicable to the necessary context within which they are applied (DeRosa 2004, 14–16).

CURRENT APPLICATIONS

Counterterrorism-related examples of large-scale data collection efforts for use with data-mining technologies and processes include the U.S. Defense Advanced Research Projects Agency's Total Information Awareness (TIA) program, the Florida state law enforcement–initiated Multi-state Anti-terrorism Information Exchange (MATRIX) program, and the U.S. Department of Homeland Security's Analysis, Dissemination, Visualization, Insight, and Semantic Enhancement (ADVISE) program. Because these systems incorporated data from sources not originally intended for these purposes, significant privacy issues arose during internal audit exercises, resulting in the eventual termination of all three programs (Chen 2006, 20–21).

Overall, data-mining tools and processes provide not only an added means of viewing and using data in general but also new perspectives on older data and significantly greater breadth when used on newly collected, and much more extensive, data sets or databases. For example, when used in combination with biometric technologies, data-mining systems and processes can provide greater analytic versatility to the end users collecting the biometric information. As well, with the exponential increase in data collected by government, law enforcement, and intelligence organizations worldwide as part of the post-9/11 global counterterrorism effort, the demand for data-mining processes, systems, and analysts is likely to follow suit (Chen et al. 2008, 197–202).

CONCLUSION

However, as beneficial as data mining may be from a procedural, organizational, systemic, analytic, or software-enhancing perspective, its continued and likely expansion and use will continue to raise parallel challenges in terms of addressing information exchange, ownership, and privacy concerns in all aspects of its application.

See also: **Volume 1, Part III:** Information Technologies to Combat Terrorism; Limitations of Technology. **Part VI:** Biometrics Technology

REFERENCES

Chen, H. *Intelligence and Security Informatics for National Security.* New York: Springer, 2006.

Chen, H., E. Reid, J. Sinai, A. Silke, and B. Ganor, eds. *Terrorism Informatics: Knowledge Management and Data Mining for Homeland Security.* New York: Springer, 2008.

DeRosa, M. *Data Mining and Data Analysis for Counterterrorim.* Washington, DC: Center for Strategic and International Studies Press, 2004.

McCue, C. *Data Mining and Predictive Analysis: Intelligence Gathering and Crime Analysis.* Amsterdam: Elsevier, 2007.

Popp, L. R., and J. Yen, eds. *Emergent Information Technologies and Enabling Policies for Counter-terrorism.* Piscataway, NJ: John Wiley, IEEE Press, 2006.

Energy-Related Counterterrorism

James David Ballard and Fred Dilger

The globalized society must face the insecurity of its energy production and distribution systems. As nation-states seek to protect their economic, social, and political interests in peacetime and in the event of war, securing necessary energy is a critical component of their strategic planning. The imperative to protect energy supplies is often referred to as energy security.

The issue of energy security is not new. In the 18th century, the English needed trees of a particular size and strength to make masts that would harvest wind power for their navy. Later, securing coal and oil supplies was a critical strategic goal during World War II. Securing shipping and vessels that carry energy supplies like crude oil and liquefied natural gas costs governments billions of dollars in military expenditures each year (Dancs 2008).

Energy security refers to the amalgamation of regional, national, corporate, and public interest in the provision of reliable sources of energy, the security of the infrastructure necessary to extract and transport that energy to market, and the protection of the final distribution mechanisms necessary to supply a nation's energy needs. The traditional sources of energy are changing with the advent of widespread use of wind, solar, and other alternative energy sources. Because these new kinds of energy sources are becoming so widely available, it is necessary to plan for the security of an ever-larger variety of energy production, transportation, and distribution efforts. In other words, energy security is a matter of a multitude of energy supply lines, and it is a matter of national security to maintain the economic health of a nation and its ability to defend itself.

Additionally, energy security planning is localized and also must occur regionally since the sources are so highly distributed. For example, the electrical grid in the eastern United States is linked with Canada, and thus security planning must be a transnational (regional) effort. Likewise, Europe's energy system is deeply interconnected, with potentially devastating cascade effects in the event of the failure of a critical component. Security observers are concerned that disruptions for one nation will affect others, and those disruptions can cause the economies of a country, a region, or even the European Union itself to grind to a halt (Choursina and Pronina 2009).

The threats to the energy supply system are also varied. War, terrorism, and natural hazards can each disrupt energy supplies, and each needs a different strategic approach. So while we may have plans in effect for a snowstorm (or heat wave), which may cause massive electrical blackouts, protecting distribution against the intrusion of cyberterrorists into the electrical grid requires different security planning.

The prominent need for a holistic security strategy to address the myriad of threats to a society's energy supplies is usually most evident during wartime, but increasingly low-intensity conflict tactics and terrorism are of concern for the security of energy. To begin a counterterrorism analysis process for such a critical infrastructure component, it is necessary to first identify the means best suited for threat identification (Sandia National Laboratories 2010).

A systematic threat identification process should be developed as part of the planning for new energy systems and the modernization of existing facilities, systems, and energy pathways. The planning needs to be proactive, not reactive, and embedded in the security for all means of energy extraction, transportation, and distribution.

TECHNIQUES OF THREAT IDENTIFICATION

Many individual social contexts exist simultaneously underlying such a discussion—shipping-lane protection against piracy, port protection for liquified natural gas, oil-head security, protection against cyberterrorism infiltration at isolated wind-farm sites, and a multitude of other issues will inform a national strategy. The following is a generic counterterrorism strategy and analysis process that can be scaled to whatever the threats are and to whatever level of infrastructure is being evaluated (e.g., local, community, state, regional, or national).

Threat identification typically begins with an asset inventory. The critical aspect to this inventory is to understand what assets, systems, subsystems, or components are important to the functioning of the immediate operation and its criticality to the energy supply and the continuation of a system of energy supply during an incident. The asset analysis should yield a facility, site, or system characterization—a specified delineation of the critical parts of the operations that are the most vulnerable and/or symbolically attractive to an adversary. It is a process of target identification and prioritization that defines which assets are critical and which, if damaged, would do the most harm.

A variety of techniques are available to conduct threat identification. Sandia National Laboratories (2010) uses a systematic methodology to assess the needs of everything from prisons to transmission mechanisms. The Sandia methodology was originally developed to meet International Atomic Energy Agency standards for the physical protection of nuclear facilities, but the Sandia process is very similar for any critical social-industrial component—water supplies, energy infrastructure, oil refineries, gas pipelines, and so on.

Other threat identification techniques include security surveys, design basis threat techniques, and adversarial vulnerability assessments. In some cases future techniques may also help in the identification of emerging threats not historically thought of as a security concern. Regardless of the methodology used, one clear indication of a more robust process is the incorporation of multiple techniques to enhance rigor, a social science approach called the triangulation of methods (Denzin 1997). Hence, the Sandia process would become more robust with the introduction of adversarial vulnerability assessments. Moreover, the security survey would be enhanced by the introduction of the straw man design basis threat techniques.

Utilizing the preceding method will hopefully yield a more reliable threat identification process and therefore a better understanding of what is important. The next question is to define what threats are best to protect against. This protection imperative can be defined using sample tactics and scenarios that embody the priorities set forth in the threat identification process.

TACTICS AND SCENARIOS

As with other security processes, it is critical to plan which tactics to defend against: Is an insider threat the most likely given the findings of your chosen threat identification process? Is a potential criminal element of most concern? Does the possibility exist that extremists may threaten the operations and delivery of the energy? Due to the economic disruption that would inevitably ensue, does a cyberattack need to be considered?

A meta-analysis of the literature and global data related to historical threats would help show a fuller range of attacks faced by energy-related concerns. These could include kidnappings, assignations, large-scale protests, deliberate accidents, sabotage, politically motivated terrorism, or other threats that have the potential to disrupt energy-related operations (Ballard and Dilger 2008b).

One means to help determine the variety of threats an energy facility may face is to produce a matrix of the threats and identify the actual infrastructure that is endangered. Another is to generate exemplar scenarios that encompass prioritizations noted in threat identification and tied to the existing and emerging threats seen globally (Ballard and Dilger 2008a). The scenarios that develop from this process are extremely useful in generating counteractions to threats.

COUNTERSTRATEGIES

In terms of counterterrorism, the strategies used to counteract threats, potential attacks, and actual incidents are myriad. Strict economic investigations would look at a cost-benefit analysis of the threats. The options available to an industry or corporation could include reducing the consequences of an attack, improving the protection provided to the energy infrastructure, deciding on operational trade-offs, and even an acceptance of the risks as they were defined in the processes noted in the preceding.

These are all strategies that a singular entity, or an industry, uses in a normalized risk assessment process, but terrorism introduces potentially high levels of violence and nation-state–level imperatives wherein governments feel compelled to act to protect national dignity, social interests, or even the reputation of a state leader/political party. For a nation-state the options to counteract threats are much different. They could include intelligence operations, military actions, economic sanctions, diplomacy, and any number of governmental options that express the collective will of the nation-state to mitigate or neutralize the threat.

States also have a need to protect vital economic interests and to ensure they have the means to wage warfare if needed. Hence, supply lines for energy are considered a national security priority and counterstrategies under such a determination could include preemptive strikes, takeover of private property, and other means to ensure future energy supplies.

SECURITY PRACTICES

Despite the reality of energy threats, security is one of the least funded and most frequently cut functional areas of corporate infrastructure.

Likewise, bureaucratic blindness can exist wherein governments stay away from corporate affairs to the detriment of national security. A trade-off thus exists between the corporate interest in profit and the nation-state's interest in securing the energy supply. At times these interests may be at odds (e.g., during an embargo of an energy supplier country), and at other times the two sides of this coin are in symbiosis.

Ultimately, the energy sector, in part or as a whole, needs to be secure, no matter the rationale, rhyme, or reason. So after the identification of potential threats, the assessment of their relative impacts on operations, and the development of scenarios that exemplify the threat environment, implementation of physical security must be initiated. Physical security has three critical systemic imperatives—detection, delay, and response. Detection of viable threats could entail intelligence but usually refers to more localized activities like intrusion detection, closed circuit television systems, electronic countermeasures, and many other technological solutions that are meant to address threats. Detection also includes access denial, entry control measures, contraband detection, alarm procedures, protection of communication lines, and various other physical and procedural means to identify and counteract threats.

Delaying actions are meant to hold off a threat or threatening intrusion until reinforcements can be summoned, mustered, and arrive at the scene. For energy facilities, the on-site security forces should be equipped in a manner that most threats can be repelled, but if they are overwhelmed, these forces should be trained to stay the course to allow time for outside assistance to arrive. This necessitates cooperative agreements between the actual physical energy site and various levels of response assets—police, fire, medical, and military. Under certain circumstances the national level of response is appropriate—for example, in the event of an attack of sufficient size, duration, and/or intensity to warrant the incident being classified as a national security threat.

Response is closely tied to delaying actions. It includes the actual physical response from needed emergency management assets like fire protection, medical services, and so on. Most important are the reinforcements provided by police or security services. In the case of governments, their responses could include technical support, military assets, unique expertise, and the provision of financial or other specific resources.

CONCLUSION

Energy security is national security, but it is also economic survival, public safety, and even face-saving efforts in the event of an attack of sufficient magnitude to warrant a governmental response. The counterterrorism aspect of a threat assessment mixes what is critical to business with what is critical to a nation-state. In both cases it is a matter of deciding what is important and what to protect against. In certain cases the state has a political imperative to respond that supersedes the interests of business. For example, to encourage the development of nuclear power, many governments indemnify businesses in the event of a catastrophe—technological or human initiated.

Energy security begins with actions that identify threats and moves to mitigation, response, and recovery. A nation-state should be aware of threats to its viability that may arise from energy attacks, but deciding at what level or at what time to intervene to protect national interests is a critical social act, one based on perceptions and rooted in political realities. The politics of energy security are international considering the scope of energy production, but they have real localized impacts. Likewise, localized threats can have an international impact. Dedication to the security of energy supplies is not an easy task; however, it is a necessary undertaking and a critical component of nation-state survival in a modern globalized world.

REFERENCES

Ballard, J.D., and F.C. Dilger. "Scenario Development in Oil and Gas Management: 'Envisioning the Future' by Means of Analytical Techniques." *Strategic Insights* 7, no. 1 (2008a). Available from the Center for Contemporary Conflict, Naval Postgraduate School. http://www.nps.edu/Academics/centers/ccc/publications/OnlineJournal/2008/Feb/ballardFeb08.pdf.

Ballard, J.D., and F.C. Dilger. "Using Social Scientific Methodological Approaches to Reducing Risk: How the Risk Reduction Approach Works with Oil and Gas Facilities." *International Journal of Social Inquiry* 1 (2008b): 105–19.

Choursina, K., and L. Pronina. "Russian Gas Flows to Europe through Ukraine Halted (Update1)." *Bloomberg.com*, January 7, 2009. http://www.bloomberg.com/apps/news?pid=20601100&sid=awMyRDM27.gI&refer=germany.

Dancs, A. *Military Cost of Securing Energy.* Washington, DC: National Priorities Project, 2008. http://www.scribd.com/doc/7788510/The-Military-Cost-of-Securing-Energy.

Denzin, N. *Sociological Methods: A Sourcebook.* New York: McGraw-Hill, 1997.

Sandia National Laboratories. "Security Risk Assessment Methodologies." 2010. May 2, 2010. http://www.sandia.gov/ram.

Global Jihad Movement

Rohan Kumar Gunaratna

The terrorist threat has steadily escalated since al-Qaeda attacked the United States' most iconic landmarks on 9/11. Despite the killing of Osama bin Laden, the leader of al-Qaeda, in Abbottabad, Pakistan, on May 1,

2011, the threat has not plateaued. Although the numerical strength of al-Qaeda has been reduced to a few hundred fighters, mostly located in the Federally Administered Tribal Areas, al-Qaeda has been able to influence three dozen groups worldwide to attack Western targets. Many of the groups in Asia, Africa, and the Middle East that have traditionally fought their local regimes and rulers perceive the United States and its allies and friends as their primary enemy.

The global terrorist threat largely stems from conflict zones such as Iraq, Afghanistan, Pakistan, Somalia, Yemen, Algeria, India (Kashmir), Russia (Chechnya), and China (Xinjiang), where Muslims are suffering. Both virulent ideologies and operational capabilities spill over from those conflict zones to neighboring regions and countries. While the bulk of the terrorist attacks will be detected and disrupted in the planning and preparation stages, a few attacks will be successful. Although the United States is the tier-one target of the global jihadists, security measures have displaced the threat to the Global South.

THE CONTEXT

Today, al-Qaeda's real power is the disparate groups and cells it had trained, financed, armed, and, most important, ideologized since the late 1980s. The al-Qaeda network (al-Qaeda group and its associated groups) and its ideologically affiliated cells comprise the al-Qaeda–led global jihad movement. The threat is not monolithic as there are Sunni groups that are operationally unconnected to al-Qaeda but steadfastly advocate global jihad. This category could be violent or nonviolent; for example, Hizb ut-Tahrir and Al Muhajiroon in the United Kingdom, and violent groups such as Laskar Jihad and Front Pembela Islam in Indonesia. Some of these groups have publicly criticized al-Qaeda, but they believe in global jihad. The groups in the Muslim territorial communities and cells in the Muslim diaspora and migrant networks present a multidimensional threat against the United States and its allies and friends. The global jihadists challenge the "infidel" (non-Muslim) and "apostate" (Muslim) regimes. The threat is both ideological and kinetic.

Considering the support for the global jihad movement in Asia, Africa, the Middle East, and elsewhere, the campaign has been a partial success. While al-Qaeda conducted one major attack every year prior to 9/11, the frequency of attacks by al-Qaeda and its associated groups grew significantly after 9/11. The key strength of al-Qaeda has been the ability of its leadership to understand both the importance and the power of modern communication. To survive and fight back, al-Qaeda used both hard and soft power but more of the latter. While investing in infrequent iconic attacks, the al-Qaeda leadership sustained communication with its actual and potential support base through Al-Sahab (the publishing arm of al-Qaeda). Many of these groups today seek to emulate the al-Qaeda tactic of suicide attacks and, more important, believe in the global jihad, targeting both the near and the distant enemy. Although bin Laden, its leader, is dead, al-Qaeda, the most hunted terrorist group in history, has completed its original mission. In addition to spawning several like-minded groups operating against the United States and its allies and friends, bin Laden successfully mobilized the Muslim communities worldwide, spawning a network of individuals and cells willing to kill and die.

BACKGROUND

During the multinational Afghan campaign against the Soviets (1979–1989), the concept of global jihad emerged. Its architect, Abdullah Azzam, a Palestinian Jordanian who came to Pakistan in 1984 for the purpose of opposing the Soviet occupation in Afghanistan, argued that wherever Muslims are oppressed and repressed, they must be liberated by the use of force. Respected as the emir of jihad, Azzam founded Maktab al Khidmat lil Mujahidin al-Arab (MAK) in 1984. Known commonly as the Afghan Service Bureau, MAK provided significant assistance to the Arab mujahideen and their families. Bin Laden, the most prominent financier of the fight, came from the richest nonroyal Saudi family. He joined hands with Azzam, who became his mentor. As MAK's principal financier, bin Laden was considered Azzam's deputy. At the height of the foreign Arab and Muslim influx into Pakistan and Afghanistan from 1984 to 1986, bin Laden spent time traveling widely and raising funds in the Arab world. Azzam recruited several thousand Arab and Muslim youth to fight the Soviet presence, and bin Laden channeled several million dollars' worth of financial and material resources to the Afghan jihad. MAK operated independently of the Western and Pakistani governments that assisted in the fight. MAK rarely interacted with the Inter-Services Intelligence of Pakistan, but it tapped into the vast Muslim Brotherhood network and the resources of the Saudi government (Jane's World Insurgency and Terrorism 2004).

A year before the Soviets withdrew, Azzam and bin Laden decided to form a vanguard group—al-Qaeda al Sulbah ("the solid base")—that could unite the whole Muslim world into a single entity. In conceptualizing al-Qaeda, Azzam drew from the pages of Islamic history. In general, what he did was to define its composition, aims, and purpose in view of the struggle of an Islamist movement after the victory over the largest land army in the world—the Soviet military. While the concept was transformed to match the changing landscape, it was never intended to be a terrorist organization (Gunaratna 2002, 3). Azzam was the ideological father and the intellectual leader, but gradually bin Laden took over ("Translation" 2004). Bin Laden's initial worldview was shaped by Azzam, formerly of the Muslim Brothers. Toward the end of the Afghan anti-Soviet campaign, bin Laden's relationship with Azzam deteriorated. The dispute over Azzam's support for Ahmad Shah Massoud, who later became the leader of the Northern Alliance, caused tension. Bin Laden preferred Gulbuddin Hekmatyar, former prime minister and leader of the Islamic Party (Hizb-i-Islami), who was both anti-Communist and anti-Western. Furthermore, together with the Egyptian members of al-Qaeda, bin Laden wished to support terrorist action against Egypt and other secular Muslim regimes. Having lived in Egypt, Azzam knew the price of such actions and opposed them vehemently. Azzam and bin Laden went their different ways. In Peshawar, Pakistan, Azzam was assassinated by the Egyptian members of al-Qaeda.

Following Azzam's death, the ideological vacuum was filled by Ayman al-Zawahiri, the leader of the Egyptian Islamic Jihad. A professional medical practitioner and a qualified eye surgeon, al-Zawahiri became both bin Laden's doctor and his mentor. After Azzam's death, bin Laden took over MAK and then transformed it. Using MAK trainers and camps, bin Laden built al-Qaeda. Al-Zawahiri, a well-known hard-liner, became his deputy and the principal strategist of the al-Qaeda–led global jihad movement. A group of 3,000 to 4,000 members, al-Qaeda gradually turned its orientation from fighting the Soviets to fighting the U.S.-led Western coalition. Having inherited and harnessed the vast global infrastructure from the anti-Soviet multinational Afghan mujahideen, bin Laden channeled the energies of the mujahideen into fighting on behalf of Muslims worldwide.

THE EVOLUTION OF THE THREAT

The real strength of al-Qaeda was not its leadership and membership per se but its overarching, highly appealing ideology. In keeping with its original mandate, its principal aim was to inspire and incite Islamic movements and the Muslim masses worldwide to attack those who threaten Islam and Muslims. In defense of Islam and its adherents, al-Qaeda conducts attacks on iconic targets of the United States and its allies and friends to inspire and instigate a perpetual campaign. Although al-Qaeda does not enjoy widespread support among the Muslim masses worldwide, it exploited the anger, suffering, and the resentment of Muslims against the United States. The U.S. lack of understanding for the Muslim world—for instance, its support for Israel, its assistance to secular Muslim rulers, and its invasion of Iraq—has given a new lease on life to terrorism and extremism.

A defining feature of the new terrorism is its networked nature. Although al-Qaeda remained a group, it worked with other groups and individuals to form a movement. Together with individual sympathizers and supporters of al-Qaeda the movement went global. Defined as the global jihad movement, al-Qaeda co-opted groups and individuals it had politicized and radicalized; in addition to training its own group and support base, al-Qaeda trained 20,000 members in its camps in Afghanistan from 1989 to 2001. Instead of building support for the group al-Qaeda, it seeks to reinvigorate the global threat. Bin Laden kept the name of al-Qaeda a public secret until the United States attacked Afghanistan in October 2001. As such, he did not focus on building support for al-Qaeda, the single group, but for the wider jihad movement throughout the 1990s and beyond. Using the core of the mujahideen who fought against the Soviets, al-Qaeda built a network of associated groups and affiliated cells globally. Since al-Qaeda attacked the United States' most iconic landmarks, the threat posed by al-Qaeda has been surpassed by the emergence of a global jihad movement consisting of al-Qaeda and other groups and individuals that advocate global jihad. The global jihad movement has three overlapping components.

First is the al-Qaeda group, established by Bin Laden, the unofficial representative of the Saudi kingdom to the Afghan jihad. Azzam, bin Laden's Palestinian-Jordanian mentor, was the ideological father of al-Qaeda. The group's global jihad ideology has great appeal both to associated groups waging the local jihad in conflict zones and to radicalized Muslim cells in the migrant and diaspora communities of the West. Also known as al-Qaeda core, al-Qaeda central, or al-Qaeda classic, the post-9/11 al-Qaeda group is operationally weak but ideologically potent.

Second, al-Qaeda's operationally associated groups consist of an umbrella of 30–40 Asian, African, and Middle Eastern groups, also known as the al-Qaeda network. Al-Qaeda provided these groups with training, weapons, financing, and ideology in Pakistan, Sudan, and Afghanistan; in conflict zones such as Bosnia, Chechnya, and Mindanao; and through the Internet. They hold declared or undeclared membership in the World Islamic Front for Jihad against the Jews and the Crusaders, formed in February 1998. They include al-Qaeda in the Islamic Maghreb (previously Salafi Group for Call and Combat), al-Qaeda in the Arabian Peninsula, Takfir Wal Hijra, al-Qaeda in Iraq (Tawhid Wal Jihad), Lashkar-e-Taiba, Jemaah Islamiyah, and the Abu Sayyaf Group.

Third, al-Qaeda's ideologically affiliated cells are operationally unconnected to al-Qaeda but driven by an ideology of global jihad articulated by it. The Supporters [of] al-Qaeda (Spanish Intelligence Service 2004)— the cell responsible for bombing the trains in Madrid on March 11, 2001— and the disrupted British cell led by Omar Khayyam (New Scotland Yard 2004) were self-financed and independent of al-Qaeda's operational control. The post-Iraq robust Islamist milieu in North America, Europe, and Australasia is transforming support cells into execution cells.

THE FUTURE

More current and future terrorist and extremist groups will emulate al-Qaeda ideology and methodology. While al-Qaeda's favored methodology is to mount suicide attacks against high-profile, symbolic, and strategic targets to inflict mass fatalities and casualties, its ideology calls for attacks against both domestic governments and Western and Israeli targets. As the near-simultaneous "no-surrender" attacks in Mumbai demonstrated in November 2008, even groups that are not part of the al-Qaeda family, such as Lashkar-e-Taiba, have adopted al-Qaeda–style attacks. Although the Lashkar-e-Taiba operatives were not suicide attackers, they staged a no-surrender (fedayeen) attack and were more militarily skilled than most al-Qaeda attackers. Long after the bin Laden era, his methodology and ideology are likely to persist.

Afghanistan and Iraq will persist as the world's defining conflict zones. The Muslim suffering, agony, and resentment will galvanize Muslims worldwide. Although only a tiny minority of the Muslims support terrorism, the majority of Muslims will be reluctant to support the Western presence in Muslim lands. The terrorist groups based in the Federally Administered Tribal Areas in Pakistan will attack not only Afghanistan but also mainland Pakistan. Increasingly, the same tactics used in Afghanistan are being replicated in Pakistan and beyond. While the high-intensity insurgency in tribal Pakistan will persist, there will be regular terrorist attacks against civilian and government targets inside mainland Pakistan. It is very likely that Pakistan will continue to suffer from attacks until the al-Qaeda–Taliban enclave is cleared.

CONCLUSION

As a result of U.S.-led global action, al-Qaeda was severely weakened. Nonetheless, the high-impact 9/11 attack, the U.S.-led coalition's intervention in Afghanistan, the U.S. invasion and occupation of Iraq, and the media reporting on Abu Ghraib and Guantánamo Bay have strengthened support for like-minded associated groups and cells as well as Islamist groups unconnected to al-Qaeda. Exploiting the suffering, resentment, and anger of the Muslims, the terrorist and extremist groups are now able to replenish their human and material losses and continue the fight. al-Qaeda has morphed from a group of 3,000 to 4,000 members in October 2001 to a movement of several tens of thousands of members, supporters, and sympathizers. Today, the global jihad movement, consisting primarily of Sunni groups, either connected or unconnected to al-Qaeda, is even more robust.

The threat posed by the global jihad movement is likely to persist in the foreseeable future. U.S. unilateral actions such as its invasion of Iraq have increased support for the global jihad movement. With the death of a million civilians in Iraq and Afghanistan, the Muslim world is angry with the West, especially the United States. To dismantle the global jihad movement, the United States and the rest of the West must work with the Muslim world. Fighting operational terrorism and its precursor, ideological extremism, is a task the United States and Europe alone cannot accomplish. Although the West has specialist resources and discipline to persist in fighting operational terrorism, it has no capacity to counter the al-Qaeda–led and –inspired propaganda. As such, a partnership of the West with the Muslim world is crucial. In addition to conducting kinetic and lethal operations to neutralize terrorist and insurgent leaders, governments worldwide must work with nongovernmental organizations and the public to build a norm against extremism and terrorism.

See also: **Volume 1, Part I:** Concept of Islamist Jihad; Global Terrorism: Post-9/11; Insurgent Terrorism; The Terrorist Threat in the 21st Century: A Global Security Problem; War on Terror. **Part III:** Military Force: Effective against Terrorists?; The United States, Iraq, and the Global Terrorism Problem. **Part IV:** Combating Religiously Based Terrorism; Lessons of Afghanistan and Iraq; Pakistan's Federally Administered Tribal Areas (FATA). **Part VI:** Afghanistan: Present and Future Challenges; Threat Convergence; Weak Link: Identifying and Attacking Terrorists' Vulnerabilities

REFERENCES

Gunaratna, Rohan. *Inside Al Qaeda Global Network of Terror.* London: Hurst, 2002.
Jane's World Insurgency and Terrorism. *Al-Qaeda.* January 9, 2004. http://jtic. janes.com.
New Scotland Yard. "Briefing on Operation Crevice (SO 13)." December 2004.
Spanish Intelligence Service (CNI). "Briefing." December 2004.
"Translation of Osama's Videotape." *Al Jazeera TV,* October 30, 2004.

Interrogation: A Multidisciplinary Approach

Matthew Alexander

Since September 11, 2001, interrogation techniques have been the subject of intense scrutiny. A multitude of opinions emerged about the legality, morality, and effectiveness of traditional interrogation techniques in the U.S. *Army Field Manual;* enhanced interrogation techniques, which evolved from survival, evasion, resistance, and escape (SERE) training; and the interrogation techniques used by law enforcement. One commonly held opinion was that the methods in the U.S. *Army Field Manual* are, as former Central Intelligence Agency (CIA) director General Michael Hayden called them, "a shot in the dark" (Mazetti 2009) when applied to al-Qaeda. Not only did the application of coercive enhanced interrogation techniques lack a foundation in science, but the experiences of other prisoners of war were that such methods of torture and abuse produced false or incomplete information.

MULTIDISCIPLINARY APPROACH

Some voices in the debate labeled law enforcement techniques as ineffective because they seek to garner a confession, whereas the objective of an intelligence interrogation is "to gather information to satisfy the commander's intelligence requirements and cross-cue other intelligence disciplines" (U.S. Department of the Army 2006, 1–4). This differentiation, however, is an artificial one. The ultimate objective of an interrogation is not a confession or tactical intelligence but cooperation. The technique is merely an avenue to a destination. To reach that destination of cooperation, professional interrogators have long borrowed from other disciplines and successfully crafted effective, noncoercive interrogation techniques against the most recalcitrant of detainees, such as Japanese prisoners of war during World War II.

Interrogation techniques in a counterterrorism or counterinsurgency context benefit from a multidisciplinary approach. The techniques are bound by legal and moral requirements but not by academic ones. In other words, interrogation techniques can, and do, borrow from other disciplines such as sales, negotiations, culture, social science, compliance, psychology, and law enforcement. Some law enforcement methods are effective against al-Qaeda or other terrorist groups simply because these groups are organized like a criminal gang or the mafia with organizational structures based on social networking rather than traditional military rank-and-file pyramids (Wilson 2010). Interrogation techniques can, therefore, take advantage of the inherent weaknesses of group dynamics, such as communications, trust, and relationships.

For example, each member of a social group is not privy to all the information of every other member of that same group. To exploit this weakness, investigators commonly use the police technique of physically separating suspects involved in a crime, asking questions, and then using statements made by each suspect against the other (a version of the so-called *prisoner's dilemma*). This method is especially effective in a battlefield interrogation scenario where ground troops desire quick and accurate information to proceed to follow-on targets before they can move. During the time immediately after capture, detainees are separated and lack the benefit of time to weigh the probability of others in their group cooperating. Thus, interrogators can use these factors along with deception to their advantage. Police detectives use this technique to discover the locations of drug dealers when they arrest more than one suspect for possession of illegal narcotics. There are endless variations of this prisoner's dilemma, including inserting false assumptions into the statements made by suspects to test them against those made by accomplices.

Another effective interrogation technique is borrowed from the fields of sales and psychology and is referred to as the *boss introduction*. Car salesmen use this technique at the end of a deal by introducing the customer to a supervisor who has the authority to negotiate the final loose ends of a contract, thereby increasing the pressure on the prospective buyer to purchase an automobile. This technique takes advantage of a known social behavior, namely, that we are "trained from birth that obedience to proper authority is right and disobedience is wrong" (Cialdini 1993). This deference to authority was demonstrated quite vividly in the Milgram Experiment at Yale University, conducted in the early 1960s (Milgram 1974), in which subjects routinely obeyed commands from an authority figure to give life-threatening electrical shocks to ailing victims (who were, fortunately, actors complicit in the experiment) despite their moral objections. Leveraging this social norm, the boss introduction introduces a second interrogator to a detainee as a person of authority with the ability to reward the detainee, thus providing a strong incentive to cooperate. This technique also borrows from the discipline of cultural studies in the following manner.

The *Army Field Manual* recommends that interrogators be knowledgeable in the culture of detainees. By using the boss introduction, interrogators take advantage of the cultural concept of *wasta* that is prevalent in the Middle East. *Wasta*, loosely defined as influence or power, is the ability of tribal sheikhs or community leaders to get things done based on their position of authority. In the interrogation scenario, a "boss" is someone with *wasta* who is able to assist a detainee and convince him to cooperate. This technique combines elements from the disciplines of sales, psychology, and culture with the *incentive approach* in the *Army Field Manual* by matching the influence of a person in a position of power with a tangible or intangible benefit. There are additional disciplinary fields from which interrogators can borrow.

Studies in the field of sports psychology have shown that mental practice enhances performance (Driskell, Copper, and Moran 1994). The technique of visualizing success before a competition has become common practice among professional athletes as well as musicians and other professionals. An interrogation technique adapted from this field involves using words to "paint" a mental picture of cooperation, and the resulting mutual benefits, in the mind of a detainee. The technique is called the *Van Gogh* (after the Dutch painter). Used together with an *emotional love approach* or a *love-of-family approach* from the *Army Field Manual*, it builds a persuasive argument for cooperation by combining powerful mental imagery with emotional incentives to reinforce the idea that cooperation is not only possible but beneficial. Again, this technique should be modified for the culture, and the mental imagery tailored to the individual detainee. In addition to borrowing from the fields of sales and psychology, other techniques in the *Army Field Manual* can be improved using versions of law enforcement techniques based on deception.

DECEPTION IN INTERROGATION

Deception in warfare is as old as warfare itself. Sun Tzu, the famous Chinese military strategist, surmised, "All war is deception." Similarly, many law enforcement interrogation techniques are rooted in the psychology of deception. For example, one technique is for investigators to present to a suspect a factual piece of information obtained from a witness or during surveillance and then to deceive the suspect into believing they have significant additional information. In the *Army Field Manual*, this approach is called *We know all*, but technical instruction on the use of deception while applying this approach is not explained sufficiently. The technique's most significant example of effectiveness is revealed in the statement of an al-Qaeda member who provided information to Iraqi interrogators leading to the deaths of the two most wanted terrorists in Iraq in 2010—Abu Ayyub Al Masri and Omar al-Bagdhadi. The al-Qaeda member, Munaf Abdul-Rahim al-Rawi, stated, "Security forces already know everything about me and my links. . . . I felt it is useless to deny or conceal information" (Abdul-Zahira 2010). Thus, the detainee admits the effectiveness of the We know all approach, which leverages deception and a prisoner's lack of complete knowledge as a legal, noncoercive method.

U.S. interrogators during World War II used deception extensively while interrogating Japanese and German prisoners of war. At two secret detention facilities, Camp Tracy outside San Francisco and Fort Hunt in northern Virginia, interrogators bugged the rooms of detainees with clandestine listening devices. They also used "stool pigeons," Japanese Americans (Nisei) and German Americans posing as prisoners of war who were inserted into the cells and engaged other prisoners in conversation, attempting to elicit secrets. While prisoners exercised, they also searched rooms surreptitiously and copied letters written home to family members, which could be examined for relevant intelligence information (Corbin 2009).

Americans were not the only ones to use deception as an interrogation technique in World War II. In England, Colonel Robin "Tin Eye" Stephens ran the British Camp 020 where captured Nazi spies were interrogated. Stephens used methods based on deception and psychology to convince prisoners to cooperate, successfully using these cooperative prisoners as double agents to penetrate German intelligence. Even the most successful German Luftwaffe interrogator from World War II, Hanns Scharff, used deception along with rapport building to elicit information from more than 90 percent of the downed Allied pilots he interrogated. Scharff used a precise and detailed database to bolster his We know all approach and often successfully feigned more knowledge than he actually possessed. This is a basic law enforcement model for evidence-based interrogation. These techniques were also used by two of the most successful American interrogators during the Vietnam War, Colonel Stuart Herrington and Orrin DeForrest, the later leveraging his previous experience as a military criminal investigator in designing rapport- and evidence-based approaches.

These deception- and evidence-based techniques have been adapted by organizations and used quite effectively. Wardens have for decades used stool pigeons and conducted clandestine cell block searches to thwart riots and prison violence. During an investigation, detectives use deception to locate additional evidence or witnesses. Ultimately, these types of law enforcement techniques are not so much about garnering a confession as they are about convincing a suspect to cooperate. It is counterproductive to erect an artificial barrier between law enforcement interrogation techniques and military intelligence interrogation techniques. It is merely the nuanced method of application that differs, not the overall objective.

Current interrogation methods can be further refined given advances in other academic disciplines. For example, international business negotiation theory has progressed to include concepts of cross-cultural communications that can be applied to intelligence interrogations. Themes from motivational speaking, marketing, and advertising (compliance) could further improve the craft. Some interrogators have suggested that even poker-playing strategies can be adapted for intelligence interrogations. Other countries, such as Indonesia, have applied a medical model that sees a detainee as a patient with an affliction requiring therapy.

CONCLUSION

Interrogation is often thought of as a static field, and complacency seduces even the most experienced interrogators into thinking that everything that can be tried has been tried before. The post–September 11 challenges faced by interrogators and headline controversies over enhanced interrogation techniques can optimistically be viewed as the mother of adversity that has inspired a modern revolutionary movement and invention. That invention includes the adoption of concepts from other disciplines to improve both the science and the art of interrogation. The time to advance interrogation techniques is now.

See also: **Volume 1, Part IV:** Detention, Interrogation, and Torture of Terrorist Suspects; Ethical and Legal Issues in Democratic Societies: National Security and Civil Liberties

REFERENCES

Abdul-Zahira, Qassim. *Militant Turncoat Leads Iraqis to al-Qaida Chiefs.* Associated Press, April 30, 2010.
Cialdini, Robert B. *Influence: The Psychology of Persuasion.* New York: Quill, 1993.

Corbin, Alexander. *The History of Camp Tracy.* Fort Belvoir, VA: Ziedon, 2009.

Driskell, James E., Carolyn Copper, and Aidan Moran. "Does Mental Practice Enhance Performance?" *Journal of Applied Psychology* 79 (1994): 481–92.

Mazetti, Mark. "Departing Spy Chief Has Few Regrets." *New York Times,* January 15, 2009. http://thecaucus.blogs.nytimes.com/2009/01/15/departing-spy-chief-expresses-no-regrets/.

Milgram, Stanley. *Obedience to Authority.* New York: Harper & Row, 1974.

U.S. Department of the Army. *Army Field Manual 2-22.3 Human Intelligence Collector Operations.* Headquarters Department of the Army, Washington, DC, September 2006.

Wilson, Chris. "Searching for Saddam: The Social Network That Caught a Dictator." *Slate Magazine,* updated February 23, 2010. http://www.slate.com/articles/news_and_politics/searching_for_saddam/2010/02/searching_for_saddam_4.html.

Multilateral Approach to Counterterrorism: Issues, Problems, Responses

Michelle Bentley

The international scope of terrorism has led politicians and security analysts to argue that counterterrorism must be a networked and multilateral response. This type of strategy requires an approach that involves the combined input of multilateral institutions. However, these institutions must first address a number of issues and challenges if counterterrorism strategy is to be successful.

ISSUES

Counterterrorism was a multilateral issue long before 9/11, albeit a relatively minor concern. Yet this became a priority after 9/11 in that the attacks on New York and Washington, D.C., highlighted a new international dimension to terrorism. Terrorism is now inherently global; organizations are internationally networked and financed and are coordinated through channels of global communication (e.g., the Internet). Consequently, any state is a potential target. Moreover, the worldwide economy means the effects of terrorism can result in detrimental consequences beyond the target state; for example, 9/11 temporarily closed the New York Stock Exchange and caused a significant drop in global markets, affecting all nations. Therefore, it is argued that a unilateral counterterrorist policy is insufficient and that states cannot realistically avoid participation in multilateral strategies, specifically where these policies and multilateral approaches address the international consequences of terrorism in a way that a state operating unilaterally cannot. Even powerful states such as the United States have pursued counterterrorism through multilateral institutions, and this is a core aspect of the strategy employed by the present Obama administration.

Indeed, the events of 9/11 marked the emergence of a comprehensively different security environment to that experienced previously. Prior to 9/11, security was fundamentally a state-centric concept. Presently, terrorism (as a form of nonstate aggression) is a key threat, specifically one incorporating new risks such as the increased lethality of asymmetric warfare and the fear that terrorists may employ weapons of mass destruction. Multilateral strategies must adapt to these changes. This is not to trivialize the continuing relevance of pre-9/11 measures, such as United Nations (UN) conventions criminalizing terrorist acts, which are still acknowledged as a core element of contemporary counterterrorist activity. However, terrorism itself has undergone a major shift, and this will affect future policy construction.

Multilateral cooperation on counterterrorism now covers a range of issues and options. These include coordination and/or sanctioning of collective military action; intelligence, such as cross-border operations to infiltrate terrorist activity and the diplomatic logistics of information sharing; formulation and implementation of international criminal law; international financial controls, such as freezing assets linked to terrorist organizations; and intergovernmental agreements related to securing trade and transportation routes from attack and preventing terrorists from acquiring weapons. Yet, increasingly, multilateral strategies have expanded beyond these measures to adopt a more holistic approach, specifically one that seeks to counter terrorism by preventing radicalism. This approach attributes radicalism to socioeconomic issues such as underdevelopment, poverty, education, and so on. If these can be addressed, the incentives to resort to terror will be eradicated. Therefore, a key issue for multilateral counterterrorism efforts is the development of strategies that focus on the removal of the conditions that may spawn terrorism and a critical assessment of where the balance/priorities lie between this and more immediate and direct methods.

PROBLEMS

International Cooperation

Multilateralism requires a very high level of international cooperation and trust. Yet collaboration between international actors is problematic. States may prioritize their own security ambitions and interests, especially where participation in multilateral counterterrorism strategies involves ceding power and control to global or regional institutions. This can be seen in the way that some regional organizations such as the Association of Southeast Asian Nations, African Union, South Asian Association for Regional Cooperation, and the Organization of the Islamic Conference have been criticized for failing to coordinate effective counterterrorism programs due to a lack of institutional cohesion and commitment by member states. Moreover, a lack of executive power within multilateral institutions means that few measures exist to force members' compliance. Indeed, these pressures may result in states bypassing the multilateral system altogether, choosing instead to pursue counterterrorism unilaterally or through bilateral relationships and coalitions. For example, the United States proceeded to intervene in Iraq despite the controversy with the UN over whether this action contravened Resolution 1441.

Moreover, this self-interested approach promotes political factionalism within multilateral fora, for example, bloc voting within the UN General Assembly and also the use of the veto in the Security Council. Underlying political disputes may affect the ability to form a consensus on counterterrorism. For example, the hostility between the Arab/Muslim bloc and the United States and Israel has been detrimental to progress in this area. Similarly, non-Western governments have felt alienated in that terrorism has been characterized as a fundamentally Western priority; conversely, non-Western states may be more concerned with issues such as poverty, underdevelopment, and health issues including HIV and malaria. Factionalism also undermines specific programs of counterterrorism, for example, intelligence-sharing initiatives. States may be reluctant to supply information on the grounds that it could compromise their own security and/or political advantage.

Fragmented Policy

Counterterrorism is an umbrella concept. Particularly within the UN, policy is not enacted through a dedicated and unified body; instead, measures are devolved across a range of departments and associated intergovernmental institutions. This is partly the consequence of the expansion of counterterrorism into wider areas of concern such as socioeconomic development, which requires the input of a variety of specialized bodies. However, it is also a structural failure to bring counterterrorism within the remit of one organization. This creates several problems. First, there is a lack of institutional coordination. There is no comprehensive blueprint or vision outlining how such a diverse range of actors should work together as part of an integrated strategy, a problem made worse by the massive—some would argue unsustainable—expansion in the number of actors involved in counterterrorism since 9/11. Indeed, there is not even a workable consensus as to what such a vision might look like as multilateral institutions are still torn by disagreement over what the aims of counterterrorism should be. This situation is exacerbated by the absence of a clear and universal definition of terrorism, which has created confusion, ambiguity, and a lack of policy cohesion. Without this conceptual clarification it is difficult to ascertain what the problem is, let alone the solution.

Second, this fragmentation generates a number of bureaucratic issues. For example, it is difficult to allocate centralized budgetary resources across such a disjointed institutional structure in which it is unclear who should receive support, how much, and for what purpose. There is also significant duplication of effort where the respective remits of different departments overlap. This is inefficient and may potentially create contradictions in policy. Measures taken to address these problems have so far been largely unsuccessful and tend to reinforce the distinctions between departments and institutions as opposed to promoting their unification. Finally, while these departments are experts in their specific fields, they are not necessarily experts in counterterrorism. "Tagging on" counterterrorism is not considered an effective strategy, and some departments have been reluctant to adopt extra responsibilities, viewing them as only vaguely related to their scope of work. This situation also precludes the professionalization of counterterrorism as a dedicated area of concern.

RESPONSES

Future strategy must take into account the issues and problems outlined here. First, there needs to be a comprehensive coordination of policy within institutions, between institutions, and between different levels of cooperation, for example, national and international. Ideally, this will also involve a rationalization of strategy around a fundamental set of aims relating to counterterrorism. This links in with demands for a single definition of terrorism in that this would alleviate confusion, promote multilateral consensus, provide a clear basis for future action, provide clarification from a legal perspective on the criminalization of terrorist acts, and help shift counterterrorism away from the near-exclusive focus on Islamic fundamentalism by opening the issue up to alternate forms of political violence. However, the need for strategic focus should not detract from calls for the development of a multifaceted approach, particularly one designed to preclude radicalism. Specifically, it is argued that such an approach must be constructed as a human rights issue. Terrorism must be stigmatized as a violation of human rights—notably the right to life, security, and dignity—in order to build effective counterterrorist strategies. Yet prohibiting terrorism in this way and making counterterrorism a compulsory aspect of the protection of human rights can succeed only where there is a universal commitment. The multilateral approach is seen as the best way of achieving this.

Second, there is the question as to who should take charge of coordinating counterterrorism strategy; the UN is frequently cited as the logical leader. At the 2005 World Summit, Malaysian prime minister Abdullah Ahmad Badawi described the UN as the only realistic forum for global counterterrorism. Indeed, the UN is seen as possessing the necessary organizational infrastructure to address many key issues, such as developing states' capacity to prevent terrorism (through improved domestic legislation, juridical training, and border controls), resolving conflicts that might otherwise constitute a "breeding ground" for terrorism, and establishing the aforementioned norm on human rights. Yet the UN needs to strengthen its capabilities. While the 2006 Global Counter Terrorism Strategy did much to improve this issue, many argue that more must be done. Suggestions include the adoption of the proposed Comprehensive Convention on International Terrorism, which would criminalize all forms of international terrorism and the provision of resources to terrorist organizations.

Moreover, there are calls for the establishment of a centralized body on counterterrorism within the UN (as opposed to the current fragmented approach), possibly as an amended version of the Counter-terrorism Committee (CTC) or through the consolidation of different departments. However, others argue that such a body should be constructed outside of the UN, away from the political and bureaucratic baggage associated with the organization. Yet moving counterterrorism outside the UN's remit would be difficult. The UN lies at the heart of a complex spider web of multilateral connections. Moving those relationships to an external environment would be problematic, particularly where this would potentially challenge the legitimacy and authority of the UN.

Finally, there must be a greater degree of transparency and accountability. For example, substantial financial resources are being invested in counterterrorism, yet there are few systems in place to monitor whether these are being used efficiently and successfully. Within this context, it must also be recognized that successful counterterrorism is difficult to measure. How do we know if it works? Did a hypothetical attack not occur because of certain policies or for other reasons? Consequently, future responses relating to counterterrorism should specify and incorporate a workable method of ascertaining their success in order to determine whether multilateral efforts are actually effective.

CONCLUSION

Since 9/11, multilateral institutions have played a key role in counterterrorism. The international dynamic of terrorism means that a multilateral response is seen as not simply desirable but inevitable. No state can take on the terrorist problem alone. However, this is a complex and difficult ambition. Effective cooperation at the intergovernmental level has always been challenging, particularly where this threatens to interfere with a state's authority over its own security. Moreover, the current fragmentation of counterterrorism activity across a range of institutional bodies is an inefficient approach. Overly broad ambitions that exceed the limitations of what can reasonably be achieved within intergovernmental institutions are destined to be limited in terms of effect. While current strategies demand the input of a range of expert and political bodies, their inclusion has been haphazard, and more needs to be done to coordinate their role into more holistic and effective strategies. This could be achieved by the creation of a dedicated counterterrorism body—possibly within the UN— but why and how this could be achieved remains to be seen.

See also: **Volume 1, Part III:** Multidisciplinary Approach to Combating Terrorism; Multilateral Sanctions against State Sponsors of Terrorism. **Part IV:** United Nations Global Counterterrorism Strategy: Significance and Limitations. **Part VI:** Combating Terrorism: A New Way Forward; Regional Challenges: Promoting Stability through Economic, Social, and Political Reforms

REFERENCES

Dhanapala, Jayantha. "The United Nations' Response to 9/11." *Terrorism and Political Violence* 17, no. 1 (2005): 17–23.
Keohane, Daniel. "The EU and Counter-terrorism." Working paper, Centre for European Reform. London: Centre for European Reform, 2005, pp. 1–38. http://library.coleurope.eu/pdf/CER/keohane.pdf.
Romaniuk, Peter. *Multilateral Counter-terrorism: The Global Politics of Cooperation and Contestation.* Abingdon, UK: Routledge, 2010.
Rosand, Eric. "The UN-Led Multilateral Institutional Response to Jihadist Terrorism: Is a Global Counterterrorism Body Needed?" *Journal of Conflict and Security Law* 11, no. 3 (2007): 399–427.
Wanadi, Jusuf. "A Global Coalition against International Terrorism." *International Security* 26, no. 4 (2002): 184–89.
Zimmerman, Doron. "The European Union and Post-9/11 Counterterrorism: A Reappraisal." *Studies in Conflict and Terrorism* 29, no. 2 (2006): 123–45.

Narco-terrorism: How Real Is the Threat?

Michelle Denise Reeves

In November 1985, Movimiento de 19 Abril (M19) guerrillas infiltrated the Colombian Palace of Justice, taking hostage the entire Colombian Supreme Court and destroying documents, many of which were U.S. extradition requests for major narcotics traffickers. A report later surfaced that

Pablo Escobar, head of the notorious cocaine-trafficking Medellín cartel, had paid the guerrillas close to a million dollars for the episode. The incident drew attention to what some U.S. and Latin American officials began to call *narco-terrorism*.

CONCEPT OF NARCO-TERRORISM

Vice President George H.W. Bush, serving as head of both the administration's task force on combating terrorism and the Southwest Florida Task Force, which aimed to detect and confiscate drug shipments crossing the U.S. border, was at the forefront of establishing the conceptual connection between terrorism and narcotics in the threat perceptions of U.S. policymakers and military officials. Less than six months after the incident, National Security Decision Directive 221 declared drugs a national security threat, widening the scope of military involvement in the drug war and linking counterinsurgency and counternarcotics in official U.S. policy for the first time.

The development of the concept of narco-terrorism occurred in the highly politicized context of the Cold War. The Reagan administration consistently charged Marxist-Leninist regimes in Latin America with trafficking in illicit drugs. According to the Reagan administration, Fidel Castro's Cuba and Nicaragua's Sandinista government had cultivated extensive ties with leftist guerrilla groups in the northern Andes in order to use the profits from drug trafficking to finance Marxist revolution in the western hemisphere and, as an added bonus, destabilize U.S. society by exacerbating the problem of drug addiction. Despite circumstantial evidence of the involvement of corrupt Cuban and Nicaraguan officials in the drug trade, however, no evidence surfaced to indicate a systematic knowledge of illicit activities in the upper echelons of those countries' governments. The evidentiary basis for Cuban and Sandinista complicity in the drug trade was similar to that for allegations of drug trafficking among the right-wing counterinsurgency forces (contras) battling the Sandinistas—charges that the Reagan administration dismissed out of hand. Funding the contras was one of Reagan's pet projects, and his administration continued to provide the guerrilla group with military and humanitarian support after allegations of the group's involvement in narcotics trafficking became public.

The Reagan administration used the term *narco-terrorism* to refer to the nexus between narcotics traffickers, political terrorists, and leftist guerrilla movements. From the beginning, however, this nexus was poorly defined. Traditionally, the definition of terrorism has been rooted in its specifically political aims. The word *narco-terrorism* was nevertheless used to designate three very different phenomena: the application of terror by narcotics traffickers to intimidate political authorities, the use of drug profits by insurgents and terrorist organizations to finance terrorist acts aimed at inducing political outcomes entirely unrelated to the narcotics trade, and the logistical network through which drugs and drug money flowed, the existence and strength of which is often dependent on official corruption. Definitions of narco-terrorism thus failed to adequately distinguish between the tactics and the goals of its practitioners. By using the term *narco-terrorism* in such an indiscriminate fashion, government officials and media commentators elided the crucial distinction between narcotics profits as a means to an end and as an end in itself.

U.S. officials were not the only ones concerned about the dangers of narco-terrorism. It was Fernando Belaunde Terry, president of Peru from 1963 to 1968 and again from 1980 to 1985, who actually coined the term. During his tenure as president, the Communist Party of Peru, or Sendero Luminoso (Shining Path), a Marxist-Leninist guerrilla movement, infiltrated the Upper Huallaga Valley, the source of the majority of the world's cocaine. The rebels had launched a Maoist-influenced guerrilla war in Peru, and the intensely brutal acts of terrorism they perpetrated had sent the Peruvian government into a state of emergency. Belaunde, like his U.S. counterpart, charged that the guerrillas of Shining Path were funded and directed from Communist countries abroad—namely, Cuba. He provided no evidence for this claim, and, indeed, no evidence existed to substantiate it. The accusation, besides being groundless, was another example of the politicized nature of the concept of narco-terrorism. Because the guerrillas posed a far greater threat to the Peruvian government than the drug traffickers, Belaunde had every incentive to appeal to the United States for help in terms that would resonate with the U.S. government and public. By the mid-1980s, the primary national security threat to the United States was perceived in terms of drugs, not leftist guerrilla insurgencies. By linking the threat of the guerrillas with the production and trafficking of narcotics, the governments of South American drug-producing countries ensured a steady supply of military and financial aid from the United States.

TERRORISM-DRUG NEXUS?

Even at the time, however, some U.S. officials were skeptical about whether the connection between narcotics trafficking and terrorism was so unambiguous. Some, like Federal Bureau of Investigation (FBI) chief William Webster, denied that such a link even existed. Others, however, acknowledged that a relationship between drug traffickers and leftist guerrillas did indeed exist, although that relationship was much more complex than the straightforward term *narco-terrorism* would suggest. Indeed, the experience of the Fuerzas Armadas Revolucionarias de Colombia (FARC; Revolutionary Armed Forces of Colombia), the oldest and most formidable of Colombia's Marxist insurgencies, demonstrated that the links between narcotics and terrorism were anything but uncomplicated. The guerrillas switched their allegiance from the Medellín cocaine-trafficking cartel to the coca-growing peasantry according to circumstances. Initially, the FARC provided the Medellín cartel with protection. As the cartel's landholdings expanded in conjunction with their trafficking network and profits from narcotics sales, tensions with the FARC, which supported the interests of the peasantry against large landholders, increased. When the Medellín cartel realized the threat FARC guerrillas posed to their trafficking organization, they promptly launched their own war against the movement.

However murky the definition of narco-terrorism, one thing is clear: U.S. policies aimed at combating the menace posed by the association of leftist guerrillas and narcotics traffickers in Latin America only exacerbated the problem. Supply-side antinarcotics policies, particularly the forcible eradication of narcotics crops, alienated the peasants, driving them to seek protection from the very leftist guerrillas whose terrorist activities so threatened the Andean governments. When the United States provided those governments with military aid and support, the guerrillas were emboldened to launch accusations of imperialism and escalate their terrorist activities in response. When the United States withdrew its support for the militaries of the Andean countries, government control over coca-producing regions was undermined, and the guerrillas were free to operate unmolested. Part of the problem was that the acknowledgment of the linkage between drugs and terrorism was not accompanied by structural changes at the bureaucratic level. Agencies operating under the jurisdiction of both the Department of State and the Department of Justice jockeyed for influence over counternarcotics policies while the military dealt with the insurgents. Institutional rivalries and a disinclination to share intelligence thus hampered the struggle against narco-terrorism.

The problem was not confined to Latin America. On the eve of the 1991 war in the Persian Gulf, allegations surfaced linking the government of Syria to drug trafficking. Lebanon's Beka'a Valley was a production site for heroin and hashish, and several Syrian officials were implicated in providing protection for the growers and traffickers. These officials purportedly provided protection and funding for the terrorist activities of Hezbollah, the Shia Islamist paramilitary organization headquartered in Lebanon. Allegations also arose concerning the involvement of Yasser Arafat and the Palestine Liberation Organization in drug trafficking. The profits from the sale of illicit narcotics were said to fund the Palestinian intifada against Israel. The Liberation Tigers of Tamil Eelam, an Indian-trained insurgency in Sri Lanka, were also accused of engaging in narco-terrorism, using the profits from opium poppy cultivation to fund terrorist acts against the Sri Lankan government. Moreover, though the collapse of the Soviet Union deprived many terrorist groups of their state sponsorship, drying up their primary source of funding and leading them to become more entangled in the drug trade, the problem itself was not new. The Soviet invasion of

Afghanistan in 1979 had brought the Russians face to face with the extensive cultivation of opium in that country and the network of traffickers and smuggling routes that was protected by corrupt government and intelligence officials in both Afghanistan and Pakistan.

A RENEWED FOCUS

Although the interregnum between the Cold War and the beginning of the global war on terror witnessed the active involvement of the U.S. military in combating the narcotics trade, in the wake of 9/11 the Defense Department has returned to its previous position of viewing the drug war as a distraction from its primary mission. But the 2001 U.S. invasion of Afghanistan brought the narco-terrorism issue into the spotlight once again. A growing body of evidence exists indicating collaboration between the Taliban, al-Qaeda, corrupt government and intelligence officials in both Afghanistan and Pakistan, and Central Asian and Chechen insurgents who control trafficking routes into Iran, Turkey, and Russia. This has led the Russian government to appeal to the Americans for a stronger and more unified effort to weaken the narcotics trade.

Nevertheless, a coordinated approach to counternarcotics and counterterrorism has proven difficult. The Pentagon has continued to insist that the role of the military is to fight the insurgents, while thwarting the opium trade is the responsibility of law enforcement. U.S. counternarcotics policy has focused more on capturing drug kingpins and less on disrupting the financial network that supports them. Further complicating the situation is the systemic corruption and the complicity of the Afghan and Pakistani governments, judiciaries, and law enforcement in narcotics trafficking. To make matters worse, although Afghanistan is the primary site of poppy cultivation, the command and control centers of the global opium trade are internationally based, including in Pakistan, which is off-limits to Western troops and law enforcement. The transnational nature of the threats of drug trafficking and terrorism demands an institutional overhaul if U.S. counterterrorism and counternarcotics policies are to succeed.

CONCLUSION

It is clear that an international infrastructure facilitating both narcotics trafficking and terrorism exists and poses a grave threat to international security. What is entirely unclear, however, is whether the conceptual framework of narco-terrorism has aided the effort to formulate a coherent strategy for shutting down this network or whether the oversimplification of complex realities has in fact hindered an effective approach. When agricultural conditions amenable to the cultivation of narcotics crops exist in countries that host insurgent populations and have weak and corrupt central governments, drug profits will inevitably fund terrorist activities. And as long as a black market for drugs exists, the profit incentive will corrupt officials, encourage the formation of smuggling cartels, and mobilize insurgents. Clearly, drug traffickers, political terrorists, and insurgents profoundly threaten international security. By labeling all of these actors *narco-terrorists*, however, we conflate key distinctions in their actions and motivations and thereby make the jobs of U.S. policymakers even more difficult. Reducing the varied manifestations of these problems to the singular concept of narco-terrorism has neither adequately advanced our understanding of these phenomena nor contributed to the creation of an effective approach to combating them.

REFERENCES

Bowden, Mark. *Killing Pablo: The Hunt for the World's Greatest Outlaw.* New York: Penguin Books, 2002.

Coll, Steve. *Ghost Wars: The Secret History of the CIA, Afghanistan, and Bin Laden, from the Soviet Invasion to September 10, 2001.* New York: Penguin, 2004.

Ehrenfeld, Rachel. *Funding Evil: How Terrorism Is Financed and How to Stop It.* Chicago: Bonus Books, 2003.

Marcy, William L. *The Politics of Cocaine: How U.S. Foreign Policy Has Created a Thriving Drug Industry in Central and South America.* Chicago: Lawrence Hill Books, 2010.

McCoy, Alfred. *The Politics of Heroin: CIA Complicity in the Global Drug Trade.* Chicago: Lawrence Hill Books, 2003.

Peters, Gretchen. *Seeds of Terror: How Drugs, Thugs, and Crime are Re-shaping the Afghan War.* New York: Picador, 2009.

Tarazona-Sevillano, Gabriela. *Sendero Luminoso and the Threat of Narcoterrorism.* New York: Praeger, 1990.

Need for Empirical Research on the Effectiveness of Counterterrorism Strategies

Teun van Dongen and Rob de Wijk

Since the events of 9/11, many states have spent vast amounts of resources on the development and implementation of counterterrorism measures, ranging from target-hardening measures to the adoption of special legislation and from media campaigns to equipment for first responders that protects them against chemical, biological, radiological, and nuclear weapons. However, the question where it got us is still left unanswered. Perhaps surprisingly, there is little research that examines the effectiveness of counterterrorism measures (Lum, Kennedy, and Sherley 2006). The problem is not that the states' counterterrorism efforts went unnoticed: there has been plenty of debate on counterterrorism, especially on the legal and ethical sides of the matter. However, there is still no framework to assess whether the newly introduced counterterrorism measures have yielded the desired results. The following sections address the question of how effectiveness in counterterrorism strategies should be measured. Prior efforts at measuring the effectiveness of counterterrorism strategies from earlier research are reviewed. The last section suggests an alternative approach that argues in favor of breaking up counterterrorism into its constituent components, each with its separate measures of success.

DIRECT CONSEQUENCES OF TERRORIST ATTACKS

Some scholars and researchers have tried to assess the effectiveness of counterterrorism by examining changes in numbers of attacks, numbers of victims, and material damage (LaFree 2006; Barros 2003; Frisch 2006, 866–67; Morag 2005, 309–11; Alexander 2002). Although terrorists need to perpetrate a certain level of violence to maintain their credibility, there are several reasons to be critical of the use of numbers of attacks as an indicator of the success of counterterrorism measures.

First, it is not clear what increases and decreases, say, about the state of the terrorist organization committing the attacks. It is possible that a group in decline initiates a wave of terrorist attacks to send a message, both to its own members and to the population at large, that it is still a viable and capable organization. The Real Irish Republican Army, following the arrest of its leader, Mickey McKevitt, is a case in point (Cronin 2009, 78). In this case, an increase in the numbers of attacks is certainly not a sign that a counterterrorism strategy is not working. An increase can also be the result of radicalization of a movement in leadership transition, when the new leaders are demonstrating their authority by organizing a spectacular event or large numbers of attacks.

A second problem with using numbers of attacks as an indicator of terrorist success or effectiveness is that they do not communicate much about the effectiveness of the overall terrorist campaign. Not all terrorist attacks are similar, and one would expect the impact of a large-scale attack that requires much preparation, resources, and operational capabilities, such as 9/11, to be far more reaching than a simple arson. Therefore, using numbers of attacks as a success indicator would ignore these differences. This can be especially confusing if terrorist organizations decide to lower the frequency of their attacks to save resources for bigger, more spectacular attacks (Byman 2003, 81). To complicate matters further, the number of terrorist attacks does not necessarily correlate with an impact favorable to a terrorist organization. Research has shown that the psychological impact of the Irish Republican Army bombings was limited to parts of the United Kingdom that were often targeted (Silke 2003). Also, bombing campaigns can turn against the terrorists. There are signs that al-Qaeda is losing popular support in the Middle East because of the bloody attacks it perpetrates (Bergen and Cruickshank 2008). An increase in the number of terrorist attacks may also be harmful to the terrorist organization's principles and objectives. Furthermore, as the impact of a single attack can be huge, terrorist organizations do not need to commit many attacks to achieve their objectives. The assassination of a government cabinet member is a single attack yet sends a very powerful message about a terrorist organization's ability to access a prominent official, thereby disrupting a country's political process. A few small attacks can yield a terrorist organization much more success than a series of larger ones. Additionally, attacks that have been thwarted by the authorities garner much attention from the international media; therefore, the organization responsible for the failed attack still gets global exposure and through the fear factor is able to impact the lives of ordinary citizens

INDIRECT INDICATORS

Instead of focusing on data that reflect the direct manifestations of terrorism, some authors have looked at indirect indicators, such as fluctuations in indicators of the general functioning of a society, that are thought to be influenced by terrorist attacks. For example, it has been argued that domestic and international support for the government executing the counterterrorism policy could serve as an indicator of the success of that policy. Similarly, the functioning of the economy has been taken as an indicator of counterterrorism effectiveness (Morag 2005; Zussman and Zussman 2006). The assumption here is that when the economy is thriving, terrorists have not managed to severely disrupt the functioning of the country. The difficulties of these approaches are obvious. Economic growth and popular support for the government are affected by many factors other than terrorism and counterterrorism. Regarding the economy, it is even questionable whether most terrorist attacks have a significant impact at all. Even the 9/11 attacks, which took place at the heart of the American economy, did not have serious long-term consequences for a financial system as vast and diversified as that of the United States (Makinen 2002, 18–19). However, a case can be made that as a result of these attacks the United States has spent billions of dollars on domestic security and two foreign wars. The jury is still out regarding the overall financial impact of the 9/11 attacks.

AN ALTERNATIVE APPROACH

The problem with the effectiveness measurements discussed in the previous sections is that the link between policy and outcome is not specified.

These effectiveness measurements do not outline a causal link between policy and effect. In the absence of this link, it is difficult to attribute a decrease in one of these indicators to counterterrorism policy. As already explained, shifts are open to various other, more plausible interpretations. Part of the difficulty in relating counterterrorism to certain outcomes is that counterterrorism measures taken together are supposed to influence one single indicator. It is often assumed, as in the examples cited earlier, that a measure of effectiveness should say something about counterterrorism as a whole (LaFree 2006; Barros 2003; Frisch 2006, 866–67; Morag 2005, 309–11; Alexander 2002). However, a counterterrorism policy is made up of various different elements, with different effects on different variables. It can include, for instance, measures to address root causes, disrupt the organization by direct action, prevent the financing of terrorist operations, and offer individual members alternatives to membership in terrorist organizations. It is difficult to find indicators that say something about such a wide range of policy instruments. Also, if such an indicator could be found, this measure of gauging effectiveness would ignore the possibility that a country is doing well on some aspects of counterterrorism and poorly on others. Therefore, a more fruitful way of tackling the effectiveness measurement problem would be to assess the effectiveness of the various components that comprise specific counterterrorism policies. This suggests that separate measures of effectiveness have to be formulated for each counterterrorism component, which will make it easier to link an outcome to a policy element. For instance, the effectiveness of rehabilitation and reintegration programs whereby former members are allowed to reintegrate back into society could be measured by the recidivism rate of those who have been exposed to various rehabilitation measures to bring this about, for example, social reintegration education and incentive packages. These programs have achieved some success in Iraq and Saudi Arabia. Taking it a step further, the influence of these programs on the morale and cohesion of the terrorist organization could be examined as well.

CONCLUSION

Measuring counterterrorism is often considered difficult or even impossible, but we should not resign ourselves to this fate. Counterterrorism effectiveness measurement is a daunting challenge that requires more focused and better research, if only because it would enhance the legitimacy of policy measures that severely impact on citizens' lives. Breaking counterterrorism down into its separate components might help us meet this challenge.

See also: **Volume 1, Part VI:** Combating Terrorism: A New Way Forward; Counterterrorism Research: Current Efforts and Future Challenges; Understanding Foreign Cultures

REFERENCES

Alexander, Y. "Introduction." In *Combating Terrorism: Strategies of Ten Countries,* edited by Yonah Alexander, 1–23. Ann Arbor: University of Michigan Press, 2002.

Barros, C. P. "An Intervention Analysis of Terrorism: The Spanish ETA Case." *Defence and Peace Economics* 14, no. 6 (2003): 401–12.

Bergen, P., and P. Cruickshank. "The Unraveling: The Jihadist Revolt against Bin Laden." *New Republic,* June 11, 2008. http://www.tnr.com/article/the-unraveling.

Byman, D. "Scoring the War on Terror." *National Interest* 72 (2003): 75–84.

Cronin, A. K. *How Terrorism Ends: Understanding the Decline and Demise of Terrorist Campaigns.* Princeton, NJ: Princeton University Press, 2009.

Frisch, H. "Motivation or Capabilities? Israeli Counterterrorism against Palestinian Suicide Bombings and Violence." *Journal of Strategic Studies* 29, no. 5 (2006): 843–69.

LaFree, G. *Efficacy of Counterterrorism Approaches: Examining Northern Ireland.* START Research Brief, 2006. http://www.start.umd.edu/start/publications/research_briefs/20061017_lafree.pdf.

Lum, C., L. W. Kennedy, and A. Sherley. "Are Counter-terrorism Strategies Effective? The Results of the Campbell Systematic Review on Counter-terrorism Evaluation Research." *Journal of Experimental Criminology* 2, no. 4 (2006): 489–516.

Makinen, G. *The Economic Effects of 9/11: A Retrospective Assessment.* Report for Congress. Washington, DC: Congressional Research Service, 2002.

Morag, N. "Measuring Success in Coping with Terrorism: The Israeli Case." *Studies in Conflict and Terrorism* 28, no. 4 (2005): 307–20.

Silke, A. "The Psychological Impact of Terrorism: Lessons from the UK Experience." In *Meeting the Challenges of Global Terrorism: Prevention, Control, and Recovery,* 189–202. Lanham, MD: Lexington Books, 2003.

Taher, Abul. "Al-Qaeda: The Cracks Begin to Show." *Times* (London), June 8, 2008.

Zussman, A., and N. Zussman. "Assassinations: Evaluating the Effectiveness of an Israeli Counterterrorism Policy Using Stock Market Data." *Journal of Economic Perspectives* 20, no. 2 (2006): 193–206.

Preemptive Counterterrorism: The Need for a Global Integrated Approach

Karunya Jayasena

There is a vital need for a global integrated approach to combating terrorism. The emerging threat of terrorism has required researchers, security officials, and policymakers to study and adopt nonconventional strategies and policies. We are in need of a global instrument that will develop and widen national, regional, and international collective efforts to counter terrorism. The common global integrated approach to fight terrorism should send a clear message that terrorism is intolerable in all its forms and manifestations. This requires us to increase our effectiveness in decision making and also in the development of concrete strategies to prevent and combat terrorism. The most effective form of preemptive counterterrorism is that which deals with the causes of terrorism and thus prevents potential terrorist acts.

DEVELOPING A CLEAR DEFINITION OF TERRORISM

The first step to a global integrated approach requires a clear definition of terrorism. "A precise, well-targeted counterterrorism strategy can only be developed if we have a *clear concept* of terrorism, i.e. when we know what it is we have to prepare ourselves to fight against" (Koechler 2002, 3). Currently, there is no universal consensus on how to define terrorism. Moreover, the lack of a clear definition is common among U.S. federal, state, and local agencies; the media; academics; policymakers; and the general public. Burgess (2003, 2) states that it is important to understand that often "a uniform definition of terrorism will not even exist across the various concerned agencies of a given country." Although there is no consensus and the concept is neither well understood nor accurately depicted, it is essential to recognize the evolution of this phenomenon. It is important to understand the difference between old and new terrorism because terrorism is a phenomenon that is grounded in an evolving historical context. To create a new social science definition, academics must recognize fundamental and recurring factors; the ways in which world systems are connected to national politics; new motives, adversaries, and rationales; and the social pressure to end terrorism.

For social scientists, defining terrorism is not merely a theoretical issue. To create a new social science definition of terrorism, academics should take the following suggestions into consideration. First, the contemporary social science definitions of terrorism must emphasize fundamental factors that recur across various forms of terrorism and attempt to understand it as a collective social phenomenon. Tilly (2004, 8) believes the "social science definitions of terrorism must exhibit some degree of causal coherence." Second, they should investigate the interconnectedness between world systems and national politics as causes for this mass violence. Consequently, we must change the way we think about terrorism, modifying our definitions as terrorism evolves. In doing so, it is important to recognize the moral implications of the concept, its history, typologies, and sociopolitical explanations, as well as counterterrorism policies.

Third, the new definitions should also consider new motives, adversaries, and rationales; however, we must not confuse the situation any further by integrating the concept with other forms of violence. Terrorism should not be confused with other types of political violence such as civil war, assassinations, or guerrilla warfare. Crenshaw (1995, 6) states, "Terrorism is an ambiguous variable not easily measured or quantified, in part because there are multiple forms of terrorism, and they are easily confused with other styles of violence." The underlying motives of terrorism run much deeper than any other forms of political violence. There is a considerable amount of social and psychological warfare behind the new terrorism. Finally, any new definitions should also recognize social pressure to stop such action. Turk (1982, 2) notes that we must send a clear message that "regarding issues of justification, it is concluded that terrorism and terror are unjustifiable" in all their forms and manifestations. Therefore, social scientists can facilitate the reduction of terrorism by developing a clear and precise definition, one that will help intelligence agents to prevent and combat terrorism through a wide array of proactive measures including increasing state capacity to counter terrorist threats.

CREATING A COMPREHENSIVE SOCIAL SCIENCE TERRORISM DATABASE

The second step to a global integrated approach requires us to develop and enhance existing methodologies. The method herein suggests a quantitative and qualitative database that includes characteristics explaining both successful and unsuccessful perpetrators and their social behaviors. The database can also store a wide array of court case information and interview transcripts, as well as newspaper and magazine articles related to the topic. It should be designed to store important chronological information from federal, state, and local law enforcement authorities, joint terrorism task forces, and foreign terrorist-tracking task forces in different countries. This database should be created to further the study of various types of micro- and macrolevel motivations—personal, tactical, political, religious, nationalist, sociological, psychological, economic, or collective—that play a role in an individual's decision to become a terrorist. It can be designed to facilitate an understanding of terrorist acts committed by men and women at both the individual level and the collective level. This database can be a significant instrument that helps a government affected by terrorism to develop strategies to deter and prevent all forms of future terrorist attacks at the state, regional, and international levels.

A new approach requires an examination of social circumstances and analyses of systematic data on male and female terrorists that demonstrates the social variables that provide an understanding of individual pathways to terrorism. We must also examine the social environment and social interaction of terrorists and question the micro/macro social forces or social events that mold them as individuals and shape their deviant behaviors. Information gathered on perpetrator demographics, victim details, and incident details should be used as basic guiding tools to combat this international problem.. The social scientific response mechanisms to combat terrorism may vary from region to region. Analysts from various fields must continuously work to identify new methods to combat terrorists and their operative cells. Researchers and intelligence agents should try not to keep the data to themselves but work collaboratively to find strategies to combat radicalization and potential recruitment for terrorism.

Policymakers should have access to the database at the cross-cultural level. This could provide a relevant comparison of terrorist attacks committed by both men and women across the globe. Additionally, the suggested methodology can be used by researchers to collect and maintain data on perpetrators, incident details, and victim details of previous terrorist attacks. When analyzing these data, researchers must focus on the individual interlocking motives of potential terrorists—religious, personal, political, sociocultural, and/or psychological predispositions that may drive individuals to commit acts of terrorism. Besides rigorous, reliable, and valid methods, one additional avenue is to develop theories that help demonstrate pathways to terrorism and to use those theories to identify global integrated strategies to capture terrorists and deter or prevent terrorism. This will not only help to identify individuals that terrorist organizations are most likely to recruit but will also help to prevent potential terrorist candidates from becoming terrorists.

ADDRESSING CONDITIONS FAVORABLE
TO THE SPREAD OF TERRORISM

The third step to a global integrated approach requires policymakers to address conditions that are favorable to the spread of terrorism. "This set of actions is intended to solve issues such as prolonged unresolved conflicts, dehumanization of victims of terrorism and the breach of human rights. Ethnic, national and religious discrimination, political exclusion, socio-economic marginalization, and lack of good governance can all lead to the spread of terrorism" (Cappe 2007, 3). A definite commitment should be made by world leaders and policymakers, individually and collectively, to strengthen existing laws at the local and national levels and help fortify the counterterrorism capabilities of civilian law enforcement and security officials.

Policymakers should pay special attention to the growth in the number of females who are involved in suicide terrorism, especially since women and girls are seen as a significant tactical component of terrorist activity. It is critical for policymakers to create policies that are more supportive of women who have experienced domestic abuse, rape crises, loss of loved ones, and violence because these social factors may make women become more vulnerable candidates for suicide terrorism. Effective implementation of policies that promote gender equality and eliminate gender discrimination will be necessary in addition to the implementation of strategies to counter terrorism on the national and regional levels.

National leaders and policymakers must also pay attention to the sociocultural environment in which the problem of terrorism arises. To build strong intergovernmental relationships policymakers should encourage community-based organizations and nongovernmental organizations to engage in assisting law enforcement organizations in implementing bilateral counterterrorism strategies within their local communities. These organizations should interact with law enforcement task forces on a regular basis, in order to receive updates on the nature and extent of the particular types of terrorist attacks being conducted in their region. Statistical data can be obtained from local researchers who use the suggested social science database as a guiding tool to maintain systematic incident details on terrorist attacks. With the help of intelligence agents these organizations can have analysts seeking to collect data on previous attacks. Therefore, it is important for policymakers to directly interact and integrate with researchers, intelligence agents, law enforcement officers, and civilians.

In addition to voicing a strong disapproval of terrorism, policymakers need to initiate efforts designed to resist any form of violent extremism. These efforts will require that policymakers and local government officials have the support of local law enforcement as well as support from nongovernmental organizations in combating terrorism. They must ask the international community for assistance and expand the concept of regional cooperation to help strengthen the country's efforts to capture and prosecute terrorists. The public should be educated about how innocent civilians can be targeted by terrorist organizations to advance their strategic goals. This would send a clear message that terrorism is unjustifiable in all circumstances. Together, they can create strategies to help both direct and indirect victims of terrorism and offer victims of terrorist acts support to cope with their personal losses of loved ones and property.

PROTECTING HUMAN RIGHTS

Policies to combat terrorism must be taken into consideration under the umbrella of international humanitarian laws, refugee laws, and human rights laws (United Nations General Assembly 2005). There should be a mutual agreement among researchers, counterterrorism agents, law enforcement officials, and policymakers to strengthen capacity and responses to terrorist threats. This will require a global coordinated strategy that will enhance the efficiency of the measures applied to the terrorism threat. The global integrated approach should promote interfaith understanding and endorse a culture of peace and tolerance among various ethnic groups. The primary responsibility of the government is to restore national peace and security and ensure human rights. The government must build strong intercultural relationships by protecting the rights and welfare of children in the nation-state who are affected by terrorism. In addition to imposing laws that give equal rights, the government should maintain up-to-date information about violations of human rights, including acts of gender-based violence.

CONCLUSION

Providing equal social, economic, and cultural rights for all is a key component in combating the terrorist threat. This would allow individuals to live with dignity and hope and have a voice in the government decision-making process. Often, in countries experiencing conflict, people are stripped of their human rights, alienated, and subjugated to various negative social circumstances. This is a potential breeding ground and recruitment haven for terrorist prospects and their sponsors. Therefore, in addition to regional corporation with neighboring countries, good governance, legitimacy, and the rule of law, the global integrated approach to countering terrorism must focus on the underlying social conditions that terrorists exploit to persuade aggrieved populations to become sympathizers with, supporters of, and ultimately active participants in terrorist groups.

REFERENCES

Burgess, Mark. "Terrorism: The Problems of Definition." Center for Defense Information. August 1, 2003. http://www.cdi.org/program/document.cfm?DocumentID=1564&from_page=./index.cfm.

Cappe, Francesco. "Security Governance Counter Terrorism Cluster UNICRI." The United Nations Counter-Terrorism Strategy, No. 105 (Suppl.) December 2007. http://www.vatican.va/roman_curia/pontifical_councils/migrants/pom2007_105-suppl/rc_pc_migrants_pom105-suppl_united-nations-cappe.html.

Crenshaw, Martha. "The Debate over 'New' vs. 'Old' Terrorism." Presented at the Annual Meeting of the American Political Science Association, Chicago, IL, August 30–September 2, 2007. http://start.umd.edu/start/publications/New_vs_Old_Terrorism.pdf.

Koechler, Hans. "Terrorism and Counter-Terrorism: Towards a Comprehensive Approach." Lecture delivered at the invitation of the National Police Commission of the Philippines. Camp Crame, Quezon City, Philippines, International Progress Organization (Online Papers). March 12, 2002. http://i-p-o.org/koechler-terrorism-counterterrorism-NAPOLCOM-Mar2002.pdf.

Tilly, Charles. "Terror, Terrorism, and Terrorists." Sociological Theory 22 (2004): 4–13.

Turk, Austin T. Political Criminality: The Defiance and Defense of Authority. Los Angeles: Sage, 1982.

United Nations General Assembly. "World Summit Outcome Report." September 15, 2005. http://www.un-ngls.org/orf/un-summit-FINAL-DOC.pdf.

Protecting Critical Infrastructure: Government/ Private Sector Alliance

Brian Houghton

Prior to the September 11, 2001, attacks, terrorists had targeted elements of infrastructure that were critical to the public. Indeed, the September 11 attacks themselves targeted two sectors of critical infrastructure: government continuity (the Pentagon) and the financial sector (the World Trade Center). Terrorists often seek to exploit vulnerabilities, and our reliance on infrastructure would have a multiplying effect on an otherwise limited attack. For example, a simple car bomb might kill dozens of people and garner major media attention; however, that same car bomb might also be used to target a unique power substation, the loss of which could cause a blackout in a city for weeks. The potential for greater damage to the public and/or government has always been tantalizing to terrorist organizations. Protecting these elements of critical infrastructure has been and continues to be a challenge to governments at all levels and demands the cooperation of the public and private sectors.

CRITICAL INFRASTRUCTURE

When we speak of *critical infrastructure*, the following areas are identified by the federal government, as in the current National Infrastructure Protection Plan: food and water systems, agriculture, health care systems, emergency services, information technology, communications, banking and finance, energy, transportation, the chemical and defense industries, postal and shipping entities, and national monuments and icons. The vast majority of the critical infrastructure that we rely on is privately owned and operated. The federal government estimates private control of infrastructure at 85 percent. This presents a unique challenge for the government, since the public expects protection from terrorism and relies on critical infrastructure to maintain their way of life, yet the government has little to no control over the systems that need to be protected. To further exacerbate the challenge, the private sector often has contradicting priorities, demanding to maintain and guard its proprietary information, while the government desires to gain more knowledge of the systems that it is mandated to protect. Even though the owners of critical infrastructure and key resources typically understand the need for protection and the importance of information sharing to assist government, their understandable inclination is to keep trade secrets, not to divulge them. Security clearances do not necessarily protect businesses' proprietary information the same way as they do national security intelligence, and the private sector has a widespread concern that the government will divulge trade secrets and otherwise compromise sensitive information.

While the threat against critical infrastructure has existed from the beginning of the modern age of terrorism, with terrorists attacking transportation, communications, energy pipelines, and other infrastructure targets, it was in the 1990s that awareness of the problem became more prevalent. Two phenomena led to this increased awareness: the rise of the Internet and major attacks on critical infrastructure. In the early 1990s the Internet went from being a tool of academia and the government to becoming integrated into many aspects of daily life. Along with the rise of the Internet came the vulnerability of this new communications medium to threats from viruses, Trojan horses, hacking, and cyberattacks.

In the same period major terrorist attacks around the world disrupted or threatened critical infrastructure. In 1993, a terrorist cell led by Ramzi Yousef attacked the World Trade Center in New York City, planting a car bomb in the North Tower's basement parking garage; the terrorists hoped to topple that structure into the South Tower. Fortunately, the bomb's effectiveness was limited; six people were killed. However, over 1,000 others were injured, mainly suffering from smoke inhalation. The second terrorist event was the March 1995 Aum Shinrikyo sarin gas attack on the subway system in Tokyo, Japan. This was one of the first terrorist attacks involving chemical weapons, sparking concerns worldwide of terrorists moving away from conventional weapons to weapons of mass destruction. In Japan 12 commuters were killed in the attack, and several thousand were injured or negatively affected by the attack. A month later the largest terrorist attack on U.S. soil up to that time took place in Oklahoma City when Timothy McVeigh detonated a powerful truck bomb, destroying the Alfred P. Murrah Federal Building. In that attack 168 people were killed, including 19 children. These three attacks, the first on the financial sector, the second on transportation, and the third on a government facility, brought to the forefront the potential impact of terrorism on critical infrastructure. A year later, President Clinton established the President's Commission on Critical Infrastructure Protection, better known as the Marsh Commission, to examine this new threat.

EFFORTS TO PROTECT CRITICAL INFRASTRUCTURE

The Marsh Commission acknowledged the growing dependence on critical infrastructure and the fact that either conventional terrorist weapons or cyberattacks could have debilitating effects on the infrastructure if targeted correctly. Recognizing the lack of both public awareness and a national focus on this, the commission recommended to the president a process of education and the start of cooperation and information sharing between industry and the government. As a result of these recommendations President Clinton signed Presidential Decision Directive 63 (PDD-63) in 1998, formally initiating the federal government's organization to protect critical infrastructure. In PDD-63 President Clinton authorized the creation of the National Infrastructure Protection Center (NIPC) within the Federal Bureau of Investigation (FBI) and specified lead agencies from the executive branch to oversee the various infrastructure sectors (e.g., the Environmental Protection Agency for the water supply, the Department of Energy for oil and gas production, and the Federal Emergency Management Agency for the continuity of government services). PDD-63 also created a National Infrastructure Assurance Council comprised of state and local government leaders and infrastructure providers to advise the president on critical infrastructure protection (CIP), as well as to promote cooperation among the private owners of infrastructure. Another institution created by PDD-63 was the Information Sharing and Analysis Center, which formally started the passing of information to and from the infrastructure providers to enhance security. The FBI also started its InfraGard program to work with private industry and other private partners in sharing information.

During the early years of CIP efforts, through the end of the Clinton presidency, the government entities tasked to overcome the challenges of information sharing and CIP across private industry enjoyed nominal success. Based on the recommendation of the Marsh Commission to provide education, the media, academia, and government agencies started to discuss the issues of CIP in various formats. However, organizations whose mission, according to PDD-63, was to safeguard critical infrastructure, such as the FBI's NIPC, did little but coordinate horizontally across the federal government with the other lead agencies, even though private industry controlled the vast majority of the nation's infrastructure. The NIPC was tasked to assist in the protection of all of the various sectors of critical infrastructure, but in practice it focused on computer investigations, neglecting the sectors (transportation, government continuity, and finance) that had been attacked just a few years prior and that had inspired the emphasis on CIP in the first place. This highlights another challenge in CIP, that of government pursuing quick victories and pet projects rather than tackling the more objectively vital aspects of the problem.

After the September 11, 2001, attacks and the subsequent creation of the Department of Homeland Security (DHS), President George W. Bush authorized Homeland Security Presidential Directive 7 (HSPD-7), which replaced PDD-63 and placed CIP in the hands of the new department. The new directive added the concept of key resources to critical infrastructure and designated 17 critical infrastructure and key resources (CIKR) sectors. The new presidential directive tasked DHS with formulating a national plan to help organize and focus the government's efforts. The National

Infrastructure Protection Plan defines the collaborative roles and responsibilities of both the government and the private sector in the task of CIKR protection, encouraging more of a public-private partnership, and reflects a risk management approach—focusing on threats, vulnerabilities, and consequences.

CONCLUSION

Currently CIP is better organized and more secure than it was 15 years ago. While the present situation is not perfect, and challenges in information sharing and the lack of full participation among the key sectors persist, there have been many real improvements. For example, DHS provides site-assistance visits in which DHS specialists conduct free vulnerability assessments of CIKR sites, assisting private industry in understanding their weaknesses and how to better protect their facilities. The department also reaches out internationally to ensure that foreign infrastructure on which the United States depends is also protected. The challenges of protecting critical infrastructure will remain for the foreseeable future. The vast majority of the infrastructure will continue to lie in the hands of the private sector. However, the government is sharing information and providing advice and other services to industry to help ensure that the vital services and facilities on which the nation relies are as safe as possible in the face of evolving terrorist and other threats.

See also: **Volume 1, Part III:** Terrorism, Counterterrorism, and the Internet. **Part VI:** Energy-Related Counterterrorism; Countering Agroenvironmental Terrorism; Public Support and Education Campaigns

REFERENCES

Bush, George W. Homeland Security Presidential Directive 7. Washington, DC: White House, 2003.

Clinton, William J. Presidential Decision Directive 63. Washington, DC: White House, 1998.

Haimes, Yacov Y., and Thomas Longstaff. "The Role of *Risk Analysis* in the Protection of Critical Infrastructures against Terrorism." *Risk Analysis* 22, no. 3 (2002): 439–44.

InfraGard. "InfraGard: A Collaboration for Infrastructure Protection." n.d. http://www.infragard.net.

President's Commission on Critical Infrastructure Protection. "Critical Foundations: Protecting America's Infrastructures." October 1997. http://www.fas.org/sgp/library/pccip.pdf.

U.S. Department of Homeland Security. "National Infrastructure Protection Plan." 2009. http://www.dhs.gov/xlibrary/assets/NIPP_Plan.pdf.

Psychological Profiling of Terrorists

Joshua Sinai

The psychological causes of terrorism and the profiling of the operatives who commit acts of terrorism have been extensively studied by psychologists and psychiatrists since the early 1970s, when terrorism became a significant international threat. The psychological profiling of terrorists involves gathering and integrating data about factors such as their psychological health based on their motives, behaviors, or social circumstances, such as family backgrounds, level of education, professional attainment, or level of religiosity, in an attempt to understand how certain individuals may be more likely than others to turn to terrorist violence, whether individually (commonly known as "lone wolves") or, more commonly, as part of a group, to achieve their political, religious, economic, or other types of objectives. For the purposes of this article, both the psychological and psychiatric (including forensic psychiatric) profiling of terrorists is referred to as *psychological profiling*.

ASSESSING PSYCHOLOGICAL TRAITS

Such a profiling task is quite difficult, since most terrorists are not available for psychoanalytic interviews or testing because of the covert and criminal nature of their activities, which are subject to government countermeasures ranging from legal prosecution to military action. Nevertheless, an extensive body of knowledge has been produced to shed light on their psychological profiles, based either on interviews with those who have been incarcerated, their associates, and others who may have disengaged from terrorism, or on fieldwork conducted in their communities to obtain a general sense of their personalities.

At the beginning of any examination intending to determine the psychological profile of a terrorist or an individual who may be heading in that direction, it is important to consider the different roles that individuals perform in a terrorist group, ranging from those in leadership positions to the lower-echelon members of a combat team. Individuals in the top echelons that establish, lead, or drive a terrorist group in certain directions, or the ones directly below them (such as ideologues, operational planners, recruiters, dispatchers who send operatives on their missions, those who manage logistics or financing, and even those who become a group's webmaster), are likely to possess different psychological traits than those who are chosen for deployment in warfare-type operations to sacrifice themselves on behalf of their group's cause.

INDUCTIVE AND DEDUCTIVE METHODS

Inductive profiling involves assuming that when a terrorist commits an act of violence, he or she is likely to exhibit a similar background and motive to others who have committed similar acts. The inductive method is useful for investigators and analysts in developing a psychological profile of an individual of concern, whether an actual terrorist or someone who may be in the process of transitioning into violent extremism, because it is a means to apply statistical data generated by academic research about past cases of a similar nature. At the beginning of the investigative process, isolated facts about an individual of concern will be combined to form a premise or hypothesis about that individual's likely psychological profile and expected future violent behavior and activities. Based on the statistical probabilities derived from previous cases, the individual who may be exhibiting such traits can now be considered to probably fit or not fit certain types of psychological profiles or expected sets of worrisome behaviors.

It is important, however, to consider that such statistical probabilities may have a built-in margin for error, which might limit their validity. Another criticism of the inductive method is that in some cases where it has been used, such as to draw generalizations about Palestinians who may be inclined to become suicide bombers, some of the researchers considered their generalizations statistically valid based on only a few cases. Finally, generalizations about the psychological profiles of Palestinian suicide bombers, even if valid for those cases, may not hold for individuals in other societies who might be drawn into becoming al-Qaeda– or Taliban-type suicide bombers.

In the deductive method, generalizations and statistical averages are avoided, with an investigator's and an analyst's own logic and reasoning applied to a given case. The conclusions reached about that subject's psychological profile are based directly on the collection and interpretation of evidence in that case, including adapting findings based on new evidence that might surface at a later time. This is also considered a type of evidence-based reasoning, because it is driven by the evidence about that subject's mindset and behavior, not by generalizations about what those who may have become terrorists in other cases are usually like psychologically or what they are likely to do.

Nevertheless, even such deductive profiling must rely to some degree on induction because induction is the beginning of the analysis about a subject under investigation and is necessary in the formation of a deductively valid argument about where such a subject may be heading, for instance, from undergoing initial radicalization to joining a terrorist group and committing violent actions on its behalf. These two types of methodologies can then be applied to profiling an individual, for example, determining whether he or she might be psychologically inclined to become a conventional terrorist (e.g., when the operative is intended to escape from the scene of the operation) or a suicide terrorist.

PSYCHOLOGICAL PREDISPOSITIONS

Both types of terrorist warfare require certain psychological predispositions on the part of their operatives who commit themselves to conducting such operations. A suicide attack is a premeditated operation in which the attacker detonates an explosive intentionally to kill himself (or herself) in order to kill a lot of people, spread fear and panic, and coerce an adversary government to concede to their demands. The crucial element is that the individuals who embark on such an operation understand that no escape from the scene of the incident is possible for them; for those who are religiously motivated, they are led to believe they will be resurrected in an afterlife and ascend to a heavenly paradise. This differs from conventional terrorism, where although the attacker is aware that his or her death is likely, he or she might still be able to escape from the scene of the incident to resume warfare later on.

It is also crucial to note that it is not only an operative's psychological predisposition that is at play here but an interplay between such operatives and the groups that transform such susceptible individuals into becoming conventional or suicide terrorists by radicalizing, recruiting, indoctrinating, and training them to conduct their operations. Some of these group-directed activities may take place on the ground or in cyberspace (i.e., the Internet).

It is not only organized terrorist groups that play a role in recruiting susceptible individuals to join their cause; a new phenomenon in Western Europe and North America is what are termed "self-starter, homegrown" violent extremists with relatively limited ties to their overseas "parent" group, such as an al-Qaeda group that might be based in Pakistan or Yemen. Based on the findings of Marc Sageman (2008), a forensic psychiatrist, these self-starter groups of friends or relatives—generally what is referred to as a "bunch of guys"—become increasingly radicalized on their own (although also influenced by frequenting extremist websites), with the result that these groups decide to take risky actions in the form of a terrorist operation, with the risks involved seeming less "frightening" because they are shared by the group (Kershaw 2010).

It is also important to note that the psychological predispositions discussed in the preceding are not sufficient by themselves to drive an individual into committing terrorist violence. Grievances against their adversaries, whether legitimate or perceived, are important drivers in individuals' (and groups') engagement in terrorist violence. Moreover, in the case of suicide terrorism, an added factor in motivating susceptible individuals to embark on such missions is their society's promotion of a cult of death through martyrdom operations, which is reinforced through indoctrination and hate propaganda in extremist religious houses of worship, schools, media, and even popular music.

Can suicide terrorists be profiled? Yes, according to Israeli psychologist and terrorism expert Ariel Merari, who finds, based on the deductive research conducted by his team (although, he admits, based on a relatively small sample of Palestinian operatives who were interviewed while incarcerated in Israeli prisons) and his own inductive reasoning, that those who are willing to kill themselves possess unique personality characteristics. In general, he writes, they are "introverted, loners, quiet, non-gregarious, and inhibited" as well as "socially marginal and downgraded by the people around them" (Merari 2010, 112–20). Becoming a martyr, he believes, provides such vulnerable individuals "an opportunity to soar to importance and fame" within their communities (Merari 2010, 120).

Unlike the susceptible suicide bombers they exploit, a terrorist group's operational managers, according to Merari, tend to be (relatively speaking) "well adjusted" and, most tellingly, are "unwilling to carry out a suicide attack themselves" (2010, 151–52). Israeli terrorism expert Anat Berko (also a former member of Merari's team) adds that a group's dispatchers have no compunction about sending others to certain death by picking a "sad guy . . . social nonentities [who lack] status but who might get recognition by dying" (Berko 2009, 7). Confirming this assessment, I know of no instances in which leaders of terrorist groups, whether Palestinian, al-Qaeda, Chechen, or others, have sacrificed either themselves or any of their children on suicide martyrdom missions. In a near exception, Hezbollah leader Hassan Nasrallah's 18-year-old son, Hadi Nasrallah, was a member of a Hezbollah armed unit, but he died in September 1997 while defending against an Israeli ambush in Lebanon, not on a martyrdom operation.

Finally, even if they had a choice, not all those deemed susceptible would embark on a suicide mission. For example, in the March 2004 bombing of trains in Madrid, which killed 191, the attacking cell did not intentionally blow themselves up at the time—they did so only later as a group effort when they were about to be captured. Similarly, Times Square bomber Faisal Shahzad attempted to escape from the scene in early May 2010, while Major Nidal Hasan apparently did not try to kill himself as a "martyr" during his shooting rampage at Fort Hood, Texas, in November 2009.

CONCLUSION

The motivation to become a terrorist results from a complex interaction between personal psychological inclinations and situational circumstances. In developing a psychological profile about an individual under concern, therefore, it is crucial to note that a single psychological trait is not sufficient by itself but may yield "red flags" that the person may be turning to terrorist activities once such traits begin to combine with other factors, especially when the person begins to associate with other individuals and groups with a nexus to terrorism.

See also: **Volume 1, Part III:** Ideology That Spawns Islamist Militancy; Multidisciplinary Approach to Combating Terrorism; Psychological Operations. **Part VI:** Biometrics Technology; Data Mining

REFERENCES

Berko, Anat. *The Path to Paradise: The Inner World of Suicide Bombers and Their Dispatchers.* Washington, DC: Potomac Books, 2009.

Bull, Ray, Claire Cooke, Ruth Hatcher, Jessica Woodhams, C. Bilby, and T. Grant. *Criminal Psychology: A Beginner's Guide.* Oxford: Oneworld, 2006.

Canter, David, and Donna Youngs. *Investigative Psychology: Offender Profiling and the Analysis of Criminal Action.* West Sussex, UK: John Wiley, 2010.

Dean, Geoff. "Criminal Profiling in a Terrorism Context." In *Criminal Profiling: International Theory, Research, and Practice,* edited by Richard N. Kocsis, 169–88. Totowa, NJ: Humana, 2010.

Kershaw, Sarah. "The Terrorist Mind: An Update." *New York Times,* January 9, 2010.

Livingstone Smith, David. *Why We Demean, Enslave, and Exterminate Others.* New York: St. Martin's, 2010.

Merari, Ariel. *Driven to Death: Psychological and Social Aspects of Suicide Terrorism.* New York: Oxford University Press, 2010.

Petherick, Wayne. *Criminal Profile into the Mind of the Killer.* London: Modern Books, 2005.

Sageman, Marc. *Leaderless Jihad.* Philadelphia: University of Pennsylvania Press, 2008.

Sinai, Joshua. *"The Fundamentalist Mindset: Psychological Perspectives on Religion, Violence and History"* [book review]. *Washington Times,* May 13, 2010.

Strozier, Charles B, David M. Terman, James W. Jones, and Katherine A. Boyd, eds. *The Fundamentalist Mindset: Psychological Perspectives on Religion, Violence and History.* New York: Oxford University Press, 2010.

Tobena, Adolf. "Individual Factors in Suicide Terrorism." *Science,* April 2, 2004, 47.

Public Support and Education Campaigns

John Preston and Magdalini Kolokitha

Terrorism has changed significantly from the Cold War to the post–Cold War era. This has also changed the nature of public support and education campaigns for counterterrorism. Historical changes have brought about a tension between education for counterterrorism at the level of international organizations (such as the United Nations) and education at the national level. At the level of international organizations, public support and education for counterterrorism are seen within a framework of education concerning human rights. At a national level, however, public support and education for counterterrorism are sometimes seen to be in conflict with broad human rights issues. A framework for the analysis of public counterterrorism education and public support campaigns that frames them in terms of pedagogy (instructional modalities) is also addressed.

THE CHANGING NATURE OF PUBLIC SUPPORT AND EDUCATION CAMPAIGNS

During the Cold War countering terrorism focused primarily on external national threats by states and particularly on the potential use of nuclear and biological weapons for military threats based on ideological and political differences between the liberal Western and the Socialist/Communist Eastern bloc. During this period public education in Europe and the United States was based on preparedness for a potential nuclear attack. Although preparedness efforts made use of national education systems, counterterrorism was, for the most part, not a mass education and public information concern. However, with the end of the Cold War signaled by the economic collapse of the Soviet Union and the fall of the Berlin Wall in 1989, the threat of terrorism, and the response to it, changed. Since 2001, terrorism has increasingly spawned discourses over ethnic, cultural, and, most important, religious struggles. Simultaneously, public support and education campaigns for counterterrorism efforts have been broadened to include issues related to organized crime, drug trafficking, and illegal immigration (Crelinsten 1998). The events of 9/11 in the United States and 7/7 in the United Kingdom have heightened government and public concern with respect to the terrorism issue and have increasingly focused counterterrorism campaigns in terms of internal threats to citizens of a state. A terrorist action is no longer identified as an external and foreign threat but rather a potential domestic-based threat requiring the awareness, compliance, and support of the public. The changes in threat and symmetry of threat have also changed the nature of public support and education campaigns for counterterrorism.

In relation to public education, for example, the United Nations via the United Nations Educational, Scientific and Cultural Organization (UNESCO) and other multilateral organizations influencing education, such as the Organization of Economic Cooperation and Development and the World Bank, have recently started focusing on ideas of multiculturalism to avoid ethnic, cultural, and religious segregation that might lead to extremism. This emphasizes a broad-based educational initiative around tolerance and acceptance of multiculturalism as an approach to prevent terrorism. Gearon (2009, 2010) observes that there is a tension between international and national conceptions of counterterrorism education. For example, there is a contrast between the United Nations citizenship and human rights education programs and the *Prevent* Agenda for counterterrorism education in the United Kingdom. While the United Nations approach focuses on conceptions of human rights, *Prevent* is explicitly designed to utilize educators in religious and citizenship education in the war on extremism and citizens in the identification and reporting of terrorist activities. Educators are also required to observe and report signs of extremism or radicalization. The increased surveillance measures implicit in public education campaigns, such as *Prevent*, sometimes request the abandonment or restriction of civic liberties.

The balance between public support for counterterrorism and civil liberties has been highly questioned and criticized. As Crelinsten (1998, 15) suggests, "The maintenance of public trust and confidence in government, achieved primarily by the fostering and nurturing of an informed public, is undermined by the trend towards a surveillance society that selectively targets certain groups deemed to be outsiders, thereby creating social divisions, moral panics and emotional swells of fear and loathing that hinders information flow and hampers public education." For example, following the events of the 7/7 attack on London's transport network in 2005, the counterterrorism campaigns on public transport attempted to balance public security and private civic liberties on the one hand and public policing and private security on the other. It is acknowledged that the 7/7 attack altered the U.K. rail network's approach to counterterrorism from passivity to an investment in and extended utilization of surveillance through the installation of close-circuit surveillance on the transport system alongside an extensive campaign of public education. The resulting guidance from the government focused on public education and information campaigns that enlisted members of the public as agents of surveillance. We can therefore see that public education for counterterrorism is increasingly politically charged with implications for human rights. Inevitably this will lead to tensions between broad-based multicultural education as a lever to counterterrorism (such as advocated by the United Nations) and more pragmatic and overt counterterrorism education measures (as advocated by the *Prevent* strategy in the United Kingdom).

FRAMING PUBLIC INFORMATION AND EDUCATION CAMPAIGNS FOR COUNTERTERRORISM

Whatever the political orientation of counterterrorism initiatives it is possible to conceptualize counterterrorist educational campaigns in terms of their employment of pedagogy. Since the early days of the Cold War, public education for counterterrorism has frequently made use of pedagogical strategies (or more often andragogical strategies, as they are most frequently aimed at adults; Brown 1988). Counterterrorism, in terms of public support and education, can be considered to be pedagogical in three ways.

First, pedagogical (or instructional) media that are used to enable citizens to prepare and respond to terrorist events can include leaflets, websites, films, reconstructions, alerting mechanisms, or warning signs. The use of a range of media for pedagogical devices is not new, and actually a wider range of elaborated media was used for counterterrorism during the early days of the Cold War. For example, films, records, mobile displays, family learning activities, games, and other popular cultural forms were used in the 1950s–1980s as opposed to the mainly text/web-based information currently in use today (McEnaney 2000).

Second, some of these pedagogical techniques that can be employed in counterterrorism might include didactic/nondidactic methods of instruction, formal/informal learning, or individual/family/community learning. These techniques will have different consequences for affect, behavior, and cognition. Rarely are pedagogical modalities solely didactic, and they can rely on active forms of learning. These techniques may be instructive through dramaturgical devices. For Davis (2007), rehearsal and display of counterterrorism is an important pedagogical device. For Preston (2009), real or fictive scenarios of terrorist attacks would, in themselves, be forms of public pedagogy (Sandlin, Schultz, and Burdick 2010): activity in the public sphere that educates the public about the correct (or incorrect) ways to respond. In terms of counterterrorism this means that terrorist scenarios (for example, the televised account of an attack on public transport) can be instructive to citizens in alternative ways to a didactic account. Related to this, Ahmed (2007, 141) considers that these dramaturgical pedagogies can carry covert messages about security procedures that were not necessarily the intention of the actors. There is, therefore, a tension between innovative pedagogical modalities in counterterrorism education and the potential loss of authorship this entails for the authorities.

CONCLUSION

Finally, a pedagogical subjectivity is created through the use of different forms of pedagogy for counterterrorism. By *pedagogical subjectivity*, we mean the ways in which the subject is defined as a "learner" of counterterrorism strategies. In contemporary preparedness initiatives, rather than individuals being passive learners, there is a desire for superreflexivity where individuals are made more aware of their own presence in real environments as a subject of security. Preparedness hence becomes a "dense" form of pedagogy as instruction through visualization and dramatization saturates our daily lives. Correspondingly, companies such as Lockheed-Martin offer "full-spectrum" preparedness products allowing for comprehensive coverage of emergencies.

See also: **Volume 1, Part III:** Combating Terrorist Recruitment, Propaganda, and Radicalization Campaigns; International Law, Human Rights, and Counterterrorism; International Media: Critical Tool in the Battle against Terrorism; Multidisciplinary Approach to Combating Terrorism; Threat, Vulnerability, and Criticality Assessments

REFERENCES

Ahmed, Sara. *Queer Phenomenology.* Durham, NC: Duke University Press, 2007.
Brown, JoAnne. "A Is for Atom, B Is for Bomb: Civil Defence in American Public Education: 1948–1963." *Journal of American History* 75 (1988): 68–90.
Crelinsten, Ronald D. "The Discourse and Practice of Counter-terrorism in Liberal Democracies." *Australian Journal of Politics and History* 44 (1998): 389–413.
Davis, Tracy. *States of Emergency: Cold War Nuclear Civil Defence.* Durham, NC: Duke University Press, 2007.
Gearon, Liam. "Religious Education and Citizenship: Guidance for Teachers." Funded by the St. Gabriel's Trust, 2009. http://re-handbook.org.uk/media/display/Religious_Education_and_Citizenship.pdf.
Gearon, Liam. "Religion, Education and Extremism: Counter Terrorism in the Classroom." Paper presented at European Educational Research Association, Helsinki, Finland, 2010. http://www.eera-ecer.eu/ecer-programmes/conference/ecer-2010/contribution/920/?no_cache=1&cHash=93629e4a8a.
McEnaney, Laura. *Civil Defense Begins at Home: Militarization Meets Everyday Life in the Fifties.* Princeton, NJ: Princeton University Press, 2000.
Preston, John. "Preparing for Emergencies: Citizenship Education, Whiteness and Pedagogies of Security." *Citizenship Studies* 13 (2009): 187–20.
Preston, J., J. Binner, L. Branicki, M. Ferrario, and M. Kolokitha. "Game Theory and Adaptive Networks for Smart Evacuations" (EP/I005765/1). Engineering and Physical Sciences Research Council. Presented at 2011 DHS Science Conference, March 31, 2011. http://www.orau.gov/dhssummit/presentations/March%2031/Day2A/Preston_Panel7.pdf.
Sandlin, Jennifer, Brian Schultz, and Jake Burdick. *Handbook of Public Pedagogy.* London: Routledge, 2010.

Regional Challenges: Promoting Stability through Economic, Social, and Political Reforms

Lee H. Igel

There is broad agreement among counterterrorism officials and professionals that it is of utmost significance to bring stability to states and regions that breed terrorism. To do this, they believe, means ridding terrorists of their safe havens and central apparatuses. Therefore, most of the strategic thinking about how to accomplish this is centered on the balance between military force, sharp policing, and intelligence gathering. Additionally, a combination of economic, social, and political reforms has also been proposed as a method to counteract terrorism. The question is, are these reforms an effective way to promote stability?

ORIGINS AND PREMISE

The objective of economic, social, and political reform is to amend or counteract prevailing conditions in states and regions that are beset by problems such as ongoing violence, lawlessness, and poverty. Much of the enthusiasm for this idea, especially in its modern form, comes from the West. In particular, it began with President Harry Truman, whose Point Four Program committed U.S. foreign aid to the economic development of poor nations throughout the world (Drucker 2003). This was soon followed by the policies of the Kennedy and Johnson administrations that purposefully sought to develop the Third World countries in Latin America and Asia, if largely as a response to the rise of Communist and extreme left-leaning movements among former subjects of colonial powers in these regions following World War II.

As economic development took hold, many nations throughout the world became industrialized. This was precisely what the plans for economic development had envisaged, for it would re-create the typical middle-class American existence throughout the Third World. Moreover, the belief was that economic development would quickly and finally eradicate poverty. Several nations, especially those in the non-Communist sphere, experienced a rapid growth of the middle class and a rise in the standard of living. However, not only did the economic development programs fail to eradicate poverty; they also seemed to continue to treat poverty as more of an economic and political problem than a social problem.

The policy of using foreign aid programs to spawn development is itself based on the Marshall Plan that followed World War II. There is, however, a significant difference: the Marshall Plan aided the Western Europeans and Japanese people, institutions, and infrastructure, all of which were entirely more competent than what exists in today's developing countries. Another difference is that that the Marshall Plan was oriented toward companies and industries, whereas foreign aid is disbursed to governments. As a result, the funds often go to the military or to projects that attract votes, often inhibiting rather than promoting economic growth.

Economic, social, and political reform policies have been proffered as a means to combat terrorism because many individuals both in government and the private sector believe that economic deprivation, low social status, and closed political systems lead to radicalization. In other words, terrorism grants its actors status and function; it gives them purpose and meaning. Indeed, lower- and middle-class populations have traditionally been receptive to terrorist ideology and lent support to these groups and their activities ("Rulers, Clerics, Radicals, Citizens" 2008). Thus, the thinking goes, overturning these dimensions could foster state stability and provide opportunities for the indigenous population.

THE COMPLICATIONS

While inveigling states to replace corrosive institutions with productive ones may be the goal, many states are considered to be "failed" or "failing." Thus, the support offered by functioning governments and nongovernmental organizations to these states is unlikely to do little more than temporarily neutralize the situation ("Where Life Is Cheap" 2011). At present, the Arab-speaking Middle East is one region in which the preceding condition may be exemplified. The use of such reforms is a direct counter to fundamentalist Islam, which justifies and inspires terrorist activities in glorification of an Islamic civilization of the past that it is hoped will return in the future ("Rulers, Clerics, Radicals, Citizens" 2008). This explains al-Qaeda and like-minded groups' desire to reestablish a caliphate—not unlike that which the Ottoman sultans ruled over until Atatürk abolished it in 1924—whereas moderates seek a union among otherwise independent Muslim states.

How this came to pass may date to around 450 years ago. It was then that the Ottoman Empire—in which Islam spread to most of the Middle East, North Africa, and parts of Europe—looked inward and rebelled against schools as the institution of advancement (Drucker 1993). Islam itself became viewed as the means to a better life, for it encompassed every aspect of the believer's being ("Rulers, Clerics, Radicals, Citizens" 2008). The religion espoused that no aspect of a person's life, whether internal or external, could be separated from Islam. This may explain why recent terrorist attacks, including the September 11 airline hijackings, were perpetrated by educated and upper-middle-class people.

Given that a large disparity in personal income, social status, and political fairness destroys mutual trust between groups and people who exist in the same space, it is understandable why there is a desire among many for economic, social, and political reforms. Yet there is, at present, little evidence to confirm whether—or to what extent—these reforms are effective. This is because there has not yet emerged one right way to implement these changes (Davis and Cragin 2009). A significant part of the problem is that, despite having become the focus of Western national security priorities since the attacks on September 11, 2001, terrorism is not the exclusive domain of fundamentalist Islam in the Middle East or of groups in Southeast Asia or Latin America (Sheehan 2008; Thomas and Thomas 2004). Nor is it any longer the case that terrorism is necessarily a tool of national policy by sovereign states (Drucker 1993). Today, terrorism—even that which is state sponsored—is increasingly conducted by private armies that range from tiny bands to organizations with hundreds of members. Then outcomes must also be considered according to variables such as diverse populations, customs, traditions, religions, classes, and governing authorities.

Further, the push for economic, social, and political reforms from the West is based on a tendency to view governments, institutions, and organizations as either autocratic or democratic. Nation-states that are perceived as in need of reform are typically tribal or ruled by an autocrat, with the latter framed around a highly centralized government and bolstered by repressive security forces. These dictators, some of whom have been in power for a few decades, are likely to have used subsidies to control the prices of goods and services like food, fuel, housing, infrastructure, and welfare ("Throwing Money at the Street" 2011). To keep domestic prices low and stagnant, as the autocrat endlessly promises to do even as world prices rise, government subsidies must be increased, which means that a larger percentage of the gross domestic product (GDP) is used. But the negative effect of such expenditure is of less consequence to the autocrat than is the provision of subsidies and other public goods because the latter furthers the autocrat's self-interests. It conserves power by at once requiring the nonruling classes to further rely on the state for basic needs, boosting cronyism among the ruling elite, and preventing the emergence of economic and political actors who might overthrow the regime or otherwise threaten its hold on power. And it provokes a question as to whether this constitutes stability or state failure.

CONCLUSION

In the very short term, reform missions often quickly gain enthusiasm among the public, both in the theater and on the home front. But as time passes, neither the economic, social, nor political landscape is likely to have improved all that much, and previous public support has waned. This brings a renewed push for reforms. The reforms are then refined and improved, yet the overall conditions improve little. Is this because it takes many years for reforms to materialize or because of something else entirely?

Uprisings throughout the Middle East during 2011 have shown that people—predominantly the young, educated, and underemployed—want change. At this writing, it cannot be determined whether the change being sought is a Western-style democracy, a Turkish-style Islamic democracy, or a different kind of polity altogether. We do know that, after years of reform efforts exacted by the mostly Western superpowers, the stability of states that produce and give refuge to major terrorist organizations has arguably become more tenuous. Since these states tend to conserve their basic economies, polities, and societies under the overlay of reform, there is debate as to whether this tactic is in need of serious restructuring. That is, there are questions about the need to reconsider reform programs so that they could be better focused on key priorities and organized around the culture and values inherent to the population. Even so, there is beneath that the question of how and to what extent the deteriorating economic, political, and social conditions of states and peoples steeped in tradition could be overhauled with any amount of success. However, if on the surface it appears that stability through economic, social, and political reforms is a reasonable tactic in counterterrorism strategy, what are the priorities, and who defines and determines them?

See also: **Volume 1, Part III:** Multidisciplinary Approach to Combating Terrorism; Role of the International Community. **Part VI:** Combating Terrorism: A New Way Forward; Multilateral Approach to Counterterrorism: Issues, Problems, Responses; Understanding Foreign Cultures

REFERENCES

Berdal, Mats, and Achim Wennmann, eds. *Ending Wars, Consolidating Peace: Economic Perspectives.* London: Routledge, 2010.

Davis, Paul K., and Kim Cragin, eds. *Social Science for Counterterrorism: Putting the Pieces Together.* Arlington, VA: RAND, 2009.

Drucker, Peter F. *The Future of Industrial Man.* New York: John Day, 1942.

Drucker, Peter F. *Post-capitalist Society.* New York: HarperCollins, 1993.

Drucker, Peter F. *The New Realities.* New Brunswick, NJ: Transaction, 2003.

"Rulers, Clerics, Radicals, Citizens: Current Trends in the Muslim World." *NYU Review of Law and Security,* New York University School of Law, No. 8–9, 2008. http://www.lawandsecurity.org/Portals/0/Documents/RLS8-91.pdf.

Sheehan, Michael A. *Crush the Cell: How to Defeat Terrorism without Terrorizing Ourselves.* New York: Crown, 2008.

Thomas, Eleanor, and Lindsay Thomas. "U.S. Southern Command (SouthCom) Struggles to Justify Its Role in the War on Terror." Council on Hemispheric Affairs, September 2, 2004. http://www.coha.org/us-southern-command-southcom-struggles-to-justify-its-role-in-the-war-on-terror/.

"Throwing Money at the Street." *The Economist,* March 10, 2011.

"Where Life Is Cheap and Talk Is Loose." *The Economist,* March 17, 2011.

Rehabilitation of Extremists:
Methods and Practice

Ami Angell and Rohan Kumar Gunaratna

Terrorist rehabilitation is a new frontier in the fight against terrorism, especially its precursor, ideological extremism. The global threat coming from violent extremist ideology requires captured terrorists to be rehabilitated before they are released. Unless they abandon the idea of violence before they are released, they will contaminate others with their ideas and will support and commit acts of violence. Over 10 percent of those released from Guantánamo Bay, where the United States failed to develop a rehabilitation program, have returned to violence. The disengagement strategy, to be effective, should incorporate incentives, reeducation, and rehabilitation.

As an essential element in the fight against extremism, detainee and inmate rehabilitation is the reverse of terrorist indoctrination. Deradicalization is both detainee and inmate rehabilitation and also community engagement. Such deradicalization initiatives can proactively and reactively counter the contemporary wave of extremism. A successful rehabilitation program must recognize all modes of rehabilitation. Within each mode of rehabilitation, there are various styles. The seven principal modes of rehabilitation are religious rehabilitation, psychological rehabilitation, social/family rehabilitation, educational rehabilitation, creative expression rehabilitation, vocational rehabilitation, and recreational rehabilitation.

CONTEXT

The global campaign against terrorism has been dominated by an overwhelming kinetic response. The lethal operations have temporarily disrupted terrorist operational infrastructures but have not disrupted the conceptual infrastructures driving extremism and terrorism. The modus operandi to catch and kill terrorists and disrupt their organizations is having a boomerang effect. Although the operational capabilities of terrorist groups have been reduced in some theaters, the motives and intentions of the terrorists to fight back have grown, protracting the fight.

In some countries, soft power has been cast aside as hard powers are wielded. The combination—smart power—is used only by very few nations. While the use of operational measures should not be disregarded, an equal amount of attention has not been given to the strategic fight—the battle of ideas. Ideological and intellectual infrastructures form the foundations of the terrorist movement. As the environment remains permissive, ideology remains the lifeblood of contemporary terrorist groups and movements. Terrorist ideologies can be delegitimized only by ideological and theological refutation. To safeguard the next generation of youth from the lure of fighting and the appeal of extremist ideology, counterideology must be incorporated into the counterterrorism toolbox. Ideally, the two counterideological prongs of community engagement and terrorist rehabilitation should be used in parallel.

Through the development of community-based programs that aim to engage indoctrinated extremists and rehabilitate operational terrorists, regeneration of violence can be prevented. These programs can be built in partnership with the government. Terrorist rehabilitation is a vital tool in the fight, through which incarcerated terrorists are engaged to recant, repent, and express remorse for their thoughts and acts of violence.

BACKGROUND

There are over 100,000 convicted and suspected terrorists languishing in prisons and detention centers from Europe to the Middle East and Asia (interview with a delegate of the International Committee of the Red Cross, January 13, 2009). Although there are vocational and educational programs to rehabilitate criminals, there are very few initiatives to rehabilitate terrorists. Though terrorist rehabilitation has been the topic of significant interest and debate from academic circles in the United States to officials in Europe, there has been very little effort to examine the concepts, processes, and outcomes of terrorist rehabilitation. Despite significant study into terrorist mindsets and the ideologies driving them, terrorist rehabilitation remains the exception worldwide, not the norm.

During the Bush presidency, the United States had a golden opportunity to start a rehabilitation program in Guantánamo Bay in Cuba. Instead, the United States earned the anger of the Muslim world through images of muffled and chained men wearing orange jumpsuits. Guantánamo Bay should have been divided into two sections, one of them being a section where detainees who cooperated received counseling and livelihood skills, played with their children, and met with their families; the other section for detainees who were uncooperative and unresponsive to the available programs. Without the benefit of the such programs, when the Guantánamo Bay detainees were released, they were more radicalized than when they were initially incarcerated. Detainees had used their time in detention to network, get ideas, and encourage each other to become more extreme. Without a rehabilitation program it is very seldom that upon release detainees will give up their ways. Guantánamo Bay illustrated this. As the battlefield of the mind was not addressed, nearly 100 former detainees have since returned to the fight. Pentagon spokesperson Geoff Morrell said the latest figures, current through December 24, 2009, showed an 11 percent recidivism rate, up from 7 percent in a March 2008 report that counted 37 former detainees as suspected or confirmed active militants (Morgan 2009).

President Obama signed a decree on January 22, 2009, commanding the closure of the detention center, but by then many might argue it was too little and too late (Priest 2009). Most countries receiving the Guantánamo Bay detainees have no rehabilitation programs, and without this benefit the detainees were encouraged to return to the economic and religious means that landed them in detention in the first place. Thus, there is an urgent need for countries to develop effective and long-term rehabilitation programs.

In the contemporary period, Egypt pioneered the idea of religious rehabilitation in the 1990s. Al Azhar scholars and other counselors as well as the historical leadership of al Gama al Islamiyah al Masri (Islamic Group of Egypt) began to influence detainees and inmates to abandon violence and build peace (Blaydes and Rubin 2008; interview with official in the Counter Terrorism Department in Cairo, April 8, 2008) Programs for rehabilitating the Communist terrorists in Malaysia and Singapore were developed in the 1960s and 1970s, but these were not elaborate. Communism in Asia was not a global threat, and religion was not the basis for the ideological mindset in that era. Resolution of the problem at the time was contextual. After realizing the scale of the threat following the al-Qaeda attacks on the United States on September 11, 2001, Singapore, Saudi Arabia, Iraq, Uzbekistan, Indonesia, and Malaysia developed national rehabilitation programs. Since then, the process of detainee and inmate rehabilitation has been gaining popularity worldwide. As a new frontier in counterterrorism practice, rehabilitation programs have provided degrees of success in countries that have adopted them. Some programs, such as those in Singapore, have been developed with community participation where clerics and scholars have volunteered to counsel detainees, and other well-meaning individuals and institutions have provided for the detainees' families. In such counterterrorism and counterextremism initiatives, participation and ownership by the community is an important first step in the right direction.

WHY TERRORIST REHABILITATION?

Rehabilitation should become a complementary strategy in the ongoing fight against terrorism and extremism. Today, many arrested terrorists arrested are not viewed as individuals requiring treatment. They are either treated as criminals or prisoners of war. However, unlike common criminals, terrorists carry an ideology. The mind is their most powerful weapon against their enemies and opponents. By unlocking the mind, a terrorist can be made to reflect on and reexamine his own ideas and thoughts. This is why terrorist rehabilitation is unique. Still in an experimental phase (Rekhi 2009), terrorist rehabilitation requires visionary leadership, a government-community partnership, and a well-resourced specialist program of dedicated and trained staff.

Terrorist rehabilitation is based on the theory that mere punishment through imprisonment is not enough to permanently reform them and facilitate their reintegration into society upon release. Particularly for terrorist detainees, ideological debate or religious counseling sessions are a very important component of the rehabilitation program. This is because their behavior and way of thinking are based on an incorrect understanding or misinterpretation of Islamic concepts. Hence, the counseling sessions serve to provide them with the correct understanding of Islam and its leading concepts. This correct understanding will not only forestall future criminal acts but also convince them that such behavior is inappropriate and misguided. Consequently, this will bring about genuine feelings of remorse and repentance, permanently removing the source of motivation for their involvement in terrorist and extremist-related activities (interview with Ustaz Mohammed Bin Ali, February 22, 2009).

FUTURE

To share global best practices, build a network, and chart the future of terrorist rehabilitation, Singapore hosted the first International Conference on Terrorist Rehabilitation on February 24–26, 2009. Organized by the International Centre for Political Violence and Terrorism Research and the Religious Rehabilitation Group of Singapore, the three-day international conference drew 200 delegates and participants from 22 countries that have existing and aspiring rehabilitation programs. The world's leading practitioners and scholars on detainee and inmate rehabilitation, including Major General Douglas Stone, the former commander of Detainee Task Force 134, presented at this conference. Security and intelligence specialists, psychologists, religious counselors, social workers, and other practitioners active in the process of rehabilitating extremists and terrorists participated in the conference. To learn from global best practices and understand the gaps in knowledge, the national programs shared their experience and future plans. The conference was designed not only as a listening and learning event but also as a forum that allowed the participants to focus on steps that should be undertaken in the near future. The understanding gained, the knowledge developed, and the networks built took rehabilitation to a national level in building support for establishing a global regime in terrorist rehabilitation (Jerard 2009). In fact, other countries—such as Libya, which hosted an event in March 2010 attended by a dozen leading experts, entitled "Swords into Ploughshares: Combating Terrorism through Debate and Dialogue"—are now engaging in similar initiatives. Likewise, Pakistan hosted the "1st Strategic Workshop on Rehabilitation and De-radicalization of Militants and Extremists" in May 2010. Both conferences aimed at brainstorming global best practices to address the upsurge of extremism in their respective countries.

CONCLUSION

The rehabilitation of terrorists and suspected terrorists in Iraq was a huge success. As the detention centers in Iraq at one point housed over 26,000 detainees, they became a breeding ground for terrorists, prompting U.S. Detainee Task Force 134, commanded by Major General Stone, to develop a multidimensional rehabilitation program. Remarkably, after the introduction and implementation of the rehabilitation programs for Iraqi detainees in the summer of 2007, violence in detention centers decreased by 50 percent. At the same time, intelligence from detainees about other Iraqis—both inside the wire and out—increased threefold. Perhaps most remarkably, the recidivism rate of detainees who participated in the rehabilitation programs was less than 1 percent. With the theater internment facilities in Iraq turned over to Iraqi authority, the United States has taken the best practices model of rehabilitation from Iraq and has applied it to the Afghan detention centers. The response has been incredible, with detainees, the military, and civilians all actively engaged in ensuring the success of the program. The Commander of Task Force 435, Vice Admiral Robert S. Harward, and Camp Parwan commander Brigadier General Mark S. Martins have worked hard to build on the Iraq model to best meet the needs and desires of the Afghan population. In detention, the strongest and most persistent voice will always win. Rehabilitation programs have the ability to become that strong voice; they have the ability to win over those in detention when the opportunity to engage is recognized and seized.

See also: **Volume 1, Part III:** Combating Terrorist Recruitment, Propaganda, and Radicalization Campaigns; Terrorist Recruitment in Correctional Institutions. **Part IV:** Combating Religiously Based Terrorism; Detention, Interrogation, and Torture of Terrorist Suspects. **Part VI:** Combating Terrorism: A New Way Forward

REFERENCES

Blaydes, Lisa, and Lawrence P. Rubin. "Ideological Reorientation and Counterterrorism: Confronting Militant Islam in Egypt." *Terrorism and Political Violence* 20, no. 4 (Winter 2008): 461–79.

Jerard, Jolene. "Conference Report on the First International Conference on Terrorist Rehabilitation." Singapore: International Centre for Political Violence and Terrorism Research, February 2009.

Morgan, David. "Pentagon: 61 Ex-Guantanamo Inmates Return to Terrorism." *Reuters,* January 13, 2009.

Priest, Dana. "Bush's 'War' on Terror Comes to a Sudden End." *Washington Post,* January 23, 2009, p. A1.

Rekhi, Shefali. "Spiritual Rehab for Terrorists." *The Straits Times* (Singapore), March 8, 2009.

Root Cause Analysis and Counterterrorism

Kamila Trochowska

Root cause analysis (RCA) is a problem-solving method that attempts to identify the core causes of a problem or event. RCA can be applied to any problem and is based on the belief that problems are ultimately solved by attempting to correct or eliminate their root causes. By directing preventive measures against the determined root causes, the likelihood of problem recurrence should be minimized or in the best-case scenario eradicated altogether. Although it is unlikely that terrorism will ever be entirely eliminated, RCA may best serve as an iterative process, a tool to be continually improved on (Okes 2009, 7).

While there are numerous methodologies for conducting effective RCA, Okes suggests a synthetic and comprehensive 10-step approach, broken down into two distinct phases. Phase one, termed the *diagnostic phase,* includes problem definition and its development, the identification of "possible causes," and data collection and analysis. Phase two is the *solution phase,* where possible corrective measures are identified, selected, and implemented. If subsequent analysis reveals that the selected remedy (or remedies) is effective, then the corrective measure is permanently incorporated into the decision-making apparatus (Okes 2009, 7–9).

TERRORISM: A COMPLEX PHENOMENON

Postmodern terrorism is a broad and complex phenomenon and as such can complicate the RCA process. While military actions, stability missions, economic sanctions, law enforcement measures, and immigration policies are essential components of international counterterrorism efforts, the focus must ultimately include actions and policies to prevent extremist groups from forming and expanding (Stern 2010). For this to be successful we should make an attempt to understand the root causes that spawn terrorist actions and the processes that drive them. Social scientists have examined many factors in an effort to understand why certain individuals gravitate to terrorist groups and activities. According to Stern (2010, 98) "the reasons that people become terrorists are as varied as the reasons that others choose their professions: market conditions, social networks, education, individual preferences."

Market conditions, poverty, and a lack of employment and educational opportunities may force mainly young people to seek solace and opportunity in identifying with a terrorist organization and hostile and extremist ideologies. In the case of suicide bombers, it is the family's future welfare that is promised. Another factor is a radicalized ideology, whether nationalistic or religious, which may provide a sense of belonging and purpose, either in marginalized Islamic communities in Europe, among refugees, or in Muslim countries where large numbers of people are stuck in a cycle of poverty, with few or no prospects of upward mobility. Moreover, young people predisposed for recruitment into terrorist groups find armed struggle and aggressive ideology as appealing as youth in the West do rap music and other subcultures. Some social scientists view terrorism as a response to a state government's actions or policies that are perceived by the people as repression, hostility, or occupation. This can include strict immigration laws, intolerance toward foreign nationals, and discrimination against refugees and immigrants in Western societies.

Terrorism has also been examined relative to values and other specific cultural characteristics. Attitudes toward the individual, the concept of human rights, and attitudes regarding issues of life and death are not static across the globe. For example, the attitude toward death varies throughout cultures. What appears to be controversial or incomprehensible behavior (e.g., martyrdom operations) in one country might seem morally appropriate in others. Other factors may include community acceptance of terrorist actions, family traditions (e.g., revenge passes on from generation to generation), mental illness, responses to real or perceived humiliation, and various unknown individual motivations.

Regarding economic conditions and education, there is little empirical data to suggest that extremism and violence are spawned by poverty and the lack of education (Stern 2010). With regard to aggressive and extremist ideologies, it might help a great deal if Muslim communities instituted deradicalization and education programs like those that have achieved some success in Saudi Arabia and Iraq. Additionally, public education, which stresses tolerance for those with diverse cultural backgrounds, specifically cultures that are prone to engendering violent and extremist behaviors, should be made available. The media might also be employed to this end. The objective is to limit the vulnerability of young Muslims who are inclined to seek out such groups. Equally important, counterterrorist actions should not be perceived as a war against a specific culture, society, or religion as this generates resistance and promulgates more violence. The ultimate goal of all peace-seeking people is to be able to live in a safe global environment free of indiscriminate violence and terrorism.

Efforts must also be initiated to limit intolerance and the marginalization of immigrants and refugees. Again, public education campaigns and the media could play a major role. Finally, from a cultural perspective, is it possible to obtain an adequate understanding of the processes underlying terrorist motivations? Access to mainstream societies where these movements are spawned could yield insight into their moral structure and other distinctive cultural aspects of a specific community of people, which is required to expand our existing knowledge base regarding various cultural traditions and sensitivities.

INTEGRATION

Following the 2004 Madrid and 2005 London bombings, Spain's Fidel Sendagorta Gomez del Campillo (of the Ministry of Foreign Affairs and Cooperation) noted that Germany's Turkish minority could not be described as integrated, yet Germany had suffered no attacks, while the perpetrators of the Madrid and London attacks had been relatively integrated. Whether integration or the lack thereof was a factor in the attacks or not, he said the most worrying trend in Europe was the growing hostility between communities. He stated, "Young people were motivated by an ideology powerful enough to point them in the direction of murder and suicide-bombings despite living in environments far removed from the more traditional scenes of violence, such as Palestine. Through attacks in Afghanistan, the United States, Spain and the United Kingdom, these young people were also given the impression that 'victories' were possible. In their eyes it was a winning strategy awakening their thirst for honour and glory, concepts he argued were no longer of relevant in European society" (Sendagorta Gomez del Campillo 2010). This is a significant and powerful statement. It advances the idea that the moral, ideological, and cultural aspects of the phenomenon should be a top priority of social scientists and others who are tasked with combating violent extremism.

CONCLUSION

Western views of what is right and just may not apply to societies whose values, beliefs, and ideals are traditionally and culturally diverse. For example, the belief that creating a fair, stable, and democratic environment in Islamic countries with equal rights and access to education will prevent radicalism and terrorist retaliation is simply false when we realize that many terrorist attacks (e.g., 9/11 or the London bombings) were perpetrated by individuals who were educated in Western countries and lived for some years in societies where they enjoyed individual rights and freedoms that are nonexistent in the repressive regimes of their native countries (Phares 2006, 18). According to this author, social processes and cultural and moral factors need to be addressed by terrorism and country-specific experts in academia and the counterterrorism community in order to effectively understand the root causes that underlie terrorist actions. The problem with applying RCA to terrorist actions is that the process works best when causal (contributory) factors are understood and those performing the analysis are in general agreement.

See also: **Volume 1, Part I:** Defining Terrorism: Issues and Problems; Definition and Dimensions of Counterterrorism. **Part VI:** Counterterrorism Research: Current Efforts and Future Challenges; Need for Empirical Research on the Effectiveness of Counterterrorism Strategies; Understanding Foreign Cultures

REFERENCES

Anderson, Stewart. "Root Cause Analysis: Addressing Some Limitations of the 5 Whys." *Quality Digest*, December 17, 2009. http://www.qualitydigest.com/inside/quality-insider-column/root-cause-analysis-addressing-some-limitations-five-whys.html.

Okes, Duke. *Root Cause Analysis: The Core of Problem Solving and Corrective Action.* Milwaukee, WI: Quality Press, 2009.

Phares, Walid. *Future Jihad. Terrorist Strategies against the West.* New York: Palgrave Macmillan, 2006.

Sendagorta Gomez del Campillo, Fidel. "Islam and Terrorism: What Can We Learn from London and Madrid Bombings." IISS Forum in Cooperation with the Wyndham Place Charlemagne Trust, May 26, 2006. http://www.iiss.org/conferences/counter-terrorism-series/islam-and-terrorism/.

Stern, Jessica. "Mind over Martyr: How to Deradicalize Islamist Extremists." *Foreign Affairs* 89, no. 1 (2010): 95–108.

Wagner, Robert. "Rehabilitation and Deradicalization: Saudi Arabia's Counterterrorism Successes and Failures." *Peace and Conflict Monitor,* University for Peace, August 1, 2010. http://www.monitor.upeace.org/archive.cfm?id_article=735.

Sun Tzu's *Art of War*: Lessons for 21st-Century Counterterrorism Practitioners

Andrew J. Waskey

Sun Tzu is believed to be the author of the Chinese military classic *The Art of War* (or *Military Strategy*). Some have questioned the authenticity of Sun Tzu, arguing that he did not exist and that the book was written by others because only a few Chinese sources discuss him, which has provided fodder for skeptics since ancient times. Whatever the merits of these debates, the book is a reality that has influenced Chinese military philosophy for millennia as part of *The Seven Military Classics of Ancient China.* Chinese generals still use it to formulate strategy for modern war.

THE ART OF WAR

The exact date of *The Art of War* is not known. It may have been written in the Spring and Autumn Period 2,500 years ago or during the Period of the Warring States 2,350 years ago. The standard edition was issued during the Tang dynasty. This version was used by Giles and Griffin as the basis of their translations. However, archaeologists' recent discoveries of Chinese military books including *The Art of War* in Han dynasty tombs have brought ancient versions to light. These are the "tomb texts" that are being translated; however, ancient Chinese is difficult to translate, and using the "tomb texts" to amend the received text presents issues that have not all been settled.

The Art of War has been known in China for millennia. It has influenced Japanese military thinking since the 700s. Knowledge of it has spread to Korea, Japan, and other Asian countries. In recent times it has become very popular in the Orient and increasingly around the world. It is being applied to many areas of life besides war, areas such as business, the martial arts, management, police work, political action, crime, economic espionage, and numerous other activities.

The reception of The Art of War in the West began in 1772 when it was translated by Father J.J.M. Amiot, a French Jesuit missionary to Beijing. Some believe that it was used by Napoleon, the Nazi High Command, and others. It was first translated into English by Captain E. F. Calthrop of the British Army in 1909. It did not, however, guide the Western military in World War I, as it relied on Karl von Clausewitz's On War. However, The Art of War was used by Mao Tse-tung, Che Guevara, and others fighting guerrilla wars, and it guided Operation Desert Storm in 1991.

Sun Tzu's topics in The Art of War are "estimates of the battlefield," "waging war," "offensive strategy," "disposition of forces," "energy," "weaknesses and strengths," "maneuver," "the nine variables," "marches," "terrain," "the nine varieties of ground," "attack by fire," and "employing secret agents." These topics are described in succinct offerings of his ideas that can be applied systematically to build and advance a position from which one can competitively advance against an enemy. There are five factors involved: philosophy, the ground, the climate, the leader, and methods. All of these are now being used by some in the war on terror.

DEFINING THE STRUGGLE

The philosophy is the thinking that is employed for defining the struggle. In the modern world the mass media were very hostile to fascism and nativist groups like the Ku Klux Klan. It was morally opposed to these groups. However, since the Vietnam War it has become "morally neutral." The result is that the way is open for terroristic groups and their supporters to play the media so that they will accept the terrorists as legitimately grieved victims. The factor of the ground means the economic grounds that support armies. For al-Qaeda it means attacking Western targets in order to attract followers and funding. The factor of climate for Sun Tzu includes all the things that cannot be controlled in war. They can be used or accepted for gain or loss.

The question whether The Art of War is known by and has been (or is being) used to guide Islamic terrorists is not yet fully answered. Some believe that its principles have been absorbed into the military thinking of Muslims in Central Asia over the centuries. Others still seek confirmation of direct use by al-Qaeda. The off-microphone comments of Imam Feisal Abdul Rauf, which were recorded and put on YouTube, suggest the use of Sun Tzu's teachings. Imam Rauf's ideas were presented in terms of coaching sports teams and the positioning of teams or the members of teams rather than armies, but their resemblance to Sun Tzu's comments on disposition of forces and offensive strategy is recognizable.

In the West the question whether *The Art of War* can be used to combat terrorism has been answered in the affirmative by some. Extremely important in the view of those applying *The Art of War* against terrorists is the definition of the struggle against terroristic violence. In the war against al-Qaeda and Islamic radicalism, more than in the fight against terroristic methods, it is a war between the ideal of freedom and the ideal of moral (Islamic) totalitarianism. This interpretation argues that Islamic terrorists are not motivated by opposition to American policies; they are driven instead by a philosophy that is much older than the United States: seeking global imposition of their ideology in the name of religion.

The view that the struggle with al-Qaeda is a war is favored by those who see it as a guerrilla war. The war is still a war even if it involves combat with small groups in an asymmetric fashion. This makes it more like the Indian wars of earlier American history. Some definitions of the war against al-Qaeda and other Islamic terrorists ignore the military part of the struggle and see it as a simply criminal matter. The use of sufficient law enforcement tools and successful prosecutions is viewed as the correct strategy. This view assumes that it will win respect for the rule of law and manifest the Western, especially American, commitment to justice.

A key element in the definition of the war is Sun Tzu's principle that one should know one's self and the enemy equally well. Understanding the type of war being fought and knowing that it is the same as the enemy's perception is vital for both generals and civilian leaders. The failure to do both can lead to defeat.

MEDIA AND INTELLIGENCE

Central to Sun Tzu's ideas is winning without fighting. This principle involves employing forces so that victory is achieved without the use of violence. It involves positioning assets where they can be seen as victims or where the enemy can be manipulated in such a way that support is crippled. For al-Qaeda this means manipulating the mass media through agents of influence or agitators so that the resolve to oppose them is weakened. It is a combination of psychological warfare and other factors that weakens the resolve of their opponents. In the end it is not battlefield victories that count (e.g., the U.S. war in Vietnam) but the outcome of the war. The American way of war as one of annihilation or attrition is applicable but may not ultimately defeat al-Qaeda because the American way is also to fight wars of short duration that have strategic value. Bearing high costs while wearing down the psychological resolve of the United States is a price al-Qaeda is willing to pay. According to Sun Tzu this is needed in war.

The last topic in *The Art of War,* gathering intelligence (spies), is vital to victory. Without the production of strong intelligence the defeat of terrorists will never be complete. It can be hampered by terrorist double agents who manipulate the American cultural belief that intelligence work is "dirty" and "antidemocratic." Allowing this belief to hamper intelligence gathering tempts intelligence agencies to become overly dependent on technology. As a consequence human intelligence is forfeited to the enemy. Without question captured al-Qaeda training manuals teach the use of deception for those who are covert agents. However, without superior intelligence the psychological advantage will be lost, and the domination of the enemy that is needed for victory will be missing.

CONCLUSION

Of significant concern for some students of the American use of Sun Tzu's philosophy is the problem of distortions that gain favor. These can lead to defeats or to the failure to attack and disrupt "an enemy's alliances and strategy," as Sun Tzu so aptly noted (Torelli n.d.).

See also: **Volume 1, Part I:** Definition and Dimensions of Counterterrorism; Defining the Enemy: Domestic-Based and International Threats; War on Terror. **Part III:** Defensive Measures against Terrorism: Military Preemption and Retaliation; Psychological Operations. **Part VI:** Psychological Profiling of Terrorists; Understanding Foreign Cultures

REFERENCES

Gagliardi, Gary. *Sun Tzu's The Art of War Plus Strategy against Terror: Ancient Wisdom for Today's War.* Seattle, WA: Clearbridge, 2004.

McNeilly, Mark. *Sun Tzu and the Art of Modern Warfare.* Oxford: Oxford University Press, 2001.

Rooney, David. *Guerrilla: Insurgents, Patriots and Terrorist from Sun Tzu to Bin Laden.* Havertown, PA: Casement, 2004.

Sawyer, Ralph D. *Sun-Tzu: The Art of War.* New York: Fall River Press, 1994.

Sun Tzu. *The Art of War.* Translated by Samuel B. Griffith. New York: Oxford University Press, 1963.

Sun Tzu. *The Art of War.* Translated by Lionel Giles. 1910. New York: Barnes & Noble, 2003.

Taber, Robert. *The War of the Flea: A Study of Guerrilla Warfare Theory and Practice.* New York: Lyle Stuart, 1965.

Torelli, Andrew. "Sun Tzu's Theory of War for Understanding the Outcomes of Terrorist Campaigns." *Sonshi: Modern Application of the Art of War.* n.d. http://www.sonshi.com/sun-tzu-terrorism.html.

Watson, Scott A. *The Art of War for Security Managers: 10 Steps to Enhance Your Organizational Effectiveness.* New York: Elsevier, 2007.

Threat Convergence

Joshua Sinai

Today we face a new category of terrorism threat that is exponentially greater in magnitude, political impact, and warfare lethality because it is converging across multiple threat dimensions that previously were largely singular in nature. These converging threat dimensions consist of (1) terrorism, especially its religious extremist category; (2) proliferation of weapons of mass destruction (WMD), including rockets and mortars; (3) criminality; (4) cyberterrorism; (5) state sponsors; (6) anarchic conditions in weak and failed states; and (7) certain enabling conditions in strong states.

THREAT DIMENSIONS

Some of the threat dimensions in this convergence are mature, such as the perpetuation for over 20 years of transnational terrorist groups such as al-Qaeda and the ascendance to political power of long-standing groups such as the Palestinian Hamas and Lebanese Hezbollah in their respective societies. Both groups also are long-term recipients of support from their state sponsor, Iran. Other threat dimensions, such as access to WMD by terrorist groups, are still nascent and have yet to fully converge. Nevertheless, the current upheavals in nuclear states, such as Pakistan, where al-Qaeda's affiliate, the Pakistani Taliban, is waging a full-scale insurgency against the government and another ally, Lashkar-e-Taiba, is supported by the government's security services, present a worrisome scenario in this regard. Other WMD states, such as Iran, may supply such weapons to Hezbollah, its Lebanese proxy, in the event of a regional conflagration with Israel or the United States. Hezbollah and the Afghan Taliban, moreover, have long-standing involvements in narco-trafficking.

In addition, growing upheavals in failing states, such as Somalia and Yemen, have enabled terrorist groups such as al-Qaeda and its affiliates to establish safe havens in those territories' ungoverned spaces. Also of concern is the current turbulence in countries such as Egypt, where the Muslim Brotherhood may come to power or at the very least have a voice in the government following elections in late 2011. Once in government, the Muslim Brotherhood will likely come to the aid of its ally, the Palestinian Hamas, in breaking the Israeli arms embargo against it, especially the importation of increasingly lethal and long-range rockets and mortars into the Gaza Strip.

Finally, all the actors in these threat dimensions are well versed in exploiting the Internet, especially its websites, chat rooms, and forums, as well as other social media tools, such as Facebook and Twitter, to advance their causes and operations. As a result, government counterterrorism organizations now have to track and counter them not only on the ground but in cyberspace as well.

As seen from the preceding examples, the convergences of these and other significant dimensions of such threats are escalating, not diminishing, thereby producing new categories of threats that are potentially more dangerous and pose a higher level of threat to regional and international stability than heretofore. Each of these threat dimensions is dangerous by itself, but what is of special concern is that when they are linked and intertwined, the terrorists' position is substantially strengthened.

CONVERGENCE

As today's terrorists converge their capabilities and linkages into a new category of heightened threat, they do not use violence only in the conventional definition to damage their government adversaries and coerce them to give in to their demands; now, they also seek to take over states, especially those deemed weak and vulnerable. In this sense, some of today's major terrorist groups aspire to become guerrilla armies and rulers of nations. This is demonstrated by the insurgencies by extremist Islamic groups such as al-Qaeda and its affiliates in Afghanistan, Pakistan, Somalia, and Yemen, which they seek to take over. As mentioned earlier, Hamas already governs the Gaza Strip, while Hezbollah has become Lebanon's de facto ruler. In Egypt, where Hosni Mubarak's regime was overthrown in February 2011, if the Muslim Brotherhood comes to power through the democratic process, it is likely to use its influence to help its Hamas affiliate in Gaza, for instance, in lifting the ban on importation of heavy weaponry, such as rockets and mortars. (Although the Muslim Brotherhood is not considered a terrorist group as such, it has a terrorist past and espouses certain ideologies that are similar to those advocated by its ally Hamas.) What is of special concern is that in a worst-case scenario such rockets could be equipped with WMD materials and agents, such as biological or chemical warheads.

Another potential actualization of threat convergence is the opportunistic cooperation between terrorists and criminal networks that provide services such as document forging, human smuggling, money laundering, and illicit drug and arms trafficking. Well-known examples include the Pakistani AQ Khan WMD smuggling network and cases of attempted smuggling of nuclear and radiological materials in the countries of the former Soviet Union. In other cases, there may not be a need for a terrorist group to cooperate with their criminal counterparts because of their own direct involvement. Hezbollah has a long history of involvement in criminal enterprises, whether illicit drug trafficking, diamond smuggling in West Africa, or petty crimes in the United States. As mentioned earlier, Hezbollah and the Taliban (whether in Afghanistan or Pakistan) have long been involved in illicit drug trafficking. Hezbollah's criminal enterprises extend to West Africa and South America's Tri-Border region, and some of its operatives have been arrested in the United States for involvement in various criminal activities. An additional example is the terrorist cell that carried out the Madrid train bombings in March 2004, which financed its operation with funds earned from trafficking in hashish and Ecstasy. The involvement of terrorist groups in criminal enterprises, however, may be calibrated at times by their operational cells' need to avoid engaging in activities that may attract the attention of law enforcement authorities. This could jeopardize an imminent terrorist attack.

In the most potentially catastrophic convergence of such threat dimensions, some terrorist groups may be attempting—or at least contemplating—the acquisition from illicit proliferation networks of WMD as their weapon of choice against state adversaries. The political upheavals in Pakistan, which are the culmination of an escalation in religious extremism and the breakdown of the country's political elites, as manifested by frequent political and sectarian killings and the full-scale insurgency being waged by the Pakistani Taliban and its allies, are an illustration of how precarious the security of nuclear weapons facilities can be in such weak and failing states.

Even strong states, such as those in Western Europe, are experiencing problems controlling portions of their own territories, whether through weak border controls, for instance, within the European Union or along the American-Mexican border, or in the form of "no-go" enclaves in certain minority-dominated communities, where local police forces exert little authority. Such "no-go" neighborhoods also serve as facilitating environments for the spread of extremist ideologies among increasingly radicalized individuals in those communities, some of whom have turned to terrorist violence to achieve their objectives. Taimour Abdulwahab al-Abdaly, whose December 2010 suicide bombing attempt failed in Stockholm, was allegedly radicalized at Britain's city of Luton, a hotbed of Islamism. The failure to fully integrate such minority communities into their larger societies, whether due to discrimination problems or resistance by some among those communities to integrate, is a significant contributor to the convergence of such threats in those societies.

Finally, it is well known that terrorists exploit the Internet for a variety of purposes, ranging from propaganda, radicalization, and recruitment of new members to fund-raising and operational command and control. They could also exploit it, however, for cyberwarfare, for instance, in launching Stuxnet-type cyberweapons against their adversaries' critical infrastructure.

CONVERGING THREATS AND VULNERABILITIES

The convergence of these seven separate threat dimensions—although additional ones could be added to the discussion—into what may turn into an entirely new category of heightened terrorist threat will require new and more comprehensive government response measures, whether by single governments or multilaterally, than merely counterterrorism measures. Focusing on the convergences of threat dimensions that are usually perceived individually, and determining whether such convergences are fully mature or are in the early stages of coalescing, is not intended to imply that each of these specific threat dimensions no longer requires tailored and customized responses. Rather, we need to broaden our thinking and conceptual approaches to effectively address the evolving intersections where these multiple threats are in the process of converging.

The converging threat dimensions, whether nascent or current, present problems as well as opportunities for the counterterrorism community. On the one hand, a multitude of facilitating conditions, whether in weak or strong states, are attracting different terrorist groups to different regions, resulting in the convergence of such threats and the overlapping of their networks. As a result of the emergent confluence of such threats and networks, counterterrorism planners now need to anticipate which emerging failed state is likely to become the next attractive safe haven for a transnational terrorist group to set up bases, training facilities, and, in a worst-case scenario, laboratories for the development of WMD and associated devices. Similarly, a new and previously unknown illicit trafficking network may emerge either in a weak state or in a strong state to provide opportunities for a terrorist group to acquire WMD. As mentioned earlier, in a worst-case scenario, certain nuclear states, such as Pakistan, may fall into the hands of terrorist groups.

CONCLUSION

Understanding how these different threats are converging also provides valuable early warning indicators of emerging vulnerabilities that may result in new categories of threats, whether as individual or as converging threat dimensions. To improve our understanding of how to respond to the challenges being generated by threat convergences, we need a comprehensive inventory of the problem areas, whether in weak, failing, or even strong states, in order to identify the threat dimensions that have the potential to converge into new categories of threats. This also provides us with the opportunity to understand which capacities need to be improved in weak states as well as strong states, such as effective governance (including opportunities for wider political participation), control over a nation's territory, provision of socioeconomic benefits to solve social ills and employment opportunities for aggrieved communities, strengthening of education to improve a population's skills to advance in society, and countering of the spread and appeal of extremist ideologies that have the potential to escalate into violence.

See also: **Volume 1, Part III:** Terrorists, Criminals, and Drug Cartels; Threat Perception and Multinational Cooperation; Threat, Vulnerability, and Criticality Assessments

REFERENCES

Baker, Pauline. "Keynote—Threat Convergence and Failing States: A New Agenda for Analysts." Carlisle, PA: Cornwallis Group, July 22, 2005. http://www.thecornwallisgroup.org/pdf/CX_2005_08-Baker-CX-July22.pdf.

Fund for Peace. "Threat Convergence: New Pathways to Proliferation? Report on the NATO EAPC/PFP Workshop within the Partnership Action Plan against Terrorism." Zurich, Switzerland, March 4–6, 2007. http://www.fundforpeace.org/tc/images/Publications/nato_eapc%20workshop%20report_final.pdf.

Sinai, Joshua. "The Evolving Terrorist Threat: The Convergence of Terrorism, Proliferation of WMD, and Enabling Conditions in Weak and Strong States." *Journal of Counterterrorism and Homeland Security International* 13, no. 2 (Summer 2007): 10–16.

Understanding Foreign Cultures

John Walsh

Most definitions of culture center on the concept of a set of values, norms, and beliefs that unite one set of people and exclude others. Norms involve the ways of behaving, including such practices as wedding gifts, specific clothing for funerals, methods of eating, and so forth. Beliefs are mostly nonverifiable assertions commonly held by one cultural group, for example, that they have a supernatural mandate to their land or way of life or that their lifestyle is innately superior to that of others. Values are lessons in how to behave in unfamiliar situations and include self-assertiveness, deference, and the propensity to smile come what may. Itemizing the different aspects of culture and documenting them in terms of prevalence and strength is an important means of understanding how people will act, how they will react in different and unexpected circumstances, and how their culture relates to various ideologies. These factors are important components in predicting behavior at the macro- and microlevels.

THE COMPONENTS OF CULTURE

A substantial number of large-scale organizational studies have been conducted to try to identify the meaningful components of culture with a view to improving cross-cultural management skills. Perhaps the most influential of these have been by Hofstede, who has distributed many thousands of questionnaires worldwide, initially to employees of IBM, and then subjected the results to statistical analysis to identify constructs. This resulted in the concepts of power distance, masculinity, uncertainty avoidance, and individuality. These measure the degree to which people of a specific culture are willing to accept high levels of vertical difference between ranks, accept gender-specific roles, tolerate ambiguity, and sub-jugate individuality to the team effort. Subsequent research in East Asia has required the addition of a long-term perspective construct. By cross-referencing people from specific countries with these constructs, it is pos-sible to identify unique profiles. For example, the United States has a high regard for individuality and an unwillingness to tolerate ambiguity, whereas Japan has very high gender-specific roles and a propensity for teamwork, and so forth. The nature of the profile of a particular culture is likely to have a significant impact on the way organizations are struc-tured and organized: for example, a hierarchy or a network, narrow or steep differences between levels, and so forth. When groups adhere to a specific ideology that is not directly correlated with a national culture, it is nevertheless possible to analyze the features of that culture with a view to predicting the behavior of its members. Such analysis also reveals insights into how individuals are likely to relate to authority figures representing alternative ideologies.

This effort and many others often seem intuitively correct and have been welcomed but suffer from the fact that people are increasingly ex-posed to internationalized best practice in business, and their workplaces are multicultural in nature. In common with most modern states, there-fore, organizations are now no longer monocultural in nature, even if ef-forts are expended to enforce a single, dominant form of culture. When that does happen, it seems to be the case that people will split their opin-ions and forms of behavior, with one persona adopted at the workplace and another exposed at other times. The idea that people have multiple different forms of personality and behavior (and hence, at least to some extent, different cultures) depending on the context in which they find themselves is quite widespread.

ESSENTIALISM AND UNIVERSALISM

It is possible to consider people as all being much the same and divided by cultural issues that are mostly quite superficial, such as dress and food.

It is also possible to consider people from different countries as being very different and to believe that, by virtue of belonging to a specific ethnic or national group, all people in that group contain within themselves a certain "essence" that makes them different from people from any other such group. There are political and religious reasons for people to adopt the first position (the universalist view) or the second position (the essentialist view). In very simple terms, some religions teach that all people are the same in the eyes of God and capable of redemption through the same means; by contrast, other religions teach that some groups of people are inherently more capable of achieving redemption (broadly defined) than other groups and that the border between the groups is impermeable. Similarly, some political ideologies promote universalism (e.g., socialism), while others promote essentialism (e.g., nationalism or fascism). Most people, of course, tend toward fairly moderate positions along this continuum and have a mixture of motivations, some contradictory in nature. Since, as already mentioned, most people have different personas in different social situations, it is evident that the terrorist persona may not be displayed in public or to most social or familial contacts. It is more likely to be displayed in situations in which the individual believes confidentiality is ensured: this explains why so many people reveal intimate personal details and opinions online that they would not express in person. However, there is an equal but opposite tendency for many people to invent lurid or even mundane details about themselves for various reasons related to self-esteem.

There is a particular issue involved when people from Western countries look at people from Asian countries, categorized by Edward Said as "orientalism." Based on accounts of the Middle East, broadly defined, during the period of European imperialism, "oriental" culture was widely understood as being characterized by weak, lazy, effeminate men and attractive, provocative, sexually available women. The institutions of such countries are constructed on the foundations of such stereotypes. Modern accounts of rich tourists or business travelers in developing countries tend to exhibit the same features. Japanese descriptions and expectations of the Philippines, for example, are reminiscent of those of American tourists in the Caribbean in this respect. Historically, the same perspective can be seen from northern Chinese visits to what is now southern China. In general, men were and are more likely to travel than women, and they are more likely to receive personal service from women in the overseas country. The orientalist mindset follows when these observations are developed into a false ideology that this is how people in the country concerned prefer to behave and have always behaved among themselves, rather than this being a response to the need to please powerful and rich visitors. The inability of disempowered people to respond as they would wish in the face of outrageous behavior by powerful patrons should also be noted in judging their actions.

COLONIAL AND POSTCOLONIAL CULTURE

The culture of a people or country can be significantly changed by colonization by another country. This is true whether the colonization involves physical conquest and the humiliation of the local people (e.g., the Japanese colonization of Korea, 1910–1945) or the extension of soft power and cultural influence without any military activity (e.g., U.S. influence over Puerto Rico). This is sometimes called *hegemony*, and determining whether it exists is a controversial subject. However the process takes place, the colonized society exhibits some similar cultural traits. First, it adopts the colonizer's styles and aspirations as its own and may import its language, clothing, and food as superior to local versions. Second, it downgrades native institutions as being backward, primitive, or otherwise undesirable. As is common in colonial situations, this is most visibly played out in the appearance and clothing of women: their desire to undergo elective cosmetic surgery and skin color–changing techniques as well as the type of clothes and accessories they prefer to wear or are encouraged or required to wear.

If colonization ends for some reason, the affected society becomes a postcolonial society and may exhibit a degree of resentment toward the previous colonists. This might manifest itself in the physical or intellectual destruction of the cultural institutions of the colonizers and the adoption of political and religious beliefs that support such an approach. In other cases, some people retain a degree of nostalgia about the past and so a penchant for retaining the cultural practices of the colonial past. Sometimes, there are both people who deeply resent the presence of colonizers and those who feel their presence brought some benefits to the country. This is the case in postcolonial India, although it is impossible to know the absolute numbers of people holding the different positions.

Many colonial histories hold long-standing miscarriages of justice that are forgotten or covered up by the colonists but that fester in the minds of some victims, who might find that their ideological sense of grievance is combined with the loss of family members or their mistreatment. Many people in the world are not members of religions that call on them to forgive past injustices. In many countries, therefore, the events of past decades or even past centuries are entirely alive in the minds of many people, particularly those who espouse violence to spawn political and social change. In some cases, state or religious agencies will keep those memories alive and fresh.

CONCLUSION

Although there are many examples of people remaining in a small area of land for generations, on the whole there has been throughout history a high level of contact among the different countries of the world and movements from one place to another. When people from different cultures encounter each other, there is an incentive for them to adopt superior practices from each other when these are practical and do not obviously contravene powerful taboos. The extent to which dietary preferences and media consumption in Western countries have changed over the last few decades of intensive globalization is evidence of this. More substantive changes can also be effected: the spread of business schools around the world offering a largely similar curriculum and body of knowledge indicates the willingness of people to exchange their traditional beliefs and values if significantly better economic opportunities are available elsewhere. Culture, in other words, changes over time and through exposure to new ideas and possibilities. Not everybody is equally open to change, of course, and many are deeply resistant.

See also: **Volume 1, Part III:** Multidisciplinary Approach to Combating Terrorism. **Part VI:** Combating Terrorism: A New Way Forward; Multilateral Approach to Counterterrorism: Issues, Problems, Responses; Public Support and Education Campaigns

REFERENCES

Badiou, A. *Saint Paul: The Foundation of Universalism.* Translated by Ray Brassier. Palo Alto, CA: Stanford University Press, 2003.
Hofstede, G. *Culture's Consequences: Comparing Values, Behaviors, Institution and Organizations across Nations.* 2nd ed. Thousand Oaks, CA: Sage, 2001.
Oderberg, D.S. *Real Essentialism.* London and New York: Routledge, 2008.
Said, E.W. *Orientalism.* London: Vintage, 1979.

Weak Link: Identifying and Attacking Terrorists' Vulnerabilities

Irena Vladimirsky

Terror has become a global phenomenon, evolving from local, national, and even regional threats into a multinational and global one. Many terrorists, regardless of their education, religion, and national and political background, look for revenge for perceived injustices and humiliations.

TERRORISM AND GLOBAL RESPONSE

The global war on terrorism includes joint efforts by governments, international organizations, private sector firms, and other organizations, including nongovernmental organizations. Although terrorism can never be entirely eliminated, a combination of different strategies against terror on the international level may lessen considerably the ability of terrorist groups to strike their intended targets. Following the terrorist attacks on the United States in September 2001, the U.S.-led war on terror was characterized by a combination of military and government legislative actions as well as the use of other professional and international resources.

Direct military attacks on terrorists' training camps are still an important tactic in the fight against terrorism. In October 2001 an international antiterrorist coalition was established to fight al-Qaeda in Afghanistan. As a result of a massive bombing campaign and simultaneous land operations by coalition forces, al-Qaeda and its affiliates were driven from numerous training camps, with many terrorists and Taliban members being killed.

Currently, terrorist actions are characterized by a shift from expensive attacks on highly protected targets such as planes, airports, and foreign embassies to attacks on less protected or "softer" targets. Operations that employ suicide bombers to attack public places such as nightclubs, railway stations, and subways have in the recent past been part of the terrorists' modus operandi. Information and intelligence sharing and cooperation between states have increased considerably since the events of 9/11. However, there remains a need for in-depth intelligence on terrorists' motivations as well as their intentions and specific funding sources. Improved information sharing between the law enforcement and intelligence communities should allow nationwide search warrants for e-mails and subpoenas for financial information. Technological breakthroughs in communications such as the Internet have ensured that information transfer is immediate. Modern technology also provides terrorists with the ability to sequence attacks and use cell phones as crude remote detonators. Many terrorist organizations and groups use the Internet to coordinate their daily activities, disseminate propaganda, and conduct operations. Some terrorist groups have more than one Internet site. International intelligence units should focus on new and innovative targets (e.g., cyberterrorism) that terrorists may attempt to exploit, such as computer databases, sites, and programs.

ATTACKING THE FINANCIAL LIFELINE

The financial war on terror likewise cannot stop any one particular terrorist attack, but it can considerably decrease terrorists' abilities to recruit members, train operatives, and restrict their capacity to acquire and transmit information. Terror groups and organizations raise funds in a variety of different ways: charity, state funding, the drug trade, intellectual property theft, human trafficking, counterfeiting, and kidnapping. The most valuable approach to defeating terrorism is that of denying terrorists resources such as financing, recruits, weapons, intelligence, support groups, and propaganda media. Antiterror strategies targeting charities must be twofold. Contributors must ensure that they know the end user of their charity funds. Governments must actively pursue charities raising money for terrorism and aggressively prosecute facilitators and known contributors. States that finance and provide other channels of support to terrorist groups must also be targeted in the anti–terror funding campaign. Strong international sanctions should be applied against states that sponsor or otherwise support domestic or internationally based terrorist organizations.

The international banking system must work to ensure that international funds cannot easily be transferred to terrorist organizations, even when such funds have a legitimate origin. Legal measures can help with the forfeiture of terrorist cash, apply freezing orders, facilitate cooperation with immigration and asylum services, and attack the problem of bribery and corruption of state public officials. The Financial Action Task Force, a 29-nation group promoting policies to combat money laundering, adopted strict new standards to deny terrorists access to the world financial system. G-20 and International Monetary Fund member countries have agreed to make public the list of terrorists whose assets are subjected to freezing and the amount of assets frozen.

WEAPONS OF MASS DESTRUCTION

One of the important tasks of the international community is to prevent terrorists from acquiring weapons of mass destruction (WMD), especially biological and nuclear weapons. Access to WMD can be treated as a supply-and-demand problem: supplies must be limited, with the current huge supplies of WMDs and component material safeguarded or destroyed. Russian stockpiles of chemical and biological weapons, the largest in the world, should be destroyed, while stockpiles of fissile material, both highly enriched uranium and plutonium, must be safeguarded. Moreover, preventing nation-states from developing or otherwise acquiring nuclear weapons and material should be a top priority of the international community. Additionally, preventing terrorists from acquiring such capabilities has become a major global concern since terrorists could conceivably obtain nuclear weapons or fissile material through theft.

To reduce the possibility of a terrorist group obtaining and using a nuclear weapon, a global deterrence system must be developed. The United Nations Nuclear Terrorism Convention makes the possession or use of nuclear weapons or devices by nonstate entities a criminal offence. An appropriate legal framework to criminalize nuclear terrorist-related offences, allowing for the arrest, prosecution, and extradition of offenders, should be adopted and recognized by the international community. Additionally, strict controls and international preventive measures should be applied to existing stockpiles of chemical and biological weapons through an expansion of the Cooperative Threat Reduction Program.

ADAPTABILITY AND PROPAGANDA

Terrorists very quickly adapt to government efforts to provide security to their citizens by using different tactics. When airplanes and airports became more protected, terrorists shifted to less protected public targets such as nightclubs, suburban trains, buses, subways, and community centers. The use of suicide bombers provides terrorist groups with live weapons that are hard to detect, deter, or defeat. It is probably not possible to completely eliminate committed suicide bombers, who represent the ultimate smart weapon, but in principle it might be possible to deter their controllers.

Many terrorists groups and organizations benefit greatly from media coverage of their activities. Terrorism is more about propaganda than violence. Terrorists pose a threat to society not only because they kill people but also, more important, because they threaten to kill people. There are several ways to cope with or lessen the influence of terrorists' propaganda. Protocols that starve the terrorist and the hijacker of the publicity on which they depend need to be established. Obviously, this would entail cooperation between government officials and the media.

Rather than impose information control on the media, it is preferable to foster a close liaison between government, law enforcement, and the media in an effort to establish guidelines and procedures that could be employed in a predetermined type of crisis incident. Violent organizations can often influence the frequency of their coverage by the nature and timing of their actions, the target chosen, and the drama and destructiveness of their deeds.

CONCLUSION

The media need to realize that its public influence is profound and therefore tailor their reporting in a way that reduces the propaganda value to the individuals or organization responsible for the attack(s). Journalists can be a positive force in the war on terror by voluntarily regulating and being more sensitive to the propaganda value of their reporting.

See also: **Volume 1, Part III:** Combating Terrorist Recruitment, Propaganda, and Radicalization Campaigns; Identifying and Combating Sources of Terrorist Financing; Ideology That Spawns Islamist Militancy; Information Technologies to Combat Terrorism; Multidisciplinary Approach to Combating Terrorism; Multilateral Sanctions against State Sponsors of Terrorism; Organizational Resilience and Counterterrorism; Psychological Operations; Role of the International Community; Target Hardening; Terrorism, Counterterrorism, and the Internet.

Part IV: Eliminating Terrorist Support Networks; Global Initiative to Combat Nuclear Terrorism; United Nations Global Counterterrorism Strategy: Significance and Limitations. **Part VI:** Sun Tzu's *Art of War:* Lessons for 21st-Century Counterterrorism Practitioners

REFERENCES

Asad, Talal. "Thinking about Terrorism and Just War." *Cambridge Review of International Affairs* 1 (2010): 3–24.

Dershowitz, Alan M. *Why Terrorism Works: Understanding the Threat, Responding to the Challenge.* London: Yale University Press, 2002.

"G-8 Leaders Statement on Countering Terrorism." 2010. http://www.whitehouse.gov/sites/default/files/g8_leaders_statement-countering_terrorism.pdf.

International Convention for the Suppression of Act of Nuclear Terrorism, New York, April 13, 2005. http://untreaty.un.org/cod/avl/ha/icsant/icsant.html.

Intriligator, Michael D. "The Economics of Terrorism." *Economic Inquiry* 1 (2010): 1–13.

Kazimirsky, Orna, Nava Grosman,-Aloni, and Alodi Sari, eds. *Heibetim al Terror uMaavak be Teror* [Terrorism and Counter-Terrorism]. Tel Aviv, Israel: Misrad ha bitachon—hotzaa laor, 2004. [In Hebrew].

Kupperman, Robert H., and Darrel M. Trent. *Terrorism: Threat, Reality, Response.* Stanford, CA: Hoover Institution Press, 1979.

Morris, Daniel R.. "Surprise and Terrorism: A Conceptual Framework." *Journal of Strategic Studies* 1 (2009): 1–27.

Narkis, Pinhas. *Teumei Hateror: Halehima ba Teror baAretz, be Artzot HaBrit ubeOlam* [Terror Twins: War on Terror in Israel, United States and in the World]. Nes Tsiona, Israel: Astrategiot ve Taktika, 2003. [In Hebrew.]

The Nunn-Lugar Cooperative Threat Reduction Program, http://lugar.senate.gov/nunnlugar/.

Index